THE TEACHING EXPERIENCE

An Introduction to Reflective Practice

Third Edition

Michael L. Henniger ■ Roxann Rose-Duckworth

Custom Publishing

New York   Boston   San Francisco
London   Toronto   Sydney   Tokyo   Singapore   Madrid
Mexico City   Munich   Paris   Cape Town   Hong Kong   Montreal

Printed in the United States of America

10 9 8 7 6 5

2008220212

JK/KL

Pearson
Custom Publishing
is a division of

www.pearsonhighered.com

ISBN 10: 0-558-33799-6
ISBN 13: 978-0-558-33799-5

Preface

Every term, college students enter courses in teacher education to explore the possibilities and problems associated with becoming a teacher. These thoughtful, inquisitive, and energetic individuals are eager to learn more about students, teachers, and schools. They bring with them their own past schooling experiences, preconceptions about teaching and learning (some accurate and some not), and a strong desire to have an impact on their world. Although there are those who have already made a commitment to the profession, most are exploring the roles and responsibilities to see if there is a good match. What these students need is a wealth of well organized and clearly written information on important educational topics, opportunities to learn about both the joys and difficulties teachers encounter on a daily basis, and the encouragement to stop and reflect on schooling issues both individually and with others.

This text was written to assist prospective teachers in this process of exploration and reflection. Through the use of an engaging writing style that speaks directly to individual readers, those considering teaching as a career are continually challenged to think critically and deeply about the abilities and attitudes of exemplary educators and compare them with their own. The content of each chapter, coupled with captivating special features in the text and on the Companion Website, provides a thorough and engaging overview of the teaching profession.

Unique Characteristics

This textbook is unique because of its efforts in:

- *Keeping costs low*—First, this text offers all the features of its more expensive competitors while keeping the pricing low to make it more affordable for students. By placing several special features of the textbook on the Companion Website and using a less expensive format, costs have been substantially lowered.

- *Tapping the power of the Internet*—Secondly, the text takes full advantage of the versatility and interactive nature of the Internet. By placing many of the text's features on the Companion Website, students can quickly and easily use a variety of Internet source materials to learn more about important topics directly linked to text content. A portfolio builder is provided for student use, as are study tools for review of chapter content.

- *Engaging the reader in active reflection*—Finally, the book is based on the belief that all good teachers must learn and use active reflection to be successful in the complex learning environments of today's classrooms. Throughout the text and in each of the features found on the Companion Website, students are guided through the active reflection process as they read about the challenges and joys of teaching and learning.

Conceptual Framework: The Process of Active Reflection

Teaching is an incredibly complex and challenging profession at all grade levels. Those who enter must be well prepared for both the difficult issues and the great joys that can be found there. This book was written to provide the reader with a thoughtful overview of teaching's complexities. By presenting prospective teachers with opportunities to reflect on their own past learning experiences, read about the realities of schooling, and discuss critical issues with others, students are led on a reflective journey that culminates in deeper insights into the teaching profession. This process of active reflection directly influences all aspects of teaching and learning, including professionalism, decision making, and accountability.

There are many factors that contribute to the complexities of schooling. At its core, however, teaching is challenging because educators are constantly required to make difficult decisions about what to do and say as they interact with students, parents, and other adults. Decisions must be made throughout the school day about issues such as strengthening student relationships, dealing with discipline problems, presenting a new concept, talking to parents, and relating to other school personnel. Unfortunately, there are no formulas for making these decisions. Because every student, parent, colleague, and situation is unique, teachers must thoughtfully consider appropriate responses to each new set of circumstances.

To be good decision makers, new teachers need to learn the complex process of active reflection. As defined in this text, the process involves the following:

- *Gather information*—It is critical that teachers learn as much as possible about teaching and learning and continue to refine this knowledge throughout their careers. These new and refined understandings can come through reading books and articles on teaching, talking to colleagues and family members, or through careful observations and assessments of students themselves.

- *Identify beliefs*—A teacher's personal belief system, developed over time through interactions with family and significant others, also influences decision making in the classroom. Although many beliefs will positively influence teaching and learning, there are some that will need to be examined in the light of new knowledge and changed so that all students have the opportunity to learn.

- *Make and implement decisions*—Part of the reflection process also includes taking time to think through the consequences of actions and then making the best possible decisions given the circumstances.

- *Assess and evaluate*—The final component of active reflection is to take the time needed to collect information on the success of decision-making (assessment) and then analyze the data collected to determine the effectiveness of efforts (evaluation).

The process of active reflection is reinforced throughout the core text and in each of the features found in the text and on the Companion Website. In each chapter, readers encounter a rich assortment of reflection strategies and are encouraged to begin developing them into *habits of active reflection* as they prepare for the day when they will be responsible for making the many difficult decisions required of all classroom teachers.

Organization of the Text

This text is organized into four major sections that guide students through an introduction to reflection and to teaching as a profession, introduce them to foundational and timely concepts and topics in education, and encourage them to consider their choice of teaching as a career. Each section is briefly described below.

Part I—*What Is Today's Context for Reflective Practice?*

In Chapters 1–5, prospective teachers are introduced to students, teachers, school settings, and issues of teacher professionalism.

- *Chapter 1* defines active reflection and identifies the benefits and challenges of teaching. It helps the reader begin the process of determining if teaching is a good career choice.
- *Chapter 2* focuses on the growing diversity among students in American classrooms and describes effective strategies for dealing with the differences that exist.
- *Chapter 3* introduces the reader to the roles and characteristics of effective teachers.
- *Chapter 4* describes the ways in which schools are typically organized and shares information on alternative forms of schooling.
- *Chapter 5* discusses the growing professional nature of teaching and the efforts being made to enhance the image of education.

Part II—*What Is Reflective Classroom Practice?*

Chapters 6–9 are designed to help the reader develop a deeper understanding of the essential elements of effective classroom teaching.

- *Chapter 6* assists prospective teachers in understanding students and the many different ways in which they learn.
- *Chapter 7* identifies the curriculum that is being taught in schools and how it has changed over time.
- *Chapter 8* describes the elements of effective instruction, including an introduction to classroom management and discipline.
- *Chapter 9* helps the reader understand the many issues surrounding the use of computers and other instructional technologies in twenty-first century schools.

Part III—*What Are the Foundations for Reflective Teaching?*

Chapters 10–14 provide prospective teachers with information about the historical, philosophical, and societal issues that influence teaching and learning.

- *Chapter 10* addresses the history of American education and describes how this past has influenced current educational practice.
- *Chapter 11* broadly defines philosophical study and describes several educational philosophies that influence teaching and learning today.
- *Chapter 12* identifies the many ways in which American society influences student behaviors and how schools are responding to these issues.
- *Chapter 13* describes the legal rights and responsibilities of teachers and students, overviews key legislation and court cases influencing schooling, and discusses ethical teaching.
- *Chapter 14* provides prospective teachers with a framework for understanding the many levels of school governance and identifies both traditional and more recent efforts being used to finance schooling.

Part IV—*How Do I Grow as a Reflective Practitioner?*

In this final section, the reader is reminded of the importance of viewing teaching as a profession that requires lifelong learning and continued growth as a reflective practitioner.

- *Chapter 15* describes what teachers can expect during their first years in the classroom and encourages prospective teachers to continue learning and growing throughout their careers.

End-of-Chapter Features

The end-of-chapter features are designed to provide students with additional opportunities to assess their knowledge of chapter topics and to develop as a professional by applying and exploring chapter concepts.

Summary. Each chapter concludes with a summary that provides a concise recap of the chapter topics and relates them to Praxis II topics covered within each chapter section.

Developing the Habit of Reflective Practice. Organized using the same focus questions used for chapter content, this section provides students with an opportunity to focus their exploration and review on each of the major sections of the chapter. Three–five review questions, portfolio activities, and field experience activities are provided. These activities are linked to the Companion Website for this text and can be completed on-line.

- *Review Questions*—Discussion and assessment questions for each major section of the chapter provide opportunities for students to discuss with each other some of the key issues raised.

- *Field Experience.* Suggested field experiences introduce students to the profession from many perspectives, providing suggestions for classroom observations of teaching and learning, interviews with teachers and school administrators, and interactions with peers.

- *Building Your Portfolio*—Portfolio-building activities are provided for each major section of the chapter, encouraging readers to create portfolio entries that can be used as a beginning assessment of their understandings and beliefs regarding teaching and learning.

Suggested Readings. Additional readings support and enhance concepts and topics presented in the chapter.

References. Complete bibliographic references are provided for each of the sources cited in the chapter.

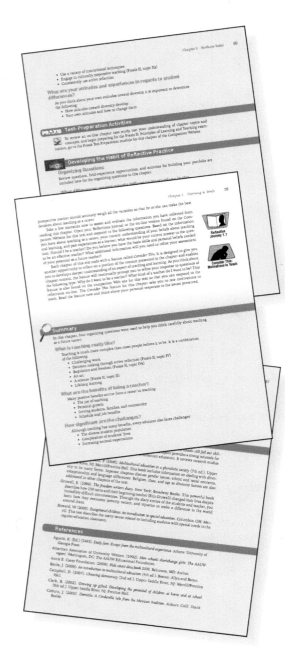

Chapter Features

With a reader-friendly writing style and frequent opportunities for reflection, this text is designed to help students in beginning teacher-education courses develop a clear understanding of all aspects of teaching as a career. A number of special features have been developed for each chapter to assist readers in this process. These features are linked to the content of each chapter with icons in the margin reminding the reader of their presence.

Reflection Opportunity. This feature, marked by an icon in the margin, encourages prospective teachers to stop at key points within the main chapter narrative and think carefully about the issues being presented. Each reflection uses a series of thought-provoking questions embedded directly in the text to help teacher-education students develop deeper insights into the issues being presented.

Engage in the Debate. Prospective teachers have the opportunity to spend additional time investigating current issues that impact teaching and learning. Each issue has been chosen because of its direct impact on schooling and its potential for controversy. After presenting some of the key elements of the debate, readers are guided through the active reflection process as they read primary source materials, conduct research on-line, and respond to the thought-provoking questions provided.

Explore Your Beliefs. This feature is designed to help prospective teachers begin to identify and analyze the beliefs about teaching and learning they currently hold. Because each student has experienced both good and bad teaching as part of their own pre-k–12 education, they bring many preconceived notions about schooling to any discussion of American education. Students are invited to bring these beliefs to the conscious level where they can be either validated or modified based on new knowledge.

Reflect on Diversity. Issues related to race, poverty, exceptionality, gender, and religion are all addressed as important aspects of diversity, allowing students to develop a deeper understanding of the impact of diversity in the schools. Through information and stories, prospective teachers are encouraged to think carefully about the similarities and differences that will exist in their classrooms and the impact they will have on teaching and learning.

Chapter Features on the Companion Website

In addition to the features found in the text, the Companion Website provides additional opportunities for readers of this text to research, reflect, and respond to other important issues. These additional features are linked to the content of each chapter. Look for icons in the margins of the text identifying each feature.

Views from the Classroom. The real world of teaching is a rollercoaster combination of joyful interchanges and difficult struggles. This feature gives readers the opportunity to hear directly from teachers in the field about what this experience is really like. Teachers at all levels share their thoughts and insights in using active reflection to address the many situations they face. These teachers have given generously of their time and effort to share with teacher-education students the realities of teaching.

Consider This. This feature is designed to give students another opportunity to reflect on a portion of the content presented in the chapter, enabling them to develop a deeper understanding of this aspect of teaching and learning. The feature prompts the reader to refine responses to questions of the following type: Why do I want to be a teacher? What kind of a teacher do I want to be? It is found on the Companion Website for this text so that students can respond to their reflections on-line.

Ian's Classroom Experiences. This feature provides an opportunity for students to read the journal entries of a teacher engaged in active reflection as he navigates the first few years of his teaching career. Ian Buchan shares with readers a variety of dilemmas and decisions that he faced as a new teacher. The decisions he makes provide a very realistic picture of the struggles of a beginning teacher who is trying to find ways to reach all of his students. Each essay is followed by reflective questions that help the reader analyze the decisions Ian made.

Key Terms. This listing of important terms covered in the chapter and their definitions is a useful review and study tool.

Test-Preparation Activities. On-line case histories and corresponding short-answer questions are formatted to connect chapter content with relevant sections of the Praxis II Principles of Learning and Teaching exam. Students can review the cases, submit their answers, and receive immediate feedback in this module of the Companion Website. In addition to being a valuable preparation activity, the exercises provide additional insight and practice in a real-world decision-making process.

MyEducationLab. This feature is new to this edition and provides links from the Companion Website for this text to videos, articles, case studies, and more that is related to the contents of each chapter. Look for the MyEducationLab logo in the margin and then follow the simple instructions to access this important content.

Chapter Study Skills. The Companion Website for this text also has a section to assist students in studying the content in each chapter. Key terms from end of chapter are presented, along with their definitions. Readers can use an electronic flashcard activity as a memory aid for learning these terms. Study guides, chapter review questions, and web links to major organizations related to the chapter are also provided.

Materials for Instructors

For those who adopt this textbook, there are several types of supplemental materials that expand upon the content of the text and assist instructors in giving students greater insights into teaching as a career.

Instructor's Manual and Multimedia Guide. These materials include suggestions for teaching the content of each chapter, uses for the materials on the Companion Website available for this text, and test items for each chapter.

Test Bank. The multiple-choice and critical-thinking questions for each chapter are available at the instructor-only section of the Companion Website.

PowerPoint Slides. Designed as an instructional tool, the slides can be used to present and elaborate on chapter content. They are available on the Companion Website for this text.

Companion Website. This Web-based resource provides instructors who adopt this text with access to an instructor-only section that provides teaching suggestions, test questions, and PowerPoint slides for each chapter.

Contents

part 1

What Is Today's Context for Reflective Practice?

Courtesy of Todd Yarrington/Merrill Education.

chapter 1

Choosing to Teach

You are embarking on an important journey that will eventually lead to the choice of a career. Throughout this text and as part of any teacher-education courses you are taking, you should begin to carefully consider what it means to be a teacher and whether teaching is the career for you. In this chapter, you will begin the process of thinking more deeply about what it means to be a teacher and how your personal abilities and attitudes may influence your success in this role. The chapter contains four sections, each with an organizing question to help guide your thinking.

Focus Questions

◀ What is teaching really like?

◀ What are the benefits of being a teacher?

◀ How significant are the challenges?

◀ Should I become a teacher?

Courtesy of Anthony Magnacca/Merrill Education.

Mrs. Henderson was the greatest teacher ever. She knew every one of her sixth grade students so well, spent extra time coming to soccer matches and concerts, and always seemed to know when a kind word and a friendly pat on the shoulder were needed. She truly enjoyed teaching and seemed to make every subject come alive for us. We loved her!

Mr. Blankenship was the pickiest teacher I have ever had. He insisted on perfectly organized proofs for geometry and logical descriptions of the work that went into the solving of algebraic equations. Mr. Blankenship had very high expectations for each of us, and kept pushing me and others to excel. At the time, I wasn't sure I liked him. Looking back, however, I realize that he always wanted the best for each of us and his persistent demands have made me a more organized learner and greatly improved my proficiency in mathematics. I'm actually thinking about majoring in either math or science when I go to college!

Mr. Palmer was the absolute worst teacher I've ever had! He never seemed to enjoy teaching any of the topics in his fourth-grade classroom. He was forever telling unrelated stories about his family or complaining about the low salaries and benefits for teachers. I think he was just putting in his time until retirement and making life miserable for students along the way. Mr. Palmer's tests were the worst. He seldom taught us anything of value and then tried to put the blame on his students by giving impossibly hard tests to "prove" that students were just getting worse every year. What a waste!

One of the interesting aspects of teaching is that we all come to the role having had a wealth of experiences in the classroom where we encountered both excellence and ineptitude. As in the above hypothetical situations, we became better educated and more fully functioning individuals following our quality interactions with some teachers, whereas our frustration, anger, and boredom multiplied from repeated exchanges with others.

This book was written so that you, the reader, can think carefully about teaching as a potential career. While using this text as part of a college or university class, you are encouraged to try on the role of teacher and see how well it fits. Do you have the motivation and interest it takes to become an excellent teacher? Can you see yourself working to develop the skills needed for competence in the classroom? Do you find schools comfortable and exciting places to be? Would the bureaucracy and paperwork be manageable or overwhelming? As you respond to these and many other questions, both individually and through discussions with others, you should begin to see a pattern emerge that will help you decide if teaching is the profession for you.

What is teaching really like?

Collectively, all of your past k–12 classroom experiences have led you to develop assumptions about what teaching is like as a career. Having watched and interacted with a variety of teachers, you unconsciously developed a sense for what it must be like to assume that role. Some of the assumptions you made about teaching are accurate, whereas others are not. For example, some of the very best educators make teaching seem effortless. As a student, you seldom saw the behind-the-scenes work that was needed to make each activity successful. It would be easy to get the inaccurate impression from these excellent teachers that little preparation and planning is needed for quality instruction.

In this section, you will begin the process of developing a more accurate understanding of what to expect as a future teacher by looking at several key characteristics of the teaching experience. You will find that some of your initial assumptions about teaching are correct, whereas others need to be reconsidered. Think carefully about the identifying characteristics of the teaching profession described below and compare them with your assumptions about this role. Table 1.1 identifies and summarizes these characteristics.

Challenging Work

As indicated earlier, one common misperception about teaching is that it is a relatively easy task. How difficult can it be, some people suggest, to know something and then share that understanding with others? If, for example, you understand the process of solving algebraic equations, shouldn't it be possible for you to teach this process to others? This relatively straightforward task becomes far more complex, however, when a variety of other factors are considered. To teach algebraic equations effectively, you need to have a strong conceptual understanding of mathematics in general and algebraic theory in particular. A good teacher would then need to be able to transform this deep knowledge of the discipline into teaching and learning activities that are understandable and motivating to students (Shulman, 1987). Effective educators are also prepared to work with students of varying abilities and those who bring with them a host of emotional and social needs that must be addressed along the way.

Teaching is further complicated by the fact that it is far more than a sharing of knowledge. William Ayers (2001) states it this way:

> Before I stepped into my first classroom as a teacher, I thought teaching was mainly instruction, partly performing, certainly being in the front and at the center of classroom life. Later, with much chaos and some pain, I learned that this is the least of it—teaching includes a more splendorous range of actions. Teaching is instructing, advising, counseling, modeling, coaching, disciplining, prodding, preaching, persuading, proselytizing, listening, interacting, nursing, and inspiring. Teachers must be experts and generalists, psychologists and cops, rabbis and priests, judges and gurus. (p. 4)

TABLE 1.1 What Is Teaching Really Like?	
Characteristic of Teaching	**Description**
Challenging Work	Rather than being easy, teaching is actually a very challenging task that requires considerable effort and skill.
Decision Making Through Active Reflection	Teaching requires daily decision making that is facilitated through the process of active reflection.
Regulation and Freedom	Although teachers work independently much of the time, it is also important that they learn to work effectively in a highly regulated system.
An Art	Like artists, teachers must creatively compose unique lessons and activities that meet the needs of all their students.
A Science	Teachers need to know and be able to use proven, research-based strategies for effective teaching.
Lifelong Learning	The best educators continue to gain knowledge and refine skills throughout their years in the classroom.

Good teachers, however, find that the complexities and challenges of teaching make the rewards of assisting children in their learning and development even more deeply satisfying.

Decision Making Through Active Reflection

Another important characteristic of your future role as an educator is that you will face numerous difficult choices every day. Although this is actually one of the things that makes teaching such an intellectually stimulating and personally rewarding profession, it also adds to its complexity. As teachers interact with students, for example, they often must choose between spending time with some students and not others during independent work times. How are these decisions made? Are they based on teachers' assessments of which students need the most help? Are there students with whom the teacher needs to build a stronger relationship? What about the students who are excelling but still need encouragement and new challenges? Similarly, teachers must make difficult choices about the content discussed each day and the teaching techniques they believe will be most effective with specific groups of students. As teachers gather information and talk through issues with others, they make complex decisions about what to do and say as they interact with students, parents, and other adults (Reagan, Case, & Brubacher, 2000). Unfortunately, there are no formulas for making these decisions. There are no textbooks that you can turn to that will have all the right answers. Because every student, parent, colleague, and situation is unique, teachers must thoughtfully consider the best responses to each new set of circumstances as they make these choices.

Effective teachers make these important decisions by taking part in **active reflection.** This process includes the gathering of information, discussing issues with others, and thinking deeply before making informed decisions. As teachers engage in active reflection, they make better decisions about what to do and say in the classroom, which in turn leads to more effective student learning. Teachers who see students engaged in more effective learning are then encouraged by these results to engage in further reflection. Throughout this text, you will be given numerous opportunities to engage in active reflection while refining your understanding of teaching and learning and thoughtfully considering a career in education. By engaging in the process of active reflection as you read this text, you will develop and refine this habit of mind, which will prove to be essential in your development as a future educator.

Each chapter of this text has a feature found on the Companion Website of this text titled *Ian's Classroom Experiences*. Look for the margin note and then consider stopping to read about a beginning teacher named Ian Buchan who is engaged in active reflection as he navigates the first few years of teaching. The thinking he uses and decisions he makes provide a very realistic picture of the struggles of a beginning teacher. The feature for this chapter provides an introduction to Ian and his essays.

Ian's Classroom Experiences: An Introduction

Defining active reflection. When teachers gather information about students, teaching, and learning; identify personal beliefs that may influence their actions; make decisions and implement actions; and then assess and evaluate the impact of their decisions on teaching and learning, they are engaging in active reflection. To help you develop the skills you will need to be a good decision maker, this textbook incorporates numerous opportunities for you to engage in each of these aspects of active reflection. All of the features for this text include focus questions organized around components of the reflection process to guide your thinking. They provide opportunities for you to think deeply and often about students and education so that you can begin to make active reflection a habitual response to the decision making required of you as a future teacher. For instance, the *Explore Your Beliefs* feature developed for each chapter of this text is an important tool that will help you bring your own beliefs to the conscious level where they can either be validated or revised based on what you are learning.

You will use active reflection in your future teaching to make all sorts of decisions about how to interact with students and which methods and materials to use in instruction. For example, Dee Edwards is planning her middle school science class for next week. After reviewing two texts that provide different presentation methods for the content she wants to teach and thinking about which strategy best fits her own teaching philosophy, Dee chooses to engage the class in a small experiment. It is designed to help them understand the concept she wants to present. She also spends time talking to a colleague who has done a similar experiment to learn about the problems and potential benefits of using this technique. Dee then thoughtfully considers the strengths and weaknesses of each of the students involved before making a decision about how she will present this task to the class. Compare Dee's approach with that of Sandra Locke, who didn't take the time to carefully think through her preparations for the same middle school science class and simply walks into the class, opens the teacher's manual for the assigned text to the appropriate page and follows the script presented there. Who do you think will be more successful with students and why? Highly skilled teachers like Dee are in the habit of thinking critically and often about the methods, materials, and activities they use so that all students can engage in meaningful learning experiences. If you are going to be successful as a future teacher, you will need to begin now to develop within yourself this same habit of active reflection.

Active reflection is an idea that has been with us for quite some time. John Dewey (1933) (see Chapters 10 and 11 for more information on Dewey) was one of the first to define and emphasize the importance of this approach to teacher decision making. He described reflection as "the active, persistent, and careful consideration of any belief or supposed form of knowledge in light of the grounds that support it" (p. 9). There are several key components to his definition:

- *Reflection is an active process.* Reflection goes beyond merely thinking about important issues to vigorously seeking solutions to the many problems that teachers face.
- *Reflection should be persistent.* It is not something you do periodically, but rather reflection is a consistent and integral part of every school day.
- *Reflection includes an examination of both beliefs and knowledge.* To make good academic decisions, teachers must think carefully and often about what they believe and how that potentially impacts their teaching. In addition, it is important to consider what is known about teaching and learning as preparations are made for new classroom experiences.

More recent writers have also provided definitions for this important concept. Cruickshank (1987) states that, "literally, to reflect is to think. However, reflection is more than merely bringing something to mind. Once one brings something to mind, one must consider it" (p. 3). Shulman (1987) emphasizes the centrality of reflection (he refers to it as reasoning) in determining the content and processes to be used in teaching. "Teaching begins with an act of reason, continues with a process of reasoning, culminates in performances of imparting, eliciting, involving, or enticing, and is then thought about some more until the process can begin again" (p. 13). Eby and Herrell (2009) discuss the importance of reflecting on beliefs and principles. They make the case that your personal beliefs will strongly influence the ways in which you teach and must be carefully examined in preparation for the many educational decisions you will make each day. Active reflection "requires a willingness to examine why you choose to do something, how you can do something better, and how your actions affect other people" (p. 8).

A rationale for reflection. It should be evident from what you have read so far that a major rationale for engaging in active reflection is that it is essential for the decision making that teachers engage in on a daily basis. Other writers have added further insights regarding its importance. Fosnot (1989) suggests that reflection leads to a sense of teacher empowerment. "An empowered teacher is a reflective decision maker who finds joy in learning and in investigating the teaching/learning process—one who views learning as construction and teaching as a facilitating process to enhance and enrich development" (p. xi). Cruickshank (1987) adds another important reason for reflection as he poses and then answers a question at the beginning of his book on reflective teaching:

> *Question:* What is more important to the beginning teacher than being readied for the first year of teaching?
> *Answer:* Being readied for all the years that follow. (p. 1)

Cruickshank then presents a strong rationale for active reflection serving as the foundational tool needed for long-term effectiveness as a teacher. He views it as the most essential component of teacher preparation. Cruickshank believes that as important as it is to get new teachers ready for their first year of teaching, it is even more crucial to develop the habit of active reflection for their long-term success in the classroom.

The reasons given above to engage in active reflection can be summarized by stating that active reflection leads to improved teaching and more effective learning. Figure 1.1 provides a graphic representation of this process. When you as a classroom teacher use active reflection, you thoughtfully determine the best possible teaching strategies for the students you will be teaching and the content being presented. This, in turn, leads to effective learning experiences for your students. When effective learning takes place both you and your students are involved in rewarding experiences that encourage you as the classroom teacher to continue to use active reflection. This creates a reinforcing cycle in which you continually reflect on ways in which you can improve your teaching so that effective learning can take place.

Figure 1.1   The Active Reflection Cycle

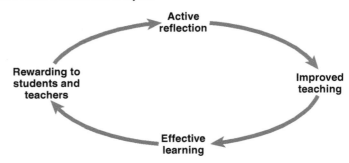

The process of active reflection. So, how does a teacher engage in active reflection? Is it simply a matter of thinking deeply and often about all aspects of teaching and learning? Or is there a process that can be studied and used as you develop the habit of active reflection? Although experienced teachers do not think about the process they go through as they use active reflection, most situations would include the four key components outlined in Figure 1.2. Teachers engage in active reflection by thoughtfully gathering information, identifying personal beliefs that may influence teaching and learning, making and implementing the best possible decisions about teaching and learning, and then assessing and evaluating the success of the options implemented. After evaluating student learning, teachers then return to one or more of the components of active reflection and continue to refine their strategies as they prepare for future teaching and learning experiences. The four elements of active reflection are described in more detail below.

- *Gather information*—It is critical that teachers learn as much as possible about teaching and learning and continue to refine this knowledge throughout their careers. These new and refined understandings can come through reading books and articles on teaching, talking to colleagues and family members, or through careful observations and assessments of students themselves. Teachers need to know as much as possible about good teaching strategies, the content they want to teach, and the students in their classrooms so that they can engage in effective decision making (Shulman, 1987).

Figure 1.2   The Process of Active Reflection

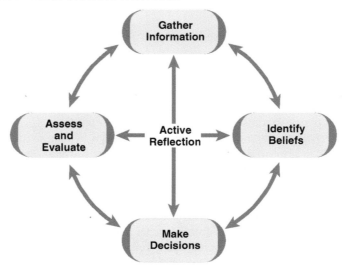

- *Identify beliefs*—Your personal belief system, developed over time through interactions with family and significant others, also influences decision making in the classroom. Your values, ideas about teaching, personal interests, and attitudes are all components of your currently held beliefs. Although many of your beliefs will positively influence teaching and learning, there are some that will need to be examined in the light of new knowledge and changed so that all students have the opportunity to learn (Dewey, 1933). This aspect of reflection requires a willingness to become a risk taker as you critically examine personal beliefs and change when needed (Eby & Herrell, 2009). A thoughtful examination of personal beliefs not only benefits the students you teach, but also leads to personal growth. As you shed outdated perceptions and develop new understandings, your own life outside of school is enriched.

- *Make and implement decisions*—Part of the reflection process also includes taking time to think through the consequences of actions on your part as the classroom teacher and then making the best possible decisions given the circumstances. Will students understand the concept being presented? Are there students who need special adaptations? What follow-up may be necessary for the development of deeper understandings? Do students' personal situations or learning styles have an impact on what you choose to do? Are there parental or community considerations that may impact your actions? These and other questions will need to be carefully thought through before decisions are made and implemented.

- *Assess and evaluate*—The final component of active reflection is to take the time needed to collect information on the success of your decision making (assessment) and then analyze the data collected to determine the effectiveness of your efforts (evaluation). In many instances, you will find that your decisions were good ones and you can move on to the next issue and begin to reflect on the best strategies to manage that situation. In other cases, your evaluation will suggest that your original problem has not been fully resolved and you will begin again the process of active reflection by gathering new information or rethinking your beliefs as you prepare to make future decisions about teaching and learning.

The following example highlights this process of active reflection. Florence Jensen teaches third grade and is preparing for class tomorrow. Her mathematics activity today on multiplication did not go as well as she had hoped, and Florence is taking the time to think about what she could do differently. She plans to gather information by talking to her teaching partner across the hall and by rereading the appropriate portion of a resource text to get some ideas about what she could do differently. Florence then identifies a personal belief as she remembers her strong desire to use manipulative materials such as Cuisenaire Rods as an aid in learning mathematical concepts. After reviewing the information gathered, Florence makes her plans and implements a revised activity for the next day. She then works to assess and evaluate her math activity by observing students as they use the Cuisenaire Rods and carefully reviewing the homework assignments as they come back the following day. Florence is pleased to see that most of the students have improved their mathematical understandings and her strategy has proven successful for this group of students. She realizes, however, that there are still three or four students that still seem to need further assistance in mastering the basic mathematical concepts presented, and Florence will spend some additional time actively reflecting on ways in which she can reach these learners.

Throughout this text you will be given the opportunity to collect your thoughts about important issues related to teaching and learning. Look for the margin note icon you see to the right throughout each chapter and consider responding to the questions you will find embedded in the text. This collection of personal reflections can eventually become a part of your **teaching portfolio.** These samples of student work and teacher activities provide documentation of your

Reflection Opportunity 1.1

growth as a future educator. Consider taking some time now to respond to the following questions for Reflection Opportunity 1.1. Do you see yourself engaging in activities similar to those of Florence Jensen as you prepare for teaching and learning in your future classroom? What do you see as the positive aspects of using active reflection? Are there potential challenges? Do you think you will be able to commit the time and energy needed to reflect on a regular basis? Is this something you think you will enjoy? Why or why not?

Throughout this text and on the Companion Website, you will read through numerous examples of active reflection and be given many opportunities to practice the processes described above. Each of the features developed for this text (and found on the Companion Website) includes guiding questions that will help you to gather information, identify beliefs, make and implement decisions, and think through the assessment and evaluation needed to determine if your reflections lead to positive results. As you engage in the process of active reflection, you will develop a much clearer understanding of what teaching is really like.

Regulation and Freedom

The regulation of teaching by local, state, and federal agencies has changed dramatically within the last 50 years. The rules that govern what takes place in the classroom have grown exponentially in that time (see Chapter 14 for more information). Such things as the length of time spent on specific subjects, the textbooks being used for instruction, requirements for being promoted to the next grade, and guidelines for teacher interactions with students are all regulated by various governing bodies.

Despite the growing number of constraints, however, most teachers find that they have considerable freedom once the doors to the classroom are closed. For most of the school day, the teacher has primary responsibility for making decisions about such things as the order and emphasis placed on each subject or topic, the specific methods of instruction, and evaluation techniques used to assess student learning. The general workday of teachers is also quite flexible. Some come to school early in the morning to plan and prepare for teaching; others stay late. Still others take work home with them in the evenings or spend time on weekends on school-related work. The flexibility and autonomy of teaching are characteristics that often attract people to the profession.

Consider taking a moment now to reflect on both the regulation and freedom of teaching. How do you think you would feel about the independence that teachers experience? Do you think you would be comfortable and confident being on your own for much of the school day, with all of the responsibility for a classroom full of students? In addition, do you see yourself as the type of person who can work in a system that is highly regulated by local, state, and national groups? Continue to think about these issues as you read further in this text and discuss the topics with others.

Reflection Opportunity 1.2

An Art

Another way to get to know what teaching is really like is to learn about how others described it. In broad terms, the education profession has been portrayed by different writers as either an art or a science. Those who think of teaching as an art see the educative process as something that cannot be easily defined or described because it changes daily based on the needs and interests of the students and the circumstances within the classroom. Good teachers, they propose, craft a lesson much as an artist takes a lump of clay and molds it into a work of art. By adding a little here, making modifications there, and using the tools of the trade to intuitively shape and form classroom activities, a creative interchange occurs between teacher and students that leads to inspired learning. Banner and Cannon (1999) describe this creative interchange as follows:

While pedagogical expertise and technical knowledge are essential to it, ultimately teaching is a creative act: it makes something fresh from existing knowledge in spontaneous, improvised efforts of mind and spirit, disciplined by education and experience. Thus, unlike a technology, in which correct application produces predictable and uniform results, teaching yields infinite surprises—infinite delights—from one moment to the next. What method can supply to teaching we know or can learn; what art can furnish out of our own selves we must imagine—and then practice. (p. 3)

Those who view teaching as an art see education as a very complicated and challenging profession that is continually changing. They believe that there is no formula for teaching that can be mastered and then applied in all circumstances to all students. Rather, as educators interact with students and plan for the curriculum, they must continually rethink, reframe, and reconfigure the content and process of teaching. This perspective is consistent with the process of active reflection discussed earlier. Educators reflect because they realize that teaching can never be merely a rote application of knowledge and skills. Although viewing teaching as an art makes the process far more difficult, it also means that the rewards are great for those who continue to work at improving what they do.

A Science

In addition to those who emphasize the art of teaching, many think of teaching as a science. Those who take this stance believe that good teachers begin with a deep knowledge of the subject matter being taught and a clear understanding of teaching and learning. This is generally referred to as the **knowledge base** of teaching. Table 1.2 briefly describes the seven types of knowledge

TABLE 1.2 The Knowledge Base of Teaching	
Content Knowledge	**An in-depth knowledge of the subject(s) taught.**
General Teaching Knowledge	Understanding the broad principles of classroom management and organization needed for good teaching.
Curriculum Knowledge	Knowledge of the organization and sequencing of the subject(s) taught.
Pedagogical Content Knowledge	Knowing how to present content to students of diverse interests and abilities so that effective learning can take place.
Knowledge of Learners	Understanding child development and its applications to teaching and learning.
Knowledge of Educational Contexts	Knowing the impact of classroom atmosphere, school climate, and community setting on student learning.
Knowledge of History and Philosophy of Education	Understanding the history and philosophy of education and their impact on teaching and learning.

Source: From Shulman, L. (1987). Knowledge and teaching: Foundations of the new reform. *Harvard Educational Review, 57*(1), 1–22.

teachers must have to be successful in the classroom. In addition to this knowledge base, teachers have also mastered the strategies needed to be successful in interactions with students. These skills needed for effective instruction can be observed, categorized, studied, and practiced by those who want to become effective teachers. A deep knowledge of subject matter, teaching, and instruction combined with the ability to use effective teaching skills are essential ingredients that teachers need to engage in active reflection and make good decisions about quality teaching and learning experiences.

Marzano, Pickering, and Pollock (2001), after a thorough review of the research literature on instructional strategies, have identified several key teaching techniques that all effective teachers display. These strategies include

- Helping students identify similarities and differences
- Providing guidance in summarizing and note taking
- Reinforcing student effort
- Providing effective homework assignments and time in class to practice what is being learned
- Helping students generate mental pictures and graphic representations of content
- Establishing clear goals for students and providing feedback on meeting those goals
- Assisting students in applying knowledge by guiding them in generating and testing hypotheses
- Helping students apply what they already know to the current learning situation.

These research-based options are discussed in more detail in Chapter 8. An important national effort to define clearly what all new teachers should know and be able to do is described in the standards developed by the Interstate New Teacher Assessment and Support Consortium (INTASC), which are summarized in Figure 1.3. For each of these standards, there are additional INTASC statements that describe the knowledge, dispositions, and performances that all beginning teachers should have, regardless of their specialty areas. Many teacher-preparation programs are specifically aligned to these standards.

To ensure that INTASC standards are being met, many states have begun to require all teacher candidates to pass a standardized test assessing their understanding of the subjects they will teach and knowledge of teaching and learning. One exam that is commonly used for these purposes is the **Praxis II.** The first part of this exam tests the subject matter knowledge of the teacher candidate. For example, mathematics teacher candidates take an exam to assess mathematics content knowledge, English teacher candidates take the English content test, and prospective elementary teachers complete a multiple subjects exam. In addition, the Praxis II assesses candidate knowledge of teaching and learning. This Principles of Learning and Teaching component is outlined in Table 1.3. It covers four broad topics: (1) students as learners, (2) instruction and assessment, (3) communication techniques, and (4) profession and community (Educational Testing Service, 2008). For web links to the Praxis examinations and an opportunity to take a practice test, go to the Companion Website for this text and click on MyEducationLab for Chapter 1.

Before completing your work for this chapter, take a few moments to read and reflect on the *Explore Your Beliefs* feature for this chapter. This feature is integrated into every chapter of this text and is designed to help you analyze your current beliefs about teaching and learning. You developed these beliefs after having had a wide range of life experiences that included exposure to both good and bad teachers, experiences of success and failure as a learner, and attitudes expressed by family members and others about teaching and learning. Because of these experiences and the way in which you perceived them, some of the beliefs you hold about teaching and learning are valid, whereas others may need to be modified based on the information being presented here. In this chapter, the *Explore Your Beliefs* feature asks you to reflect on whether teachers are born or made. Having read the past two sections on the art and science of teaching, spend some time

Figure 1.3   INTASC Standards

Standard #1: The teacher understands the central concepts, tools of inquiry, and structures of the discipline(s) he or she teaches and can create learning experiences that make these aspects of subject matter meaningful for students.

Standard #2: The teacher understands how children learn and develop and can provide learning opportunities that support their intellectual, social, and personal development.

Standard #3: The teacher understands how students differ in their approaches to learning and creates instructional opportunities that are adapted to diverse learners.

Standard #4: The teacher understands and uses a variety of instructional strategies to encourage students' development of critical thinking, problem solving, and performance skills.

Standard #5: The teacher uses an understanding of individual and group motivation and behavior to create a learning environment that encourages positive social interaction, active engagement in learning, and self-motivation.

Standard #6: The teacher uses knowledge of effective verbal, nonverbal, and media communication techniques to foster active inquiry, collaboration, and supportive interaction in the classroom.

Standard #7: The teacher plans instruction based upon knowledge of subject matter, students, the community, and curriculum goals.

Standard #8: The teacher understands and uses formal and informal assessment strategies to evaluate and ensure the continuous intellectual, social, and physical development of the learner.

Standard #9: The teacher is a reflective practitioner who continually evaluates the effects of his/her choices and actions on others (students, parents, and other professionals in the learning community) and who actively seeks out opportunities to grow professionally.

Standard #10: The teacher fosters relationships with school colleagues, parents, and agencies in the larger community to support students' learning and well-being.

Source: Model standards for beginning teacher licensing and development: A resource for state dialogue, by Interstate New Teacher Assessment and Support Consortium, 1992. Retrieved October 6, 2008 from: *http://www.ccsso.org/content/pdfs/corestrd.pdf.* Reprinted with permission.

reading and thinking about this feature so that you can explore your beliefs on this issue. The complete feature is found on the Companion Website for this text so that you can read about the issue and respond to the questions on-line.

Explore your beliefs: Teachers are born, not made

A common assumption held by many people is that someone with strong academic skills and an ability to relate well with others needs very little further preparation to be a teacher. Those with this perspective feel that the need for formal teacher preparation is minimal and can be accomplished very quickly and easily when candidates for the profession have the needed academic and interpersonal skills.

Teach for America (TFA) is one current example of a program grounded in these beliefs. Each year, the Teach for America program accepts up to 1,000 college graduates nationwide, puts them through an intensive 5-week summer training program, and then places these new teachers in urban and rural settings where it is typically difficult to find certified teachers.

Despite strong personal qualifications and a desire to be of service through teaching, many TFA teachers find they are unprepared for the challenges of the classroom. One Yale University graduate had this to say about her Teach for America experience: "I—perhaps like most TFAers—harbored dreams of liberating my students from public school mediocrity and offering them as good an education as I had received. But I was not ready. . . . As bad as it was for me, it was worse for the students . . . I was not a successful teacher and the loss to the students was real and large." (Schorr, 1993, pp. 317–318)

Despite the fact that the Teach for America program recruits applicants with strong academic credentials and effective interpersonal skills, many TFA teachers end up becoming frustrated and leave the profession. The research evidence suggests that a high proportion of these teachers leave during the first 2 years, with departure rates nearly three times the national average (Darling-Hammond, 2000).

Other studies of teachers admitted to the classroom with less than full preparation (including options other than TFA) find that these teachers have greater difficulties in planning, teaching, assessing, and managing classroom activities (Darling-Hammond, 2000). Further evidence indicates that students also suffer when teachers have received inadequate training before entering the classroom. For example, a Texas study found that students in districts where lower percentages of teachers had completed traditional teacher certification programs were less likely to pass the mandated state achievement tests (Fuller, 1999).

Developing the Habit of Reflective Practice
Gather Information

1. Do an Internet search for "Teach for America" and read about the Teach for America program.

2. How long has Teach for America been in existence? What are its goals?

3. How does Teach for America work? How do they recruit candidates for TFA? What kind of training do TFA teachers get prior to and during their teaching?

Identify Beliefs

1. What is your reaction to the statement "teachers are born, not made"? Do you believe that it is true, partially true, or not at all a true statement? Give your reasoning for the position you take.

2. Do you think that teacher training makes a difference? Should all prospective teachers be required to take an extensive training program? Why or why not?

Make Decisions

1. If you had the opportunity to participate in a teacher certification program that was much shorter than a traditional certification program, would you take that opportunity or not? Why or why not?

2. If you were living in a community where there was a shortage of teachers, would you support your school district in hiring teachers from the TFA program? Why or why not?

Assess and Evaluate

1. If your district began hiring teachers from the TFA program, how would you recommend they assess and evaluate the effectiveness of this kind of teacher recruitment and training?

2. When choosing a teacher certification program, what characteristics would you use to assess and evaluate the program?

Sources

Darling-Hammond, L. (2000). How teacher education matters. *Journal of Teacher Education*, *51*(3), 166–173.

Fuller, E. (1999). Does teacher certification matter? *A comparison of TAAS performance in 1997 between schools with low and high percentages of certified teachers.* Austin: Charles A. Dana Center, University of Texas at Austin.

Schorr, J. (1993). Class action: What Clinton's National Service Program could learn from "Teach for America." *Phi Delta Kappan, 74*(4), 315–318.

Lifelong Learning

Another important characteristic of the education profession is that it requires continued learning and growth on the part of teachers. Even though you have developed insights about teaching just by being a part of the educational system for many years and will learn a great deal more by the time you receive teacher certification, mastering the art and science of teaching is a never-ending process. Education is a very complex but rewarding profession that requires continued learning.

One of the main reasons that teachers must continue to grow and learn is that no two students and no two teaching situations are ever identical. You will need to begin again to reconstruct the ingredients for effective teaching each time you start working with a group of students by continually engaging in the process of active reflection. As Parker Palmer (1998) states in his book, *The Courage to Teach:*

> I have taught thousands of students, attended many seminars on teaching, watched others teach, read about teaching, and reflected on my own experience. My stockpile of methods is substantial.

TABLE 1.3 Praxis II—Principles of Learning and Teaching Test	
Topic	**Components**
I. Students as Learners	(a) Student Development and the Learning Process (b) Students as Diverse Learners (c) Student Motivation and the Learning Environment
II. Instruction and Assessment	(a) Instructional Strategies (b) Planning Instruction (c) Assessment Strategies
III. Communication Techniques	(a) Effective Verbal and Nonverbal Communication (b) Effect of Culture and Gender on Communication (c) Questioning Strategies to Stimulate Discussion
IV. Profession and Community	(a) The Reflective Practitioner (b) The Larger Community

Source: Principles of teaching and learning: Test at a glance. Retrieved October 7, 2008 from *http://www.ets.org/Media/Tests/PRAXIS/pdf/0524.pdf*

myeducationlab
The Power of Classroom Practice

MyEducationLab 1.1

But when I walk into a new class, it is as if I am starting over. My problems are perennial, familiar to all teachers. Still, they take me by surprise, and my responses to them—though outwardly smoother with each year—feel almost as fumbling as they did when I was a novice. (p. 9)

Although this notion of beginning again with each new group of students and never really perfecting the act of teaching may seem daunting at first glance, it is also a major reason why educators find their work so rewarding and fulfilling. Each day is filled with new possibilities, unique interactions with students, and formidable challenges that must be met. For example, Marta has just enrolled in your tenth-grade American history class after recently moving to your community from Mexico. Marta has limited English skills and struggles to communicate with you and with other students in the class. Although it is a major challenge for you to plan successful activities for her, the sense of satisfaction and accomplishment you and she both experience are indeed rich. The best teachers accept the challenges of students like Marta and are always thinking, anticipating, feeling, and acting to meet the many demands of the job. If you seek a work environment that is always changing and continually challenges you to try harder, one that requires you to think more creatively, and one that needs people who care deeply about each new student, then teaching may be just the career for you.

Learning to teach can be viewed as a lifelong process that consists of four main phases. These phases are outlined in Table 1.4. You may be surprised to know that you have already completed the first phase based on earlier experiences as a learner in elementary through high school classrooms and other formal learning settings since that time. These experiences have given you many opportunities to learn about both positive and negative teaching. Although providing you with good insights into becoming an effective educator, your observations and participation in these settings have more than likely led to misperceptions as well (Feiman-Nemser, 1999). You will need to begin now to think carefully about the ideas you have developed about teaching and learning from your own experiences and be sure that you are approaching teaching with accurate perceptions of what it takes to be an effective educator.

The second phase in learning to teach is the one you are just beginning. **Initial teacher certification** through colleges and universities requires a minimum of a bachelor's degree and

TABLE 1.4 Phases in Learning to Teach	
Phase	**Description**
Experience as a Learner	Your own experiences in elementary through high school classrooms have allowed you to observe and informally learn about teaching
Initial Teacher Certification	The courses in subject-matter content, teacher education, and classroom applications required to receive an initial teaching certificate
Teacher Induction	The first few years in the classroom you will be learning on the job as you work with students and receive guidance from mentor teachers and others
Continuing Professional Development	The course work, degrees, advanced certification, and both individual and group reflections that will help you continue to grow as an educator throughout your career

typically includes course work in the subject matter to be taught, teacher education courses, and several experiences working in public school classrooms. The last component of most programs is called the *internship* or *student teaching experience,* where you will spend up to a full year in a classroom developing skills as an educator.

Once you complete initial teacher certification, it will be time to find that first teaching job and begin working with students. But the task of learning about teaching is far from complete. In many ways, it has just begun. The first few years in the classroom are often referred to as the period of **teacher induction.** During this time, new teachers are spending long hours in on-the-job training as they refine their knowledge and skills in teaching. For this induction period, most teachers are assigned an experienced educator who serves as their **mentor.** The mentor, along with other colleagues, provides guidance and support regarding all aspects of teaching, including your growing skills in using active reflection. More information on teacher induction and mentoring can be found in Chapter 15.

After this period of teacher induction, most teachers are beginning to feel like they can breathe a little easier. Although much remains to be learned, they believe that the hardest part is behind them and that life can begin to settle down a bit. During this phase of **continuing professional development,** teachers refine their skills by engaging in additional learning experiences offered through local school districts and in university settings. For example, in most states the initial teacher certification is only good for a few years, after which it must be replaced with a permanent or more advanced teaching credential. This typically requires teachers to engage in further formal and informal learning experiences. Many teachers combine the work needed for a permanent teaching credential with a master's degree to add to their knowledge of teaching and learning.

What are the benefits of being a teacher?

Teaching is a very personal activity that attracts people to it for a variety of reasons. Some love the content and want to share that excitement with their students. Others have a passion for working with students and want to do all they can to assist in their growth and development. Most people find that a combination of reasons attracted them to, and keep them in, the teaching profession. Before reading about what others have said are the benefits of teaching, take a moment to think about what attracts you to teaching at this time.

The Joy of Teaching

The transmission of knowledge to a new generation of students is a time-honored component of education at all levels. All teachers should see this as a significant aspect of their responsibilities in the classroom. For many, this also becomes a major reason for the excitement they experience throughout each school day. For example, a survey of new teachers by Public Agenda, a nonprofit public opinion organization based in New York City (Farkas, Johnson, & Duffett, 2003), found that 96% of all educators surveyed indicated that teaching is work they love to do.

This love of teaching is generally seen as consisting of two main components. The first is a passion for the subject matter being taught. Many middle school and secondary school teachers are attracted to those levels because of the excitement they feel as they think about and discuss with others the specific subjects they teach. Although elementary teachers are generalists in the sense that they are responsible for all subjects, many educators at this level are also attracted to the profession because of their enthusiasm for the subjects they teach.

Another component of this love of teaching is the delight found in teaching others. Many educators find that the subject matter itself, although interesting, provides less excitement and challenge than does assisting others in understanding and applying new knowledge. They talk about the pleasure they experience when they see students' faces light up as they finally make the connections that are needed for understanding new concepts. For example, Sarah, who teaches middle school physical-education classes, just finished helping Jeremy, who is paralyzed from the waist down and uses a wheelchair, to refine his basketball techniques. It has been truly exciting to watch him develop into one of the best free-throw shooters in the class. Sarah feels a deep sense of accomplishment as Jeremy successfully completes his free-throw skills test. Teachers like Sarah find that the rewards of helping students develop their knowledge and skills make all the struggles and effort worthwhile.

Before completing work for this chapter, consider reflecting on how you would feel about teaching subject matter and working with students at the grade level of your choice. Do you see yourself getting excited about the subjects you would teach? What evidence do you have from prior experiences to verify your response? How would you feel about the relationships you would have with students? Are you the type who genuinely enjoys being with students and assisting them in their growth and development? Although you may need more information and further experiences in the classroom before you can answer these questions accurately, your responses will help you determine if teaching is the career for you.

Reflection Opportunity 1.3

Personal Growth

Personal growth can come from a number of different sources. For a teacher, one option for growth is the need to continually know more about students and teaching. Another form of personal growth for teachers comes from knowing oneself. The earlier discussion of active reflection makes it clear that when you consistently think about teaching and learning, you will grow not only in your knowledge of students and teaching but also in your understanding of self. Parker Palmer (1998) makes the case for the importance of knowing oneself as a teacher when he writes:

> After three decades of trying to learn my craft, every class comes down to this: my students and I, face to face, engaged in an ancient and exacting exchange called education. The techniques I have mastered do not disappear, but neither do they suffice. Face to face with my students, only one resource is at my immediate command: my identity, my selfhood, my sense of this "I" who teaches—without which I have no sense of the "Thou" who learns . . . In every class I teach, my ability to connect with my students, and to connect them with the subject, depends less on the methods I use than on the degree to which I know and trust my selfhood—and am willing to make it available and vulnerable in the service of learning. (p. 6)

Personal understanding and growth are not only necessary prerequisites to good teaching and learning, they are also rewarding for teachers themselves. The challenge to grow and change as an individual is part of the excitement that draws people to continue to put in the long hours and endure the many frustrations that accompany meaningful teaching.

Serving Students, Families, and Community

Many educators find that another major benefit of teaching is that it provides numerous opportunities to serve students, their families, and the broader community that go well beyond the sharing of content knowledge described above. David Hansen, in his book *Exploring the Moral Heart of Teaching* (2001) and an earlier work titled *The Call to Teach* (1995), makes a strong case for teaching being viewed as a **vocation** or calling. This level of service implies a deep commitment to students, families, and community that influences all other aspects of the teaching/learning process:

> The Latin root of vocation, vocare, means "to call". It denotes a summons or bidding to be of service. It has been used to describe both secular and religious commitments. For example, some persons have felt called or "inspired" by divine purposes to join a religious order and to serve faithfully a given community. They have become ministers, nuns, priests, rabbis, missionaries, or pastors. Others have felt impelled to serve not divine purposes but rather human ones. They have felt called to human society with its manifold needs and possibilities.

Many nurses, doctors, politicians, lawyers, and teachers have felt the kind of magnetic pull toward a life of service exemplified in the idea of vocation. (Hansen, 1995, p. 1)

As American society continues to grow more complex, fast paced, and impersonal, difficult social issues abound. Drug and alcohol abuse, violence, poverty, discrimination, and child abuse and neglect are among the many challenges that students, families, and communities face (see Chapters 2 and 12 for more information). Add to these the challenges that come from the normal stresses of growing into adulthood and it becomes increasingly clear that viewing teaching as an opportunity to serve the human and personal needs of students and others is essential. Teachers often find themselves plunged into the midst of these difficult issues, and they must make every effort to do what they can to interact with students and others in caring ways. Rather than seeing these challenges as a burden, teachers view them as positive opportunities for personal and professional growth. For example, Brenda Morrow, a third-grade teacher in El Paso, Texas, describes three of the many students she has taught and the positive benefits of serving these students and their families:

> For Rika, who spoke little English after only six months in this country, at first too timid to try, won an honorable mention in a citywide poetry contest—in English. For her triumphant smile of accomplishment, I teach.
>
> For Sean, who always knew he could do anything, who had a supportive and loving family, who, now in his second year at a prestigious university, has his eyes set upon a Senate seat or the Oval Office. For Sean, I teach.
>
> For Jerry, who, after his father was brutally murdered, found the classroom the haven of peace and safety that a small boy craves when his childhood has forever been robbed by the wickedness of the world. For Jerry, I teach. (Levine, 1999, p. 103)

Schedule and Job Benefits

Although not as altruistic as the call to serve students and their families, the schedule and job benefits of teachers are often considered important pluses for the profession. The flexibility and security of teaching are viewed as positives that help compensate for some of the frustrations that are also associated with working in school settings.

Schedule. Without question, quality teaching takes hard work and numerous hours of planning, preparation, and assessment. Although this leads to long workdays, especially during the first few years of teaching, many educators appreciate the fact that they have considerable flexibility in completing their tasks. Beyond a minimum number of hours that teachers are contracted to be in the school building each day, they can work at a time and place of their choosing. Some teachers arrive early in the morning to prepare, and others choose to stay in their classrooms after the students have left to complete their preparations for the following day. Still other teachers find that getting away from the school setting and working from the comfort of their own homes is a more relaxing and productive option. This flexibility, which helps satisfy the individual work preferences of educators, also enables many teachers to blend work and family responsibilities more effectively.

Another aspect of the teacher's schedule that is important to consider is the summer vacation time. Although some schools are moving to a year-round schooling format (see Chapter 4), the period from mid-June through mid-August is still considered a time away from the classroom for most teachers. It allows for a change of pace from the rigors of classroom teaching and time to engage in other activities. Some take this opportunity to slow down, become reenergized, and engage in their favorite hobbies and activities. Others may supplement their teaching income through additional work experiences. Still others use the time to take course work through their local colleges or universities to increase their knowledge and understanding of teaching and learning. Once again, the teaching schedule allows considerable flexibility in determining how to make use of a substantial portion of time during the calendar year.

Figure 1.4 Average Teacher Salaries by State

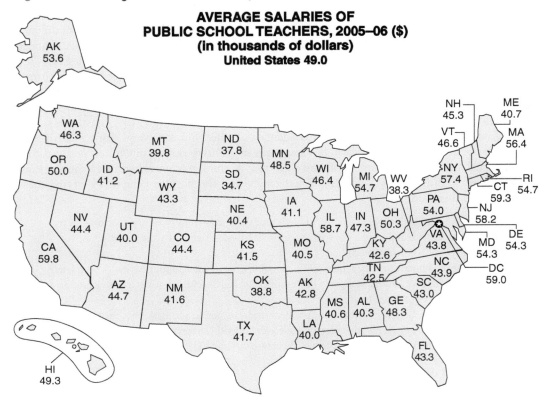

**AVERAGE SALARIES OF
PUBLIC SCHOOL TEACHERS, 2005–06 ($)
(in thousands of dollars)
United States 49.0**

Source: From National Education Association. (2007). *Rankings and estimates.* Washington, D.C.: Author.

Job benefits. Although improvements have been made in teacher salaries during the last several years, most educators still find that they are below the income levels found in other occupations. The latest data available from the American Federation of Teachers (2007) indicates that teacher salaries are below those of many occupations, including accountants, buyers, programmers/analysts, and engineers. Another concern surrounding teacher salaries is that although average teacher salaries have risen from slightly over $38,000 in 1995–96 to over $49,000 for the 2005–06 school year, when these salaries are adjusted for inflation, the average increase for this same 10-year period is only 1.9 percent (National Education Association, 2007). Figure 1.4 provides a look at average teacher salaries by state for 2005–06.

Despite these salary concerns, most teachers find at least three other job benefits that make teaching attractive:

- *Health- and dental-care benefits.* Compared to other occupations, teachers typically have higher-quality health and dental coverage available to them at an affordable cost.

- *Secure retirement plan.* Teachers' contributions to their individual retirement plans are typically matched with monies from the state to provide a secure and generous retirement plan that can begin as early as age 50 with a minimum number of years of service.

- *Job security.* Even though economic downturns may influence future pay increases and the costs of health- and dental-care benefits, once a teacher is tenured (see Chapter 13) there is a high level of job security in teaching as compared with other occupations.

Each chapter of this text has a feature called *Engage in the Debate,* which is designed to provide you with additional information on current issues that affect teaching and learning. Issues are chosen because of their impact on schooling and their potential for controversy. After presenting some of the key elements of the debate, you will be asked to reflect on the issue and state your own views. The *Engage in the Debate* feature in this section addresses the topic of male teachers in elementary schools. In addition to presenting reasons for the low number of male elementary teachers, the feature goes on to describe a rationale for their importance. Read the *Engage in the Debate* feature and clarify your ideas on this controversial topic.

Engage in the debate: Male elementary teachers

Current national statistics indicate that approximately 75% of all teachers today are women (National Education Association, 2007). Men are definitely in the minority, especially in elementary schools, where only about 9% are male (NEA, 2008). Many men avoid teaching altogether because of the low wages and the difficulties of supporting a family on a teaching salary. Those who do choose to teach tend to gravitate to the middle and high school levels so that they can teach specific subject matter content.

Some men avoid elementary teaching because of role stereotyping. They think that women are better at interacting with young children. Others feel that society in general thinks that men who want to work with younger children are "strange" and worry about being accused of child molestation. Some men also find it easier to relate to older students or want to be able to coach so that they can supplement their income (National Education Association, 2008).

Despite the low numbers of male teachers, many people believe that it is beneficial to have men in the elementary classroom. These teachers can serve as role models for children from single-parent families who have fewer interactions with men. Boys, especially, may relate better to male teachers and be more successful in the classroom as a result.

Developing the Habit of Reflective Practice

Gather Information

1. Research this topic; make a list of the benefits of having male teachers for younger students. What challenges do male teachers face that make it difficult for them to consider teaching at the elementary level?

2. What are some of the programs or efforts being made to recruit more males as elementary school teachers?

Identify Beliefs

1. What do you consider to be the benefits of having male teachers in elementary schools?

2. Should teacher training programs and school districts make a concerted effort to recruit more men to teach at the elementary level? Why or why not?

Make Decisions

1. If you were an elementary school principal with two equally well qualified candidates for a teaching position (one male and one female), would you give preference to the male candidate? Why or why not?

2. If you were serving on the school board of a district that had only 4% men in its elementary teaching staff, what would you do to try to raise that percentage? Or would you do anything at all?

Sources

National Education Association. (2008). Wanted: More male teachers. Retrieved October 10, 2008 from *http://www.nea.org/teachershortage/03malefactsheet.html:*

National Education Association. (2007). *Rankings and estimates*. Washington, D.C.: Author.

How significant are the challenges?

As you begin to think seriously about teaching as a career, it is important to be aware of more than just the benefits that come from working in the classroom. It is also necessary to understand the potential difficulties you will face. By discussing the issues that make teaching more complex, you can develop a more balanced perspective on the realities of the teaching profession. This perspective should then help you make the best personal decision about teaching as a future career option. Each of the issues discussed below is addressed in more detail in Chapters 2, 5, and 12.

Diverse Student Population

Without question, one of the challenges you will face if you choose to teach is the diversity of students found in virtually every school across the nation. This diversity can be categorized into five main areas: cultural, racial, and ethnic diversity; family diversity; diverse student abilities; economic diversity; and gender diversity. The very real differences that can be found among each of these groups of students have important implications for teaching and make your work in the classroom both more rewarding and more complicated (see Chapter 2 for more details).

Each chapter of this text includes an important feature called *Reflect on Diversity,* which is designed to help you understand the impact on teaching and learning of issues related to race, ethnicity, economic status, exceptionality, gender, and religion. Through information and stories, you will be asked to think carefully about the similarities and differences among people and the impact of this diversity on schooling. The *Reflect on Diversity* feature in this section looks more closely at poverty and its influence on schooling. Poverty is a growing phenomenon in American society that has a major impact on families, including the very real possibility of becoming homeless. In this feature, you will hear from a mother of two children who experiences divorce, significant illness, loss of her job, and then becomes homeless. Read the feature to learn more about this mother's struggles and reflect on the ways in which homelessness will influence your future teaching.

Reflect on diversity: The road to homelessness

Here, in the words of a homeless parent, is the story of one family's experience in moving from a relatively comfortable life situation to one of hardship and strife (Ferguson, 2001):

Canton is my hometown. I graduated from the practical nurse program of the Canton City Schools System. I have worked for the past fifteen years as an LPN, including the past eight years at the Pines Nursing Center. I married and have two children—Aaron, who is eighteen, and Jasmine, who is nine. When my husband and I were together, we made decent money.

Everything began to unravel last summer. My husband and I separated. At the same time, I began missing work due to illness. Eventually, I had to take a leave of absence. It took all summer for my physician to diagnose me with a very serious heart condition. This diagnosis couldn't have come at a worse time. I had just switched employers—one that provided better health insurance. But the diagnosis occurred when I was between coverage, and so I had no means to pay my huge health care expenses. With my husband gone and my physician having instructed me to stop working, I had no way to pay the rent for our apartment. Jasmine and I were evicted in October.

We moved in with my sister. That arrangement lasted only a week and a half, because she had to move as well. Then, we were really in a jam. A friend assisted me in locating the YWCA of Canton Homeless Shelter, where Jasmine and I have been staying since November. We live together in a single room. We've managed to hold onto our clothes and some personal belongings, but all of our furniture and house wares are long gone.

Jasmine has changed schools during this period, and that has been a big thing for her. She misses her old friends and teachers. School gives her something to do and keeps her mind off of the stress in our lives right now. I dread if we are still homeless in the summer.

Developing the Habit of Reflective Practice

Gather Information

1. Learn more about homelessness in this country and the barriers that children who are homeless face in regards to education at
http://www.nmha.org/homeless/childrenhomelessnessfacts.cfm

2. Explore the resources available to the homeless residents of your community by making a list of the local agencies that assist homeless individuals, children, and families.

Identify Beliefs

1. If you were Jasmine's teacher in the story above, how would you feel about helping her through this difficult time in her life?

2. Do you think that teachers should be assisting homeless children and their families in finding the resources they need to function effectively? Why or why not?

3. What stereotypes of homeless people do you have? How would these beliefs impact how you worked with homeless students?

Make Decisions

1. As a teacher of homeless children, what would you personally be willing to do to support children and their families?

2. How as a teacher would you help your students have more compassion and understanding of families who are homeless?

Assess and Evaluate

1. How could a school find out what kind of impact homelessness has on students' education? What kinds of data could they look at to help them predict and react to the impact?

2. How do you think schools for homeless children should evaluate their effectiveness?

Source

Ferguson, L. (2001). Oral Testimony of Lois Ferguson on Behalf of the National Coalition for the Homeless. Retrieved August 24, 2004, from *http://www.nationalhomeless.org/experiences/ lois.html*

Not only will you work with students like Jasmine, described in the *Reflect on Diversity* feature, but you will also find many other diverse students in your future classrooms. Take, for example, the fifth-grade classroom of Sandra Thornton. In terms of diversity, Sandra's class is fairly typical for her school. Of the 27 students, 4 are Hispanic, 3 are African American, 2 are of Asian descent, and 18 students are Caucasian. Fourteen live in families with two parents, 12 come from families where the biological parents have divorced (with 9 of these parents having remarried), and 1 student lives in a family situation that includes two female parents. Furthermore, 5 of the families live at or below the poverty level, 19 families are considered middle class, and 3 would be classified as upper middle class in terms of income. Sandra's students are divided fairly evenly by sex, with 15 boys and 12 girls. The teaching challenges she faces are further complicated by the ability levels of students placed in her classroom. Two students with special needs and four that have been classified as gifted are part of the mix that Sandra must plan for every day. See if you can imagine yourself in Sandra's classroom facing both the challenges and opportunities of her diverse group of students.

The rich diversity of a classroom like Sandra's provides many opportunities for interesting interactions between the teacher and students. For example, one of her African American students is Muslim, providing opportunities for both Sandra and her class to gain insights into another religious tradition. At the same time, however, teaching a diverse group of students is definitely more challenging. To take just one small example, Sandra must plan six separate sets of activities for the mathematics curriculum she is required to teach. In addition to the primary activities planned for the majority of the class, individual plans must be made for each of the students with special needs and enrichment activities must be provided for those students who are moving more quickly in their development of mathematical concepts.

Views from the Classroom: An Extreme Makeover

Each of the chapters in this text also includes a feature called *Views from the Classroom* that describes real stories from the lives of real teachers. Each story highlights an important issue from the classroom and explains how the teacher used active reflection to develop strategies to deal with the problem encountered. The feature for this chapter (found on the Companion Website for this text) tells the story of a young homeless boy named Jason and his teacher's efforts to understand and support Jason through this difficult time. Having read and responded to the *Reflect on Diversity* feature earlier in this chapter, you know that homelessness is a significant problem and one you will face as a classroom teacher. The *Views from the Classroom* feature now gives you a concrete example of a teacher's positive and caring response to a homeless child. As you read this feature, reflect on how you would respond to similar circumstances in your own future teaching.

Complexities of Students' Lives

In addition to the growing diversity of students and families, many societal factors contribute to the complexities of students' lives today and make teaching a more challenging profession (see Chapter 12 for more information). These factors include poverty, teen pregnancy, AIDS/HIV, child abuse and neglect, suicide, violence, alcohol and drug abuse, and school dropouts. Teachers cannot be expected to solve these complex problems on their own, but they need to be aware of the extent of the problems and contribute time and energy when possible in an effort to help students and their families find solutions.

The students in Jim Masterson's high school chemistry classes exemplify the many complex issues that students face. Four seniors were recently arrested outside the high school gym during a basketball game for substance abuse. Three were caught drinking beer and the fourth was smoking marijuana. A junior in one of his classes tried to commit suicide and needs to be watched carefully for any signs that might indicate another imminent attempt. Jim also reported one suspected case of child abuse early in the school year when a sophomore student came to class with unexplained bruising on his arms and face. In addition, one of his students is an unmarried teen mother. The father is also a member of the same chemistry class. Think about your personal beliefs and how you would feel as a teacher working in this classroom setting.

Although it should be clear that Jim cannot expect to fully resolve any of these difficult issues on his own, he can work to support and encourage students as opportunities arise. For example, he made a point to work harder to understand and relate to the student who had tried to commit suicide. As he gathered additional information, Jim found that she was frustrated with her chemistry assignments and needed additional help in completing them. He suggested an after-school tutoring session with two other classmates and the student agreed. Jim checks in with her regularly to see if there is anything else he can do to help her feel better about her academic accomplishments. The extra attention has helped her open up a bit more and she is starting to share with her tutors some of the frustrations she has had in her home life.

Increasing Societal Expectations

Another challenge facing teachers today is the increasing number of expectations being placed on them by community, state, and federal groups. In addition to the expectation that teachers assist students in dealing with the kinds of social forces described above, four other pressures are adding new challenges to working with students:

- Teaching special-needs children in the regular classroom
- Increasing graduation rates
- Expanding the teaching role
- Helping students develop stronger skills in core academic areas

The first of these challenges is brought about because of the effort to *include students with special needs* in the classroom. The passage of several pieces of federal legislation during the past 30 years has led to growing numbers of students with special needs being placed in regular education classrooms. Although there are many benefits to this approach for teachers and all students, it also brings new challenges. For example, despite the fact that most teachers have had only limited training in working with students with special needs, they are expected to plan activities for them when they are in the regular classroom.

Another expectation that teachers must address is the pressure to *increase graduation rates.* Teachers at all levels are being encouraged to do everything they can to keep students in school through high school graduation. Despite the fact that graduation rates have increased significantly during the past 50 years (see Table 1.5), the pressure is on to help every student receive a high school diploma. What this means is that some students who would have opted out of formal education to join the workforce in the past are now expected to stay in school. Many of these students are more difficult to teach for a variety of reasons: they may have learning difficulties, lack the motivation to learn, and/or are unable to see the relevance of the learning activities presented.

A third expectation that may increase teacher stress comes from an *expansion of the teaching role.* For a variety of reasons, many teachers today are expected to teach an expanded curriculum. At the elementary level, for example, the social issues referred to above have made it necessary for teachers and schools to take the lead in educating students in new ways. Some examples of this are sex-education units, discussions about the problems of drug use, helping students develop strong self-esteem, and the implementation of violence-prevention programs.

A final pressure that teachers face today is to *help students develop greater proficiency in basic skills.* At the same time that teachers are expected to do everything they can to keep students in school, they are asked to help them develop stronger skills in core curriculum areas such as science, mathematics, social studies, and literacy. Individual state governments and the legislative branch of the federal government are consistently mandating higher standards that students must meet to move through the educational system. In many states, students who fail to

TABLE 1.5   High School Completion Rates

Year	Percentage of students who graduated
1910	13.5%
1940	38%
1970	55%
1988	86%
1994	88%
1999	90%

From: McLaughlin, M. (1990). *High school dropouts: How much of a crisis?* Washington, D.C.: The Heritage Foundation; and Annie E. Casey Foundation. (2004). *Kids count data book.* Baltimore, MD: Author.

meet targeted levels of achievement are forced to take summer school programs or are retained in a grade so that they can have additional time to develop the needed skills. Teacher and school performance ratings are also being tied to the success rates of students as measured on tests of basic skills.

Each of the societal expectations described above strengthens the need for teachers to use active reflection as they plan and implement daily learning experiences. For example, the inclusion of special-needs students in classrooms means that teachers will need to gather new information about each special-needs student by talking to other specialists and searching available academic resources. Teachers must also be sure to identify and reflect on their personal attitudes about working with special populations so that these beliefs do not hamper effective student learning.

Occupational Status

Another challenge you will face if you choose to enter teaching relates to the attitudes of others toward education as a profession. Unfortunately, many people still view teaching as a rather easy job that requires only minimal academic preparation and limited skills in working with people. Those who have not experienced the challenges of the classroom often fail to see the true complexities of teaching. This fairly common attitude can be summarized in the often-heard phrase "those who can't, teach." The assumption inherent in this statement is that people who enter the teaching profession would probably be unsuccessful in other occupations and therefore choose the "easy" task of teaching.

Ayers (2001) provides three indicators of the low status of teaching as a career. One that has already been mentioned is the issue of *salary*. The relatively low pay of teachers may well reflect the general attitude of society toward the education profession. A second indicator is the *high percentage of women* in the profession. Because men have historically dominated virtually every high-status occupation, teaching was one of a limited number of alternatives open to women. The third indicator of the low occupational status of teachers is the attempts by many to *make curriculum materials "teacher-proof."* By providing a teacher's guide with step-by-step directions and frequently even the words teachers should use in instruction, many publishers of teachers' guides are implying that educators lack the skills needed to design lessons and activities on their own.

Lack of Support

A final challenge that faces many teachers entering the profession is the low level of economic and emotional support they receive as educators. Economic support for teaching covers such things as money to purchase teaching materials, equipment, and supplies used in the classroom. For example, the costs associated with a textbook series to teach a single high school subject such as biology can run several thousand dollars. Not surprisingly, it is difficult for school districts to continually update these books and, consequently, teachers must often make do with materials that are out of date. Equipment for use in the classroom, ranging from such things as computers and high-power microscopes to maps, is often in short supply due to limited budgets for these items. Even regular consumable materials such as test tubes, petri dishes, and chemical supplies for science laboratories may be difficult to purchase in some schools facing tight financial constraints. Teachers often find it necessary to dip into their own pockets for the money needed to support the many interesting projects they want to bring into the classroom. As one first-year teacher put it: "The students are so needy. And, there's no budget. I had to do everything without money and beg, borrow, or steal" (DePaul, 1998, p. 3). Although this lack of support is real, many teachers are finding creative ways of dealing with the problem. Writing small grants for money and materials from state agencies and corporations, asking parents for support in developing needed curriculum materials, and working with local community businesses are some of the many options available to you.

In addition to the low level of economic support for materials and supplies, most teachers find that it can be lonely in the classroom, with few opportunities to discuss successes and problems with others. Although other teachers and administrators are well meaning and would truly like to spend time assisting you and others with the difficult tasks that will help you grow into strong teachers, the realities of teaching are such that there is little time to engage in this kind of support and encouragement. One first-year teacher, when asked if she felt isolated, responded: "Not physically, but certainly mentally. Sure, the other teachers are nice. But they didn't seem to want to get to know me or make sure everything was going OK" (Boss, 2001, p. 3). The establishment of teacher mentoring programs (see Chapter 15 for more information) is one recent development that is designed to provide new teachers with more effective support and encouragement.

Think about the challenges described in this section. What are your initial reactions? Do you get energized or discouraged? Would you envision yourself getting up each day excited about the prospects of facing complex intellectual and social issues or does this scenario make you feel overwhelmed? Continue to reflect on these issues as you read more about these topics in future chapters. If you consistently respond to these challenges without becoming overwhelmed or discouraged, then teaching is more likely to be a fulfilling profession for you.

Reflection Opportunity 1.4

Should I become a teacher?

As indicated earlier in this chapter, people choose the teaching profession for many different reasons. Despite the significant challenges that every teacher must face, the benefits make it a very attractive option for many people. Sharon Draper, the 1997 National Teacher of the Year, wrote in a letter to prospective new teachers:

> As you consider teaching as a career, I'd like to offer my own personal response to teaching as a profession. My students often ask me, "Why are you a teacher?" implying that teaching is a terrible career choice. I tell them in response, "I teach because I need you as much as you need me. I teach because once upon a time a teacher made a difference in my life, so I am here to make a difference for you." . . . I never wavered in my desires and determination to become not just a teacher, but a really good teacher who made memories in the minds of children . . . I continued to try to make a difference—one child at a time. For our greatest accomplishments in education are not the plaques and awards, but the smiles and hugs and memories of children touched today and somehow influenced tomorrow. (Council of Chief State School Officers, 2008, p. 20)

Sharon Draper's passion and commitment to teaching are clearly evident in the above letter. Not all who enter the profession, however, find this level of fulfillment. And because teacher preparation is a long and arduous task, you should make every effort to determine as early as possible whether or not teaching is the career path for you. Although some people "just know" from a very early age that teaching is where they are to be, most future educators need to spend a significant amount of time and energy thoughtfully considering life in the classroom before they can make the right decision about teaching as a career. Use the active reflection process described earlier in this chapter and summarized in Figure 1.2 to gather more information about teaching, identify your beliefs about teaching and learning, make and implement decisions, and assess and evaluate the decisions you make.

Gather Information

One way in which you can gather information about teaching as a career is to observe teachers as they engage in their craft. Unfortunately, it is not always convenient to travel to the schools. If you do have the opportunity, however, consider taking time now to see first hand what teaching is really like.

Another strategy that you can use to gather further information about teaching as a career is to think about the motives you have for considering the education profession. A decision about a career is a complicated one that is seldom based on a single motive, but rather is a mix of factors that come together to guide one's choice. As you read further in this chapter, try to make sense of your own motives for considering teaching as a career. If you are approaching education for the right reasons, it is much more likely that you will find the profession a satisfying one and students will learn and grow from their interactions with you.

The positive reasons for entering teaching closely parallel the benefits of being an educator described in an earlier section of this chapter. They include an excitement for the teaching–learning process, acceptance and adaptation to the teaching lifestyle, interest and expertise in the subject being taught, and caring for and connecting with the clientele. Table 1.6 provides a summary of these motives. All four are important for successful teaching. It is difficult to imagine, for example, that a person could be successful in the classroom without getting significant pleasure from the many daily interactions a teacher has with students. Similarly, if you don't get excited by the content you teach, each day would be hard to endure rather than a stimulating experience. What does vary from one teacher to the next, however, is the relative strength of each of these motives. Some may see assisting students in

TABLE 1.6 Motives for Teaching

Excitement and intrigue with the teaching–learning process.	The teacher finds it very rewarding to help others learn. Learning is viewed as a process and it is understood and appreciated that each person learns differently. The teacher sees him/herself as a learner as well and enjoys the role of student as much as the role of teacher.
Acceptance of and adaptation to the teaching lifestyle.	The teacher appreciates the public life of being a teacher. He/she sees teachers as being leaders in the community. The teacher actually enjoys putting in the extra hours necessary for effective assessment and planning. He/she is able to balance teaching responsibilities with a personal life outside of school.
Interest and expertise in the subject being taught.	The teacher has a passion for the subject matter he/she is teaching. He/she is very proficient in the subject and is continually learning more about the subject. He/she believes that his/her subject is relevant and important to students.
Caring for and connection with the clientele.	The teacher enjoys the group of students he/she is assigned to teach. He/she appreciates the unique characteristics of this specific group (e.g., students with special needs, students living in poverty, students who are English-language learners, students who are Native American, students who are incarcerated, middle school students, etc.).

TABLE 1.7 Skills Influencing Teaching

Skill	Examples
People Skills	Seeing the perspectives of others Remaining calm in emotional situations Getting along with others Looking for the best in others
Organizational Skills	Giving clear directions Anticipating steps to accomplish tasks Managing time efficiently Keeping effective records
Intellectual and Linguistic Skills	Understanding the subject(s) to be taught Using effective verbal communications Using effective written communications

their growth and development as the most important reason to teach, whereas others may find a shared love of learning to be a highly motivating reason to teach.

Another important area in which you can gather information that can be used to determine if teaching is a good career option is to carefully consider the skills that you bring to the profession and the impact these personal characteristics may have on your potential effectiveness as a teacher. You may want to organize your thinking by considering three broad categories of skills that can have a far-reaching influence on your success as a future teacher (see Table 1.7). The first of these is your people skills. Because teaching is about working with people, you will need the ability to establish and maintain strong relationships with others. A second broad category is your organizational skills. Teachers need to think carefully about the ways in which they organize and present the concepts to be learned in their classrooms. In addition, effective organizational skills are needed in such areas as planning the school day, providing equitable interactions with all students, and developing meaningful assessments of student progress. Third, you will need strong intellectual and linguistic skills to understand and effectively communicate the concepts to be shared with students. To watch an interview with a first year teacher, go to the Companion Website for this text and click on MyEducationLab for Chapter 1.

While this issue is fresh in your mind, consider taking a few moments to make a list of the skills you would bring to the teaching profession. As you reflect on the list you created, what impact do you think each of these items might have on the ways in which you teach? You may also want to discuss your skills with classmates or a current teacher to gain further insights about their potential impact on your role as a teacher.

Identify Beliefs

As indicated earlier, your own past experiences as a learner have helped shape your current beliefs about teaching and learning. The successes and failures you have had, the interactions you have had with teachers, and the influence of significant others in your growing-up years have led to your current belief system. Some of these beliefs may change as you learn and grow in future interactions with others. Taken together, these personal beliefs are important indicators of your potential for success as a future teacher. Your beliefs about subject matter, students, learning, and self all influence the decisions you will make in the classroom. These beliefs are summarized in Table 1.8.

Your beliefs about the subjects you teach influence not only the specifics of what you teach and how, but also significantly affect student enthusiasm for these subjects. When you view

MyEducationLab 1.2

**Reflection
Opportunity 1.5**

TABLE 1.8   Beliefs Influencing Teaching

Belief	Description
Beliefs About Subject Matter	• Subject-matter knowledge not fixed, but complex and evolving • Knowledge is developed from the vantage point of the learner • Subject matter is intellectually interesting
Beliefs About Students	• Students have diverse talents that should be respected • All students can learn • Students should be respected as individuals
Beliefs About Learning	• Learning should be intrinsically motivated • Establishing a climate for effective learning is essential • Students learn in different ways
Beliefs Regarding Self	• Values critical thinking • Committed to lifelong learning • Willing to grow personally and professionally • Seeks help from others

subject matter as intellectually stimulating, students are much more likely to feel the same way. A second set of beliefs that directly influences your teaching are those you hold about students. If you truly believe that all students can learn and that each student brings a unique set of talents to the learning situation, there is a much greater likelihood that quality learning will occur in your classroom. Thirdly, your beliefs about learning also influence your effectiveness as an educator. Good teachers see the importance of creating the right climate for learning and recognize that students learn in different ways. Finally, your beliefs about yourself impact your teaching. Valuing critical thinking and wanting to learn and grow throughout your life are important beliefs associated with effective teachers.

Consider taking some time to reflect on the contents of Table 1.8. What subject matter areas do you enjoy and why? Do you truly believe that all children can learn? At this point, what do you believe about learning? Can you identify beliefs about yourself that may impact your future role as a teacher? Are there specific individuals in your life that have influenced the beliefs you currently hold that influence teaching? What were these people like?

Reflection Opportunity 1.6

Make and Implement Decisions

Although you do not need to make and implement a final decision now regarding teaching as a career, you may consider taking some actions that can help you make a more informed decision in the future. One strategy you may wish to consider implementing is to spend time observing and working in school settings. This kind of first-hand experience will provide you with practical information about what it is really like in the classroom. You may want to consider spending time observing and working in a broad range of classrooms so that you have a more complete picture of teaching in k–12 schools. Another decision you could make is to spend time talking with teachers and administrators in the field. Educators from your local community are often willing to spend time talking about their work in schools. They can provide you with additional insights about both the positive and negative aspects of a career in education. A third possible strategy you could implement is to commit to reading the stories of inspirational educators so that you can gather further insights about teaching. For example, the book by Esmé Codell (1999), titled *Educating Esmé,* paints a clear picture of what one beginning teacher in an inner-city school experienced. Reading this book would provide you with additional thoughts about a career in education. You can undoubtedly think of other strategies on your own that would help you in this decision-making process. As you implement these options and others, you will add information and insights that will allow you eventually to make the best possible decision about teaching as a future career.

Assess and Evaluate

The decision to become a teacher is not one to be taken lightly. Teachers have the potential to impact the lives of large numbers of students over the courses of their careers. Take, for example, a secondary educator who teaches five periods a day with an average of 25 students in each class. Each term, that teacher works with approximately 125 students. Multiplied by three terms a year and a career that could span 30 years or more, this educator has the opportunity to influence the lives of over 100,000 students. Although elementary teachers work with fewer students, they can often develop stronger relationships with their students and have an even greater impact on their lives. Because of this potential to positively or negatively influence so many students, every prospective teacher should seriously weigh all the variables so that he or she can make the best decision about teaching as a career.

Take a few moments now to assess and evaluate the information you have collected from reading this chapter. Open your Reflections Journal or the on-line version found on the Companion Website for this text and respond to the following questions. Based on the information you have about teaching as a career, your current understanding of your beliefs about teaching and learning, and past experiences as a learner, what would be your current answer to the question: Should I be a teacher? Do you believe you have the basic skills and personal beliefs needed to be an effective teacher? What additional information will you need to refine your assessment of your potential as a future teacher?

Each chapter of this text has another feature called *Consider This* found on the Companion Website for this text. It is designed to give you another opportunity to reflect on a portion of the content presented in the chapter and enables you to develop a deeper understanding of an aspect of teaching and learning. As you think about chapter content, the feature will continually prompt you to refine your response to questions of the following type: Why do I want to be a teacher? What kind of a teacher do I want to be? The *Consider This* feature for this chapter asks you to rate motivations to teach. You may want to read the feature now and think about your personal responses to the issues presented.

**Reflection
Opportunity 1.7**

**Consider This:
Motivations to Teach**

Summary

In this chapter, four organizing questions were used to help you think carefully about teaching as a future career:

What is teaching really like?

Teaching is much more complex than most people believe it to be. It is a combination of the following:

- Challenging work
- Decision making through active reflection (Praxis II, topic IV)

- Regulation and freedom (Praxis II, topic IVa)
- An art
- A science (Praxis II, topic II)
- Lifelong learning

What are the benefits of being a teacher?

Many positive benefits accrue from a career in teaching:
- The joy of teaching
- Personal growth
- Serving students, families, and community
- Schedule and job benefits

How significant are the challenges?

Although teaching has many benefits, every educator also faces challenges:
- The diverse student population
- Complexities of students' lives
- Increasing societal expectations
- Occupational status
- Lack of support

Should I become a teacher?

As you begin to think about the possibility of teaching as a career, it is important to use a variety of strategies to clarify your perspectives:
- Gather information
- Identify beliefs
- Make and implement decisions
- Assess and evaluate

PRAXIS   Test-Preparation Activities

 To review an on-line chapter case study, test your understanding of chapter topics and concepts, and begin preparing for the Praxis II: Principles of Learning and Teaching examination, go to the Praxis Test Preparation module for this chapter of the Companion Website.

inTASC   Developing the Habit of Reflective Practice

Organizing Questions

Review questions, field-experience opportunities, and activities for building your portfolio are included here for the organizing questions in this chapter.

What is teaching really like?

Review Questions

1. What are three characteristics of active reflection?
2. What are the key components of active reflection?
3. How are teachers both independent and connected with others?
4. What are the phases in learning to teach?

Field Experience

Find a teacher who is working at a grade level that may be of interest to you and spend time discussing education with that person.

- Ask for information on why he or she entered the profession.
- Also find out what this person sees as the benefits and challenges of teaching.
- Write a summary of your interview and share with others the insights developed from your discussion.
- How did the teacher's responses affect your feelings or motivation for becoming a teacher?

Building Your Portfolio: *Experiences with Students*

INTASC Standard 2. Identify all experiences you have had to date working with students.

- These experiences need not be in formal educational settings and should include babysitting, summer camps, and past jobs that have allowed you opportunities to interact with preschool through high school students.
- Give detailed information that includes the approximate dates, kinds of experiences, and the names of any contact people who could help clarify the tasks you performed.
- In a separate document, briefly describe something you gained from each experience, and consider how these experiences can contribute to your success as a teacher.
- Plan to update this portfolio entry as you engage in new experiences with students.

What are the benefits of being a teacher?

Review Questions

1. What are the two components associated with a love of teaching?
2. How would you define *vocation?*
3. What are the job benefits that most teachers find attractive?

Field Experience

Talk to four or five adults who do not work in school settings.

- Ask them to identify another occupation or two that they think requires skills comparable to those of teaching. Probe to find out why they feel this way.
- Also ask these adults to describe their views on the importance of teaching to the greater society.
- Once you have collected this information, spend some time reflecting on your findings. From your discussions, what other occupations were identified as requiring skills similar to those of teachers?
- What does this experience tell you about the status of teaching? How did these adults view the importance of teaching? Discuss what you found with others.

Building Your Portfolio: *A Case for Teaching*

INTASC Standard 9. Based on your current understandings of education, make the strongest/ most persuasive case you can for someone else becoming a teacher.

- What do you see as the potential benefits?
- How can the problems be minimized?
- Make sure you include in the rationale your understanding of the importance of teachers to society at large. Revisit your response after you have read the last chapter of this text.

How significant are the challenges?

Review Questions

1. Describe the diversity you can expect to find in American schools.
2. What are some of the stresses students face?
3. How are societal expectations for teachers and schools changing?

Building Your Portfolio: *Special Talents*

INTASC Standard 9. One thing that may help you make a decision about teaching as a career is to think about the special talents you possess that would help you meet the challenges of being a teacher.

- Create a list in which you identify special talents you have and describe how they could be put to use in the classroom.
- There are many possibilities for this list, including athletic skills/experiences, musical and/or artistic talents, writing skills, special aptitudes in subject-matter areas, theatrical skills, speaking abilities, and other hobbies or talents.

Should I become a teacher?

Review Questions

1. What personal skills and beliefs are important for you to have as a future teacher?
2. Identify the positive motives for entering the profession.

Building Your Portfolio: *Perceptions of Others*

INTASC Standard 9. Select four or five friends and/or family members and ask them for an honest assessment of why they think you should or should not consider teaching as a career.

- Have them identify specific personality characteristics that they think would enhance your chances of success in the classroom as well as those that may cause you difficulties. Record their responses.
- Honestly assess yourself in the same manner and record your responses.
- Carefully consider the responses of your friends and family and compare them with your own responses. Summarize your findings along with any insights you gained into your potential as a future teacher.

Suggested Readings

Ayers, W. (2001). *To teach: The journey of a teacher* (2nd ed.). New York: Teachers College Press. This book challenges teachers and teachers-to-be to emphasize caring and giving in their relationships with students at the same time that they help develop academic and life skills. The author makes it clear that although excellent teaching is a constant challenge, it can also be one of the most rewarding of professions.

Barone, T. (2001). *Touching eternity: The enduring outcomes of teaching.* New York: Teachers College Press. The author of this book emphasizes the positive long-term impact that good teachers have on their students. A case study of a high school art teacher and his former students is used to help the reader reflect on the importance of highly effective teachers in American society.

Graves, D. (2001). *The energy to teach.* Portsmouth, NH: Heinemann. The basic premise of this book is that quality teaching requires a great deal of energy. Although many people enter the profession with a strong commitment to students and a willingness to expend the energy necessary to be successful, many end up feeling worn out. Graves provides encouragement to teachers by helping them understand what they can do to get the energy they need to be successful and what actions or activities they should avoid so that they will not end up physically and emotionally exhausted.

Levine, S. (Ed.). (1999). *A passion for teaching.* Alexandria, VA: Association for Supervision and Curriculum Development. This edited book contains a wealth of stories and poems from master teachers that describe the reasons for their continued passion for teaching. Reading them helps clarify the many positive benefits of the teaching profession.

References

American Federation of Teachers. (2007). *Survey and analysis of teacher salary trends.* Washington, D.C.: Author

Ayers, W. (2001). *To teach: The journey of a teacher* (2nd ed.). New York: Teachers College Press.

Banner, J., & Cannon, H. (1999). *The elements of teaching.* New Haven, CT: Yale University Press.

Boss, S. (2001). Facing the future. *Northwest Education, 7*(2), 3–9 and 41.

Codell, E. (1999). *Educating Esmé. Diary of a teacher's first year.* Chapel Hill, NC: Algonquin Books.

Council of Chief State School Officers. (2008). *Voices for the future.* Retrieved 2008, from *http://www.ccsso.org/projects/National_Teacher_of_the_Year/Voices_for_the_Future/*.

Cruickshank, D. (1987). *Reflective teaching. The preparation of students of teaching.* Reston, VA: Association of Teacher Educators.

DePaul, A. (1998). *What to expect your first year of teaching.* Washington, DC: U.S. Department of Education.

Dewey, J. (1933). *How we think: A restatement of the relationship of reflective thinking to the educative process.* Boston: D.C. Heath and Company.

Eby, J., & Herrell, A. (2009). *Teaching in the elementary school. A reflective action approach.* (5th edition). Columbus, OH: Merrill.

Educational Testing Service. (2008). *Praxis II overview.* Princeton, NJ: Author. Retrieved October 7, 2008, from *http://www.ets.org/*.

Farkas, S., Johnson, J., & Duffett, A. (2003). *Stand by me.* New York: Public Agenda.

Feiman-Nemser, S. (1999). *From preparation to practice: Designing a continuum to strengthen and sustain teaching.* New York: Supporting and Strengthening Teaching Project.

Fosnot, C. (1989). *Enquiring teachers, enquiring learners: A constructivist approach to teaching.* New York: Teachers College Press.

Hansen, D. (1995). *The call to teach.* New York: Teachers College Press.

Hansen, D. (2001). *Exploring the moral heart of teaching.* New York: Teachers College Press.

Levine, S. (Ed.). (1999). *A passion for teaching.* Alexandria, VA: Association for Supervision and Curriculum Development.

Marzano, R., Pickering, D., & Pollock, J. (2001). *Classroom instruction that works: Research-based strategies for increasing student achievement.* Alexandria, VA: Association for Supervision and Curriculum Development.

National Education Association. (2005). *Rankings and estimates.* Washington, D.C.: Author.

Nelson, F., Drown, R., & Gould, J. (2002). *Survey and analysis of teacher salary trends 2001.* Washington, D.C.: American Federation of Teachers.

Palmer, P. (1998). *The courage to teach.* San Francisco: Jossey-Bass.

Reagan, T., Case, C., & Brubacher, J. (2000). *Becoming a reflective educator* (2nd ed.). Thousand Oaks, CA: Corwin Press.

Shulman, L. (1987). Knowledge and teaching: Foundations of the new reform. *Harvard Educational Review, 57*(1), 1–22.

Think about the diversity encountered in your own k–12 learning experiences. Were they more or less diverse than Kathy Klein's classroom described above? Depending on the level of diversity experienced, do you think you will be more or less receptive to diversity in your own classroom? Do you expect the students you teach in the future to be more or less diverse than the ones in Kathy's classroom? Is the diversity described here something that excites you or makes you nervous? Describe the feelings you have.

As we begin the 21st century, a very visible change that is taking place in America's schools is the growing **diversity** of students and their families. From rural America to the big city, schools are no longer populated with primarily White, Anglo-Saxon, Christian students of average and above-average abilities. Less than half of today's children come from two-parent homes in which dad earns a wage and mom raises the children (Annie E. Casey Foundation, 2008). Students bring diverse languages, income levels, cultural traditions, sexual orientations, religions, family support systems, learning styles, and abilities to the classroom. Although student diversity adds complexities to the teaching role, it also creates an even more stimulating teaching and learning environment and provides greater rewards for those who rise to the challenges presented.

What differences (and similarities) among people influence interactions in the classroom?

Before beginning a discussion of the differences that you will find among students in your future classroom, it may be important to take a moment and reflect on the many similarities that also exist. To personalize this issue, think about someone you currently know or have known reasonably well who is of a different race, sex, sexual orientation, or ability. What does this person have in common with you? Construct a list of similarities. Are there things you both like or dislike? Do you share some common values with this person? What shared experiences have you both had? If you think hard, it is likely that you will construct a fairly long list of things that you both have in common. This person who is different from you in some significant way is also much the same.

In much the same way, the students you will teach have a great deal in common with each other and with you, despite the differences that exist. They have many similar needs, interests, experiences, and attitudes. For example, Chapter 6 describes several common student needs that influence learning, such as the need to belong and to feel safe and secure. Even though students are different in many ways, it is important to remember first the many ways in which they are all alike.

In addition to remembering the similarities that all students share, please realize that the information presented here describes in general terms the conditions of different groups of students found in American schools. Although it is useful to be aware of these averages and percentages, students in your future classrooms will be unique individuals and will seldom neatly fit the national norms being shared here. Your job as a teacher is to balance an understanding of this general information with the more-specific knowledge gathered about each of the individual students you teach. As you gather new information about student similarities and differences and actively reflect on it, you will develop important insights that significantly influence your plans for teaching and learning.

Race and Ethnicity

Racial and ethnic differences between people have had a long-standing impact on interactions in the classroom. The term **race** refers to the category to which people assign individuals on the basis of physical characteristics, such as skin color or hair type, and the generalizations and stereotypes made as a result. Although diverse definitions exist, **ethnicity** may be defined as the identification with population groups characterized by common ancestry, language, and customs.

The U.S. Census Bureau has traditionally identified five main racial groups: Caucasian (White), Hispanic, African American (Black), Asian, and Native American. More recently, these racial categories have been called into question, in part because so many people do not readily fit into a single racial category. Despite this blurring of the lines between groups, race continues to be one of the most powerful and destructive forms of social categorization. Landsman (2004), for example, describes interviews with school administrators and teachers where she learned that many adults have low expectations for students of color, particularly Black and Latino students. These racist attitudes seriously impact students' opportunities for success in school:

> Principals have told me about teachers who say openly that black boys are impossible to work with because they are hyperactive and uncontrollable. These same teachers ignore the behavior of white boys who are acting out. Teachers have told me that they avoid their faculty lounge because the talk behind closed doors is offensive to them, full of negative assumptions based on race. One teacher told me that it is like "witnessing the chances for kids diminish right before your eyes." (p. 28)

Studies of population trends indicate that racial and ethnic diversity in the United States has grown dramatically in the last several decades and is projected to change even more in the years ahead (Forum on Child and Family Statistics, 2008). One reason for these changes is that birth rates vary between subgroups within our country. For example, birth rates for Hispanic women in the United States are higher than those for African American women, which in turn are higher than those for Whites (U.S. Census Bureau, 2004). The second main reason for this growth in diversity is the continued immigration of people from around the world to the United States. Whereas earlier immigrant populations came primarily from European countries, larger numbers are now entering the United States from Asia and Central and South America. For both of the above reasons, then, the projected percentage of the total U.S. population who will be non-White will increase by the year 2050 from approximately 19 percent currently to nearly 28 percent (U.S. Census Bureau, 2004). These population trends are having a significant impact on racial and ethnic diversity in the schools.

Looking more specifically at the racial composition of classrooms (see Figure 2.1), population statistics indicate that the percentage of U.S. children of color has increased during the last several decades and will continue to increase in the years ahead (U.S. Census Bureau, 2004). In many urban areas such as Chicago, New York, and Los Angeles, students of color already make up more than 50% of the student population in many schools. The large numbers of immigrants and high birth rates of Hispanic families have led to rapid growth in the Hispanic student population. At the same time, growth in the African American student population is less than that for other groups, and their percentage of the total population is projected to remain relatively constant in the next two decades. Similarly, the percentage of American Indian/Alaska native students should remain relatively constant. Finally, the number of Asian and Pacific Islander students, while small, is expected to grow by 50% by the year 2020 (U.S. Census Bureau, 2004).

This increasing racial diversity of schools and classrooms has led to significant changes in what is taught. For example, it is important for teachers to help students understand the important similarities and differences that exist among students from different racial and ethnic groups and assist them with communicating and interacting in positive ways. Teachers must also be aware of the perspectives and contributions of different racial groups to American life and share this information with students. These strategies and others are part of what has come to be called **culturally responsive teaching.** More will be said about this important component of teaching later in the chapter.

When addressing the diverse races and ethnicities represented in our schools, some people refer to this phenomenon as a melting pot. Most educators do not use this term, nor advocate for what this term implies. A **melting pot** is a metaphor for the way in which heterogeneous societies develop, in which the ingredients in the pot are processed until they lose their unique identities and yield a final product of uniform consistency and flavor, but which is quite different from the original ingredients. Educators do not aim to make all students similar—but rather to build tolerance within the school community and create an educational environment that accepts and celebrates

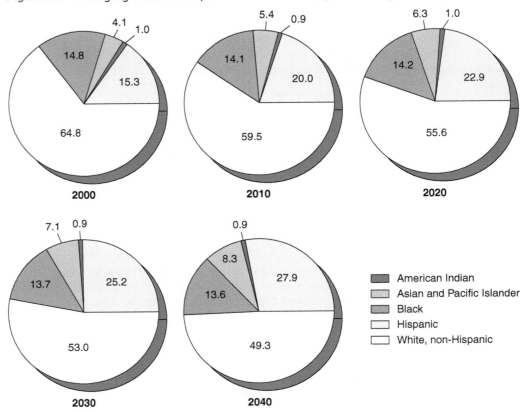

Figure 2.1 Changing Racial Composition of Schools, by Percentage, 2000–2040

Legend:
- American Indian
- Asian and Pacific Islander
- Black
- Hispanic
- White, non-Hispanic

2000
- 4.1
- 1.0
- 14.8
- 15.3
- 64.8

2010
- 5.4
- 0.9
- 14.1
- 20.0
- 59.5

2020
- 6.3
- 1.0
- 14.2
- 22.9
- 55.6

2030
- 7.1
- 0.9
- 13.7
- 25.2
- 53.0

2040
- 0.9
- 8.3
- 13.6
- 27.9
- 49.3

Note: Percentages for 2010 and 2030 do not equal 100% due to rounding.
Source: National Population Projections, by U.S. Census Bureau, 2003. Retrieved March 13, 2003, from *http://www.census.gov/population/www/projections/natproj.html*

MyEducationLab 2.1

differences. Assimilation can have negative implications for minority cultures, causing the distinctive features of the minority culture to be minimized and even disappear altogether. Educators today aim for **cultural pluralism,** which is a viewpoint that emphasizes and encourages acceptance of the unique characteristics of each culture, aiming to address similarities and differences between groups of people. To watch a video interview of a Laotian high school student and her mother, go to the Companion Website for this text and click on MyEducationLab for Chapter 2.

Gender

There is little question that male students differ from their female counterparts in many of their emotional, social, and behavioral traits. From pre-kindergarten settings through high school grades and beyond, male and female students are very different in terms of temperament, interests, and needs. Educators seem to agree that these differences are influenced by society, culture, and educational experiences. Some researchers like Leonard Sax, a physician and psychologist, purport that there are distinct genetic differences in the way male and female brains function. In his book, *Why Gender Matters* (2005), he states that boys seem to benefit from math instruction that uses a straightforward presentation of numbers from the beginning. Sax goes on to say that girls use a different portion of their brain to perform mathematical operations and benefit from mathematical exercises that are more connected to language.

Another gender-related issue brought about by the women's movement and gender-related federal legislation is the need for schools to treat boys and girls more equitably. Although much progress has been made in this regard, subtle forms of gender bias still exist within American society and the schools. For example, the American Association of University Women (AAUW) published a controversial report in 1992 that described how girls were being shortchanged in American schools. They stated that girls "do not receive equitable amounts of teacher attention, they are less apt than boys to see themselves reflected in the materials they study, and they often are not expected or encouraged to pursue higher-level mathematics and science courses" (p. 147). This report and the research on which it was based led to a renewed emphasis by the schools to provide more equitable educational opportunities for girls. It appears that efforts in this area are beginning to close the gender gap, particularly in the sciences (Sanders and Nelson, 2004). Girls are more likely than before to excel in mathematics and most sciences. More girls than ever before are enrolling in college. In fact, females outnumber male graduates in 4-year university degrees. However, women still lag behind in high-tech degrees.

Although most of the research and writing to date has focused on educational inequities for girls, concern for boys and their performance is growing (Gurian and Stevens, 2004). Boys get poorer grades than girls in school, drop out more frequently, and are referred to special education classes more often. Furthermore, boys score considerably lower than girls on national reading tests and are 5–10 times more likely to be disciplined in elementary and middle school (Pollack, 1998). School personnel will need to work hard to make sure that boys are more successful in these problem areas. Because boys tend to have a strong interest and aptitude in computer technology, some teachers are integrating the use of computers into subjects where boys tend to lag behind girls. It has also been found that boys tend to learn best when they are allowed to move around and manipulate objects (Grubb, 2001).

Learning Styles

Strategies used by students to actually gather and internalize information about the world will vary between individuals. These **learning styles** are important for you to understand as you plan lessons and activities for the classroom. Learning styles are simply different approaches or ways of learning. Many educators break learning styles into three categories: visual learners, auditory learners, and tactile/kinesthetic learners. Of course, all learners use visual cues, auditory information, and kinesthetic experiences to receive information (unless a disability prevents this). However, one or more of these receiving styles is normally dominant. This dominant style defines the best way for a person to learn new information by filtering what is to be learned. This style may not always be the same for all tasks. The learner may prefer one style of learning for one task and a combination of others for another task. Visual learners learn through seeing. These learners need to see the teacher's body language and facial expression to fully understand the content of a lesson. They tend to prefer sitting at the front of the classroom to avoid visual obstructions (e.g., people's heads). They may think in pictures and learn best from visual displays including diagrams and videos. During a lecture or classroom discussion, visual learners often prefer to take detailed notes to absorb the information. Auditory learners learn through listening. They learn best through verbal lectures and discussions. Auditory learners are quite skilled at interpreting the underlying meanings of speech through listening to tone of voice, pitch, speed, and other nuances. Written information may have little meaning until it is heard. These learners often benefit from reading text aloud and using a tape recorder. Tactile/kinesthetic learners learn through moving, doing and touching. Tactile/kinesthetic persons learn best through a hands-on approach, actively exploring the physical world around them. They may find it hard to sit still for long periods and may become distracted by their need for activity and exploration.

Information on learning styles is important to your future teaching because it helps explain why students are so very different in the ways they learn. Knowing about these differences allows teachers to plan a variety of experiences to take advantage of these styles. For example, a teacher discussing a medieval play could use a PowerPoint slide show to attract the interest of visual learners, small-group discussions for those who prefer an auditory mode for learning, and sample costumes with a role play for those who benefit from kinesthetic experiences.

Sexual Orientation

Another important and highly controversial difference that exists between people concerns their sexual orientation. It is highly likely that in addition to the many **heterosexual** students in your classrooms, you will either teach **gay** and **lesbian** students or work with parents with these sexual orientations. For example, Matt is a typical 11th-grade student in many ways. He is doing well in all his classes, is well-liked by his peers, and participates in two varsity sports. Yet, Matt is different in one significant way—he is gay. Although he has not openly admitted his sexual preference to his friends, recent experiences with other young men have made it clear to Matt that he is definitely gay. Having developed a particularly strong relationship with his French teacher, Matt has shared his hopes, dreams, and fears with her. He has felt considerable relief in being able to share this part of himself with another person. Matt is thinking about talking to his parents and is also wondering if he should share his sexual orientation with some of his closest friends. Although there are undoubtedly many students like Matt in today's schools, it is difficult to estimate the percentages of the population who are either gay or lesbian due to the powerful stigma attached to homosexuality and the tendency of this group to remain silent concerning their sexual orientation. Data, for example, regarding the numbers of gay and lesbian families varies from approximately two million to as many as eight million families (National Gay and Lesbian Task Force, 2004).

Teachers and schools are becoming increasingly involved in the issues surrounding sexual orientation for two main reasons. First of all, gay and lesbian students deserve the same opportunities as heterosexual students to learn in an environment that is both safe and supportive. If you choose to teach at the middle school or high school level, you will need to understand the additional stresses that gay and lesbian students face and be prepared to support and encourage them in every way possible as they spend time in your classroom. (Of course, issues related to homosexuality are not just limited to middle and high school students, even preschool educators need to know how to deal with biases and gender issues.) The second reason that you and others will need to be involved in supporting gay and lesbian students is that you are legally required to do so. The 14th Amendment to the U.S. Constitution requires equal treatment of all people, including gay and lesbian individuals (see Chapter 13 for more information on legal responsibilities). Attitudes towards gay and lesbian individuals are often deeply rooted and can significantly impact relationships. The *Explore Your Beliefs* feature for this chapter describes some of the ways in which teachers and others engage in harassment of gay and lesbian students. As you read this information, think about your current beliefs on sexual orientation and how they may influence your interactions with gay and lesbian students or parents.

Explore your beliefs: Anti-gay harassment in schools

While the majority of educators would not allow a racist slur to go unnoticed, some teachers do not use the same standards for those remarks made at the expense of lesbian and gay people. These slurs often do not even get recognized as being hurtful and are considered by many to be socially acceptable. Many young people use terms such as "lezzy", "faggot", "homo" "sissy" or "queer" when referring to gay and lesbian people or to people who they don't like or respect. This behavior attacks the self-esteem of lesbian and gay youth and teaches all young people that hatred of homosexuals is condoned by our society. Educators who downplay, excuse, or ignore this kind of name-calling encourage the perpetrators to feel as though they can harass others without any consequences; while the students they target feel scared, helpless, and abandoned by the very adults who are supposed to ensure their well being. Numerous surveys attest to the heavy toll that name-calling takes on lesbian, gay, bisexual, and transgender (LGBT) youth. For example, the 1999 Massachusetts Youth Risk Behavior Survey concluded that students who described themselves as gay, lesbian, or bisexual were significantly more likely than their peers to report attacks, suicide attempts and drug and alcohol use. When compared to peers, this group was: over 4 times more likely to have attempted suicide, over 3 times more likely to miss school because of feeling unsafe and over 3 times more likely to have been injured or threatened with a weapon at school.

Indifference to name-calling among faculty and staff greatly increases the likelihood that incidents will snowball and intensify. Educators should strive to create a cooperative learning environment where **all** students feel safe to express themselves in all their diversity.

Developing the Habit of Reflective Practice

Gather Information

1. Go to the Safe Schools Coalition website and research bullying, harassment, and school-based violence.
2. Go to the National Mental Health Association website and research bullying of gay youth.

Identify Beliefs

1. Do you think bias against gay and lesbian students is a significant issue? What makes you feel this way? Have you seen or heard examples of bias?
2. How would you feel about teaching students who are openly gay or lesbian or have parents who are openly gay or lesbian?

Make Decisions

1. What should a teacher do to prevent this kind of harassment?
2. What should a teacher do or not do when reacting to this kind of harassment?

Assess and Evaluate

1. What risks does a teacher take when he/she confronts students who are name-calling with such terms as "fag", "gay", "homo" and "lezzy"? What risks does the teacher take if he/she ignores the behavior?
2. How could a teacher know if there were problems with anti-gay harassment with his/her students? Is observation of student behavior enough? Why? Why not?

Resource

Massachusetts Department of Education, (2000). Massachusetts state youth risk behavior study. Taken from the Worldwide Web at *http://www.glsen.org/cgi-bin/iowa/all/library/record/18.html* on October 15, 2008.

Diverse Student Abilities

Another major factor influencing diversity in American schools is the large variance in student abilities. Students with exceptional needs, normally developing students, and those who are gifted and talented create a mix of abilities and needs that significantly influence the ways in which you will teach. A typical classroom of 25 students, for example, could easily have 3 or 4 students with exceptional needs and an equal number of students categorized as gifted and talented. Students with special needs are often categorized as either disabled or gifted. **Students with exceptionalities** include those with speech and language difficulties, physical–motor handicaps, intellectual impairments, social–emotional problems, and health-related disabilities.

These are the definitions of the 13 categories of disabilities (Heward, 2006) identified by the federal government (listed in order of prevalence within U.S. schools):

1. *Specific learning disabilities:* A disorder that impacts a students' understanding of or the ability to use language, spoken or written, that may manifest itself in an imperfect ability to listen, think, speak, read, write, spell, or use mathematical calculations.

2. *Speech or language impairments:* Problems in communication due to delays and disorders ranging from simple sound substitutions to the inability to understand or use language.

3. *Mental retardation:* A disability characterized by significant limitations in both intellectual functioning and conceptual, social, and practical adaptive skills.

4. *Emotional disturbance:* An inability to build or maintain satisfactory interpersonal relationships with peers and teachers. The student displays inappropriate types of behavior or feelings under normal circumstances.

5. *Other health impairments:* Having limited strength, vitality or alertness, due to chronic or acute health problems such as leukemia, alcohol dependency, severe allergies, arthritis, ADD, and asthma.

6. *Developmental delay:* Children ages 3–9 who are experiencing developmental delays in one or more of the following areas: physical development, cognitive development, communication development, social/emotional development, or adaptive development.

7. *Autism:* A developmental disability significantly affecting verbal and nonverbal communication and social interaction, generally evident before age 3, that adversely affects educational performance.

8. *Multiple disabilities:* Simultaneous impairments (such as mental retardation and blindness), the combination of which causes such severe educational challenges that the child cannot be accommodated in a special-education program solely for one of the impairments.

9. *Hearing impairments:* A hearing impairment, whether permanent or fluctuating, that adversely affects a child's educational performance. The term includes both children with partial hearing and those who are deaf.

10. *Orthopedic impairments*: A severe orthopedic impairment that adversely affects a child's educational performance. The term includes impairments caused by a congenital anomaly (e.g., clubfoot or absence of a limb), impairments caused by disease (e.g., poliomyelitis, bone tuberculosis), and impairments from other causes (e.g., cerebral palsy and amputations).

11. *Visual impairments:* A visual impairment that, even with correction, adversely affects a child's educational performance. The term includes children with partial sight and those with blindness.

12. *Traumatic brain injury:* An injury to the brain caused by an external physical force, resulting in total or partial functional disability or psychosocial maladjustment, or both, which adversely affects educational performance.

13. *Deaf–blindness:* Simultaneous hearing and visual impairments, the combination of which causes such severe communication and other developmental and educational problems that a child cannot be accommodated in special-education programs solely for children with deafness or children with blindness.

According to the U.S. Department of Education (*Education Week,* 2004), over 6.5 million of the nation's schoolchildren receive special-education services. Not all children who have a disability require special education; many are able to attend school without any program modification. Most students with disabilities, whether identified as special-education students or not, spend the majority of their time in the regular classroom. **Gifted students** perform exceptionally well in one or more aspects of schooling and often need specialized help to meet their potential.

As a teacher, one of the significant challenges you will face is to plan lessons and activities that meet the needs of all students' different ability levels in your classroom. One type of lesson that teachers use when trying to meet the needs of students with a wide range of abilities is a simulation. For example, instead of just reading about pioneers traveling west, the students would be assigned roles and have decisions to make about packing, travel directions, and survival. This type of learning experience benefits all learners, helping exceptional learners connect with the ideas, helping to make the vocabulary concrete to English language learners and aiming to spark some creative problem solving in gifted learners.

Students with disabilities. As you begin to think about working with students with disabilities, remember that they are people first and only secondarily require special services. As indicated in the earlier discussion of similarities among all people, students with disabilities are more like their peers than they are different from them. Approaching them with this attitude will make it more likely that they will receive the experiences they need for healthy development. For example, Evan is an elementary child with Down syndrome. He has the same needs for positive social interactions with his peers and affirmation from his teacher as any of the other students in his class. Evan also needs appropriate learning opportunities that match his abilities and interests. Although his disability means that learning may require more time and effort than it does for other students, Evan is more similar to his classmates than he is different and should be treated as such. Notice how when Evan was described, he was identified as a child with Down syndrome. This is different than identifying him as a Down-syndrome child. Putting the special-education label after the child implies that this is just one characteristic of the student rather than the overall description. The *Reflect on Diversity* feature for this chapter highlights this important point through the stories of six accomplished students with special needs.

Reflect on diversity: Yes I can!

Sometimes, when people think about students with disabilities the things that stand out in their minds are what these students can't do. It is important, however, that as a future teacher you remember that students with disabilities are capable of a great many accomplishments. Each year the Council for Exceptional Children and the Yes I Can Foundation present awards to 35 students with disabilities for their academic, artistic, athletic, community service and employment achievements.

Here are five descriptions of highly accomplished students who were previous "Yes I Can" award recipients:

Andrea, a high school student with Down syndrome, works 5–6 days each week at Fisher Foods and continues to attend school on a daily basis. She rides the bus independently from school to work and clocks in on time. She communicates well with fellow employees and customers. Her job coach reports that she consistently does more than expected.

Michael suffered a severe brain injury when he was 8-years-old, leaving him hemiplegic (paralyzed on one side of the body). He was determined not to let this injury overcome his educational goals. Today, he is on the honor role and is an active, well-spoken student. Michael's academic progress is exceeded only by his determination and positive attitude.

Despite multiple impairments which cause many reading difficulties, Olivia independently formed a book club at school and created a catering service with her older sister.

Benjamin has never been able to see the piano keys he practices at daily nor read the musical notes he plays, but he is a highly accomplished pianist. At the age of 8, Benjamin plays almost 50 musical pieces by listening and memory.

Nick does not let Cerebral Palsy or blindness keep him from playing the drums. As a member of the varsity band at his high school, Nick has performed for hundreds in his community. Audience members not only love to hear Nick play, but are inspired by his ability and obvious love of music.

Developing the Habit of Reflective Practice

Gather Information

1. Do an Internet search for the "Yes I Can Foundation" and read about the most recent recipients of this award.

Identify Beliefs

1. What stereotypes and fears do you have (or have observed other people having) of people with disabilities?
2. How should students with disabilities be treated in our school system?

Make Decisions

1. How can schools help students with disabilities accomplish all they are capable of achieving?
2. How can teachers change stereotypes that people have about those with disabilities?

Assess and Evaluate

1. How could a school assess their strengths and areas for improvement for working with students with disabilities?
2. How prepared are you to work with students with special needs? What could you do to become more prepared?

Historically, the vast majority of students with disabilities were educated in separate classrooms. Those with severe disabilities were frequently placed in institutions where they had little or no contact with more normally developing children (Friend, 2005). Through the advocacy efforts of parents and concerned others, federal legislation was passed in the 1970s that made it mandatory to include children with disabilities in the regular school classroom whenever possible. The term inclusion is used to describe the educational services provided to students with disabilities in regular schools and classrooms. **Inclusion** recognizes every individual's right to be treated equally, and to be accorded the same services and opportunities as everyone else. In a school setting, full inclusion involves educating all children in regular classrooms all of the time, regardless of the degree or severity of a disability. Effective inclusion programs take place in conjunction with a planned system of training and supports for all faculty and staff members. Such programs usually involve the collaboration of a multidisciplinary team that includes regular and special educators (or other personnel such as a social worker) as well as family members and sometimes even the student being served.

Special-education legislation and laws. Four individual pieces of federal legislation have collectively had a major influence on the inclusion of students with special needs in the regular classroom. The first of these was the *Education for All Handicapped Children Act* (Public Law 94–142), which was passed into law in 1975. The most significant provision of this law was that all students with disabilities were guaranteed a free and appropriate education. In addition, children between the ages of 3 and 18 were to be educated in regular classrooms with students without disabilities whenever possible. This process of mainstreaming and inclusion has gradually led to higher levels of participation by children with disabilities in the regular classroom. In 1990, the U.S. Congress amended Public Law 94–142 and renamed it the *Individuals with Disabilities Education Act* (I.D.E.A., Public Law 101–476). This law expanded the coverage of the original law from age 18 to age 21 and modified the categories of disability to include such things as autism and attention deficit disorders (ADD). The third important law influencing students with disabilities is the *Americans with Disabilities Act* (Public Law 101–336), which was also enacted in 1990. This piece of legislation was designed to end discrimination against individuals with disabilities in employment, public services (including education), public accommodations, and transportation. In essence, this law mandates the inclusion of people with disabilities into all aspects of American life. The fourth and most recent piece of federal legislation that impacted special education was The *Individuals with Disabilities Improvement Act of 2004* was signed into law by President Bush in late 2004. New requirements for special education included:

- States and schools must take positive steps to eliminate the problem of students being inappropriately identified as having a disability, largely due to their race or ethnicity. States are required to develop policies and procedures to prevent the disproportionate representation by race and ethnicity of children as having a disability.

- Parents should not be forced to medicate their children as a condition of the child attending school and school personnel should not attempt to make medical diagnoses that should rightly be made by trained medical personnel (e.g., teachers should not be diagnosing children as having attention deficit disorder or requiring parents to place their child on Ritalin).

- The federal government plays a supporting role in funding education and shaping overall policy goals, but state and/or local educational agencies should make all decisions regarding achievement standards, assessments, and programs of instruction.

With most schools using an inclusion model for special-education services, you will most likely be working with children who have exceptional needs. As an educator, you are required by law to provide the **least-restrictive environment (LRE)** for exceptional learners. This means that exceptional learners should be placed in a school setting most like the one in which other students are educated as long as the child who has the disability can succeed. The presumption in current law (IDEA) is that the LRE for most students is the general education classroom.

Classroom teachers working with students who have exceptional needs are not solely responsible for their education. They have the support of special-education teachers and any other professionals who provide related services to students with disabilities, such as speech/language pathologists, bilingual special educators, school psychologists, school counselors, social workers, school nurses, educational interpreters, and paraeducators (depending upon student needs). The general education teacher works with the multidisciplinary team (team of teachers, specialists, administrators, and parents) to assess the student's individual needs, to determine eligibility for special-education services, and to develop an **individualized education program** (IEP). The IEP is a document that specifies a student's level of functioning and needs, the instructional goals and objectives for the student, and how the student will be assessed and evaluated. The IEP outlines the nature and extent of special education services that will be provided and any supplementary aids the student will receive. (Each student's IEP is updated annually.) An example of a piece of information one might find on an IEP is the listing of **assistive technology.** Assistive technology is a term used to describe devices that improve the functional capabilities of students with disabilities. IDEA requires that students have access to assistive technology as needed. For example, a student with cerebral palsy might use special communication devices called communication boards that can "speak" words or phrases as students tap on a picture. Another student who has low vision might use a beeping ball to help her participate in physical education class and recess.

Before moving to the next section, take a few minutes to read and reflect on the *Views from the Classroom* feature found on the Companion Website for this text. Jemal is a good example of

Views from the Classroom: Jemal

the type of student with special needs that you will encounter in your future classroom teaching. Read about his teacher's approach to working with Jemal and reflect on your feelings about working with students with special needs.

Gifted and talented students. A small, but important, percentage of students in American schools can be classified as gifted and talented. These students are often identified early in their schooling for having demonstrated a level of accomplishment well beyond what others of the same age can do. Traditionally, high levels of intellectual functioning have been viewed as the primary form of giftedness. Consequently, standardized intelligence tests were the primary tools used to identify people who are gifted. More recently, however, giftedness has been more broadly defined to include exceptional skills in other areas, such as leadership, social skills, creativity, and verbal expression. These kinds of skills do not lend themselves well to being measured with a standardized test (Clark, 2002).

Unlike students with disabilities, gifted students have limited legal rights under state and federal law (Council for Exceptional Children, 2008). There is no federal legislation, for example, that mandates educational opportunities for gifted students. *The Jacob K. Javits Gifted and Talented Students Act of 1994,* although providing for model programs and projects, does not give gifted students legal rights similar to those for children with disabilities. Approximately 37 states, however, do require that special services be provided to gifted students (Council for Exceptional Children, 2008).

Perhaps the best framework for understanding categories of giftedness is the work of Howard Gardner, a faculty member at Harvard University. Gardner (1983) has promoted a view of intelligence or giftedness that he calls his **theory of multiple intelligences** (see Table 2.1). He identifies eight distinctly different intelligences. Using these as a framework for understanding how students learn helps teachers to realize that there are many students with exceptional skills in every classroom. It also clarifies the need to modify instructional strategies to meet the varying intelligences of different students. Howard Gardner encourages teachers to assess all learners in a way so that instead of finding out "who is smart?," the teacher aims to find out "how are my students smart?" His theory helps educators and students understand that individuals have many talents that can be useful to society. In 1999, his original list of seven intelligences was expanded to eight when he added the naturalist intelligence. He has considered adding a ninth intelligence, existential intelligence, but has yet to do so (Gardner, 2005).

How do school, family, and life experiences impact teaching and learning?

Reflection Opportunity 2.3

Every student brings a unique blend of family and life experiences to the classroom. These include an assortment of religious traditions, first-language experiences, family income levels, and family structures. Think about your own family and life experiences. What is your religious, linguistic, economic, and family history? What aspects of this history are unique? Think about the beliefs and experiences that you have in common with others around you. How do you think that your history will influence your ability to work with students in your classrooms? Continue to reflect on these questions as you read the following sections about the family and life experiences of students.

Religion

From its earliest days, America has been a nation in which Christianity has been the primary form of religious expression. As indicated in Table 2.2, this is still very much true today. Despite its acceptance by an overwhelming majority of the population, however, Christianity itself has a

TABLE 2.1 Gardner's Multiple Intelligences

Intelligence	Description
Linguistic Intelligence	People who speak or write creatively and with relative ease
Logical–Mathematical Intelligence	People who demonstrate strong reasoning skills and effectively engage in mathematical and scientific inquiry
Spatial Intelligence	People (such as engineers and sculptors) who form refined mental models of the spatial world around them
Musical Intelligence	Those who are especially talented in singing or playing a musical instrument
Bodily Kinesthetic Intelligence	This intelligence helps people (like athletes and dancers) solve problems and fashion products using their body or body parts
Interpersonal Intelligence	A particularly strong ability to understand other people
Intrapersonal Intelligence	Allows people to be particularly insightful about themselves
Naturalistic Intelligence	A special ability to recognize differences in the natural world

TABLE 2.2 Top 10 Organized Religions in the United States

Religion	Estimate of Adult Population	Percent of Population
Christianity	159,030,000	76.5%
Judaism	2,831,000	1.3%
Islam	1,104,000	0.5%
Buddhism	1,082,000	0.5%
Hinduism	766,000	0.4%
Unitarian Universalist	629,000	0.3%
Wiccan/Pagan/Druid	307,000	0.1%
Spiritualist	116,000	—
Native American Religion	103,000	—
Baha'i	84,000	—

Source: From "Largest Religious Groups in the United States of America" by Adherents.com. Retrieved November 10, 2008 from http://www.adherents.com/rel_USA.html#religions.

diversity of beliefs and traditions. For example, the beliefs of Seventh Day Adventists and Roman Catholics differ significantly from Protestant groups such as Lutherans, Baptists, and Presbyterians, which differ from most evangelical Christian churches. Knowing about these similarities and differences may be important to you as a future teacher. In addition to the differences in beliefs that exist within Christianity, a growing number of your future students will have non-Christian religious backgrounds. As greater numbers of immigrants from non-European countries have found their way to the United States, they brought with them an increasingly diverse set of religious traditions. Among the largest of these are the Buddhist, Muslim, and Hindu religions. According to Diana Eck (2001), "The United States has become the most religiously diverse nation on earth" (p. 4).

Religious beliefs and traditions can potentially impact life in the schools in any number of ways. For example, should Muslim or Jewish public-school teachers be allowed to wear head coverings as expected in their religious traditions? If schools acknowledge Christian holidays, what should be their response to the holidays of other religious groups? Should a Sikh student be allowed to wear the kirpan, a symbolic knife required of all initiated Sikhs, to school? Should birthdays be celebrated in the classroom when students who are Jehovah's Witnesses do not celebrate birthdays? Should Halloween be celebrated in the classroom when some evangelical Christians see this holiday as a satanic holiday? These and many other dilemmas must be addressed by schools and teachers in the 21st century.

Some teachers make these decisions on a case-by-case basis, but it is becoming more common for school districts and states to have policies and laws that address issues related to religion in school. One such example is a student teacher who passed out Valentine cards to her fourth-grade students. The school was acknowledging Valentine's Day with a class party in each classroom on February 14th. Most teachers and student teachers in the building gave Valentines to their students. But this particular student teacher chose to hand out Valentines that had Bible verses printed on them. As it turned out, this was against school district policy because the school district viewed this as a teacher using influence to promote her religious beliefs. The student teacher faced disciplinary actions due to this decision.

How will you as a future teacher respond to the religious diversity you encounter? The first step is to recognize your initial reaction to people who look and dress differently from yourself:

> *After race, the most visible signal of difference is dress, and this is where religious minorities become visible minorities. Many Muslim women wear hijab, either a simple head scarf or a full outer garment. A few even wear a face covering called nikab. Muslim men may wear a beard, and Sikh men may wear not only a beard but also a turban wrapped around their uncut hair. Jewish men may wear a yarmulke or skullcap. Buddhist monks may wear saffron, maroon, black, brown, or gray robes.* (Eck, 2001, p. 297)

For many people, the first response to visible differences of religion is suspicion, fear, curiosity, or discomfort. What do you think your reactions will be to differences in dress due to religious beliefs?

You should also reflect on your attitudes toward those whose religious beliefs differ from your own. A good place to begin this line of thinking is to assess your own religious beliefs. How have family members and other significant people in your life influenced your beliefs? Take a few moments to write down the basic elements of your religious beliefs. How strongly do these beliefs influence your actions? If others' beliefs are in conflict with your own, can you look beyond these religious differences and work to help each individual within your classroom learn and grow? Would your religious convictions make it difficult for you to work with parents whose beliefs are different from your own? These are not easy questions to answer and may require careful thought as you prepare to enter the teaching profession.

**Reflection
Opportunity 2.4**

Language

Just as religious beliefs are growing increasingly diverse within the United States, the languages spoken by students are also becoming more varied. Immigrant families bring with them a variety of languages spoken at home, with Spanish, Chinese, Tagalog (Filipino), Korean, Vietnamese, Arabic, Hindi, and Russian being some of the more common (Banks, 2008). Many students from these immigrant families haven't yet mastered English and are defined by the schools as **English language learners (ELL).** For example, Natalia is a third-grade student who recently immigrated to the United States with her family from Russia. She speaks Russian fluently at home and has developed a basic understanding of English from earlier schooling experiences. Although Natalia understands quite a bit of English, she struggles with some concepts because it is her second language. Her teacher and school have determined that Natalia is an English language learner and are providing some specialized language services. Students like Natalia, whose first language is not English, are often placed in a **bilingual education** or an **English as a Second Language (ESL) program** where they may receive some instruction in their native language and special assistance in learning English language skills.

Data from the National Center for Education Statistics (2008) indicate that the number of school-aged children who speak a language other than English at home rose from 3.8 million (9% of the total school population) in 1979 to 10.8 million (20%) in 2006. Statistics also indicate that over a third of these students have limited English proficiency. Eighteen states had their numbers of students with limited English proficiency rise by more than 200% from 1992 to 2002 (Zehr, 2005).Considerable differences exist between ELL students in American schools and their English-proficient peers. One difference is that approximately 45% are foreign born. Frequently, parents of ELL students immigrated to the United States when the children were very young. Another difference is that many ELL students have had inadequate preparation for starting school ready to learn. They are less likely than their English-speaking peers to have attended preschool, been read to regularly by parents (who are often non-English speaking), or played extensively with educational games and toys. Finally, many ELL students live in poverty settings where poor nutrition, inadequate health care, and safety concerns are common (Zehler et al., 2003).

To help students who are English language learners become more successful in school, the federal government passed the *Bilingual Education Act of 1968,* which provided money to schools for the operation of bilingual education programs. Further motivation for offering such programs came from the 1974 Supreme Court ruling in *Lau v. Nichols* in which the court held that Chinese-speaking students in San Francisco were being discriminated against because the schools were not helping students deal with their language difficulties. With the passage of the *No Child Left Behind Act of 2001,* bilingual education was renamed English language acquisition and is now funded under this newer law.

Although states such as California, Texas, Florida, and New York are seeing the greatest influx of English language learners, the growing numbers nationwide mean that you can expect to have several in your future classrooms. This change will impact your teaching in several ways. One example of this is the way in which you communicate with parents. Because of language differences, newsletters sent home to non-English-speaking parents may need to be written in their native language and, similarly, some parent–teacher conferences will require the services of an interpreter. Another challenge you will need to overcome as you work with English language learners is the tendency to focus primarily on low-level repetitive drills rather than on higher-level content (Zehler et al., 2003). In addition to being less likely to hold the attention of English language learners, these activities fail to challenge them to build on what they know. A third challenge you will face is to look more deeply at the language skills of your English language learners. Many, like in the example of Natalia above, appear to have a working knowledge of English but may lack the more complex language skills they will need to be successful in school.

Family Income

Another difference that exists between students is the amount of income earned by their families. As you might expect, there are great variances in incomes and these differences can have a significant impact on student learning. In general, families with incomes near or below the poverty level are of the most concern to teachers and schools. A total of a little over one-third of all children in the United States live in low-income families where total earnings are less than $42,400 for a family of 4 in 2008. A family of four with an income of $21,200 met the 2008 federal definition of poverty. The highest rates of poverty in the United States are for families with children under the age of 3 (National Center for Children in Poverty, 2008). The estimated 2.7 million children in this category are more likely than their more financially advantaged peers to have increased exposure to a number of risk factors such as inadequate nutrition, environmental toxins, fewer adult interactions due to maternal depression, trauma and abuse, lower-quality child care options, and substance abuse by parents. Children who grow up in poverty are more likely to drop out of school, have children out of wedlock, and be unemployed (Annie E. Casey Foundation, 2008). Although low-income families do not typically exhibit all of the risk factors listed for families at or near the poverty level, they often face many of the same challenges. Table 2.3 describes some characteristics of these low-income children and families.

As a future teacher, you will work with many students who come from low-income families. In addition to limiting the school-related financial burdens of these children and their families, you should work to provide support in whatever ways you can. For example, Venus Jones is a student in Adele Robert's fifth-grade classroom. Venus is from a single-parent family and her mother is currently unemployed. Adele has provided support to the family in several important ways. Last winter, when she overheard Venus talking to a classmate about her younger sister's need for a winter coat, Adele contacted a local community organization that was able to help. In preparation for the upcoming field trip to the city zoo, Adele also made sure that scholarship money was allocated for Venus's zoo entrance fee. Finally, at the parent–teacher conference last month, Venus's mom admitted to being discouraged about her unemployment and Adele recommended a community employment service that could assist her in finding a new job. Although you will never be able to fully resolve many of the problems faced by low-income students and their families, options are available that can be pursued to assist in meaningful ways, such as making referrals to community agencies and providing a clothing bank within the school.

TABLE 2.3 Low-Income Children	
Characteristic	**Percent Low Income**
Race of Child	
White	38%
Black	22%
Latino	33%
Ages of Children	
Infant/Toddler	43%
Preschool	43%
Kindergarten	42%
Elementary	39%

Source: Basic facts about Low-Income Children: Birth to age 18 (2008) by the National Center for Children in Poverty. Retrieved November 17, 2008 from *http://www.nccp.org/publications/pdf/text_845.pdf*

Individuals and families with low-income jobs and those who have lost their jobs sometimes find themselves at least temporarily homeless. More and more frequently, teachers find they need to talk about this difficult topic with students. To view a lesson on homelessness, go to the Companion Website for this text and click on MyEducationLab for Chapter 2.

Ruby Payne works with educators to get them to see how the impact of poverty goes deeper than the pocketbook. In her book, *Framework for Understanding Poverty* (2001), she describes how individuals accustomed to personal poverty think and act differently from people in the middle and upper economic classes. As you read in Chapter 1, most teachers today come from middle-class backgrounds. Economic class differences between teachers and students often make both teaching and learning challenging. Sometimes teachers do not understand why a student from poverty is chronically acting out or is not grasping a concept even after repeated explanations. At the same time, the student does not understand what he/she is expected to produce and why. Payne shares "hidden rules" that govern how we think and interact in society—and the significance of those rules in a classroom. For example, families living in poverty tend to view money as something that should be spent, middle class families tend to view money as something that should be managed, and wealthy families tend to view money as something that should be conserved and invested. A teacher who is shocked that her student spent the money that was collected for the school's jogathon might get some insight by thinking about these hidden rules.

One of the issues you will face with students living in poverty is that they have fewer opportunities to work with computers in their homes. In addition, many low-income students attend schools that also have limited technology options. Because of this lack of access, many low-income students have limited technology skills and may be hesitant to use computers when they have the opportunity. The *Engage in the Debate* feature for this chapter talks about how this lack of digital equity for low-income students, students of color, students who are English language learners, and students with special needs influences their learning and development. Read this feature now so that you can better understand the implications of these inequities.

myeducationlab
The Power of Classroom Practice

MyEducationLab 2.2

Engage in the debate: Digital equity

In simple terms, digital equity means all students have adequate access to information and communication technologies for learning and for preparing for the future—regardless of socioeconomic status, physical disability, language, race, gender, or any other characteristics that have been linked with unequal treatment (Solomon, 2002, p 18).

With the rapid growth in computer and technology use, the issue of equal access to this important teaching and learning option has become increasingly important. Many students come to school with fewer opportunities to engage in technology use. In 2001, 5- to 17-year-olds whose families were in poverty were less likely to use the Internet at their home than 5- to 17-year-olds whose families were not in poverty—47 percent compared with 82 percent (DeBell and Chapman, 2003). Similarly, 36% of Black families as compared to 50% of White families have Internet access (Solomon, 2002).

Schools are becoming increasingly important sites for providing greater digital equity. Unfortunately, injustices continue to exist here as well. Schools in low-income areas, for example, tend to have less money to invest in computers and Internet access and lag behind many wealthier districts in technology use and computer to student ratios. Most schools have also found it difficult to provide the hardware and software needed for students with disabilities to effectively use computers. Students with limited English proficiency make up another group that has had difficulty receiving equitable technology opportunities. Educators agree that these situations must be remedied, but the challenges to doing so are many.

Developing the Habit of Reflective Practice

Gather Information

1. Go to the TechLearning Website and read about digital equity.
2. Go to the International Society for Technology in Education Website and research digital equity.

Identify Beliefs

1. Are computer and Internet skills vital for success in learning?
2. Do you think that digital equity is a major concern in education today? Why or why not?

Make Decisions

1. What can schools and individual teachers do to minimize the digital inequities that currently exist?
2. What role should computer and Internet skills play in learning?

Assess and Evaluate

1. How could a school assess its digital equity amongst students?
2. What approaches seem to have the most impact: those at the federal, state, district, school or classroom level?

Sources

DeBell, M., and Chapman, C. (2003). *Computer and Internet use by children and adolescents in 2001* (NCES 2004–014). U.S. Department of Education. Washington, DC: National Center for Education Statistics.

Solomon, G. (2002). Digital Equity: It's not Just About Access Anymore. *Technology and Learning*, 22, (9), pp 18–26.

Family Structure

Another difference that students bring with them to the classroom is the family unit from which they come. By 1995, the traditional two-parent family with one wage earner was in the minority. In its place, various other family configurations are becoming more common. Table 2.4 summarizes the home living situations of students that you will likely see as a future teacher. For example, the number of *single-parent families* now totals approximately 32% (Annie E. Casey Foundation, 2008). Another more common family situation today is to have *parents who are considerably older or younger than the norm.* A small but growing number of couples are waiting until later in life to have children. First-time parents who are in their late thirties or early forties are more common today than in the past. Conversely, many young women in their teens continue to have children. The percentage of teen mothers has improved somewhat in the past few years, but there are still over 414,000 children born each year to teen mothers between 15 and 19 years of age. (Annie E. Casey Foundation, 2008). Another common family situation is to have *both parents work.* In homes with two parents, the growing trend is for both parents to work. Current statistics indicate that in approximately one-third of two-parent families both parents work (Forum on Child and Family Statistics, 2008). Numbers are also growing for families in which *children live with grandparents.* Approximately 2.5 million children in the United States under the age of 18 live with their grandparents (U.S. Census Bureau, 2000). Finally, as indicated earlier, the numbers of *gay and lesbian families* are increasing (National Gay and Lesbian Task Force, 2004). Teachers can expect to have students in their classrooms living in all of these different

TABLE 2.4 Family Structures

Family Type	Description
Two-Parent Families	The traditional family, consisting of a father, mother, and one or more children, is now in the minority in the United States.
Single-Parent Families	Family units headed by a single mother are the most common, but single-parent families headed by a single father are growing.
Families with Older Parents	Growing numbers of couples are waiting until their 30s and 40s to have children. Their life experiences are often much different from parents who have children in their 20s.
Families with Teen Parents	A significant number of parents have children as teenagers. These parents are struggling to grow into adulthood at the same time they are expected to be adults in interactions with their children and others.
Children Living with Grandparents	Grandparents are more regularly called upon to serve as parents of their grandchildren when the actual parents are unable to assume that role.
Gay and Lesbian Families	A small but growing number of gay and lesbian couples are opting to raise children.

family constellations and more. Read *Ian's Classroom Experiences* on the Companion Website for this text to learn more about a student named Raphael and the struggles he faced due to a difficult family situation.

As a future teacher, you will need to think about the diversity of the family situations you encounter and adapt your interactions with these families accordingly. Begin by thinking about your personal attitudes toward these various family units. Do you, for example, have negative reactions toward single-parent families or gay/lesbian families? If so, can you change your attitudes or set them aside so that your interactions with the students involved will be positive? How will you change the interactions you have with students' families knowing the diversity you will find? One simple change many teachers have made in recent years is to address written communication to "families" or "caregivers" rather than to "parents."

Ian's Classroom Experiences: Raphael

Reflection Opportunity 2.5

How should teachers respond to student diversity?

As a future teacher, you will need to work hard to respond effectively to each student entering your classroom door. As the discussion in this chapter indicates, these students will have a diverse mix of abilities, beliefs, socioeconomic status, and races. Educators must recognize that every child deserves access to educational opportunities. Teachers must aim to identify and eliminate barriers to success. It will be your responsibility to address the unique needs of all of your students. In addition to your personal commitment to meeting these students' needs, two recent federal laws make it clear that teachers must make every effort to support the learning and development of all students:

- *No Child Left Behind Act* (NCLB). This important piece of federal legislation (see Chapter 5 for more information) is designed to improve the learning of all children. As the title states, its primary goal is to ensure that all students learn. The law emphasizes the critical importance of planning and preparing for the diverse students in your classrooms so that no child is left behind.

- *Individuals with Disabilities Education Act* (IDEA). This federal law, which was reauthorized by Congress and President Bush in December 2004, was mentioned earlier in this chapter. In addition to mandating the inclusion of people with exceptional needs into all aspects of American life, it is designed to provide exceptional learners with disabilities quality educational experiences that are integrated into the regular public school classroom whenever possible.

Teaching a diverse group of students in the same classroom means that you, the teacher, must be thoughtful and creative in the ways in which you interact with students and organize for instruction. Although adding to the complexities of teaching, it also brings an excitement to the process that would not be available otherwise. As you read each of the following sections, think about your own willingness to respond to diverse students in these ways (see Table 2.5). If your reactions are positive, this is another good indicator that teaching is a good career choice for you.

TABLE 2.5 Responses to Diversity

Response	Description
Create a Climate of Acceptance	A classroom in which students feel accepted by both adults and their peers
Eliminate Gender Bias	This deeply rooted bias will need to be addressed personally, with students in your classes, and with parents and community members
Use a Variety of Instructional Techniques	Such strategies as individualized instruction, cooperative learning, and project learning will help you meet the needs of all students
Implement Multicultural Education	By making the curriculum more inclusive of different cultural perspectives and contributions, raising the academic achievement of minority students, improving intergroup relations, and helping students understand and deal with social and structural inequities in society you are engaging in multicultural education
Engage in Active Reflection	Active reflection allows you to identify and meet the needs of all students in your classrooms

Create a Climate of Acceptance

Good learning takes place in classrooms where all students are valued and encouraged to do their best work. To accomplish this, you will need to create a classroom climate in which students feel accepted by both adults and their peers. Students of all races, cultures, religions, socioeconomic backgrounds, sexual orientations, and abilities should feel welcomed and included. Glasser (1990) describes this as a **friendly workplace.** In these environments, people are polite to one another and work well together. Diversity in the classroom may make the goal of a friendly workplace more difficult to attain. Just as you can probably identify areas of prejudice in your own thinking and actions, students in your classroom will have similar issues that may lead to negative feelings and problem behaviors.

When necessary, you should plan to take the time to discuss any problem behaviors or negative attitudes that are expressed. Often, this will need to be done individually to avoid embarrassment and potential confrontation. At other times, it may be helpful to discuss these issues as a class. In either case, even though the content of these discussions may not relate to the subject(s) you teach, you will need to work through the concerns and conflicts before addressing the content of your lesson plans.

One example of a strategy that you could use to help create a climate of acceptance is to think carefully about the rules that you and your students will live by in your future classroom. Because rules create a framework for helping students understand both acceptable and unacceptable behaviors, you may wish to include one or more rules that emphasize the importance of responding positively to the differences that will exist among your students. One such rule would be "respect the ideas and beliefs of others." When this rule is highlighted as important in your classroom and carefully discussed so that students understand what is meant by it, you have begun the process of creating a classroom that is accepting of differences. Can you remember classrooms from your own school experiences in which you felt there was a climate of acceptance? What did the teacher do or say to create this climate?

Eliminate Gender Bias

The effort to eliminate gender bias from the schools will require the continued involvement of students, teachers, parents, and administrators during the next several decades. Deeply rooted attitudes such as this one and others discussed in this chapter change slowly and require constant work on everyone's part. As a classroom teacher, your role is multifaceted. Here are some suggested steps you can take:

- *Identify your own gender bias.* Although we all want to think we are without bias, the little things we do often subtly influence both boys and girls in our classrooms. For example, in the dress-up area in a kindergarten room, a teacher provides clothing that would typically appeal to girls such as dresses, feather boas, and high heels. This is likely to encourage only girls to dress up and have imaginative play in this area of the classroom. In the same classroom, the teacher has two closets for children, one labeled "girls" and one labeled "boys". Why assign closets based on gender?

- *Confront the bias of students.* Many of the students you will teach bring gender bias to the classroom from television viewing, parental attitudes, and life experiences. An example of a bias frequently displayed is that girls are not good at math and science and should not be encouraged to get involved in rigorous study of these disciplines. Attitudes like this need to be identified and discussed in nonthreatening ways. One of the easiest ways to do this is to read biographies and autobiographies of people who challenge common gender stereotypes. Reading about the astronaut Sally Ride and the scientist Rachel Carson can help students see that women can be successful in careers that require a strong understanding of math and science.

- *Educate parents and community members.* Many people outside the schools are unaware of the extent of gender bias and its harmful effects. It is important to take the opportunities that are presented to educate others. For example, talking about specific examples of gender bias and their effects at a school open house might help parents begin to see the negative impact of this thinking.

- *Select appropriate curriculum materials.* Many instructional materials are sexist and portray women and girls in very stereotypic ways. These options should be avoided when possible. For example, a puzzle depicting community helpers, all of whom are white males, would be inappropriate to use with young children. For older students, written materials that describe career options for students should avoid sexist language such as "fireman" and "postman" and instead use more inclusive language such as "firefighter" and "mail carrier".

- *Provide equitable learning opportunities.* Make sure you give both boys and girls equal chances to answer questions and fully participate in classroom activities. Consider videotaping or audiotaping yourself to make sure you are allowing equitable opportunities.

Use a Variety of Instructional Techniques

It should be obvious that students with diverse abilities have different academic needs that you as the classroom teacher must work to meet. A gifted student, for example, may excel when engaged in individualized learning tasks, whereas other students may require more directed instruction to be successful. A variety of instructional strategies should be considered when working with diverse students. Table 2.6 summarizes four important options. The first is **individualized instruction.** Some students may work best when given instructional activities that are specifically prepared for them and that are different from the assignments given to other students in the class. By modifying the level of difficulty and challenge provided by these tasks, students are more likely to have their academic needs met.

Another instructional strategy to consider is **cooperative learning.** Students are placed in small groups in which each student has a specific role that allows for positive contributions to the group. In this environment, students support one another more effectively in their learning.

A third instructional strategy that can work effectively with many students is called **project-based learning.** Teachers using this approach allow small groups of students to do in-depth investigations of interesting topics related to the classroom curriculum and real-world problems. For example, a group of students may work to figure out a way to eliminate littering around their school property, or students may use the public bus schedule to figure out how the class could go to the local museum. Chapter 8 provides more information on these and other teaching strategies.

Effective teachers aim to **differentiate instruction.** Differentiating instruction means adapting what goes on in the classroom so that students have multiple choices for taking in information, making sense of ideas, and expressing what they have learned. A teacher who is differentiating instruction provides different avenues for students to acquire content, process ideas, and develop products.

Engage in Culturally Responsive Teaching

Gay (2000) defines **culturally responsive teaching** as using the cultural knowledge, prior experiences, and performance styles of diverse students to make learning more appropriate and effective for them; it teaches to and through the strengths of students. An educational institution that is meeting the academic and personal needs of diverse students is likely to be engaged in multicultural education. For a variety of reasons, multicultural education is an essential part of culturally responsive teaching (Gollnick & Chinn, 2006). Banks (2008) has identified two broad goals for

TABLE 2.6 Instructional Techniques

Technique	Description	Example
Individualized Instruction	Instructional activities that are designed to be completed by a single student working on his/her own.	A second grade student who independently reads a book of her choice and then prepares a book report to share with the whole class.
Cooperative Learning	Small groups of three–five students are given work projects where the teacher has identified specific roles for each student. The group then works together to complete the task.	Three students in a high school history class are to gather information on World War I, develop a timeline of major events, and make a report to the class of their findings. Each student is assigned specific roles as part of the project.
Project-Based Learning	Small groups of students select a topic of interest to them, collect information, summarize their findings in an interesting way, and share the information with others.	Three middle school science students are interested in studying friction. They collect information from a variety of sources, plan three demonstrations that show the properties of friction, and then share their findings with the rest of the class.
Differentiated Instruction	Adapting instruction so that students have a variety of choices for taking in information, making sense of ideas, and expressing what they have learned.	Students in a fourth-grade class come together as a group to begin a study of mammals. After developing some common understandings, the teacher breaks students into small groups where they are given tasks with differentiated goals for learning.

multicultural education. The first of these is to improve educational equality for young women and men, students from varying ethnic and cultural groups, and students with special needs. Secondly, multicultural education should help all students (including those who are Caucasian) build the knowledge, skills, and attitudes they need to be successful in a diverse American society.

Teachers and schools should plan on implementing a variety of strategies to meet these goals. Campbell (2004) identifies four main components to multicultural education:

1. *Making the curriculum more inclusive of different cultural perspectives and contributions.* For example, a course on American history should include relevant information and discussion of the contributions of Native Americans, African Americans, and Hispanic people to the time periods being studied.

2. *Raising the academic achievement of minority groups.* Although many large-scale government projects (such as Project Head Start for preschool children) have had limited

TABLE 2.7 The Achievement Gap

| | Mathematics—Grade 4 | | | Reading—Grade 4 | |
Race	Year	*Scale Score	Year	Scale Score*
White	1992	220	1992	224
	2007	248	2007	231
Black	1992	188	1992	192
	2007	222	2007	203
Hispanic	1992	200	1992	197
	2007	227	2007	205
Asian/Pacific Islander	1992	225	1992	216
	2007	253	2007	232
American Indian	1992	217	1992	211
	2007	228	2007	203

*Scores on the National Assessment of Educational Progress.
Source: National Center for Education Statistics (2007). *The nation's report card.* Retrieved October 17, 2008 from: *http://nces.ed.gov/nationsreportcard*

success in improving the academic performance of minority students, every teacher must commit to helping students grow academically, regardless of race or ethnicity. Table 2.7 identifies the gaps in achievement that currently exist between racial groups at grade 4. Unfortunately, these gaps continue to widen as students proceed through their schooling.

3. *Improving intergroup relations.* Teachers need to use materials and techniques in their classrooms that break down thinking and actions that are prejudicial, stereotypic, and discriminatory.

4. *Helping students understand and deal with social and structural inequities in society* (such as racism, sexism, and class prejudice). For example, although racism may not be exhibited in your classroom, it is important for students to know that it exists and that strategies are available that can be used to minimize its consequences.

Individually, each of these four components of multicultural education has merit in the classroom. It appears, however, that a combination of all four would be the most beneficial in meeting the academic, social, and emotional needs of all students.

To avoid marginalizing the importance of multicultural education, you will need to infuse the curriculum with activities that validate the importance of different racial, cultural, ethnic, gender, and ability groups. This infusion process requires more than simply adding diverse perspectives to the academic content. It also means that teachers need to take the time to work on building intergroup relationships consistently. Discussing current events that have racial, cultural, ethnic, and gender significance is another option that can be worked into many classrooms. Identifying prejudices exhibited in the classroom and then working to break them down is yet another aspect of infusing the curriculum with multicultural issues.

One prominent way that many educators bring multicultural views into the classroom is through their use of literature. For example, Rhonda, a second-grade teacher, read the traditional Cinderella story to her students. Rhonda did her research and found out that this story appears to date back to a Chinese version in the 9th century! After checking some books out from the library, she read the following versions of the Cinderella story to her students:

- *Chinye: A West African Folk Tale* (Onyefulu, 1994)
- *Sootface: An Ojibwa Cinderella Story* (San Souci, 1994)
- *Domitila: A Cinderella Tale from the Mexican Tradition* (Coburn, 2000)
- *Angkat: The Cambodian Cinderella* (Coburn, 1998)

She helps her students discover that most renderings of this popular story include an evil step-mother and stepsister(s), a dead mother, a dead or ineffective father, some sort of gathering such as a ball or festival, mutual attraction with a person of high status, a lost article, and a search that ends with success. Rhonda is weary of the gender biases in this traditional tale and is happy to find out that Cinderella, in many of her original forms, was a self-reliant, strong woman who was not looking for a prince to rescue her. Rhonda is also careful with the stereotypes associated with stepfamilies in many of these tales and helps her students to recognize and challenge the accuracy of this stereotype.

Consistently Use Active Reflection

The process of active reflection defined in Chapter 1 and integrated throughout this text is another important response that you can make to the diverse students you will face in future classrooms. Consider again the exciting mix of students you will teach each and every year. They will be a unique blend of religions, family incomes, native languages, genders, sexual orientations, abilities, ethnicities, learning styles, and races/ethnicities. No one approach, no single set of teaching plans, no magic formula can be plucked from a book or Internet source to meet the diverse needs of your future students.

Even the 2003 National Teacher of the Year, Betsy Rogers, has faced challenges meeting the needs of diverse learners. After her year as Teacher of the Year ended, Betsy (a White, middle-aged woman) returned to the classroom. Instead of returning to the school where she taught when she received national recognition for her teaching, she chose to teach at a school that faced many challenges. Eighty-four percent of the student population was African American, and 16% were Hispanic. Nearly all of the students qualified for the federally funded free and reduced-price lunch program. The school had a history of low scores on the state standardized test. The building was in disrepair and did not even have a working computer lab or swingset. Snakes commonly made their way into classrooms. Rogers kept a computer blog describing her experiences during the 2004–2005 school year. Some of the excepts from her Web log show that even the most experienced, dedicated, and skilled teacher can feel challenged by student diversity (Rogers, 2005):

- I had no idea the stress involved in working under these conditions. I actually thought I had the answers needed to turn this school around. The afternoon of the first day, I began to understand how little I knew.

- Daily I question myself, "Am I the right person to work at this school? Can I really help and have an impact? Do I have what it takes?" . . . I just know that I want to be at this school.

To be successful in responding to student diversity and meeting the intent of legislation such as the *No Child Left Behind Act* (NCLB) and the *Individuals with Disabilities Education Act* (IDEA), you will need to spend time engaging in active reflection, just as Betsy Rogers does on a regular basis. As you gather information, identify beliefs, make decisions, and assess and evaluate the results of your decisions, *all* students in your classrooms will have the chance to learn in meaningful ways. It is not an easy path to follow, nor will you always be successful, but engaging in the process of active reflection significantly improves your ability to work effectively with diverse groups of students.

What are your attitudes and experiences in regards to student differences?

Teaching students from diverse backgrounds is a situation full of stimulation and change. Imagine having a classroom, for example, that includes a student in a wheelchair, two students with learning disabilities, a gifted student, and one Russian, two African American, and three Hispanic students. With the additional diversity that comes from different religious beliefs, languages spoken, income levels, and family structures, it is easy to see that the typical classroom of students is full of differences. For teachers who love students and get excited about the challenges each one presents, this kind of diverse classroom provides a wonderfully stimulating set of experiences. Each new day is filled with the promise of struggles, the hope of success, and the joy of connecting with students from all walks of life.

Although student diversity should be viewed primarily as an exciting opportunity, it also presents new challenges to you as a future teacher. The first obstacle is to understand your own personal feelings and attitudes about people who are different from yourself. How do you think you will feel about having diverse cultures in your classroom? Do you have any negative feelings about working with different family configurations (single-parent families, gay parents, etc.) or teaching children with special needs? Are you ready to commit the extra time and energy it will take to make diversity a positive experience in your classroom rather than a negative one? These are not easy questions to answer and should be thoughtfully considered both now and throughout your teacher-preparation program.

Reflection Opportunity 2.6

The Development of Attitudes

As you begin to think about your attitudes toward students and adults who are different from yourself, it is important to understand how these attitudes develop. There are many influential factors, but one of the most important is the *attitudes of parents and family members*. Starting as early as $2\frac{1}{2}$ years of age (Banks, 2008), children develop attitudes about diversity by watching and listening to family members interact with and talk about diverse people. Can you identify family members in your life that have influenced your attitudes towards diversity? In what ways did they influence your views?

The *stereotypes of diverse people presented in movies and television* also significantly influence attitudes. Students spend many hours each day watching movies and television in which diverse people are often portrayed in negative and stereotypic ways. See if you can identify a current movie or television program that that you feel portrays diverse people in stereotypic ways. Why did you pick this movie or program? In what ways is it stereotypic? Do you think that television programs and movies have a significant impact on attitudes towards diversity? Why or why not?

Reflection Opportunity 2.7

The *attitudes of peers* also shape the values and beliefs of others. Students notice how their peers talk about and interact with those who are different from themselves. For example, Paul is a popular high school junior who plays two sports and is vice president of the Associated Student Body. He is also very intolerant of gay and lesbian students. Yesterday, just as he was passing by a known gay student in the cafeteria, he stated loudly "They really shouldn't let fags in the lunchroom. It's enough to make us lose our appetites." It is likely that those students who want to be part of Paul's social group will be influenced by his negative attitudes. They may imitate his words and actions in an attempt to be a part of the group. Can you remember instances in which your attitudes toward diversity were influenced either positively or negatively by your peers?

Your Attitudes

Are you able to identify attitudes you hold toward people who are different from yourself? If you are like most people, some will be obvious and easy to understand, whereas others are far more subtle. In this section, you will be given some guidelines to assist you in the process of under-

TABLE 2.8 Understanding Your Attitudes Toward Diversity

Guiding Question	Description
Who am I as a person?	Take time to reflect on your race, sex, sexual orientation, ability, religion, language(s), family income, and family structure to better understand your own background.
What kinds of diversity experiences have I had?	Think about the diverse people you have spent time with over the course of your lifetime and their influence on your thinking about diversity.
What do I know about diversity?	Consider what you currently know and what you need to learn to be able to understand and work with people from diverse backgrounds.
How can I grow and change?	Think about spending additional time with people different from yourself and also making the effort to learn more about others so that you can grow in your understanding and acceptance.

standing your personal attitudes toward diversity. Four questions, each with suggested activities that should help you begin the process of understanding your own attitudes toward diversity, are presented here. Table 2.8 summarizes this process. Although you should begin now to understand and improve your attitudes toward diverse people, this is an issue that most teachers must continue to address throughout their careers.

The first guiding question that should help you better understand your attitudes is simply *Who am I as a person?* Throughout this chapter you have been given information on the differences that exist among students. Race, gender, sexual orientation, ability, religion, language, family income, and family structure play major roles in determining who you are as an individual. Think about the importance to you of each of these aspects of your life. For example, how important are your religious beliefs to the ways in which you think and interact with others? It may also be useful to jot down some more specific characteristics for each aspect of your life. For example, if you are of average ability, describe academic areas in which you struggle and those in which you excel. As you respond to each of these items, you will begin to develop a better understanding of your personal history and who you are as a person. In turn, this should help you better understand the basis on which you evaluate these characteristics in others. If possible, discuss your thoughts with another person or a small group to help you refine your thinking.

A second guiding question to consider is *What kinds of diversity experiences have I had?* Think about the people you have met and spent time with over the course of your lifetime that were different from yourself. Were these experiences that led to positive attitudes or less favorable ones? It may be beneficial to also consider ways in which you could create opportunities for additional meaningful experiences with diverse people. Although a deeper understanding cannot be accomplished in a brief interaction, doing something like volunteering to tutor a student who is an English language learner for a semester may give you important insights into diversity issues. Once you have reflected on the diversity experiences you have had, consider discussing them with another person or small group.

Reflection Opportunity 2.8

Reflection Opportunity 2.9

A third guiding question that should help you better understand your attitude toward diversity is *What do I know about diversity?* You can add to your knowledge by reading about theoretical perspectives and research results that relate to diverse people. Although there are many resources from which to choose, three books that can add much to your understanding are *Teaching/Learning Anti-Racism* (Derman-Sparks & Phillips, 1997), *The Light in Their Eyes—Creating Multicultural Learning Communities* (Nieto, 1999), *Exceptional Lives: Special Education in Today's Schools* (Turnbull, Turnbull, & Wehmeyer, 2007). Consider reading some information from one or more of these books and then writing about what you learn. In addition, you can learn a great deal from reading the stories of people with diverse backgrounds. Two good resources for essays of this type are *Daily Fare: Essays from the Multicultural Experience* (Aguero, 1993) and *The Politics of Reality: Essays in Feminist Theory* (Frye, 1983). Choose two or three essays of interest to you, read them carefully, and then spend some time writing about your reactions to these perspectives.

A final question to ask is *How can I grow and change?* As mentioned earlier, we all need to grow in our understanding and acceptance of diverse people. Undoubtedly, the best way to do this is to spend time with diverse people and work hard to understand how they are both similar to, and different from, yourself and others. Take every opportunity to celebrate the similarities and respect the differences you will find. In addition, you could consider reading about how others have grown and changed in their understandings of diversity. Nieto (1999) provides several essays of this type that give the reader ideas about strategies that may be effective to try.

The *Consider This* feature for this chapter asks you to reflect on the experiences you have already had with diverse people. Take some time now to think about how extensive these experiences have been, what you have learned, and additional experiences that will be important for you to have as you prepare to be a teacher. Go to the Companion Website for this text and respond to this feature on-line.

**Consider This:
Diversity Experience**

Summary

In this chapter, four organizing questions were used to guide your thinking about students today:

What differences (and similarities) among people influence interactions in the classroom?

Although it is important to remember that there are many similarities between students, some important differences include these:
- Race and ethnicity (Praxis II, topic Ib)
- Gender (Praxis II, topic Ib)
- Sexual orientation (Praxis II, topic Ib)
- Abilities and learning styles (Praxis II, topic Ib)

How do school, family, and life experiences impact teaching and learning?

Student differences are also related to family and life experiences:
- Religion (Praxis II, topic Ib)
- Language (Praxis II, topics Ib, IIIa)
- Family income (Praxis II, topics Ib, IIIa)
- Family structure (Praxis II, topic Ib)

How should teachers respond to student diversity?

There are several important actions that teachers can take in response to student differences:
- Create a climate of acceptance (Praxis II, topic Ic)
- Eliminate gender bias (Praxis II, topic Ic)

- Use a variety of instructional techniques
- Engage in culturally responsive teaching (Praxis II, topic IIa)
- Consistently use active reflection

What are your attitudes and experiences in regards to student differences?

As you think about your own attitudes toward diversity, it is important to determine the following:
- How attitudes toward diversity develop
- Your own attitudes and how to change them

PRAXIS Test-Preparation Activities

To review an on-line chapter case study, test your understanding of chapter topics and concepts, and begin preparing for the Praxis II: Principles of Learning and Teaching examination, go to the Praxis Test Preparation module for this chapter of the Companion Website.

Developing the Habit of Reflective Practice

Organizing Questions

Review questions, field-experience opportunities, and activities for building your portfolio are included here for the organizing questions in this chapter.

What differences among people influence interactions in the classroom?

Review Questions

1. Why is the racial composition of American schools changing?
2. What does it mean when a student with disabilities is described as a person first and only secondarily as one with special needs?
3. Describe Gardner's theory of multiple intelligences.

Field Experience

Spend some time observing a student with special needs in the regular classroom and as this student receives special services.
- What accommodations does the regular classroom teacher make to involve this student in the learning process?
- Where does this student receive special services and what are they?
- Talk to the classroom teacher and the special services provider(s) to learn more about how this student's needs are being met.

Building Your Portfolio: *Knowledge of Diverse People*

INTASC Standard 3. Choose a subgroup of people within American society and spend some time researching characteristics of this group.
- In what ways are their traditions, family interactions, attitudes, and behaviors similar to ones you have? Identify ways in which this group of people differs from you.
- Describe the impact the differences you found may have on your feelings toward this group of people and your ability to teach them in your classroom.
- Include a summary of this information in your portfolio.

How do family and life experiences impact teaching and learning?

Review Questions

1. How is religious diversity influencing teaching and learning in the classroom?

2. In what ways does poverty affect student learning?

3. How does family diversity shape the interactions you will have with students and their families?

Building Your Portfolio: *Lesson Plan for Diverse Students*

INTASC Standard 3. When you begin the process of writing lesson plans, it is important to clearly identify strategies you can use to meet the needs of diverse students (ability, cultural/racial, family, or gender differences).

- Consider the group of Americans you identified and researched in the previous portfolio activity and create a list of well-described strategies you could use to meet the needs of these students in your classroom.
- As you continue throughout your career, add additional good examples of this planning to your portfolio.

How should teachers respond to student diversity?

Review Questions

1. Develop a list of five things you can do to create a climate of acceptance in your future classroom.

2. Identify several subtle ways in which gender bias exists in classrooms today.

3. What are the goals of multicultural education?

Field Experience

Talk to a classroom teacher to get additional perspectives on the impact of diversity on teaching and learning.

- How does the teacher describe the diversity that exists within his or her classroom?
- What are the strengths and problems associated with diversity?
- What does she or he do to meet the needs of diverse learners?

Building Your Portfolio: *Experiences Working with Diverse Students*

INTASC Standard 3. As you begin your teacher-preparation program, start the process of documenting the experiences you have with diverse students.

- Describe what you did, the diverse students you worked with, and the results of your interactions.
- Review the different types of diversity described in this chapter and create a file for each. Continue to seek out experiences with diverse populations with which you are less familiar or comfortable.
- Keep a journal or other written record of your interactions to add to this portion of your portfolio.

What are your attitudes toward student differences?

Review Questions

1. How are attitudes toward diversity developed?

2. What can you do to improve your attitudes toward diverse students?

Building Your Portfolio: *Your Diversity Background*

INTASC Standard 9. Summarize the diversity experiences you have had as part of your day-to-day life in a family and community.

* Was your family experience diverse in some way?
* Describe experiences you had in school with children who were culturally, racially, and ethnically different from yourself.
* Have you traveled to or lived in another country?
* Can you speak a second language?
* Describe how your diversity experiences have influenced your attitudes toward student differences.

Suggested Readings

American Association of University Women. (1998). *Gender gaps: Where schools still fail our children. Washington, DC: AAUW Educational Foundation.* This report provides a strong rationale for continued efforts to remove gender bias from American education. It reviews research studies as a basis for its conclusions.

Gollnick, D., & Chinn, P. (2006). *Multicultural education in a pluralistic society* (7th ed.). Upper Saddle River, NJ: Merrill/Prentice Hall. This book includes information on dealing with diversity in its many forms. Separate chapters discuss gender issues, ethnic and racial concerns, exceptionality, and language differences. Religion, class, and age as diversity factors are also addressed in other chapters of the text.

Gruwell, E. (1999). *The freedom writers diary.* New York: Broadway Books. This powerful book describes how 150 teens and their beginning teacher (Erin Gruwell) changed their lives despite incredibly difficult circumstances. Through the diary entries of the students and teacher, you learn how they overcome poverty, racism, and injustice to make a difference in the world around them.

Heward, W. (2006). *Exceptional children: An introduction to special education.* Columbus, OH: Merrill. This text describes the many issues related to including students with special needs in the regular-education classroom.

References

Aguero, K. (Ed.) (1993). *Daily fare: Essays from the multicultural experience.* Athens: University of Georgia Press.

American Association of University Women. (1992). *How schools shortchange girls: The AAUW report.* Washington, DC: The AAUW Educational Foundation.

Annie E. Casey Foundation. (2008). *Kids count data book 2008.* Baltimore, MD: Author.

Banks, J. (2008). *An introduction to multicultural education* (4th ed.). Boston: Allyn and Bacon.

Campbell, D. (2004). *Choosing democracy* (3rd ed.). Upper Saddle River, NJ: Merrill/Prentice Hall.

Clark, B. (2002). *Growing up gifted: Developing the potential of children at home and at school* (6th ed.). Upper Saddle River, NJ: Prentice Hall.

Coburn, J. (2000). *Domitila: A Cinderella tale from the Mexican tradition.* Auburn Calif: Shen's Books.

Coburn, J. (1998). Angkat: *The Cambodian Cinderella*. Auburn, CA: Sheri's Books.

Council for Exceptional Children. (2008). Information center on disabilities and gifted education. Retrieved November 13, 2008 from: http://ericec.org/faq/gt-legal.html

Council for Exceptional Children. (2004, May 14). CEC disappointed in lack of full funding in Senate IDEA bill (press release).

Derman-Sparks, L., & Phillips, C. (1997). *Teaching/learning anti-racism—A developmental approach*. New York: Teachers College Press.

Eck, D. (2001). *A new religious America: How a "Christian country" has become the world's most religiously diverse nation*. San Francisco: Harper.

Forum on Child and Family Statistics. (2008). *America's children: Key national indicators of well-being, 2008*. Vienna, VA: National Maternal Child Health Clearinghouse.

Education Week. (2004). *Quality counts 2004: Count me in: Special education in an era of standards*. Washington, DC: Author.

Friend, M. (2005). *Special education: Contemporary perspectives for school professionals*. Boston: Allyn and Bacon.

Frye, M. (1983). *The politics of reality: Essays in feminist theory*. Trumansburg, NY: Crossing Press.

Gardner, H. (1983). *Frames of mind: The theory of multiple intelligences*. New York: Basic Books.

Gardner, Howard (1999). *Intelligence reframed. Multiple intelligences for the 21st century*. New York: Basic Books.

Gardner, H. (2005). FAQ on multiple intelligences. Retrieved August 23, 2005 from: http://www.howardgardner.com/FAQ/faq.htm

Gay, G. (2000). *Culturally responsive teaching: Theory, research, & practice*. New York: Teachers College Press.

Glasser, W. (1990). *The quality school: Managing students without coercion*. New York: Harper and Row.

Gollnick, D., & Chinn, P. (2006). *Multicultural education in a pluralistic society* (7th ed.). Upper Saddle River, NJ: Merrill/Prentice Hall.

Grubb, J. (2001). Research briefing on boys and underachievement from the TES. National Literacy Trust [On-line]. Retrieved May 15, 2005 from: www.literacytrust.org.uk/research/boyact.html

Gurian, M., and Stevens, K. (2004). With boys and girls in mind. *Educational Leadership, 62*(3), 21–26.

Heward, W. L. (2006). Exceptional children: An introduction to special education. Pearson: Upper Saddle River, NJ.

Landsman, J. (2004). Confronting the racism of low expectations. *Educational Leadership, 62*(3), 28–32.

National Center for Children in Poverty. (2008). *Basic facts about low income children: Birth to age 18*. Retrieved November 14, 2008 from: http://www.nccp.org/publications/pdf/text_845.pdf

National Center for Education Statistics. (2008) *The condition of education 2008*. Washington, D.C.: Author.

National Gay and Lesbian Task Force. (2004). Lesbian, gay, bisexual and transgender (LGBT) parents and their children. Retrieved October 13, 2008 from: http://www.thetaskforce.org/downloads/LGBTParentsChildren.pdf

Nieto, S. (1999). *The light in their eyes—Creating multicultural learning communities*. New York: Teachers College Press.

Onyefulu, O. (1994). *Chinye: A West African folktale.* N.Y.: Viking.

Pollack, W. S. (1998). *Real boys: Rescuing our sons from the myths of boyhood.* New York: Random House.

Rogers, B. (2005). Betsy Rogers' blog. Retrieved May 20, 2005 from: http://blogs.edweek.org/teachers/brogers

Sanders, J., & Nelson, S. (2004). Closing gender gaps in science. *Educational Leadership, 62*(3), 74–77.

San Souci, R. (1994). *Sootface: An Ojibwa Cinderella Story.* NY: Bantam Doubleday Dell.

Sax, L. (2005) *Why gender matters: What parents and teachers need to know about the emerging science of sex differences (pp. 11–38).* Garden City, NY: Doubleday.

Steinberg, J. (2000, August 20). Increase in test scores counters dire forecasts for bilingual ban. *New York Times.*

Turnbull, A., Turnbull, R., & Wehmeyer, M. (2007). *Exceptional lives: Special education in today's schools.* (5th ed.) Upper Saddle River, NJ: Prentice Hall.

U.S. Census Bureau. (2004). U.S. interim projections by age, sex, race, and Hispanic origin. Retrieved November 13, 2004 from: http://www.census.govipc/www/usinterimproj/>

U.S. Census Bureau. (2000). *Census 2000.* Washington, DC: Government Printing Office.

Zehler, A., Fleischman, H., Hopstock, P., Stephenson, T., Pendzick, M., & Sapru, S. (2003). *Descriptive study of services to ELL students and ELL students with disabilities.* Washington, DC: U.S. Department of Education.

Zehr, M.A. (2005). Newcomers bring change, challenge to region. *Education Week, 24*(34), 1, 17, 19.

Each year, the Disney Learning Partnership honors outstanding American teachers. The quotes above are from some of the 2001 honorees. They emphasize some of the key elements of their teaching philosophies and highlight how these outstanding teachers interact with their students. Although they take very different approaches to the profession, these award-winning teachers share a commitment to meeting the needs of students and engaging in outstanding instruction in the classroom.

Who are our teachers?

Schooling consists of many parts, each of which has an important role to play in the overall success of students. The many physical elements of school, such as books, desks, school supplies, teaching materials, school buses, and even the school buildings themselves, significantly impact teaching and learning. Support personnel, such as janitors, cooks, teachers' aides, secretaries, counselors, and principals, also provide many valuable services to students and teachers. As important as these elements are to schooling, they are still far less vital to student success than the teachers who serve in classrooms across America. To a large extent, teachers determine whether or not students learn and grow. Excellent teachers tend to overcome whatever negative circumstances they face and guide students into quality learning experiences. Conversely, even in the best of conditions, poor teachers are seldom capable of fostering good education.

Lowell Milken, of the Milken Family Foundation, had this to say about the importance of excellent teachers in the introduction to a recent report (Milken, 2002):

> There is a critical need to attract, retain and motivate the best talent to the American teaching profession. Quality teachers are absolutely central to assuring excellence in the educational experience of every young person in America. Indeed, good teachers are to education what education is to all other professions. They are the indispensable element—the sunlight and oxygen—the foundation on which everything else is built. That is why we, as a nation, must make it a national goal to place a talented teacher in every classroom in America. Access to a high quality teacher is a right that every student and every parent deserves (p.3).

Before looking carefully at the skills and attitudes that you will need to become an excellent teacher, you will first have the opportunity to understand more clearly what teachers are like as a group. In this section, you are going to look at several descriptors of America's teachers. By reviewing this information, you can grow in your understanding of the profession and the people who are essential to its success. As you think about the women and men who serve as educators in America's schools, try to envision yourself working alongside those being described here. Can you see yourself fitting easily and well into this teaching community?

Teachers' Ages and Years of Service

Bill Holmgren has been teaching middle school mathematics for over 25 years. He began his career at age 24 and has been going strong ever since. Bill still loves the challenges associated with teaching middle school students. Their enthusiasm and energy help balance the constant struggle he faces in keeping them focused on learning mathematical concepts. Bill's work is never easy or dull, but is always rewarding. Despite his love of teaching, Bill has decided to retire at age 54 when he has completed 30 years in the classroom. At that point, his retirement benefits are maximized and he can move on to other interests with no financial worries. Bill has mixed feelings about this impending change.

National statistics indicate that there are increasing numbers of teachers like Bill in classrooms across the country. Beginning in 1960, the National Education Association (NEA) has conducted surveys every 5 years to assess the status of American public school teachers. In its most recent survey published in 2003, the NEA found that the average age of teachers is 46, with nearly 70% over the age of 40 and approximately 10% under 30 years of age. This trend toward an older and more experienced workforce has been in progress since the mid-1970s, with approximately half of all teachers having more than 20 years of experience. In addition, the median years of experience for America's teachers has increased from 8 in 1976 to 15 in 2001 [National Education Association (NEA), 2003].

One consequence of a more mature teaching force is that America's schools benefit from having increasingly more experienced educators guiding student learning. A large portion of America's teachers are seasoned veterans who have accumulated a wealth of knowledge and experience in working with students. A second implication of these statistics is that the educational workforce is gradually aging, leading to greater numbers of retirements in the years ahead as teachers complete their classroom careers. This "graying" of the teaching profession is one of the primary reasons for the teacher shortages currently being experienced in many regions of the country.

Although the majority of teachers got into the field more than 20 years ago, 23% entered the profession within the last five years. As experienced teachers retire, they are likely to be replaced by young, inexperienced teachers, who are more likely to leave the field of teaching than mid-career teachers (Center for Strengthening the Teaching Profession, 2005). More than one-third of all new teachers leave the profession within 3 years and almost one-half leave within 5 years. The percentages are even higher for minority teachers, male teachers, and teachers under 30. It is hypothesized that many new teachers leave the teaching profession because of poor working conditions and low salaries (NEA, 2007). Aiming to encourage new teachers to remain in the profession, many states and school districts have launched programs to support people new to the teaching profession. Currently more than half of the states require mentoring for entry-level teachers. Mentoring provides new teachers with support and also helps build long-term relationships that can lead to classroom success. Mentoring programs offer new teachers a practical way to overcome the many hurdles they face in their critical first year (NEA, 2007).

How do you feel about the possibility of having a mentor as you begin a career in education? Do you think that beginning teachers should be required to have a mentor or should it be a choice? How do you think mentor teachers should be selected?

**Reflection
Opportunity 3.1**

Degrees Earned

Another set of statistics that should further clarify your understanding of America's teachers is the degrees they have earned (see Table 3.1). Most teachers are highly educated, with nearly 50% holding a master's degree and an additional 1% having earned their doctoral degrees (National Center for Education Statistics, 2007). Since the early 1960s, dramatic increases have been seen in the numbers of advanced degrees earned by teachers.

TABLE 3.1 Teachers' Highest Degrees Held								
	1966	**1971**	**1976**	**1981**	**1986**	**1991**	**1996**	**2003**
Less than Bachelor's	7%	2.9%	0.9%	0.4%	0.3%	0.6%	0.3%	N/A
Bachelor's	69.6%	69.6%	61.6%	50.1%	48.3%	46.3%	43.6%	50.8%
Master's or Specialist Degree	23.2%	27.1%	37.1%	49.3%	50.7%	52.6%	54.5%	46.9%
Doctorate	0.1%	0.4%	0.4%	0.3%	0.7%	0.5%	1.7%	1.2%

Adapted from: National Center for Education Statistics. (2007). *Digest of educational statistics*. Washington, D.C.: U.S. Government Printing Office.

Sherrie Jacobs is a good example of this trend. She has been teaching third grade for 8 years now and has decided to enroll in a master's degree program in the fall. The program is designed to assist teachers in developing stronger theoretical and practical knowledge of literacy learning. Sherrie will complete her degree by taking weekend and summer courses that blend well with her teaching schedule. Her main motivation for taking on this additional workload is the desire to learn more about teaching reading and language arts to her diverse group of elementary students. Sherrie is looking forward to putting into practice the information she will gather about teaching literacy. Many of today's teachers are working to develop strong academic credentials to assist them in dealing with the complexities of the classrooms in which they teach. As in the example of Sherrie above, are you prepared to learn and grow as a future teacher?

Gender

If you haven't already done so, take a careful look at the gender of the students in your college's education classes. Do you find more men or women represented? Unless the program you are in is unusual, you will find more women than men. Women are more likely than men to enter and complete teacher-education programs. Low salaries relative to other professions appear to have an influence on the low percentage of men in the teaching profession. Recent statistics also support the observation that the number of women teachers continues to grow. The percentage of women engaged in K–12 teaching has gradually increased over the last four decades to its current level of 77% of the total (Freeman, 2004). Male teachers made up about one-third of the teaching force in the 1960s, 1970s, and 1980s, but their numbers slid through the 1990s and hit the low of 21% in the 2003 NEA teacher survey.

Historically, women taught almost exclusively at the elementary level, while the opposite was true for men, who typically taught at the secondary level. Those trends have changed somewhat, with more women found in secondary schools and greater numbers of men teaching in elementary classrooms. In terms of overall numbers, however, there has been a steady increase over the years in the percentage of women teaching in America's schools. The recruitment of more men into teaching, particularly at the elementary level, may be a difficult task, but one that could benefit many students. Many young people come to school without having a father at home, and when they are able to have access to a male teacher as a positive role model, it can be beneficial.

Racial Diversity

In the last chapter, you learned about student diversity and its impact on schooling. The growing number of students of color is one aspect of this diversity. At the same time that the student population is becoming more racially diverse, however, the teaching ranks remain predominantly White. Recent survey data indicate that approximately 9% of all teachers are Black, 0.7% are Native American, 5.2% are Hispanic, and 1.3% are Asian/Pacific Islander (National Center for Education Statistics, 2007). In total, 90% of roughly 3 million teachers are White, whereas almost 40% of students are minorities. Other data suggest that there has been little overall change in minority teacher percentages since 1971 (National Education Association, 2003).

The NEA and others are pursuing ways to improve teacher diversity. They are aiming to improve college access for minorities and are encouraging classroom aides to pursue teacher certifications. Despite the efforts of the NEA, public-school systems, and colleges to encourage minority teachers, little change has been seen in the numbers of minority teachers finding their way into America's classrooms. Shawna Robinson is a good example of the difficulties that K–12 schools and colleges face in recruiting minority teachers. She is a bright African American student beginning her first year of college. Shawna's prior work in chemistry has already made her a strong contender for a continuing full scholarship in that discipline. She has been approached by the department chair and encouraged to continue her studies in chemistry. Meanwhile, the mathematics department is trying to get Shawna to consider a joint mathematics/technology degree that would prepare her for graduate study in either area. Although members of the education program have also spent time with her and would like to see Shawna consider teaching, the lure of greater financial rewards and the promise for more support during the college years from the other college departments will make it hard for her to seriously think about education as a career choice. Clearly, schools and teacher-training institutions need to redouble their efforts to attract qualified minority candidates such as Shawna into the teaching profession because it is important that young people in our schools have the opportunity to have a minority as a role model. For more information on the benefits and challenges of recruiting teachers of color, read the *Engage in the Debate* feature for this chapter.

Engage in the debate: Recruiting teachers of color

As indicated in Chapter 2, our nation's students are growing increasingly diverse. Unfortunately, the same cannot be said for the diversity of school teachers. Nationally, minorities represent only about 16 percent of the teacher workforce, but a third of our public school's student population are minority (National Center for Education Statistics, 2007) and this proportion is expected to increase significantly. Many schools have no minority teachers at all. It is quite possible that students today could go through their entire K–12 education without ever seeing a teacher of color.

Although educators and others recognize the critical importance of increasing the diversity of America's teachers (Banks, 2008), the challenges of recruiting minority educators are great. Because the status of teaching as a profession is still relatively low (see Chapter 5), minority candidates who would make fine teachers tend to look elsewhere for job opportunities. The competition for these students is very strong at colleges and universities, talented students of color are often inundated with offers from more prestigious programs. For others, higher education in general, with its predominately White student and faculty populations, becomes a difficult environment in which to learn. Many students of color drop out before completing a degree.

One unique strategy that some school districts are implementing is a paraprofessional-to-teacher program. Many ethnic employees are already working in school systems in such positions as instructional assistants and other support service positions. Given their knowledge and experience, such individuals have the potential to become effective classroom teachers. Many of them, however, have never been encouraged or guided to become teachers, and they may not have the financial resources to attend a university while supporting their families and maintaining their current jobs. Paraprofessional-to-teacher programs link a school district with a university's education department to provide guidance, scholarships, and sometimes the promise of a teaching contract upon completion of the training.

Developing the Habit of Reflective Practice

Gather Information

1. Based on your experience with schools right now, how ethnically diverse is the teacher population? Approximately what percentage of teachers in these schools are people of color?

2. Read the most recent *Digest of Education Statistics* published by The National Center for Education Statistics at *http://nces.ed.gov/programs/digest* to get a demographic overview of today's teachers.

Identify Beliefs

1. Do you think students benefit from having teachers who are racially and culturally diverse? Explain your response.

2. Do you think that preservice teachers of color should be given extra support in some way as they complete their teacher preparation programs and begin their careers? Why or why not?

Make Decisions

1. From your perspective, what should be done or recruit people of color into the teaching profession?
2. If you were serving on the school board of a district, what would you do to try to raise that percentage of minority teachers?

Assess and Evaluate

1. How could a school district assess how well they were doing with attracting and retaining teachers of color?
2. How is America's public school system doing with increasing the percentage of minority people in the field of teaching?

Sources

An Introduction to Multicultural Education, 4th ed., by J. Banks, 2008, Boston: Allyn and Bacon; "Recruiting Teachers of Color" by Northwest Regional Educational Laboratory, 2001, Northwest Education, 7 (2), pg. 28; "Urban Teacher Corps/East Valley Teacher Corps" at (retrieved December 28, 2004 at *http://coe.asu.edu/oss/urbaneast.php*); Lenhardt, B. (2000). *The preparation and professional development of teachers in the Northwest: A depiction study.*

Banks, J. (2008). *An introduction to multicultural education.* Boston: Allyn and Bacon.

National Center for Education Statistics. (2007). *Digest of Education Statistics.* Washington, D.C.: Author.

What are their roles?

Whereas most people not associated with education tend to think of teaching solely in terms of sharing information and skills with future generations, those who have been in the classroom understand that this is only one of several key roles that teachers assume as they work with their students. The best teachers deal with more than just the learning task; they provide support as students struggle with personal and interpersonal issues, guide students and families to resources needed to help resolve conflicts and problems, and serve as role models for their students in virtually all aspects of life. Table 3.2 summarizes these roles.

TABLE 3.2 Teaching Roles

Facilitate Learning	Helping students grow in their knowledge of the world
Support Emotional and Social Development	Assist students in dealing with emotions and interacting with others
Guide to Resources	Direct students and their families to resources that help reduce or remove stress
Role Model	Use of actions and words that show students positive ways of interacting in the world
Reflective Practitioner	Engaging in active reflection facilitates success in other roles.

Facilitator of Learning

A traditional view of education would have teachers spending most of their classroom time sharing their accumulated wisdom with less knowledgeable students who were expected to internalize this information for future use. This "factory model" of teaching and learning (Glasser, 1990) implies that teachers should serve as dispensers of information and, conversely, that students are rather passive recipients of this content.

Although this model may be appropriate in some educational circumstances, it is being replaced in many classrooms with an approach in which the teacher becomes more of a facilitator of learning. In this facilitator role, teachers recognize the necessity of students having a significant role in their own learning. Teacher facilitators provide a variety of resources and guide students as they work to build their own understandings of the world. This **constructivist approach to learning** is grounded in the writings of theorists such as John Dewey and Jean Piaget (see Chapter 10) and is gaining acceptance in many K–12 classrooms. For example, Mike Beranek's third-grade classroom is described as follows:

> "Under Construction" yellow tape and flashing hazard signs are part of the empty classroom that students discover the first day of school, as they become active participants helping to construct their learning environment for the year. Mike works hard to assure that students become actively engaged in learning by identifying projects and activities they wish to study. (Disney Learning Partnership, 2002)

The learning that takes place in these settings can be richer and more meaningful to students. A love of learning and a lifelong interest in growing as a person often result when this approach is used. A good teacher knows when to act as the "sage on the stage" and when to act as a "guide on the side." The effective educator strives to take on more of the latter. Can you see yourself being a facilitator of learning rather than the more traditional dispenser of knowledge?

Supporter of Emotional and Social Development

A second role that teachers assume in their work with students is that of support person for social and emotional development. For a variety of reasons (see Chapter 12 for details), students today encounter stressors that complicate their lives. Because of this stress, teachers are an important source of support to many students in their classrooms as they struggle with complex emotional and social dilemmas. Esmé Codell (1999) describes one such emotionally troubled student in a diary summarizing her first year of fifth-grade teaching:

September 30
Shira is Filipino and speaks mostly Tagalog. Sometimes she goes into fetal position under her desk. She has four brothers, named Vincent I, Vincent II, Vincent III, and Vincent IV. (p. 35)

December 13
Shira heard "I Saw Mommy Kissing Santa Claus" as I was trying to find something on a cassette. She came out of a fetal position and started to dance in front of the whole class, shaking and everything, with all these Polynesian-like hand movements. All of us watched in utter astonishment. When she finished, we went wild with applause. She did it again and again and again, crying and laughing at the same time. It was the weirdest thing. Then she hugged me. . . . She has not gone into a fetal position since and does not cry as much and is making all sorts of friends, smiling all the time. (pp. 67–68)

As in the preceding narrative, it is often hard to know when and how our supportive actions will benefit students emotionally and socially. Yet those actions can and do have a very powerful effect. Teachers in schools across America are providing encouragement that is helping students develop both emotionally and socially. Sometimes, students themselves are aware of the impact teachers have had in their lives. Others may not be able to verbalize the results of this support for many years, if at all. But, without question, both students and teachers are often deeply impacted by this important role in the classroom.

For many students in your future classroom, social and emotional development will be significantly influenced by their cultural heritage. When this heritage is understood and valued by teachers and other classmates, students will develop healthier personalities and be more socially responsive in relationships with others, as seen in the example of Shira above. For example, 8-year-old Samuel and his family are recent immigrants from Mexico. Because he is learning English as a second language and having difficulties communicating with others, he feels lonely and isolated. His teacher can help Samuel's development by knowing about and supporting his cultural heritage in the classroom. By teaching the class some Spanish terms, studying about Samuel's former home, and valuing his traditions, the teacher can significantly influence his social and emotional development. The *Reflect on Diversity* feature for this chapter gives an example of one teacher's efforts to better understand and support the cultural heritage of her students.

Reflect on diversity: It takes a village

Pam Johnson has been teaching for over 20 years. She teaches kindergarteners, 1st graders and 2nd graders at a K–12 public school in Koliganek, Alaska. Koliganek School has 84 students, all of whom qualify for free/reduced lunch. The average class size is 14 students. The school is located in a remote area of the state. 98 percent of the population is Yup'ik Eskimo. She came to the district over 20 years ago as an "outsider" and every year she learns something new about the Yup'ik culture.

At the beginning of each school year, she asks herself this question: "If someone were to walk into my classroom, would she/he be able to tell that my students lead a subsistence life style, and that their Yup'ik culture is of great value?" This question helps her to keep focused on the culture of her students. She implements the Yup'ik worldview and Yup'ik teaching model in her daily plans. She labels her classroom in both English and Yup'ik and involves the elders of the community in her classroom whenever possible to recreate the *qasgiq* (the place of learning that was used before the traditional western school moved into their area). The elders are the teachers and the students learn by listening and watching their elders.

The traditional *qasgiq* method is used in her classroom to introduce the concept of respect. Students learn about respect from the elders while participating in a variety of cultural activities, such as native dance, ice fishing, plucking ducks, splitting fish and skinning beaver. The students then share their newly gained knowledge with parents and elders via a presentation and potluck.

Over the years, Pam has learned how passionately the parents and elders feel about their native culture and language, and that formal school-based education was not always a positive experience for many of the people in the community. She has heard from elders and parents who, as students, were punished if they spoke their native language. Many of the parents were shipped out to boarding schools in the lower 48 states and in Alaska. These discussions made Pam realize how much influence teachers have on cultures and communities. This makes her even more determined to try to incorporate the Yup'ik culture and community into her classroom. She believes that involving the entire community is necessary to educate her students. Pam also believes that it takes a whole community to educate its teachers. She advocates that the purpose of education is to show students how to accept differences, how to work together and see themselves as people who can make a difference in their rapidly changing world. Pam says, "Students that are allowed to experiment, manipulate, and take risks in a safe environment become the creative thinkers and problem solvers needed for the future of their village, state, country and world."

Developing the Habit of Reflective Practice
Gather Information

1. Go to *http://doe.sd.gov/octa/ddn4learning/themeunits/alaska/yupik.htm* to learn more about the Yup'ik culture by researching this topic on the internet.
2. Go to the Alaska Teacher Placement website at *http://alaskateacher.org/* to learn about becoming a teacher in Alaska.

Identify Beliefs

1. Is it important for a teacher to connect with his/her students' families? Why or why not?
2. In what ways should a teacher strive to connect with the community where he/she teaches?

Make Decisions

1. Would you choose to teach in a remote village such as the one where Pam Johnson teaches? Why or why not?
2. If you were recruiting teachers to teach in Yup'ik villages in Alaska, what characteristics and qualifications would you look for?

Assess and Evaluate

1. How could a teacher know if his/her classroom was supportive of the students' culture(s)?
2. If you were asked to visit Koliganek School to assess and evaluate the way the teachers are connecting with the community, what evidence would you seek?

Source

Interview with Pam Johnson, December 2004.

Guide to Resources

Although caring teachers can assist students in dealing with many of their problems and concerns, some problems are too large or complex for teachers to manage on their own. In these circumstances, teachers can still help by knowing—and sharing with students and their families—information about school, community, state, and national resources that are available to meet a variety of needs such as mental illness, drug addiction, and sexual abuse. Table 3.3 provides some examples of the types of resources you may be able to share with students and families to help them address their complex needs. This role of guiding students and families to available resources can be better understood through an example. Assume that Rhonda is a student in your seventh-grade social studies class. She is living in low-rent housing with her mom and her mom's boyfriend. You have recently found out that the boyfriend is dealing drugs and has offered "samples" to Rhonda on several different occasions, which she has reluctantly accepted. You have a good relationship with Rhonda and she has confided to you that she is worried that she may become addicted to one of the drugs being used or that she will be permanently harmed by the ones she has taken. This issue is a complex one that you feel needs to

TABLE 3.3 Resources for Students and Families

Resource	Description
School Resources	The school counselor, librarian, principal, staff specialists, and other teachers may all be potential resources to support students and their families
Community Options	Community counselors, service organizations such as those sponsored by United Way, and churches are examples of community resources
State and Federal Programs	Websites on the Internet, crisis hotlines, and state and federal support agencies are all available for a variety of student and family needs

be addressed by more knowledgeable personnel. Rhonda agrees to meet with you and the school-district specialist who counsels students about the harmful effects of drugs. This could be an important first step in assisting her with a potentially serious drug problem. You let Rhonda know that you are committed to continuing to help her with this issue. After some reflection, you commit yourself to finding out more about drug use with teens as a way to make yourself aware of other students who may be struggling with this dilemma. You look within your curriculum to see where you can address this issue with students during class time. Effective educators make themselves knowledgeable of local, state, and/or national resources that would be available to support students and their families through difficult times. What kind of awareness and experience do you have with such resources?

Role Model

Another powerful tool that teachers have as they interact with students is the ability to influence others through example. What teachers do often has a more powerful impact on students than what they say. Genuine excitement about learning, taking extra time to listen and respond to students' problems and concerns, and a demonstration of positive attitudes about diverse students and their families are some examples of ways in which teachers serve as role models for their students.

Imagine being a student in a health class where the teacher instructs you to make healthy life choices such as remaining tobacco free and maintaining a low body-fat percentage. Yet you smell cigarette smoke on the teacher's clothing and you notice he is at least 40 pounds overweight as you watch him eat his daily doughnut and guzzle his favorite cola drink. What kind of an impact will this have on your learning about healthy lifestyles?

The following scenario provides another example of how teachers serve as role models for their students. Calista, an elementary school teacher, e-mailed the school librarian the previous day to let the librarian know that her class would not be at their library class this week due to a guest teacher coming into the classroom. Right after the guest speaker leaves, the librarian steps into the classroom and speaks to Calista, who is across the room. "You had no right to schedule a guest speaker during my instructional time with your students. You have just told your students that my time with them doesn't really matter. You should show me some respect!" All of Calista's students sit quietly in their seats to watch their teacher's reaction. Calista is a bit flustered and embarrassed so she has a hard time coming up with an immediate response. At this point, the librarian turns and leaves the room, slamming the door. Calista gathers herself and realizes that she did make a mistake to infringe upon the school librarian's instructional time. But she also realizes there is a bigger issue here. This conflict has just occurred in front of her students. Calista understands the importance of being a positive role model and decides to take advantage of this "teachable moment." She decides to scrap her planned writing lesson and instead decides to model how to write an apology letter. She shares her regret for her actions with her students and then shares how this will impact her future decision making. She sends the apology note to the librarian via e-mail and drops into the library the following morning to resolve the issue. Calista follows up with her class the next day to let them know how the problem was resolved. Calista has turned an unfortunate event of the librarian losing her temper in front of the class into an incredible teaching opportunity. She did this because she embraces the prospect of being a role model for her students.

To personalize this aspect of the teacher's role, think back to a teacher from your own schooling experiences that had a significant impact on your life. What did this person do or say that influenced you? Can you remember specific examples of this teacher's behavior or attitudes they conveyed that had an influence on you? Try to remember aspects of this teacher's personality that made him or her attractive to you. Describe those traits.

**Reflection
Opportunity 3.2**

Reflective Practitioner

Take a moment to look back at each of the teacher roles defined in this section. As a future educator, which of these roles can be facilitated through your use of active reflection? Think carefully about each of these roles as you respond to the following questions. Can you be an effective facilitator of learning without engaging in active reflection? How might active reflection assist you in your role as supporter of emotional and social development? Does active reflection influence your ability to assist students and their families in locating needed resources? Is there a connection between being a role model and active reflection?

Reflection Opportunity 3.3

It should be clear from your responses to the above questions that active reflection is an essential tool that you can use to be successful in the many roles you will assume as a future teacher. Three important national organizations provide support for this idea by emphasizing the value of active reflection in key publications:

- *National Council for Accreditation of Teacher Education* (NCATE). This national organization is responsible for making sure that teacher education programs meet high standards as they prepare new teachers. In their professional standards document they state: "They (teacher education students) are able to reflect on and continually evaluate the effects of choices and actions on others and actively seek out opportunities to grow professionally." (National Council for Accreditation of Teacher Education, 2002, p. 18).

- *Interstate New Teacher Assessment and Support Consortium* (INTASC). This working group of the Council of Chief State School Officers developed an important document in which they clearly defined 10 standards that all new teachers should meet before they enter the classroom (see Figure 1.3 for a list of these standards). Standard nine states: "The teacher is a reflective practitioner who continually evaluates the effects of his/her choices and actions on others (students, parents, and other professionals in the learning community) and who actively seeks out opportunities to grow professionally. (Interstate New Teacher Assessment and Support Consortium, 1992, p. 31).

- *National Board for Professional Teaching Standards* (NBPTS). This national organization provides advanced certification for teachers who are seeking recognition for high levels of accomplishment in teaching. One of the five core propositions that form the basis for this advanced certification states: "Teachers think systematically about their practice and learn from experience." (National Board for Professional Teaching Standards, 2008, p. 4).

What skills and attitudes are characteristic of effective teachers?

Peggy Myers is a middle school science teacher honored by the Disney Learning Partnership as an American Teacher Award Honoree for 2001. Her teaching is described as follows:

> Peggy never liked science when she was in school; however, science became her favorite subject when she started teaching. Peggy sees herself as a "salesman" trying to sell curiosity and a love of learning to her students. Using real world examples, connecting new learning to prior learning and integrating other subjects, she strives to have her students personalize and internalize science. Peggy likes to involve her middle school parents by having students demonstrate and explain photographs and charts to their parents at home. (Disney Learning Partnership, 2002)

Reflection Opportunity 3.4

Think about your own likes and dislikes as a student and future teacher. Like Peggy above, are there subject areas that are your least favorite as a student? Can you imagine being an effective teacher of this content? What educational experiences will influence how you work with students? What skills and attitudes will you bring to the education profession? How will these skills and attitudes impact student learning?

During the last several decades of the 20th century, educational researchers and theorists have worked to identify a core set of skills and attitudes that effective teachers like Peggy possess. In this section, you will begin to learn more about these common characteristics.

Skills Common to Effective Teachers

An effective teacher plans instruction consistent with state standards to facilitate high levels of learning for all students. After a thorough analysis of current research, Danielson (2007) has developed a broad framework for understanding the key skills needed for effective teaching. She suggests four main skill areas in this framework.

Effective teachers:

- Engage in quality planning and preparation
- Prepare a positive classroom environment
- Use proven instructional techniques
- Exhibit professional behavior.

Each of these skill areas is described in more detail in the sections that follow. Additional information on effective teaching can also be found in Chapter 8.

Engaging in quality planning and preparation. Many people assume that the only real challenge in teaching comes from understanding the content to be taught. They seem to think that once this has been mastered, it is simply a matter of telling others what you know. In reality, subject-matter knowledge is only the beginning point of the instructional process. Teachers who possess a thorough understanding of what is to be taught then must spend considerable time and energy in planning the activities, materials, and evaluation elements that are necessary to successfully help others develop new understandings. The elements needed to engage in successful planning for instruction include:

- Knowledge of content and pedagogy
- Knowledge of students
- Selecting instructional goals
- Knowledge of resources
- Designing instruction
- Assessing student learning

Effective teachers carefully orchestrate these elements into a coherent plan for student learning. Table 3.4 presents a summary of these needed elements.

Preparing a positive classroom environment. Have you ever stopped to reflect on the many behind-the-scenes activities that must take place if a stage play is to be successful? The lighting crew, prop assistants, makeup and costume workers, and special-effects crew are just a few of the possible groups that work unobserved to make sure all parts come together to create a smoothly flowing performance. In much the same way, effective teachers do considerable behind-the-scenes work in planning the classroom environment in ways that allow for positive student learning experiences. The key elements that a teacher must work on to create this environment are:

- Creating an environment of respect and rapport
- Establishing a culture for learning

TABLE 3.4 Engaging in Quality Planning and Preparation

Skill	Description
Knowledge of Content and Pedagogy	Teachers know the subjects they teach and the appropriate methods of instruction
Knowledge of Students	Teachers know the typical patterns of student learning and development and can apply that knowledge to individual students
Selecting Instructional Goals	Teachers set appropriate learning expectations for lessons and activities
Knowledge of Resources	Teachers can locate the materials and people needed for instruction
Designing Instruction	Teachers plan lessons that are organized for effective learning
Assessing Student Learning	Teachers engage in fair and meaningful evaluation of student learning

- Managing classroom procedures
- Managing student behavior
- Organizing physical space

Table 3.5 briefly summarizes the key aspects of each of these elements.

Jacob Nelson provides an example of this effort as he prepares a Civil War unit for his high school American history class. In preparation for this unit of study, he has organized several experiences and activities for students. These include the participation of a local group of Civil War enthusiasts who will come to class in costume to describe key battles and the horrendous loss of human life for both sides in the conflict. Jacob has also located a Black civil rights activist

TABLE 3.5 Preparing a Positive Classroom Environment

Skill	Description
Creating an Environment of Respect and Rapport	Developing caring teacher–student and peer relationships
Establishing a Culture for Learning	An environment in which learning is valued and meaningful experiences occur
Managing Classroom Procedures	Successful management of classroom routines
Managing Student Behavior	Effectively responding to appropriate and inappropriate student behaviors
Organizing Physical Space	Positive use of classroom space to facilitate learning

who has agreed to come and discuss the long-term impact of slavery on African Americans today. They are planning to meet at least twice to plan carefully for the discussion of this volatile topic. Jacob has also located three videos on the Civil War that he will review and consider for use and has identified numerous Internet resources that students can explore as they start to collect additional information on topics of interest to them.

Nora Flanagan, a nationally recognized high school teacher from Chicago, shared how she establishes a positive environment in her classroom:

> The real "Three Rs" of education are respect, rapport and relationships. I treat my students with the respect they deserve as young men and women and I nurture in them a respect for themselves that is denied to them by too many facets of our society. I build a rapport with all my students that is based on this respect, along with trust and compassion.

It is obvious that Nora works to create a positive classroom environment for her students (Disney Learning Partnership, 2002).

Teachers also create a positive classroom environment when they provide opportunities for diverse students to interact in ways that will help facilitate understandings between groups and improved peer relationships. Sometimes it is the small things that teachers and schools do that contribute to the development of these positive environments. The *Explore Your Beliefs* feature for this chapter describes a national effort to mix up the normal seating arrangements in the school cafeteria so that diverse groups of students who don't normally interact can have the opportunity to do so in a non-threatening environment. This seemingly small effort is having positive results in creating classrooms and schools that are more positive places for teaching and learning. Take some time now to read about this opportunity for diverse groups of students to get to know one another. As you read this information, think about how important you think this and other similar efforts are for your future teaching. Record your responses on-line.

Explore your beliefs: Mix it up at lunch day

Mix It Up at Lunch Day is a project that supports student efforts to identify, question and cross social boundaries within their schools and communities. Since 2001, The Southern Poverty Law Center (a non-profit organization that combats hate, intolerance and discrimination through investigation, litigation and education) has promoted *Mix It Up at Lunch Day* each November.

This national event encourages students to swap seats in the cafeteria, widely viewed as the most segregated area of many schools. Each year millions of students across the country are breaking the "rules" that tell them where to sit and who to hang out with at lunch. *Mix It Up at Lunch Day* is designed to give all members of the campus community an opportunity to have some fun while meeting other students from different backgrounds and cultures. All student groups on campus are invited to participate in the event and faculty, staff, and administrators are invited to lunch with new faces as well. For many schools, *Mix It Up at Lunch Day* merely marks the kick-off of ongoing projects aimed at making lunchrooms, hallways and classrooms more welcoming for all students.

For many students, social boundaries are a troublesome, daily constant. Although the types of boundaries may vary from school to school, *Mix It Up* surveys have shown (Southern Poverty Law Center, 2008):

- A majority of middle and high school students said that schools were quick to put people into categories.
- Many admitted that they had rejected someone from another group.
- Others said it's hard to become friends with people in different groups.

The *Mix It Up* event encourages students to take a fresh look at their school environments and ask why the barriers that divide groups exist. Social boundaries can create divisions and misunderstandings in our schools. By working to cross these barriers through programs like *Mix It Up*, students can help create environments with less conflict and fewer instances of bullying, harassment and violence.

Developing the Habit of Reflective Practice

Gather Information

1. Go to *www.tolerance.org* to read more about *Mix It Up at Lunch Day*.
2. Interview at least 5 people about their memories of middle and high school cafeterias. Do they remember social boundaries/groups? How did that impact him/her?

Identify Beliefs

- How do you think social boundaries in schools affect students?
- Is it possible to break down social boundaries in a school setting? Is it something to strive for? Why or why not?

Make Decisions

1. If you worked in a school with social boundaries, would you advocate implementing a program like *Mix It Up at Lunch Day*? Why or why not?
2. How would you go about promoting this program at a school where social boundaries are very prevalent? How would you get students willing to take the social risk involved in an event like this?

Assess and Evaluate

1. If your school did participate in this program, how would you evaluate its impact for yours students and faculty?
2. How could you communicate the impact of this program to the community?

Source

Southern Law Poverty Center. (2008). Mix it up at lunch day. Retrieved October 24, 2008 from *http://www.tolerance.org*

Using proven instructional techniques. Marilyn Wilson is preparing for an upcoming unit on chemical reactions for her eighth-grade general science class. She is in the process of planning several hands-on experiments in which her students can safely mix different chemicals and note their reactions. As students work in pairs, they will make hypotheses and test them out with their equipment and supplies over the next several classes. Students always seem to enjoy these opportunities to experiment and explore. Marilyn must be sure she has clearly defined the tasks to be accomplished and identified the questions she will use to get her students focusing on the appropriate aspects of the experiments. She plans to be available to answer questions as they come up and will give suggestions and hints to help those who are struggling. Marilyn captivates the interests of students and motivates them to learn by using proven instructional strategies.

These techniques (often described as **best practices** by educators) are briefly summarized in Table 3.6. Do you remember teachers who have used these proven instructional strategies? Did quality learning take place when these strategies were used? To watch a video of a high school teacher engaged in good instructional practices, go to the Companion Website for this text and click on MyEducationLab for Chapter 3.

myeducationlab
The Power of Classroom Practice

MyEducationLab 3.1

Exhibiting professional behavior. Teaching is a complex occupation requiring continued professional growth and responsibilities that go beyond traditional classroom instruction. Effective

TABLE 3.6 Proven Instructional Techniques

Skill	Description
Communicating Clearly and Accurately	Use of strong verbal and written communication skills
Using Effective Questioning and Discussion Techniques	Questioning and discussion strategies that expand student understanding and get them actively involved
Engaging Students in Learning	Actively involving students in significant learning
Providing Feedback to Students	Giving students continued information about their progress in learning
Being Flexible and Responsive	Spontaneously modifying lessons based on student needs and interests

TABLE 3.7 Professional Teaching Behaviors

Behavior	Description
Reflecting on Teaching	Thoughtful consideration of what should be taught and how
Maintaining Accurate Records	Keeping written records to document student learning
Communicating with Families	Staying in written and verbal contact with families to support student learning
Contributing to the School and District	Supporting the smooth functioning of the school and school district
Growing as a Professional	Taking courses and workshops and talking to others about teaching and learning
Showing Professionalism	Serving as advocates for students and their families

teachers exhibit the professional behaviors summarized in Table 3.7. Effective teachers engage in professional conduct and strive to become true professionals by improving their understandings of teaching and learning, honing their instructional skills, and making significant contributions to their school, district, and community. For example, Kara Sorenson has been teaching history at the high school level for the past 15 years. In addition to completing her master's degree, Kara has taken numerous workshops and participated in regular professional-development activities provided by her school and district. Kara spends long hours thinking about, and planning for, instruction and student evaluation. She also works collaboratively with the school counselor, special-education staff, and building administrators to meet the needs of her students. Kara is engaged in the work of being a professional. Kara is a typical teacher according to the 2003 NEA teacher survey, which found that teachers typically spent 50 hours a week on their duties and put up $443 of their own money to help students during the school year. Fifty-seven percent hold at least a master's degree, and 77% took courses through their school districts during the year.

Consider taking a moment to reflect back on the skills common to effective teachers presented in this section. As you picture yourself in the teaching role, which of these skills do you think you can readily develop? Are there others that may be more difficult for you? What aspects of your personality will make it either easier or more difficult to develop these skills? Have you had experiences that gave you opportunities to develop the foundations for good teaching? Your personality and experiences will influence the ways in which you develop the skills needed in teaching.

**Reflection
Opportunity 3.5**

Attitudes of Effective Teachers

Although every teacher brings his or her own unique personality to the classroom, effective teachers do share several common attitudes. These attitudes are summarized in Table 3.8. First of all, teachers are real people who share their humanity with students. Second, they have a desire to know themselves as individuals so that they can build on their strengths and compensate for weaknesses as they work with students in the classroom. Third, excellent teachers think positively of their students and work to treat each one with dignity and respect. Fourth, they are excited about learning and can share that joy with students. Finally, they have a positive attitude about working closely with other adults to make sure that every student has the greatest likelihood of success in the classroom.

Effective teachers are real. Some people enter teaching for the wrong reasons. One example of a poor reason to become an educator is to "show others how smart I am." Have you experienced a teacher of this type? They often appear aloof, arrogant, and proud. Students are often viewed as second-class citizens who should be honored to be learning in the presence of a great mind. In reality, these teachers may be trying hard to cover up a poor self-image by giving the impression of strong academic prowess. With few exceptions, they are ineffective in the classroom

TABLE 3.8 Attitudes of Effective Teachers

Attitude	Description
Effective Teachers Are Real	Teachers share their true selves with students
Effective Teachers Seek Self-Understanding	They know their own strengths and limitations, understand what is meaningful to them, are in touch with their emotions, and know their personal likes and dislikes
Effective Teachers Have Positive Expectations for Students	Teachers have realistic, yet challenging expectations for individual students and their learning
Effective Teachers Care About Their Students	They have an attitude of prizing, acceptance, and trust in relation to their students
Effective Teachers Are Excited About Learning	Teachers demonstrate to students their love of learning
Effective Teachers Are Willing to Collaborate with Other Adults	They see themselves as part of an educational team, take time to maintain and strengthen relationships, and value these relationships

and are generally disliked by students. Teachers of this type are not being authentic because they have failed to share their true selves with their students.

Rogers (1969) puts it this way:

> When the facilitator (teacher) is a real person, being what he is, entering into a relationship with the learner without presenting a front or a façade, he is much more likely to be effective. This means that the feelings which he is experiencing are available to him, available to his awareness, that he is able to live these feelings, be them, and able to communicate them if appropriate. It means that he comes into a direct personal encounter with the learner, meeting him on a person-to-person basis. It means that he is being himself, not denying himself. (p. 106)

The teachers that Rogers describes are the ones that students enjoy being around and can relate to because of their genuineness. These qualities in a teacher give students the confidence to be real themselves and expect to be understood. This atmosphere of openness and trust is critical for effective learning. Can you envision yourself being real in relationships with students?

Self-understanding. In the hustle and bustle of life, how often do you go beyond the tasks of the moment to reflect on who you are as a person or why you do the things you do? This introspection takes time and effort and is frequently avoided by many people. The best teachers, however, somehow find time for this important task because it is so critical to success in the classroom. This makes sense when you realize that teachers can only help others learn and grow as individuals when they have first taken the time to do this for themselves.

This process of self-awareness for teachers is a lifelong process that consists of four main components:

- *Knowing your strengths and limitations as a person*
- *Reflecting on what is meaningful to you as a person*
- *Understanding your emotional life*
- *Knowing your likes and dislikes about people*

Effective teachers have an awareness of their strengths and limitations. Genetic inheritance and life experiences combine to determine your personal strengths and weaknesses. You come to teaching with a unique mix of both. Through personal reflection and discussion with others, you can determine your strengths and weaknesses and begin to build your teaching style with this information in mind. For example, if one of your strengths as a person is using humor in your interactions with others, you will want to decide how this can be used to your advantage as a future teacher. Take a moment to identify your strengths and weaknesses. How will these impact your role as an educator?

Effective teachers take time to reflect on what is meaningful to them. To understand yourself, you must determine the things, activities, and interactions that bring meaning to your life. Jersild (1955), in a classic text on teachers' search for self-understanding, states:

> The search for meaning is not a search for an abstract body of knowledge, or even for a concrete body of knowledge. It is a distinctly personal search. The one who makes it raises intimate personal questions: What really counts, for me? What values am I seeking? What, in my existence as a person, in my relations with others, in my work as a teacher, is of real concern to me, perhaps of ultimate concern to me? (p. 4)

Views from the Classroom: Should I Stay or Should I Go?

Although this reflection is a difficult task, teachers who expect to guide their students in their search for meaning must first work at coming to grips with this issue themselves. This careful self-analysis may lead you to question your desire to teach. The *Views from the Classroom* feature for this chapter tells a teacher's own story of the struggles she faced regarding this issue. Go to the Companion Website for this text and read her reflections.

Quality educators strive to understand their emotional life. Without question, interactions between teachers and students evoke many emotions from both parties. For example, how would you react to a student who snickers at a statement you just made as the classroom teacher? How would you feel about a student making a racist or sexist statement aimed at another student or at you? What emotions would you experience if a student were to give you a big hug on the way out the classroom door at the end of the day? Understanding your emotional responses and what triggers them can help you deal with the many emotion-filled situations you will face as a future teacher. It will also give you empathy and understanding as you guide students in managing their own emotions (Greenberg, 1969).

A final component of self-understanding is knowing your likes and dislikes about people. Our values, beliefs, experiences, and personality create for each of us a very strong attraction to some students we teach and a definite aversion to others. Greenberg (1969), in a classic text titled *Teaching With Feeling,* tells us:

> It is impossible to feel the same way toward all children. Human beings inevitably react uniquely and specifically to other human beings . . . Appearances, manners, gestures, ways of speaking and relating to others, all affect our likes and dislikes . . . Factors we dislike in ourselves can influence our dislike for others. (pp. 39–40)

**Reflection
Opportunity 3.6**

When these personal attitudes toward others are recognized, teachers can work hard to be more equitable in interactions with students, their families, and other adults associated with the schools.

Based on the information presented in this section, how well do you know yourself? Consider spending a few moments now to reflect on your personal strengths and limitations. Describe those aspects of your personality that you think will be assets to you as a future teacher. What are some weaknesses that may negatively influence your success? Can you identify values that you hold that may impact the way in which you teach? How would you describe your emotional life and its potential influence on your role as a teacher? Are there others you could talk to who would give you insights into your understanding of self? If so, talk to them and then write down their insights.

Positive expectations. In addition to understanding themselves, teachers need to recognize clearly the attitudes they hold toward students and the significant influence these attitudes have on student learning. Positive attitudes create a climate in which effective schooling can take place, whereas negative ones lead to destructive relationships and diminished opportunities for learning. Good and Brophy (2003) describe this attitude in terms of **teacher expectations** for student learning.

Take, for example, Mary, who is beginning her third year teaching high school mathematics. Two students in her second-period algebra class highlight the influence of teacher expectations. Mary understood from another teacher that Amy R., who has just transferred into the class, was a difficult student and would do poor work. Although Amy's performance in class has been fine so far, Mary is expecting problems from her. Ron, another student in the same class, has been turning in only about a third of his assignments, often stares out the window as if he is bored, and got a D grade on the first exam. Mary expects that Ron will continue to be a low performer in her class.

Although Mary's expectations are understandable, the effects of her attitudes may be problematic. Good and Brophy (2008) suggest that one possible effect is that her attitude may become a **self-fulfilling prophecy.** In the case of Amy R., Mary received erroneous information. The other teacher had been talking about Amy D. rather than Amy R. Because Mary expects poor performance, however, she may well find that Amy R. achieves only to the level of her expectations. Research suggests that in many circumstances, the teacher's expectations can either positively or negatively influence student performance (Brophy, 1983).

Caring attitude. Andy Baumgartner is one of the Council of Chief State School Officers' National Teachers of the Year. In an open letter to new teachers, he states:

> "How does one sort through the many and confusing descriptors of life as an educator, in order to plot a successful and rewarding career in teaching?" you ask. I can only relate what I have observed about my colleagues:
> - The effective teacher always considers the needs of his/her students first!
> - The truly successful teacher knows and cares about students as individuals and worthy members of a school community. (Council of Chief State School Officers, 2008)

Ian's Classroom Experiences: Death of a CO_2 Car

Although Mr. Baumgartner's list of ingredients for successful teaching consists of several more elements beyond the two listed here, these two are clearly essential. This attitude of caring and working to meet the needs of students is at the heart of excellent teaching. Read the *Ian's Classroom Experiences* feature for this chapter on the Companion Website and see the impact of an inadvertent lack of caring on the part of a teacher on a student's behavior.

Similarly, Rogers (1969) describes the importance of teachers having an attitude of prizing, acceptance, and trust in relation to their students. He suggests qualities that teachers must possess to facilitate learning in the classroom. One of these qualities is the teacher's attitude toward students:

> There is another attitude which stands out in those who are successful in facilitating learning. I have observed this attitude. I have experienced it. Yet, it is hard to know what term to put to it so I shall use several. I think of it as prizing the learner, prizing his feelings, his opinions, his person. It is a caring for the learner, but a non-possessive caring. It is an acceptance of this other individual as a separate person, having worth in his own right. It is a basic trust—a belief that this other person is somehow fundamentally trustworthy. (p. 109)

Teachers who bring this attitude of prizing, acceptance, and trust to their relationships with students create a climate in which students feel good about themselves. When teachers value students, encourage them as individuals, and expect them to be successful in their efforts, conditions are optimal for learning. Noted educator and author Haim Ginott wrote this often quoted passage in his book, *Teacher and Child* (1972):

> I have come to a frightening conclusion.
>
> I am the decisive element in the classroom.
>
> It is my personal approach that creates the climate.
>
> It is my daily mood that makes the weather.
>
> As a teacher I possess tremendous power to make a child's life miserable or joyous.
>
> I can be a tool of torture or an instrument of inspiration.
>
> I can humiliate or humor, hurt or heal.
>
> In all situations, it is my response that decides whether a crisis will be escalated or de-escalated, and a child humanized or de-humanized (pp. 15–16).

One can see that a teacher who operates from this premise would definitely have a caring attitude to his/her students.

Excitement for learning. The principal has just walked into Mark's fourth-grade class to observe his teaching casually. She watches as Mark leads students in a group discussion related to recycling of household materials. Students have brought materials from their trash at home that could potentially be recycled. Mark and his students are talking animatedly about the items exhibited and the ways in which they could be reused or recycled. It is obvious that he feels strongly about this topic and students are responding with enthusiasm. Mark is excited about his students' learning and it is contagious.

Mark is demonstrating an attitude toward learning that is critical for teachers at all levels to possess. When teachers get excited about learning, the enthusiasm usually spreads to students and meaningful educational experiences abound. While some may find it difficult to maintain a consistent level of excitement toward learning, the best teachers seem able to do so. And when they get excited, teaching becomes a much more rewarding experience for everyone involved. Memorable teachers are often passionate about their work. Sylvia Ashton-Warner (1963) exemplifies this passion as she responds to her editor's request for a "few cool facts" about her celebrated teaching techniques with young Maori children in New Zealand:

> A "few cool facts" you asked me for . . . I don't know that there's a cool fact in me, or anything
> else cool for that matter, on this particular subject. I've got only hot long facts on the matter
> of Creative Teaching, scorching both the page and me. (p. 23)

Effective collaboration. Although it is true that teachers have considerable autonomy in their work with students, a number of other adults also play important roles in student learning and development. As a future teacher, you will need to work with a long list of other people to maximize student learning and development. This list includes school administrators, counselors, special educators, educational assistants, and parents, among others. To watch an interview with a special education teacher, go to the Companion Website for this text and click on MyEducationLab for Chapter 3. The roles will vary in each circumstance, but the attitude effective teachers have in their interactions with this diverse group of adults is one of professional collaboration to best serve the needs of students. The necessary components of effective collaboration include:

MyEducationLab 3.2

- Seeing yourself as part of an educational team.
- Taking time to maintain and strengthen relationships.
- Prizing, accepting, and trusting adults.

See Table 3.9 for a summary of these components. Although these professional relationships require time and energy from all participants, they are critical elements of effective teaching and learning.

TABLE 3.9 Effective Collaboration	
Component	**Description**
See Yourself as Part of an Educational Team	Effective teachers realize that their students can be most successful when a variety of adults work collaboratively on behalf of students. By taking advantage of the insights and talents of other adults, teachers and others have a much greater chance of positively influencing students' lives.
Take Time to Maintain and Strengthen Relationships	Teachers who collaborate with other adults find the time to maintain and strengthen their rapport. The essential ingredient in this process is effective communication through such things as face-to-face contacts, telephone calls, e-mail messages, and written documents.
Prize, Accept, and Trust Other Adults	When teachers set aside their own prejudices and pre-conceived notions and work to understand and value the contributions of other adults, many opportunities for productive collaboration on behalf of students will result.

Some schools use **Critical Friends Groups** (CFGs), to increase the collaboration and effectiveness of their faculty members. The CFGs identify student learning goals that make sense in their school, look critically at practices intended to achieve these goals, and collaboratively examine teacher and student work in order to meet these objectives (Dunne, Nave, & Lewis, 2000). Each Critical Friends Group has at least one coach, who guides the group members (teachers within the same school or district) as they develop a collegial culture that promotes close reflection on teaching practices and student work, with a constant focus on improving student learning. To create this culture, CFG coaches use a variety of protocols—examining student and teacher work, solving problems, discussing professional and student texts, observing peers, setting goals, building teams, and creating teacher portfolios.

Can effective teachers have different teaching styles?

Good teachers do indeed differ in the ways in which they interact with students. This statement should not be particularly surprising, because every teacher is an individual and brings his or her own unique combination of strengths, weaknesses, and attitudes to the task. Guild and Garger (1998) state:

> When we accept that people really are different, we also must accept that teachers will bring their own unique qualities to the way they teach. We call this "teaching style," and it means we will see teachers' personalities reflected in their professional behavior. We will see differences in the way teachers relate to students. We will see differences in how teachers structure and manage their rooms. We will see differences in the mood and tone that teachers set in their classrooms. We will see differences in the methods and materials teachers use to help students learn. We will see differences in curriculum interests and emphases. We will see differences in expectations for student work and in priorities and strategies for evaluating student learning. (p. 90)

Many different writers and researchers during the last several decades have written about teaching styles. Although some have carefully identified and described these styles for better understanding and future research, others have used metaphors to help others grasp the essential differences in teaching styles. Table 3.10 summarizes some key examples from this latter group. Goodlad (1984) described teachers using sports metaphors including coach and quarterback to summarize different teaching styles. Rubin (1985) drew on the arts to identify teaching styles that he referred to as artist and actor, whereas Rogers (1969) saw teachers as counselors, and Glasser (1990) likened teachers to managers in business. Although these teaching-style metaphors have overlapping characteristics, they help clarify the differences that exist among equally effective teachers.

Teacher as coach. One teaching style that is common in the schools is the **teacher as coach.** A coach knows his or her sport, makes most of the decisions about plays and players, instructs team members on how to play the game, and exhorts the team to give their all. Coaches control the activities of the participants as they work to ensure victory over their opponents. Many educators have a coaching teaching style in which they exhibit strong content knowledge, make most of the decisions about what is to be taught, share their expertise with students, and encourage students to learn. A charismatic teacher, like a good coach, leads his or her students to greater levels of understanding through direct involvement in the learning process.

Teacher as quarterback. Other educators use a style described as **teacher as quarterback.** A quarterback is a member of the team who serves as the key leader on the field of play. He calls the plays and directs the team from within the game itself. Unlike the coach who directs from the

TABLE 3.10 Teaching Styles

Style	Description
Teacher as Coach	Actively involved from outside the learning experience in giving directions, providing instruction, and motivating students to learn
Teacher as Quarterback	Active member of the learning team working to facilitate learning through personal excitement and example
Teacher as Artist	Using a deep understanding of the components of learning to create unique lessons and activities that facilitate student learning
Teacher as Actor	Making learning exciting and meaningful through actions and words
Teacher as Counselor	Making the support of students' social and emotional development central to teaching
Teacher as Manager	Creating a supportive learning environment in which students are eager to work individually and in groups

sidelines, the quarterback is actively engaged in the sport along with the other players. Teachers using this style view themselves as co-learners along with their students and work to facilitate learning through their take-charge attitude, an excitement about learning, and through example. In addition, just as a quarterback sometimes changes the play at the last moment, teachers also adjust their activities to meet the needs and interests of students.

Teacher as artist. A third teaching style can be identified as the **teacher as artist.** Artists take raw materials and with imagination, skill, and a touch of the unexplainable create an object of beauty. They know the characteristics of the materials used well and can transform them into objects of beauty. Teachers using this style are often hard to analyze because it is difficult for others to see how they took the building blocks for learning and blended them in creative ways into a meaningful experience for students. This little bit of magic is difficult to teach others, but is found in abundance in many teachers.

Teacher as actor. Another important approach to teaching can be described as **teacher as actor.** Actors engage their audiences in two primary ways. Through their words and actions they either entertain or get their audiences to think deeply about complex issues. Similarly, teachers engage their students by entertaining them or by motivating them to reflect on difficult topics. Some people dislike this metaphor because actors are not genuine and real when they play a part, but it should be obvious that teachers are in a sense performers who each day step onto the classroom stage to share with the audience through their actions and words. Part of the time, these performances are designed to help students think deeply about important topics. On other occasions; their role is to entertain in an effort to motivate students to learn. Some teachers are better than others at getting excited about this role and at hamming it up a bit with their students. These teachers truly love the opportunity to be in the limelight and can use their time to motivate student learning through their daily performances.

Teacher as counselor. The teaching style of some teachers can best be described as the **teacher as counselor.** A counselor is trained to assist others in their social and emotional development. By spending time listening carefully, asking effective questions, and letting others know they care, counselors have a significant impact on healthy development. As discussed earlier in this chapter, an important role that all teachers assume to some degree is supporting students' social and emotional development. Some teachers, however, despite a lack of training, find this aspect of teaching extremely important and make it a high priority in their interactions with students. They enjoy the opportunity to assist students in their social and emotional development and do an excellent job of listening to and guiding students as they struggle with a variety of difficult and stressful issues.

Teacher as manager. A final teaching style to be identified is the **teacher as manager.** A good manager in business and industry today is considered a person who creates a supportive atmosphere where employees are eager to do their jobs and work as a team for the good of the group. These managers have established a good rapport with employees, get them involved in the decision-making process, and provide them with the support they need to be productive in their work efforts. Teachers who see themselves as managers serve as guides to student growth by preparing an environment that is rich in potential learning possibilities. Managing teachers give students the opportunity to make at least some of the decisions that are relevant to their own learning. In addition, they work to foster positive teacher–student and peer relationships.

**Reflection
Opportunity 3.7**

After having read through the descriptions of teaching styles presented in Table 3.10 and described above, think about teachers you have known and try to identify the styles they exhibited. As you reflect on their abilities and personalities, were there differences in the ways in which they approached the challenges of teaching? Think about which style or styles you responded to favorably as a student. Which teaching style or styles do you think were most effective in promoting your learning and development? Do you think other students prefer different styles?

Because students come to the classroom with varying learning styles (Guild & Garger, 1998) and diverse needs and interests, schools benefit when they can hire effective teachers with a variety of teaching styles. There is no one style that is the best. In fact the most effective teachers combine a variety of these teaching styles. Each style has its strength, and each is needed in every classroom. Consider which styles seem appealing to you at this time. What do you like about these teaching descriptions? Take a look now at the *Consider This* feature found on the Companion Website for this text and see if you can identify the teaching style of an effective teacher you had in your K–12 education.

**Consider This:
Effective Teachers**

Summary

In this chapter, four questions were used to clarify your thinking about America's teachers:

Who are our teachers?

A number of characteristics help define teachers today:

- Teachers' ages
- Years of teaching experience
- Degrees earned
- Gender
- Racial diversity

What are their roles?

The many roles of teachers today make education a challenging, yet exciting career. These roles include the following:

- Facilitating learning (Praxis II, topics IIa, IIb)
- Supporting social/emotional development (Praxis II, topics Ia, IIIa)
- Sharing resources for growth and development
- Serving as a role model

What skills and attitudes are characteristic of effective teachers?

All good teachers share a common set of skills and attitudes, such as these:

- Engaging in quality planning and preparation
- Preparing a positive classroom environment
- Using proven instructional techniques
- Exhibiting professional behavior (Praxis II, topic IVa)
- Being real
- Seeking self-understanding
- Having positive attitudes toward students (Praxis II, topics Ia, Ib)
- Getting excited about learning
- Collaborating with other adults (Praxis II, topic IVb)

What teaching style(s) do effective teachers implement?

Because teachers bring their own personalities to teaching, effective teachers often have very different styles. Metaphors have been used to describe these styles:

- Teacher as coach
- Teacher as quarterback
- Teacher as artist
- Teacher as actor
- Teacher as counselor
- Teacher as manager

PRAXIS Test-Preparation Activities

To review an on-line chapter case study, test your understanding of chapter topics and concepts, and begin preparing for the Praxis II: Principles of Learning and Teaching examination, go to the *Praxis Test Preparation* module for this chapter of the Companion Website.

Organizing Questions

Review questions, field-experience opportunities, and activities for building your portfolio are included here for the organizing questions in this chapter.

Who are our teachers?

Review Questions

1. What is the typical educational level of teachers today?
2. What are some factors influencing the low numbers of minority teachers in America's schools?

Building Your Portfolio: *My Personal Identity*

INTASC Standard 9. Spend some time reflecting on your own age, sex, and race.

- How do you see the above-mentioned factors influencing your relationships with students in the classroom?
- Do you think they will have a positive or negative impact on your interactions with parents and other school personnel?
- Describe in writing these aspects of your personal identity and their potential impact on teaching and learning.

What are their roles?

Review Questions

1. Identify the teaching roles discussed in this chapter. From your own educational experience, describe an example of a teacher assuming each of these roles.

2. What resources are available to help you support students and their families?

Field Experience

Spend some time talking with a classroom teacher of your choice about the planning and preparation needed for effective teaching. Ask this teacher the following questions:

- Ask the teacher to identify and describe the roles he or she assumes in the classroom. (Share the roles described in this text if necessary.)
- Ask the teacher which role is most challenging? Find out why the teacher finds this role so challenging.
- Discuss your findings with others in your class.

Building Your Portfolio: *Teaching Roles*

INTASC Standard 2. For an age/grade/subject matter area of your choice, identify one of the teaching roles presented in this chapter.

- Describe how you will accomplish it as a future teacher.
- What personal strengths will help you be successful in the role?
- What limitations will you need to overcome?
- Describe what you see to be the importance of the role you chose for this portfolio entry.

What skills and attitudes are characteristic of effective teachers?

Review Questions

1. Outline the process of preparing a positive classroom learning environment.

2. What are the behaviors you will need to exhibit to engage in professional teaching?

3. Identify the attitudes of effective teachers.

Field Experience

Observe a teacher working with students in the classroom.

- What strategies were used to stimulate student learning?
- Describe the efforts made to maintain and build teacher–student and peer relationships.
- Did you see the teacher interact with parents or other school personnel? Describe these interactions. (If you did not get an opportunity to observe these types of interactions, try to spend time talking with the teacher about how they communicate with their students' families and school colleagues.)
- What do your observations tell you about the skills and attitudes needed for effective teaching?

Building Your Portfolio: *Positive Attitudes*

INTASC Standard 9. Write down in list format the attitudes of effective teachers defined in this chapter.

- As you reflect on this list, consider adding others of your own choosing.
- Once your list is complete, write down your own interpretation of how effective you will be in maintaining each of these attitudes as you work with students.
- Describe any problem areas you see and how you will work to overcome them. Save this list and your responses to it as an entry in your portfolio.

What teaching style(s) do effective teachers implement?

Review Questions

1. Why are metaphors useful in helping others understand differences in teaching styles?
2. How can teachers with different styles be effective?

Building Your Portfolio: *Teaching Style*

INTASC Standard 9. Choose one of the metaphors for teaching style described in this chapter or come up with one of your own (examples: teacher as gardener; teacher as conductor) that you feel describes the teaching style you would like to have.

- Describe in more detail what you see as being the characteristics of this teaching style.
- How will your personal strengths and limitations influence your use of this style? Save your responses to these questions as an entry in your portfolio.

Suggested Readings

Ashton-Warner, S. (1963). *Teacher.* New York: Bantam. In this classic book a passionate educator describes her methods and shares her love for teaching. Whether or not you agree with her methodology, you will be inspired by the joy she found in teaching and the caring attitude she had toward children. Ashton-Warner's teaching style has been an encouragement to a great many over the years.

Guild, P., & Garger, S. (1998). *Marching to different drummers* (2nd ed.). Alexandria, VA: Association for Supervision and Curriculum Development. This text provides an excellent overview of student diversity due to culture, brain differences, and learning styles. Several chapters also deal with the issues of teaching styles and the importance of finding one's personal style and building on its strengths.

Jersild, A. (1955). *When teachers face themselves.* New York: Teachers College Press. Jersild, in this classic text, describes the importance of teachers' self-understandings in effective education. He makes a strong case for self-understanding being a foundation to effective teaching and learning.

Rogers, C. (1969). *Freedom to learn.* Columbus, OH: Merrill. Rogers, in another classic text, proposes an approach to education in which teachers create an atmosphere where students are free to learn. Teachers do not simply turn students loose to do what they please, but rather carefully create a caring environment in which "significant, self-initiated, experiential learning is possible". (p. 9)

References

Archer, J. (1999). New teachers abandon field at high rate. *Education Week, 18*(27), 1, 20–21.

Ashton-Warner, S. (1963). *Teacher.* New York: Bantam Books.

Baker, D.P., & Smith, T. (1997). Trend 2: Teacher turnover and teacher quality: Refocusing the Issue. *Teachers College Record, 99,* 29–35.

Brophy, J. (1983). Research on the self-fulfilling prophecy and teacher expectations. *Journal of Educational Psychology, 75,* 631–661.

Center for Strengthening the Teaching Profession. (2005). *Teacher retention and mobility.* Silverdale, WA: Author

Codell, E. (1999). *Educating Esmé. Diary of a teacher's first year.* Chapel Hill, NC: Algonquin Books.

Council of Chief State School Officers. (2002). *Voices for the future.* Retrieved October 17, 2008 from: http://www.ccsso.org/.

Danielson, C. (2007). *Enhancing professional practice: A framework for teaching.* (2nd ed.) Alexandria, VA: Association for Supervision and Curriculum Development.

Disney Learning Partnership. (2002). *American Teacher Award honorees.* Retrieved July 16, 2002, from: http://disney.go.com/disneylearning/ata

Dunne, F., Nave, B., Lewis, A. (December, 2000). *Critical friends groups: Teachers helping teachers to improve student learning.* Research Bulletin: Phi Delta Kappa Center for Evaluation, Development and Research. Retrieved August 7, 2005 from: http://www.pdkintl.org/edres/resbul28.htm

Freeman, C. (2004). *Trends in educational equity of girls & women: 2004.* Retrieved November 27, 2004 from: http://nces.ed.gov/pubs2005/2005016.pdf.

Ginott, H. (1972). *Teacher and child. A book for parents and teachers.* New York: Macmillan.

Glasser, W. (1990). *The quality school: Managing students without coercion.* New York: Harper and Row.

Good, T., & Brophy, J. (2008). *Looking in classrooms* (10th ed.). Boston: Allyn and Bacon.

Goodlad, J. (1984). *A place called school.* New York: Macmillan.

Guild, P., & Garger, S. (1998). *Marching to different drummers* (2nd ed.). Alexandria, VA: Association for Supervision and Curriculum Development.

Greenberg, H. (1969). *Teaching with feeling.* Indianapolis, IN: Pegasus.

Interstate New Teacher Assessment and Support Consortium. (1992). *Model standards for beginning teacher licensing, assessment and development: A resource for state dialogue.* Washington, DC: Council of Chief State School Officers.

Jersild, A. (1955). *When teachers face themselves.* New York: Teachers College Press.

Milken, L. (2002). Growth of the Teacher Advancement Program: Teaching as the opportunity. Retrieved November 7, 2008 from: http://www.mff.org/pubs/lm_tap_book.pdf

National Board for Professional Teaching Standards. (2008). *What teachers should know and be able to do: The five core propositions of the National Board.* Retrieved October 21, 2008 from http://www.nbpts.org/userfiles/file/what_teachers.pdf.

National Center for Education Statistics. (2007). *Digest of Education Statistics, 2007.* Retrieved November 27, 2008 from: http://nces.ed.gov/programs/digest/d07/tables/dt07_064.asp

National Council for Accreditation of Teacher Education. (2002). *Professional standards for the accreditation of schools, colleges, and departments of education.* Washington, DC: Author.

National Education Association (NEA). (2003). *Status of the American public school teacher 2000–2001.* Washington, D.C.: Author.

National Education Association (NEA). (2007). *Rankings & estimates: Rankings of the states 2006 and estimates of school statistics 2007.* Retrieved October 20, 2008 from: http://www.nea.org/

North Carolina State Board of Education. Troops to teacher program. Retrieved August 9, 2005 from: http://www.ncpublicschools.org/troops/

Rogers, C. (1969). *Freedom to learn.* Upper Saddle River, NJ: Merrill/Prentice Hall.

Rubin, L. (1985). *Artistry in teaching.* New York: Random House.

What matters most: Teaching for America's future (1996). Retrieved June 7, 2005 from: http://www.tc.edu/nctaf/publications/whatmattersmost.html

There are many parents like Matiul and Happy who struggle with the task of finding the best schools to meet the needs of their children. Statistics indicate that more students than ever before are enrolled in schools that their parents have selected. As this trend toward increasing educational options for students continues, parents will be faced with even greater challenges in determining the best choices for their children.

In this chapter, you are going to read about different levels and types of schooling and the people that work in each setting. The main purpose for this chapter is to help you begin to identify which programs, grade levels, and subject-matter areas best fit your personality and interests. In other words, what teaching role(s) are you attracted to and why? You will need to decide what subjects and ages of students appeal to you. As you read the following sections, reflect on your feelings about each of the schooling options presented. If possible, spend some time observing and participating in a variety of school settings. After reading about and getting involved in several classrooms, you will find some that feel right, others that seem an unlikely match, and a few that are definitely out as possibilities. While finding the right school and classroom match may take several years to complete, it is important to begin now to identify your place in the educational system.

How are schools traditionally organized?

Although you spent many years attending schools during your public or private education, you may not have a clear understanding of the different ways in which schools are organized. Having a good overview can help you understand the system better and assist you in making good choices some day about school preferences and desired teaching experiences. Even though you think a particular grade or subject interests you the most at this point, think carefully about all the different possibilities presented here. You may find that other options become more attractive as you study them in more depth. Figure 4.1 provides a visual summary of the common configurations found in schools. Each of these schooling options will be discussed in more detail below.

Although there is great diversity in the ages and grades of students included in school buildings, there are four common configurations. The first is **early-childhood education (ECE),** which has been defined by the National Association for the Education of Young Children (NAEYC) as including children from birth through 8 years of age (National Association for the Education of Young Children, 2008). This definition means that children through Grade 3 are considered part of early-childhood education. In many instances, children from birth through age 5 are housed in special facilities for young children, whereas kindergarten through Grade 3 students are most commonly found in elementary schools. The second traditional grouping of students is **elementary education,** which includes children from kindergarten through fifth or sixth grade. In most school districts, students move from their elementary experiences to a middle or junior high school. **Middle school** is most commonly organized for children beginning in the fifth or sixth and continuing through the eighth grade, and **junior high schools** typically consist of the seventh, eighth, and ninth grades. The final level is the **senior high school,** which is organized to accommodate students beginning in the 9th or 10th and continuing through the 12th grades.

Early-Childhood Education

Programs in early childhood education have shown steady growth during the last several decades. One reason for this increase is the large number of mothers with young children in the workforce (Annie E. Casey Foundation, 2008). Another major factor is the recent research evidence that supports the importance of the early years for overall child development (Mead, 2004). Early-childhood programs can be divided into three subgroups:

- *Infant/toddler programs*—serve children from birth to 2 years of age;
- *Pre-kindergarten programs*—support learning and development for 3- and 4-year-olds;
- *Primary education*—serves children from 5 through 8 years of age.

Figure 4.1 Typical School Organizations

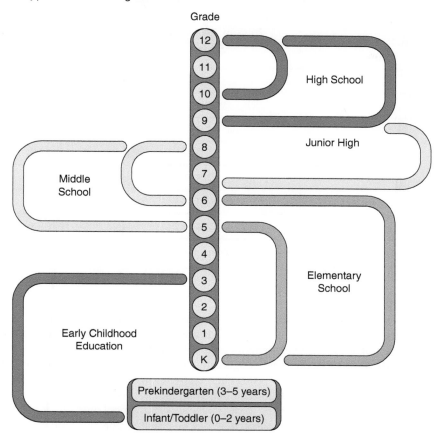

Infant/Toddler Education. Programs for infants and toddlers are not yet a common part of public education because quality programs are expensive to implement (Massachusetts Cost and Quality Study, 2004). At the same time, however, close to three-quarters of all families are placing their very young children in child-care settings on a regular basis (Honig, 2002). Options for children with special needs at this age, however, are becoming more widespread in many communities and are starting to find their way into public-school settings. Another option that is available in some high schools is an infant/toddler program combined with a parent-education program for teens. Maggie Wilson, for example, teaches high school social studies but also spends part of her day teaching a course in child development and coordinating the infant/toddler program offered for teen mothers and fathers. She has seven children in the program, with mothers and fathers spending time each day working with the infants and toddlers as part of the requirements for the course in child development.

Pre-kindergarten Education. Children 3 and 4 years of age are increasingly involved in pre-kindergarten education. Table 4.1 provides data on these enrollment trends since 1965. Most of these students are taught in two main types of privately operated pre-kindergarten programs that are open to all families who can afford to pay the costs of tuition. **Preschool** programs typically operate 2 or 3 half-days each week and provide play opportunities and enrichment experiences that help prepare children for K–12 education. **Day-care** programs provide services for employed parents who need education and care for their children during the workday and normally offer care from around 7 a.m. until approximately 6 p.m.

TABLE 4.1   Enrollment in Pre-kindergarten Programs

Year	Percent 3-Year-Olds	Percent 4-Year-Olds
1965	4.9	16.1
1975	21.5	40.5
1985	28.8	49.1
1990	32.6	56.1
1995	35.9	61.6
1998	37.6	66.6
2000	39.2	68.9
2006	42.4	68.8

Adapted from *Digest of Education Statistics,* by National Center for Education Statistics, 2008. Washington, DC: U.S. Government Printing Office.

In addition to the private pre-kindergarten options, some 3- and 4-year-olds are participating in programs housed in U.S. public schools. Approximately 35% of all public schools have either full-day or part-day programs located in their buildings (Wirt et al., 2004). Many of the pre-kindergarten programs housed in public schools are designed to meet the needs of special populations of young children. The Head Start program for young children from low-income families is probably the best known of these options. Preschools for children with special needs are also growing in numbers because of federal legislation mandating these programs within school districts.

In order to better understand what it is like to teach at the pre-kindergarten level, the following scenario describes a typical pre-kindergarten center. Although the program is hypothetical, data from a real center were used in preparing this scenario. As you read about this setting, try placing yourself in the situation as a new teacher. How would you feel about working with pre-kindergarten students? Think about personal strengths and limitations that might make it easier or more difficult for you to work at this level.

Brookhaven Head Start Child-Care Center. The Brookhaven Head Start Child-Care Center has provided quality services to low-income children and their families for the past 7 years. It is one of eight centers in this community of 75,000 and is part of a growing number of Head Start programs that offer full-day child care for those who participate. Funded through a combination of federal, state, and local housing authority monies, Brookhaven is open from 6:30 a.m. until 6:30 p.m., 49 weeks of the year. A total of 34 4- and 5-year-old children from low-income families are enrolled.

A Head Start program supervisor for the community oversees the education curriculum and basic child services provided at each of the Head Start centers, including Brookhaven. In addition, the center supervisor coordinates student and family services on-site. Three teachers work 40 hours each week planning, preparing, and implementing educational experiences for their students. Each teacher is also responsible for conducting regular home visits with 10–12 families. During these contacts, teachers share suggestions with parents about working with their children at home and identify resources to help meet a variety of family needs. An assistant to the center supervisor, four teaching assistants, and a cook are also employed at Brookhaven. Three times each year, the Interfaith Coalition sponsors a health and dental screening program. Children who are found to have medical or dental needs are referred to appropriate community services.

Figure 4.2   Brookhaven Daily Schedule

6:30–8:00 A.M.	Opening/safety checklist/setup/early morning snack/limited center activities
8:00–9:00 A.M.	Learning Center choices
9:00–10:00 A.M.	Cleanup, toileting, snack time, tooth brushing, transition to group time
10:00–11:00 A.M.	Circle time, small-group times (language, math, science, gross motor), cleanup, cooperative group skill development
11:00 A.M.–12:15 P.M.	Learning areas, large- and small-group activities, cleanup
12:15–1:00 P.M.	Hand washing, lunch, cleanup
1:00–2:30 P.M.	Tooth brushing, bathroom, nap preparation, nap time/quiet time
2:30–3:15 P.M.	Outdoor time
3:15–4:45 P.M.	Transition to classroom, Learning Center choices
4:45–5:30 P.M.	Small motor activities, journals
5:30–6:30 P.M.	Cleanup, story, departure

The Brookhaven Center consists of two large rooms that are organized into learning centers. Each center is equipped with toys and materials that children use during free-choice times throughout their school day. The learning centers include art, books, blocks, computers, writing materials, dramatic play materials, manipulatives, and music. Materials in each center are organized on low shelves so that children can easily access them and can readily return materials to their proper places at the end of their playtimes. Figure 4.2 gives the daily schedule for the center.

Sue Sandford has been a teacher at Brookhaven for the past 3 years. She has a bachelor's degree in elementary education and is working toward her endorsement in early childhood education. Sue spends 6 hours each day in the classroom working with children in the center. In addition, she sets 2 hours aside for daily planning and the conducting of home visits with families participating in the Head Start Center programs. Although the center opens at 6:30 a.m., teachers stagger their times in the classroom and Sue is responsible for children beginning at 12:30 p.m. and remains until the center closes at 6:30 p.m.

Have you spent time as an adult in a pre-kindergarten classroom? If so, what was it like? What was the teacher's role in the classroom? Was the classroom set up in learning centers? How did it compare to the Brookhaven Center described here? If you have not been in a prekindergarten setting as an adult, have you spent any time with young children of this age? What were your reactions to these children? Do you have an interest in learning more about teaching at this level? What would you need to do or see in order to better know how you would feel about teaching at the prekindergarten level?

**Reflection
Opportunity 4.1**

Elementary Education

Traditional elementary education, from colonial times through the early part of the 20th century, consisted of Grades 1–8. Students completing elementary school then moved directly into 4-year high schools. Three sublevels were common to this traditional elementary school: primary education (Grades 1–3), the intermediate grades (4–6), and upper elementary (Grades 7 and 8). This pattern of organization slowly changed at both ends, with kindergarten programs being added to the beginning and the fifth or sixth through eighth grades moving to junior high or middle school buildings.

Teachers in elementary schools typically have what are referred to as **self-contained classrooms.** For the most part, this means they are responsible for teaching all subjects and that students remain in the same classroom for most of the school day. The common exceptions to this self-contained format are the teaching of music, art, and physical education by specialists in areas outside the regular classroom. For example, Josh Anderson's fifth-grade students spend 30 minutes twice each week with the physical education specialist and receive music and art instruction on alternate weeks. If he chooses to do so, Josh can then supplement these experiences with his own physical education, art, and music activities throughout the week.

With the many different educational responsibilities of elementary teachers, it is often helpful to have assistance from parents and community members in preparing for, and teaching at this level. To watch a video of an interview with a teacher and parent regarding parent involvement, go to the Companion Website for this text and click on MyEducationLab for Chapter 4.

myeducationlab
The Power of Classroom Practice

MyEducationLab 4.1

Kindergarten. Kindergarten programs typically serve 5-year-old children and prepare them for the academic curriculum of first grade. These programs began in Germany in the middle part of the 19th century under the leadership of Friedrich Froebel (1886) and gradually became an option for American children. Chapter 10 provides additional information on the history of kindergarten education.

Traditional kindergarten programs emphasized the development of social and emotional skills while also preparing students for a first-grade program that included reading, writing, mathematics, science, and social studies learning. The importance of social and emotional development in kindergarten is idealized in a popular book by Robert Fulghum (1989) titled *All I Really Need to Know I Learned in Kindergarten*. He states that in kindergarten he learned the most important lessons in life, which include:

> Share everything.
>
> Play fair.
>
> Don't hit people.
>
> Put things back where you found them. Clean up your own mess.
>
> Don't take things that aren't yours.
>
> Say you're sorry when you hurt somebody.
>
> Wash your hands before you eat.
>
> Flush.
>
> Live a balanced life.
>
> When you go out into the world, watch out for traffic, hold hands, and stick together.
>
> Be aware of wonder. (pp. 6–7)

To develop these social understandings and prepare for the more academic subjects of first grade, traditional kindergarten programs provided large blocks of time for children to play. Through their interactions with dolls, blocks, other toys, and each other, students were able to develop many of the basic skills needed for success in later schooling.

More recently, kindergarten programs have evolved into classrooms where much of the school day is spent on traditional academic subjects. Teachers are working with students in large and small groups to guide the development of skills needed for success in reading, mathematics, and other academic subjects. With the current emphasis on getting children ready to learn that comes from the *No Child Left Behind Act of 2001,* it is more difficult for kindergarten teachers to justify the playful activities that were more commonly a part of the school day. Consequently, children in kindergarten programs today typically have fewer opportunities to engage in this valuable learning experience.

Primary Education. The first–third grades are an important time for developing the basic academic skills needed for success in later schooling. The teaching of reading, writing, spelling, arithmetic, science, and social studies forms the core of the curriculum. Typically, students spend an hour or more daily in literacy learning, a similar amount of time in mathematics instruction, and have two or three weekly opportunities for science and social studies learning. Children who successfully master these fundamental skills develop attitudes and expertise that will help them throughout their schooling. Those who fall behind or struggle at this level may well find their future academic progress hindered.

Those teaching in the primary grades often feel torn between the teaching approaches common to early-childhood education and those used in the more traditional elementary-school classroom. In early-childhood education, more emphasis is placed on active learning and teaching that integrates mathematics, science, and literacy learning into activities that are of interest to children (see Chapters 7 and 8 for more information). Traditional elementary education at the primary level is more subject based, and teachers typically have separate times during the day when they engage students in science, mathematics, and literacy learning.

One of the newer strategies being used at the primary level to assist young children in their learning and development is the multiage classroom where children of different ages are taught in the same setting. There are many benefits to this strategy, including the possibility of one teacher working with the same children for several years. To read an article on multiage classrooms, go to the Companion Website for this text and click on MyEducationLab for Chapter 4.

myeducationlab
The Power of Classroom Practice
MyEducationLab 4.2

Intermediate Grades. The fourth through the fifth or sixth grades (ages 9–11) are an important time for students. They spend this time refining the basic academic skills learned during the preceding years and begin to pursue special interests in more depth. Students are becoming more self-aware and learning more about their own personal strengths and limitations. During this time, students also begin to separate emotionally from their families and peer influence grows.

While remaining self-contained, some intermediate classrooms become more specialized when two or more teachers work together to provide instruction. For example, Sharon White and Alyssa Franklin, two fifth-grade teachers, are sharing the teaching responsibilities for their respective classes of 25 and 27 students. Sharon teaches both groups mathematics, and Alyssa takes responsibility for all language arts instruction. The teachers have adjoining classrooms and simply switch rooms when it becomes necessary to do so. This option allows them both to teach subjects they enjoy and accommodates their individual strengths. Students and parents both seem to like this approach to instruction. In the following description of another hypothetical school setting, you will learn more about what it is like to teach at the elementary-school level.

Trentwood Elementary School. Trentwood Elementary is a K–5 school with just over 300 students. It is nestled into a quiet neighborhood of predominantly lower-middle-class families. Some students are close enough to walk to school, but many ride school buses and begin arriving around 8:30 a.m. for the 8:55 a.m. through 3:30 p.m. school day. The school has 14 classroom teachers, 2 special-education teachers, a music specialist, a physical education teacher, and 2 reading specialists. Years of teaching experience vary from 2 to 32, with the average being 18 years in the classroom. In addition, there are 9 part- or full-time instructional assistants who provide support for classroom instruction, English as a Second Language (ESL), and special education. Other staff members include the school principal, secretary, school psychologist/student-support specialist (two-thirds time), library/media specialist, library assistant, two cooks, two custodians, and a school nurse (1 day a week).

Although most teachers spend considerably more time than the minimum required in their contracts, they are expected to be in the elementary school building between 8:30 a.m. and 4 p.m. daily. A typical schedule for a third-grade classroom at Trentwood Elementary is presented in Figure 4.3. Planning lessons, preparing materials for classroom use, evaluating student

Figure 4.3   Trentwood Elementary Schedule, Grade Three

8:55–9:45 A.M.	Opening, daily oral language, spelling
9:45–10:30 A.M.	Mathematics, PE (Monday, Wednesday)
10:30–10:45 A.M.	Recess
10:45 A.M.–12:00 P.M.	Literacy block
12:00–12:45 P.M.	Lunch
12:45–1:45 P.M.	Sustained silent reading, library (Friday)
1:45–2:45 P.M.	Science, PE (Thursday)
2:45–3:30 P.M.	Social studies, music (Tuesday, Thursday)

performance, communicating with parents, and meeting with other teachers generally occur outside the regular school day.

Steve Brenner, in his second year of teaching at Trentwood Elementary, is already involved in a number of extracurricular activities at the school. In addition to the biweekly staff meetings called by the school principal, he is a member of the professional development committee, which helps plan the in-service training activities that will occur throughout the year. Steve also participates in the technology and literacy study group and meets once a month with fellow teachers to collaborate and plan for these two important parts of the curriculum. In addition, he is involved in individualized education program (IEP) and multidisciplinary team (MDT) meetings for children with special needs. Finally, Steve organizes an after-school art club that meets for 6 weeks every spring. With the exception of music and physical education, Steve teaches all subjects to his class of 26 8-year-olds. Even though Steve is just in his second year of teaching, he has already developed a strong following of students and parents who greatly appreciate him as a teacher.

Reflection Opportunity 4.2

Views from the Classroom: Changing Grade Levels

Consider spending a few minutes to reflect on teaching at the elementary-school level. How well do you relate to elementary-age children? Are you comfortable communicating with them, or is it awkward to try to hold a conversation with a young child? What does your response tell you about how effective you would be as an elementary school teacher? How would you feel about teaching all subjects in an elementary classroom? Could you get excited about all subject-matter areas or are there some that would be hard to teach? Can you see yourself enjoying a career working at this level? What makes you feel this way?

You may find that even though you think that elementary teaching is an option you want to pursue, it is difficult to narrow down your choice of grade levels. Some veteran teachers find that changing grade levels can be a positive move that adds new meaning to teaching responsibilities. The *Views from the Classroom* feature for this chapter is one teacher's perspectives on changing grade levels. Go to the Companion Website for this text and read her reflections.

Junior High and Middle Schools

Beginning in the early 20th century, the combination of a burgeoning school population and an increasingly complex curriculum led to the growth of new schooling options. Junior high school programs for students in Grades 7–9 appeared in the early part of the 20th century. By midcentury, they were common in most American school districts. Beginning in the late 1960s, middle schools for Grades 6–8 provided yet another option for schools. Today, middle schools are now the more common bridge between elementary and secondary education. Middle schools continue to grow in number, whereas junior high options continue to decline, as indicated in Table 4.2.

TABLE 4.2   Public Junior High and Middle Schools

Year	Middle Schools	Junior High Schools
1970–1971	2,080	7,750
1975–1976	3,916	7,521
1980–1981	6,003	5,890
1990–1991	8,545	4,561
1995–1996	10,205	3,743
1997–1998	10,944	3,599
2005–2006	12,545	3,249

Adapted from *Digest of Education Statistics,* by National Center for Education Statistics, 2007. Washington, DC: U.S. Government Printing Office.

Junior High Schools. Typically, junior high schools include Grades 7 through 8 or 9 and serve as a period of transition between elementary and secondary education. Educators at the beginning of the 20th century gave three main reasons for the creation of junior high schools (Pulliam & Van Patten, 2003):

- Educators desired to extend the academic curriculum of the high school downward into the upper elementary grades (seventh and eighth grades).
- The needs of older elementary students were not being met by the traditional elementary school.
- A new school structure was needed to smooth the transition from childhood to young adulthood.

Another more practical and less student-oriented reason for the movement to junior high school programs was the need to alleviate a school-building shortage at the elementary level due to increasing enrollments. Many school districts decided to build new high schools and then use the vacated school buildings to house junior high programs for the seventh through the ninth grades. Although this approach was effective in managing the large elementary school enrollments, it did not provide a good rationale for quality programs at the junior high school level.

Although some teachers at the junior high level are responsible for teaching a block of courses such as the language arts (reading, writing, and English) over a longer part of the school day (2–3 hours), junior high schools are usually departmentalized, meaning teachers specialize in one or more subject areas and teach those subjects to groups of students for 45–50 minute periods. For example, Bill North spends his day teaching mathematics at the junior high level. He has two integrated mathematics classes, two groups of beginning algebra students, and one geometry class in addition to his planning period. In addition to the core academic subjects of mathematics, social studies, science, and the language arts, junior high school teachers often provide opportunities to explore other courses, including business, agriculture, physical education, home economics, and vocational education.

In an effort to make junior high schools friendly places for students, a number of different strategies are being tried. One option is to create a system of social houses to improve school climate. To read an article on this topic, go to the Companion Website for this text and click on MyEducationLab for Chapter 4.

MyEducationLab 4.3

Ian's Classroom Experiences: Advocate Without

Middle School Programs. Middle schools typically serve students in Grades 5 or 6 through Grade 8. One very positive feature of the typical middle school is the effort made to transition students from the self-contained teaching typically found in elementary schools to the departmentalized format they will see in high school. Fifth- and sixth-grade teachers at the middle school level typically spend about half of their day with the same group of students and then have the opportunity to do more departmentalized teaching for the remainder. For example, Tanya Jacobs teaches sixth grade in a middle school and spends her mornings teaching the same group of students an integrated language arts curriculum. Her afternoons are then spent teaching social studies to three classes of sixth graders. Seventh- and eighth-grade teachers in Tanya's building, on the other hand, spend most of their time instructing four or five different groups of students in a more specialized curriculum. In comparison to traditional junior high schools, middle school programs have tended to place greater emphasis on career counseling, personal counseling, and relevant learning experiences. You may want to read *Ian's Classroom Experiences* for this chapter to get further insights into middle school teaching.

Efforts are currently under way by middle school educators to establish a better balance between the counseling and relevant learning experiences approach and a more academic emphasis. Reform efforts emphasize seven key ingredients (Jackson & Davis, 2000):

- A rigorous yet relevant curriculum based on how students at this age learn best
- Instructional methods that help all students achieve high standards and develop into lifelong learners
- Teachers who are well prepared to understand and instruct young adolescents
- A caring community of learners developed through strong adult–student relationships
- Democratic governance of schools through the participation of all staff members
- A safe and healthy school environment that promotes academic performance and personal development
- Parent and community involvement in supporting student learning

Hoover Middle School. The following scenario describes Hoover Middle School, a hypothetical setting that should help you understand what teaching at this level would be like. Hoover is one of the older buildings in the school district, having been built in 1953. It was originally constructed as the high school for a community of approximately 15,000. As the city grew and needs changed, Hoover eventually became a middle school and now houses approximately 650 sixth-, seventh-, and eighth-grade students. The staff includes 28 teachers, 4 special educators, 1 library media specialist, 1 counselor, 2 administrators (principal and assistant principal), 2 certified support staff (a psychologist and a speech and language pathologist), and 15 classified support personnel (instructional assistants, office personnel, custodians, and food service staff).

Although the building is showing signs of wear, the teachers and staff at Hoover are enthusiastic and motivated. They have adopted a teaming model, and six interdisciplinary teams work cooperatively to teach integrated studies (language arts and social studies), science, and mathematics. Students with special needs are included within each of the six groups and special education teachers are assigned to each grade level to support students with disabilities who have been placed in the regular education classroom.

Teachers at Hoover Middle School are contracted to be in the school from 8:00 a.m. through 3:30 p.m. daily, with lunch breaks and planning periods free from student responsibilities. Figure 4.4 gives a sample teaching schedule for Hoover Middle School. In addition to teaching responsibilities, each interdisciplinary team meets for 2 hours each week outside the regular school day to jointly plan future activities. Meetings of the entire school staff are held after school on the third Tuesday of each month.

Figure 4.4 Sample Teaching Schedule, Hoover Middle School

8:25–9:33 A.M.	Block I (integrated language arts and social studies)
9:37–10:41 A.M.	Block II (integrated language arts and social studies)
10:45–11:49 A.M.	Block III (integrated language arts and social studies)
11:54 A.M.–12:24 P.M.	Lunch
12:29–1:00 P.M.	Block IV (reading)
1:04–2:09 P.M.	Block V (integrated language arts and social studies)
2:13–3:02 P.M.	Planning period (students in enrichment activities)

Mary Franklin is in her 12th year at Hoover. Her teaching responsibilities include language arts, reading, and social studies. Mary is part of the seventh-grade interdisciplinary team and works with five other science, mathematics, and special education teachers to implement an integrated curriculum for just over 100 seventh-grade students in the school. In addition to her responsibilities in the classroom, Mary has chosen to get involved in several extracurricular activities. She is head coach for the track team, assists with girls' basketball, and is part of the faculty group that coordinates the after-school study lab. Mary receives extra pay for each of these assignments and has a supplementary contract with her school district for the delivery of these services.

Reflect on the information presented above on middle and junior high schools. Think first about your own personal experience. Which type did you attend? What do you remember from these years? Based on your current understandings of both settings, what do you see as the strengths and limitations of each school type? If you were a parent of a seventh-grade student, would you rather they attended a middle school or a junior high school? What is your rationale for this decision? Can you see yourself teaching in a middle school like the one described above? Why or why not?

**Reflection
Opportunity 4.3**

Senior High Schools

For much of their history, senior high schools consisted of Grades 9–12 for those students who were able to continue their education following 8 years at the elementary level. With the addition of junior high schools in the early part of the 20th century, high schools more typically enrolled students in Grades 10–12. Currently, both organizational structures are found. Districts using a middle school model usually have 4-year high schools, whereas those with junior high programs generally have 3-year high schools.

Initially, high schools were privately supported through parental tuition and served one primary purpose: to prepare students for a college education. It was not until the late 1800s that publicly funded high school programs began to appear. Gradually, as a high school education became more available to all, the focus became more comprehensive. **Comprehensive high schools** offer some students the education they need to be prepared for college, while at the same time providing others with course options that will better prepare them for a job. For instance, Shawn Smith and Jerry Baldwin, good friends who teach at the same high school, are typical of the very different teaching assignments that exist at most high schools. Despite their friendship, they rarely see each other during the school day. Shawn's classroom is in the industrial technology wing where he teaches principles of technology and manufacturing technology. Many of his students will complete their high school degrees and then attend the local community college for more specific vocational–technical preparation. Jerry, on the other hand, teaches science in a separate campus building that houses both the science and mathematics departments. He has three periods of general science and two biology classes each term. Typically, Jerry's students are more likely to go on to a 4-year college after their high school experience. School-wide meetings, which occur infrequently, are generally the only time when Shawn and Jerry see one another at school.

This move to comprehensive high schools has been accompanied by considerable controversy. Critics argue that high schools need a core curriculum that all students should complete. Vocational–technical education is seen as "watered down" academic programs that don't adequately prepare students for the world of work. These concerns led to three key reform reports from the 1980s. Each proposed significant modifications in the high school curriculum. These reports are summarized in Table 4.3.

Despite the criticisms over what is being taught in American high schools, the majority of young people attend and successfully complete a secondary education degree. At the same time, however, the number of students who fail to complete a high school education or its equivalent is troublesome. Although the percentage of dropouts has declined from over 27% in 1960 to just over 9% in 2006 (National Center for Education Statistics, 2008), far too many young people still fail to complete what has become the basic level of education necessary to result in reasonably good job opportunities.

Sentinel High School. The following scenario describes a typical high school setting so that you can reflect on what it would be like to teach at this level. Sentinel High School, constructed in 1966 to meet the growing educational needs of a suburban community, is now a large campus housing more than 1,600 students in grades 9 through 12. Sentinel has four full-time administrators, including the school principal, two assistant principals, and an activities and athletics director. The 82 certificated faculty are organized by area of expertise, with 3 in business education, 5 in the career/counseling center, 11 English educators, 3 faculty in family and consumer education, 6 in the fine arts (music, art, and drama), 7 world language educators, 1 library media and technology specialist, 9 mathematics faculty, 5 faculty in physical education, 8 science educators, 7 social studies instructors, 2 technology faculty, 7 staff in the specialized instruction department, and 8 faculty in interdepartmental instructional programs (alternative school, driver

TABLE 4.3   High School Reform Efforts

Reform Title	Description
The Paideia Proposal	Adler (1982) proposed a more classic high school curriculum based on the Great Books that would allow students virtually no elective course work.
A Nation at Risk	This influential report (National Commission on Excellence in Education, 1983), suggested that all high school students be required to take four years of English, and three years each of mathematics, science, and social studies.
American High School Study	In a proposal parallel to that of the *Nation at Risk* report, this study recommended an increase in the academic core required for graduation from one-half to two-thirds of the total credits. More course work in English, history, science, mathematics, foreign language, and civics was recommended (Boyer, 1983).

education, ESL, drug counseling, and gifted/talented). An additional 38 classified staff support the educational efforts of the school (secretaries, food services staff, custodians, interpreters, and instructional assistants).

Whereas a traditional high school schedule typically consists of the same six or seven 50-minute classes each day, students at Sentinel participate in what is generally referred to as partial block scheduling. Figure 4.5 provides an overview of the block schedule for Sentinel High School. In exchange for longer class periods of 1 hour and 50 minutes 2 days a week, students take only half of their scheduled subjects on those days. For the rest of the week, students follow a more traditional schedule in which all of their subjects are taught.

Jeff Conners is in his eighth year of teaching social studies at Sentinel High School. After receiving his secondary education certification and a bachelor's degree in history, Jeff taught for 5 years at the middle school level before transferring to the high school. Along with the rest of the school staff, he is contracted to be in the school from 7:15 a.m. until 2:45 in the afternoon. Despite being in his second decade of teaching, Jeff still finds it difficult to leave the building before 4:30 p.m. each day. In addition to class preparation, grading, and communicating with parents, he has biweekly meetings with other members of the social studies faculty, is currently serving on the Task Force on Student Violence, and is chairing the school's efforts to revise the parent handbook sent out each year. Jeff currently teaches one period of economics, two U.S. history classes, one period of world history, and a class in government. This semester, the second period is his planning and preparation time.

Now that you have read more about teaching at the high school level, stop and think about the possibility of teaching at this level. What would appeal to you about working in a high school setting? What do you see as the drawbacks? Are there particular subjects that you think you would enjoy teaching and could teach effectively? What makes you think this? Do you think high school students would relate well to you? Why or why not? What personal characteristics do you think would either make you a strong or a weak teacher at this level?

Reflection Opportunity 4.4

Figure 4.5   Weekly Schedule, Sentinel High School

Schedule A	Period 1	Break	Period 3	Period 5		
1, 3, 5 (Tuesday)	7:45–9:35 A.M.	9:35–9:55 A.M.	9:55 A.M.–12:20 P.M. (includes lunch)	12:25–2:15 P.M.		
Schedule B	Period 2	Break	Period 4	Period 6		
2, 4, 6 (Wednesday)	7:45–9:35 A.M.	9:35–9:55 A.M.	9:55 A.M.–12:20 P.M. (includes lunch)	12:25–2:15 P.M.		
Schedule C	Period 1	Period 2	Period 3	Period 4	Period 5	Period 6
Monday, Thursday, Friday	7:45–8:39 A.M.	8:45–9:44 A.M.	9:50–10:44 A.M.	10:50 A.M.–12:14 P.M. (includes lunch)	12:20–1:14 P.M.	1:20–2:15 P.M.

**Reflection
Opportunity 4.5**

Before continuing on to the next section of the text, consider reflecting on all the teaching levels presented in this portion of the chapter. Think about the levels of education that interest you. Pre-kindergarten, elementary, middle school/junior high, and high school teaching are all possibilities for you to consider. At this point, which of these levels holds the greatest appeal for you? What is it about the students at this level that you find most inviting? If you were teaching at this level, which subject or subjects would you enjoy sharing with others? Do any other aspects of working at this level make it more attractive than others? Are there levels of schooling that you definitely feel are not of interest to you? Give a rationale for your response.

What specialized educational experiences exist in schools?

In addition to the levels of education described above, there are four other groupings of specialized educational experiences commonly found in American schools. One or more of these settings may be of interest to you as a future teacher. Table 4.4 provides a summary of these services. They include:

- *Special education.* Educational opportunities for students with special needs. Can be found at each of the four educational levels described above.
- *Bilingual education.* Instruction provided in many school districts to meet the needs of students whose primary language is other than English and who come to school with limited English proficiency.
- *Gifted and talented programs.* Typically begin during the elementary school years and continue through high school. Instruction specifically designed for students who are identified as gifted and/or highly talented.
- *Vocational–technical education.* Options are generally associated with the senior high school, but may be introduced earlier in some settings. Vocational/technical course work provides students with the skills they need to enter business and industry.

Special Education

For much of American history, special-education services were provided in segregated programs housed away from regular classrooms. Children in these settings were isolated from virtually any contact with their more normally developing peers. Beginning in the 20th century, classes for children with milder disabilities were gradually located in regular public-school buildings.

TABLE 4.4 Specialized Educational Services	
Service	**Description**
Special Education	Educational efforts on behalf of students with disabilities, many of which are provided in the regular classroom
Bilingual Education	Programs designed to help students with limited English proficiency (LEP) to develop language skills in English
Gifted and Talented Education	Programs for students who are identified as gifted and talented offer opportunities to meet their interests and needs
Vocational–Technical Education	Programs at the middle and high school levels designed to provide educational experiences that lead more directly to employment following high school rather than to higher-education settings

Although the number of students receiving special education services has increased during the last 3 decades, segregated special-education programs for all levels of disabilities have decreased markedly as greater numbers of children with special needs have been placed in regular-education classrooms for part or most of their school day. This inclusion of special-needs students in regular classrooms, although not without its opponents, has proven to be a critically important direction for special education (Heward, 2006). Do you remember students with disabilities in your K–12 schooling experiences? Were these students integrated into the activities of your classrooms or isolated in separate classes?

Marissa Davis is an example of a special-education teacher at the middle school level. Her daily routine is typical of many special educators. Marissa begins by working one on one with a variety of students with special needs. For example, she visits and spends time with a seventh-grade student with autism, two eighth-grade students with physical handicaps, and three others who have various learning disabilities. Marissa travels throughout the school building to work with each of the students assigned to her. Sometimes, she takes the student out into the hallway for a brief lesson, other times she provides assistance within the regular classroom. In the afternoons, Marissa has her own classroom and small groups of students come in for specialized instruction.

Much of Marissa's work each day is determined by the Individualized Education Program (IEP) written for each student with special needs. This document is initially written and revised annually through the collaborative efforts of parents, regular education teachers, special educators, involved school personnel, and the student (where appropriate). The IEP defines the student's current level of performance, annual goals, assessment strategies, and special services to be provided. "The IEP is a system for spelling out where the child is, where she should be going, how she will get there, how long it will take, and how to tell if and when she has arrived" (Heward, 2006, p. 70). Marissa meets regularly with the classroom teachers and other school services personnel to collaboratively plan activities to meet the goals of each student's IEP.

During the past 25 years, the costs of providing programs for children with special needs and the number of students being served have increased dramatically. Federal spending has grown from approximately $100 million in 1975 to $8.5 billion in 2003 (Sack, 2004). For this same time period, state and local allocations have grown proportionately, with each continuing to be several times larger than the federal commitment. The growth in services for students with special needs has been both a blessing to the students and a major problem for the schools. The students themselves appear to benefit from opportunities to interact with peers in educational settings that allow for optimal growth. Schools, on the other hand, struggle to accommodate students with disabilities in the regular classrooms, find it difficult to hire enough qualified staff to work with these students, and scramble to locate the funding needed to implement mandated programs (Sack, 2004).

If you choose to become a regular-education teacher, the inclusion of special-needs students in regular-education classes will give you numerous opportunities to work with these students and their families. To be effective, you will need to better understand what these families feel and experience. The *Reflect on Diversity* feature for this section tells a moving story of what it is like for a parent to discover that his or her child has a disability. Typically, there are a range of emotions, including shock, grief, anger, and disbelief. For many, however, this is eventually replaced by the realization that although life will be different, there are a great many new experiences and joys as well. Stop now and read this story and reflect on what it must be like to find that your journey into parenting has led in an entirely unexpected direction.

Reflect on diversity: An unexpected trip

When her son, Jason, was born with Down syndrome in 1974, Emily Perl Kingsley became an activist to help Jason and other children with special needs fulfill their potential. *Welcome to Holland*, her inspirational essay below, has been reprinted in many languages all over the world.

Reprinted by permission of the author.

Welcome to Holland

I am often asked to describe the experience of raising a child with a disability—to try to help people who have not shared that unique experience to understand it, to imagine how it would feel. It's like this. . .

When you're going to have a baby, it's like planning a fabulous vacation trip—to Italy. You buy a bunch of guidebooks and make your wonderful plans. The Coliseum. The Michelangelo David. The gondolas in Venice. You may learn some handy phrases in Italian. It's all very exciting.

After months of eager anticipation, the day finally arrives. You pack your bags and off you go. Several hours later, the plane lands. The stewardess comes in and says, "Welcome to Holland."

"*Holland?!?*" you say. "What do you mean, Holland?? I signed up for Italy! I'm supposed to be in Italy. All my life I've dreamed of going to Italy."

But there's been a change in the flight plan. They've landed in Holland and there you must stay. The important thing is that they haven't taken you to a horrible, disgusting, filthy place full of pestilence, famine, and disease. It's just a different place.

So you must go out and buy new guidebooks. And you must learn a whole new language. And you will meet a whole new group of people you would never have met. It's just a *different* place. It's slower-paced than Italy, less flashy than Italy. But after you've been there for a while and you catch your breath, you look around and you begin to notice that Holland has windmills...and Holland has tulips. Holland even has Rembrandts.

But everyone you know is busy coming and going from Italy...and they're all bragging about what a wonderful time they had there. And for the rest of your life, you will say, "Yes, that's where I was supposed to go. That's what I had planned." And the pain of that will never, ever go away...because the loss of that dream is a very, very significant loss.

But . . . if you spend your life mourning the fact that you didn't get to Italy, you may never be free to enjoy the very special, the very lovely things . . . about Holland.

Developing the Habit of Reflective Practice

Gather Information

1. Visit the National Association for Down Syndrome at *http://www.nads.org/* to read more about children with Down syndrome and their families.

Identify Beliefs

1. What challenges do you think parents and educators of children with special needs face?

2. What joys do you think parents and educators of children with special needs face?

3. How does the essay, "Welcome to Holland", relate to educators?

Make Decisions

1. If you were hiring a teacher, what personality traits and qualifications would you be looking for in potential candidates who would be working in inclusive educational settings?

2. If you were working with a family who had a child with exceptional needs, would you share this essay with them? Why or why not?

Assess and Evaluate

1. How are you currently prepared to work with children who have exceptional needs such as Down syndrome?

2. What can you do to better prepare yourself for working with children who have exceptional needs?

Take out your Reflections Journal or open the on-line journal found on the Companion Website for this text and think about teaching in a special-education setting. Have you had experiences working in a special-needs classroom or with an individual student with special needs? If so, describe the experiences and what you learned from them. If not, consider taking the time to participate in this setting. Can you see yourself working exclusively with students with special needs? Why or why not? What personal characteristics do you have that would either make you an effective teacher in this setting or that you think would make it difficult for you to work with special-needs students?

**Reflection
Opportunity 4.6**

Bilingual Education

Another specialized educational experience found in most American schools is bilingual education. You may find you have an interest in teaching bilingual education. If not, knowing about this educational option will help you work with the students you do have that are learning English as a second language. Traditionally, bilingual education has been viewed as an opportunity to help students whose native language is other than English to learn a second language. These **limited English proficient (LEP)** students have English language skills lower than those typically needed for success in the classroom and are taught for at least a portion of the day in their native language before moving to strictly English-speaking classes. This approach still exists, but considerable controversy surrounds its necessity and effectiveness. Those opposing bilingual education suggest that students should simply be immersed in English language classrooms and given extra assistance in that setting to master the language. Students in these programs are often referred to as English language learners (ELLs). Those who support a more traditional bilingual education approach suggest that this sink or swim option for ELL students is unfair and leads to far greater numbers of failures and dropouts. In June 1998, the state of California became a major proponent of the immersion approach with the passage of *Proposition 227*. This measure virtually ended the state's traditional bilingual education programs in favor of a 1–year English-immersion option. Initial research on the effectiveness of this approach, although controversial, seems to support its use. Rossell (2005), for example, studied the impact of California's immersion model on English language learners and found that students in these programs scored better on tests of reading and mathematics abilities than did others in more traditional bilingual education programs.

With the growing linguistic diversity of students in states such as Arizona, California, and Texas (see Table 4.5), providing assistance to English language learners is becoming an increasingly important component of education at all levels within American schools. Educators need to

Year	Arizona		California		Texas	
	Total Enrollment*	LEP Enrollment*	Total Enrollment*	LEP Enrollment*	Total Enrollment*	LEP Enrollment*
1992–1993	748	83	5,749	1,151	3,714	344
1997–1998	833	112	5,727	1,406	3,981	507
2005–2006	1,094	152	6,259	1,571	4,525	640

TABLE 4.5 Limited English Proficient Students in Selected States

*Enrollments in thousands

Source: Adapted from *NCELA's State Resource Pages,* by National Clearinghouse for English Language Acquisition & Language Instruction Educational Programs, 2004. Retrieved October 28, 2008 from: *http://www.ncela.gwu.edu/stats/3_bystate.htm*

know how to implement quality programs. Montecel and Cortez (2002) have identified these key components of successful programs for LEP/ELL students:

- Supportive and informed district and school leadership
- Clear goals for LEP students
- Safe and orderly school climate
- Fully credentialed bilingual teachers
- Parent involvement in bilingual programs

José has been team teaching in a two-way bilingual education program at the elementary level for the past 3 years. He arrived in the United States as a child and followed his parents as they moved around the country picking apples, cutting asparagus, preparing and harvesting strawberries, and working in the grape vineyards. After struggling for several years in elementary school to learn English while also trying to keep up his studies in other subjects, José finally mastered his second language and vowed in high school to get through college and become a teacher for others who needed help learning English as a second language. Half of the students in José's class are English speaking and are taught primarily by his co-teacher, Tia. Tia was a Spanish major in college and works with her students to immerse them in learning Spanish as a second language while also teaching them other academic skills. José works mostly independently with his group of Spanish-speaking students to teach them English while at the same time working to enhance their reading, mathematics, social studies, and science understandings. Tia and José co-teach for parts of the day as they integrate linguistic and academic learning for both groups of students. Together, they are assisting the entire class to become bilingual at the same time that they are being taught the traditional elementary school subjects. Participation in the class by English-speaking students is entirely voluntary and there is a long waiting list of those wanting admission. Many English-speaking parents understand the value of learning a second language and want their children to have this experience.

Reflection Opportunity 4.7

Stop and think about teaching in a bilingual-education setting. How important is it for students whose first language is other than English to have quality opportunities to learn English while at the same time retaining use their first language as part of the teaching/learning process? What does your response tell you about your willingness to work in a bilingual setting? Do you have the language skills that you would need to work in a bilingual classroom? If not, would you be willing to develop the skills you would need to teach in a bilingual setting? Why or why not?

Gifted and Talented Education

A third specialized educational experience found in most schools is gifted and talented education. These programs are designed for students like Adam. Adam is finishing his last term of high school classes and is preparing for college in the fall. He is a hard-working student who is liked by both classmates and teachers. Adam has taken challenging courses in mathematics, the sciences, social studies, and English throughout his schooling and always seems to do well. He has never received an end-of-term grade lower than an A. Adam has always scored within the top 5% on the standardized tests administered by the school district. Some of his elementary and secondary teachers consider him gifted, whereas others attribute his success to an outstanding work ethic. Depending on the definition used for giftedness and the availability of programs, students like Adam may or may not be involved in gifted education programs during their elementary and secondary schooling. Were you, or someone you knew, a part of a K–12 gifted and talented program? What did students do in this program that was different from what others were doing?

Gifted and talented education varies widely by state. This is evident in two main ways. First of all, the percentages of students identified as gifted and talented are considerably different across states. Although on average 6.7% of all U.S. students are classified as gifted and talented, states vary from a high of 14% of students in Oklahoma to a low of 0.8% in Vermont. States also vary widely in their legal commitment to gifted and talented students. Only 26 states have a full or partial mandate to serve gifted and talented students (National Center for Educational Statistics, 2008). Those with partial mandates provide identification only or, at best, minimal services as deemed appropriate by local education agencies.

In many ways, gifted and talented students are the least well served group of students in our educational system. Without clear legal rights and because of the general emphasis on lower-achieving students, they are frequently overlooked (DeLacy, 2004). Already overworked teachers often find it difficult to prepare all of the special activities needed to challenge the gifted and talented students in their classrooms. To combat this problem, many school districts and states have developed program options to meet the special needs of this student population. For example, Kendra James is a teacher of gifted and talented students at the upper elementary and middle school levels for a smaller school district. Students who have been identified as gifted and talented come from all over the district to participate in her program one day a week. Kendra works with fifth graders on Monday, sixth-grade students on Tuesday, and seventh- and eighth-grade students on Wednesday and Thursday, respectively. She plans creative and challenging tasks that stretch each group as they spend a day in her classroom. Last month Kendra's sixth-grade students studied classical architecture and compared what they found to buildings in the local area.

Consider the possibility of teaching in a gifted and talented program. What kind of a learner are you? Does learning come easily or are you a person who struggles to learn at least some subjects? What might this tell you about your success in working with gifted and talented students? What other personal characteristics would make it either easy or difficult for you to work in a gifted and talented program? Do you think that gifted and talented students need and want special educational programs designed especially for them? What makes you feel this way?

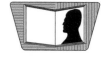

**Reflection
Opportunity 4.8**

Vocational–Technical Education

Vocational–technical education has been an important option for many students throughout most of the 20th century. With the recent move toward more rigorous academic programs at the high school level, these programs have suffered an image problem. Consequently, vocational–technical education programs are lower priorities for most local schools when budgets get tight. This sentiment is also being expressed at the federal level. (Cavanagh, 2003).

Despite the concern over its status, some middle schools and most high schools offer students the opportunity to participate in vocational–technical education. Table 4.6 provides a summary of the numbers of vocational courses taken by students within American high schools. These courses introduce students to career possibilities in business and industry and provide them with initial educational experiences needed for success. Career counseling for vocational–technical job options is also readily available at the high school level. Students at the middle school/junior high school level may have the opportunity for exploratory experiences in vocational–technical education as well. Career guidance and counseling at the middle school/junior high level also provide additional information regarding these job opportunities.

Jennifer is a business education instructor at Travis High School. She works with two other faculty members and together they teach an assortment of courses. Together, they assist their students in engaging in the planning, organizing, directing, and evaluating tasks that are necessary for productive business operations. In addition to basic business education courses, they also provide opportunities for their students to learn about software programs to prepare presentations, develop spreadsheets, publish newsletters, and enhance digital photos. Jennifer's special interests are in 3D modeling and video-game programming and she teaches these subjects as well.

Think about teaching in a vocational–technical classroom. First of all, are vocational–technical programs important options for middle school and high school students to have? Why do you think this way and how would your feelings about vocational–technical education influence your thinking about teaching in this area? Have you taken vocational–technical courses that

**Reflection
Opportunity 4.9**

TABLE 4.6   Vocational-Education Courses Taken in High School

Student Characteristics	Average Number of Courses
Male	4.60
Female	3.82
White	4.34
Black	4.29
Hispanic	3.83
Asian	2.82
American Indian	4.79
Academic Track	2.28
Vocational Track	9.56

Note: The number of courses is measured in Carnegie units, with one unit representing the completion of a 1-year course.

Source: Adapted from *Digest for Education Statistics,* by National Center for Education Statistics, 2003. Washington, DC: U.S. Department of Education.

were of particular interest to you as part of your own schooling experience? If so, would you consider teaching that subject some day? Why or why not? If you haven't taken any vocational–technical courses, consider visiting a local school and either observing in a classroom or talking to a teacher who works in a vocational–technical program. Use this experience to make a decision about the possibility of teaching in this setting.

What are the alternatives to traditional public schools?

Although the levels of schooling and the specialized educational settings described above are the most common configurations found in schools today, students and their families are experiencing many alternative forms of education. Some of the more prominent options include magnet schools, charter schools, year-round schools, private schools, and alternative schools. Many of these programs are physically and administratively housed in the public schools, others have loose connections to public education, and yet others have no direct relationship. As you read about these various options, see if any are of particular interest to you as a site for your future teaching.

Magnet Schools

Magnet schools were designed primarily as an option to give students with significant talents in an academic area a more specialized curriculum. While providing a well-rounded education, magnet schools allow for deeper explorations in the area of interest. For example, magnet high schools often emphasize mathematics, science, or the arts and attract students from a relatively large geographic area interested in pursuing study in that specialty. In addition to their specialized curricula, magnet schools were originally seen as an important strategy in America's efforts to desegregate its schools. During the 1970s, magnet schools became popular options in large urban areas as a tool to reduce the exodus of White families from inner city schools to the surrounding suburbs. By attempting to stem this White flight from the inner city, magnet schools were seen as a voluntary option to aid in desegregation efforts (Jones, 2002). Unfortunately, this effort on the part of magnet schools has been relatively unsuccessful (Merelman, 2002).

Despite its limited success as a tool in desegregation, magnet schools have proven to be a popular option for both students and their families. From just a few schools in the 1970s, their numbers have grown to more than 4,000 elementary and secondary schools (Magnet Schools of America, 2008). One reason for their popularity is that parents and students have some control over the school attended. Although waiting lists are often long, the opportunity to choose a school with a specific area of emphasis is attractive to many. Teachers with skills and interests in the magnet-school curriculum are also eager to get involved in these programs, making for a strong and motivated faculty. An example of a magnet school is Aviation High School in Seattle, Washington (Gilman, 2005). Students who enroll in the school have a common interest in everything having to do with aviation and the entire curriculum revolves around this topic. The school has a strong emphasis on mathematics, science, and technology, which provides students with the foundational understandings needed for a broad array of future occupations including aeronautical engineer, pilot, avionics technician, and astronaut. Begun in 2004, the school had approximately 200 students a year later. Each student must complete several written essays and a face-to-face interview before they can be admitted to the program. Once enrolled, they tackle a rigorous college-prep curriculum that includes four years of both mathematics and science.

Charter Schools

A second alternative school option is the **charter school.** The movement began in the 1990s as another choice for parents who wanted alternatives to the traditional public schools that could help boost their children's academic achievement. The following description highlights its key elements:

> Charter schools are by definition independent public schools. Although funded with taxpayer dollars, they operate free from many of the laws and regulations that govern traditional public schools. In exchange for that freedom, they are bound to the terms of a contract or "charter" that lays out a school's mission, academic goals, and accountability procedures. State laws set the parameters for charter contracts, which are overseen by a designated charter-school authorizer—often the local school district or related agency (Education Week, 2008, p. 1).

By freeing charter schools from many of the local and state regulations currently in place and allowing families to choose this educational option, the expectation was that in 3 to 5 years these programs could show results that surpassed those of traditional schools.

There has been rapid growth in the number of U.S. charter schools, growing from 253 in 1995–1996 to an estimated 3400 in 2004–2005 (Vanourek, 2005). By the 2002–2003 school year, a total of 39 states had passed legislation allowing for the creation of charter schools (Finnigan et al., 2004). Currently, an estimated 2% of all students nationwide are enrolled in charter schools, with 42% of these students concentrated in three states (Arizona, California, and Florida). One of the main reasons cited for this rapid growth is the desire to have an alternative to traditional programs, which were seen as lacking ingredients that could help students reach their true academic potential (Education Week, 2008). The second most common reason for starting a charter school was to better assist special populations of students who are currently underserved, particularly minority, low-income, and special-needs students. Although students with special needs are served at about the same percentage as public schools in general, Vanourek (2005) reports that 59% of students enrolled in charter schools are minority. In addition, 49% are eligible for free and reduced-price lunch. Read the *Engage in the Debate* feature to reflect in more depth on the benefits and problems of this schooling option.

Engage in the debate: The debate over charter schools

Charter schools are becoming more prevalent every year, as are the debates regarding their effectiveness. Those in favor of charter schools propose that our public schools work well for many children, but not all. Advocates say that charter schools reduce bureaucracy and empower teachers and principals to innovate. They believe charter schools can act as laboratories of reform, identifying successful practices that could be replicated in other schools. Proponents argue that charter schools get results because they receive state funding only if families choose them. Through school choice, competition within the public school system is created, pressuring school districts to reassess their educational practices.

Those opposed to charter schools state we should not spend public money on expensive, risky propositions. To improve our schools, they say, we should reduce class sizes and put a well-qualified educator in every classroom rather than using money to support charter schools. Opponents claim that charter schools, due to their small size and limited numbers, will provide only *some* families with public school choice options, thereby raising issues of fairness and equity. Those against charter schools also have concerns about accountability. Because they are freed from rules and regulations intended to ensure quality in public education, charter schools have an unfair advantage when competing against other public schools.

Developing the Habit of Reflective Practice

Gather Information

1. Go to *http://www.uscharterschools.org* to find out more about charter schools. Check to see which states have legislation that permit charter schools. Read about the state's regulations for charter schools.

2. Go to *http://nces.ed.gov/* and read the summary of the most recent study of America's charter schools.

Identify Beliefs

1. Are all students given the same opportunities for a quality education in our country's public school system? Give evidence to support your answer.

2. What are the benefits and pitfalls of getting teachers more involved in decision making within schools?

Make Decisions

1. Should charter schools be allowed? Why or why not?

2. How much freedom from state regulations should charter schools have? What exceptions and accountability should charter schools have?

Assess and Evaluate

1. How should the effectiveness of charter schools be assessed and evaluated?

2. Will charter schools be as prevalent, more prevalent or less prevalent in 10 years as compared to now? Defend your prediction.

Year-Round Schools

Another alternative education option that is gaining in popularity is the **year-round school.** Districts that move to the year-round model reorganize the academic calendar by breaking up the summer vacation into shorter, more frequent breaks throughout the school year. Figure 4.6 provides an example of a school calendar for a year-round school and compares it with a more typical school calendar. According to data collected by the National Association for Year-Round Education (2008), in the 2006–2007 school year there were 3,000 schools in the United States that operate on a year-round schedule, and together they serve more than 2 million students.

Figure 4.6   Sample School Calendars

Year-Round School Calendar

Mid-July	School year begins. Students begin classes 3 days after teachers return.
Mid-September	Fall break, approximately 3 weeks.
October to Mid-December	Remainder of fall term.
Mid-December to New Year	Christmas break.
January to end of March	Winter term.
Early April	Spring break, 2 weeks
Mid-April through May	Spring term.
June through Early July	Summer break.

Typical School Calendar

Early September	School starts
Late December–Early January	Winter break
Late February	Mid-winter break
Mid-April	Spring break
Late June–Early September	Summer break

Three main reasons are cited for the move to year-round schools (McGlynn, 2002). The first is a *concern about student achievement.* Teachers have long been frustrated by the losses in learning that tend to occur over the traditional summer vacation. Younger children, especially, need to re-learn at least a portion of what they had mastered in the previous academic year. Year-round schools are seen as a way to eliminate this problem. A second reason frequently cited is the *over-crowding of classrooms.* School districts that are short on classroom space are giving year-round schools a try as one way to alleviate the space crunch. By operating on a staggered, multi-track schedule, schools can accommodate larger numbers of students in the same physical space. Finally, year-round schools give more opportunities to *work with students who fall behind.* Summer school offerings for students who are at risk of failing have extended the school year for many. Rather than promoting students before they are ready, these summer programs (often mandatory) are designed to give these students extra assistance to keep them from falling behind their peers. As a future teacher, do you think you would like the year-round school model? Why or why not?

Corporate Landing Elementary School, in Virginia Beach, Virginia is an example of a year-round school (Virginia Beach City Public Schools, 2008). It has the same number of school days each year as other schools in the district, but they are distributed across 12 months, rather than the more typical 10 months of most schools. Students are taught the same subjects as those in other schools, but instruction is grouped into 45-day segments with 5–15-day breaks between each block distributed throughout the year. During the breaks, "students who have not mastered the learning objectives for the previous instructional block will be strongly encouraged to attend the next intersession for special help. Other students may wish to attend intersessions for enrichment activities to broaden or deepen their learning" (Virginia Beach City Public Schools, 2008, p. 1). Students who are involved in remedial learning during break times do not pay any fees for this service, whereas parents may be charged nominal fees for enrichment activities.

Private Schools

Private schools are an alternative schooling option in which the tuition paid by families covers most of the costs for schooling. For example, the expenses associated with classroom space, books, educational supplies, and teacher salaries are all paid through non-governmental funds for students in these settings. Throughout much of American history, private schools were the most common educational option available to students and their families, especially at the secondary level. Beginning in the 19th and 20th centuries, however, publicly funded education gradually became more plentiful and enrollments in private schools slowly declined. According to data from the National Center for Education Statistics (2008), currently there are more than 5 million students, or about 10% of school-age children who attend private schools in the United States.

Private schools can be grouped broadly into two categories: those that have religious affiliation and those that do not. By far the largest percentage has religious affiliation. Catholic schools enroll the largest number in this category, with approximately 2.2 million students nationwide in over 7,600 schools (National Center for Educational Statistics, 2008). There are roughly 7,000 private schools without religious affiliation which serve approximately 925,000 students.

The *Explore Your Beliefs* feature for this chapter describes another private-school alternative that has remained popular in some settings: single-sex schools. Although there are a handful of public single-sex schools, the vast majority of them are private. Read about the potential benefits and problems of this schooling option and reflect on your beliefs regarding single-sex schools.

Explore your beliefs: Single-sex schools

Until recently, most single-sex schools were private institutions catering to wealthy parents able to afford what they consider a classic model of excellent education. In 2006, however, the United States Department of Education published new regulations governing single-sex education in public schools. (NASSPE, 2008). They allow coeducational public schools (elementary and secondary) to offer single-sex classrooms when schools:

1. Develop a rationale for offering a single-gender class in that subject.
2. Provide a coeducational class in the same subject at the same school.
3. Conduct periodic reviews to determine whether single-sex classes are still needed.

In recent years, there has been significant attention given to single sex schools such as Thurgood Marshall Elementary School in Seattle, Washington where Principal Benjamin Wright reinvented his school as a gender-separate academy (NASSPE, 2008). This elementary school has one of Seattle's highest percentages of minority and low-income pupils. In the fall of 2000, Wright divided the 343-student school into separate all-boys and all-girls classes. Test scores rose dramatically. Only 10 percent of the boys met state standards for reading when the school was coed; but after just one year of single-sex education, 66 percent of boys met the standards. Girls' test performance improved as well, although less dramatically. Before the split, discipline referrals were averaging thirty students per day, mostly boys. After the change to single-sex education, discipline referrals dropped to one or two per day.

Those against single sex schooling argue that people work and live in a society that integrates men and women and boys and girls and that by separating our students out by gender we are actually doing them a disservice. Those in favor of single sex education cite studies that indicate students in single sex schools make greater academic gains than those in co-educational settings (Viadero, 2002).

Developing the Habit of Reflective Practice

Gather Information

1. Go to *http://www.singlesexschools.org/* to read more about single sex schools.

2. Try to find someone who has been educated in a single sex environment. Interview them and get details about the experience. Was it a positive one? Why or why not?

Identify Beliefs

1. Look at your own educational experience. How did single sex or co-ed learning environments impact your learning?

2. Which is more preferable in your mind – a single sex educational setting or a co-educational setting?

Make Decisions

1. To what degree would you like to see single sex education implemented? Not at all, at the classroom level, at the school level, at the district level, or at the state level?

2. Which level of schooling would you predict most benefits from single sex schooling? Elementary schools, middle schools or high schools?

Assess and Evaluate

1. If you were asked to help evaluate the effectiveness of a single sex school, what kinds of evidence would you seek to find?

2. Based on the current research that supports and questions the validity of single sex education, do you support or challenge the regulations set by the US government?

Sources

National Association for Single Sex Public Education (NASSPE). 2008. Single-sex education. Retrieved on November 13, 2008 at *http://www.singlesexschools.org/*

Viadero, D. (2002). Evidence on single-sex school is mixed. *Education Week,* June 12, 2002, p. 8.

Alternative Schools

The 1960s and 1970s in America represented a time of awakening civil rights, a questioning of leadership and the status quo, and a period of growing concern for the effectiveness of all public institutions. Schools, as a major public institution, came under fire for being uncaring and rule bound. One attempt made during these years to rethink how schools should operate was the creation of programs that served as alternative places of learning for students who were unsuccessful in more traditional settings or those who may be better served in nontraditional classrooms (Graba, 2004). These options have come to be known as **alternative schools.**

Alternative schools are nontraditional options available to students and their families in a variety of forms, some of which have already been discussed in this section. For example, the charter school movement is often described as a form of alternative education (Graba, 2004). Other types of alternative schools include:

- **Free school**—An option where students choose what they want to learn and when to learn it (Galley, 2004). A. S. Neill (1960), in his book titled *Summerhill,* described an early British school modeled on these principles.

- **High-tech school**—A specialized school where teachers engage in less face-to-face instruction. In its place, students spend extended parts of their school day using technology as a major learning tool (Hurst, 2003).

- **Home schooling**—An option growing in popularity, home schooling occurs when parents choose to teach their own children in the home setting. Within parameters defined in each state, children can be home schooled throughout all or part of their formal educational experiences. Chapter 13 provides further information on this topic.

- **Boarding school**—A private school option for students who need 24-hour care. They are designed to assist students who are struggling with such things as drug abuse, depression, defiance, school failure, and self-esteem issues.

Who works in schools?

As discussed above, one strategy that you can use to determine if teaching is the best career choice for you is to think carefully about school settings and educational experiences to see if there are options that appeal to you. Another strategy that may help in your decision making is to consider the people you would be working with if you were to enter teaching. In addition to the many highly qualified teachers, schools have:

- **Support staff** such as cooks, bus drivers, instructional assistants, custodians, and secretaries. They assist teachers and schools in providing services needed for effective teaching and learning.

- **Educational specialists,** including counselors, technology specialists, librarians, family support specialists, and nurses. Educational specialists have received intensive training that helps them assist students in growth that extends beyond traditional school subjects.

- **Administrators** such as assistant principals, principals, assistant superintendents, superintendents, and other central office administrators. They assume leadership roles in hiring and evaluating teachers and staff, guiding the overall directions of teaching and learning, and managing school budgets.

These people have important roles to play in the educational process. You will need to establish good working relationships with them so that together you can meet the needs of all your students. In the following section, you will learn more about each of these potential colleagues so that you can better answer this question.

Support Staff

At all levels of schooling, numerous support staff engage in important tasks for the well-being of students and others at the school. In general, the larger the school, the greater the number of support staff you will find there. Your success as a teacher is more dependent on each of these people than you might initially think. Some of the key roles of support staff and their impact on what you do in the classroom are presented below:

- *Cooks*—Low-income students receive breakfasts and lunches for free through federal programs (U.S. Department of Agriculture, 2005). When cooks prepare nutritious foods that students are willing to eat, you are much more likely to have students who are able to engage in quality learning experiences.

- *Bus drivers*—Getting students to school and home on time and safely is an important task. It is a positive step toward good relations with parents and helps ensure better school attendance.

- *Instructional Assistants*—Also called teachers' aides and para-educators, instructional assistants work in classrooms to help students needing special assistance. They provide one-on-one and small-group instruction that is so badly needed for some students to succeed.
- *Custodians*—By keeping the classrooms and school facilities in good working order, custodians provide important assistance in creating a quality learning environment.
- *Secretaries*—In addition to providing support to the administrators in the school, secretaries are a wealth of information about how to get things done. They serve as the school clearinghouse on such things as making photocopies, seeking small grants for school supplies, understanding school safety policies, and procedures for field trips.

Educational Specialists

In addition to the support staff you will find in schools, there will be many different educational specialists that can assist you in meeting the needs of each student in your class. These specialists have typically completed at least a bachelor's degree in their area of expertise and assist students in the following ways:

- *Counselors*—Schools are hiring counselors to serve two important roles. First, they work with students struggling emotionally and/or socially to develop the skills they need to be successful in the classroom. Secondly, counselors help students make initial decisions about career choices and provide basic information about college admissions procedures. Traditionally, counselors were found primarily at the high school level. More recently, middle/junior high schools and elementary schools find that it is important to have counselors at these levels as well.
- *Technology Specialists*—As computers and technology options become even more important parts of school operations, many schools are hiring specialists who maintain and update computer systems as needed. They may also work with students and other educators to assist them in being able to use the latest software and hardware options available to them.
- *Librarians*—School libraries are important centers for the sharing of information. Librarians have traditionally been responsible for organizing and maintaining the books and other print materials students and teachers need in their classrooms. With the increased use of computers and the Internet as information sources, the roles of librarian and technology specialist have often been combined and one person may serve both functions.
- *Family Support Specialists*—A relatively new position found in schools today is the family support specialist. Trained either as an educator or in a human services profession, this specialist works to engage families in the life of the school. By serving as a resource to families and encouraging their involvement in the educational process, they are strengthening important home–school relationships.
- *Nurses*—School nurses help patch up students' cuts and bruises, isolate sick children before they are sent home, make the initial determination about emergency medical care, and screen students for medical, dental, optical, and hearing problems. In most schools, nurses are the only school personnel allowed to administer prescribed medications to students.

Administrators

A final group of people that you will work with if you choose a career in teaching is administrators. Those that you have regular contact with in your school play a direct and significant role in your success as an educator. For example, the *principal,* as school leader is responsible for creating a caring school environment in which all students have the opportunity to learn. He or she must find ways in which staff, teachers, specialists, and administrators can work together to support student learning. When this caring school environment exists, the school is an exciting and safe environment for all. Many schools also have one or more *assistant principals* to help with the many administrative functions needed for effective teaching and learning. For example, an assistant principal may be responsible for school safety. This may include helping develop an earthquake preparedness plan that helps teachers and students know what to do in case this natural disaster strikes. Another function typically assigned to an assistant principal is the coordination of school management and discipline policies.

Although school-based administrators may have the most direct influence on your work in the classroom, central district administrators such as program directors, assistant superintendents, and the superintendent of schools will all have an impact on your work. For example, the *program director* responsible for special education helps determine the allocation of instructional assistants who work with students with special needs. Because you will likely have students with special needs in your future classroom, the allocation of instructional assistants could have a significant impact on how well you are able to work with these students. Your role as a teacher could also be influenced by the *assistant superintendent* responsible for business and operations. If this person were to create a small grants program that allowed teachers to apply for some money that could be spent for equipment and materials, he would have created an opportunity that could provide you with much needed resources for your classroom. Finally, the *superintendent,* as the person responsible for the overall direction of the entire school district, could also impact your work in the classroom. For example, if she were to work with the school board and parents to make arts education a stronger emphasis in the school system, what you teach and the resources you have available to you could either be increased or decreased based on this decision.

Take a moment now to look at and reflect on the *Consider This* feature for this chapter found on the Companion Website for this text.It is designed to help you think about and record the past experiences you have had with students and how those experiences have influenced your comfort level with each group. Also consider taking time to add new experiences with students so that you can better determine the teaching situation that best matches your needs and interests.

Consider This:
Evaluating
Experiences with
Student Populations

Summary

In this chapter, three organizing questions were presented to help you develop a better understanding of schools today:

How are schools traditionally organized?

There are four major levels of schooling and four additional groupings of specialized educational experiences found in most school districts:

- Early-childhood education
- Elementary schools
- Junior high and middle schools
- Senior high schools

What specialized educational experiences exist in schools?

There are four main specialized educational experiences that you will find in schools:

- Special education (Praxis II, topic Ia)
- Bilingual education (Praxis II, topic Ia)

- Gifted education (Praxis II, topic Ia)
- Vocational–technical education

What are the alternatives to traditional public schools?

Virtually every school district has a number of alternatives to traditional formats for schools, including these:
- Magnet schools
- Charter schools
- Year-round schools
- Private schools
- Alternative schools

Who works in schools?

If you choose to teach, you will be working with a variety of important individuals beyond the teacher colleagues you will have:
- Support staff
- Educational specialists
- Administrators

PRAXIS Test-Preparation Activities

 To review an on-line chapter case study, test your understanding of chapter topics and concepts, and begin preparing for the Praxis II: Principles of Learning and Teaching examination, go to the Praxis Test Preparation module for this chapter of the Companion Website.

inTASC Developing the Habit of Reflective Practice

Organizing Questions

Review questions, field-experience opportunities, and activities for building your portfolio are included here for the organizing questions in this chapter.

How are schools traditionally organized?

Review Questions

1. What are the student ages and groupings within early childhood education?
2. How is the typical middle school different from a junior high school?
3. What is a comprehensive high school?

Field Experience

Select what you currently think to be your first choice for a teaching position (elementary, middle school, secondary, special education, etc.).
- Spend as much time as you can (2 or 3 full days would be best) in the teaching setting you select.
- Study students at that level, thinking particularly about how well you see yourself relating to them.
- Take time to review the materials available for the subject(s) being taught and think about how interesting this content is to you.
- Pay particular attention to the role of the teacher and how you see yourself fitting into a similar position. Discuss what you find with others.

Building Your Portfolio: *Special Education*

INTASC Standard 3. Whether or not you choose to become a special education teacher, you will need to be aware of the many issues surrounding working with children with special needs.

- For a level of education that interests you, contact an appropriate school and ask for written information about its special-education programs.
- After reviewing these materials, write a one- or two-page summary of special education efforts in that setting.

What specialized educational experiences exist in schools?

Review Questions

1. What is inclusion and how will it affect you as a future teacher?
2. In what ways do bilingual education programs assist LEP students to learn?
3. Why do programs for gifted and talented students vary significantly by state?
4. What is the main purpose for vocational–technical education?

Field Experience

Choose one of the four specialized educational experiences described in this text and arrange to observe a teacher in this setting.

- What roles did the teacher perform and how were they similar to, and different from, those of a regular classroom teacher?
- Talk to the teacher to find out their perceptions of the benefits and problems of working in this setting.
- Share what you found with others.

What are the alternatives to traditional public schools?

Review Questions

1. How is a charter school different from a regular public school?
2. Why are year-round schools becoming more popular?
3. What kinds of students are typically served in an alternative school?

Field Experience

Choose one of the alternatives to traditional public schools described in this chapter and spend some time in a representative program.

- What do you like and dislike about this option?
- What are the strengths and weaknesses for both students and teachers?
- Can you see yourself teaching in this setting? Discuss what you find with others.

Building Your Portfolio: *Alternative Education*

INTASC Standard 4. Do some research on one of the alternative education options presented in this chapter.

- This may include spending time in a local program, collecting written materials from local and state options, and doing an Internet search for articles and Websites about existing programs.
- Once you have collected these data, summarize your findings in a short paper describing the strengths and limitations of this form of alternative education.

Who works in schools?

Review Questions

1. How might a school secretary be helpful to you as a future teacher?
2. What are the roles of a technology specialist?
3. In what ways does the school principal influence teaching and learning?

Field Experience

Choose one category of support staff identified in this section of the text to get to know better.

- Take some time to interview a person working in this role in the schools to find out what they do.
- Ask them to identify ways in which the work they do influences teaching and learning in the school.
- Share the results of your interview with others.

Suggested Readings

Davis, G., & Rimm, S. (2004). *Education of the gifted and talented* (5th ed.). Boston: Allyn and Bacon. This book provides information on strategies used by teachers and other school personnel to determine which students are gifted and talented and describes programs that are successful in meeting their diverse needs.

Garcia, G. (2005). *English learners: Reaching the highest level of English literacy.* Upper Saddle River, NJ: Prentice Hall. This text outlines strategies for teaching English to second language learners. It provides a clear rationale and framework for these efforts.

Henniger, M. (2009). *Teaching young children: An introduction* (4th ed.). Upper Saddle River, NJ: Merrill/Prentice Hall. This book provides a description of children and families during the early childhood years. It presents an overview of teaching and learning at this level.

Turnbull, A., Turnbull, R., & Wehmeyer, M. (2007). *Exceptional lives: Special education in today's schools* (5th ed.). Upper Saddle River, NJ: Merrill/Prentice Hall. This text provides a thorough overview of special education and prepares future teachers for their role in the education of students with special needs.

Wonacott, M. (2002). *The impact of work-based learning on students.* ERIC Digest No. 242. This summary document provides evidence of the value of vocational education for secondary students in American schools.

References

Adler, M. (1982). *The Paideia proposal: An educational manifesto.* New York: Macmillan.

Annie E. Casey Foundation. (2008). *Kids count 2008.* Baltimore, MD: Author.

Boyer, E. (1983). *High school: A report on secondary education in America.* New York: Harper.

Cavanagh, S. (2003, March 12). Advocates criticize Bush Voc. Ed. proposal. *Education Week,* p. 26.

DeLacy, M. (2004, June 23). The "No Child" law's biggest victims? An answer that may surprise. *Education Week,* p. 41.

Education Week. (2008). Charter schools. Retrieved October 27, 2008 from: *http://www.edweek .org/rc/issues/charter-schools/*

Education Week. (2002). In early childhood education and care—Quality counts. In *Quality Counts 2002* (pp. 8–9). Washington, DC: Author.

Finnigan, K., Adelman, N., Anderson, L., Cotton, L., Donnelly, M., & Price, T. (2004). *Evaluation of the public charter schools program: Final report.* Washington, DC: U.S. Department of Education.

Froebel, F. (1886). *Education of man* (J. Jarvis, Trans.). New York: Appleton-Century-Crofts.

Fulghum, R. (1989). *All I really need to know I learned in kindergarten.* New York: Villard Books.

Galley, M. (2004, May 12). Free rein. *Education Week,* p. 36.

Gilman, R. (2005). Going sky high. *Edutopia, 1*(7), 20–21.

Graba, J. (2004). Creating new schools: Promising strategy for change? Speech given at the Grantmakers for Education and the Philanthropy Roundtable, May 26, 2004, Denver, Colorado. Retrieved January 7, 2005 from: *http://www.educationevolving.org*

Heward, W. (2006). *Exceptional children: An introduction to special education* (8th ed.). Columbus, OH: Merrill/Prentice Hall.

Honig, A. (2002). Research on quality infant/toddler programs. *Clearinghouse on Early Learning and Parenting.* Retrieved October 30, 2005 from: *http://ceep.crc.uiuc.edu/eecearchive/digests/2002/honig02.html#in*

Hurst, M. (2003, September 17). Philadelphia and Microsoft planning high-tech school. *Education Week,* p. 23.

Jackson, A., & Davis, G. (2000). *Turning points 2000: Educating adolescents in the 21st century.* New York: Teachers College Press.

Jones, R. (2002). Defining diversity. *American School Board Journal, 189*(10), 4–5.

Magnet Schools of America. (2008). Resources and articles. Retrieved October 27, 2008 from: *http://www.magnet.edu/modules/content/index.php?id=6*

Massachusetts Cost and Quality Study. (2004). *The cost and quality of full-day year-round early care and education in Massachusetts: Infant and toddler classrooms.* Washington, D.C.: Administration for Children and Families.

McGlynn, A. (2002, March). Districts that school year-round. *School Administrator.* Retrieved December 27, 2004 from: *http://www.aasa.org/publications/sa/2002_03/mcglynn.htm*

Mead, S. (2004). *Open the preschool door, close the preparation gap.* Washington, D.C.: Progressive Policy Institute.

Merelman, R. (2002, February 6). Dis-integrating American public schools. *Education Week,* pp. 36–52.

Montecel, M., & Cortez, J. (2002). Successful bilingual education programs: Development and dissemination of criteria to identify promising and exemplary practices in bilingual education at the national level. *Bilingual Research Journal, 26*(1), 1–21.

Murray, V., & Groen, R. (2005, January 5). Survey of Arizona private schools: Tuition, testing, and curricula. *Policy Report,* No. 199. Retrieved October 23, 2005 from: *http://www.heartland.org/pdf/17097.pdf*

National Association for the Education of Young Children. (2008). *About NAEYC.* Retrieved October 27, 2008 from: *http://www.naeyc.org/about/*

National Association for Year-Round Education. (2008). *Statistical summaries of year-round education programs: 2006–07.* Retrieved October 27, 2008 from: *http://www.nayre.org/*

National Center for Education Statistics. (2008). *Digest of education statistics.* Washington, D.C.: U.S. Government Printing Office.

National Commission on Excellence in Education. (1983). *A nation at risk: The imperative for educational reform.* Washington, DC: Government Printing Office.

Neill, A. (1960). *Summerhill: A radical approach to child rearing.* New York: Hart.

Pulliam, J., & Van Patten, J. (2003). *History of education in America* (8th ed.). Upper Saddle River, NJ: Merrill/Prentice Hall.

Rossell, C. (2005). Teaching English through English. *Educational Leadership, 62*(4), 32–36.

Sack, J. (2004). The funding fix. In *Quality counts 2004: Count me in.* Bethesda, MD: Education Week.

Thomas, D., Enloe, W., & Newell, R. (2005). *The coolest school in America: How small learning communities are changing everything.* Lanham, MD: Scarecrow Education.

U.S. Department of Agriculture. (2005). Child nutrition programs: National school lunch program. Retrieved October 2, 2005 from: *http://www.ers.usda.gov/Briefing/ChildNutrition/lunch.htm*

Vanourek, G. (2005). *State of the charter movement.* Washington, DC: Charter School Leadership Council.

Virginia Beach City Public Schools. (2008). Corporate Landing Elementary. Retrieved October 27, 2008 from: *http://www.corporatelandinges.vbschools.com/*

Wirt, J., Choy, S., Rooney, P., Provasnik, S., Sen, A., & Tobin, R. (2004). *The condition of education 2004* (NCES 2004–077). Washington, D.C.: U.S. Government Printing Office.

Zehr, M. (2004, March 31). Private schools, Catholic closings. *Education Week,* p. 6.

chapter 5

The Teaching Profession

If you choose a career in teaching, you are doing more than just committing to doing your best to educate the students walking through your classroom door. You will enter a profession that has both rights and responsibilities associated with it. In this chapter, you will learn more about teaching as a profession and reflect on your responsibilities as a future educator. Three questions will guide your thinking.

Focus Questions

1. What makes teaching a profession?

2. How is teacher professionalism changing?

3. What are my professional responsibilities?

Courtesy of Anthony Magnacca/Merrill Education.

Trina and her husband Rod, both teachers in the local schools, are attending a neighborhood Christmas party. The conversation, as it often does in this kind of social situation, has focused on the latest developments in people's lives at work. The guests' occupations are varied and include a carpenter, nurse, bank teller, lawyer, grocery clerk, medical doctor, physical therapist, and a salesman. A rather natural human tendency in this situation is to mentally compare the benefits, drawbacks, and status of your occupation with the others being discussed. During the conversation, Marcie, a doctor in general practice, talks about the growing complexities of childbirth from a physician's perspective. Suzanne describes the back strain she is getting from standing all day in her job as a grocery clerk. Randy shares some insights on the latest issues in corporate law, his specialty. David, a bank teller, describes the humorous interactions he has had recently with people regarding money. At one point in the conversation, someone mentions the upcoming state-wide school testing efforts and both Trina and Rod share their concerns about the school district's overreliance on standardized tests to assess student progress.

If you were a participant in the above party, how would you compare teaching with the other occupations identified? Based on its importance to society and status among other professions, where do you see education fitting? How do you think others at the party might view Trina and Rod's careers in teaching when compared with the other occupations represented? Would they see teaching as closer in status and benefits to the nurse and bank teller than to the lawyer or doctor? Why do you feel this way? Based on its importance to society and status among other professions, what do you see as the professional status of teaching? Is it close to the top, in the middle, or nearer the bottom in comparison with other occupations? In all likelihood, both you and they would see teaching as closer in status and benefits to the nurse and bank teller than to the lawyer or doctor. Take out your Reflections Journal or open the on-line journal and record your responses to these questions.

What makes teaching a profession?

Although very few people deny the critical importance of education to a healthy American society, the professional status of teaching is not as high as it can and should be. The expression "those who can't, teach" is a highly inaccurate but widely held sentiment many people believe to be true. The common perception is that teaching is a rather easy job that nearly anyone with a little training can do well. A widely distributed newspaper cartoon strip published in 2004 highlights this misperception. In it, a young boy comes home from school and shares his report card with his mother. Mom is shocked to see that he is failing in every subject. He consoles his mother and tells her that everything will work out in the end. Still upset, however, the mother wonders aloud what the boy will do once he graduates. The boy's response: He will become a teacher! These and other indicators make it clear that there is much work that needs to be done before the general public as well as those involved in education view teaching as a true profession.

Without further information, you may find it difficult to decide how well teaching measures up against other professions. Teaching is similar in some ways to other clearly defined professions, but also seems to be different from them as well. In the next section, you will read about the characteristics common to all professions so that you will have a better idea of what makes an occupation a profession. This is then followed by a critique of teaching based on these criteria common to all professions. Once you have read and reflected on the information in the following two sections, you will have a better understanding of the professional status of teaching.

Defining a Profession

Have you ever stopped to wonder what makes an occupation a profession? Most people would agree that a profession requires advanced education and training and strong intellectual skills. For example, the practice of medicine is almost universally thought of as an important profession. Fewer, however, would consider bricklaying a professional occupation. Despite the bricklayer's obvious talents and the value of the work performed, bricklayers are usually considered highly skilled laborers rather than professionals. But what factors have led our society to view doctors as part of a profession while talented bricklayers are not? The seemingly simple task of defining a profession is actually a rather complex one.

It makes sense to begin by identifying the common traits of all professions before specifically looking at teaching to determine its professional status. Several writers who have studied this issue have identified a list of common characteristics of professions (Lagemann, 2004; Rowan, 1994; Webb, Metha, & Jordan, 2007). Although the lists that have been generated are somewhat different, a profession:

- *Requires strong intellectual skills.* Members of professions must use their intellectual abilities to investigate issues, problem solve, and effectively communicate their findings to others.

- *Involves complex interactions with people and/or information.* For example, both social workers and engineers have highly complex interactions: the former with people and the latter with information.
- *Provides an essential service.* Professions offer services to clients that are vital to their health and well-being. For example, one characteristic of police work is that it provides a service that is essential to society.
- *Requires extensive specialized training.* Several years of education and practical experience with the essential elements of the profession are necessary for entry.
- *Allows autonomy in decision making.* Professionals are given the freedom to apply their knowledge of the profession to the specific requirements of individual clients in making decisions about what is best for them. Psychiatry is a good example of an occupation that allows individual practitioners the autonomy to make decisions that are best for their clients. You may want to read *Ian's Classroom Experiences* feature found on the Companion Website for this text and think about Ian's autonomy in decision making in this situation.
- *Emphasizes service to its clients.* Professionals dedicate themselves to meeting the needs of the people they serve. They are obligated to always do what is in their clients' best interests.
- *Identifies standards of behavior.* Professions have developed codes of ethical conduct that state acceptable and unacceptable professional behavior. These written documents are typically broad in scope and outline only in general terms what is considered ethical behavior.
- *Assumes individuals are responsible for their own actions and decisions.* Members of a profession accept the fact that they are personally responsible for their own behavior in relationship to their clients. In business, for example, top management meet this requirement of a profession while the typical office worker often does not.
- *Engages in self-governance.* Professional groups see themselves as responsible for independently monitoring admission, retention, and exclusion from the profession. The legal profession, for example, is responsible for determining who may become a lawyer and also has strategies in place to censure and/or bar individuals from continuing to practice law.

**Ian's Classroom
Experiences:
Points of View**

When all characteristics are present in the occupation, it is clearly a profession. On the other hand, when several characteristics are missing, the occupation is less likely to be considered a profession. Figure 5.1 provides a summary of these characteristics. After reviewing these

Figure 5.1   Characteristics of a Profession

A profession:

- Requires strong intellectual skills.

- Provides an essential service.

- Requires extensive specialized training.

- Allows autonomy in decision making.

- Emphasizes service to its clients.

- Identifies professional standards of behavior.

- Assumes individuals are responsible for their own actions and decisions.

- Engages in self-governance.

characteristics again, can you name several occupations that you would consider professions? Are there others you would list as not being a profession? Keep these thoughts in mind as you read the next section and see how teaching measures up to these criteria.

Teaching as a Profession

Throughout the history of American education, teaching has slowly but steadily moved toward greater professionalism. In colonial days, teachers had no formal teacher preparation and frequently knew little more than the students they taught. Many viewed education as merely a stepping stone to a better position. Salaries were very low, and often were no better than wages paid for common manual labor (Cubberley, 1934). By the mid-1800s, teachers began to receive specialized training before entering the classroom. Teacher-education institutions referred to as **normal schools** became more common across the United States. Initially, the education received there by future teachers was exclusively in the academic disciplines and provided no instruction regarding the principles of good teaching. The salaries of teachers remained low, exemplifying the low status of education.

Following the Civil War, teacher preparation began to improve. The growth in numbers of secondary schools led to an increasing demand for teachers with strong academic preparation. In addition, an expansion of the knowledge regarding teaching and learning led to the gradual inclusion of this content in teacher-education programs. The 20th century saw additional progress made toward teacher professionalism. The length of teacher preparation programs slowly moved from 2 to 4 years, and by the 1950s the requirement of at least a 4-year college degree for teaching was common. National professional organizations such as the **National Education Association (NEA)** and the **American Federation of Teachers (AFT)** grew in size and number. These organizations further promoted rigorous teacher-preparation programs, lobbied for better salaries and benefits, and developed guidelines for professional conduct (Pulliam & Van Patten, 2007).

Despite the progress that education has made in becoming more professional, most would argue that it has not fully reached the goal of being a profession. Over the last several decades, this perspective has been evident in writings about education. Etzioni (1969), for example, called teaching a *semi-profession*. Howsam, Corrigan, Denemark, and Nash (1976) identified teaching as an *emerging profession*. Goodlad (1990) suggested that teaching should be considered a *not-quite profession*. Based on the characteristics presented earlier, arguments can be made both for and against considering teaching a profession. These arguments are summarized in Figure 5.2 and described in more detail below.

Arguments for Teaching as a Profession. There are several good reasons to consider teaching a profession. One is that it *requires strong intellectual skills*. The mathematics, reasoning, and language skills required of teachers compare well to other selected occupations. Particularly in the areas of reasoning and language, teachers need intellectual skills similar to those of other professions. Reformers of teacher education have recognized this need for strong intellectual skills and have helped implement a steady rise in the academic requirements for entering and exiting teacher education programs (National Center for Education Statistics, 2007). To view a video showing a grade level meeting of teachers in an elementary school making a variety of difficult decisions, go to the Companion Website for this text and click on MyEducationLab for Chapter 5.

Another argument in support of teaching as a profession is that it *involves complex human interactions*. In research comparisons with other occupations, teachers' human-interaction skills are rated as more complex than those of accountants, registered nurses, and secretaries, but somewhat less complex than those of physicians and lawyers (Rowan, 1994). One aspect of these complex human interactions is the need for teachers to assist students of different races and ethnicities in understanding each other and working together effectively. The *Reflect on Diversity* feature for this chapter provides additional insights on this topic from the perspective of

myeducationlab
The Power of Classroom Practice

MyEducationLab 5.1

Figure 5.2   On Balance: Teaching as A Profession

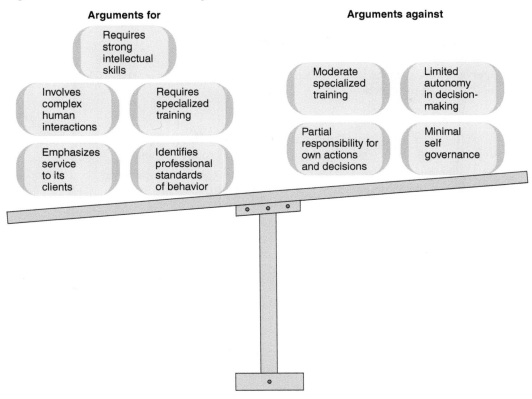

a student of color. Read the feature and reflect on the complex human interactions you will encounter as a future teacher.

Reflect on diversity: Being an incognegro

Amber Musser was an African American student at Harvard University. She saw herself "as a solitary black face in a sea of white, I am an incognegro" (Musser, 2000, p. 1). Using a play on words, Amber saw herself as moving through Harvard incognito, with her true identity hidden or disguised. Despite her many efforts to share her heritage and "blackness" with others, she believed that her peers truly did not recognize or understand her.

Amber's life history is full of stories about her Caribbean heritage and how it was misunderstood by others. In elementary school, for example, the first time she lost a tooth in class everyone crowded around to see what color her blood would be. It was assumed by her peers that it would be much darker than theirs. Amber also talks about one of her first memories of being called Black. She responded by indicating that the asphalt was Black, but that her skin color was tan. Amber was beginning to learn that others didn't see things the same way she did.

Race became a conscious issue for her in high school when she moved to a new school. As with all students her age, friendships were critically important to Amber. Luckily, she was able to establish a close friendship with another Black student and in time came to know her Black friends. They all ate lunch together at a table dubbed "Little Africa". But through this experience she also began to realize that because of her Black friends, White students were hesitant to spend time with her. Timid hellos and brief conversations were the extent of Amber's interactions with others in the school. While there was no overt racism, there was also little opportunity for Amber to share her true self with others whose skin color was different from hers. She was moving through her schooling as an incognegro.

Developing the Habit of Reflective Practice

Gather Information

1. Read more about diversity issues at
   http://www.hcs.harvard.edu/~dnd/archive.shtml

2. Interview someone who was considered a minority in their school setting. Question him/her about the experience.

Identify Beliefs

1. Would the "Mix It Up Lunch" as described in Chapter Three's *Explore Your Beliefs* have had an impact on Amber's schooling experience? Defend your reasoning.

2. Do you think that African American students continue to have experiences common to what Amber Musser describes? Defend your reasoning.

Make Decisions

1. As a teacher, you overhear a conversation between two students. The conversation is much like what Amber describes when someone calls her Black for the first time. How do you react to that interaction? Do you respond then? Later? Never? What do you say or do, if anything?

2. As a teacher, how could you make every student feel like a valued member of your class?

Assess and Evaluate

1. How are you currently prepared to work with students who have a different racial background from your own?

2. What can you do to better prepare yourself for working with students who have a different racial background from your own?

Source

Musser, A. (2000). Confessions of an incognegro. *Diversity and Distinction*, Winter 2000, pp 1-4.

Several other factors can be identified that strengthen the case for teaching as a profession. One such factor is that teaching *provides an essential service* to society. Teachers and schools play a critical role in educating and supporting the overall development of children and youth. These young people then have a direct impact on the future well-being of society. Another reason to consider teaching a profession is that it *requires specialized training*. The educational requirements for teachers have become more complex during the past several decades, making teaching comparable to many other professions in the length of its vocational preparation. Teaching also can be viewed as *emphasizing service to its clients*. One of the reasons that teaching is such a complex task is that educators actually must serve several clients simultaneously. Students, of course, are primary clients. Teachers serve students by working hard to meet their individual and collective learning needs. In addition to students, however, parents and community are also important clients that teachers can and do serve. The *Views from the Classroom* feature for this chapter describes one teacher's efforts to involve a parent and the positive impact this involvement had on the child. Go to the Companion Website for this text and read this feature now. Finally, teaching *identifies professional standards of behavior*. Several codes of ethical conduct guide the practicing teacher. Table 5.1 gives a brief overview of four different codes of ethics developed by professional education associations. A link to each document is provided on the Companion Website for this text.

As you read these different codes of ethics, you will notice that each is broad in scope and outlines only in the most general terms what is expected of ethical teachers. Wagner (1996)

Views from the Classroom: Never Say Never

TABLE 5.1   Codes of Ethics

Organization	Description
National Education Association	The best-known and most frequently cited code. It contains two principles: the teacher's commitment to students; and commitment to the profession.
Council for Exceptional Children	This code describes eight components of ethical behavior for teachers of students with special needs.
National Association for the Education of Young Children	This document includes a statement of six core values and a description of ethical responsibilities in four professional relationships (children, families, colleagues, and community/society).
International Reading Association	This code is an example of a specific content area professional organization and its statement of ethical conduct.

Links which display these codes of ethics can be found on the Companion Website for this text.

emphasizes that such codes "do not provide a set of 'do's and don'ts' for every possible situation. The point of a code of ethics is not to tell the professional what to do in each and every instance, but to draw his or her attention generally to the most important moral considerations . . . Professionals must create their own 'do's and don'ts' by considering the moral tradition of their profession" (p. 10). Codes of ethics merely provide a starting point for the many moral deliberations that teachers face. Chapter 13 will provide further insights on ethics and teaching.

Arguments Against Teaching as a Profession. Although much progress has been made, more work must be done before educators can truly be considered part of a profession. Several arguments are frequently cited as reasons for considering teaching as a developing profession. The first of these is that teaching *requires only moderate specialized training.* For example, students who want to be lawyers must complete a rigorous doctoral program called the Juris Doctorate or J.D. before entrance into the profession. Although teacher preparation has grown stronger over time, its length and intellectual rigor still lag behind that of many other professions. The competition for entrance into teacher education programs and later into the teaching ranks has also typically been minimal, leading many to question the qualifications of new teachers. The relatively recent adoption of standardized tests for entrance into, and exit from, teacher-training programs is an attempt to remedy this situation (Education Commission of the States, 2003). Unfortunately, however, some teachers are failing these standardized tests.

A second reason often cited for education's lack of professional status is that teaching *allows limited autonomy in decision making.* Although it is true that teachers make many decisions each day that impact the lives of students and their families, they frequently have limited input into the overall directions of teaching and learning. In the medical profession, doctors make independent decisions about medicines and medical procedures based on an understanding of the symptoms and past histories of individual patients. Teachers, on the other hand, must work within the confines of school policies, state regulations, and federal mandates as they work to meet the needs of their students.

Another reason that teaching has not yet reached the status of a profession is that teachers assume only *partial responsibility for their own actions and decisions*. Until very recently, teachers were not held accountable for how and what they taught. If students didn't learn, rather than being something the teacher might have done or said, it was often assumed to be due to issues such as student motivation or a lack of parental involvement. With the passage of the *No Child Left Behind Act (NCLB) of 2001,* however, both the public and the field itself are seeing the importance of teachers taking more responsibility for their own actions (see Chapter 4 for more information on NCLB). Both teachers and schools are being held more accountable for student learning. The NCLB act, for example, requires a **statewide assessment** in both reading and mathematics for Grades 3–8 (Robelin, 2002). These paper-and-pencil tests, generally in the form of multiple-choice or true/false questions, are administered to all students in the state to determine student progress in these subjects. The law also mandates that states improve academic achievement for all students and implements consequences for schools that do not meet the expected levels of progress. This puts pressure on teachers to make sure their students learn. In some cases, this is complicated further by linking teacher salaries to their performance. The *Explore Your Beliefs* feature for this chapter describes a hypothetical story of a dentist whose performance is rated by the number of cavities of his patients. This analogy may give you insights into the complexities of rating teacher performance based on student learning.

Explore your beliefs: Performance pay for teachers

Performance pay for teachers is a strategy being tried in some school districts to motivate teachers to engage in effective instruction by offering them pay increases for improved student performance. This highly controversial approach prompted John S. Taylor, a district superintendent in South Carolina, to write an essay titled "Absolutely the Best Dentist", which is reprinted in part here:

My dentist is great! He sends me reminders so I don't forget checkups. He uses the latest techniques based on research. He never hurts me, and I've got all my teeth, so when I ran into him the other day, I was eager to see if he'd heard about the new state program. I knew he'd think it was great.

"Did you hear about the new state program to measure the effectiveness of dentists with their young patients?" I said.

"No," he said. He didn't seem too thrilled. "How will they do that?"

"It's quite simple," I said. "They will just count the number of cavities each patient has at age 10, 14 and 18 and average that to determine a dentist's rating. Dentists will be rated as Excellent, Good, Average, Below Average and Unsatisfactory. That way parents will know which are the best dentists. It will also encourage the less effective dentists to get better," I said. "Poor dentists who don't improve could lose their licenses to practice in South Carolina."

"That's terrible," he said.

"What? That's not a good attitude," I said. "Don't you think we should try to improve children's dental health in this state?"

"Sure I do," he said, "but that's not a fair way to determine who is practicing good dentistry."

"Why not?" I said. "It makes perfect sense to me."

"Well, it's so obvious," he said. "Don't you see that dentists don't all work with the same clientele; so much depends on things we can't control?

"For example," he said, "I work in a rural area with a high percentage of patients from deprived homes, while some of my colleagues work in upper-middle class neighborhoods. Many of the parents I work with don't bring their children to see me until there is some kind of problem and I don't get to do much preventive work.

"Also," he said, "many of the parents I serve let their kids eat way too much candy from a young age, unlike more educated parents who understand the relationship between sugar and decay.

"To top it all off," he added, "so many of my clients have well water which is untreated and has no fluoride in it. Do you have any idea how much difference early use of fluoride can make?"

Reprinted from "Absolutely the Best Dentist," by John Taylor, *The School Administrator,* June 2000.

Developing the Habit of Reflective Practice

Gather Information

1. Do an Internet search for "Absolutely the Best Dentist" and read John Taylor's entire essay.

2. Interview at least 5 people to see what their opinions are on the idea of performance pay for teachers.

Identify Beliefs

1. What motivates you to do quality work? What role does money have in stimulating your performance?

2. What are the positive and negative outcomes that could result from linking student performance on standardized tests to increased salaries for teachers?

Make Decisions

1. Do you think teachers should be given pay increases based on their ability to raise student scores on standardized tests? Why or why not?

2. Do you think teachers should receive reduced pay if their students fail to achieve required test scores? Why or why not?

Assess and Evaluate

1. How does John Taylor's analogy between dentists and teachers work for you?

2. How do you think essays like this one would be perceived if printed in your local newspaper? Are essays like this a good way to influence the public about issues such as performance pay for teachers?

Source

Taylor, J. (2000). Absolutely the best dentist. *The School Administrator* June 2000.

Finally, full status as a profession eludes education partly because teaching has *minimal self-governance*. Admission criteria for teacher-education programs are typically created and monitored by state education agencies with little input from teachers themselves. Similarly, retention in the teaching ranks is typically based on the observations and evaluations of local school administrators based on school or district policies. Removing ineffective teachers from the classroom is often a very difficult task once **tenure** has been achieved. Tenure provides teachers with a binding contract that helps ensure a place for them in the schools in future years. Legal proceedings that substantiate grossly inappropriate actions on the part of the teacher are generally the only way in which tenured teachers can be removed. Chapter 13 provides additional information on teacher tenure.

Consider writing down your thoughts about teaching as a profession. After reading about the arguments for and against teaching as a profession, how would you describe its professional status? What do you see as the most significant reasons for identifying teachers as professionals? What must yet be done to further the development of the teaching profession? When reflecting on your personality and skills, can you see yourself as a professional educator? Why or why not?

Now that you have a better understanding of the issues surrounding teaching as a profession, you may wonder how the status of teaching has changed over time. Is it becoming more like other professions? If so, what is some evidence that demonstrates that this has taken place? Are there

**Reflection
Opportunity 5.2**

additional strategies that can be implemented that will help teaching continue growing as a profession? The next section will help provide answers to these and other similar questions.

How is teacher professionalism changing?

Although teacher professionalism has been growing steadily throughout America's history, recent activities in three areas have led to an even greater emphasis on moving teaching closer to professional status. The first of these areas is the educational reform efforts that began in the mid-1980s. These activities focused national attention on many issues related to professionalism. Higher standards for students in recent years have also had an impact on professionalism. Finally, more rigorous teacher-certification standards have helped create better-prepared educators for America's classrooms.

Educational Reform Reports

You are probably aware of the considerable debate in public and professional circles about the health of the American educational system. Many suggest that it is in crisis and major educational reform is needed in order for the system to remain viable. These changes in the system are needed, they say, so that teachers can do a better job of teaching and students can increase the level of their learning. Others believe that although much can be improved, American education is doing well and the criticisms being leveled against the system are exaggerated. Typically, it is the former position that gets the most publicity both within educational circles and in the popular media.

The most recent efforts to implement major reform in American education began in the early 1980s when President Reagan established the National Commission on Excellence in Education. The commission's 1983 report, *A Nation at Risk: The Imperative for Educational Reform,* identified many serious problems with American education. Citing a "rising tide of mediocrity," the report emphasized the importance of rigorous academic programs, proposed that teacher-preparation programs be strengthened, and promoted the introduction of more sophisticated school management procedures.

In addition to the report issued by the National Commission on Excellence in Education, several other writers and researchers added their voices to the call for reform during this same time frame. Responses, although varied, were unified in their strong criticism of the current educational system and their insistence on the need for major change. Educational reform proponents such as John Goodlad (1984), Theodore Sizer (1984), William Glasser (1986), and Ernest Boyer (1983) emphasized the importance of restructuring the ways in which schools are operated and suggested alternatives such as site-based management, improving school climate, identifying teachers as facilitators of learning, encouraging parent participation in education, and implementing school choice. In response to these proposals and the original report from the National Commission on Excellence in Education, individual states initiated changes in two major areas. They began implementing higher graduation requirements for students and increased their testing of both students and teachers. These efforts are summarized in Table 5.2 and described in more detail below.

Higher Standards for Students

Initially, you may see little connection between increasing expectations for students in American schools and the issue of professionalism. But consider the impact of higher standards on teachers themselves. As students are expected to learn more and perform at higher levels, the quality of teaching required must also improve. Teachers who are successful in encouraging higher performance in their students are therefore perceived as more competent and professional.

Efforts to increase standards for students have taken three main directions. The first is a focused attempt to get students to take more rigorous course work, particularly at the high school level. In 1987, then U.S. Secretary of Education William J. Bennett proposed the creation

TABLE 5.2 Education Reform Efforts	
Emphasis	**Description**
Higher Standards for Students	• Focused efforts to get students to take more rigorous course work • Development of broad standards for core subjects • Increased use of standardized testing
More Rigorous Teacher Certification	• Testing requirements for entrance into, and exit from, teacher-education programs • Improving the curriculum students in teacher education must take • Mandating continuing education following initial teacher certification

of a **core curriculum** for all high school students that called for 4 years of English; 3 years each of mathematics, science, and social studies; 2 years of foreign language study; and other requirements that limited the number of electives students could take to approximately a quarter of their total time. Many states responded to this proposal by increasing their requirements for high school graduation.

The second direction taken to increase expectations for students was the development of broad **standards for core subjects** such as mathematics, science, language arts, and social studies (Marzano, 1998). With the support of the federal government, professional organizations such as the National Council of Teachers of Mathematics, the National Association for the Advancement of Science, the National Council of Teachers of English, and the National Council for the Social Studies developed reports that identify the essential knowledge and skills expected from students in each of these areas. These efforts have led to a clearer definition of the core competencies needed by all students in specific disciplines.

The final direction that has led to higher standards for students is the increased use of **standardized testing** to determine how well students are doing in learning the essential content and skills of each discipline. These tests are typically multiple-choice questions that are administered to large numbers of students and then used to compare their academic performance. The California Standards Tests (California State Government, 2005) are examples of this type. They test California students' academic knowledge in English–language arts, mathematics, science, and history–social science. During the last 20 years, states have passed legislation mandating standardized testing at different grade levels. These data are then used to compare students from year to year in the same state and with others around the nation to see if student performance has increased.

Although these tests have value, the heavy emphasis on standardized testing has often been criticized (Abrams & Madaus, 2003; Amrein & Berliner, 2003). One key problem is the tendency for educators to spend their time teaching students content they will need to be successful on the tests. This "teaching to the test" mentality places too much emphasis on the rote memorization of facts and deemphasizes problem solving and process-oriented learning. Many are critical of standardized tests because they are not effective in assessing the problem-solving abilities and higher-level thinking skills needed by students to be successful in today's world. Students who are expected to learn in these circumstances often lack motivation and are less likely to be successful. Another issue is the concern that standardized tests fail to assess the diverse student populations served in the schools accurately. They tend to discriminate against females, minorities, and students from lower socioeconomic groups. Tests, critics argue, contain information that is typically learned outside the school setting and is based more on family circumstances than on a student's native intelligence or ability. For example, research suggests that standardized tests favor high-income families and that students can expect to score an additional 30 points on the Scholastic Aptitude Test (SAT) for every $10,000 in family income (Sacks, 2001).

Higher Standards for Teachers

In addition to mandating standardized tests for students, educational reform efforts have been a factor in creating higher standards for teachers as well. These reform efforts originated primarily in individual states. Because teacher certification is a state responsibility, the framework for the teacher-education program you are entering was largely determined by an education agency in your state. If you were to move to another part of the country, you would encounter at least a few differences between your current state's and your new state's requirements for initial and continuing teacher licensure. Despite these differences, trends indicate that all future teachers are completing more rigorous preparation programs than in the past and are engaging in more continued professional development. Four major changes have been implemented during the last two decades that influence teacher professional development.

The first change has been in the *testing requirements* for entrance into, and exit from, teacher-education programs (Education Week, 2008). Standardized tests are again the primary method of evaluation and the most commonly used exam for teachers in training is the **Praxis series.** Many states require completion of the Praxis I exam (see Table 5.3) for entrance into their teacher-education programs and passing scores on the Praxis II exam (see Chapter 1) prior to issuing a teaching certificate. As with standardized exams in general, these tests discriminate against minorities and low-socioeconomic status college students and therefore tend to exclude these important groups from the teaching ranks. A second criticism of the teacher testing requirements is the low scores required by many states for entrance into, and completion of, teacher-education programs. These low scores, critics emphasize, are not effective in screening out teacher candidates who have low academic skills (Walsh & Snyder, 2004; Wang, Coleman, Cohen, & Phelps, 2003).

TABLE 5.3 Praxis I: Pre-Professional Skills Tests	
Test	**Description**
Reading	This test measures a person's ability to understand and evaluate written statements of lengths varying from one or more sentences to passages of approximately 200 words.
Mathematics	This test measures a person's understanding of key mathematical concepts expected of an educated adult. It assesses conceptual and procedural knowledge, measurement and informal geometry, and formal mathematical reasoning.
Writing	This test measures a person's ability to use grammar and language appropriately in written communications. It includes a multiple choice section on the use of standard English and an essay written on a specified topic.

Source: Adapted from *Tests at a Glance,* Educational Testing Service. Retrieved January 6, 2005 from: *http://www.ets.org/praxis/prxtest.html*

The second major change that has been implemented to enhance teacher professional development has been to *improve the curriculum* students must complete for initial teacher preparation. In many states, these changes have included a stronger emphasis on liberal arts as a component of teacher preparation. For example, some states now require substantial formal coursework in the subject area(s) taught in addition to the teacher-education course work required for certification (Education Week, 2008). Another major modification in teacher preparation has been the implementation of early field experiences to give preservice teachers a variety of opportunities to work with students. These early and regular contacts with P–12 students help build the skills and confidence needed to be successful in the student teaching experience and beyond.

The third effort to strengthen teacher professional development has focused on *continuing education following initial certification.* During the past two or three decades, states have generally moved away from giving lifetime teaching certificates and instead have implemented systems in which licenses require periodic updating. In most cases, this updating comes in the form of additional college or university credits every few years. For example, in many states teachers who now receive initial certification will be required to take an additional 10–15 credits within the next 3–5 years to avoid having their certificates expire. Other states require educators to complete a master's degree or a specific plan of further study to receive a permanent teaching credential that replaces the initial certificate. Forty percent of states require teachers to complete a **professional teaching portfolio** to demonstrate their competence for a teaching credential (Wilkerson & Lang, 2003). This portfolio is a collection of lesson plans, student assignments, video and audiotapes, and testing results that help demonstrate teacher effectiveness.

The final effort to improve teacher professional development was initiated at the national level by the National Board for Professional Teaching Standards. As mentioned in Chapter 3, this organization offers advanced certification for teachers seeking acknowledgment for high levels of performance in the classroom. This voluntary program is called **National Board Certification** and is considered the highest level of teacher accomplishment for those working in P–12 classrooms. Teachers who seek National Board Certification complete a rigorous program that includes teaching portfolios, student work samples, videotapes and thorough analyses of the candidates' classroom teaching and student learning. (National Board for Professional Teaching Standards, 2008). Most teachers who go through the National Board Certification process have 5 or more years of teaching experience and less than half of those who do apply are successful their first try. Currently, 38 states offer financial rewards of several thousand dollars to teachers who successfully complete National Board Certification (Education Week, 2008).

Do you know what your state requires for a permanent teaching credential? Spend some time researching this issue on your state department of education Website and describe your findings. Do you feel your state is doing a good job of strengthening teacher certification? What do you like about what your state is doing? Are there things you would like to see changed? If you are required to continue your education to receive a permanent teaching credential, does this prospect excite or frustrate you? Why do you feel this way? Do you see yourself as the type of person who would be excited about pursuing National Board Certification at some point in your career? Explain why you feel this way.

Reflection Opportunity 5.3

Unfortunately, these efforts to strengthen the rigor of teacher certification programs and professional development are coming at a time when states are experiencing shortages in many areas and have begun implementing strategies to put less qualified personnel in K–12 classrooms (Walsh & Snyder, 2004). For example, the use of emergency certificates to meet the demand for teachers in urban areas and for mathematics, science, and special education teachers has grown during the last several years. Although the need for teachers in these areas is undoubtedly great, these efforts fail to support the move toward increased professionalism in teaching.

What are my professional teaching responsibilities?

Although the above discussion about the growth of teaching as a profession is interesting and can lead to lively discussions, it has little real value unless you personally begin to apply this information to your own future career. If you choose to enter teaching, it is essential to see yourself as continuing to grow both personally and professionally throughout your career. You may not have much direct impact on the overall course of teacher professionalism, but you do have ultimate control over your own personal actions. Consider engaging in five categories of behavior that can markedly enhance your own interactions with students and others: using active reflection, conducting yourself in a professional manner, continuing your professional development, participating in professional organizations, and accepting leadership roles.

Using Active Reflection

As described initially in Chapter 1, a major emphasis of this book has been on the importance of using active reflection as an integral part of your teaching. It is through active reflection that you will continue to grow in your understanding of students and in your ability to plan activities to meet their many needs. As you gather information, identify beliefs, make decisions, and assess and evaluate the results of your actions, the teaching and learning in your classroom will remain dynamic and move in positive directions.

Several national initiatives provide additional support for the importance of engaging in active reflection. Together, these initiatives define a national climate for reflection that clearly supports the value of thinking deeply and often about teaching and learning as you continue to grow as an educator:

- *No Child Left Behind Act of 2001 (NCLB).* This important piece of federal legislation is designed to improve the learning of all children. To accomplish this task in our increasingly diverse society, it is critical for teachers to reflect daily on every aspect of their educational efforts so that no child is left behind.

- *Individuals with Disabilities Education Act (IDEA).* This federal law (Chapter 2 describes the act in more detail) is designed to provide students with disabilities quality learning experiences that are integrated into the regular public school classroom whenever possible. To provide the best education for students with disabilities, teachers must again think deeply and often about effective methods, materials, and activities that can be used to stimulate quality learning experiences.

- *National Council for Accreditation of Teacher Education (NCATE).* This national organization is responsible for making sure that teacher education programs meet high standards as they prepare new teachers. In their professional standards document they state: "They (teacher-education students) are able to reflect on and continually evaluate the effects of choices and actions on others and actively seek out opportunities to grow professionally" (National Council for Accreditation of Teacher Education, 2008, p. 22).

- *Interstate New Teacher Assessment and Support Consortium (INTASC).* This working group of the Council of Chief State School Officers developed an important document in which they clearly defined 10 standards that all new teachers should meet before they enter the classroom (see Chapter 1 for a list of these standards). Standard 9 states: "The teacher is a reflective practitioner who continually evaluates the effects of his/her choices and actions on others (students, parents, and other professionals in the learning community) and who actively seeks out opportunities to grow professionally" (Interstate New Teacher Assessment and Support Consortium, 1995, p. 5).

- *National Board for Professional Teaching Standards (NBPTS).* As mentioned earlier, this national organization provides advanced certification for teachers who are seeking recognition for high levels of accomplishment in teaching. One of the five core propositions that form the basis for this advanced certification states: "Teachers think systematically about their practice and learn from experience" (National Board for Professional Teaching Standards, 2005).

Conducting Yourself in a Professional Manner

Another strategy you can use to grow as a professional is to begin right now to learn more about teacher professionalism and start engaging in appropriate interactions with others. Find out if your teacher-preparation program has created a statement on professional behavior and make sure you understand the implications of such a document. If your institution does not have such a document, consider proposing that it be developed and discussion initiated to clarify its implications. Figure 5.3 shows a sample professionalism statement. You can also find and read the

Figure 5.3   Sample Professionalism Statement

Students are expected to familiarize themselves with, seek clarification of, and adhere to the expectations of university faculty, school principal, and classroom teachers regarding:

1. Conducts self ethically
   1.1 Maintains confidentiality of privileged information
   1.2 Interacts with students in an adult professional manner
   1.3 Displays sensitivity and balance when treating controversial issues

2. Works productively
   2.1 Makes expected contributions to solving student academic/conduct problems
   2.2 Makes expected contributions to maintaining communications with parents
   2.3 Maintains professional manner in dealings with parents, faculty, and others

3. Displays initiative by using a variety of resources
   3.1 Maintains expected teacher hours/schedules
   3.2 Submits plans and other requested information punctually
   3.3 Attends school and department/grade level meetings
   3.4 Adheres to established standards for dress and grooming

4. Initiates personal growth in subject area(s), learning theories, and/or instructional practices; establishes goals for professional improvement
   4.1 Sets goals for learning
   4.2 Solicits and considers suggestions from others
   4.3 Completes any prescribed training or self-study to attain goal
   4.4 Meets university expectations

5. Utilizes knowledge of families and community resources to enhance support for children and families, including those from diverse racial and ethnic groups
   5.1 Demonstrates an awareness of factors such as family structure, lifestyles, culture, and special challenges/stressors that can make an impact on parent participation/involvement
   5.2 Demonstrates awareness of agencies/resources available to support families and knowledge regarding access to such services

Source: The professionalism statement of the Woodring College of Education, Western Washington University. Reprinted with permission.

codes of professional conduct written by organizations such as the NEA (see Table 5.1). Make sure that you take time to discuss the implications of these documents with others.

A discussion of issues related to professionalism should be a regular part of your teacher-preparation program. For example, seminars associated with field experiences provide excellent opportunities to discuss professional interactions with students, teachers, parents, and other school personnel. Most of your university course work should also address professionalism issues from time to time. When you discuss these issues with peers and others, you will experience many opportunities to grow in your understanding of, and engagement in, professional behavior.

Reflection Opportunity 5.4

Consider reflecting on the issue of professionalism. What are some examples of professional behaviors as teachers interact with the students they teach? Can you also identify nonprofessional behaviors? Think about teacher professionalism in relationship to parents and community members. What does being professional mean in these relationships? Can you see yourself engaging in professional behaviors in your future interactions as a teacher? Are there areas in which you may have more difficulty in being professional?

Continuing Your Professional Development

If you've spent much time in the K–12 schools, you know that there is seldom a dull moment in teaching. New strategies for teaching, changes in the curriculum, and the challenges of unique students are just some of the things that keep life interesting. In responding to these challenges, the best teachers are continually seeking out new information from sources such as colleagues, university courses and workshops, and professional publications so that they can do the best job possible in their interactions with students and others.

It may be difficult to imagine at this point in your teacher-preparation program, but your quest for knowledge about teaching and learning has only just begun and will continue throughout your career. You can begin now to establish the mind-set needed to be successful in growing as a teacher by first *seeking advice from others you respect*. Teachers you have met, university professors, and classmates are all valuable resources that can assist in your professional development. By beginning now to reach out to others you respect, you will be much more likely to continue this as a future teacher.

In addition, you should plan for *continuing your education following your initial teacher certification*. Although this may be the last thing you want to think about at this point in time, you need to mentally prepare yourself for this important eventuality. Find out what your state requires for continuing certification and then consider how you can most effectively grow through additional university course work. You may want to think about working toward additional teaching endorsements once you get your first teaching job. In some cases, these endorsements strengthen your ability to teach at a given level (i.e., a reading endorsement strengthening your work with primary-aged children), and other endorsements give you the flexibility to teach a completely new subject or grade level (i.e., adding a mathematics endorsement to supplement your science teaching certificate). In many situations, working toward a master's degree also makes good sense. You may wish to talk to a faculty advisor who can give you more information about this option. In any case, begin thinking about some goals for longer-term professional development that can be met through future university course work.

Reflection Opportunity 5.5

Can you see yourself getting excited about continuing your professional development throughout your career as an educator? Will you enjoy seeking out advice from others you respect? Is the thought of continuing to take college course work appealing to you? Are there aspects of continuing professional development that are not as exciting to you?

Participating in Professional Organizations

Another important step you can take now as part of your professional responsibilities is to participate in one or more professional organizations. There are literally hundreds of different national organizations associated with education from which you can choose. Virtually all have student memberships that allow you to get involved now at a reduced rate and receive many of the benefits of full membership. Most organizations hold an annual national meeting where members come together to learn more about various aspects of education and to network with others in the field. In addition, many organizations publish materials related to teaching and learning, and spend considerable time and energy advocating at all levels on behalf of students and teachers.

Two professional organizations that you will become familiar with as a teacher are the National Education Association (NEA) and the American Federation of Teachers (AFT). These two organizations strive to improve the professional lives of all teachers. Both organizations share the same two purposes. One objective of both the NEA and AFT is to serve as a strong teacher's union, with collective bargaining, strikes, and sanctions used to better the working conditions of all teachers. The other purpose is to assist in the continuing professional development of all teachers through the sponsorship of local, regional, and national conferences and the development of timely publications on issues related to education. One of the controversies surrounding NEA and AFT is that although joining a teacher's union is not mandatory, it is necessary to pay that portion of the dues that covers the costs of collective bargaining activities. Because the teacher's union acts on behalf of all teachers in districts it represents, this is seen as justifiable. The *Engage in the Debate* feature for this chapter gives you the opportunity to gather more information on union dues and think through your thoughts on this issue.

Engage in the debate: Should teacher union membership be compulsory?

Fifty years ago, almost every teacher belonged to local teachers' associations but membership in the state and national teacher unions was voluntary and not widespread. Then, in the late 1950s, states began enacting laws granting unions in public education the privilege of being the exclusive representatives of all teachers in bargaining salary and benefits with school districts.

In about half of the states, laws exist which allow teacher union officials to enforce compulsory union dues from teachers. In many school districts, the union will become the "exclusive representative" for every teacher in the district, whether that teacher voted for the union or not. If a teacher does not agree with the contract, he/she has no choice but to abide by the contract or quit their job. Teachers, however, must pay for these services with dues. The annual dues are generally over $700.

If a teacher objects to the political or ideological activities of their union, s/he may choose to opt out. Teachers who choose this alternative are not required to pay for non-bargaining activities and are eligible for a refund of this portion of their dues. *Non-bargaining* activities include political, social and ideological functions. The union will still represent that teacher in collective bargaining, contract management, and grievance processing, but that teacher will no longer have to contribute to political causes he/she does not support.

Compulsory union dues are a hot topic in the news in some states. In fact there have been lawsuits accusing state unions of spending dues that were supposed to be spent on bargaining activities on other activities such as political fundraising.

Developing the habit of reflective practice
Gather Information

1. Go to the Public Service Research Foundation to read about reasons for not joining a teacher's union: *http://www.psrf.org/issues/teachers.jsp*
2. Go to the teacher union websites (NEA; AFT) to read their perspectives on union membership: *http://www.nea.org/ http://www.aft.org/*
3. Interview three educators to find out their opinions and experiences with teacher unions.

Identify Beliefs

1. What benefits do teacher unions bring to teachers? What benefits do teacher unions bring to students?

2. What difficulties or pitfalls do teacher unions bring to teachers? What difficulties or pitfalls do teacher unions bring to students?

Make Decisions

1. Should teacher unions be mandatory for teachers to join? Why or why not?

2. How much freedom should teacher unions have when it comes to how they spend their money?

Assess and Evaluate

1. What advice would you give to a beginning teacher as to how involved he/she should be with the teachers' union? Give a rationale for your advice.

2. Will teacher unions be as prevalent, more prevalent or less prevalent in 10 years as compared to now? Defend your prediction.

National Education Association (NEA). By far the largest professional organization for teachers, the National Education Association is a complex institution serving more than 3.2 million members (NEA, 2008). Although teachers are the most prominent affiliates of the NEA, administrators, teacher aides, professors, guidance counselors, librarians, and college students are also involved. Operating at the national, state, and local levels, the NEA exerts a powerful influence on teachers and schools.

The NEA offers a wealth of services to teachers and others. In addition to publishing numerous books and pamphlets on educational topics, the organization regularly produces *NEA Today, Today's Education,* and the *NEA Research Bulletin* to update members on current issues in education. The NEA also has personnel who give local affiliates and members assistance with their collective bargaining and lobbying efforts. Finally, members can receive benefits such as life and health insurance coverage, credit cards, and mortgages through the national organization.

The National Education Association was founded in 1857 to "elevate the character and advance the interests of the profession of teaching and to promote the cause of education in the United States" (National Education Association, 2008). To further this goal, the NEA sees itself as a leader in the school reform efforts of the past and present. The association promotes the importance of every student having access to a quality education in a safe and caring setting. The NEA's central purpose has led to active involvement in politics at the local, state, and national levels. Because of its size and the quality of its membership, the NEA has had a significant impact on political campaigns and issues ranging from teacher salaries and benefits to such topics as providing public funds for private schooling.

American Federation of Teachers. The American Federation of Teachers is somewhat younger and smaller than the NEA. Founded in 1916, the AFT currently has about 1.4 million members, many of whom are teaching in key urban areas such as Chicago and New York. The organization is affiliated with the American Federation of Labor–Congress of Industrial Organizations (AFL-CIO), a voluntary alliance of 57 national and international labor unions, and sees itself as an important part of the American labor movement. The mission statement of the AFT gives as its purpose:

> to improve the lives of our members and their families, to give voice to their legitimate professional, economic and social aspirations, to strengthen the institutions in which we work, to improve the quality of the services we provide, to bring together all members to assist and

support one another and to promote democracy, human rights and freedom in our union, in our nation and throughout the world. (American Federation of Teachers, 2008)

Over the years, the AFT has unflinchingly viewed itself as a labor union for teachers and has worked hard to improve their working conditions. Collective bargaining and strikes (when necessary) are used to negotiate increasingly better teacher contracts. Though sometimes accused of being unprofessional and too concerned with issues benefiting teachers, the AFT has been very successful in improving the salaries, benefits, and general working conditions of the teachers it serves.

While maintaining its involvement in union activities, the AFT has broadened its focus in recent years to include other interests. It is now very much an advocate for a variety of educational reforms. Examples of current interests include the following:

- providing quality health care in school settings
- improving the status and qualifications of paraprofessionals
- identifying world-class standards for schools
- involving higher education in raising academic standards,
- supporting the National Board for Professional Teaching Standards (American Federation of Teachers, 2008).

Other Professional Organizations. In addition to the NEA and AFT, four other types of professional organizations are available that you may want to join. Table 5.4 provides examples of each type. One group of associations focuses on a *specific educational level*. For example, early childhood educators who work with prekindergarten and primary children often join the National Association for the Education of Young Children (NAEYC). Other professional organizations have a *subject-matter focus*. For example, if you choose to be an elementary educator and spend a significant part of your school day engaged in reading instruction, the International Reading Association (IRA) would be a good choice for a subject-matter specialty organization. A third group of organizations has a *specialty focus* and are often the best choices for educators interested in a specific teaching focus. For example, special educators, bilingual teachers, teachers of the gifted and talented, and vocational–technical educators all have specialty organizations they can join. A final type of professional organization can best be categorized as *generalist* and appeals to a broad

TABLE 5.4 Professional Organizations for Teachers	
Type	**Examples**
Educational Level	National Association for the Education of Young Children (birth–age 8) National Middle School Association
Subject Matter	National Council for Teachers of Mathematics National Council for the Social Studies National Council for Teachers of English
Specialty	National Association for Gifted Children Council for Exceptional Children National Association for Multicultural Education
Generalist	Association for Supervision and Curriculum Development Phi Delta Kappa International

range of educators. For example, you may find an organization such as Phi Delta Kappa (PDK) of interest as a future teacher. Phi Delta Kappa is an honorary society whose members have demonstrated high academic achievement, completed at least 15 semester hours of graduate course work, and shown a commitment to educational service. None of these professional organizations would be considered a union; instead, they see themselves as groups of educators with common interests who communicate through regularly scheduled conferences and publications.

Reflect on the professional organizations described above. What benefits do you think professional organizations might have for you as a future teacher? Do you see yourself getting actively involved in several of them? Which ones appeal to you the most? Are there types of organizations that do not interest you? If so, why do you feel this way?

Reflection Opportunity 5.6

Accepting Leadership Roles

One final aspect of your professional responsibilities as a future teacher is to take on leadership roles in educational settings. As a teacher, you will automatically accept an important leadership role in guiding the learning of each student in your classroom. Beyond that, however, you will also need to move outside the classroom and use your expertise and growing understandings of teaching and learning to help lead your school, district, and the broader educational community to continued improvement. Although this may take you beyond your current comfort zone, it is essential that you see yourself as eventually taking on these leadership roles. Danielson (2007) has identified four components of professional practice. One component is the domain of professional responsibilities. It includes the following elements:

- Service to the school
- Participation in school and district projects
- Service to the profession
- Advocacy

Your leadership roles in the school, district, and profession will be unique to you and build on your strengths. For example, Antasia is a high school mathematics teacher. She is now in her fifth year of teaching and has gained the confidence she needs to begin moving beyond her classroom to help others in her school and district. Last year, Antasia volunteered to lead an after-school tutoring program that provides assistance to all students in the school who need extra help with their mathematics courses. This fall, Antasia accepted the assignment of department chair for mathematics at her high school. She is working with her counterparts at the two other high schools in the district to implement a new mathematics program. Next year, Antasia is considering serving as vice president of the state mathematics education group. If elected, she will be a part of a 13-member team working to assess how well the state is meeting its established performance standards in mathematics. Antasia is engaged in several leadership roles based on her unique skills and interests. Although your skills and interests may be different from Antasia's, as you mature as an educator, be prepared to step forward and assume leadership responsibilities in your school, district, and the profession. If education is to continue to grow as a profession, its members (including you) must be willing to make the effort needed to work for positive change.

Your future leadership role in education also includes becoming an **advocate** for students and their families. An advocate is someone who speaks or writes in support of others. As a teacher, you will need to actively support the needs and interests of students and their families. It is your professional and ethical responsibility to become an advocate. The NEA Code of Ethics states: "The educator strives to help each student realize his or her potential as a worthy and effective member of society" (National Education Association, 1975). To help students reach their full potential, you will need to serve as their advocate. To read a student teacher's journal about the challenges of advocating and reaching one student, go to the Companion Website for this text and click on MyEducationLab for Chapter 5.

myeducationlab The Power of Classroom Practice

MyEducationLab 5.2

Attempts to move teaching closer to professional status will only occur when people associated with education speak out at every opportunity for changes that can make a difference. Again, it is important for you to begin now to advocate for positive change. It is often the little things you and others do today that make a difference in the long run. For example, when parents, neighbors, or friends ask you about your future, speak proudly and intelligently about teaching. Share your thoughts about the value of having quality educational programs and what it will take to make these programs a reality. Be informed so that you can help others know the good things that are happening in classrooms throughout your community. Take the opportunities that present themselves to share with others both the importance of quality teaching and the challenges encountered daily in educational settings. Make sure that you know and can articulate to others the things that need to happen to move teaching closer to professional status.

One other way in which you can serve as an educational advocate is to encourage others to consider teaching as a career. Perhaps you are involved in teacher preparation right now because a teacher or another significant adult encouraged you to consider it as an option. You should now consider it your responsibility to begin noticing other capable individuals who might find teaching a rewarding career. Taking a few minutes to share your perspectives on teaching could help them decide to give it a try. Starting now, make it your goal to seek out individuals that have the needed skills and attitudes and suggest that they consider teaching as a career.

Stop and think for a moment about what advocacy means to you. How would you define it? Do you see the value of engaging in advocacy efforts? Does the idea of advocacy excite or frighten you? Why do you think you feel this way? Try to identify several specific examples of advocacy that teachers of all backgrounds and abilities can do. Do you see yourself getting involved as an advocate for teaching and learning in these and other ways?

After having read this chapter, take some time now to reflect again on teaching as a profession. The *Consider This* feature found on the Companion Website for this text gives you the opportunity to rate teaching in three areas that have been identified as important aspects of any profession. Read the information provided and give your own assessment of the current status of teacher professionalism.

Reflection Opportunity 5.7

Consider This: Teaching as a Profession

Summary

In this chapter, three questions were identified to help you better understand the issues surrounding teaching as a profession:

What makes teaching a profession?

It is important to know what it means to be a profession and how teaching matches up with these criteria:

- Defining a profession
- Teaching as a profession (Praxis II, topic IVa)

How is teacher professionalism changing?

Teaching is growing toward greater professionalism through these means:

- Educational reform efforts
- Higher standards for students
- Higher standards for teachers

What are my professional responsibilities?

Your professional responsibilities include the following:
- Using active reflection
- Conducting yourself in a professional manner (Praxis II, topic IVa)
- Continuing your professional development
- Participating in professional organizations (Praxis II, topic IVb)
- Accepting leadership roles (Praxis II, topic IVb)

PRAXIS   Test-Preparation Activities

To review an on-line chapter case study, test your understanding of chapter topics and concepts, and begin preparing for the Praxis II: Principles of Learning and Teaching examination, go to the Praxis Test-Preparation module for this chapter of the Companion Website.

Developing the Habit of Reflective Practice

Organizing Questions

Review questions, field experience opportunities, and activities for building your portfolio are included here for the organizing questions in this chapter.

What makes teaching a profession?

Review Questions

1. What are the characteristics of a profession?
2. What arguments are usually given for teaching being considered a profession?
3. In what areas is teaching considered less professional?

Field Experience

Review the characteristics of a profession cited in this chapter and then spend time observing a teacher during his or her school day.
- Look for specific indicators of professional behavior on the part of the teacher.
- What was said or done that indicated the teacher was part of a profession? Share your insights with others.

Building Your Portfolio: *Teaching as a Profession*

INTASC Standard 9. Review the arguments presented in this chapter both for and against teaching as a profession.
- Take a stand either for or against teaching as a profession and write a clear rationale for the position you take.
- Discuss either what is needed for teaching to become a profession or strategies that would help strengthen its position as a profession.

How is teacher professionalism changing?

Review Questions

1. What efforts have been made to increase the expectations for students in American schools?
2. In what ways has teacher certification become more rigorous?

Building Your Portfolio: *Teacher Certification Requirements*

INTASC Standard 9. Research the requirements for initial and continuing teacher certification in your state. The Internet Website for your state department of education should be a good source of information.

- What entrance and exit exams, if any, will be required of you?
- Describe the content knowledge, understandings of students and teaching, and practical experiences in the classroom required by your state for the level at which you want to teach.
- In reference to the requirements in your state, will you also be expected to take further college and university courses to receive a permanent teaching certificate? Write up your findings for your portfolio.

What are my professional responsibilities?

Review Questions

1. What can you do to conduct yourself in a professional manner?
2. Describe the strategies you can use to continue your professional development.
3. In addition to teacher unions, what professional organizations exist and what are their purposes?
4. How can you serve as an advocate for your chosen profession?

Field Experience

Attend a local meeting of a professional organization of interest to you.

- What was the content of the meeting?
- What did you learn from participating in the meeting?
- Talk to one or two members after the formal meeting about the benefits of the organization. What did you learn? Share what you learned with others.

Building Your Portfolio: *Professional Teaching Responsibilities*

INTASC Standard 9. Think back to teachers you have had who you feel were especially professional in their interactions with you and other students.

- Describe the behaviors they engaged in that made you feel that they were being professional.
- How can you make sure that you engage in similar activities as a future teacher?
- Summarize your responses in a brief paper.

Suggested Readings

Boyer, E. (1983). *High school: A report on secondary education in America.* New York: Harper and Row. In a report to the Carnegie Foundation for the Advancement of Teaching, Boyer recommended strengthening the academic core curriculum in American high schools. His proposal was widely adopted in the 1980s and 1990s.

Glasser, W. (1990). *The quality school: Managing students without coercion.* New York: Harper and Row. Glasser advocates moving away from the current model of teacher-directed learning to experiences that are teacher facilitated. By removing the element of coercion and allowing students to engage in cooperative learning, schools can become stimulating environments for student learning and development.

Goodlad, J. (1984). *A place called school.* New York: Macmillan. This book is a summary of a study entitled "A Study of Schooling" funded by several major foundations. From his research, Goodlad found that improving schooling requires changing many components at the same time: teacher behaviors, administrative interactions, curricula, school organization, and school–community relations. In his book, he lays out a plan for accomplishing positive school reform.

Sizer, T. (1984). *Horace's compromise: The dilemma of the American high school.* Boston: Houghton Mifflin. After spending 2 years visiting high schools throughout the United States, Sizer found that good teachers are being hampered in their efforts to engage in quality instruction by the school environments themselves. He proposes several changes that can help high school teachers engage in more effective instruction.

References

Abrams, L., & Madaus, G. (2003). The lessons of high-stakes testing. *Educational Leadership, 61*(3), 31–35.

American Federation of Teachers. (2003). *Survey and analysis of teacher salary trends 2003.* Washington, DC: Author. Retrieved January 6, 2005 from: Wide Web at *http://www.aft.org/salary/index.htm*

American Federation of Teachers. (2008). *About AFT.* Retrieved January 8, 2005, from: http://www.aft.org/about/index.htm

Amrein, A., & Berliner, D. (2003). A research report—The effects of high-stakes testing on student motivation and learning. *Educational Leadership, 60*(5), 32–38.

Bennett, W. (1987). *James Madison High School: A curriculum for American students.* Washington, DC: U.S. Department of Education.

Boyer, E. (1983). *High school: A report on secondary education in America.* New York: Harper.

California State Government. (2005). *California Standardized Testing and Reporting (STAR) program.* Retrieved November 4, 2005 from: *http://star.cde.ca.gov/star2004/aboutSTAR.asp*

Cubberley, E. (1934). *Public education in the United States.* Boston: Houghton Mifflin.

Danielson, C. (2007). *Enhancing professional practice: A framework for teaching.* (2nd ed.) Alexandria, VA: Association for Supervision and Curriculum Development.

Education Commission of the States. (2003). *Eight questions on teacher preparation: What does the research say?* Denver, CO: Author.

Education Week. (2008). The teaching profession. In *Quality Counts 2008,* pp. 50–56.

Etzioni, A. (1969). *The semi-professions and their organization: Teachers, nurses, social workers.* New York: Free Press.

Glasser, W. (1986). *Control theory in the classroom.* New York: Harper and Row.

Goodlad, J. (1984). *A place called school.* New York: Macmillan.

Goodlad, J. (1990). *Teachers for our nation's schools.* San Francisco: Jossey-Bass.

Howsam, R., Corrigan, D., Denemark, G., & Nash, R. (1976). *Educating a profession.* Washington, DC: American Association of Colleges for Teacher Education.

Interstate New Teacher Assessment and Support Consortium. (1995). *Next steps: Moving toward performance-based licensing in teaching.* Retrieved June 16, 2005 from: *http://www.ccsso.org/publications/index.cfm*

Lagemann, E. (2004). Toward a strong profession of education. *Harvard Graduate School of Education News.* Retrieved January 1, 2004 from: *http://www.gse.harvard.edu/news/features/lagemann01012004.html*

Marzano, R. (1998). What are the general skills of thinking and reasoning and how do you teach them? *Clearinghouse, 71*(5), 268–273.

National Board for Professional Teaching Standards. (2008). About NBTS. Retrieved November 7, 2005 from: *http://www.nbpts.org/about/index.cfm*

National Center for Education Statistics. (2007). *Digest of education statistics.* Washington, DC: Government Printing Office.

National Commission on Excellence in Education. (1983). *A nation at risk: The imperative for educational reform.* Washington, DC: Government Printing Office.

National Council for Accreditation of Teacher Education. (2008). *Professional standards for the accreditation of teacher preparation institutions.* Washington, DC: Author.

National Education Association. (2008). *NEA fact sheet.* Washington, DC: Author. Retrieved November 19, 2008, from: *http://www.nea.org/presscenter/neafact.html.*

National Education Association. (1975). Code of ethics of the education profession. Retrieved November 4, 2005 from: *http://www2.nea.org/code.html*

Pulliam, J., & Van Patten, J. (2007). *History of education in America* (9th ed.). Upper Saddle River, NJ: Merrill/Prentice Hall.

Robelin, E. (2002, January 9). An ESEA primer. *Education Week,* pp. 28–29.

Rowan, B. (1994). Comparing teachers' work with work in other occupations: Notes on the professional status of teaching. *Educational Researcher, 23*(6), 4–17, 21.

Sacks, P. (2001). *Standardized minds: The high price of America's testing culture and what we can do to change it.* Cambridge, MA: Perseus Books.

Sizer, T. (1984). *Horace's compromise: The dilemma of the American high school.* Boston: Houghton Mifflin.

Wagner, P. (1996). *Understanding professional ethics.* Bloomington, IN: Phi Delta Kappa Educational Foundation.

Walsh, K., & Snyder, E. (2004). *Searching the attic: How states are responding to the nation's goal of placing a highly qualified teacher in every classroom.* National Council on Teacher Quality. Retrieved January 4, 2005 from: *http://www.nctq.org/nctq/images/housse_report_2.pdf*

Wang, A., Coleman, A., Cohen, R., & Phelps, R. *Preparing teachers around the world.* Educational Testing Service. Retrieved from: *http://www.ets.org/research/pic*

Webb, L., Metha, A., & Jordan, K. (2007). *Foundations of American education* (5th ed.). Upper Saddle River, NJ: Merrill/Prentice Hall.

Wilkerson, J., & Lang, W. (2003). Portfolios: The pied piper of teacher certification assessments. *Education Policy Analysis Archives, 11* (45). Retrieved November 18, 2008 from *http://epaa.asu.edu/epaa/vlln45/*

"Self Actualized" can stand uncertanty, realize potential, deep relationships

Ex. teachers

Us informally

I believe you can

self Respect

good about life course

Respect,
Competence, Confidence, Success

part 2

What Is Reflective Classroom Practice?

Courtesy of Mary Kate Denny/PhotoEdit.

Have you noticed that significant differences exist in the ways students learn? Some pick up information quickly and with relative ease, whereas others seem to struggle mightily to make the same connections. Certain students learn best when they engage in physical manipulation of objects; others prefer to discuss things verbally with their peers. And although many students seem independently motivated to learn, others need constant feedback from the teacher to get even the simplest tasks accomplished. What causes these and other differences and how do these differences influence the ways in which you will interact with students? This is a complex question that will require in-depth study at some point in your teacher-preparation program. You will probably have at least one course that focuses on these issues in greater depth. At this point, however, you will begin by looking at the multifaceted nature of student learning.

Do student needs affect learning?

As you begin to think about student needs and how they might influence learning, consider the story of Kendra. Kendra is a 16-year-old student in your sophomore biology class. She attended the first parent–teacher conference of the year with both of her upper-middle-class parents. It was frustrating to hear how Kendra's dad, in particular, seemed to feel that she was never doing work that met his expectations. Perhaps this explains her hesitation to try new things. When new concepts or skills are introduced in class, Kendra often displays self-defeating behaviors saying things like "I can't do this," or "I'll never get this." Once Kendra learns the material, which takes a lot of work on your and her behalf because she is so convinced that she can't learn it, she is quite successful. As her comfort level with the new material increases, she is able to meet all standards. Kendra's behavior has you concerned that if she continues to believe that she can't face new challenges her learning will be negatively impacted. Already, her peers are becoming annoyed with her when they work as partners or in groups; she tends to shy away from sharing equal responsibility in group tasks. Although her classmates accuse of her "slacking," you suspect her lack of effort in group projects probably is related to her self-defeating behaviors when facing new challenges. She may also be worried that one of her peers may be critical of her efforts, as her father tends to be. You have noticed that she is willing to take on a leadership role within groups when the concept is one that she feels very confident about. You're trying to figure out how to help her believe in herself and how to convince her that mistakes are part of the learning process.

Every student brings personal needs to the classroom that influence how they learn. In some cases, like that of Kendra, these needs may significantly hinder school performance. Your job as a future classroom teacher will be to understand what those needs are for each student and to develop strategies to help meet them whenever possible. This is another challenging aspect of teaching, but one that will make a big difference in student learning.

Basic Human Needs

Basic human needs have a profound impact on student learning. For example, you can probably remember times in your life when inadequate nutrition or a lack of sleep for even a short period of time significantly influenced your ability to learn. Other needs, such as these for affection and love, are less obvious but still essential to effective learning. Theorist Abraham Maslow (1968) identified a categorization scheme for human needs that effectively describes them and their relationships to one another. He suggests a hierarchy that graduates from basic needs at the bottom to higher-level ones. Figure 6.1 provides a visual depiction of this hierarchy. It is important to know that the most fundamental needs have priority over those at a higher rank for healthy development. In other words, basic physical needs such as food, shelter, and clothing must be satisfied before higher-level needs such as being valued by others can be met.

You might initially think that although meeting basic human needs is an important issue, it is a family or community concern rather than something that will impact your future life as a teacher. In reality, it is a vitally important issue that significantly impacts classroom learning.

Figure 6.1   Maslow's Hierarchy of Needs

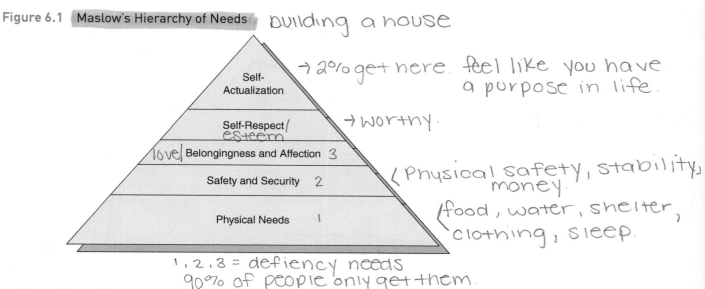

Handwritten annotations:

building a house

→ 2% get here. feel like you have a purpose in life.

→ worthy.

love

(Physical safety, stability, money.

(food, water, shelter, clothing, sleep.

1, 2, 3 = deficiency needs
90% of people only get them.

Pyramid labels (top to bottom):
Self-Actualization
Self-Respect/esteem
Belongingness and Affection   3
Safety and Security   2
Physical Needs   1

Maslow makes it clear that students who come to the classroom with unmet lower-level needs are going to struggle academically. If learning is going to take place, it becomes necessary for teachers to assist students in meeting basic physical, safety and security, and belongingness and affection needs. It is only then that students can engage in effective learning and support their higher level needs for self-respect and self-actualization. For example, the elementary school teacher who keeps a box of crackers and some peanut butter available for students who come to school without having had breakfast is helping to meet a basic physical need. The middle school teacher who refers his students' families to various community resources such as the food bank, clothing banks, free dental clinics and counseling is helping to meet the basic needs of his students. The secondary teacher who works hard to create a safe, caring classroom atmosphere is assisting students with feeling a sense of belonging. Once lower level needs are met, students are ready to learn.

Need for Social Acceptance

Another need that all students have is the need for social acceptance. In the school setting, this means acceptance by peers, teachers, and other school personnel. Typically, students in the early elementary grades have a greater need for acceptance by adults than do those at the middle school and high school levels. Over time, the need for peer acceptance begins to outweigh the desire for acceptance by significant adults (Charles, 2008). In most cases, students who find it difficult to feel socially accepted tend to have greater trouble dealing with the academic aspects of schooling. Their energy and efforts are diverted into other areas and little is left for intellectual pursuits.

Consider writing down your thoughts on social acceptance in school settings. Think back to your own schooling experiences. What did others do or say to be more socially accepted by either their peers or classroom teachers? Do you remember both positive and negative behaviors by students? Can you remember one or more students who struggled with being accepted by either their peers or classroom teachers? What do you remember them doing or saying? For those you remember who had difficulty being socially accepted, were these students successful academically? What does this tell you about the importance of social acceptance to student learning?

Rudolf Dreikurs and others (Dreikurs, Grunwald, & Pepper, 1971) add further insights into our understanding of the personal needs students bring to the classroom. They suggest that the need for social acceptance is an important one for all students. When students feel unacceptable to either peers or teachers, they become behavior problems in the classroom (Charles, 2008). They mistakenly choose to engage in problem behaviors while attempting to gain social

**Reflection
Opportunity 6.1**

acceptance. Dreikurs identifies a downward spiral of misbehaviors on the part of students engaged in this struggle for approval:

1. attention seeking,
2. exerting power over others,
3. seeking revenge, and
4. engaging in displays of inadequacy (giving up).

Students who choose these options are causing themselves and others difficulty in the classroom. Even when overt problems are not evident, some students spend so much time and energy working to be socially accepted that they have little left for learning. Teachers must work to prevent the overt problems and assist students in developing appropriate ways of interacting with others. Until their need for social acceptance is met, students will find it difficult to learn.

Self-Esteem Needs

How students feel about their own capabilities also influences their ability to learn. For example, Jay is the kind of student teachers love to have in their classrooms. As a junior in high school he has already distinguished himself academically, socially, and on the athletic fields. Academically, he has taken all of the available higher-level mathematics courses, two advanced science classes, 2 years of Japanese language study, and advanced placement English. Socially, Jay has been elected junior class president and is well liked by both classmates and teachers. Jay is also a 2-year letterman in both football and wrestling. As you talk to him, he appears confident, relaxed, and positive about life. Jay is said to have high **self-esteem.** His feelings of self-worth make it much easier for him to succeed in all aspects of school life.

Not all students will have the high level of self-esteem that Jay brings to the classroom. Consider, for instance, Aleetha. Just entering the second grade, she is already showing signs of poor self-esteem. Yesterday, the physical education teacher had a very difficult time getting Aleetha to even try to play the game planned for the day. She complained of not being able to move quickly because of a sore ankle, but an examination by the school nurse showed no signs of an injury. Aleetha was brought to school today by her mom and sobbed uncontrollably as she clung to her on leaving. During an art activity, her hand slipped and caused the paintbrush to skew out of control across the page. Aleetha was furious at herself and just sat and fumed for the rest of the activity.

The self-esteem of students, especially when it is low, is yet another factor that will influence the interactions you have with students. Stanley Coopersmith (1967) is generally credited with being one of the first to write about the importance of self-esteem in people's lives. He identified the elements needed for the development of positive self-esteem and described the problems that occur when individuals have poor self-perceptions. More recently, Kostelnik, Whiren, Soderman, Stein, & Gregory (2009) have identified three dimensions to self-esteem: competence, worth, and control:

- *competence* is the belief that you can accomplish tasks and achieve goals.
- *worth* can be viewed as the extent to which you like and value yourself.
- *control* is the degree to which people feel they can influence the events around them.

You will have many opportunities as a teacher to either positively or negatively influence each of these three dimensions of self-esteem. For example, teachers who have high expectations for their students and clearly communicate confidence in them are building each student's sense of competence. Or, teachers who spend time learning about student interests and genuinely enjoying them as individuals are enhancing their sense of worth. On the other hand, teachers who fail to give students choices about what they do in the classroom and make all their educational decisions for them are negatively influencing their sense of control.

As you might expect from the example of Jay presented earlier, students with high self-esteem are generally more confident in their learning abilities and tend to display greater interest and motivation in school (Schunk, 2008). Students with low self-esteem, on the other hand, are characterized by feelings of inadequacy, fear of rejection, dependence on others, and loss of control over events (Kostelnik et al., 2009). This confidence level may be affected, however, by the content being learned. Some writers are suggesting that self-esteem may be hierarchical and that although general self-concept can be high (or low), student perceptions of their abilities in specific subject-matter areas may vary (Marsh & Shavelson, 1985). So, for example, a student with generally high self-esteem may view himself as only average in his mathematics capabilities.

Responding to Student Needs

Once you understand the importance of student needs, the next step is to identify those that are influencing classroom learning. This can be accomplished in two main ways (Jones & Jones, 2007). One option is to carefully observe students to determine their needs. By listening to conversations with others and watching what students do and how they interact, you can learn a great deal about needs. The second technique is to ask students directly what they require to be more successful in learning. Students are surprisingly good judges, so taking the time to talk with them about needs can be very productive. For example, asking students about their favorite lesson in a recent unit of study can tell you a lot about students' needs as learners. For older students, a questionnaire addressing these same issues can also be used to collect information. Rick Wormeli (2003), a middle school teacher from Virginia, uses a variety of strategies to get to know his students and their needs:

- First day advice. As students enter his classroom on the first day of school, they find an index card on their desks. Students are asked to: *Give me advice on how to be the best teacher you've ever had in this subject.*

- Interest surveys. Wormeli hands out interest surveys with questions like: *What is a favorite book from your childhood? Why do you like that book? Who is someone you admire and why? What are two common activities you do after school? What is a responsibility you have?*

- Learning profiles. Wormeli also uses various learner profiles, some of which are free to teachers and some of which charge a fee. He recommends the Dunn and Dunn Learning Style Inventory and the Myers-Briggs Personality Type indicators.

Wormeli emphasizes that gathering information about your students isn't as important as actually using it. It is easy to spend time gathering data, but it takes work and dedication to make use of the it. Some strategies for meeting needs are directly related to your teaching roles. For example, as you create a classroom environment that encourages students to learn and grow, you are also helping meet students' needs for safety and security. Similarly, as you get to know all students better so that you can plan activities based on their interests, you are also helping meet their need for social acceptance.

It is important to realize that although you can assist in meeting many personal student needs, the issues are frequently too difficult or time consuming for the average teacher to resolve on his or her own. Take, for example, the need for safety and security as described by Maslow. It is possible for teachers to take responsibility for meeting these needs while students are in the classroom, but there is little that teachers can do when students are at home. Similarly, the need for belongingness and affection can be addressed by you as the classroom teacher, but it is not possible to meet this need completely. John, a third-grade teacher, has discovered this in his classroom. He has six children this year who are in single-parent families headed by mothers. Four of these children seem in particularly need of affection and caring from John as a significant male figure. Despite his many efforts to have positive interactions with each one as regularly as possible, they never seem to be able to get enough personal time from him. One option that John may want to consider is encouraging these students' mothers to sign them up for the Big Brothers program.

Another factor you must consider in meeting student needs is that every teacher will have different personal limits about getting involved in nonacademic issues. For example, spending some of your lunch break building a stronger relationship with a student may help meet his need for social acceptance but take away important break time for you as a teacher. Attending a special concert or sporting event would be a very meaningful way to show a student you care about her; but your involvement in this activity would mean a night away from home and missed opportunities for quality time with your own family. You will need to decide just how involved you can be in meeting student needs without resenting it, getting burned out, or having it negatively impact aspects of your personal life.

Can you see yourself engaged in the kinds of activities described in this section to meet student needs? Are there some that you would see as more appropriate than others? Will you feel good about helping meet student needs or resent the time and effort required? How do you think you will feel about the parents and families of students that need help in meeting basic needs? Will you be able to work effectively with these families?

Reflection Opportunity 6.2

How does development influence learning?

Two broad perspectives have been used to describe human learning, one emphasizing the factors within the individual that influence learning and a second stressing the importance of external factors. Table 6.1 summarizes these two perspectives. In this section, the internal factors will be described.

Imagine you are preparing for a road trip across the United States. What would you do to prepare for this adventure? In all likelihood, you would begin by getting out some maps and plan-

TABLE 6.1 Perspectives on Learning

Perspective	Described In	Definition
Internal factors (within the individual) have the greatest influence on human learning	Developmental theories	Movement through predictable stages in development that are determined primarily by heredity
	Developmental norms	Typical behaviors that can be expected at a given age and stage of development
	Learning Styles	Individual's preferred method of learning; varies primarily due to genetics
External factors (outside the individual) have the greatest influence on human learning	Learning theories	Learning from the ways in which people and things in the environment respond to their actions
	Social learning theory	Learning that occurs from watching what others do and say

ning a route to follow, deciding how many miles to travel each day, and determining where to stay at night. The road maps allow you to plan for a successful trip.

In much the same way, an understanding of human development provides teachers with a road map that describes in detail the journey of students to physical, emotional, intellectual, and social maturity. By knowing the normal paths that most students follow as they learn and grow, and by understanding the implications of this information for your teaching, you will be more successful in your work in the classroom. Because of the complexities of human behavior, however, it is important to remember that there are no simple, universally accepted descriptions of development for all students in every circumstance.

Those who focus on internal factors are emphasizing the importance of *heredity* in human learning. They see genetic programming as the best explanation for the changes that occur and propose **developmental theories** to describe them. In addition, those with this perspective have identified typical patterns of behavior common to specific ages called **developmental norms.** These norms help give teachers and parents information about what can be expected of children at different ages. Finally, those emphasizing internal factors and their influence on development also suggest that the strategies used by students to actually gather and internalize information about the world will vary between individuals. These **learning styles** are also important for you to understand as you plan lessons and activities for the classroom. The following sections describe the influences of these internal factors on learning.

Developmental Theories

One of the first to popularize developmental theories was Jean Jacques Rousseau (1979), whose writings in the mid-18th century ushered in a radically different view of children and development. In his book, *Emilé,* first published in 1762, Rousseau described what he saw as the natural characteristics of children at different ages and the type of education appropriate for each level. For example, he felt young children learned primarily through their senses:

> Since everything that comes into the human mind enters through the gates of sense, man's first reason is a reason of sense–experience. It is this that serves as a foundation for the reason of the intelligence; our first teachers in natural philosophy are our feet, hands, and eyes. To substitute books for these does not teach use of reason, it teaches us to use the reason of others rather than our own; it teaches us to believe much and know little. (Rousseau, 1762/1979, p. 90)

Other noted developmental theorists include Arnold Gesell (Gesell & Ilg, 1949), Sigmund Freud (1920), Jean Piaget (1950), and Erik Erikson (1963). All of these researchers' theories of human development suggest that people pass through a series of predictable stages as they mature. People at the same stage share common characteristics and typically enter and exit the stage at similar ages. Many feel that these developmental stages significantly influence learning (Schunk, 2008). Knowledge of developmental theories can help you understand students' learning needs and plan for more effective instruction. The psychosocial theory of Erik Erikson and the cognitive–developmental theory of Jean Piaget will be briefly described here as examples of important developmental theories.

Psychosocial theory of development. Erik Erikson (1963) provides a description of human development referred to as a **psychosocial theory.** He identifies stages in a person's psychological growth, each of which is influenced by interactions with the social environment. Erikson suggests that humans pass through a series of eight stages from birth through old age. These stages are briefly summarized in Table 6.2. Each stage has a major issue that must be resolved and which Erikson refers to as a *psychosocial crisis.* As the person successfully works through the crisis of the current stage, he or she is better prepared for the challenges of the next developmental period. The psychosocial theory of development suggests that positive relationships with significant others are critical at each stage of development. Read the *Ian's Classroom Experiences*

relationship = important

**Ian's Classroom
Experiences:
A Moment in Time**

These are not linear!

TABLE 6.2 Stages of Psychosocial Development

Stage	Description
Stage I: *trust vs. mistrust* (birth–1 year)	Young children are dealing with the trustworthiness of their primary caregivers. When parents and others provide consistent care and meet the child's physical and emotional needs, a sense of trust begins to develop.
Stage II: *autonomy vs. shame and doubt* (1–3 years)	Children make initial attempts at doing some things for themselves. Feeding and dressing, for example, helps give children a sense of independence.
Stage III: *initiative vs. guilt* (3–5 years)	Children develop a sense of initiative by making plans, setting goals, and working hard to accomplish tasks. Parents and teachers must encourage the child's natural curiosity so that initiative will grow.
Stage IV: *industry vs. inferiority* (6–12 years)	Children are working on learning the skills necessary for success in society. If they are struggling in their mastery of these skills, children start to think of themselves as inferior.
Stage V: *identity vs. confusion* (13–19 years)	Young people are working to identify their vocational and professional orientation. If they fail to find this identity, they become confused and directionless.
Stage VI: *intimacy vs. isolation* (young adult)	People are seeking a love relationship which leads them to personal intimacy. Failing that, they become more isolated.
Stage VII: *generativity vs. stagnation* (mature adult)	Adults find themselves more involved in helping relationships through parenting, supporting others, and taking on civic responsibilities.
Stage VIII: *integrity vs. despair* (older age)	Older adults reflect back on their accomplishments. If they can accept the positives and negatives they find, a sense of integrity is found.

Handwritten annotations: confident; start ideas; get stuff done or be inferiority; competence = believe you can; fidelity = being true to yourself; sometimes can't commit; mom!!!; feel good about life; mid life crisis; 12–25 years

Source: *Childhood and Society* (1963) by E. Erikson. New York: W. W. Norton.

feature for this chapter on the Companion Website for this text to learn more about the positive influence of relationships in teaching.

Each stage of psychosocial development has applications for teaching. If you intend to work at the high school level, for example, you would want to pay particular attention to Erikson's fifth stage of development. He calls the psychosocial crisis at this stage *identity vs. confusion* and describes it as the adolescent's struggle to find a vocational and professional focus. As a high school teacher, part of your informal interactions with students would probably include information and guidance as they engage in beginning attempts at vocational decision making. For example, you might suggest an advanced chemistry course for a student considering entering the medical profession while encouraging another student to take a foreign language. In addition, you would want to make clear connections between the subject matter you are teaching and real-world occupations that students may enter so that they can begin to make informed decisions about the knowledge and expertise needed for various careers.

Cognitive–developmental theory. Over a long and productive career, Jean Piaget created an influential **cognitive–developmental theory** that explains intellectual or cognitive growth. In it he suggests that each person passes through a series of four stages as they grow to maturity. These stages, summarized in Table 6.3, occur at approximately the same ages for every person, so knowing about them helps adults understand the ways in which students think and learn. Piaget (1950) suggests that the ways in which people understand the world vary significantly from one stage to the next. At about age 2, children make one of their most significant shifts in thinking:

> It is during the preschool years that the human mind performs its greatest magic: the child is freed from dependence on sensory–perceptual–motor experience as the sole channel of communication with his environment. The evolution of the capacity to deal with experience symbolically represents the key extensor process of the maturing organism. It manifests itself in every medium of expression known to man, and runs the full course from the simplest gestural representations to advanced levels of abstraction. (Biber, 1964, pp. 90–91)

Each of Piaget's four stages of cognitive development has direct implications for teaching. If, for example, your teaching interests are at the primary level in elementary school, you should pay careful attention to Piaget's stage of preoperational development. Juwanda, a first-grade student, exemplifies the characteristics of this stage. She is making good progress in her ability to think symbolically, so the many symbols associated with her mathematics activities (such as the symbolic equation $3 + 2 = 5$) and reading are beginning to make sense to her. Juwanda still struggles, however, to take into consideration multiple features of a more complex problem. For the science activity last week, for example, she had difficulty realizing that the items being used on the balance beam varied in both size and density, both of which were factors in determining the weights of these objects. Another example of an important active learning experience during the preschool and primary years is the field trip. To view a video about field trips, go to the Companion Website for this text and click on MyEducationLab for Chapter 6.

myeducationlab
The Power of Classroom Practice
MyEducationLab 6.1

TABLE 6.3 Stages of Cognitive Development

Stage (Age)	Description
Sensorimotor intelligence (birth–2 years)	Children learn about the world through sensory experiences and motor activity. An infant's sucking and shaking of various objects are examples.
Preoperational intelligence (2–7 years)	Children begin to use symbolic thinking rather than exclusively learning through sensory and motor interactions with the world. Children make initial attempts at being logical, but are unsuccessful by adult standards. They have difficulty seeing things from any perspective other than their own.
Concrete operations (7–12 years)	Children think more logically and systematically, especially when dealing with concrete objects. They recognize that matter doesn't change in quantity or mass when moved or manipulated. There is more ability to see the perspectives of others.
Formal operations (13 years on)	This stage marks the beginning of adult thinking. The abstract and logical thought necessary for scientific investigation are possible.

Source: *The Developmental Psychology of Jean Piaget* (1963), by J. Flavell. New York: Van Nostrand.

Developmental theories tend to emphasize typical patterns of development. Some students, however, do not follow all of these patterns because of hereditary or environmental complications. So, for example, a student with a hearing impairment or a student born addicted at birth to crack cocaine will follow typical developmental patterns in some areas, but will likely be delayed in others. The *Reflect on Diversity* feature for this chapter describes some of the additional challenges faced by exceptional students.

Reflect on diversity: Twice exceptional

The behavioral and attitudinal changes occurring with Lisa Greim Everitt's son Mark were baffling. The same student who a few years earlier had been reading articles in National Geographic as a 5-year-old was now having significant difficulties in first and second grade (Fine, 2002).

Rather than being a delight to his teachers as he was in earlier years, Mark had now become a "problem student." Instead of participating in group activities and following teacher directions, Mark began to retreat into his own little world. His refusal to answer questions, even when he clearly knew the answers became a real frustration to his teachers. And despite his exceptional abilities in reading, Mark had significant difficulties doing even the simplest of writing tasks.

School personnel went so far as to label Mark as "emotionally disturbed." They strongly encouraged his mother to seek out an alternate school setting for him. Unfortunately, there were no options locally that could serve Mark's unique needs. None of the private schools in the area felt that they could help him be successful. And despite his exceptional reading abilities, none of the gifted education programs felt equipped to help Mark deal with his problem behaviors.

Students like Mark are now being called "twice exceptional." He is considered gifted by his school district, but also has been identified as having attention deficit hyperactivity disorder, bipolar disorder, and nonverbal learning disabilities. Programs for students such as Mark are very rare.

Although this story may seem unusual, many gifted students have considerable difficulty adjusting to life in the schools. For example, "Despite Einstein's brilliance, as a schoolboy he had behavioral problems, was a rotten speller, and had trouble expressing himself. His report cards were dismal" (Fine, 2002, p. 39). It seems that many gifted students struggle to be successful in traditional educational settings.

Developing the Habit of Reflective Practice
Gather Information

1. Do an Internet search for "Hogiesgifted.org" to read more about twice exceptional children.

2. Think back and see if you can identify a classmate who might have been twice exceptional. How did this person do in school or in life? Were there special services available to assist this person?

Identify Beliefs

1. Why do you think twice exceptional students are often neglected or misdiagnosed when problems arise?

2. Some educators are critical of parents who say their child who is struggling behaviorally and academically in the classroom is "gifted". Do you think that parents tend to leap to this explanation more than teachers?

Make Decisions

1. What are some of the challenges twice exceptional students face in schools? How can schools and teachers better meet the needs of these students?

Assess and Evaluate

1. If you were visiting a school to assess and evaluate how the staff was addressing the needs of gifted and talented students, what evidence would you look for in classrooms to show that the needs of these students was being met?

Source

Fine, L. (2002). Research: Diamonds in the rough. *Education Week* October 24, pp 38, 39, 41.

Developmental Norms and Teaching

In addition to important developmental theories such as the two described above, researchers over the years have collected considerable information that describes the typical behaviors of children at different ages. These characteristics are often referred to as developmental norms. If you understand the typical social, emotional, cognitive, physical, and linguistic abilities of the students you teach, it becomes much easier to plan effective learning experiences for them.

For example, Tanya, a middle school mathematics teacher, took two courses on child development and learning as part of her teacher-preparation program. In addition, the district has conducted several workshops during the last few years that have focused on developmental issues and teaching. Because of this training and experience, Tanya understands what typical middle school students can be expected to do and she builds her class activities around this information. For example, she understands that most of her students still find it difficult to grasp abstract mathematical concepts and plans to use some manipulatives called Cuisenaire rods to help her advanced classes visualize some basic algebraic concepts. Similarly, other students are benefiting from some overheads she developed to help them conceptualize fractions and decimals.

Learning Styles

How would you describe your preferred learning environment? Do you study best when you listen to music while curled up in a favorite chair? Is it more effective for you to work alone or in a small group? As you read a chapter in your textbook for an upcoming class, do you find it easier to learn when the material is carefully organized or can you dig out the key information even when the author's writing style is less structured? When a question is asked in class, do you need time to reflect before giving a response or are you quick to answer?

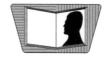

Reflection Opportunity 6.3

Your answers to the above questions help identify components of a personal learning style. The ways in which you perceive, organize, process, and remember information are often different from those of the person sitting next to you in class (Schunk, 2008). The components of individual learning styles are presented in Table 6.4. Each of your future students will have their own combination of the components described that make up their preferred strategies for learning. For example, one student may prefer to learn through auditory input, tend to think globally, categorize objects by function, and respond quickly to questions. A second student may prefer to learn visually, think analytically, categorize objects by physical attributes, and prefer to reflect before responding to questions. Knowing more about the attributes of learning styles will help you plan more effective learning experiences for all your students.

Information on learning styles is important to your future teaching because it helps explain why students are so very different in the ways they learn. Knowing about these differences allows teachers to plan a variety of experiences to take advantage of these styles. For example, a high school English teacher discussing a medieval play could use overhead transparencies to attract the interest of visual learners, small-group discussions for those who prefer auditory learning, and sample costumes for those who benefit from kinesthetic experiences. The *Views from the Classroom* feature for this chapter gives one educator's perspective on teaching hands-on science to take advantage of learning styles. Go to the Companion Website for this text to read her thoughts.

Views from the Classroom: Teaching Hands-on Science

TABLE 6.4   Components of Learning Styles

Component	Description
Sensory Modality Preference	Students vary in terms of their preferred sensory mode for learning. Some choose auditory input, others like visual stimuli, and another group learns best through touching and moving objects in the real world.
Field Dependence–Independence	Field-dependent learners tend to think more globally, while field-independent thinking is more analytical. Both learning styles have their own strengths and drawbacks in classroom settings.
Categorization Style	This learning style refers to the ways in which learners see objects as similar to others. Different learners choose to categorize objects in terms of their functions, physical attributes, or category.
Cognitive Tempo	Some students respond quickly to questions or information they are given; others choose to reflect on the data before proceeding.

Source: Learning Theories: An Educational Perspective, 5th ed. (2008), by D. Schunk. Upper Saddle River, NJ: Merrill/Prentice Hall.

What is the impact of the environment on student learning?

Learning is a complex process that is difficult to understand. Because it occurs within the minds of individuals who vary greatly in terms of personality, genetic inheritance, and environmental experiences, no one theory can adequately explain its many facets. In the last section, you were given information about the internal factors that influence learning. Here you will learn more about the effects of the environment. You may want to refer back to Table 6.1 for a summary of this perspective. Two separate but interrelated theories help explain how external factors impact learning. **Behavioral learning theory** describes how responses made by the environment to actions taken by the learner determine whether or not the acts will occur again in the future. If the responses are positive, then the behaviors are more likely to reoccur. **Social learning theory** emphasizes the importance of learning from the actions of others. When learners see these behaviors being encouraged, it increases the chances that they will also engage in the same activities. Both of these theories provide deeper insights into the learning process.

Before reading about these two learning theories, however, take a few moments to read the *Explore Your Beliefs* feature for this chapter and think carefully about the issues presented there. A strong case is made for teachers taking greater responsibility when students fail to learn. Rather than assuming that students who are unsuccessful in school are responsible for their own failures, the best teachers recognize that they significantly influence opportunities for learning.

Explore your beliefs: Failure to learn is the student's fault

Despite the efforts that teachers put into their instruction, some students are still unsuccessful in learning the content or skills. Even though it feels very good to know that many students have learned and grown from their teaching, most teachers find it frustrating when not all are engaged in the learning process.

What causes this failure? If you've invested considerable effort into the learning situation, a rather natural reaction is to assume that it was the student's low level of motivation that led to the lack of success. Although this may be true in some circumstances, there are other important causes for a student's failure to learn.

Effective teachers strive to teach the whole child, aiming to address what Brian Cambourne (1988) has identified as the *Conditions of Learning*. Cambourne identified specific conditions that must be present in a classroom for natural learning to take place. An example of a teacher applying these conditions of learning will help you understand their importance. Mr. Alexander's class publishes a weekly newsletter for families and uses the following conditions of learning to ensure success:

- Students are immersed in writing about their lives by describing past and future events in the classroom. They write every day.
- Mr. Alexander models the complete writing process by authoring articles for the newsletter and sharing his work from rough drafts to final copy with the class.
- Students are told that mistakes in their writing are normal, and they learn how to improve their writing from first to final draft.
- Students feel a sense of obligation to complete the newsletter each week since they have an authentic audience (their families) and a genuine purpose (to inform and entertain their readers).
- Mr. Alexander expects students to do their best writing and meet the publication deadlines.
- Students are practicing their writing on a regular basis and for an authentic purpose.
- Students not only get feedback from the teacher and classmates, but also from the readers of their newsletter—their family members.

Developing the Habit of Reflective Practice

Gather Information

1. Do an Internet search for "Conditions of Learning" to read more on this topic.
2. Think back on something you learned recently (e.g. learning how to change a tire, how to put in contact lenses, or how to prepare a certain food entrée). Consider how Brian Cambourne's conditions of learning played a role in learning.

Identify Beliefs

1. What motivates you to get engaged in a learning experience? Do you agree with Brian Cambourne's conditions of learning?
2. What is the problem with assuming that failure to learn is basically the students' fault?

Make Decisions

1. Do you think it will be important for you to discover the reasons for failure in your future students? Why or why not?

Assess and Evaluate

1. Think about a time when you were not engaged in a learning situation. How did this lack of engagement affect your performance? How did the teacher respond? How could Brian Cambourne's conditions of learning have been applied to increase your engagement and improve your learning?

Source

Cambourne, B. (1988). *The Whole Story: Natural Learning and the Acquisition of Literacy in the Classroom.* Katona, NY: R. C. Owen Publishers.

Behavioral Learning

John B. Watson was an early 20th-century proponent of behavioral learning theory. He believed that through careful control of the environment, you could guide learning and development in whatever direction desired. One of his most famous quotes summarizes this attitude:

> Give me a dozen healthy infants, well-formed, and my own specified world to bring them up and I'll guarantee to take any one at random and train him to become any type of specialist I might select—doctor, lawyer, merchant—chief, and yes, even beggarman and thief, regardless of his talents, penchants, tendencies, abilities, vocations, and race of his ancestors. (Watson, 1924, p. 5)

By far the best known and most influential behaviorist is B. F. Skinner (1953), whose writings have had a major impact on educational thought and practice (Schunk, 2008). Learning, according to his work, is explained by the impact that environmental events have on people. Rather than viewing internal cognitive structures and developmental stages as factors, behaviorists believe that learning can be described by the positive and negative interactions that the learner has with people and things in the environment. The basic elements of behavioral learning theory are presented in Table 6.5. For example, a parent using these principles to toilet train a child rewards him with candy and praise as external incentives to get the child to use the toilet. Similarly, the elementary teacher who uses behaviorist theory in the classroom rewards students with praise, time for fun activities, and stickers when they engage in behaviors the teacher is working to promote.

Behaviorism assumes that the motivation to learn is external to the individual. That is, the reactions of people or the consequences of events determine whether or not a person will be more or less motivated to learn in the future. For example, Rachel received praise from her teacher and positive feedback from her classmates after her science project was placed on display near the high school office. These experiences will positively motivate her to engage in future science activities.

Social Learning

A second approach to explaining the impact of the environment on human learning suggests that people acquire knowledge, skills, strategies, and attitudes by observing others. Social learning theory suggests that people gain knowledge of the world by watching others and how the environment reacts to their actions. Without actually engaging in these tasks at the time of learning, they are able to internalize the actions and perform them at some future time. Albert Bandura (1977) is generally credited with developing this theory of learning. He describes two essential elements to his model: vicarious learning and modeling, which are summarized in Table 6.6.

TABLE 6.5 Elements of Behavioral Learning Theory	
Element	**Example**
Positive Reinforcement	Spending positive time with students Candy and special treats (such as free time) Verbal praise Smiles, hugs, high-fives, pat on the shoulder
Punishment	Verbal warnings Removing student from group to regain control "Paying back" wasted instructional time through the use of noninstructional time such as recess
Ignoring	Giving no verbal or nonverbal responses to a student engaged in an inappropriate attention-getting activity

TABLE 6.6 Elements of Social Learning Theory

Element	Description
Vicarious Learning	Watching others and indirectly learning specific information and skills from their successes and failures
Modeling	Developing more general attitudes and skills through repeated observations of a role model

Bandura (1986) suggests that much of human learning occurs indirectly through what he calls **vicarious learning,** as the learner watches the behavior of others and how the environment responds to this action. Learning in this way is faster than having to perform the behavior in order to master it. Students can also gain understanding without having to suffer any negative consequences associated with certain behaviors. For example, watching a film about the negative effects of cocaine can help students avoid the harmful results of drug use. There are a number of different sources for vicarious learning. They include: *live people* such as parents, teachers, and peers; *electronic sources* such as television, computers, and videotapes; and *printed materials* including books and magazines.

The concept of **modeling** is the second critical component of Bandura's theory. Rather than being a more direct demonstration of a specific skill, modeling tends to be an informal expression of attitudes and skills that can be taken in by the observer only through repeated exposure to the model. Learning takes place when the observer displays new behaviors that wouldn't occur without having been exposed to the model. So, for example, when you are consistently excited and enthusiastic about the subjects you teach, many of your students will observe this behavior and will demonstrate similar interests themselves. Also, the ways in which you deal with errors in logical thinking or the wrong answers students give to questions asked will be carefully observed and imitated by students as well.

Vygotsky, a developmental theorist and researcher who worked in the 1920s and early 1930s, was another person of significance who aimed to explain the impact of the environment on human learning (Forman & Cazden 1986). He advocated that human beings are products not only of biology, but also of their human interactions. He believed that children learn from interacting with the adults and other children around them. His theory encourages teachers to plan learning activities at points where students are challenged (he refers to this as the **zone of proximal development**). Teachers applying his theory plan lessons that build on the language of students' everyday lives through familiar examples and behaviors, analogies and metaphors, and the use of commonly found materials. Teachers demonstrate, do parts of the task students cannot do, work collaboratively with students where they need help, and release responsibility to students when they can perform the task independently. He refers to this gradual release of responsibility as **scaffolding.**

Consider writing down your thoughts about the influences of internal and external factors on student learning. Although some people believe almost exclusively in the importance of either hereditary or environmental influences, most would suggest that both play a role in human growth and development. Take a moment to reflect on your own past learning experiences. Can you identify situations in which you felt learning was influenced by your level of developmental understanding? Conversely, what can you remember about learning that was significantly influenced by the people, places, and things around you? Do you remember situations in which both internal and external factors influenced your personal growth and development? What do these reflections suggest to you about the relative influences of heredity and environment on human growth and development?

**Reflection
Opportunity 6.4**

What is the role of assessment in learning?

How are you at test taking? If you study hard and have a good idea of the format and content of the exam, do you normally do well? Or are you one of those people that struggle through every test despite your level of preparedness? Tests are one of many forms of **assessment** frequently used to evaluate student learning. In your future classroom, you will use many different assessment strategies in your work with students. Some of the more common options used include:

- *Tests.* Some tests are used to determine students' grades, others help teachers decide what concepts need to be retaught, and yet others measure levels of achievement or intelligence compared to other students. Some tests are open ended, with essay questions or other opportunities for students to show what they know. Still others offer selected responses such as multiple choice, matching, or true/false questions.

- *Informal observations.* Informal observations strategies get used most often because they can be easily accommodated into the teaching day. The high school Spanish teacher who listens unobtrusively to the conversations of small groups is engaged in informal student observations.

- *Formal observations.* One example of a formal observation is the **anecdotal record,** consisting of brief written notes by the classroom teacher. It includes the date and time of the observation, a description of who was observed, what the students were doing, and the words spoken. A second technique that provides teachers with many insights about learning is the **checklist.** To use, the teacher merely places a check beside the items observed. For example, a fifth grade teacher may be walking around the room as her students work on various activities that help them explore fractions. As she observes students problem solving, she checks off what understandings they demonstrate such as equivalent fractions, mixed numbers, adding fractions, and reducing fractions.

- *Written responses.* One of the most common assessments of student learning is in the form of written responses on homework, in-class assignments, papers, and projects. Most of these written assessments are developed and evaluated by the classroom teacher.

- *Oral responses.* Throughout the school day, teachers evaluate the questions students ask and mentally critique the responses students give to questions posed by the teacher. These oral responses provide important assessment information.

- *Self-reports.* When students rate their own learning, they are engaged in self-reporting. The most common form for these reports is a questionnaire that the teacher develops.

- *Portfolios.* A portfolio is a collection of student work (including such things as papers, tests, audio- and videotapes of student activities, pictures, and drawings) and teacher-generated assessments that collectively are used to evaluate student learning.

- *Authentic Assessment.* Assessments that tasks require students to perform real-world tasks that demonstrate meaningful application of essential knowledge and skills are called **authentic assessment.** For example, a fourth-grade teacher may ask her students to help plan a future field trip to a local museum. She will be assessing how they read and interpret the city bus schedules, how they determine the necessary budget for transportation and admittance to the museum, how they recruit parent volunteers, and how they work together to set goals and accomplish the necessary tasks. For more information on authentic assessment, go to the Companion Website for this text and click on MyEducationLab for Chapter 6.

Think about the list of assessments presented above. Which of them do you remember teachers using in your educational experiences? Do you think some were more or less successful in measuring your learning in the classroom? Do you remember other students who either had dif-

MyEducationLab 6.2

**Reflection
Opportunity 6.5**

ficulties with the assessments used or who seemed to thrive through their use? What does this tell you about effective assessment?

Over the last several years, assessment of student learning has become an even more important part of the schooling process. One of the main reasons for this emphasis is the *No Child Left Behind Act of 2001*. This major piece of federal legislation mandates that states and local school districts be able to demonstrate that students are making adequate progress toward established learning goals. The success of these efforts is measured through the administration of standardized tests of academic achievement. When schools are not able to demonstrate an adequate level of educational progress for students, they are given assistance in bringing scores up to more acceptable levels. If, over time scores still do not improve, significant penalties can be imposed on both schools and students. For example, 20 states have decided that students may not be allowed to graduate if their individual test scores are too low (Education Week, 2004). Because these assessments have significant consequences for students and schools, they are often referred to as **high-stakes tests.** Read the *Engage in the Debate* feature for this chapter to learn more about this controversial issue.

Engage in the debate: High stakes testing

One assessment strategy that has received considerable criticism over the years has been the standardized test. Some believe that these tests make it possible to compare the achievements of students from different schools, eliminating bias from grade inflation. Others contend that these tests are inaccurate and put African American and most other minority students at a disadvantage in school because they score much lower than Whites (Education Week, 2004).

While they have many detractors, standardized tests are now being used by many states in ways that make them high-stakes. "A test is high-stakes when its results are used to make important decisions that affect students, teachers, administrators, communities, schools, and districts (Au, 2007)." In other words, low scores on high-stakes tests may mean that students don't graduate, teachers get poor evaluations, or schools receive less funding.

Educator and author, Alfie Kohn (2008), believes that the current emphasis on high-stakes testing is leading to sacrifices in other areas. He shares these examples:

- Science and social studies have been severely trimmed in states that do not include those subjects on standardized tests.
- Recess has been cut back in many schools as a result of testing pressures.
- The arts and music have all but disappeared from many schools.
- There are fewer opportunities to learn outside the classroom—many schools have cut back on field trip experiences so that students have more time for test-preparation in the classrooms.

Developing the Habit of Reflective Practice
Gather Information

1. Do an Internet search for "high-stakes tests" and read some additional information about this growing phenomenon.
2. Do an Internet search for "AlfieKohn.org" to read more about Alfie Kohn's concerns about high-stakes testing.

Identify Beliefs

1. What is your opinion about the use of standardized tests in general? Do they have a place in schools?
2. What are your beliefs about the strengths and limitations of using standardized tests in high-stakes decision making?

Make Decisions

1. Imagine that you are on a committee in a school district. This committee is formed to decide on what the graduation requirements should be. Will you advocate that passing a standardized test should be on of the graduation requirements, why or why not?

Assess and Evaluate

1. Do you think that high-stakes testing is a good approach to educational reform? Why or why not?

Sources

Au, W. (2007). High-stakes testing and curricular control: A quantitative metasynthesis. *Educational Researcher, 36,* 258–69.

Kohn, A. (2008). The case against "tougher standards". Retrieved from *http://www.alfiekohn.org/standards/rationale.htm* December 5, 2008.

In addition to being used for the high-stakes decisions described above, assessments of student learning are important for two main reasons. First, they provide teachers with a progress report on student learning while they are still engaged in a particular unit of study. This type of evaluation is referred to as **formative evaluation** and serves as an informal spot check of student progress that enables teachers to adjust, modify, and reteach content as they proceed through a particular unit of study (Miller, Linn, & Gronlund, 2009). For example, a secondary history teacher who asks the class a series of questions following a discussion of World War I is engaging in formative evaluation. He will use the responses the students give to help him decide what modifications need to be made for the discussions on World War I planned for the next day. Also, the sixth-grade teacher giving a practice spelling test is using formative evaluation to gather information that will help her decide if further instruction is needed prior to the actual test next week.

The second main purpose for assessing student learning is to evaluate what students have learned or accomplished. This is called **summative evaluation** and is completed after instruction has ended (Miller, Linn, & Gronlund, 2009). The physical education teacher observing student performance in a game of soccer is using a form of summative evaluation. She uses her observations to evaluate the soccer unit she has just completed. The secondary mathematics teacher who tests student knowledge of geometric proofs following instruction by administering an hour-long exam is also using summative evaluation. Both formative and summative evaluations are used extensively in school settings.

Assessment is something educators are engaged in on a daily basis. While this can have negative effects on student learning, assessment can actually encourage independence and increased motivation in students. When classroom assessment focuses on assessment *for* learning rather than assessment *of* learning, students benefit (Stiggins, 2002). There is a huge difference between assessment for learning and assessment of learning. Both play a role in education; but it is the assessment for learning that gets students to buy into doing their very best. Table 6.7 summarizes this notion of using assessment for learning rather than assessment of learning.

Let's look at how the common educational tool of a rubric changes when the focus is on assessment for learning, rather than assessment of learning. A **rubric** is a scoring tool that lists specific criteria that the teacher expects for a piece of student work. It also identifies gradations of quality for each level of performance. For example, a fourth- and fifth-grade multiage classroom contributes a weekly article for the local newspaper (an example of authentic assessment). The "Pet of the Week" articles focus on a pet available for adoption at the local Humane Society. (This service learning project made sense for this class to take on because the school is about 1 mile away from the animal shelter.) Each week, two students visit the animal shelter with a parent volunteer. They get their photo taken with a "difficult to adopt" animal. Then they

TABLE 6.7   A Comparison of Rubric Use: Assessment of and Assessment for Learning

Assessment *of* learning	Assessment *for* learning
The teacher develops the rubric.	The class develops the rubric by discussing what a quality product or performance looks like. Examples and nonexamples are used to encourage dialogue.
The purpose of the rubric is to give a score or a grade. The student does not see the rubric until the teacher uses the rubric for scoring.	The purpose of the rubric is to help students meet the learning goals. The rubric helps the learner throughout the learning process.
The rubric is written for teachers, parents, and administrators to understand.	The rubric is written in student-friendly language. The jargon used in the rubric is commonly used in classroom discussions.
The rubric is only used by the teacher.	The rubric is used to help the teacher and student assess progress in collaboration. Students use the rubric for self-assessment and peer assessment.

take notes on the breed, personality, appearance, background and skills of the pet. They then return to the school where over the course of the next few days, they work together to compose a persuasive piece of writing that encourages community members to adopt this pet and/or visit the Humane Society. The teacher uses the Pet of the Week project to focus on assessment for learning. The rubric for this task is found in Table 6.8.

It is important to note that this rubric (Table 6.8) was developed as a class. Students looked at some previous Pet of the Week examples and answered the question, "What is a quality Pet of the Week article?" When they first began this project, they didn't have previous examples to look at so they used other examples of persuasive writing to give them ideas. It was important that they clarify who their audience was and the purpose for their writing. Once they established that the majority of their readers would be adults living in their community and the purpose was to persuade them to adopt this or another pet from the Humane Society, it became easier to figure out what was important to consider for this piece of writing. Rubric changes were made throughout the year as students learned more about writing. As students worked on their articles, they kept the rubric handy to guide them in the writing process.

One common concern with rubrics is that they can stifle creativity, indicating a possible lack of motivation and independent thinking. When the focus is on assessment for learning, this is less likely to occur. For example, when a group of middle school students created and used a rubric (see Table 6.9) for their poetry recital; many went beyond what the rubric outlined as a quality performance. Many students used props and costumes even though the rubric did not mention the use of such materials. The focus of their performance was on entertaining their audience. The rubric was used to help them fine-tune their performances. Although students did receive a grade, that was not what motivated them. They were consumed with doing their best for their audience. For weeks prior to the recital, students were motivated to select and memorize a poem. They were interested in learning how to portray moods, meaning, and feelings to their audience. They understood that memorization and public speaking skills were important. If the poetry recitals had been all about earning a grade, it is less likely that students would have gone beyond what the rubric outlined as exceptional. If the performances were only about earning a grade, it is not likely

TABLE 6.8   Pet of the Week Rubric

Area of Performance (Criteria)	Degrees of Performance (Quality)		
	Does not meet Standards	**Meets Standards**	**Exceeds Standards**
Conventions	Frequent errors in conventions interfere with readability	One–two errors with conventions	Correct spelling, punctuation, capitalization and grammar
Organization	Difficult for reader to get main point	Introduction and conclusion used	Introduction and conclusion, flows smoothly with transitions
Persuasion	The reporter does not appear to persuade the reader to adopt the animal	Recommends adopting the pet	Clear statement for adoption recommendation with supporting details
Word Choice	Limited vocabulary and redundant words	Adequate and functional words	Specific, accurate, natural, and effective language
Fluency	Incomplete or run-on sentences, choppy sentences	Varied sentence beginnings	Varied sentences beginnings and lengths

that students would have been so excited to invite family members to attend. This resulted in 100% of the students and their families showing up for an evening performance at a school where this was not typical for family events! The students were so motivated to do their best that they decided to videotape themselves on stage prior to both performances and critiqued their work.

When a teacher focuses on assessment *for* learning:

- Students often go beyond the expectations, they aren't consumed with "what counts" for their grade but rather what makes quality work.
- Student work is unique. One student's work does not look like a carbon copy of another student's work.
- Students participate in formal and informal assessment opportunities.
- Students can talk about the importance of assessment to their learning.
- Students focus on what they know and can do. They are able to clearly articulate what they are working on as a reader, writer, mathematician, scientist, artist, etc.

Assessment *of* learning will always be a part of schooling. Teachers will continue to give tests and grades as a way of reporting academic progress to their students' families and administrators. Students will continue to participate in district-wide and state-wide standardized tests as a means of accountability. There is value in both assessment *of* and assessment *for* learning;

TABLE 6.9   Poetry Recital Rubric

Criteria	"C" Performance	"B" Performance	"A" Performance
Did the student introduce the poem?	No introduction	Introduction shared title and author	Introduction got the audience's attention
How did the student sound?	Hard to understand speaker	Showed some confidence	Clear, loud, fluent, expressive voice
How did the student look?	Body language interfered with audience's appreciation of the poem	Showed some confidence	Posture and body motions showed confidence and preparation
How accurate was the recital?	Some noticeable errors and/or needed some prompts to continue	A few noticeable errors or pauses to remember	No noticeable errors
How challenging was the poem?	The chosen poem(s) is less than the requirement of 100 words	The chosen poem(s) is considered appropriate for this recital	The chosen poem(s) is considered challenging to memorize and recite

but it's the daily classroom assessment practices that will impact the success of students and the degree to which students will become independent learners.

Think about the difference between assessment of and assessment for learning. Which of them do you remember teachers using in your educational experiences? What traditional assessment practices would need to be changed to focus on assessment for learning? What happens when a teacher focuses only on assessment of learning? What happens when a teacher focuses only on assessment for learning? If there was a formula for how to divide assessment for and assessment of learning, what percentage of each would you recommend? Do these recommendations change as students get older?

Reflection Opportunity 6.6

As discussed in Chapter 1, assessment is an essential element of the active reflection process emphasized in this text. In order to thoughtfully plan your instruction for the highest levels of student learning, you will need to use an array of effective assessment strategies to evaluate student learning. When you collect information from a variety of sources on students' levels of learning, think carefully about the implications of this data, and consider your findings in relation to the other steps in the active reflection process, it becomes possible to plan creatively and well for future teaching activities.

The *Consider This* feature for this chapter asks you to apply what was discussed earlier in this chapter on understanding and responding to student needs. Go to the Companion Website for this text and take some time now to reflect on these issues before completing your work for this chapter.

Consider This: Understanding And Responding To Students' Needs

Summary

In this chapter, four organizing questions were identified to assist you in developing a better understanding of student learning:

Do student needs affect learning?

A number of student needs influence student learning:
- Basic human needs (Praxis II, topic Ic)
- Need for social acceptance (Praxis II, topic Ic)
- Self-esteem needs

How does development influence learning?

Factors from within the individual help explain many aspects of learning:
- Developmental theories (Praxis II, topic Ia)
- Developmental norms and teaching (Praxis II, topic Ia)
- Learning styles (Praxis II, topic Ia)

What is the impact of the environment on student learning?

Environmental factors explain many aspects of student learning:
- Behavioral learning
- Social learning

What is the role of assessment in learning?

There are many different types of evaluation, each of which has value in teaching and learning:
- Types of assessment (Praxis II, topic IIc)
- Role in learning (Praxis II, topic IIc)

PRAXIS   Test-Preparation Activities

To review an on-line chapter case study, test your understanding of chapter topics and concepts, and begin preparing for the Praxis II: Principles of Learning and Teaching examination, go to the Praxis Test-Preparation module for this chapter of the Companion Website.

Developing the Habit of Reflective Practice

Organizing Questions

Review questions, field-experience opportunities, and activities for building your portfolio are included here for the organizing questions in this chapter.

Do student needs affect learning?

Review Questions

1. What happens when students feel socially unaccepted by either peers or teachers?
2. How does self-esteem impact student learning?
3. What is your role as a teacher in responding to student needs?

Building Your Portfolio: *Meeting Student Needs*

INTASC Standard 2. Choose one of the personal student needs described in this chapter.
- For this need, describe how you will plan to help students meet it for the age/grade you are interested in teaching.
- If you are aware of any school or community resources available to help meet this need, include that information as well.

How does development influence learning?

Review Questions

1. What is a developmental theory?
2. Describe the usefulness of developmental norms to a classroom teacher.
3. In what ways should an understanding of learning styles influence the ways in which you teach?

Building Your Portfolio: *Create a Developmental Profile*

INTASC Standard 2. For the age/grade you think you want to teach:
- Create a developmental profile that outlines the typical abilities of students at that age.
- After referring to one or more child development texts, describe the key intellectual, social, emotional, and physical attributes of that age/grade.

What is the impact of the environment on student learning?

Review Questions

1. How is behavioral learning theory different from developmental theory?
2. In what ways do teachers engage in modeling as they spend time in their classrooms?

Field Experience

Observe a teacher engaging students in learning experiences.
- As you watch students working to gain knowledge, which of the developmental or learning theories presented in this chapter best describes their efforts?
- What did you see or hear that makes you think this?
- Discuss your thoughts with others.

Building Your Portfolio: *Social Learning*

INTASC Standard 2. Remember back to your own K–12 learning experiences.
- Identify a situation in which you learned from observing someone else's behavior.
- Describe what happened and why you learned from this other person's actions.
- Based on what you remember from this situation and others, write a short essay describing what you see as both the strengths and weaknesses of social learning.

What is the role of assessment in learning?

Review Questions

1. What other forms of assessment besides tests are available?
2. Describe the differences between formative and summative evaluation.

Field Experience

Spend some time in a classroom of your choice.
- Make several anecdotal record observations of a single student. It would be best if you could do this task with a partner so that you can compare notes about what is being observed.

- Refine your ability to see and record accurate details of what this student says and does as you talk through what you observed with your partner.
- After completing your observations, write a summary in which you discuss your interpretation of what you observed.

Building Your Portfolio: *Student Portfolios*

INTASC Standard 8. Conduct some research on student portfolios.
- Do some reading about the use of portfolios with students.
- You may also wish to talk to a classroom teacher about the effectiveness of portfolios as an evaluative tool.
- Once you have done your research, describe both the strengths and limitations of portfolios for the age/grade you would like to teach.

Suggested Readings

McDevitt, T., & Ormrod, J. (2007). *Child development and education*. (3rd ed.). Columbus, OH: Merrill. This is a comprehensive child development text written especially for educators. Using a topical approach, this book provides teacher candidates with artifacts and other evidence of the developmental processes of children and their implications for teachers.

Miller, D., Linn, R., & Gronlund, N. (2009). *Measurement and assessment in teaching* (10th ed.). Upper Saddle River, NJ: Merrill/Prentice Hall. This text provides an excellent overview of the problems and benefits of measurement and assessment and gives information about the elements necessary for good teaching. It provides clear guidance in the development of different assessment instruments for use in the classroom.

Schunk, D. (2008). *Learning theories: An educational perspective* (5th ed.). Upper Saddle River, NJ: Merrill/Prentice Hall. As the title implies, this text does a thorough job of describing the major theories of learning. There are separate chapters on the behavioral and social learning theories.

References

Bandura, A. (1977). *Social learning theory.* Upper Saddle River, NJ: Prentice Hall.

Bandura, A. (1986). *Social foundations of thought and action: A social cognitive theory.* Upper Saddle River, NJ: Prentice Hall.

Biber, B. (1964). Preschool education. In R. Ulich (Ed.), *Education and the idea of mankind.* New York: Harcourt Brace.

Charles, C. (2008). *Building classroom discipline* (9th ed.). Columbus, OH: Merrill.

Coopersmith, S. (1967). *The antecedents of self-esteem.* San Francisco: W. H. Freeman.

Dreikurs, R., Grunwald, B., & Pepper, F. (1971). *Maintaining sanity in the classroom.* New York: Harper and Row.

Education Week. (2004). Standards and accountability, in *Quality Counts 2004,* pp. 108–109. Bethesda, MD: Author.

Erikson, E. (1963). *Childhood and society* (2nd ed.). New York: W. W. Norton.

Forman, E. A., & Cazden, C.B. (1986). Exploring Vygotskian perspectives in education: The cognitive value of peer interaction. In J. V. Wertsch (Ed.), *Culture, communication, and cognition: Vygotskian perspectives.* New York: Cambridge University Press.

Freud, S. (1920). *A general introduction to psychoanalysis.* (J. Riviere, Trans.). New York: Liveright.

Gesell, A., & Ilg, F. (1949). *Child development: An introduction to the study of human growth.* New York: Harper & Brothers.

Jones, V., & Jones, L. (2007). *Comprehensive classroom management: Creating communities of support and solving problems* (8th ed.). Boston: Allyn and Bacon.

Kostelnik, M., Whiren, A., Soderman, A., & Gregory, K. (2009). *Guiding children's social development.* (6th ed.) Albany, NY: Delmar.

Marsh, H., & Shavelson, R. (1985). Self-concept: Its multifaceted, hierarchical structure. *Educational Psychologist, 20,* 107–123.

Maslow, A. (1968). *Toward a psychology of being.* Princeton, NJ: Van Nostrand Reinhold.

Miller, D., Linn, R., & Gronlund, N. (2009). *Measurement and assessment in teaching.* (10th ed.). Upper Saddle River, NJ: Prentice Hall.

Piaget, J. (1950). *The psychology of intelligence* (M. Piercy & D. Berlyne, Trans.). New York: Harcourt, Brace.

Rousseau, J. (1979). *Emile* (A. Bloom, Trans.). New York: Basic Books. (Original work published 1762.)

Schunk, D. (2008). *Learning theories: An educational perspective* (5th ed.). Upper Saddle River, NJ: Merrill/Prentice Hall.

Skinner, B. F. (1953). *Science and human behavior.* New York: Macmillan.

Stiggins, R. (2002, June). Assessment crisis: The absence of assessment for learning. *Phi Delta Kappan,* pp. 758–765.

Watson, J. (1924). *Behaviorism.* New York: Norton.

Wormeli, R. (2003). *Day one and beyond.* Portland, ME: Stenhouse.

chapter 7

Developing Curriculum

One of the important tasks you will engage in as a future teacher is determining what should be taught. Although it is possible to simply follow what is outlined in a textbook, the best teachers spend considerable time and energy tailoring content and activities to meet the needs and interests of different groups of students. In this chapter, four organizing questions will help you better understand the excitement and challenges of developing your teaching curriculum.

Focus Questions

1. What influences curriculum development?

2. How has curriculum changed over time?

3. What factors influence curriculum decisions?

4. What are current curriculum trends?

Courtesy of Anthony Magnacca/Merrill Education.

Sarah Hanson has just gotten the last of her fifth grade students out the door and is relaxing for a few moments before tackling her next project. It is 3:30 on a beautiful Friday afternoon and she would love to be working in her garden or going for a leisurely walk. Before she can leave school, however, Sarah must spend some time planning for the coming week. Having just finished a unit on decimals, next week she will begin a discussion of problem-solving strategies in mathematics. After reviewing the relevant standards from the National Council of Teachers of Mathematics, her state's goals for problem solving, and the school's mathematics textbook, Sarah makes plans for the content she wants to present on this topic. In addition to her preparations for mathematics, Sarah will need to make similar plans for the writing, science, social studies, and reading content she will be addressing with her students. As usual, there will be no time for leisure this afternoon. Sarah is busy developing the curriculum for the coming week.

Can you imagine yourself getting excited about teaching if all you had to do day after day was to simply pick up a textbook and follow the detailed plan described there? If you used this approach and strictly adhered to the content and sequence of topics listed in the text, the end result might well be a series of uninteresting teaching experiences for both you and your students. "For today's science lesson, students, please begin by reading pages 43–48. We will then discuss questions 1-5 listed on page 48 and near the end of the hour I will assign homework problems from those listed on page 49." This approach leads to a very mechanical approach to teaching that requires little imagination or thought. It would also be considerably less likely to meet students' needs and interests or excite them about learning in general.

A more creative approach to teaching and learning occurs when you take the time to develop your own teaching plans from a variety of resources and with the needs and interests of your students in mind. When compared to the "teaching from the textbook" method, this approach is far more difficult. It requires greater amounts of time and mental effort to do well. Working to create your own curriculum, however, is one of the many exciting intellectual endeavors that make teaching such a rewarding experience. Furthermore, your involvement in detailed curriculum planning will do much to motivate your students to learn the meaningful content you have organized. This chapter is designed to provide an overview of curriculum planning and development. It begins with a discussion of issues that influence this process.

What influences curriculum development?

Before looking at what influences curriculum development, it is important to understand how curriculum is defined. The **curriculum** is all that is taught, both knowingly and unknowingly, in the schools. It is a multifaceted and complex aspect of schooling. Teachers typically spend a major portion of their planning time working on developing curricula for their classrooms. They are influenced as they engage in this process by various school, district, state, and national guidelines that are in place for each subject taught.

Curriculum Defined

Although curriculum has been described as having many different elements, in this chapter it will be defined as having four main components: the formal curriculum, an informal curriculum, the hidden curriculum, and the null curriculum. Table 7.1 provides an overview of these four components. Teachers are primarily responsible for helping develop and implement the formal curriculum. They may also influence, either directly or indirectly, the other three components.

TABLE 7.1 Components of Curriculum

Component	Description
Formal curriculum	Every subject that the schools intend to teach their students
Informal curriculum	Activities, interest groups, clubs, and sports programs offered within the schools
Hidden curriculum	Everything that the schools indirectly teach students through the attitudes and behaviors of teachers and staff
Null curriculum	All the potential subjects and topics that are *not included* in the curriculum

Formal curriculum. The **formal curriculum** consists of every subject that the schools intend to teach their students. It includes more traditional subject matter content in areas like mathematics, reading, science, social studies, music, the arts, and health and fitness. In addition, the formal curriculum includes such things as learning about different cultures, drug and alcohol awareness, sex education, and violence prevention. This formal curriculum is often identified at the national level, defined more specifically within individual states, and further refined at the district, school, and classroom levels. For example, the *No Child Left Behind Act* of 2001 is a recent piece of federal legislation that has important implications for public education. One portion of this act identifies reading as an essential element in the primary grades by stating that all children should learn to read by the end of the third grade. Based on legislation such as this and input from educators and professional organizations, individual states then determine somewhat more specific goals for the reading curriculum. For example, the Nebraska Department of Education has defined beginning reading, word identification, comprehension, vocabulary, and work/study skills expected from all children in the state. A sample of the expectations for fourth-grade students reads: "By the end of the fourth grade, students will demonstrate the use of multiple strategies in reading unfamiliar words and phrases" (Nebraska Department of Education, 2008, p. 3). School districts, schools, and finally individual classroom teachers then work to make these broad statements into more specific curriculum plans for students. So, Belsa Martinez, a fourth-grade teacher in Nebraska, incorporates this state expectation into her reading curriculum. She has worked with her class to develop a list of various strategies effective readers use when they come across an unfamiliar word or phrase in their reading. The list posted in her classroom includes:

- Look at illustrations to get clues.
- Think about what word makes sense there.
- Reread the sentence or paragraph, get a running start.
- Find a small word inside the larger word.
- Think about if you know a word similar to that word.
- Sound it out or pull it apart.

As she works with students individually, in small groups or as a whole class, she continues to refer to the list of strategies. She often facilitates discussions where students share the strategies they use and how the strategies help them as readers. She emphasizes that there are a variety of strategies that readers use when faced with words or phrases that cause them to stumble.

Informal curriculum. Ramona Zarelli teaches high school social studies. In addition to her regular teaching load, she has taken on coaching responsibilities for the girls' volleyball team. Ramona receives extra pay for this extracurricular assignment. Two other teachers in her department also have taken on additional assignments. Jeremy Black is involved in driver's education classes after school, and Vanessa Williamson works with the chess club. Each of these teachers is participating in the informal curriculum of the school.

Every school has an **informal curriculum** that supplements the formal classes and content taught. At the elementary level, for example, students may choose to come to school early or stay late for supplemental studies in learning a foreign language, extending mathematical understandings, or refining writing skills. These activities are viewed as enjoyable enrichment times for children with special interests and talents in these areas. Often structured as clubs for students, they may include competitions or special events that serve as culminating experiences. In addition to these and other enrichment activities, middle schools and high schools offer students the opportunity to participate in a number of organized sports. This part of the informal curriculum also provides important learning opportunities for students. Extracurricular activities promote citizenship and sportsmanship, teach lessons about teamwork and self-discipline, and facilitate the physical and emotional development of students while instilling a sense of school and community pride (Youniss and Yates, 1997). These activities can also provide opportunities for students to build helpful and supportive relationships with staff members. These relationships with faculty members positively affect students' academic development and lifelong learning attitudes while increasing the likelihood going beyond a high school education. To accommodate students who have after-school obligations such as jobs or family commitments, it is recommended that schools offer some of their informal curricular activities before school, during lunch periods, or during special activity periods set aside by the school during the regular school day (Wimberly, 2002).

Reflection Opportunity 7.1

Consider writing about your experiences with the informal curriculum. Did you participate in any aspects of the informal curriculum described above as part of your P–12 experiences? What do you remember about these activities? Were they beneficial to you? How would you compare the benefits of the informal curriculum you participated in to the more formal curriculum you were a part of? What does this tell you about the value of each curriculum? As a future educator, can you see yourself teaching or leading any of the clubs, activities, or sports that have been described as part of the informal curriculum?

Hidden curriculum. Bill Hornberger is in his 27th year of teaching middle school mathematics. Although he was enthusiastic and effective as a teacher for many of those years, Bill is tired of working with the high-energy students in his classes. He plans on retiring at the end of this year and he is basically "going through the motions" as he finishes up his career. He tends to be abrupt and aloof in his interactions with students and spends a minimum of time in planning and evaluating his curriculum. Bill's attitude is having an impact on his students' attitudes about mathematics and middle school life in general. He is influencing the **hidden curriculum** of his classroom and school. The hidden curriculum is generally described as everything that the educational system indirectly teaches students through the attitudes and behaviors of teachers and staff (Parkay, Anctil, & Haas, 2006).

As a future teacher, you will strongly influence what is learned in the hidden curriculum. Attitudes toward learning, values, ways of interacting with students, and feelings about diversity issues are just a few of the many things that students learn indirectly from their teachers. Although the hidden curriculum engages students in indirect learning and may seem to have limited influence, it actually has a significant impact. Think back to your own P–12 learning experiences and identify one teacher who you remember as particularly outstanding. What do you recall learning from this person that could be considered part of the hidden curriculum? How did this teacher share this part of the curriculum with you? Were there other teachers who may have shared less positive aspects of the hidden curriculum with you? Most people find that they remember attitudes, ways of thinking, and perspectives more often than the actual content taught. The potential for having a long-term impact on students' lives through the hidden curriculum is great.

Reflection Opportunity 7.2

Null curriculum. Elliot Eisner (2002) identifies the **null curriculum** as all potential curriculum topics that are not included in the classroom. These topics tend to be avoided for two main reasons: They are either too controversial or the perceived value to students is low. Topics such as religion, homosexuality, creationism, and abortion rights are all examples of controversial issues typically avoided by the schools. For these topics and others, it is difficult for schools and individual teachers to engage students in impartial learning experiences that add to their understandings while being sensitive to the diversity of attitudes that students and their families have regarding them. For this reason, they are typically not part of the curriculum.

The second set of topics contained in the null curriculum consists of those not addressed because they are seen as less important to students. An example of this type at the elementary level is art education. Most school districts support the value of art education, but few actually hire full-time art educators for elementary schools. At the same time, many elementary teachers find that they are consumed by the demands of what they and others consider the core curriculum and consequently devote little time for the teaching of art. By default, then, art instruction becomes a part of the null curriculum.

Approaches to the Curriculum

As you develop curricula for your classroom, you will manage the task in one of two distinct ways. The more traditional approach at most educational levels is typically referred to as the **subject-centered curriculum.** Teachers using this strategy see the curriculum as best organized around the logical order of the discipline. In the elementary mathematics curriculum, addition is taught before subtraction, followed by multiplication and then division. From this perspective, the discipline itself determines the order of the curriculum. Other planners engage in a **student-centered curriculum.** Teachers who use this methodology first determine student needs and interests before identifying content to be taught. Instead of deciding on curriculum content and then seeing how this information can best be taught to students (the subject-centered approach), the student-centered curriculum planner looks at the developmental abilities and interests of a particular class of students and then matches that with relevant content.

Subject-centered approach. Marv Kinsley teaches seventh- and eighth-grade science and mathematics at Compton Middle School. Today he is planning for the coming week's science activities. Having just completed Chapter 7 in the science text, the class will be starting a new unit on chemical changes as an introduction to the study of chemistry. Chapter 8 in the text for science suggests a sequence of activities that Marv modifies to better match his own thinking about how the activities should be sequenced. Next, he plans strategies that he can use to make this content interesting and exciting for his students. Marv is using a subject-centered approach to curriculum planning. Do you remember teachers who used the subject-centered approach to curriculum development? What was your reaction to this approach?

Student-centered approach. In the above example, if Marv Kinsley were teaching using a student-centered curriculum approach, he would begin by determining his students' needs and interests regarding science. He can gather this information through observations of the class, asking them directly, or by knowing what typical seventh- and eighth-grade students are interested in learning about science. Once this information is determined, Marv then begins to identify what will be taught in the coming week. He collects information from a variety of sources, including the school text for science, and begins to develop more specific curriculum plans. Although this approach is more responsive to student needs and interests, it should be clear that using this strategy for curriculum development is also more time consuming and challenging for teachers.

Consider both the subject-centered and the student-centered curriculum. Both approaches can be effectively used by teachers, but one will probably be more attractive to you. Which do you think sounds most appealing at the present time? What is it about this approach that you like? Can you identify personality characteristics that may make one approach a better "fit" for you than the other? Think about the implications of this preferred approach for teaching and learning in your future classroom.

**Reflection
Opportunity 7.3**

Sometimes, the curriculum approach you want to use may be in conflict with approaches of other teachers. Others may be skeptical that your ideas will work. The *Views from the Classroom* feature for this chapter shares the reactions of one teacher when faced with the comment from others "it will never fly." Go to the Companion Website for this text and read this teacher's responses to those who told him his strategies would not work.

**Views from the
Classroom: It Will
Never Fly, Orville**

National, State, and District Influences on Curriculum

Curriculum development is a complex process that includes input from a great many sources. You will need to make decisions about what should be taught after examining information from a variety of levels. National curriculum standards, state curriculum goals, and school-district curriculum materials all directly influence what you will actually teach in the classroom.

Before looking at each of these influences, however, it is important to distinguish the difference between curriculum and standards. **Standards** are statements about what students should know and be able to do, what they might be asked to do to give evidence of learning, and how well they should be expected to know or do it. **Curriculum** is the program devised by educators to prepare students to meet standards. It consists of activities and lessons at each grade level, instructional materials, and various instructional techniques. In short, standards define what is to be learned at certain points in time and curriculum specifies the details of the learning and assessment opportunities.

National influences on curriculum. Many national professional organizations (see Chapter 5 for more information on these organizations) help shape the curriculum by developing standards that describe in broad terms the content these groups feel is important for P–12 students to know. Although these **curriculum standards** do not identify specific content for P–12 classrooms, they create a conceptual framework on which this curriculum can be based. Although they are not mandated, curriculum standards provide a focal point for constructive dialog among educators and offer guidelines to states and school districts as they work on developing curriculum guides, creating assessment tools and purchasing instructional materials. Some examples of standards are listed in Table 7.2. You may want to review the Websites of professional organizations such as the National Council of Teachers of Mathematics (2008), the National Council for the Social Studies (2008) and the Music Educators National Conference (2008). For additional information on current state and national standards, go to the Companion Website for this text and click on MyEducationLab for Chapter 7.

Judy Gulledge (Ritchhart, Moran, Blythe, & Reese, 2002), a middle school science teacher from Norfolk, Virginia, has found a way to keep standards and testing in perspective as she develops and implements her science curriculum. She states that standards may contribute to "what" is taught; but they should never be the sole reason "why" something is taught. At the

myeducationlab
The Power of Classroom Practice

MyEducationLab 7.1

TABLE 7.2 Sample National Curriculum Standards

Organization	Sample Standard	Subcomponents of Standard
National Council for Teachers of Mathematics (NCTM)	Number and Operations	• Understand numbers • Understand meanings of operations • Compute fluently
National Council for the Social Studies (NCSS)	Culture and Cultural Diversity	• Human beings create, learn, and adapt culture • Culture helps us understand ourselves as individuals and members of groups • Cultures exhibit both similarities and differences
Music Educators National Conference (MENC)	Singing, Alone and with Others (Grades 9–12)	• Sing with expression and technical accuracy • Sing music written in four parts • Demonstrate well-developed ensemble skills

beginning of every school year, she is required to submit an overview of her science curriculum for the year. As she prepares this document, the last resource she uses is the list of standards. She begins the planning of her curriculum by examining current events. Judy then looks for issues that will encourage her students to take action within their own community. Once the primary issues for the curriculum are established, she then composes overarching understandings that can be reapplied throughout her students' lifetime. Finally, Judy looks at the standards her students are required to meet. Because her curriculum is based on broad, timely, and enduring goals, it is easy to link the required standards to the curriculum. For example, one year the local newspaper in her community featured an article discussing the possibility of introducing a new strain of Japanese oyster into the Chesapeake Bay to help replenish depleted native stocks. Her seventh-grade students debated whether a nonnative oyster should be introduced to the bay. While preparing for the debate, the students met the required standards and also deepened their understandings about how human activities can alter the equilibrium of an ecosystem and learned that the survival of all organisms depends on the physical conditions existing in the environment.

The *No Child Left Behind (NCLB) Act of 2001* is another example of a national influence on curriculum. It has had a significant impact on instructional practices. NCLB has put enormous pressure on teachers to improve student performance as measured by yearly standardized exams. Testing under NCLB does not begin until third grade, but teachers in the earlier grades, including kindergarten, are being pressured to focus more on basic academic skill acquisition in preparation for these tests. Even preschool teachers are beginning to feel this pressure. Under NCLB, schools are held accountable for making progress toward state-set goals, and their federal funding could eventually be withdrawn if they fail to meet these goals. Many educators worry that this focus on test scores means that little time and energy is left for teachers to plan creative and motivating activities for students.

Another impact of NCLB is that teachers are devoting more class time to core subjects such as reading and mathematics, because these are the required subjects being tested. As a result, subjects such as social studies, health and fitness and the arts are experiencing a decrease of curriculum resources and instructional time. In March 2005, Education Week hosted a Web forum (Education Week, 2005) where these questions were posed to their readers: "Is the No Child Left Behind Act's emphasis on reading and math squeezing social studies out of the curriculum? What role should social studies play in schools today? How can curriculum demands be balanced?" One respondent wrote: "The traditional academic core subjects should take precedence over the other subjects if we are to remain a viable country. We cannot afford another generation of poorly educated students."

The late child psychologist and Holocaust survivor, Haim Ginott (1972) would likely disagree with this perspective and argue for schools valuing social studies as an essential component of the curriculum:

> My eyes saw what no person should witness: gas chambers built by learned engineers. Children poisoned by educated physicians. Infants killed by trained nurses. Women and babies shot by high school and college graduates. So, I am suspicious of education. My request is: help our children become human.

The Washington-based Center on Education Policy (2005) reported that 27% of school systems say they are spending less time on social studies, and nearly 25% say they are spending less time on science, art, and music. It appears that teachers will vary in how NCLB affects these aspects of the curriculum.

State influences on curriculum. Every state has a centralized office that deals with issues associated with P–12 education. Often called the office of the superintendent for public instruction or simply the state department of education, these state organizations play a significant role in the development of a framework for conceptualizing the curriculum that is taught in the schools.

Although the curriculum standards developed by states are generally broad and nonspecific, they define the parameters that schools use in developing curricula. Typically, states outline what students are expected to learn at each grade level within each subject area. Sample state curriculum standards are shown in Table 7.3.

District influences on curriculum. Although national and state standards create the framework on which curriculum is based, local school districts have primary responsibilities for developing and/or adopting more specific curriculum plans and activities. School boards, administrators, and teachers all have important roles to play in this activity. These roles are outlined in Table 7.4. Typically, school boards serve as approval-giving bodies for curricula that are adopted district-wide. School board members generally listen to the concerns voiced by others regarding the existing curricula and then empower groups within the district to develop or review alternative programs for potential approval by the board. For example, a new mathematics curriculum for grades P–12 that has been carefully studied by teachers, administrators, and community members would be implemented only after receiving the approval of members of the school board.

Depending on their management style, superintendents, assistant superintendents responsible for curriculum, and building principals may either take leadership in developing new curricula or empower teachers and community members serving on curriculum committees

TABLE 7.3 Sample State Curriculum Standards

State	Standard	Sample Content Standard	Sample Benchmarks
Michigan	Mathematics: Geometry and measurement	Shape and shape relationships	High school: 1. Use shape to identify plane and solid figures, graphs, loci, functions and data distributions. 2. Determine necessary and sufficient conditions for the existence of a particular shape and apply those conditions to analyze shapes.
Washington	Reading: Understands and uses different skills and strategies to read	Use word recognition and word meaning skills to read and comprehend text	Grade 4: 1. Apply phonetic principles to read including sounding out, using initial letters, and using common letter patterns to make sense of whole words. 2. Use meaning, context, and pictures to comprehend story.

Sources: From Michigan Department of Education. (2005). Grade level content expectations. Retrieved July 11 2005 from: *http://www.michigan.gov/mde/0,1607,7–140–28753 33232—,00.html.*

Office of the Washington Superintendent for Public Instruction. (2005). Essential academic learning requirements. Retrieved July 11, 2005 from: *http://www.k12.wa.us/curriculumInstruct/reading/ealrs.aspx.*

TABLE 7.4 District Influences on the Curriculum

Group	Roles
School Boards	Serve as approval-giving bodies for curricula that are adopted district-wide
Administrators	Take leadership in developing new curricula in the school or district or empower teachers and community members serving on curriculum committees to create their own curriculum plans and materials
Teachers	Serve on curriculum development and review committees both within their own school building and for similar groups meeting for district-wide projects

to create their own curriculum plans and materials. The former is typically referred to as **top-down curriculum development,** and the latter style leads to **grassroots curricular reform.** Top-down curriculum development is exemplified by an assistant superintendent for curriculum who works primarily with principals and other district administrators to develop a new music program. Teachers are then informed of the curriculum changes and asked to implement them in their classrooms.

An example of grassroots curriculum development would be an assistant superintendent for curriculum calling together a group of teachers and community members to develop a drug awareness and prevention curriculum. After clarifying the task and providing the group with resources, the administrator then gives the committee the time and resources needed to develop the curriculum. Which type of curriculum development (top-down or grassroots) would you be most comfortable with as a teacher?

Your Role as a Teacher in Curriculum Development In addition to serving on curriculum committees within your school building and district, you will be expected to make specific long- and short-term plans for the curriculum of your classroom. Working within the established curricula for your school and district, and taking into consideration state and national guidelines, you will plan an organized and motivating curriculum for your students. When you engage students in meaningful interactions with relevant content, they are much more likely to become motivated learners.

As you begin the curriculum-development process for your students, four key elements are essential to your success. The first is *meeting the needs and interests of individual students.* After reading Chapter 6, you should be aware that every student has unique abilities and needs. They differ in terms of preferred learning styles. Student interests also vary. A major task you will face in planning curriculum, then, is to include strategies that will allow you to vary such things as content emphasized, skills to be mastered, and learning materials used to meet individual student needs and interests (Drake & Burns, 2004). For example, a middle school social studies teacher who listens carefully to student comments and chooses to study student rights as part of a unit on democracy is building on student interests to plan her curriculum. By providing opportunities for small group work and a choice of projects that students can complete to demonstrate their understandings, she is also helping to meet individual students' needs. Of course, as teachers use students' needs and interests to guide instructional planning, they need to balance this with curriculum requirements. For example, a high school English teacher who finds out a great number of his students are interested in surfing cannot just opt to take his students on a surfing field trip. He can, however, take that interest and adapt the curriculum requirements to this special interest. For example, his class might interview competitive surfers either in person or via e-mail. These interviews can then be summarized into biographical posters that can be put on display in the school hallway and local surf shops. Through this activity, his students are learning about interview techniques and writing biographies as mandated by his district's curriculum guide.

The second key to your success in curriculum planning is *helping students recognize the connections between disciplines.* Learning outside the classroom is seldom organized into neat little boxes that carry labels such as "mathematics knowledge" or "reading skills." It is much more likely to be integrated around a topic of interest to the learner. Yet, this compartmentalization of learning is often the way in which we teach these subjects in school settings. You will need to work hard to help students make the connections between disciplines through your organization and presentation of content, the use of real-world applications, or clear explanations of the connections that exist among disciplines. So, for example, a fourth grade teacher who has chosen to study astronomy as part of the science curriculum can prepare instructional strategies in such a way that students use mathematics and writing as integral parts of their investigation of the heavens. In addition, he can plan to include a study of historical artifacts and beliefs about astronomy to add further insights.

A third key element of curriculum development is *making learning relevant* to life outside the classroom. Teacher planning needs to include an emphasis on why the information, skills, and thought processes emphasized are important. If, for example, you taught algebra at the high school level, it would be important for you to share how some occupations rely on algebra and higher-level mathematics knowledge as foundational to the work they do. In addition, the same logical thinking and problem-solving strategies needed for solving algebraic equations is critical to a great many more occupations. Sharing this information with students will help them understand the relevance of the content and processes you are teaching.

A final element of successful curriculum development is *seeing yourself as an important part of positive curriculum change.* The standards movement and high-stakes testing trend occurring across the United States has increased the curriculum mandates found in American schools. Some teachers take an active part in the decision-making process, whereas others feel as if they have no voice in these decisions (Riddle Buly and Rose, 2001). Whether teachers feel they have a voice or not, there are bound to be tensions and struggles with any curriculum change. Teachers who successfully work with curriculum mandates tend to view change from the inside out rather from the outside in:

> By viewing change from the inside out, the professional does not blindly accept and support a change. Rather, the professional continues to be a reflective practitioner, first learning the principles of the mandated instructional framework, then questioning based on prior knowledge and expertise, and finally feeling secure enough to modify the vehicle to further meet the needs of the students. (Riddle Buly and Rose, 2001, p. 5).

**Reflection
Opportunity 7.4**

Think about the grade and/or subject you think you will want to teach. What will be the content of the curriculum for that age/grade? How well do you know the content yourself? Are there gaps in your understanding? Is a deep understanding of the content important to being able to plan the curriculum for your future classroom? For the curriculum you will teach, can you see yourself meeting the needs and interests of your students, making connections between disciplines, and making learning relevant to your future students?

How has curriculum changed over time?

The curriculum taught in American schools has changed dramatically since colonial times. For much of the 17th and 18th centuries, most of the decisions about content were made locally by teachers based on an understanding of what was important for students to know. The 19th and early 20th centuries saw growing involvement on the part of national figures and professional

TABLE 7.5 Historical Trends Influencing Curriculum

Trend	Dates	Key Aspects
Religious Emphasis	1620–1780	• Emphasized religious training • Mostly private schools • Primarily available to upper class families
Citizenship Emphasis	1780–1820	• Help students become productive citizens • More public school options • Developing a sense of American identity
Common School Revival	1812–1865	• Equal opportunity led to more public schools • Primary growth was in elementary school options • Broad, general curriculum began to emerge
Public High Schools	1880–1920	• Free public high schools become available • Shift to a more comprehensive curriculum
Meaningful Curriculum Content	1890–1930	• Public begins to question content of curriculum • Growing desire to make curriculum meaningful

organizations as a more uniform curriculum began to evolve. Table 7.5 summarizes key historical trends that have influenced curriculum development.

More recently, six major reform efforts have shaped the curricula offered in America's schools. These efforts are summarized in Table 7.6 and described in more detail below. In general, these efforts can be seen as focusing on either a student-oriented approach to curriculum planning or a subject-oriented one. The pendulum has swung from one extreme to the other in an attempt to create either relevant or rigorous content for students at all levels within the P–12 system. Hopefully, curriculum planners for the 21st century can avoid the "either/or" mentality demonstrated in the efforts described next and instead create new options that are rigorous and relevant while still ensuring accountability and fair treatment for all students.

Progressive Education

One of the early efforts of this century to change the content of curricula came to be known as the **progressive education** movement. Growing primarily from the philosophy of education promoted by John Dewey (1929), who is discussed more thoroughly in Chapter 11, the progressive movement sought to develop curricula that were based on the needs and interests of students. Students were seen as experiencing beings who learned the most when they were engaged in "learning by doing." They were encouraged to spend classroom time manipulating real-world materials and learning from their conversations with teachers and peers. In 1919, this child-centered approach became a formal organization called the Progressive Education Association (PEA).

Sputnik and Curricular Excellence

In the 1950s, advances in Russian technology caused a panicked American public to call for change in American schooling. The 1957 launch of the *Sputnik* satellite, apparently placing Russia

U.S. Secretary of Education William Bennett proposed a more rigorous academic curriculum for America's high schools in his 1987 book titled *James Madison High School: A Curriculum for American Students*. Ernest Boyer published *High School: A Report on Secondary Education in America* in 1983 with a similar focus and published a follow-up book in 1995 titled *The Basic School: A Community for Learning*.

One unfortunate outcome of the back-to-the-basics movement is the de-emphasis of other important curriculum areas. If teachers are spending more time with reading, writing, mathematics, science, and social studies there will be fewer opportunities for other subjects such as the arts. There are many who would suggest, however, that this de-emphasis is a serious problem. The *Engage in the Debate* feature for this chapter makes a strong case for the inclusion of the arts as a critical part of schooling. Read the feature now and respond to the reflection questions posed.

Engage in the debate: Arts education

At all levels, when budgets get tight or a more "basic" curriculum is emphasized, one of the first parts of the school curriculum to be scrutinized for cuts is the arts. The visual and performing arts are sometimes looked upon as superfluous or only extra curricular, not part of a "real education". In the popular 1996 movie, *Mr. Holland's Opus*, the lead character (Mr. Holland), says to his principal who cut the arts in favor of just reading and writing, ". . . without the arts there will be nothing to read or write."

Within recent years there has been a renewed interest in making the arts more valued components of the curriculum. In 1998, then first lady, Hillary Rodham Clinton hosted a White House special event titled "Recognizing the Power of Arts in Education" The arts were applauded as unique means of expression that are essential to include in K–12 education (Boss, 1999).

"The Value and Quality of Arts Education: A Statement of Principles," is a 2002 document (Music Educators National Conference, 2008) from the nation's ten most important educational organizations, including the American Association of School Administrators, the National Education Association, the National Parent Teacher Association, and the National School Boards Association. It begins with this statement: "Every student in the nation should have an education in the arts." The report lists benefits conveyed by arts education into four categories:

- **Success in society:** Every human culture uses art to carry forward its ideas and ideals.
- **Success in school:** Students learn many important skills through the arts such as thinking skills, social skills, and communication skills.
- **Success in developing intelligence:** Neurological research has proven that participation in the arts can actively contribute to brain development:
- **Success in life:** The arts positively affect students in the areas of creativity, cooperation, discipline, diligence and self esteem.

Our schools are being challenged to make sure "no child is left behind" as they strive to help all students reach the level of achievement essential for success in school, work and life in the 21st century. Proponents of arts education emphasize the role that the arts should play in helping our schools achieve this goal.

Developing the Habit of Reflective Practice
Gather Information

1. Search the Internet for the National Art Education Association and Music Educators National Conference websites to read more about arts education.

2. What role did arts education play in your K–12 education? Did the schools you attend value the arts? How well were the arts supported financially and conceptually in your K–12 education? Did your schools have qualified, full-time arts education instructors?

Identify Beliefs

1. Do you think that arts education is as important as the more standard components of the curriculum such as mathematics, science and social studies? Why or why not?

2. Should arts education have a higher priority in K–12 education? What is your rationale for the position you take?

Make Decisions

1. Imagine that you are a committee in a school district. This committee is formed to decide on where to make necessary budget cuts. The committee has narrowed it down to 2 choices: cut the arts funding or cut the athletics funding. If you had to choose one of the two, which of the two would you opt to cut and why?

Assess and Evaluate

1. What strategies can be employed to help maintain an arts education curriculum in the schools?

2. Why do you think some educators do not support arts education?

Sources:

Boss, S. Applauding the arts. In *Arts education: Basic to learning*. Portland, OR: Northwest Regional Laboratory.

Music Educators National Conference (2008). The value and quality of arts education. Retrieved December 10, 2008 from *http://www.menc.org/about/view/the-value-and-quality-of-arts-education*

Concept–Based Curriculum

As teachers work to align their curriculum with state and national standards, many are turning toward an approach that takes learning beyond the facts. Teachers using a concept-based curriculum (Erickson, 2002) work to help students develop and deepen their understandings. A common approach taken by educators using a concept-based curriculum is called **Understanding by Design (UbD).**

UbD, developed by Grant Wiggins and Jay McTighe in the late 1990s, utilizes a three-stage "backward planning" curriculum-design process (2005). UbD advocates that teachers begin with the end in mind. Educators work through a curriculum design process that includes three stages:

- Stage One: Identify the desired results (goals and standards).
- Stage Two: Figure out how students will show evidence of learning the identified desired results (performance and assessment).
- Stage Three: Design learning opportunities that will promote understandings and equip students to perform successfully (lessons and instruction).

During Stage One, teachers identify the enduring understandings that they want their students to develop at the completion of the learning sequence. Enduring understandings go beyond facts and skills and instead focus on larger concepts, principles, or processes. In Stage Two, teachers develop performance tasks that help them determine facets of student understanding (Wiggins & McTighe, 2000). During Stage Three of Understanding by Design, teachers plan lessons that will help their students accomplish the performance tasks chosen.

Teachers using a concept-based approach to curriculum development like Understanding by Design tend to use an interdisciplinary approach to learning, weaving subject areas together.

Steven Levy, an award-winning elementary educator and educational consultant and author, writes in his book, *Starting from Scratch* (1996):

> Compartmentalized learning does not help children reach our highest educational goals because it does not correspond to the way human beings experience life . . . presenting the world broken up into subjects puts it into a form already abstracted and shaped—predigested, if you will. It's like giving the children a coloring book or a paint-by-number set rather than a blank piece of paper . . . How do we learn naturally about the world? In reality, we experience the world whole, not broken into discrete chunks. (pp. 19–20)

Ian's Classroom Experiences: How Does Assessment Inform Instruction?

Teachers who are using this approach to curriculum planning are careful to go beyond facts, helping students to grasp transferable concepts (Erickson, 2002). The *Ian's Classroom Experiences* feature for this chapter (found on the Companion Website for this text) discusses Understanding by Design and the role of assessment. You may want to read this feature now.

What factors influence curriculum decisions?

The reform efforts just described have had a significant impact on curriculum planning for America's schools. In addition, other less obvious factors have influenced this process. The textbooks used in P–12 schools, the technology found in classrooms, diversity in American society, and parent and community influences have also been important factors that have shaped the content taught in the schools.

Textbook Selection

The textbook selection process varies between states. In Texas and California, for example, the state governing body for P–12 education selects the textbook options from which school districts can choose. After receiving input from interested citizens, these states determine the best textbooks for all subjects at all grade levels. In other states, however, textbook decisions are left to individual school districts after input from parents and interested community members.

Regardless of the methods of adoption, textbooks play a significant role in curriculum planning and implementation. For example, in 2002, the popular textbook series approved for use by California in K–6 reading curriculum was *SRA/Open Court Reading,* published by SRA/McGraw Hill (California Department of Education, 2008). Teachers who use this series are influenced in several ways as they develop curricula for their classrooms. First, the organization of the texts will likely determine the order and presentation of the elementary reading lessons and activities. The stories, vocabulary, chapter objectives, learning activities, and evaluation strategies are other components of the textbook package that often influence the teaching and learning of reading in the elementary classrooms in which they are used. Priscilla Eide, a third-grade teacher, shared her struggles when working with this reading series (Eide, 2001):

> The difficulty for me has been in dealing with the rigid time limitations set by the program. I recognize that time limitations are necessary in order to replicate a program such as this. I also realize that there is a real tension for me between developing deep thinking in students and in moving on to the next reading experience . . . (p. 17)

Research shows that between 80 and 90% of classroom and homework assignments are textbook-driven (Jones, 2000). Some educators even argue that the four largest textbook publishers in the United States have established a *de facto* national curriculum. Because of this, it is critical that school districts choose carefully when adopting a textbook. Many are beginning to question the role that textbooks should play in the curriculum.

Technology in the Classroom

When you think about the word technology, what is the first thing that comes to mind? If you are like most people, your thoughts probably focus on computers. Although the computer is one of the more recent and clearly an important technological advance, technology actually includes much more than this. The International Technology Education Association (2005) states:

> Broadly speaking, technology is how people modify the natural world to suit their own purposes. From the Greek word *techne,* meaning art or artifice or craft, technology literally means the act of making or crafting, but more generally refers to the diverse collection of processes and knowledge that people use to extend human abilities and to satisfy human needs and wants. (p. 2)

When first introduced to the schools, technological innovations as diverse as chalkboards (early 1800s) and educational television (1950s) were promoted as having the potential to radically change teaching and learning in the K–12 classroom. Yet, time has demonstrated that these important and useful technologies have failed to truly revolutionize education.

Similar claims have been made about the potential of computers to completely change the content and process of education. Seymour Papert (1980), in his classic book *Mindstorms,* stated:

> This book is about how computers can be carriers of powerful ideas and of the seeds of cultural change, how they can help people form new relationships with knowledge that cut across the traditional lines separating humanities from sciences and knowledge of the self from both of these. It is about using computers to challenge current beliefs about who can understand what and at what age. (p. 4)

Thirteen years later, in *The Children's Machine* (1993), Papert was still optimistic that computers would change the educational landscape in new and dramatic ways.

It is still too early to determine the long-term impact that computers will have on reshaping American education, but it is becoming clear that teachers who use computers regularly are changing the content of their classroom curricula (Kellner, 2005). The increased availability of high-quality software programs, CD-ROM materials in all subject areas, and Internet access for growing numbers of schools (Education Week, 2004) are changing both the quantity and quality of information that teachers and students can use in the classroom. Chapter 9 provides more in-depth information on technology options in the classroom and their influence on learning.

Reflect on your personal attitudes toward using computers and other technology in learning. Do you see yourself as a person who embraces these options and gets excited about using them yourself? Or, are you a little more resistant to trying out new alternatives? Will your personal attitudes toward technology influence your willingness to incorporate it into your future classroom? Why or why not?

**Reflection
Opportunity 7.5**

Diversity in American Society

Another factor influencing the direction of curriculum planning in the United States is the increased emphasis on recognizing and valuing the diversity that exists in every part of society. As you develop curricula for your future classroom, you will need to ensure that you emphasize the contributions of diverse people to academic disciplines. For example, most science textbooks now include information about how men and women, people with handicapping conditions, and people from different cultures have all helped shape the content and direction of the sciences. As a future teacher you will be encouraged by your school, district, and state to be more sensitive about including this information in your classroom.

Another way in which our diverse society influences the curriculum is through the recognition that the diverse learners in today's classrooms require more individualized and personalized curricula. An obvious example of this type is that non-English-speaking students need instruction in English as a second language. Similarly, when students with special needs are included in the regular classroom, curriculum modifications are often needed. Perhaps not so obvious, however, is the need to structure the curriculum and classroom experiences so that girls have more equitable opportunities to learn mathematics (National Science Foundation, 2005). In each of these instances, and more, the needs of diverse learners have led to a richer, more diversified curriculum.

In order to meet the needs of the diverse learners in classrooms, teachers are engaging in **multicultural education.** One element of multicultural education is to make the curriculum more inclusive of different cultural perspectives and contributions. By doing this, teachers are helping students better understand and appreciate our diverse world. The *Reflect on Diversity* feature found in this section provides additional insights into multicultural education by identifying and discussing four different levels that can be found in classrooms.

Reflect on diversity: The dimensions of multicultural education

James A. Banks, perhaps the most influential scholar in the field of multicultural education, proposes that studies of diversity typically take place at one of four levels:

Level 1—Contributions: This is sometimes called the "heroes and holidays" approach. The school focuses on heroes, holidays, food, and other discrete cultural elements. In a school that operates on this level, the curriculum would remain the same except for a few lessons added around special events such as Martin Luther King Day.

Level 2—Additive: Teachers using this approach simply add content to include multicultural perspectives; it appears to be an afterthought. A school adds a unit or course on a particular ethnic group without any change to the basic curriculum, adding, for example, a unit on Native Americans or "The Immigrant Experience".

Level 3—Transformation: Schools using this approach actually undergo significant curricular revision. Teachers infuse various perspectives, frames of reference, and content material from diverse groups to extend student understanding of the nature, development, and complexity of our world. For example, if a class was learning about Westward Expansion in the 1800s, they would look at this from not only the viewpoint of pioneers and explorers, but also the viewpoint of Native Americans of that time period.

Level 4—Decision Making and Social Action: At this level, schools and teachers include all of the elements from level 3 above but also encourage students to make decisions and take action related to the concepts, issues, or problems they have studied. For example, the class that researched the biases surrounding Columbus might write letters to publishers and organizations that seem to carry on the inaccurate legend. Schools that develop this kind of multicultural curriculum strive to help students develop a vision of a better society and acquire the knowledge and skills necessary to bring about constructive social change.

Banks states that a multicultural curriculum should have three major goals: to know, to care and to act. Transforming a school's curriculum to level 3 and 4 is no easy task, but definitely worth the time and effort.

Developing the Habit of Reflective Practice
Gather Information

1. Do an Internet search for "EdChange.org" and read more about multicultural education.
2. Think back on your own education. Which level of multicultural education did you experience?

Identify Beliefs

1. How do you define multicultural education? What should it look like in classrooms?
2. Are there certain populations of students that need a multicultural education more than others? If yes, which populations and why? If no, why not?

Make Decisions

1. What are some of the challenges schools face when aiming to develop a curriculum at levels 3 and 4?
2. If you could go back to your own schooling, what is one change you would make to improve your own multicultural education?

Assess and Evaluate

1. If you were visiting a school to assess and evaluate how the curriculum is taking a multicultural approach, what evidence would you look for in classrooms and throughout the school to show the level of multicultural curriculum integration.
2. Why do you think some educators are "turned off" or intimidated by creating and implementing a multicultural curriculum? What could be done to change their opinions?

Sources

Banks, J. (2008). *An Introduction to Multicultural Education* (4th ed.). Boston: Allyn, and Bacon.

Banks, J. (2009). *Teaching strategies for ethnic studies.* (8th edition). Boston: Allyn and Bacon.

Parent and Community Influences

Public schools, by definition, exist to meet the educational needs of children as identified by individual states and local communities. It should come as no surprise, then, that both parents' and community members' opinions about the content of the curriculum influences what you will teach. Particularly at the local level, parents and community members discuss their views of curriculum content with individual teachers, participate in curriculum planning efforts in the schools, and attend school board meetings to share their opinions about curriculum matters.

Parents and community members often want to have the things they value emphasized in the school curriculum. For example, parents often work hard to have certain books either included or excluded from the curriculum because they are in agreement with, or in opposition to, their viewpoints. The American Library Association keeps track of books that are challenged in schools each year. The 10 most challenged books of 2007 included (American Library Association, 2008):

- *The Chocolate War* a novel by Robert Cormier. Challenged for sexual content, offensive language, religious viewpoint, being unsuited to age group, and violence.
- *The Golden Compass,* a book by Phillip Pullman, for religious viewpoint.
- *I Know Why the Caged Bird Sings,* by Maya Angelou for being sexually explicit.
- *The Adventures of Huckleberry Finn,* by Mark Twain for racism.

In addition to questioning the materials used in curriculum, school districts also must deal with concerns about the content of curriculum. Community members, with strong commitments to having children learn content in such areas as art, music, the "basics," care for the environment, drug prevention education, sex education, and AIDS education, work to communicate their beliefs to teachers and schools so that this content can also be addressed in the curriculum.

Reflection Opportunity 7.6

Think about how you will react to parents and community members who try to influence school curricular. First, do you believe this is a task that they should be engaged in? How will you feel about parents and community members whose curricular views differ from your own? For example, consider a controversial issue such as birth control. Many people believe that all students should be aware of the variety of birth control options available to them, including abstinence. Others feel that abstinence is the best and only strategy that should be discussed in school settings. If you had a parent or community member whose beliefs on this topic were different from your own, how would you react? Would you be able to set aside your differences in other circumstances so that you could have effective parent–teacher conferences and positive interactions with this parent or community member?

What are current curriculum trends?

The significant shifts in curriculum described above combined with the opinions of parents and community members have led to constantly changing notions about what should be taught in America's schools. Despite these past swings, current curriculum planners at the national, state, and local levels seem to be drawing closer to agreement on the content that students should be encountering in the classroom. In this section, an overview of current trends for eight curriculum areas is given.

Language Arts and English

Certainly one of the most basic and important skills that all students must have in order to be productive members of society is the development of strong expertise in reading and writing. And although the content for these basic skills may seem easy to define, there actually has been considerable controversy about what should be taught.

In reading, for example, a long-standing debate concerns the relative values of teaching phonics versus what is called a whole-language approach. For the last several decades, literacy experts have debated the relative merits of **phonics instruction** (teaching the relationships between sounds and sound combinations to their written counterparts) and **whole-language learning** (helping children construct reading and writing understandings from meaningful literacy activities). More recently, many researchers and writers have begun to suggest that reading instruction must integrate both phonics and the whole-language approach to be successful. No one approach has proven successful with all students (International Reading Association, 2008).

Similarly, the writing curriculum has changed to a more integrated approach. The traditional emphasis on teaching grammar and spelling has been combined with a more natural emphasis on meaningful writing experiences to create a stronger overall curriculum for students at all grade levels. An example of a popular approach to teaching writing that follows this more integrated approach is the **six-trait writing process** (Spandel, 2009) outlined in Table 7.7. By identifying six qualities or characteristics of successful writers and helping students develop proficiency in using them as they engage in meaningful writing experiences, better writing from more motivated students is obtained.

In addition to reading and writing, curriculum in the language arts also includes listening, speaking, and viewing. Due to television, advertising, the Internet and other popular media influences, visual literacy is getting more attention from many educators (Burmark, 2002). Students in today's world need to know how to process both words and pictures. Many people assume that American children are already visually literate because they spend many hours each day watching TV, surfing the net, and playing video games. Tad Simons (Burmark, 2002) challenges us to rethink this notion:

> Just as one does not learn to write by reading, or learn to play the guitar by listening to the radio, one does not become visually literate by simply looking at images. Visual literacy is a learned skill, not an intuitive one. (p. 5)

TABLE 7.7 The Six-Trait Writing Process

Trait	Description
Ideas	Quality writing begins with a clear point, a theme, or story line that is backed up with good details.
Organization	The structure and order of the writing is important.
Voice	The writer's personal style combined with concern for the needs and interests of the audience helps create good writing.
Word Choice	Carefully chosen words and phrases make for more interesting reading.
Sentence Fluency	How sentences sound and "fit together" when read aloud is important.
Conventions	The importance of such things as spelling, grammar, capitalization, and punctuation are emphasized.

Adapted from: Northwest Regional Education Laboratory. (1998). *Dear Parent: A Handbook for Parents of 6-Trait Writing Students*. Portland, OR: Author.

When students learn about visual literacy, they become more effective communicators. It is important that students learn to express ideas clearly and quickly and often the best way to do this is through an image. Communication has moved from using images as a decorative element to an integral part of the message.

Mathematics

Historically, the K–12 mathematics curriculum consisted of two main components. First, students were expected to memorize facts related to the mathematical content being learned. In elementary schools, for example, addition, subtraction, multiplication, and division facts were memorized. Second, students were taught the computational skills they would need to solve mathematical problems. So, at the secondary level, learning the procedures involved in solving quadratic equations was a typical task.

Although these facts and procedures are needed and should be taught, they are not enough for students to truly understand mathematics. They fail to help students understand the structure and broad concepts that are essential to the discipline. Beginning in the 1960s with Bruner's (1960) inquiry-based approach to the curriculum, more effort has been made to help students understand the structure of the discipline. The National Council of Teachers of Mathematics (2008) makes it clear that the "basics" in mathematics education today, while including the learning of computation facts and procedures, should also include applications of computation to real life, an understanding of what computation means, a deeper knowledge of computational procedures, skills in communicating mathematically, and mathematical topics that prepare students for success in the 21st century. Oliver Wendell Holmes (Burke, 1999) introduced us to the idea of three-story intellects:

There are one-story intellects, two-story intellects, and three-story intellects with skylights. All fact collectors who have no aim beyond their facts are one-story men. Two-story men compare, reason, generalize, using the labors of fact collectors as well as their own. Three-story men idealize, imagine, predict—their best illumination comes from above, through the skylight.

Many educators use this idea, as adapted by Bellanca and Fogarty (1991) and aim to have students use all three levels of their mathematical thinking:

- *Level One:* Students count, describe, match, and name.
- *Level Two:* Students compare, sort, solve, and explain.
- *Level Three:* Students predict, estimate, evaluate, and apply principles.

One of the primary ways that teachers are encouraging students to move to the third level of their mathematical thinking is by encouraging students to reason with numbers in their own way. The traditional method of teaching students algorithms for arithmetic operations is being rethought by many educators (Parker, 2004). An **algorithm** is a set of rules for solving a particular kind of problem. Most of us were taught that there is one right algorithm for solving each type of computation problem. Yet many other countries use different algorithms than those we use in the United States. In today's schools, instead of focusing on memorizing the standard algorithm most of us learned in school, many students are being asked to invent and/or try diverse procedures. They are encouraged to make sense of what they are doing and to explain their reasoning. A big concern with teaching algorithms prematurely is that students do not understand when they have a wrong answer; they have no way of determining the reasonableness of their answer.

Teaching mathematics today may be very different from the ways in which you were taught. To view a virtual room tour and an interview with a current middle school mathematics teacher, go to the Companion Website for this text and click on MyEducationLab for Chapter 7.

MyEducationLab 7.2

Science

The elementary science curriculum has typically focused on helping children understand the world around them. The natural world of plants and animals is often addressed first, followed by the study of such things as electricity, simple machines, and magnetism. Middle school science tends to address these same topics in greater depth and is followed by a high school curriculum that typically includes multiterm courses in general science, biology, chemistry, and physics. What do you remember studying in your own P–12 science classes? Were they positive learning experiences?

Trends in the science curriculum parallel those described above for mathematics. Science educators, criticized for their emphasis on the learning of facts and isolating science from other disciplines and the real world, have begun to make changes in the curriculum to include more emphasis on understanding science concepts in the context of meaningful learning experiences. The American Association for the Advancement of Science has created Project 2061 (the expected year of return for Halley's comet) to identify the common knowledge that all K–12 students must possess in order to understand the nature of science. This project is credited with increasing science literacy within the United States (Koppal & Caldwell, 2004).

Social Studies

The social studies curriculum includes a broad variety of disciplines whose main purpose is to understand people and their interactions with one another. Although history is often viewed as a cornerstone of the social studies curriculum, geography, political science, sociology, psychology, economics, and anthropology are also important elements. Portions of the content of each of these disciplines can be effectively taught at all levels within the K–12 educational system.

An issue that is having significant impact on current directions in social studies education is the inclusion of diverse perspectives in the content being addressed. In history courses, for example, educators are working hard to make sure that a variety of cultural perspectives are included when discussing historical events. When addressing early colonial times in America, for example, it is appropriate to go beyond the perspectives of the European people who immigrated to this country and include discussions about the attitudes and feelings of the Native American people and the African men, women, and children who were brought to America as slaves. Rather than approaching history using a strictly **eurocentric curriculum,** educators are adding insights from the diverse peoples around the world who have had a major influence on American society.

Another issue that is having a significant impact on the social studies curriculum is the extent to which values should be taught in relation to the topics being addressed. Although there are mixed opinions on **character education** in the schools, it is gaining in popularity in many areas. The *Explore Your Beliefs* feature for this chapter takes a more in-depth look at this component of the social studies curriculum. Read this information now and assess your beliefs about character education.

Explore your beliefs: Character education

According to a report by the Josephson Institute (2008), cheating, stealing and lying by high school students remains at high levels. Following a benchmark survey in 1992, the Josephson Institute has conducted a national survey of the ethics of American youth every two years. The following summarizes the significant findings of the 2006 survey:

- In the last year, over one in four high school students admitted to having stolen something from a store.
- Sixty percent of the students reported having cheated on a test in the last year.
- One student in three admitted to having used the Internet to plagiarize an assignment during the past year.

Studies like these get educators, politicians and community members talking about the importance, relevance and appropriateness of character education. Over the years, two opposing views have emerged. One view, based largely on the theory and writings of Lawrence Kohlberg (1981), suggests that there are values common to all people and they should be directly taught to students in K–12 classrooms. Advocates for character education say that educators are shaping the character of their students, whether it is intentional or not. Character education is evident in the way teachers talk, the attitudes they model, the behaviors they tolerate, the deeds they encourage, and the expectations they have of their students. Proponents for character education argue that the question is really whether schools choose to teach character education by design or by default.

A second perspective, influenced by the writing of Simon, Howe, and Kirschenbaum (1972) in the book *Values Clarification* (1972) strongly discourages the teaching of specific values in school settings. This point of view sees the development of values as a personal decision in which teachers and the schools must remain neutral. Many people who argue against character education worry that it may be used as a vehicle to introduce religious values into the public schools.

Despite many vocal opponents, character education is becoming the norm in schools across the country. Lawmakers in many states have passed laws to require that their schools incorporate some form of character education into their curriculum. This trend is expected to continue.

Developing the Habit of Reflective Practice
Gather Information

- Do an Internet search for "character education." Go to *http://www.urbanext.uiuc.edu/ schoolsOnline/charactered.html* to read more about this important topic.
- Think back on your own education. Was character education explicitly taught to you in your schooling experience?

Identify Beliefs

- Do you think character education (or its nonexistence) in your own education had an impact on your own character development?
- What role should schools have in influencing the moral development of their students?

Make Decisions

1. What core values do you think would be appropriate for a character education program? What core values do you think should only be addressed by students' families?
2. Do you think states should mandate character education be in the public schools? Why or why not? Who should make this decision?

Assess and Evaluate

1. Think of a teacher you had that seemed to encourage particular values within his/her classroom. What impact did this have on your learning?

Resources

Josephson Institute. (2008). The ethics of American youth: 2006. Retrieved December 12, 2008 from *http://charactercounts.org/programs/reportcard/2006/index.html*

Simon, S., Howe, L., & Kirschenbaum, H. (1972). *Values clarification. A handbook of practical strategies for teachers and students.* New York: Hart Publishing Co.

Many educators are using service learning to help their students apply their social studies learning in a real-world context. **Service learning** provides students an opportunity to perform community service work that compliments their classroom activities (Billig, 2000). There are three levels of service learning, each of which comes with its own challenges and benefits:

- *Direct-Service Learning:* Students have personal contact with those receiving services.
- *Indirect-Service Learning:* Students channel resources to those who are in need.
- *Advocacy as Service Learning:* Students lend their voices and talents to advocate for those who are in need.

The Arts

The arts are generally thought of as including art, music, dance, and theatre. Although there are exceptions, most P–12 schools have demonstrated a low level of commitment to a strong arts curriculum. In most elementary schools, for example, the regular classroom teacher is expected to teach most of the arts curriculum, with help from either volunteers or specialists who travel between schools offering limited additional instruction. At the middle school and high school levels, students have more access to specialists who teach a variety of courses in art, music, drama, and dance. Unfortunately, most of these courses are considered electives by the schools and students take fewer of them or none at all.

Often considered frills during hard economic times, the arts have typically been the first components of the curriculum to be cut. In addition, when educators emphasize a back-to-the-basics curriculum, the arts are often overlooked. Finally, if you compare the number of faculty hired to teach the arts in P–12 classrooms with those engaged in mathematics, language arts, science, and social studies instruction, it is clear that as the schools work to meet state and national curriculum standards, they have placed most of their teaching resources in areas other than the arts.

Reflect on the importance of the arts in education. What experiences have you had in the arts and how do you think this influences your thoughts on their importance? What are the values of

Reflection Opportunity 7.7

the arts from your perspective? Should they have a higher importance than they currently do? If you were a school district administrator faced with certain budget cuts, how would you prioritize the different curriculum areas taught in the schools? What would you value the most? Where would you place the arts on your list of priorities? Would the arts be one of the first or last areas to be cut? Give a rationale for the position you take.

Physical Fitness and Health

The physical education curriculum in the P–12 schools has many components, all of which are growing in importance as Americans become increasingly more sedentary. Recent national statistics indicate that the percentage of overweight children has increased from approximately 4% in the 1960s to more than 15% currently (Ogden, Flegal, Carroll, & Johnson, 2002). Table 7.8 provides percentages of overweight children by race and age. These figures emphasize the crucial importance of exercise and fitness in the schools. The National Association for Sport and Physical Education (NASPE) recommends that students in elementary schools receive 150 minutes of physical education each week, and that secondary students need 220 minutes per week (Tonn, 2005). Unfortunately, only about 8% of elementary schools and 7% of secondary schools provide this level of participation. In addition to exercise and fitness, the physical education curriculum includes physical skills development, health, recreation, and dance. Organized sports and recreation programs are also offered by schools as extracurricular activities. At the elementary school level, specialists in physical education work with individual classes of students once or twice each week for approximately 30 minutes each session on aspects of this broad curriculum. Classroom teachers are then expected to supplement this instruction with additional content in physical education. Physical education specialists teach the entire curriculum at the middle school and high school levels. Most secondary schools offer both elective and required courses in physical education. As with the arts curriculum, physical education courses tend to have a lower priority in most school districts. This comes at the same time that the reauthorized *Child Nutrition Act of 2004* states that by 2006–2007, school districts must have student wellness plans in place (Richardson, 2006). These wellness plans must include a physical education component. With these thoughts in mind, should school districts be committing more resources to the physical education curriculum?

Vocational-Technical Education

Historically, vocational–technical education has emphasized the preparation of students for entry-level work in jobs that required less than a 4-year college degree. The back-to-the-basics reform movement and the growing complexity of most entry-level occupations have led to more comprehensive vocational–technical preparation programs. Students now take a balanced curriculum that includes a combination of academic, vocational, and technical

TABLE 7.8 Overweight Children

Age Range	All	White	Black	Hispanic
2–5	10.4%	10.1%	8.4%	11.1%
6–11	15.3%	11.8%	19.5%	23.7%
12–19	15.5%	12.7%	23.6%	23.4%

Source: Ogden, C., Flegal, K., Carroll, M., & Johnson, C. (2002). Prevalence and trends in overweight among U.S. children and adolescents, 1999–2000. *Journal of the American Medical Association, 288*(14), 1728–1730.

course work (National Center for Education Statistics, 2003). In addition, more students who complete high school vocational–technical programs go on to complete postsecondary programs as well.

At the same time that more students are completing vocational–technical courses, the financial support for these programs is in jeopardy. For example, former President Bush proposed that the entire $1.3 billion federal funding be eliminated from the 2006 budget (Cavanagh, 2005). Although federal support is a relatively small portion of the total funding for vocational–technical education, it is a signal of the relative value placed on these programs. Vocational–technical education finds itself in the difficult position of defending its worth and competing with other important programs for funding at the local, state, and national levels. Have you taken any vocational–technical education courses? What value would you place on any courses you completed?

Foreign Languages

Although students in America's schools are increasingly involved in foreign-language learning, they lag far behind their peers from around the world who frequently engage in learning additional languages from the beginning of their schooling experiences. The push to increase academic standards for graduation from high school has increased the number of courses in foreign-language study that students take (National Center for Education Statistics, 2008). In 1982 students averaged 1.1 years of foreign language study. This average increased to 2 full years in 2004. Still, American students are involved in far less foreign language study than students in other countries. Most European countries, for example, require students to learn both their native language(s) and English at a high level of proficiency.

As the world becomes increasingly more interconnected, the need to have American students trained in foreign languages will continue to grow. Many educators and others are strongly suggesting that we begin foreign-language learning in the elementary grades so that students can have opportunities to develop deeper understandings of one or more other languages. Cutshall (2005) states the case this way:

> Beginning language learning at an early age is crucial to increasing our language capabilities.
> A primary difference between the United States and nations that boast greater language
> strengths is the latter countries' emphasis on learning languages at younger ages. (p. 22).

It appears clear from this and other sources, that while American foreign-language learning has progressed over the last several decades, we have much work to be done before the United States can become competitive with other nations around the world. With the growing globalization of business and the many benefits of second-language learning (Cutshall, 2005), this is an important direction to take.

Consider This: Your Own Academic Preparation

As you complete your reading of this chapter, stop and review the *Consider This* feature found on the Companion Website for this text. It is asking you to think about your own academic preparation and to critique both the subject areas in which you feel competent and those that are weaker. How many of your successes and problems can be attributed to your own motivation (or lack thereof)? Conversely, how much do you think your teachers and schools influenced your academic performance and abilities?

Summary

In this chapter, four organizing questions were presented to help you develop a better under-standing of developing curriculum:

What influences curriculum development?

Curriculum takes a variety of forms and is influenced by a number of different groups:
- Curriculum defined
- Approaches to the curriculum
- National, state, and district influences (Praxis II, topic IIb)
- Your role as a teacher in curriculum development (Praxis II, topic IIb)

How has curriculum changed over time?

Throughout American history, the curriculum has continued to change based on various social influences:
- Progressive education
- Sputnik and curricular excellence (Praxis II, topic IIIa)
- The inquiry-based curriculum
- Questioning curriculum options
- Back-to-the-basics movement
- Concept-based curriculum

What factors influence curriculum decisions?

Four factors have a significant influence on curriculum decisions:
- Textbook selection (Praxis II, topic IIa)
- Technology in the classroom (Praxis II, topic IIa)
- Diversity issues (Praxis II, topic Ib)
- Parent and community influences (Praxis II, topic IVb)

What are current curriculum trends?

All of the factors identified above have influenced the current status of curriculum:
- Language arts and English (Praxis II, topics Ib, Id, Ie)
- Mathematics (Praxis II, topic IIb)
- Science (Praxis II, topic IIb)
- Social studies (Praxis II, topic IIb)
- The arts (Praxis II, topic IIb)
- Physical fitness and health (Praxis II, topic IIb)
- Vocational–technical education (Praxis II, topic IIb)
- Foreign languages (Praxis II, topic IIb)

PRAXIS Test-Preparation Activities

To review an on-line chapter case study, test your understanding of chapter topics and concepts, and begin preparing for the Praxis II: Principles of Learning and Teaching examination, go to the Praxis Test Preparation module for this chapter of the Companion Website.

Developing the Habit of Reflective Practice

Organizing Questions

Review questions, field-experience opportunities, and activities for building your portfolio are included here for the organizing questions in this chapter.

What influences curriculum development?

Review Questions

1. How important are the informal, hidden, and null curricula when compared with the formal curriculum of the schools?
2. What are the differences between the subject-centered and student-centered curricula?
3. Describe the national, state, and district influences on the curriculum.

Field Experience

Spend some time talking to an administrator in a school of your choice. Seek information from this person about the informal curriculum.

- What options are available at that school?
- How many students participate in the various activities? Who serves as instructors for these programs?
- Which are paid positions and which are assignments for adult volunteers? Discuss what you found with others.

Building Your Portfolio: *State Curriculum Guidelines*

INTASC Standard 7. For the state in which you currently live, or the one where you plan to eventually teach, locate and study the state curriculum guidelines that have been developed for all students. In many instances, this information is available on state department of education Web sites.

- If possible, make a hard copy of these documents for inclusion in your portfolio.
- After reviewing the available materials, summarize their contents and include this information in your portfolio.

How has curriculum changed over time?

Review Questions

1. How did the subject-centered and student-centered approaches to curriculum development influence curriculum reform in the 20th century?
2. What is the inquiry-based curriculum?
3. How did the social and political unrest of the 1960s and 1970s influence curriculum change?

Building Your Portfolio: *Curriculum Reform Effort*

INTASC Standard 1. Choose one of the five major curriculum reform efforts described in this chapter and research it in more depth.

- What were the forces that led to the reform?
- How was the proposed reform different from what already was happening in the schools?
- Are there aspects of this reform effort that are still evident today? Write up your findings for a portfolio entry.

What factors influence curriculum decisions?

Review Questions

1. In what ways do textbooks influence curricula in the schools?

2. How has an increased emphasis on diversity issues impacted school curricula?

Field Experience

Review the textbook(s) used in a classroom of your choice. Critique the content being presented.

- What is included and what has been omitted?
- Also analyze the directions provided for teachers to help them present this content to students.
- Are there specific directions or more general guidelines for teachers to consider?
- Look at things like pictures, boxed features, and special interest-getting tools used to help motivate students to read and use the text. Share your findings with others.

Building Your Portfolio: *Parent and Community Influences on Curriculum*

INTASC Standard 10. Attend a school board meeting with the purpose of observing how parents and community members influence the curriculum of the schools. You may also want to talk to a school board member, principal, or district administrator to find out additional information.

- Describe the meeting you attended. What was discussed and who participated in that discussion?
- From your observations and discussions, what impact do parents and community members have on the curriculum? Give specific examples where possible.

What are current curriculum trends?

Review Questions

1. Describe the current debate over literacy learning in America's schools.

2. What have been the major criticisms of mathematics and science instruction during the last several decades?

3. What disciplines are associated with social studies?

Building Your Portfolio: *Subject-Area Curricular Trend*

INTASC Standard 1. Choose one of the curriculum areas discussed in this chapter and spend some time studying in more detail the emerging trends for this discipline. You may wish to locate one of the appropriate national curriculum organizations (such as the National Council of Teachers of Mathematics) and review information on this organization's Website to obtain the needed information.

- Describe the emerging trends you found for the discipline you studied.
- For the grade level of your choice, summarize the implications of these curriculum trends for your portfolio.

Suggested Readings

Bennett, W. (1987). *James Madison High School: A curriculum for American students*. Washington, DC: U.S. Department of Education. Bennett argues for a stronger emphasis on the basics in American high schools and proposes a core curriculum that all students should complete.

Bruner, J. (1960). *The process of education*. New York: Random House. In this classic book, Bruner identifies the inquiry-based curriculum and presents a rationale for this approach to curriculum planning.

Neill, A. (1960). *Summerhill: A radical approach to child rearing.* New York: Hart Publishing Company. As the title implies, this book documents a radical approach to schooling. It is one in which the students themselves define the curriculum.

Silberman, C. (1970). *Crisis in the classroom.* New York: Random House. Silberman is often considered a spokesperson for those who were dissatisfied during the 1970s and 1980s with the unimaginative and lackluster curriculum of the schools. He outlines the perceived problems and presents suggestions for improvement.

References

American Library Association. (2008). The 10 most challenged books of 2007. Retrieved December 10, 2008 from: *http://www.ala.org/ala/oif/newspresscenter/news/pressreleases2008/penguin.cfm*

Bellanca, J. A., & Fogarty, R. (1991). Blueprints for thinking in the cooperative classroom. Palatine, IL: Skylight.

Bennett, W. (1987). *James Madison High School: A curriculum for American students.* Washington, DC: U.S. Department of Education.

Billig, S.H. (2000). Research on K–12 school based service learning: the evidence builds. *Phi Delta Kappan, 81,* 658–664.

Boyer, E. (1983). *High school: A report on secondary education in America.* New York: Harper.

Boyer, E. (1995). *The basic school: A community for learning.* Princeton, NJ: Carnegie Foundation for the Advancement of Teaching.

Bruner, J. (1960). *The process of education.* New York: Random House.

Burke, K. (1999). *How to assess authentic learning.* Arlington Heights, IL: Skylight Professional Development.

Burmark, L. (2002). *Visual literacy: learn to see, see to learn.* Alexandria, VA: ASCD.

California Department of Education. (2008). *Reading/language arts/ELD publishers list.* Retrieved December 10, 2008 from: *http://www.cde.ca.gov/ci/cr/cf/rla2002pub.asp*

Cavanagh, S. (2005, February 23). Vocational education's new job: Defend thyself. *Education Week,* p. 1, 18.

Center on Education Policy (2005). *From the capital to the classroom: Year 3 of the No Child Left Behind Act.* Washington, DC: Author.

Cutshall, S. (2005). Why we need "the year of languages." *Educational Leadership, 62*(4), 20–23.

Dewey, J. (1929). *Democracy and education.* New York: Macmillan.

Drake, S., & Burns, R. (2004). *Meeting standards through integrated curriculum.* Alexandria, VA: Association for Supervision and Curriculum Development.

Education Week. (2004). *Technology counts 2004.* Washington, DC: Author.

Education Week. (2005, March 16). Is NCLB making history of social studies? Retrieved October 22, 2005 from: *http://www.edweek.org/tb/2005/03/15/111.html*

Eide, P. (2001, January). Coping with change: Educational reform in literacy practice. *Primary Voices K–6, 9*(3), 15–20.

Eisner, E. (2002). *The educational imagination: On the design and evaluation of school programs* (3rd ed.). Upper Saddle River, NJ: Merrill/Prentice Hall.

Erickson, L. (2002). *Concept-based curriculum and instruction: Teaching beyond the facts.* Thousand Oaks, CA: Corwin Press.

Ginott, H. (1972). Teacher and child. New York: McMillan.

Holt, J. (1964). *How children fail.* New York: Dell.

International Reading Association. (2008). *Making a difference means making it different: Honoring children's rights to excellent reading instruction.* Retrieved December 10, 2008 from: *http://www.reading.org/resources/issues/positions_rights.html*

International Technology Education Association. (2005). *Standards for technological literacy.* Retrieved December 10, 2008 from: *http://www.iteaconnect.org/TAA/PDFs/xstnd.pdf*

Jones, R. (December, 2000). Textbook troubles. American School Board. National School Boards Association. Retrieved October 21, 2005 from: *www.asbj.com/2000/12/1200coverstory.html*

Kellner, D. (2005). The changing classroom: Challenges for teachers. *Technological Horizons in Education.* Retrieved March 2005 from: *http://www.thejournal.com/magazine/vault/A5261.cfm*

Kohl, H. (1969). *The open classroom.* New York: Random House.

Koppal, M., & Caldwell, A. (2004). Meeting the challenge of science literacy: Project 2061 efforts to improve science education. *Cell Biology Education.* Retrieved March 17, 2005 from: *http://www.project2061.org/publications/articles/articles/cellbioed.htm*

Levy, S. (1996). *Starting from scratch: One classroom builds its own curriculum.* Portsmouth, NH: Heinemann.

Music Educators National Conference. (2008). *Performance standards for music: Grades pre-K–12.* Retrieved December 10, 2008 from: *http://www.menc.org/resources/view/performance_standards_for_music_preface*

National Center for Education Statistics. (2003). Public high school students who participated in vocational/technical education. Retrieved December 10, 2008 from: *http://nces.ed.gov/pubsearch/pubsinfo.asp?pubid = 2003024*

National Center for Education Statistics. (2008). *Special analysis 2007. High school coursetaking.* Retrieved December 10, 2008 from *http://nces.ed.gov/programs/coe/2007/analysis/sa02a.asp.*

National Council for the Social Studies. (2008). *Expectations of excellence: Curriculum standards for social studies.* Retrieved December 10, 2008 from: *http://www.socialstudies.org/standards*

National Council of Teachers of Mathematics. (2008). *Principles and standards for school mathematics.* Retrieved December 10, 2005 from: *http://standards.nctm.org/*

National Science Foundation. (2005). *Weaving gender equity into math reform.* Retrieved March 17, 2005 from: *http://www.terc.edu/wge/home.html*

Nebraska Department of Education. (2008). *Nebraska reading/writing standards.* Retrieved December 17, 2008 from: *http://www.nde.state.ne.us/ndestandards/documents/ReadingWriting Standards_000.pdf*

Ogden, C., Flegal, K., Carroll, M., & Johnson, C. (2002). Prevalence and trends in overweight among U.S. children and adolescents, 1999–2000. *Journal of the American Medical Association, 288*(14), 1728–1732.

Papert, S. (1980). *Mindstorms: Children, computers, and powerful ideas.* New York: Basic Books.

Papert, S. (1993). *The children's machine: Rethinking school in the age of the computer.* New York: Basic Books.

Parkay, F., Anctil, E., & Haas, G. (2006). *Curriculum planning: A contemporary approach* (8th ed.). Boston: Allyn and Bacon.

Parker, R. (2004). Thinking about algorithms and procedures. Retrieved October 26, 2005 from: *http://www.mec-math.org/public/rutharticle1.pdf*

Postman, N., & Weingartner, C. (1969). *Teaching as a subversive activity.* New York: Delacorte Press.

Rickover, H. (1959). *Education and freedom.* New York: E. P. Dutton.

Rickover, H. (1983, February 3). Educating for excellence. *Houston Chronicle,* p. 8.

Riddle Buly, M., & Rose, R. R. (2001, January). Mandates, expectations and change. *Primary Voices K–6, 9*(3), 3–6.

Richardson, J. (2006). *Child nutrition and WIC legistation in the 108th and 109th Congresses.* Washington, DC: Congressional Research Service.

Ritchhart, R., Moran, S., Blythe, T., & Reese, J. (2002). *Teaching in the creative classroom: An educator's guide for exploring creative teaching and learning.* Burbank: Disney Learning Partnership & Project Zero, the Harvard Graduate School of Education.

Silberman, C. (1970). *Crisis in the classroom.* New York: Random House.

Spandel, V. (2009). *Creating writers through 6-trait writing assessment and instruction* (5th ed.). Boston: Allyn and Bacon.

Tonn, J. (2005, January 19). Federal dietary guidelines encourage physical activity. *Education Week,* p. 9.

Wiggins, G., & McTighe, J. (1998). *Understanding by design* (1st ed.). Alexandria, VA: Association for Supervision and Curriculum Development.

Wiggins, G., & McTighe, J. (2005). *Understanding by design* (2nd ed.). Alexandria, VA: Association for Supervision and Curriculum Development.

Wiggins, G., & McTighe, J. (2000). *Understanding by design study guide.* Alexandria, VA: Association for Supervision and Curriculum Development.

Wimberly, G. L. (2002). School relationships foster success for African American students: ACT policy report. Iowa City: ACT.

Youniss, J., & Yates, M. (1997). Community service and social responsibility in youth. Chicago: The University of Chicago Press.

chapter 8

Using Effective Teaching Strategies

Excellent teachers have a variety of different styles and use an array of strategies to motivate students to learn. Despite the many differences, however, good teaching has a common core that all effective teachers know and use. In this chapter, four organizing questions will help you better understand both the similarities and differences that exist among teachers.

Focus Questions

▪ Why are strong relationships with students and other adults important?

▪ What does research tell us about effective instructional strategies?

▪ What instructional models can I use?

▪ What skills will I need in management and discipline?

Courtesy of Anthony Magnacca/Merrill Education.

"The rewards I find in teaching are rooted in the joy of not only watching but also being part of my students' learning and development" (stated Michele Forman, the National Teacher of the Year for 2001). "A good teacher needs not only a good understanding of what he or she teaches, but also a sense of excitement in learning and a clear vision of how the key elements of a subject can be conveyed to students."

With this philosophy Forman emphasizes an incredibly strong teacher and learner relationship. "Without mutual trust, students are wary of accepting the risk and vulnerability of learning," she said. "For them, the threat of feeling or appearing inept or incompetent is best overcome with the support of a teacher in a caring, accepting and respectful relationship."

Among Forman's many beliefs about education, she is especially passionate about classes that include students with varied backgrounds and ability levels. "Education is enriched for all students when learners bring their different experiences, perspectives and skills to the group," she said (Council of Chief State School Officers, 2005).

Michele Forman, who teaches social studies at Middlebury Union High School in Middlebury, Vermont, has been honored as an outstanding educator by being named the National Teacher of the Year for 2001 by the Council of Chief State School Officers. But what makes her such an excellent teacher? After rereading the opening scenario, see if you can uncover some of the characteristics that have made Michele such a fine teacher. What does she believe about teacher–student relationships? How important is content knowledge to effective teaching from her perspective? What are the challenges that Michele defines in her work? Are you energized and excited about addressing the challenges she presents?

Although Michele Forman is a unique individual with a teaching style that is hers alone, she shares many elements in common with other outstanding educators. This chapter is designed to build on Ms. Forman's insights regarding the elements of effective teaching and help provide you with a better understanding of both the similarities and differences that exist between all good teachers. Please realize, however, that the information presented here is only a brief overview of these important topics. You will need to learn a great deal more before you truly understand the complex task of teaching.

Why are strong relationships with students and other adults important?

Teaching can be successful only when several key ingredients are present. Many would suggest that the most fundamental of these is the ability to establish and maintain effective working relationships with students and other adults. It is the humanity of the teacher, the ability to be real and make connections with students and others that often determines whether or not learning takes place in the classroom. In his classic book, Greenberg (1969) states it this way: "The human, emotional qualities of the teacher are the very heart of teaching. No matter how much emphasis is placed on such other qualities in teaching as educational technique, technology, equipment, or buildings, *the humanity of the teacher is the vital ingredient if children are to learn*" (p. 20).

Developing Positive Relationships with Students

Consider writing down your thoughts about positive relationships with students. Think back to your K–12 schooling experiences. Do you remember a teacher who was well loved by her or his students? What was it that this teacher did to attract students to him or her? Can you remember aspects of this teacher's personality that were attractive to you? How did she or he interact with students? Try to remember some specific things this teacher did that made it enjoyable to be nearby. Most people have fond memories of one or more teachers that fit this category. These remarkable educators always seem to have time to spend listening and responding to both the joys and sorrows of their students' lives while approaching teaching and learning with an enthusiasm that is infectious. The strong relationships these teachers develop are at the heart of good teaching.

One writer who emphasized the importance of effective teacher–student relationships is Thomas Gordon (1974). He has identified several characteristics of successful interactions between teachers and students:

> The relationship between a teacher and a student is good when it has (1) *Openness or Transparency*, so each is able to risk directness and honesty with the other; (2) *Caring*, when each knows that he is valued by the other; (3) *Interdependence* (as opposed to dependency) of one on the other; (4) *Separateness*, to allow each to grow and to develop his uniqueness, creativity, and individuality; (5) *Mutual Needs Meeting*, so that neither's needs are met at the expense of the other's needs. (p. 24)

Nel Noddings (1992) is another educator who, more recently, has emphasized the importance of caring in relationships with students. She identified four components to this caring process. The first component she calls *modeling*. Teachers' interactions with students provide examples of the caring relationships students should have with each other and with adults. Secondly, teachers and students need to engage in *dialogues* that are open-ended discussions with no predetermined outcome. Caring relationships also require *practice*. Students need opportunities to practice caring in their relationships with others. Community-service projects are one example of this type. The final component of caring relationships is *confirmation*. Teachers need to find ways to validate student progress in developing caring relationships.

Teachers build strong relationships with students in one of two main ways. First, they take the time and effort needed to have authentic, meaningful interactions with students. When teachers engage in the simple act of greeting students warmly as they arrive at the classroom door, they are engaged in this process of relationship building. A second option for strengthening teacher–student relationships is to engage students in planned activities that can systematically provide for more positive interactions. Table 8.1 outlines several simple activities that can help build these relationships. By actually including these activities during the school day or after hours, teachers can become more purposeful in building relationships with students. This is particularly important for those students who are quiet and unassuming or for those who are more difficult for the teacher to like.

Although building relationships with students may sound like a relatively simple and straightforward task, there are many situations in which this is not the case. For example, building relationships with English language learners may be more difficult than first anticipated.

TABLE 8.1   Planned Activities for Building Relationships

Activity	Description
Eating Lunch with Students	Particularly at the elementary level, teachers can schedule times to visit informally with individual students over lunch.
Arranging Interviews	Students interview teachers to learn more about them as individuals.
Sending Letters and Notes to Students	Letters of introduction and positive notes to individual students help build relationships.
Using a Suggestion Box	Teachers can show their interest in student ideas by having a suggestion box where students can anonymously share their thoughts.
Participating in School and Community Events	Events such as carnivals, musical and dramatic productions, sporting events, and debates are opportunities for teachers to relate to students outside the classroom.
Getting Involved in Playground Time	At the elementary level, teachers can spend some enjoyable time with students on the playground
Sending Birthday Cards	Knowing student birthdays and sending a card is a good way to build relationships

Source: From Jones, V., & Jones, L. (2007). *Comprehensive classroom management: Creating communities of support and solving problems* (8th ed.) Boston: Allyn and Bacon.

The *Reflect on Diversity* feature for this chapter tells a story about a young English language learner and his teacher's interactions with him. This surprising but true story challenges us all to make the effort to build effective relationships with students. Read this story respond to the reflection questions posed.

Reflect on diversity: His name is Michael

He appeared at my classroom door in the middle of a busy morning gripping the hand of a harried school secretary. He was a tiny child with carefully combed hair, wearing a crisply pressed shirt, tightly clutching his lunch money. The secretary handed this child to me and rattled off the institutional essentials: "His name is Michael. He is a bus rider. He doesn't speak English." Not much of an introduction, but that's how it happens in schools . . .

We did all the usual new-kid things that day. We played the name game. The kid of the day gave him the grand tour of our room. He got to sit on the couch even though it wasn't really his turn. The children insisted that Michael have a buddy for absolutely everything—learning buddy, recess buddy, bathroom buddy, lunch buddy, cubby buddy, line buddy, water buddy, rug buddy, bus buddy . . .

Michael existed marginally on the outside of the group. Sometimes he was on the outside looking in; sometimes he was on the outside looking out. I often saw him with his eyes closed—looking somewhere hidden. He was well-mannered, punctual, respectful, cute-as-a-button—but completely detached from me, from the children, and from the learning.

I met with the bilingual resource teacher to chat about concerns and possibilities. She told me she could come do an informal observation "a week from tomorrow." It was a long wait, but that's how it is in schools. She came. She watched. She listened. On her way out she said, "You might have better results, dear, if you call him Miguel."

Miguel didn't stay with us for long. His family moved on to follow their own calendar of opportunities. We didn't get to say goodbye, but that's how it happens in schools.

Miguel's paperwork arrived about three weeks after he had moved away. I was going through the folder, updating it for his next teacher, when I noticed something that made me catch my breath. His name wasn't Michael. It wasn't Miguel. His name was David.

Reprinted from "His Name is Michael," by Donna Marriott, *Education Week,* October 9, 2002.

Developing the Habit of Reflective Practice

Gather Information

1. Search the Internet for additional information on "working with English Language Learners."

2. Think back on your own education. How were the needs of English Language Learners met?

Identify Beliefs

1. What adjustments in teaching should be made for learners who do not speak English as their first language?

2. Is it important to have people in the schools who can communicate with students like "Michael" in their native language? Why or why not?

Make Decisions

1. Identify two or three ways in which the teacher could have verified "Michael's" name.

2. What actions could the teacher have used to make David's transition into the classroom more successful?

Assess and Evaluate

1. If you were visiting a school to assess and evaluate how the faculty and staff is working with English Language Learners, what evidence would you look for to determine their effectiveness?

2. Why do you think some students are "lost in the shuffle"? How can you as a teacher keep this from happening?

Source

Marriott, D. (2002). His name is Michael. *Education Week,* October 9, 2002.

Gary Rubenstein (1999), a nationally recognized high school educator, states that if teachers really want to understand their students, they need to see each student as an individual. Although it can be helpful for a teacher to read about a culture (e.g., Hispanic, Vietnamese), he reminds educators that the learning should not stop there:

> That's why I talk to students every day before, during and after class. When students are doing some activities at the beginning of class, I check roll by calling each student's name and saying something to each one ("How's your brother?" Or "Nice game yesterday.") The more I learn about a student, the better teacher I become. (p. 137)

In a book entitled *Learning to Trust: Transforming Difficult Elementary Classrooms Through Developmental Discipline* (2003), educator and author Marilyn Watson shares how elementary teacher, Laura Ecken, develops collaborative, trusting relationships with even her most challenging students. At the beginning of the school year, Laura incorporates a wide array of activities that help her connect with her students including charts, graphs, and Venn diagrams describing their characteristics. They also draw self-portraits and make a quilt displaying important facts about everyone in their class. As the school year progresses, her get-to-know-you activities become more academic in nature. For example, when students share their favorite part of a story or the most interesting fact they learned in a research project, she still is getting to know her students better.

Working With Parents

Linnea Wilson, who teaches middle school language arts, is preparing for parent–teacher conferences in 2 weeks. She has sent home information with her students about the content and format of these meetings and made personal telephone calls to the parents she particularly wants to see. In addition, she has created a survey for parents so that they can share questions, concerns, and praises prior to the conference. The surveys help Linnea prepare for each family's unique needs and concerns. Next week she will prepare an agenda for each of the scheduled appointments so that the conference time can be as productive as possible. During the conference, Linnea makes sure that part of the time is spent actually looking at the child's work. She also remembers that just as parents can learn from her, she can learn from each of her student's parents. Linnea aims to encourage two-way communication rather than just talking to the parents. Linnea is in her fourth year of teaching and has found that parent conferences are an excellent format for gathering and sharing information about schooling with parents. Like Linnea, you will want to build strong working relationships with parents and families through the use of parent conferences and other involvement strategies.

There has been a growing emphasis in America's schools on the importance of establishing good working relationships with students' parents and guardians. A topic that was seldom mentioned 30 years ago, working with parents has become a significant research issue and an important component of many teacher-preparation programs (Berger, 2008). Teachers, parents, and children all benefit when positive communication and interaction take place between the home and school (Gestwicki, 2007). Teachers benefit from increased support in the classroom and at home. Parents develop a better understanding of their own children and strengthen their own parenting skills. In addition, good home–school relationships increase student performance and enhance student self-concept. Meeting and talking with students' parents or caregivers throughout the year can help educators understand their students' lives outside of school (Watson & Ecken, 2003). Watching how students interact with the most influential adults in their lives can help teachers understand their students' academic and social behaviors. For example, when teacher Judy Mulhair hears the interaction between her student, Dirk, and his father, she begins to understand why Dirk is so hesitant to take risks in the classroom. As Dirk shows his father a story he wrote in class, his father points out every grammatical and spelling error in the paper and fails to comment on the content of the story. Dirk's initial excitement over the story he wrote about his dad's new hunting dog was flattened because of his dad's reaction to the story. Judy uses this opportunity to model for Dirk's father a positive reaction to the story. She also plans to provide extra encouragement to Dirk in the classroom because of the interaction she observed between father and son.

In addition to the quality interactions you will have with parents during conferences, you will need to be aware of and use a variety of other communication strategies. Traditional options such as brief notes home, telephone calls, newsletters, and parent meetings (i.e., school-wide open house, classroom meeting for interested parents) are all effective ways for teachers to communicate with parents and families. More recently, teachers have been taking advantage of modern technologies to improve interactions between home and school. Table 8.2 suggests some ways in which technology can help facilitate communications with parents.

| TABLE 8.2   Using Technology to Communicate with Parents ||
Communication Tool	Description
Electronic Mail	For the growing number of parents who have computers and Internet access, sending a quick e-mail message is a very convenient and easy way to communicate with parents.
Video/Audiotapes	Many parents can't come visit the classroom as often as they would like, but would still like to see/hear what is going on there. Making a video/audio tape of classroom activities that can be then checked out by parents can help keep them involved.
Websites	Many schools and some teachers now have their own Websites that parents can access for a great deal of information about school/classroom activities. Technology options have made this a relatively easy option for schools and teachers to consider using.
Homework Hotline	Hardware and software is now available that allows individual teachers to record a daily message for parents and students regarding homework for the next day. Parents can call the school and find out what assignments are due and details regarding their completion.

Think about this aspect of your future teaching. How do you think you will feel about taking the time to communicate and interact with parents in positive ways? Do you think you will be comfortable in talking and working with them? Can you see some of the benefits of these interactions? Are there some parents you may be more comfortable with than others? What could you do to strengthen relationships with those parents who are harder to relate to?

**Reflection
Opportunity 8.3**

Other Collaborative Relationships

You might have assumed from past educational experiences that as a future teacher, you will generally operate independently as you plan for and teach your future students. That is, once the school day begins, you will be the primary person responsible for educating those under your care. Although there is considerable truth to this assumption, teaching is becoming an increasingly collaborative profession. For example, because of the needs of your students, you may find yourself working with the speech language pathologist (SLP) (formerly known as speech therapist), school counselor, school nurse, special education teacher, the English language learner (ELL) instructor, and others on a regular basis. The principal and vice principal are other school personnel who are actively involved in working with teachers to implement effective management and discipline procedures and assist in curriculum planning. You will want to collaborate with them as well. For example, Jorie Steele, a fifth-grade teacher, works in a school where collaboration among educators is the normal way of doing business. Each Friday, the school hires a substitute teacher to roam between classrooms throughout the day. This teacher arrives at Jorie's classroom at 11:00 in the morning to teach an art lesson that Jorie has prepared. Jorie gathers her assessment data and student work samples and reports to the special-education classroom, where the special-education teacher, English language learner teacher, and reading teacher are waiting. These educators have 30 minutes to sit and plan strategies for supporting Jorie's students in their learning for the next week. They talk about students' successes and problems during the current week and goals for the coming week. Once Jorie returns to her classroom, the substitute teacher moves on to the next classroom so that the teacher there can attend a collaborative work session with another set of colleagues. Once a month, the principal joins these work sessions and the meeting times expand to 40 minutes.

Rick Wormeli (2003) reminds educators that collaborating with colleagues can also be facilitated without meeting face to face. He suggests establishing a faculty portfolio of ideas by placing a box near the photocopying machine. The box can be filled with folders for each subject taught in the school. Then when staff members photocopy materials for use in their classes, they are encouraged to make one additional copy and place it in the appropriate folder in the box. By sharing copies of tests, projects, vocabulary lists, classroom policies, class newsletters, behavior contracts, graphic organizers, parent letters, field-trip forms, and articles, the isolation that teachers often experience can be dissipated.

A third type of collaborative relationship you will want to establish is with community members. When you, for example, take the time to share with a local businesswoman your rationale for using a new curriculum approach, you have created an ally who can assist you in telling others about the important work you are doing. In addition, some teachers even include community members in their curriculum. For example, Roxann Rose, one of the authors of this text and a former elementary school teacher, linked each of her students with a community member through a mentor pen pal program. Roxann collaborated with a local Rotary Club to create a list of professionals from the community who were willing to mentor her students by becoming their pen pals. The students chose a mentor by selecting from a list of interesting career options (e.g., veterinarian, architect, judge, author, bakery owner, dentist). Throughout the year, the student and Rotary Club volunteer communicated with each other. In addition to having authentic opportunities to refine their writing skills, students were challenged to think seriously about careers that many of them had never considered.

It should be clear from the above examples that you will need to establish good relationships with a variety of different colleagues, your students' families, and community members in order to be successful in your work as a teacher. As with any relationship, taking the time to build rapport, engaging in regular and effective communications, and respecting differences are all essential in each of these relationships.

What does research tell us about effective instructional strategies?

You may be surprised to learn that the area of systematic, scientific study of effective teaching strategies is only about 40 years old. In the early 1970s, researchers began to study the effects of different instructional skills on student learning. During the last three decades of the 20th century, research evidence slowly began to mount and a clear pattern has emerged regarding the strategies individual teachers use to positively influence student learning. The Mid-continent Research for Education and Learning (McREL) group completed a review of this research (Marzano, Pickering, & Pollock, 2001) and identified instructional techniques that have proven successful in boosting academic performance. These strategies are summarized in Table 8.3.

TABLE 8.3   Instructional Strategies Influencing Student Achievement

Category	Description
Identifying Similarities and Differences	Effective teachers help students identify similarities and differences. Researchers have found these mental operations to be basic to human thought.
Summarizing and Note Taking	Effective teachers explicitly teach students how to summarize the information being learned and strategies for effective note taking.
Reinforcing Effort	Good teachers help students understand the importance of effort and guide them in seeing its impact on individual performance.
Homework and Practice	The assignment of an appropriate amount of homework (increasing with age) and opportunities to practice new and developing skills are necessary for effective learning.
Nonlinguistic Representations	Good teachers help students generate mental pictures and provide graphic representations of the information being learned.
Goal Setting and Providing Feedback	Effective teachers establish a direction for learning and give students feedback about how well they are doing.
Generating and Testing Hypotheses	Good teachers help students apply knowledge by guiding them in generating and testing hypotheses.
Activating Prior Knowledge	Teachers need to help students remember and use what they already know through the use of cues or hints, effective questioning strategies, and advanced organizers.

From: Marzano, R., Pickering, D., & Pollock, J. (2001). *Classroom instruction that works: Research-based strategies for increasing student achievement.* Alexandria, VA: Association for Supervision and Curriculum Development.

Identifying Similarities and Differences

The ability to identify similarities and differences is a broad skill that enables students of all ages to engage in problem solving and information processing that is basic to all aspects of learning (Medin, Goldstone, & Markman, 1995). Take, for example, Mrs. Jackson's American history class (Marzano et al., 2001). As a part of their study of the 1960s, her students were reading and discussing Martin Luther King, Jr.'s "I Have a Dream" speech. Knowing that her students had been exposed to this speech several times in the past, Mrs. Jackson wanted to help her students understand it in a different way, so she presented them with an incomplete analogy:

"I Have a Dream" was to the Civil Rights Movement as _____ was to _____.
In small groups, students were to complete the analogy using another historical event or document in the first blank and a movement or event in the second blank. The students were asked to be ready to explain their completed analogy to the entire class.
To Mrs. Jackson's surprise, students were quite adept in designing and explaining their analogies. To the students' surprise, this activity deepened their understanding of the effect the "I Have a Dream" speech had on the Civil Rights Movement. (Marzano et al., 2001, p. 13)

Through the use of analogies, Mrs. Jackson enabled her students to engage in a complex process of identifying similarities and differences that helped them deepen their understanding of American history.

Summarizing and Note Taking

A second category of research-based strategies that effective teachers use is assisting students in summarizing what they have learned and engaging in effective note taking. To effectively summarize or take good notes, students must first decide what information is worth knowing and what should be omitted and then determine a method of organization. Teachers at all levels can help their students develop effective summarizing and note-taking strategies. You can assist in this process by providing an organizational framework to assist students in summarizing or by periodically providing your students with teacher-prepared notes. Contrary to what you might predict, summarizing and note taking can and should be taught to even very young children. Yeabsira Obed, a second-grade teacher, helps his students summarize stories by modeling a note-taking strategy as they read together. He writes down key events of each story on sticky notes. Then after completing the story, students help him organize the notes into the correct sequential order. Yeabsira makes sure that his students understand that quality story summaries include characters, setting, a problem and a solution.

Reinforcing Effort

Rather than attempting to directly build students' cognitive skills, reinforcing effort focuses on students' attitudes and beliefs (Marzano et al., 2001). Good teachers work to strengthen positive attitudes about effort by talking about its effects and helping students to see its impact. Teaching about effort can include such things as personal stories about times when perseverance paid off for you, having students share their own examples of effort and its impact on their lives, or reading and discussing stories that demonstrate the value of effort (e.g., *The Little Engine That Could* for primary children). By periodically providing students with scoring guides that help them rate their own effort and corresponding level of achievement, you can also help students see that their efforts do result in higher levels of achievement.

Traditionally, teachers have frequently reinforced student efforts through the use of praise. Saying "good job" and its many derivatives is common practice for educators who want to reinforce the good work that is occurring in their classrooms. Some researchers and writers suggest, however, that saying "good job" has unintended negative consequences. The *Explore Your Beliefs* feature for this chapter looks at this issue in more depth. Take a few moments now to read this information and think about your own attitudes towards this form of reinforcement.

Explore your beliefs: Good job!

Visit any school and there's one phrase you are bound to hear over and over again: "Good job!". There are even websites that offer other ways that teachers can send the same message using different words. Many teachers work hard to give students frequent, and varied, verbal praise.

Despite common usage in the schools, Alfie Kohn (2001), aims to persuade educators to stop using so much praise. He advocates for supporting and encouraging students, but suggests teachers do so in other ways. His concerns about verbal praise include:

- When teachers praise students, they are aiming to manipulate them.
- The more kids are praised, the more praise they need to feel successful.
- Instead of saying, "I did it!"; over-praised students tend to say, "Was that good?"
- Scientific research has shown that the more we reward people for doing something, the more they tend to lose interest in whatever they had to do to get the reward.
- Praise can actually encourage students to do something for the wrong reason. For example, do we want students to wait in a line for the slide because they get praised for this behavior or because they see the value in taking turns?

Instead of always praising students, Kohn recommends that teachers:

- *Say nothing.* Kohn questions the idea that students will only repeat behaviors for which they are praised, and encourages teachers to just remain quiet.
- *Say what you saw.* A teacher might say "You put your shoes on yourself." or "You used a lot of purple today."
- *Ask questions.* For example, "What was the hardest part to draw?" or "How did you figure out how to make the feet the right size?"

Kohn concludes that some compliments and thank-yous are appropriate when they are not being used to manipulate future student behaviors.

Developing the Habit of Reflective Practice

Gather Information

1. Search the Internet for "ways to say good for you."
2. Think back on your own education. How did your teachers use verbal praise? Did you or someone you knew become a "praise junky," needing verbal praise to do your work?

Identify Beliefs

1. What effect do you think praise has on student performance and behavior?
2. Do you agree with Alfie Kohn's thoughts on praise? Why or why not?

Make Decisions

1. Identify two or three ways in which you will give students in your future classrooms feedback on their performance.
2. Will you choose to use limited verbal praise or a lot in your future classroom?

Assess and Evaluate

1. If you were visiting a school to evaluate how they encourage students, what evidence would you look for to show that the school has created a positive learning environment for their students?

2. How would you know if you have used too much or too little verbal praise in your classroom?

Resource

Kohn, A.(2001). Five reasons to stop saying "good job." *Young Children 56* (5), 24–28.

Homework and Practice

Homework has become a common component of American education that begins for most students in the early elementary school years. Because a relatively small portion of a student's waking life is actually spent in school, homework provides an opportunity to extend learning experiences beyond the classroom. Research conducted on the benefits of homework suggests that academic gains are smaller in the early years and gradually grow in significance throughout the high school experience (Cooper, 1989). In addition to the potential academic benefits, proponents indicate that homework helps students develop good study habits, promotes positive attitudes toward school, and encourages the realization that learning takes place in a variety of settings.

Think about the homework experiences you have had. How much homework did you typically do? Do you think it was too much or too little from your perspective? Do you think homework helped you become a better student? Why or why not? Were there some homework assignments that were more beneficial than others? What did these beneficial assignments have in common?

**Reflection
Opportunity 8.4**

Most of the skills being learned in schools need considerable practice for them to be perfected. That may seem most obvious with a physical skill such as handwriting or keyboarding. It is equally true, however, with cognitive skills such as reading, written communications, mathematics, and the scientific method. These are all complex skills that require many repetitions in order to master. The old adage "practice makes perfect" contains a great deal of truth. The challenge for teachers is to provide opportunities to practice developing skills in ways that are both interesting and meaningful to students. It takes a surprisingly large number of repetitions to achieve a relatively modest level of competence in using new skills (Anderson, 1999), so teachers need to be sure to provide a variety of interesting practice experiences. Playful activities and ones that allow students to apply their developing skills in meaningful situations are examples of ways in which teachers allow for more interesting practice.

Nonlinguistic Representations

Paivio (1990) suggests that when people acquire new information, it is coded and stored in both a linguistic and an imagery mode. We create "mental word strings" and either mental pictures or actual physical sensations to store new information. These latter two categories are referred to as nonlinguistic representations. An example of this type would be the mental imagery readers engage in as they create "pictures" of the actions and settings described in print. Using both linguistic and nonlinguistic representations enables students to better process and remember what they are learning.

You will have a variety of strategies to choose from to help students use nonlinguistic representations in their learning (Marzano et al., 2001). One example would be the use of *physical models*. They represent in concrete terms the concepts being studied. For example, rectangular sticks of varying lengths known as Cuisenaire rods are used in many elementary school mathematics classrooms to represent arithmetic operations. Another nonlinguistic representation is the use of *pictures and pictographs*. Drawing a picture of a flower and its major parts or using symbols and symbolic pictures to describe the process of photosynthesis helps students understand and remember what they are studying. A third example of a nonlinguistic representation is *physical movement*. Young children learning to write the letters of the alphabet can trace sandpaper representations of each letter and thereby create a physical memory that helps them remember the motions needed to write them.

Goal Setting and Providing Feedback

Setting broad goals for learning and giving students regular feedback about how well they are attaining these goals are two additional strategies that effective teachers use to enhance instruction. Educational research supports the many benefits associated with both strategies (Walberg, 1999). The process of goal setting is like consulting a road map before starting a trip in the car. It provides opportunities for teachers and students to set directions for the learning process. And although there are many possible pathways to the same end result, knowing the chosen direction helps both students and teachers prepare for and achieve the desired goal. When students know where they are going, it makes it much more likely that they will reach both their short-term and long-term objectives.

After analyzing literally thousands of studies on teaching, Hattie (1992) found that providing students with feedback on their performances was a powerful strategy that effective teachers use to enhance achievement. This feedback should tell students both what they are doing well and what needs to be done differently. Corrective feedback, when shared in a timely way, provides the greatest opportunities for student improvement (Marzano et al., 2001). One effective strategy for providing feedback is through the use of a rubric. Rubrics, such as the one shown in Figure 8.1, provide students with specific feedback on their individual levels of knowledge and skill development.

Teachers should strive to provide feedback that will help students answer three questions about their learning: Where am I going? Where am I now? How can I close the gap between the two? (Chappius, 2005). Students need to come to an understanding that where they are now in their learning is an okay place to be, but not an okay place to stay. Mistakenly, many teachers believe that the grades they give their students provide this feedback. Tony Winger, an instructional coach and social studies teacher from Colorado, makes it clear that this is not the case. She points out that grades give little feedback regarding students' academic strengths and weaknesses and

Figure 8.1   Rubric for Fourth-Grade Science Experiment

	4	3	2	1	0
Content Is there a clear description of the science content learned?					
Process Was the scientific process followed as described in class?					
Written Description Is the report easy to read? Does it have clear sentences, good spelling, and appropriate grammar?					
Points Earned					

Key: 4 = excellent; 3 = good; 2 = needs improvement; 1 = unacceptable; 0 = no judgment possible.

Comments:

can even be counterproductive (Chappius, 2005). For example, a student who is earning an A in science class may be reluctant to improve her lab reports. She may say, "Why improve? I'm already earning an A on each lab report."

Generating and Testing Hypotheses

Although generating and testing hypotheses is often associated with scientific investigations, it is actually a part of most fields of study. For example, a historian investigating Native American cultures in the years prior to the 1400s would need to generate hypotheses about what life was like and then seek to verify them through careful study of existing artifacts and the writings of others. Or a political scientist studying colonial governments in America would first generate hypotheses about what factors influenced the structure of government in each of the colonies and then read various accounts of this period to test these hypotheses. Generating and testing hypotheses are skills that can be learned by students of all ages. You can assist your future students in learning this important skill by first modeling it for them and then providing settings in which students can practice this learning strategy. For example, a group of fourth-grade students are working with math manipulatives that show halves, thirds, fourths, fifths, sixths, sevenths and eighths. The teacher writes these fractions on the board: $\frac{1}{3}$, $\frac{1}{5}$, $\frac{1}{8}$, $\frac{1}{6}$, and $\frac{1}{2}$ and asks the students to identify the smallest fraction. The class comes to a quick agreement that $\frac{1}{8}$ is the smallest fraction. Although many teachers would stop at that point, it is important to ask students to explain their reasoning. A student might explain by saying "Well, $\frac{1}{8}$ is the smallest fraction there is, nothing is smaller than $\frac{1}{8}$," as other students nod in agreement. By having students explain their reasoning, the teacher can see that students have mistakenly hypothesized that the manipulatives used to study fractions represent all of the fractional parts that exist. The teacher knows that she will need to set up an experience to help students rethink this hypothesis (Burns, 2005).

Activating Prior Knowledge

When teachers help their students remember what they already know regarding a specific topic, they are activating prior knowledge. Teachers typically use cues, questions, and advance organizers to accomplish this task. Although these strategies have much in common, each is useful in helping students call to mind what they already know. *Cues* are hints from the teacher about what is to be experienced and how it relates to what has already been learned. Marsha Harvey cues her second-grade class as they prepare for their upcoming field trip to the seashore by reminding them that they have studied local sea life and will be seeing some forms they investigated while discovering new ones as they explore the tide pools and beach area.

Questioning is another strategy teachers use frequently to activate prior knowledge. Questioning accounts for a high percentage of the time teachers spend interacting with students. Research indicates that teachers use between 45 and 150 questions for every half hour of teaching in the classroom (Nash & Shiman, 1974). When teachers use skilled questioning, they encourage their students to reflect on their understandings and to consider new possibilities (Danielson, 2007). Effective questions rarely require a simple right or wrong response, but rather have many possible correct answers. Teachers skilled at questioning give their students time to think (referred to as wait time) before they are asked to respond to a question and encourage all students to participate in the discussion. Teachers who are proficient at questioning often probe a student's answer while encouraging students to clarify and elaborate by asking questions such as: Could you give an example of that? Would you explain further what you mean by? Does anyone see another possibility? Who would like to comment on that idea?

Advance organizers are a third strategy for activating prior knowledge and were originally identified as an important educational approach by David Ausubel (1968). He viewed them as introductory materials that were presented prior to the actual learning experience to "bridge the gap between what the learner already knows and what he needs to know before he can successfully learn the task at hand" (p. 148). One common advance organizer that teachers use is a

Know–Want–Learned (KWL) chart. Students create an individual chart with three columns. The first column is labeled "What do I already know? The second column is for "What do I want to know?" And the third column allows the students to describe "What did I learn?".

As you reflect on all of the instructional strategies described above, remember that the amount of emphasis you place on any one strategy will be dependent on the group of students you are teaching. For example, if you are teaching English language learners, you may find that using more nonlinguistic representations may be helpful in assisting these students in their learning. The *Engage in the Debate* feature for this chapter describes some of the other controversies surrounding this unique group of learners. Read this information and think carefully about how you will teach these students.

Engage in the debate: Educating English language learners

The number of English Language Learners (ELLs) is increasing steadily in American schools. These children contribute a great richness of diversity and cultural heritage, but at the same time bring considerable challenges. Students for whom English is their second language are both learning a new language and mastering the content being taught. The best way to educate students for whom English is their second language is something that Educators are having a hard time coming to agreement on the best ways to educate these ELL students.

Two major approaches are currently being used for English Language Learners. The first, referred to as native language emphasis, advocates teaching ELL students initially in their native languages. All academic instruction is provided in the students' native language while English is taught as a separate subject. As the students show competency in English, they are integrated back into regular education classrooms.

The second common approach, called sheltered-English, offers education within a English speaking classroom, but at a level that is "sheltered", meaning the instruction is constantly modified to make sure the student understands it. In this approach, English Language Learners are immersed in English in a supportive way. Through the use of visuals, manipulatives and hands-on experiences, the teacher aims to teach content and the English language simultaneously.

Educating English Language Learners is a political hot topic. In 1998, California (the state with the largest percentage of English Language Learners), decided that classrooms with native language emphasis should be eliminated and replaced with one-year, sheltered English classes. In 2000, Arizona passed a similar law that prohibits native-language instruction for most English Language Learners children in public schools. These state laws have garnered criticism because they override parental choices, the judgment and experience of professional educators, and decisions made by local school boards.

Developing the Habit of Reflective Practice
Gather Information

1. Search the Internet for the "National Clearinghouse for English Language Acquisition" and read more information on ELLs.
2. Think back on your own K-12 education. How were English Language Learners taught at the schools you attended? What impact did these instructional practices appear to have on student success?

Identify Beliefs

1. Should decisions about educating English Language Learners be made by law makers and/or voters? Why or why not? Why should make these decisions?
2. What are the benefits and potential problems of assisting ELL students with their language learning?

Make Decisions

1. Imagine that you are a committee in a school district. This committee is formed to decide on which instructional approach will be used for English Language Learners in your school district. What information will you need to help you make the best decision?

2. Which of the two approaches presented here do you think is the best way to teach English Language Learners? Give a rationale for your opinion.

Assess and Evaluate

1. Why do you think some educators advocate for or against native language emphasis?

2. Why do you think some states have passed laws banning and/or restricting native language instruction in their schools?

Source

Lessow-Hurley, J. (2009). *The foundations of dual language instruction*. (5th ed.) Boston: Allyn & Bacon.

What instructional models can I use?

In addition to the more specific instructional strategies described above, researchers and writers have worked to identify the different styles teachers use to interact with their students. For more than 40 years, Bruce Joyce and Marsha Weil (Joyce & Weil, 2009) have been influential educators engaged in this process of studying promising approaches to teaching. They have found many different models and organized them into four broad groups: the behavioral systems model of instruction, the personal model, the information processing model, and the social model of instruction. These four groups of models are outlined in Table 8.4 and described in more detail below. As you go through your teacher-preparation program, you will learn more about these models and begin making decisions about which approaches you will want to use in your work with students.

TABLE 8.4   Models of Instruction

Model	Description	Example(s)
Behavioral Systems Model	Students learn as they modify behavior in response to environmental feedback	Direct Instruction Mastery Learning
Personal Model	Each individual must take responsibility for their own learning while striving to reach their full potential	Nondirective Teaching
Information-Processing Model	Students make sense of their world as they are assisted in organizing the information around them	Constructivist Education
Social Model	Students learn as they interact with peers and teachers in learning communities	Cooperative Learning

Joyce, B., Weil, M., & Calhoun, E. (2004). *Models of teaching* (7th ed.). Boston: Allyn and Bacon.

Behavioral Systems Model of Instruction

The basic premise behind the **behavioral systems model of instruction** is that human beings of all ages learn from the ways in which the environment around them responds to their behaviors. For example, a student chooses to work on difficult geometric proofs because she has received praise for her past efforts from both the classroom teacher and her parents. A second example of behavioral systems learning would be when a student observes a classmate receiving some free time on the computer after having completed his math assignment and decides to complete her own work in the hope of earning a similar reward. In both examples students are engaging in behaviors because of the perceived benefits received from those around them for these actions.

The theoretical basis for this approach is often referred to as *behavior modification* and is rooted in the work of Thorndike (1913), Pavlov (1927), Watson (1924), and B. F. Skinner (1953). These behaviorists and others have developed an approach to teaching that relies on observable behaviors, carefully crafted learning tasks, and highly organized systems for reinforcing appropriate student behavior and discouraging inappropriate ones. The behavior systems model has been viewed as an attempt to develop a more scientific approach to teaching and learning.

One important example of the behavioral systems approach to instruction is referred to as **direct instruction.** It is generally viewed as a highly organized, carefully planned teaching methodology. Teachers using direct instruction tend to place a strong emphasis on academics, engage in considerable direction and control over student learning, have high expectations for student progress, and have developed an organized system for managing instructional time (Joyce & Weil, 2009). Jill Bielenberg, a high school math teacher, begins her direct instruction lesson by sharing the objective of her lesson with her students, "Today you are going to learn how to convert pounds to kilograms so that you will be prepared to do the nursing module we begin tomorrow." She then spends 5 minutes reviewing what students learned in earlier lessons. They reexamine the definitions of pounds and kilograms and recall previous lessons where they used these measurements of weight. Jill then takes the next 5 minutes to give a clear rationale for this learning task, reminding students that they will be completing a nursing module later in the week where they need to convert patient weights from pounds to kilograms so that they can determine correct medication dosages. Following this, Jill then spends about 10 minutes demonstrating how to convert pounds to kilograms. After completing her instruction, students are given about 20 minutes to practice the skill on a worksheet. As students work through the problems, Jill walks around the room and helps students when necessary (this is referred to as **guided practice).** The last 10 minutes of class is spent summarizing the day's activities. Jill calls on a few students to review the steps necessary for the weight conversion. She reminds them that they'll be using this skill tomorrow and then excuses them as the bell rings. Direct instruction probably sounds quite familiar to you because it is a very prevalent instructional method in American schools (Arends, 2007).

Personal Model of Instruction

The first thing to come to mind when most people think of teaching is the major role that teachers play in sharing knowledge with their students. The study of mathematics, investigating the social studies, science learning, an appreciation for the arts, and developing skills in reading are among the many things that effective teachers address. Yet teaching is much more than this. It also includes helping students develop physically, emotionally, and socially so that they can become productive members of society.

The **personal model of instruction** emphasizes the development of the selfhood of each individual student. In its purest form, this approach deemphasizes the importance of the teacher's role in intellectual development and instead promotes each student's self-understanding and social/emotional well-being. Teachers using the personal model of instruction believe that as students grow in self-understanding, they will be able to engage more effectively in academic learning. The emphasis, therefore, is on assisting students in their personal growth. The theoretical underpinnings of this approach come from the work of people such as Stanley Coopersmith (1967), who wrote about student self-esteem, Abraham Maslow's (1968) work on basic human needs and growth towards self-actualization, and most specifically from the writings of Carl Rogers (1969), whose work on nondirective counseling was applied to teaching. In the prologue to his book *Freedom to Learn,* Rogers gives the following rationale for **nondirective teaching,** the best example of the personal model of instruction:

> I want to speak to them (educators) about *learning.* But *not* the lifeless, sterile, futile, quickly forgotten stuff which is crammed into the mind of the poor helpless individual tied into his seat by ironclad bonds of conformity! I am talking about LEARNING—the insatiable curiosity which drives the adolescent boy to absorb everything he can see or hear or read about gasoline engines in order to improve the efficiency and speed of his "hot-rod." I am talking about the student who says, "I am discovering, drawing in from the outside, and making that which is drawn in a real part of *me.* (1969, p. 3)

Personal models of instruction are infrequent in classrooms today. But many teachers use elements of this approach to create a learning environment that is more responsive to student needs, that involves students in determining what should be learned, and that encourages self-understanding. In other words, many teachers use the personal model as a framework for their instructional efforts and then incorporate other instructional strategies to meet the needs of students. For example, as Jennifer O'Toole (Roberts, Kellough, & Moore, 2006) teaches her sixth-grade students about Manifest Destiny, one student asks, "Why isn't the United States still adding states? Because Jennifer is using the personal model of instruction, she would not attempt to answer this question, but instead would encourage students to find their own answers to this question. Jennifer would assist students as they explore this topic in more depth. For example, she could help them discover the political and social ramifications of adding states. Jennifer will remain open to changing topics and class activities as she works to meet the needs and interests of her students.

The *Ian's Classroom Experiences* feature for this chapter, found on the Companion Website for this text, discusses the fragility of a student's social/emotional well-being. Read it now to see the powerful influence teachers have on the lives of their students.

Ian's Classroom Experiences: Laughter Is a Sometimes Bitter Pill

Information-Processing Model of Instruction

Each of us is bombarded daily with a wealth of information that must be understood and categorized. The basic job of teachers using the **information-processing model of instruction** is to give students the tools they need to make sense of these data. In this model students are seen as innately motivated to seek out information from the world around them and make sense of it. Joyce & Well (2009) describe several different examples of this type.

One information-processing model of instruction is referred to as **constructivist education.** Grounded in the developmental theories of Jean Piaget (1950) and Lev Vygotsky (1978), this approach to education is based on the notion that students process information differently depending on their stage of intellectual development. Teachers using the constructivist approach promote the idea that students build or construct their own understanding of the world through activities based on personal interests. As they manipulate real-world objects and interact with the people around them, students create for themselves an understanding of the world. Perkins (1999) describes three main types of learning that take place in constructivist education. The first of these is *active learning.* Rather than passively taking in information, students engage in discussion, research topics, and get involved in tasks that involve them physically and intellectually. Second, constructivist education engages students in *social learning.* Students learn through their social interactions with peers, teachers, and other adults. Finally, students engage in *creative learning.* Rather than simply taking in new information, students actually create or recreate knowledge for themselves.

To view a video of a first grade teacher engaged in a hands-on science activity, go to the Companion Website for this text and click on MyEducationLab for Chapter 8.

Veronica Morris teaches third grade and uses constructivist teaching in her classroom. Just this past fall, she organized her room into five centers, each with a separate emphasis on mathematics, science, literacy, the arts, and technology. During much of the school day, students are allowed to move freely between centers and engage in projects that Veronica has planned for their consideration. She also encourages students to actively pursue issues that are of interest to them and often finds that many student-designed projects last for several months. They frequently work in teams to research their special interests, write reports, and create physical artifacts that demonstrate what they have learned. Constructivists like Veronica aim to create schools that do both: make instruction student-centered and successfully prepare students for their adult years (Brooks & Brooks, 1993). Veronica works to apply the concept of the zone of proximal development (ZPD), another key constructivist idea from Vygotsky (Arends, 2007). Vygotsky proposed that learners have two different levels of development: the level of actual development and the level of potential development. The *level of actual development* is the current intellectual capability of a student. They are able to work independently when performing at this level. On the other hand, the *level of potential development* is the level a student can perform at with assistance. The zone between the learner's actual level of development and the level of potential development is referred to as the ZPD. Veronica works to make sure that her centers provide appropriate challenges and assistance so that students are moved forward into their ZPD, where new learning occurs. For example, she works to make sure that students are reading books at their level of actual development when they are reading independently. Veronica has prepared baskets filled with books at their independent reading level as determined by an earlier assessment. While students are moving through the centers, Veronica meets with small groups of students for reading instruction. The books she uses for these small group lessons are books at their level of potential development. These are books that students would not be able to read independently, but can be managed with just a bit of assistance from the teacher. By doing this, her students are continually improving their reading skills.

Another example of Veronica's constructivist approach can be seen each afternoon as the class focuses on investigations with the use of the *problem-based instructional strategy.* Currently, the class is investigating the problem of litter on school property. The students noticed this problem and chose to use class time to find a solution. They gathered information to see why littering was occurring. Students spent time in groups brainstorming and then selecting a proposed a solution to the problem. As a class, they decided more garbage cans painted bright colors were needed on school property. The class is currently discussing strategies for obtaining and then painting the needed garbage cans. After implementing their solution, they will analyze its effectiveness as the last step in the problem-solving process.

Across the hall from Veronica is Hector Juarez, who teaches math to sixth-grade students. The school has bought a new math textbook series that includes mathematical crossword puzzles integrated into each chapter. Hector has noticed that his students have struggled with completing the crossword puzzle assignments and has decided to help his students understand the unique characteristics of crossword puzzles. For example, his students wonder why there is a 1-across clue and a 4-across clue—but no 2-across or 3-across clue. They also need to learn the strategies of completing a crossword puzzle. For example, they need to know that you use the answers within other clues to help you determine the answer for an unknown clue. Also, students need to know that a good strategy is to first answer the questions you are sure of and then return to the questions that need further study. Hector, using the information-processing model of instruction, plans to follow the *gradual release of responsibility* strategy in his teaching. (Pearson and Gallagher, 1983). He explicitly presents crossword puzzle strategies and then gradually hands over responsibility for learning to the students. First, he models the strategies used in completing a crossword puzzle by demonstrating the reading, writing, and mathematical problem solving he uses when solving these puzzles. Hector then demonstrates how to use classroom tools such as glossaries, dictionaries, calculators, and rulers to solve the puzzles. In addition, he gives students ideas for what to do when you come across a clue you cannot solve. Hector continues to support and guide students through the completion of several more crossword puzzles before gradually turning additional responsibility for learning over to the students. When the time seems right, Hector breaks the class into small groups and steps back from direct participation. He then monitors student progress and then uses the assessment data he gathers to determine whether further demonstrations are needed. Finally, when he feels that his students have a strong sense of how to solve crossword puzzles, Hector has his students work independently on the crossword puzzle assignments.

Social Model of Instruction

In the **social model of instruction,** it is assumed that students learn best when they engage in social interactions with their peers and with teachers. Although many theorists have promoted social interactions as essential to effective learning, the writings of John Dewey (1929) have had the most significant impact on current educational thinking. Through the communications that take place in social interactions, Dewey stated:

> Not only is social life identical with communication, but all communication (and hence all genuine social life) is educative. To be a recipient of a communication is to have an enlarged and changed experience. One shares in what another has thought and felt and in so far, meagerly or amply, has his own attitude modified. (1929, p. 6)

Teachers who want to develop a climate conducive to social learning must create **learning communities** in which students work cooperatively in small and large groups to grow in knowledge through their interactions. These learning communities require effort on the part of the teacher to establish. Students must be provided with strategies that enable them to communicate effectively with each other, be given opportunities to build good working relationships, and have clearly defined educational tasks before they can be successful as a community of learners.

The best known example of a social learning model is **cooperative learning.** Students engaged in cooperative learning work in small groups organized by the teacher to complete tasks that require them to learn as a team. The 1970s and 1980s showed a growing interest in cooperative learning, with considerable research and writing being done during these years (i.e., Johnson & Johnson, 1975; Slavin, 1983).

For cooperative learning to be successful, teachers must first make sure they monitor student behavior during small-group times. This helps keep students engaged and gives the teacher important information for future activities and evaluation. In addition, as groups work to complete their tasks, the teacher needs to give students feedback on ineffective and effective use of social skills. When needed, activities designed to teach additional social skills are taught to ensure smooth functioning of the groups (Ellis & Whalen, 1990). The development of strong social skills is critical to student success in later job situations. Research indicates that the most frequently cited reason for individuals getting fired from their first job is not lack of job-related skills, but rather their poor interpersonal skills (Kagan, 1997). It is therefore essential that schools provide learning experiences that allow students to work cooperatively with their peers.

An example of cooperative learning called **jigsaw** can be found in Annie DeBunce's seventh-grade history class. Jigsaw is a cooperative instructional approach where each student's learning is essential for the completion of the experience. Annie's students are studying the Civil War time period. She breaks her class into 5 groups of 6 students. Within each group, she assigns each student a separate task:

- *Student 1* researches Abraham Lincoln's perspective and experiences of the war.
- *Student 2* researches Ulysses S. Grant's perspective and experiences of the war.
- *Student 3* researches Frederick Douglass's perspective and experiences of the war.

- *Student 4* researches Sojourner Truth's perspective and experiences of the war.
- *Student 5* researches Harriet Tubman's perspective and experiences of the war.
- *Student 6* researches Robert E. Lee's perspective and experiences of the war.

As the students complete their research, Annie groups students according to their research topic. The Abraham Lincoln group meets and shares their information with one another; the Ulysses S. Grant group meets and shares their information with one another and so on. Having students meet with other students who have identical research assignments increases the chances that each report will be more accurate and complete. The exercise finishes when Annie puts students back into their original groups where there is one expert on each key person from the Civil War. Each student then educates the whole group about her or his specialty. The jigsaw cooperative learning strategy encourages listening, engagement, and empathy by giving each member of the group an essential part to play in the academic activity (Aronson, 2005).

In addition to cooperative learning, another common way that teachers implement the social model of instruction is through **Socratic classroom discussions** (Copeland, 2005). Named after one of the world's greatest educators, this method of facilitating classroom discussion centers around the teacher's use of six different types of questions:

- *Concept clarification:* These questions get students to think deeply. Examples: Can you give me an example? Can you rephrase that? How does this relate to what we've been discussing?
- *Probing assumptions:* These questions help students rethink assumptions and beliefs that are the foundation of their answers. Examples: What else could we assume? How can you verify or disprove that assumption? What would happen if . . . ?
- *Questioning viewpoints:* These questions encourage students to acknowledge that there are other and sometimes equally valid perspectives. Examples: How could you look another way at this? How is it better than . . . ? What is the difference between . . . and . . . ?
- *Probing implications:* These questions help students predict the consequences to their answers. Examples: Then what would happen? How does . . . affect . . . ? How could . . . be used to . . . ?
- *Reflective questions:* These questions turn students' questions back on themselves. Examples: What was the point of you asking that question? What does that mean? Why did you ask that question?

Socrates felt that it was not enough simply to learn or memorize facts. To truly know, and to seek wisdom, one must work toward understanding. The Socratic method of leading class discussions, sometimes referred to as Socratic circles, is a way to help students come to a deep understanding of a particular issue. Imagine a middle school class that has been studying the Holocaust. It would be easy to focus students' learning on just the facts, but consider how their understanding would be impacted if the teacher led a Socratic discussion on the topic of the Holocaust or on the topic of prejudice.

After reading about the behavioral systems, personal, information-processing, and social models of instruction, consider spending a few minutes thinking carefully about each of them. Which do you find appealing and why? Can you see yourself using them in the classroom someday? Are there one or more options that you think you may not be comfortable with? What makes you feel this way? Can you identify personality characteristics in yourself that may make it easier or more productive to use one or more of the models identified?

**Reflection
Opportunity 8.5**

What skills will I need in management and discipline?

Part of any good teacher's repertoire of skills is the ability to deal with the routines of teaching. Such things as passing out papers, moving students physically and psychologically from one activity to the next, and making sure the lesson moves at a rate that keeps students interested in what is going on are referred to as **management** skills. This ability to organize and coordinate learning experiences is an essential talent you will need to possess. Equally important is the teacher's ability to respond positively to the problem behaviors that students produce. When students talk out of turn, fail to complete their work, or demean fellow students, you will need to be prepared with effective **discipline** strategies. Management and discipline skills are frequently discussed together because they share much in common, and both are necessary to create an environment that is conducive to learning. Both new and experienced teachers will tell you that successful management and discipline make a very big difference in teacher effectiveness (Long & Morse, 1996). Table 8.5 lists some important components of effective management and discipline.

When people talk about discipline and **punishment,** they often use the two words interchangeably. Educators, however, make significant distinctions between them. Good discipline is designed to assist students in making better behavioral choices. Punishment, on the other hand, is used to eliminate undesirable behaviors. In other words, discipline emphasizes what a student *should do,* whereas punishment emphasizes what a child *should not do.* Discipline can be seen as an ongoing process, whereas punishment is a one-time occurrence. Discipline fosters the student's ability to think, whereas punishment tends to encourage obedience without thinking. Discipline bolsters self-esteem by communicating that the student is capable of doing better, whereas punishment tends to lower self-esteem in that it suggests that the student needs the teacher to behave

TABLE 8.5 Components of Effective Management and Discipline	
Component	**Description**
Understanding current research and theory	Research and theory has grown extensively over the last several decades and is useful in understanding and responding to both positive and negative student behaviors.
Recognizing and responding to students' personal and psychological needs	Teachers who are aware of unmet student needs can provide understanding, assistance, and/or resources that in turn help eliminate problem behaviors.
Developing strong teacher–student and peer relationships	When teachers work to create classrooms that are "caring communities," learning is enhanced and problem behaviors diminish.
Implementing effective instructional strategies	When students are engaged in quality educational experiences, they are less likely to misbehave.
Using proven classroom organization and management skills	The physical organization of the classroom indirectly tells students a great deal about teacher expectations. When combined with effective management of classroom routines, student misbehavior declines.
Dealing effectively with inappropriate student behavior	Because of the characteristics of individual students and each unique situation, teachers need a variety of strategies to deal with misbehaving students.

Source: From Jones, V., & Jones, L. (2004). *Comprehensive classroom management: Creating communities of support and solving problems* (7th ed.). Boston: Allyn and Bacon.

appropriately. In summary, discipline leads students to self-control, whereas punishment actually undermines independence and reinforces engaging in behavior to please the teacher.

Problem-Prevention Strategies

Many of the management strategies that teachers use are designed to prevent problems from occurring in the first place. In fact, the best overall strategy for classroom management and discipline is to engage first and foremost in **problem-prevention strategies** (Sergiovanni, 1994). An example of this type discussed earlier in the chapter is the importance of building strong teacher–student relationships. The careful preparation of the classroom environment and developing clear rules for students are other important problem prevention strategies.

Meredith Jacobsen, a teacher of seventh- and eighth-grade English at Eisenhower Middle School, provides an example of the importance of preparing the classroom environment. Prior to beginning her fifth year of teaching, Meredith spends some time organizing her classroom space. Every classroom in the building is equipped with individual student desks. Meredith wants a wider aisle down the middle of these desks so that she can move easily through the room. She plans for an even number of desks on each side of this aisle so that students can work in pairs during parts of each class period. A note to the custodian will help her maintain this desired arrangement. Meredith has two computers and wants to have them both easily available to students during class time without being disruptive to others. A collection of novels used in several of her classes will also need to be shelved in such a way that students can have ready access to them. Meredith has several posters and numerous quotes that she will want to display around the classroom as well. These elements, and more, must be organized prior to the first day of school. To view a virtual classroom tour and an interview with an kindergarten teacher, go to the Companion Website for this text and click on MyEducationLab for Chapter 8.

MyEducationLab 8.2

Another important problem-prevention strategy is the development of clear rules for student behavior (Good & Brophy, 2008). When students understand the value of behavior standards and agree to follow them, many misunderstandings and problems between teachers and students can be avoided. How rules are developed may differ depending on the level at which you teach. Elementary teachers often find that engaging students in the rule-making process is helpful in promoting ownership (Evertson & Emmer, 2009). Secondary teachers generally do not want to develop a separate list of rules for five or six classes and prefer instead to create their own rules and ask each class for additional ideas that may be helpful (Jones & Jones, 2007). Table 8.6 presents some helpful strategies to use in developing classroom rules.

Managing Instruction

Adam Barclay, in his second year of teaching high school mathematics, is struggling with group instruction. Getting students' attention before beginning the lesson, setting a good pace for his instruction, and making sure a variety of students participate in discussions are examples of the problems he faces. It is discouraging to prepare interesting lessons for his classes and have only modest success in presenting them. After observing Adam during two separate lessons, his principal has suggested that in addition to the interesting lessons, focusing on improving the management of his teacher-led activities will enhance his instruction. Adam's *classroom-management skills* need work.

The importance of strong skills in the management of instruction was first researched by Kounin (1970). After identifying two groups of classroom teachers, one acknowledged as highly effective and the other as struggling with their teaching, Kounin collected several thousand hours of videotapes of their interactions with students. Careful analysis of these tapes led to the finding that successful teachers were able to prevent many problems from occurring through the use of strong management skills. These skills, which are outlined in Table 8.7, allow effective teachers to manage teacher-led activities smoothly and without getting off track.

To effectively manage instruction, teachers must first understand the student population they are teaching (Danielson, 2007). One aspect of this understanding is the realization that stu-

TABLE 8.6 Developing Classroom Rules

Guideline	Description
Keep the list short	Four to six rules are all that are necessary. Too many rules make the list difficult to remember and create an unwanted feeling of rigidity.
Make rules broad in focus	Rules should identify broad categories of behavior that you expect in the classroom, rather than specific ones. Listing all your behavioral expectations is both difficult and unnecessary.
State rules positively	Rather than saying, "don't hurt others," it is more appropriate to state your rules more positively: "treat each other with respect." Positive rules tell students what *to do,* rather than what *not to do.*
Identify rules the first day of class	Rather than waiting for problems to present themselves, expectations should be clarified the first day of school.
Develop rules consistent with your school/district	Make sure that the rules are in agreement with written policies of the school and district in which you teach.
Create rules that apply to you as well	Classroom rules are meant primarily for students but should also apply to you as the teacher.

dents' prior experiences will have an impact on how they learn and behave. Students will have misunderstandings and be influenced by their families' opinions and experiences. For example, some kindergarten children may learn from their home experiences that instructions given by an adult do not need to be listened to until they have been repeated multiple times. Duong Trong uses *sponge activities* during transition times with his kindergarten students to reach those who need multiple repetitions of instructions effectively. Sponge activities (Hunter, 1994) are designed to produce learning during transitional times. Sponge activities during transitions "soak up" these otherwise wasted moments to make effective use of them. Duong, instead of continuing to nag his students, announces once that it's time to move from tables to the rug, goes himself to the rug area, and begins playing a counting game with students. This sponge activity makes good use of this transitional time while also letting students know that directions are given only once.

Think about the management skills described in Table 8.7. Do you remember a teacher who had poor management skills? How did this influence her/his teaching? Conversely, did you have teachers who used strong management strategies? Do you remember these teachers as effective? Based on these reflections, how important do you think management strategies are to effective classroom instruction? Do you think you will be able to develop strong management skills? Why or why not?

**Reflection
Opportunity 8.6**

Options for Discipline

Although every teacher works to avoid student misbehavior by using problem prevention and classroom management strategies, misbehaviors still occur. Unmet student needs, poor self-image, and testing behaviors are just some of the reasons why even the best prepared teachers still have misbehaving students. Teachers need a variety of strategies that they can use to respond to these problems. Although many more discipline approaches are available than can be discussed here, four options are introduced briefly below. Table 8.8 provides an outline of the key elements of each approach.

TABLE 8.7   Management Strategies

Type	Strategy	Description
Preventing Misbehavior	Withitness	Dealing with small misbehaviors before they escalate into bigger ones by recognizing and dealing quickly with them
	Overlapping	Addressing two or more events at the same time rather than dropping one and focusing entirely on the other
Managing Movement	Momentum	Speeding up and slowing down the rate of instruction to maintain the right pace for learning
	Smoothness	Staying focused rather than wandering through instruction, which can confuse and frustrate many students
Maintaining Group Focus	Group Alerting	Making sure that students in the group are paying attention to, and are ready to engage in, the discussion and interactions
	Encouraging Accountability	Letting students know that their participation will be noticed and evaluated in some manner
	High-Participation Formats	Finding ways to keep students actively involved even when they are not responding directly to a teacher's questions

Source: From Kounin, J. (1970). *Discipline and group management in classrooms.* New York: Holt, Rinehart, and Winston.

TABLE 8.8   Discipline Options

Option	Key Elements
Problem-Solving Approaches	• Teacher-guided problem-solving approach • Classroom meetings • Peer mediation • Peace tables
Teacher Effectiveness Training	• Problem ownership • I-message • No-lose method of problem solving
Dreikurs's Approach	• Importance of social acceptance • Natural consequences • Logical consequences
Behavior Modification	• Positive reinforcement • Punishment • Ignoring

Problem-solving approaches. More than 30 years ago, William Glasser (1969) described an approach to discipline that has become a part of the strategies used by many teachers to resolve problems that occur in their classrooms. Based on his own theory for treating behavior problems (called *reality therapy*), Glasser's **problem-solving approach to discipline** actively involves students in planning for better behavior. When a problem occurs, the teacher sits down and guides the student through a process that culminates in a plan for better behavior. The student and teacher first identify the problem behavior, brainstorm together more productive alternatives, create a plan to improve behavior, and then commit to making the plan work. More recently, Glasser (1986, 1990) has refined his initial thinking to include the importance of instructional strategies and classroom climate in dealing with discipline issues.

Another strategy that Glasser has promoted extensively in his work is the importance of holding regular **classroom meetings.** He believes that gathering students together to discuss issues that impact the whole group is both an effective discipline strategy and a positive way to build rapport between students and their teacher. He identifies three types of classroom meetings:

- *Problem-solving meetings*—These meetings provide opportunities for students to discuss social behaviors that impact the whole class. The problem-solving approach described above is used to help students identify problems and plan for more positive interactions.

- *Open-ended meetings*—Students and teacher engage in conversations on intellectually important subjects that are of interest to all.

- *Educational–diagnostic meetings*—At these meetings, teachers develop strategies for assessing how well students understand the concepts of the curriculum (Glasser, 1969).

Barbara Coloroso, a nationally recognized educational consultant who focuses on issues related to classroom behavior management, advocates problem-solving practices that are compatible with Glasser's approach. She proposes that teachers do the following when disciplining their students (Charles, 2008): Show students what they have done wrong; Give them ownership of the problem; Provide ways to solve the problem, including win–win solutions; Leave their dignity intact.

Coloroso has developed what she calls the three R's to help students take responsibility for their actions: Restitution, Resolution, and Reconciliation. For example, when getting a drink from the water fountain, Carla puts her finger against the spout, causing the water to spray. She had intended for the water to hit a friend, but instead it hits a nearby bulletin board and damages a poster made by a classmate. For *Restitution,* she needs to correct any harm that was done. With the teacher's help, Carla decides to recreate the poster, aiming to duplicate what her classmate had originally created. For *Resolution,* the teacher helps Carla to see that she needs to determine what caused the misbehavior and then take steps to make sure that it will not happen again. Carla realizes that she was trying to show off to her friends and that she was not following the rules for using the water fountain. She promises to remember the rules in the future and also pledges to think about the consequences before she tries to entertain her friends. For *Reconciliation,* Carla needs to heal the relationship with the person who was hurt. After discussing her options with the teacher, she chooses to apologize to her classmate.

Coloroso also suggests that her problem-solving model can assist educators in helping put an end to bullying (Coloroso, 2003). She points out that bullying always includes three elements: an imbalance of power, the intent to do harm, and a threat of further aggression. Coloroso proposes options to assist bullies in changing their behaviors, suggestions to support the victims, and ideas for engaging those who see bullying taking place. The bullies themselves need to have their negative energy redirected into positive leadership activities. Secondly, the victims can be helped by bringing attention to their particular strengths and talents. Finally, the bystanders can be encouraged to stand up against the injustices brought about by bullying.

In addition to problem-solving approaches such as those of Glasser and Coloroso, many schools are implementing strategies to help students resolve their own conflicts. Two important problem solving options being used are **peer mediation** and **peace tables.** Peer mediation is a process by which students volunteer to receive training on how to intercede in conflicts between peers. Peer mediators then help classmates find fair solutions to their conflicts (Zirpoli, 2008). Schools using peer mediation report less teacher stress due to classroom management, more time for academic instruction, and increased student capacity to solve their own disputes (Lane & McWhirter, 1992). In addition, schools using peer mediation report fewer incidences of physical violence and an increase in student cooperation (Johnson & Johnson, 1996).

Schools using peace tables begin by educating all students about the steps in the conflict-resolution process. Peace tables are then set up throughout the school as places where students can go to resolve their problems. Peace tables generally have a list of helpful hints and reminders of the steps that students can take to solve problems. For younger children, the table may even contain props such as puppets for students to use during the conflict-resolution process.

Teacher effectiveness training. A second program to have a significant impact on classroom management and discipline was developed by Thomas Gordon (1974). His approach was first developed to assist parents and was called *parent effectiveness training* (Gordon, 1970). Using the same basic techniques, *teacher effectiveness training* promotes the idea that teachers must create an atmosphere in which shared decision making is used to solve classroom problems. Gordon encourages teachers to give up their authoritarian power over students in favor of a more equitable approach to classroom management and discipline. He believes that when students and teachers work together to resolve conflicts, the end result is more satisfying and effective for all parties.

Gordon (1974) suggests two strategies to use in working through conflicts. The first he calls an **I-message.** An effective I-message consists of three parts: (1) the personal pronoun *I*, (2) the feelings experienced by the adult, and (3) the effect the student behavior has on the teacher. For example, Rachelle, a second-grade child in your classroom, interrupted the math instruction three times today with inappropriate comments. Following the lesson, you take her aside and respond using an I-message: "I get frustrated when you interrupt my teaching with comments that aren't related to the lesson." Gordon's second strategy for dealing with problem behaviors is his *no-lose method of problem solving.* In situations in which I-messages haven't worked or are inadequate, this problem-solving strategy is implemented in much the same way as Glasser's approach discussed earlier.

Dreikurs on discipline. Another major contributor to the field of classroom management and discipline is Rudolf Dreikurs. His approach, like that of Gordon, was first applied to parenting and later to teaching (Dreikurs, Grunwald, & Pepper, 1971). Dreikurs believes that when students feel unacceptable to either their peers or teachers, they become behavior problems in the classroom (Charles, 2008). They mistakenly choose undesirable behaviors in an attempt to gain social acceptance. Dreikurs identifies a downward spiral of misbehaviors on the part of students: (1) attention seeking, (2) power over others, (3) seeking revenge, and (4) displays of inadequacy (giving up).

Susan McCloud, an elementary school principal in Kentucky, suggests strategies for helping students feel accepted (McCloud, 2005). She points out that when teachers greet students by name and chat with them respectfully, students feel safe and comfortable—even loved. Susan found that when students at her school began to feel honored and safe, they stopped misbehaving and teachers had more time to focus on teaching. She and her staff changed the student population from a rowdy, irresponsible noncooperative, disrespectful group to one that valued a calm environment, responsible behavior, cooperation, and respect. By helping her students feel a strong sense of belonging, her staff was able to help students become problem solvers rather than problem producers.

Dreikurs et al. (1971) identify two important discipline strategies for teachers to use in their work with students. They are both designed to help students recognize the fact that their inappropriate classroom behaviors have related consequences.

Natural consequences follow automatically from the student's behavior and require no adult intervention. For example, Alicia has been warned several times that tipping her chair back on two legs may lead to falling down. Rather than punishing her for this behavior, the teacher decides to allow the natural consequence to occur. Although Alicia may be slightly hurt or embarrassed, this natural consequence may help her choose to eliminate the behavior in the future. **Logical consequences** are teacher-determined outcomes that are directly related to the student's behavior. For example, Angela has been drawing patterns on her desk during eighth-grade English class. You have decided that she will need to come back during her free time and scrub her desk clean. The consequence for Angela's behavior is directly related to the behavior itself and is a logical consequence.

Behavior modification. The final discipline approach to be discussed here is called *behavior modification*. Based primarily on the theory of operant conditioning developed by B. F. Skinner (Skinner, 1953), this approach is based on the premise that human behavior is either encouraged or discouraged by the responses from the environment that immediately follow it. Behavior modification consists of three strategies that teachers can use to manage student behavior. The first of these is referred to as **positive reinforcement.** Typically, this is defined as anything that immediately follows a behavior and increases the likelihood that the behavior will occur in the future (Kameenui & Darch, 1995). A smile, a pat on the back, spending time with a child, and positive comments about student work are all examples of potentially reinforcing actions. A second behavior-modification technique is called **punishment** and can be defined as anything that follows a behavior that is intended to decrease the likelihood that the behavior will occur again in the future. For example, Julian has just interrupted you for the third time during the math lesson to ask an unrelated question. Having reminded him about the importance of appropriate questions the first two times he disturbed your teaching, you now implement a mild punishment by telling Julian that he owes you 5 minutes from the upcoming recess. During this time owed, Julian will sit at his desk and work on assignments not yet completed. The final behavior-modification technique is usually referred to as **ignoring** (Sprick, Sprick, & Garrison, 1992). Ignoring occurs when no response is given to a student behavior. Although this may sound easy, it is actually a skill that requires practice. To truly ignore a behavior, you must give no verbal or nonverbal feedback. Eye contact, sighing, and moving closer to a student who is engaged in an undesirable behavior are all responses that are avoided when ignoring is used.

Developing Your Own Management and Discipline Style

For much of American educational history, the decision on which discipline approach to use was a simple one. Paddling and other punishment strategies associated with behavior modification were used almost exclusively. It was not until the late 1960s that other options became available for use in the classroom (Jones & Jones, 2007). The variety of approaches available today is both a blessing and a potential problem. The problem comes from needing to identify which options you will use. As you grow in your understanding of teaching styles and student learning, you will also need to identify management and discipline strategies that you feel good about using and are compatible with the teaching style you want to use with students. The *Views from the Classroom* feature for this chapter describes one teacher's efforts to create her own set of strategies for management and discipline. Go to the Companion Website for this text and read her thoughts and then respond to the reflection questions presented.

As you begin thinking about creating your own management and discipline style, you should know that many schools are developing and instituting school-wide discipline policies (Marzano,

Views from the Classroom: S.M.I.L.E.

2003). These policies do not usually preclude teachers from using some of their own individual strategies, but they do communicate to students and their families that the faculty and staff are speaking with one voice on how discipline should be addressed. Some school-wide discipline policies include a way of collecting data on student behavior. For example, The School-Wide Information System (SWIS) is a Web-based software system for recording, entering, organizing and reporting discipline referrals (Walker, Ramsey, & Gresham, 2004). The discipline referrals may then be summarized and analyzed for individual students, for groups of students who share certain characteristics, or for the entire student body over a given time.

In addition to being aware of school-wide discipline policies, you should also spend time learning more about existing management and discipline programs so that you can begin to make good decisions about which approach(es) will work for you. One factor that may help you in this selection process is the extent to which each approach is based on control strategies (Burden, 2003). Methods from the behavior-modification approach, for example, are generally considered high control because of their emphasis on external rewards and punishments to influence student behavior. *Assertive Discipline* (Canter & Canter, 2002), a widely used management model, would be considered a high-control option because of the program's emphasis on the teacher's right to reinforce desired behaviors and establish clear consequences.

In contrast to the Assertive Discipline approach, *Teaching with Love and Logic* (Fay & Funk, 1998) would be considered a low-control model because it is based on the philosophical belief that students have primary responsibility for controlling their own behavior. With guidance from the teacher, students are viewed in this approach as having the capability and motivation to make wise decisions. Teachers using Love and Logic strive to share control with their students and balance consequences with empathy. Although it may sound fairly easy to share control with students, many teachers find it difficult because of their own personality traits and long-held ideas of what teaching should be like. Teachers typically want to take charge, and find it harder to share the control of classroom activities with students.

Some teachers, rather than choosing high- or low-control programs, opt for management and discipline models that have a moderate level of control. One such approach is called *Discipline with Dignity* (Curwin & Mendler, 2001). In this approach, teachers establish social contracts and teach students how to make responsible choices. Current research suggests that low- to medium-control methods of management and discipline are more effective than high-control methods. Not only are they more effective in regulating student behavior, but they also improve student achievement (Darling-Hammond & Bransford, 2005).

You will want to know about and be able to use a variety of discipline techniques, because every student and situation is unique. The distinctiveness of each child and situation will make it necessary for you to think carefully about the problem and implement an appropriate solution. Students will come to your classroom with their own set of experiences, attitudes, abilities, and personalities. It should not be a surprise, then, that a discipline strategy that works for one student may not help a second. Similarly, every discipline situation has its own unique set of players and circumstances, thus making it difficult to use a single approach.

To develop your own management and discipline approach, you will also need to know yourself. Each of the discipline options identified in this chapter has the enthusiastic support of many good teachers around the country. For example, some very good teachers find that behavior-modification techniques are their primary discipline strategies, whereas others select Glasser's method as their major approach. These successful teachers have studied the available discipline options, looked at their own personal strengths, weaknesses, and preferences, and then selected approaches that best fit their personality and teaching style. Your challenge will be to do the same analysis for yourself. Take out your Reflections Journal or open the on-line journal found on the Companion Website for this text and respond to the following questions. What personal strengths

**Reflection
Opportunity 8.7**

and weaknesses do you have that will influence the ways in which you discipline students? Which of the approaches discussed in this chapter are most interesting to you? What attracts you to this option? Can you see yourself using more than one of the approaches presented? At some point within the next few years, you will want to select discipline techniques that fit you and use them to deal with students' problem behaviors.

    After reading this section on management and discipline strategies, the *Consider This* feature for this chapter will give you an opportunity to try out an option that has proven effective for many educators. Go to the Companion Website for this text and spend some time creating your own enforceable statements, and then reflect on their value as you complete your reading for this chapter.

**Consider This:
An Effective
Management
Strategy**

Summary

In this chapter, four organizing questions were identified to clarify your thinking about effective teaching strategies:

Why are strong relationships with students and other adults important?

Effective relationships are essential to good learning. They can be encouraged by:
- Developing positive relationships with students (Praxis II, topics Ic, IIIa)
- Working with parents (Praxis II, topic IVb)
- Encouraging other collaborative relationships (Praxis II, topic IVa)

What does research tell us about effective instructional strategies?

Research has identified several strategies that effective teachers use in their work with students:
- Identifying similarities and differences (Praxis II, topic IIa)
- Summarizing and note taking (Praxis II, topic IIa)
- Reinforcing effort (Praxis II, topic IIa)
- Homework and practice
- Nonlinguistic representations (Praxis II, topic IIa)
- Goal setting and providing feedback (Praxis II, topic IIa)
- Generating and testing hypotheses
- Activating prior knowledge (Praxis II, topic IIa)

What instructional models can I use?

Four broad models of instruction are used in classrooms:
- Behavioral systems model of instruction (Praxis II, topic IIa)
- Personal model of instruction (Praxis II, topics IIa, IIIc)
- Information-processing model of instruction (Praxis II, topic IIa)
- Social model of instruction (Praxis II, topic IIa)

What skills will I need in management and discipline?

Effective teachers need both management and discipline skills to create a positive atmosphere for learning:
- Problem-prevention strategies (Praxis II, topic Ic)
- Managing instruction (Praxis II, topic Ic)
- Options for discipline (Praxis II, topic Ic)

PRAXIS   Test-Preparation Activities

 To review an on-line chapter case study, test your understanding of chapter topics and concepts, and begin preparing for the Praxis II: Principles of Learning and Teaching examination, go to the Praxis Test-Preparation module for this chapter of the Companion Website.

inTASC   Developing the Habit of Reflective Practice

Organizing Questions

Review questions, field-experience opportunities, and activities for building your portfolio are included here for the organizing questions in this chapter.

Why are strong relationships with students and other adults important?

Review Questions

1. What are some of the characteristics of effective teacher–student relationships?

2. How do teachers, parents, and children benefit from positive home–school relations?

3. Give some examples of the collaborative relationships with other adults that will be important to you as a future teacher.

Field Experience

After spending some time observing in a classroom of your choice, pick out a student with whom you would like to develop a good working relationship. Try to select someone who you are not drawn to naturally.
- Develop a list of strategies that you could use to build your relationship.
- If possible, try them out to see how they work.
- Discuss your experiences with others.

Building Your Portfolio: *Working with Parents*

INTASC Standard 10. One of your future roles as a teacher will be to develop good working relationships with the parents and guardians of your students and work to get them involved in the educational process. After having reviewed a book on parent involvement in education (see Suggested Readings for an example):
- Describe five strategies that you would use to communicate more effectively with parents.
- Identify five strategies for involving parents in the learning of their children.

What does research tell us about effective instructional strategies?

Review Questions

1. What are the keys to good note taking?

2. What benefits are often associated with homework?

3. What is a rubric and how is it used?

Field Experience

Spend some time observing a teacher at work in the classroom.
- What strategies did you observe from the list of research-based instructional techniques described in this chapter?

- How would you assess the effectiveness of the strategies you observed?
- Did you observe instructional strategies that you felt were ineffective?

Building Your Portfolio: *Developing a Rubric*

INTASC Standard 5. Identify a specific writing project that would be appropriate for the grade and subject you are considering as a future teacher.
- For the writing project identified, develop a scoring rubric that would give students completing the assignment clear feedback on the criteria being used for evaluation.
- Place a copy of the writing project and the scoring rubric developed in your portfolio.

What instructional models can I use?

Review Questions

1. How does a teacher use direct instruction in the classroom?
2. What is the primary emphasis of the personal model of instruction?
3. What types of learning are attributed to constructivist education?
4. What is the primary mode of learning in the social model of instruction?

Building Your Portfolio: *Investigate an Instructional Model*

INTASC Standard 5. Choose one of the instructional models described in this chapter that is of interest to you and spend some time researching this option further.
- Use the references found in the text, do an Internet search using key names, and spend some time in the library to gather information on the model you chose to review.
- Write a summary of the strengths and limitations of the instructional model for inclusion in your portfolio.

What skills will I need in management and discipline?

Review Questions

1. Describe examples of the management skills needed by teachers.
2. What are the key ingredients for developing effective rules?
3. What is an I-message and how is it used?

Field Experience

Talk to a classroom teacher about her or his discipline procedures. What does the teacher do or say to deal with inappropriate student behavior? Discuss with the teacher the ingredients needed for effective discipline in the classroom. Share your findings with classmates.

Building Your Portfolio: *Classroom Rules*

INTASC Standard 5. For an age/grade of your choosing:
- Develop a list of classroom rules that you would use for that age group.
- Why did you include the rules you did?
- How would you introduce these rules to the class?
- Do any of the rules need clarification for students? If so, how would you go about doing this?

Suggested Readings

Berger, E. (2008). *Parents as partners in education* (7th ed.). Upper Saddle River, NJ: Merrill/Prentice Hall. This book presents an excellent overview of the steps needed to build effective relationships with parents. The principles presented apply to all relationships in the classroom.

Jones, V., & Jones, L. (2007). *Comprehensive classroom management: Creating communities of support and solving problems* (8th ed.). Boston: Allyn & Bacon. This book provides strong content and an excellent framework for creating a comprehensive program for classroom management and discipline.

Joyce, B., & Weil, M. (2009). *Models of teaching* (8th ed.). Boston: Allyn & Bacon. In this text, the authors share their extensive knowledge of different models of instruction. The book has been in print over 20 years and is generally considered one of the best descriptions of models of teaching.

Marzano, R., Pickering, D., & Pollock, J. (2001). *Classroom instruction that works: Research-based strategies for increasing student achievement.* Alexandria, VA: Association for Supervision and Curriculum Development. This book provides a thorough overview of the research that has been done on effective teaching strategies. Many good examples illustrate the strategies being discussed.

References

Anderson, J. (1999). *Learning and memory: An integrated approach* (2nd ed.). New York: Wiley.

Arends, R. I. (2007). *Learning to teach.* (7th ed.) Boston: McGraw Hill.

Aronson, E. (2005). *Jigsaw classroom: Overview of the technique.* Retrieved November 7, 2005: www.jigsaw.org/overview.htm

Ausubel, D. (1968). *Educational psychology: A cognitive view.* New York: Holt, Rinehart & Winston.

Berger, E. (2008). *Parents as partners in education* (7th ed.). Upper Saddle River, NJ: Merrill/Prentice Hall.

Brooks, J. G., & Brooks, M. G. (1993). *In search of understanding: The case for constructivist classrooms.* Alexandria, VA: ASCD.

Burden, P. R. (2003). *Powerful classroom management strategies: Motivating students to learn.* Thousand Oaks, CA: Corwin Press.

Burns, M. (2005). Looking at how students reason. *Educational Leadership, 63*(3), 26–31.

Canter, L., & Canter, M. (2002). *Assertive discipline: Positive behavior management for today's classroom.* Los Angeles: Canter and Associates.

Chappius, J. (2005). Helping students understand assessment. *Educational Leadership, 63*(3), 39–43.

Charles, C. (2008). *Building classroom discipline* (9th ed.). New York: Longman.

Coloroso, B. (2003). *The bully, the bullied, and the bystander: How parents and teachers can break the cycle of violence.* New York: HarperCollins.

Cooper, H. (1989). Synthesis of research on homework. *Educational Leadership, 47*(3), 85–91.

Coopersmith, S. (1967). *The antecedents of self-esteem.* San Francisco: W. H. Freeman.

Copeland, M. (2005). *Socratic circles: Fostering critical and creative thinking in middle and high school.* Portland, ME: Stenhouse.

Council of Chief State School Officers. (2005). Michele Forman 2001 National Teacher of the Year. Retrieved March 22, 2005, from: *http://www.ccsso.org/projects/National_Teacher_of_the_Year/ National_Teachers/126.cfm*

Curwin, R., & Mendler, A. (2001). *Discipline with dignity.* Columbus, OH: Merrill. Education.

Danielson, C. (2007). *Enhancing professional practice: A framework for teaching.* (2nd ed.) Alexandria, VA: ASCD.

Darling-Hammond, L., & Bransford, J. (2005). *Preparing teachers for a changing world: What teachers should learn and be able to do.* San Francisco: Jossey-Bass.

Dewey, J. (1929). *Democracy and education.* New York: Macmillan.

Dreikurs, R., Grunwald, B., & Pepper, F. (1971). *Maintaining sanity in the classroom.* New York: Harper and Row.

Ellis, S., & Whalen, S. (1990). *Cooperative learning: Getting started.* New York: Scholastic.

Evertson, C., & Emmer, E., (2009). *Classroom management for elementary teachers* (8th ed.). Boston: Allyn and Bacon.

Fay, J., & Funk, D. (1998). *Teaching with love and logic: Taking control of the classroom.* Golden, CO: Love and Logic Institute.

Gestwicki, C. (2007). *Home, school, and community relations* (6th ed.). Albany, NY: Delmar.

Glasser, W. (1969). *Schools without failure.* New York: Harper and Row.

Glasser, W. (1986). *Control theory in the classroom.* New York: Harper and Row.

Glasser, W. (1990). *The quality school: Managing students without coercion.* New York: Harper and Row.

Good, T., & Brophy, J. (2008). *Looking in classrooms* (10th ed.). Boston: Allyn and Bacon.

Gordon, T. (1970). *Parent effectiveness training.* New York: New American Library.

Gordon, T. (1974). *Teacher effectiveness training.* New York: Wyden.

Greenberg, H. (1969). *Teaching with feeling.* Indianapolis, IN: Pegasus.

Hattie, J. (1992). Measuring the effects of schooling. *Australian Journal of Education, 36*(1), 5–13.

Hunter, M. (1994). *Discipline that develops self-discipline.* Thousand Oaks, CA: Corwin Press.

Johnson, D., & Johnson, R. (1975). *Circles of learning.* Upper Saddle River, NJ: Prentice Hall.

Johnson, D. W., Johnson, R. T., & Holubec, E. (1988). *Cooperation in the classroom.* Edina, MN: Interaction Book Company.

Johnson, R. T., & Johnson, D. W. (1996). Conflict resolution and peer mediation programs in elementary and secondary schools: A review of the research. *Review of Educational Research, 66,* 459–473.

Jones, V., & Jones, L. (2007). *Comprehensive classroom management: Creating communities of support and solving problems* (8th ed.). Boston: Allyn and Bacon.

Joyce, B., & Weil, M. (2009). *Models of teaching* (8th ed.). Boston: Allyn and Bacon.

Kagan, S. (1997). *Cooperative learning.* San Clemente, CA: Kagan Cooperative.

Kameenui, E., & Darch, C. (1995). *Instructional classroom management.* White Plains, NY: Longman.

Kounin, J. (1970). *Discipline and group management in classrooms.* New York: Holt, Rinehart, and Winston.

Lane, P., & McWhirter, J. (1992). A peer mediation model: Conflict resolution for elementary and secondary school children. *Elementary School Guidance and Counseling, 27,* 15–21.

Long, N., & Morse, W. (1996). *Conflict in the classroom: The education of at-risk and troubled students*. Austin, TX: Pro-Ed.

Marzano, R. J. (2003). *What works in school: Translating research into action*. Alexandria, VA: Association for Supervision and Curriculum Development.

Marzano, R., Pickering, D., & Pollock, J. (2001). *Classroom instruction that works: Research-based strategies for increasing student achievement*. Alexandria, VA: Association for Supervision and Curriculum Development.

Maslow, A. (1968). *Toward a psychology of being*. Princeton, NJ: Van Nostrand Reinhold.

McCloud, S. (2005). From chaos to consistency. *Educational Leadership, 62*(5), 46–49.

Medin, D., Goldstone, R., & Markman, A. (1995). Comparison and choice: Relations between similarity processes and decision processes. *Psychonomic Bulletin & Review, 2*(1), 1–19.

Nash, R., & Shiman, D. (1974) The English teacher as questioner. *English Journal, 63*, 42–45.

Noddings, N. (1992). *The challenge to care in schools: An alternative approach to education*. New York: Teachers College Press.

Paivio, A. (1990). *Mental representations: A dual coding approach*. New York: Oxford University Press.

Pavlov, I. (1927). *Conditioned reflexes: An investigation of physiological activity of the cerebral cortex*. London: Oxford University Press.

Pearson, P., & Gallagher, M. (1983). The instruction of reading comprehension. *Contemporary Educational Psychology, 8*, 317–344.

Perkins, D. (1999). The many faces of constructivism. *Educational Leadership, 57*(3), 28–33.

Piaget, J. (1950). *The psychology of intelligence* (M. Piercy & D. Berlyne, Trans.). New York: Harcourt, Brace.

Roberts, P. L., Kellough, R. D., & Moore, K. (2006). *A resource guide for elementary school teaching: Planning for competence*. Upper Saddle River, NJ: Pearson Education.

Rogers, C. (1969). *Freedom to learn*. Upper Saddle River, NJ: Merrill/Prentice Hall.

Rubinstein, G. (1999). *Reluctant disciplinarian: Advice on classroom management from a softy who became (eventually) a successful teacher*. Fort Collins, CO: Cottonwood Press.

Sergiovanni, T. (1994). *Building community in schools*. San Francisco: Jossey-Bass.

Skinner, B. F. (1953). *Science and human behavior*. New York: Macmillan.

Slavin, R. (1983). *Cooperative learning*. New York: Longman.

Sprick, R., Sprick, M., & Garrison, M. (1992). *Establishing positive discipline policies*. Longmont, CO: Sopris West.

Thorndike, E. (1913). *The psychology of learning: Volume II. Educational psychology*. New York: Teachers College Press.

Vygotsky, L. (1978). *Mind in society: The development of higher psychological processes*. Cambridge, MA: Harvard University Press.

Walberg, H. (1999). Productive teaching. In H. C. Waxman & H. J. Walberg (Eds.) *New directions for teaching practice and research* (pp. 75–104). Berkeley, CA: McCutchen.

Walker, H. M., Ramsey, E., & Gresham, F. (2004). *Antisocial behavior in school: Evidence based practices*. Belmont, CA: Thomson Wadsworth.

Watson, J. (1924). *Behaviorism*. New York: Norton.

Watson, M., & Ecken, L.(2003). *Learning to trust: Transforming difficult elementary classrooms through developmental discipline.* San Francisco: Jossey Bass.

Winger, T. (2005). Grading to communicate. *Educational Leadership, 63*(3), 61–65.

Wormeli, R. (2003). *Day one and beyond: Practical matters for new middle-level teachers.* Portland, ME: Stenhouse.

Zirpoli, T. (2008). *Behavior management: Applications for teachers.* (5th ed.) Upper Saddle River, NJ: Prentice Hall.

chapter 9

Integrating Technology

As a future teacher, you will have many opportunities to use computers, the Internet, and other technologies in support of teaching and learning. You will need to understand technology's potential and be able to effectively use it in the classroom. Four organizing questions will help you more fully understand the changing relationships between education and technology.

Focus Questions

1. How has technology been used in the classroom?

2. What are schools doing to enhance technology use in the curriculum?

3. What is the impact of computers on teaching and learning?

4. What issues must be resolved to strengthen technology's impact?

Mrs. Simpson's fifth-period social studies class has just begun and Kelly, Angie, and Megan have gathered in a small group to talk about their upcoming presentation to the class about ancient Greek architecture. These seventh-grade students have spent time searching the Internet, reading appropriate information from the class CD-ROM encyclopedia, and finding books from the school library on their chosen topic. Kelly located some interesting digital images on the Internet that the group wants to share with the class. Angie used the school's digital camera to photograph local architectural designs for comparison with those from ancient Greece, and the group is now thinking about a PowerPoint® multimedia presentation that will allow them to share what they have learned with their classmates. With Mrs. Simpson's assistance, the girls excitedly plan the next steps as they prepare for the class presentation.

Although the scenario just described is not common in all classrooms, it is becoming more prevalent in most schools. Teachers are working to develop the skills they need to integrate technology into their instruction at the same time that students are engaged in using these options at school and in the home to learn more about the world around them. As computers and the Internet become increasingly more available in school settings, these technologies and others are strongly influencing teaching and learning in America's schools.

How has technology been used in the classroom?

In Chapter 7, **technology** was broadly defined as any device or tool that can be used to extend human abilities. Using that definition, can openers, paper clips, hammers, and telephones are all examples of technology. Similarly, in education the overhead projector, video camera, and the ruler are all technology options commonly found in many classrooms. Although we tend to think of the computer as being synonymous with technology, many other tools have in fact been used over the years to assist teachers and students in the learning process.

As you read this section, think about technological innovations you remember from your own schooling. What made the technology you used in school either successful or unsuccessful? Were computers a part of your educational experience? If so, how were they used? What changes occurred in the ways computers were used during your pre-K–12 classroom experiences? Reflect on and describe the changes you might expect to see in the next decade.

**Reflection
Opportunity 9.1**

Early Technology Options

The introduction of new technology in the classroom has often been viewed as a quick and easy solution to very complex educational problems. Near the beginning of the 20th century, for example, the radio was seen as an important new technology that would allow teachers to supplement classroom teaching, update the information found in school textbooks, and expose students to a wider array of topics and information than the classroom teacher could do on his or her own (Trotter, 1999).

Some technological advances have had little impact on schooling, but others have been very successful in transforming teaching and learning. For example, radio, telephone, and television are among the many technologies that were initially seen as tools that would dramatically change education but never lived up to that potential. On the other hand, the mimeograph machine, videocassette recorder, and overhead projector have all had a significant influence on America's classrooms. Tyack and Cuban (2000) suggest that new technologies are successful when they are flexible tools that assist the teacher in managing the traditional aspects of their classroom lives, but that they are relatively ineffective when they require teachers to change dramatically their interactions with students.

Television

When educators began experimenting with television for the delivery of courses in the 1940s, many predicted that this technology would revolutionize schooling (Trotter, 1999). Administrators saw television as an option that would allow the schools to deliver courses to a growing student population without hiring large numbers of new teachers. Others felt that with a few top-quality teachers developing courses for delivery via television, more students would receive the best possible instruction. In addition, many teachers were enthralled by the glamour of television broadcasting.

Not everyone, however, was enthusiastic about the use of the television in the classroom. Some teachers were concerned about the implications for their jobs, whereas others felt that the impersonal nature of television viewing detracted from the educational experience. Before the advent of the VCR, the coordination of class schedules needed to allow students opportunities to view live broadcasts left still other teachers and administrators frustrated. Hardware breakdowns and insufficient numbers of television sets were additional administrative hurdles that caused many to react negatively to the proposed addition of this new technology (Tyack & Cuban, 2000). Television programming has also been criticized for reinforcing negative stereotypes (Williams, 2004) and desensitizing children and youth to violence (American Academy of Child and Adolescent Psychiatry, 2008). These issues and more make it difficult for teachers to use television in the classroom successfully.

Although television has not lived up to early expectations as a transforming method of teaching and learning, it is still viewed as having a positive impact in the classroom in several ways. The Corporation for Public Broadcasting (2004), after reviewing educator surveys and research, suggests that educational television:

- Reinforces reading and lecture material
- Aids in the development of a common base of knowledge among students
- Enhances student comprehension and discussion
- Provides greater accommodation of diverse learning styles
- Increases student motivation and enthusiasm
- Promotes teacher effectiveness (p. 2).

Television has proven valuable in classrooms when quality video tapes and DVDs are on hand for use. With these resources, schools are able to provide educational opportunities to students that would not otherwise be available. For example, some schools that do not have qualified instructors to teach foreign languages may choose to use language video programs such as Saludos and Salsa (Rhodes & Pufahl, 2003). Although there is no doubt that students benefit most from having a teacher who is a fluent foreign language speaker, foreign language video programs can be an effective way for students to learn a second language when this option is not available.

Computers

The most recent technology to gain momentum as a tool to reform teaching and learning is the computer. From the 1980s to the present, the numbers and quality of computers and software available to students have continued to grow. The number of students per computer, a long-standing measure of computer access, decreased from 125 in 1981 (Tyack & Cuban, 2000) to 3.8 in 2006 (Education Week, 2008).

Because computers have been a relatively new addition to America's schools, it is still unclear whether or not they will have a major influence on teaching and learning. On the one hand, most teachers have moved beyond a minimum level of competence with computers and are beginning to use them more regularly in their classrooms (Education Week, 2008). At the same time, a smaller number have the advanced skills necessary to integrate computer technology into the classroom day effectively. Time will tell whether computers will follow educational television as a short-lived educational technology phenomenon or become as invaluable as the photocopier in assisting teachers in the delivery of instruction.

Teacher uses. Regardless of their long-term impact on instruction, teachers are putting computers to use in a variety of important ways. The most common option for teachers is *word processing*. They create handouts for students, write letters to parents, and respond to administrators' requests for information. Another common use is for *record keeping*. Grade files for students, standardized test results, and lesson planning are among the many options for record keeping. Most teachers also use computer technology for *communicating* via e-mail with other teachers, administrators, and parents. Another strategy a growing number of schools use is an assortment of *Web-based services* to post grades, list homework assignments, and communicate with parents. Finally, teachers are using technology for *assessment*. Teachers and schools are using a number of different strategies for incorporating technology into their assessment efforts. Some teachers, for example, are using test generating software to create their own exams to use with students. In addition, some schools use assessment programs that allow parents with the appropriate password to view their child's grades via the Internet (Garten, 2005). Computers are also influencing classroom assessment as teachers and schools implement digital portfolios. For example, student products that are difficult to place in a hard-copy portfolio (such as a performance with puppets or a diorama) can be photographed with a digital camera. Students can then write captions for the photos and add these documents to their portfolios. In addition, computers are essential when teachers and schools have students keep **digital portfolios** as an assessment strategy. Like their hard-copy counterparts, digital portfolios are collections of student work kept in a digital format. They are used to demonstrate progress toward district, state, and national standards (Niguidula, 2005).

Instructional uses. In addition to the teacher-productivity tools mentioned above, the number of instructional uses for the computer is growing. A wealth of software options provide students with a variety of learning experiences on the computer. Table 9.1 gives several examples of typical software available for classroom use. One available option is called **drill and practice software** and is used by students to practice what they have already learned in other ways.

Another option found in many classrooms is **simulation software.** Students using this type of software assume roles and reenact events as they manipulate scenarios created by the software. A third software program being used by students is **word-processing software.** Used for writing tasks such as papers, reports, and creative-writing assignments, good word processing software is available for all grade levels. **Encyclopedia software,** generally available on CD-ROM, is another common option. Several excellent programs serve as the electronic equivalents of encyclopedias. Students can use these sources to gather information for class projects and report writing. A final software type that is available in limited quantity is **creativity software.** Although many software products falsely advertise their creative potential, some pieces actually are available that encourage students to actively engage in creative thinking.

The Internet

Are you a regular Internet user? If so, you are aware of the vast quantities of information available from the Internet. Although some Internet sites are either of low quality or contain information that is inappropriate for student use, a great deal of information is available that both students and teachers can productively use to facilitate teaching and learning. As a future teacher, you will want to be aware of both the strengths and limitations of Internet use in the classroom.

Just as computers are beginning to have an impact on schools in America, the rapid growth in Internet use is also influencing teaching and learning. In simple terms, the **Internet** is a worldwide collection of interconnected computers. Using technology referred to as the **World Wide Web,** Internet users are able to quickly and easily move between sites using a simple visual format (Provenzo, Brett, & McCloskey, 2005). Growth in worldwide Internet use has been very rapid, with 20 million users in 1993 and over 1.2 billion in 2006 (Computer Industry Almanac, 2007), with the United States having the largest number of users. Table 9.2 identifies the top 10 countries in the world in Internet use. China has shown the greatest growth, having doubled the number of users in the last few years (Computer Industry Almanac, 2007).

The Internet has opened up a huge world of new information to both teachers and students. Teachers, for example, are using it to create at least a portion of their lesson plans. Education Week (2005) found that 77% of all schools nationwide have a majority of teachers who use the Internet for instruction. Only 19% of schools have a majority of teachers who are considered beginners in terms of technology use. Most teachers are also engaged in sending e-mail, and some are creating their own Websites to share positive teaching experiences and student work with others. Students are also very involved in Internet use. Most use it at least occasionally as an information-gathering tool for school assignments. More than 70% of students have been given classroom instruction in

TABLE 9.1 Software Options

Type	Example	Description
Drill and Practice	Mighty Math Astro Algebra	Teaches students in Grades 7–9 basic concepts and problem solving strategies for algebra
Simulation	The Oregon Trail	Students lead a wagon train through the many challenges facing the early American pioneers
Word Processing	Microsoft Word	Allows students of all ages to create letters, papers, and projects for classroom projects
Encyclopedia Software	Encyclopedia Britannica	The CD-ROM equivalent of paper encyclopedias with a wealth of information, charts, data, and pictures
Creativity Software	Imagination Express	Encourages elementary and middle school students to create puppet shows, illustrated books, multimedia presentations, movies, and videos

using an Internet search engine to find information for their work at school (Meyer, 2001). Many students are also using the Internet to communicate with others via e-mail or creating accounts on social networking websites such as Myspace and Facebook to communicate with groups of friends.

Roblyer (2006) suggests that the Internet benefits students and teachers in many ways. Among the benefits listed are:

- *Easy and rapid communication*—The use of e-mail, in particular, has increased the rapidity and ease with which students and parents communicate with teachers. It is important to remember, however, that teachers must use caution when sharing information electronically. Because there is no assurance of confidentiality, teachers should not use last names of students when sharing information about grades or concerns about behavior. In many instances, a face-to-face discussion would be a more beneficial and respectful situation in which to share this information.

- *Access to expert resources and information*—Experts and information not available locally can be readily accessed via the Internet. Using reliable sources can greatly expand the availability of important information for a variety of tasks.

- *Provide up-to-date information*—Although there is a lag time of several months or years between when an article or book is written and when it appears in print, the Internet provides users with more up-to-date resources.

- *Easy sharing of information and work*—Using the Internet, students and teachers can share information with each other as they work together to complete projects and papers.

- *Support for cooperative group work*—The Internet's wealth of information and ease of access motivate students as they work together on common projects.

One significant problem that many teachers face when they encourage students to use the Internet is cyber cheating. It is an old problem (plagiarism) presenting itself in a new technology. The *Explore Your Beliefs* feature for this chapter asks you to think more deeply about this growing

TABLE 9.2   Top 10 Countries in Internet Use

Rank	Country	Users (millions)
1	United States	210.2
2	China	131.1
3	Japan	90.9
4	India	67.6
5	Germany	50.3
6	United Kingdom	37.9
7	South Korea	35.0
8	France	32.0
9	Italy	31.6
10	Brazil	29.5

Source: From "Worldwide Internet users top 1.2 billion in 2006" by Computer Industry Almanac, 2007. Retrieved December 15, 2008 from: http://www.c-i-a.com/pr0207.htm.

problem. Read this feature now and respond to the questions presented so that you can learn more about your own feelings on this topic.

Explore your beliefs: Cyber cheating

Working to prevent cheating is not a new task for teachers. Today, however, technology has altered this challenge. For example, today's students are not likely to write notes on their hands; instead they use programmable calculators, handheld computers, digital watches, and cell phones to hold their crib notes. In addition, students who are motivated to plagiarize now possess a more sophisticated set of electronic aids that include paper mill Web sites from which whole papers can be easily purchased or traded.

Christine Pelton, a teacher from Piper, Kansas, (Simpson, 2002) required her 118 science students to collect and study 20 different leaves, and to prepare a written report about each. The assignment would count for 50% of their final grade. While evaluating student work, Pelton noticed that some of the written reports contained identical passages. So she used a plagiarism detection computer program and discovered that 28 students had copied substantial portions of their reports directly from Web sites.

The punishment for first offense cheating, according to her school district's policy, was no credit for the assignment. So the 28 students who plagiarized their reports received a zero, which would result in a failing grade for the class. Many of these students' parents were upset and eventually went to the school board and demanded the teacher be overruled. The board agreed and made the Leaf Project count for much less of the total grade. All the kids who failed the class for cheating would now pass. Pelton, feeling that her authority had been completely undermined resigned soon afterwards.

Today, many educators aim to create a set of conditions in which it is unlikely that plagiarism will occur. Not only do they review the consequences for students caught cheating, they also avoid assignments that require students to simply gather facts. Instead, they assign projects that engage students in problem solving where they are making personal choices. In addition, many teachers require that students turn in a series of drafts and revisions before the final paper is accepted.

Developing the Habit of Reflective Practice

Gather Information

1. Search the Internet for "cyber cheating in schools" and read more on this problem behavior.
2. Think back on your own education. How were students cheating? How did teachers prevent and react to cheating behaviors?

Identify Beliefs

1. What effect do you think cheating has on student learning, performance and behavior?
2. Do you agree with the consequences that Christine Pelton tried to give her students for cheating?

Make Decisions

1. If you were a school board member, would you have voted to support Christine Pelton's decision? Why or why not?

Assess and Evaluate

1. How could Christine Pelton's assignment be altered so that students would be less likely to cheat?

Source

Simpson, M. (2002). Taking a stand for integrity. *NEA Today*, May 1, 2002. Retrieved July 16, 2005 from *http://www.nea.org/neatoday/0205/rights.html*

Think about how you have used the Internet as a learning tool either in your pre-K–12 or college classes. What information do you find useful on the Internet? What aspects of the Internet do you find distracting and/or of little value? Based on your responses to these questions, consider the potential usefulness of the Internet for the future students you plan to teach. For the grade or subject you plan to teach, how might students use the Internet as a learning tool?

Reflection Opportunity 9.2

What are schools doing to enhance technology use in the curriculum?

If computers and Internet use are to be more than just another marginalized technology option, they must be carefully integrated into the everyday life of the schools. Rather than being on the periphery, computers need to be used daily in all subject matter areas as important tools for teaching and learning. This complex task requires the schools to carefully plan and implement strategies that can make increased computer use a reality.

Reflection Opportunity 9.3

The integration of computer technology into the classroom will require extended effort on the part of teachers. As you begin reading this section, reflect on the relative merits of this task. Is it worth doing? In addition, think about your willingness as a future teacher to commit the time and energy needed on your part to integrate technology into your teaching. How do you think you will feel about engaging in this task? Do you think you will enjoy it or is it something you may struggle to fit into an already busy schedule?

Classroom Computers with Internet Access

When computers were first introduced into the schools, they were generally grouped together in a computer lab. Because only a few machines were available, creating a lab allowed for better access by students throughout the school. It also made it possible for the one or two trained computer "experts" to teach others how to use the equipment and software. Unfortunately, this setup also meant that students typically only had access to computers for a few minutes each week.

As computers became more commonly available and a growing number of teachers started to use them on a regular basis in their teaching, this technology has increasingly been placed in individual classrooms. Currently, over 90% of all U.S. schools have Internet-connected computers in one or more classrooms. On the other hand, even though more computers are being placed directly in classrooms, the ratio of students to classroom computers still remains relatively high at 7.6 students per computer (Education Week, 2005).

Gail McGoogan (McGoogan, 2002) provides an excellent example of how teachers are using computers and the Internet to improve their teaching. Each year, she works with colleagues to create a unique videoconferencing opportunity for the first–fifth grade students at her elementary school. About 80 students, assisted by parent volunteers and their teachers, spend the night at school to communicate with children around the world. This exercise helps students see how closely their lives are tied to what is happening around the world. Prior to this culminating event, students use their reading and writing skills to research countries and brainstorm questions. Students e-mail more than 200 classrooms in their search for schools with videoconferencing capabilities. Students develop a schedule for the night, taking time zones into consideration when planning conversation times. One year, Gail's students were excited to find out that their peers in Scotland were hoping for a day off from school because it was snowing there. Then they were surprised to find out that their peers in Australia were just returning from their summer vacation! To learn about life in other areas of the world firsthand from children who live there makes social studies relevant and meaningful to these students.

Another good example of how computers and the Internet are influencing teaching and learning is the use of **WebQuests** in the classroom (March, 2004). WebQuests began in 1995 as the brainchild of Bernie Dodge and Tom March. They are inquiry-oriented activities in which some or all of the information comes from resources on the Internet. WebQuests are designed to effectively use learners' time by focusing their energies on using information rather than just looking for it. WebQuests also encourage learners to analyze, synthesize, and evaluate the information they find. An example of a WebQuest comes from a group of middle school teachers who asked their students to determine the group with the best claim to the bones of Kennewick Man (Baglio, Hiller, & Zehnder, 2005). Kennewick Man is a skeleton found near the Columbia River in Kennewick, Washington in 1996. Eight anthropologists, including two from the Smithsonian Institution, filed a legal action to halt the return of this 9,000-year-old skeleton to Native American tribes living in the region where the bones were found. The tribes believed that nature should be left to take its course with the remains. The scientists, on the other hand, argued that the study of these bones would benefit the entire country. They pointed out that the Kennewick Man was one of the oldest skeletons ever discovered in the United States. The middle school teachers who initiated the WebQuest suggested a scenario in which the students would be grouped into teams. Their job would be to determine who had legal rights for ownership of these bones. Each student team was to write a legal brief that explained the issue, described the claimants and their viewpoints, identified the pertinent laws, and explained the group's decision. Groups also gave a mock press conference where they answered questions from reporters (their classmates).

A final area in which computers and the Internet are having an impact on teaching and learning is the ease of access to primary source materials that can deepen students' understandings of historical events while capturing their imagination. For example, the Smithsonian Institution's Website (*www.smithsonianeducation.org*) offers primary source materials with accompanying lesson plans to teachers at no charge. Andy Holland, a sixth-grade teacher, is beginning his annual unit on the Wright brothers. But instead of using the social studies textbook as his primary guide, he divides his class into five groups and distributes copies of relevant primary and secondary source documents found on the Smithsonian Website (Norby, 2004):

- *Group one* receives Orville Wright's journal entry from December 17th, 1903; the day the Kitty Hawk first took flight.
- *Group two* looks at the telegram Orville sent his father describing the first successful flight.
- *Group three* reads a letter the Wright brothers' father wrote to a reporter who was documenting the December 17th flight.
- *Group four* reads an account of a bystander who was injured on the ground when the plane collided with him upon landing from the historical flight.
- *Group five* reads a newspaper article appearing in a newspaper the day after the first flight of the Kitty Hawk.

As students discuss what they have read as a large group, they are amazed to find that their sources often contradict each other. This experience allows Andy's students to investigate an important event in the same way historians do. The Smithsonian Website and others like it make primary resources easily accessible to educators and their students. These sites open up to schools resources that were once available only to those who lived physically near to review the original documents. Now teachers have access to educational resources such as the National Aeronautics and Space Administration (NASA), Plymouth Plantation, the White House, and Mount Rushmore.

Schools that have invested in computers and Internet access find that they are able to serve their students in new and important ways. Access to the Internet gives students greater curriculum options for specialty courses. Cyber learning provides choices that can expand schooling experiences far beyond the walls of the school. The *Reflect on Diversity* feature found later in this chapter describes how rural areas can strongly benefit from this option.

Quality Software

Another issue that schools must face if they are to increase effective computer use effectively is to have quality instructional software available for students and teachers to use in their work. What might sound like a rather simple task is actually a very difficult one. Because instructional software is a commercial product with potentially huge revenues, there are literally thousands of options to choose from. It is difficult to sort through all of the many options to find the best ones for a given educational situation. Although there are several good sources for reviews of instructional software, even finding the time to sort through and read the many reviews can be a challenge. Children's Technology Review (2008), for example, has reviewed over 8000 different software programs that are available for use at home and in the school setting.

Take, for example, Tom Harding. He is interested in finding some new software to use on the five computers that were recently purchased for his fifth-grade classroom. Tom is particularly interested in locating some software for mathematics instruction. But after reviewing the software catalogs in the school office, Tom is unsure how to proceed. He found 22 pieces of software from different publishers that look good in the catalogs and seem to meet his requirements. Tom needs some assistance in making good selections from the many options available to him. Table 9.3 provides suggestions for evaluating software.

What is the impact of computers on teaching and learning?

There are a variety of opinions on the impact that computers will have on teaching and learning. Some believe that it will have a transformational influence. The Blue Ribbon Panel on Technology convened by Learning Point Associates (2004), for example, engaged in a series of activities that helped them create a vision for what technology in education will look like in the future. They state:

> The central theme of this vision is *technology transformation*, not technology integration.
> Technology should be used to do fundamentally different things in education rather than

TABLE 9.3   Evaluating Software

Characteristic	Criteria
Goals and Objectives	Does the software match with your overall curriculum? Will it meet the needs of your particular group of students? Rather than reading the software documentation, you will need to review the software itself.
Content	Does the software meet your instructional objectives? Review the software to make sure it has content that is developmentally appropriate for your students and follows a logical learning sequence.
Methodology	Are the methods of instruction used in the software consistent with sound learning theory? Are you comfortable with the approach used and does it fit with your own instructional methodologies?
Utilization	Determine the ease of use of the software. Can students operate it with minimal adult assistance? Is the software easy to enter, exit, and use? Can the teacher have some control over the program (e.g., turn off the sound if desired)?

Source: From Provenzo, E., Brett, A., & McCloskey, G. (2005). *Computers, curriculum, and cultural change* (2nd ed.) Mahwah, NJ: Lawrence Erlbaum.

enhance what is already happening in the classroom. In some cases, technology will drive the transformation while in others it will facilitate long-standing ideas (p. 1).

Another proponent of transformational change through the use of computer technology is Seymour Papert (2000). Papert is the developer of a computer programming language for children called LOGO. He believes that computers are already in the process of completely reforming education.

Neil Postman (2000), on the other hand, argues for a more cautious approach to the use of computers in the classroom. He sees other issues as being more important to address:

I am not arguing against using computers in school. I am arguing against our sleepwalking attitudes toward it, against allowing it to distract us from more important things, against making a god of it. This is what Theodore Roszak (1986) warned against in The Cult of Information: "Like all cults," he wrote, "this one has the intention of enlisting mindless allegiance and acquiescence. People who have no clear idea of what they mean by information, or why they should want so much of it, are nonetheless prepared to believe that we live in an Information Age, which makes every computer around us what the relics of the True Cross were in the Age of Faith: emblems of salvation (p. x)." To this I would add the sage observation of Alan Kay of Apple Computer. Kay is widely associated with the invention of the personal computer, and certainly has an interest in the use of computers in schools. Nonetheless, he has repeatedly said that any problem the schools cannot solve without computers, they cannot solve with them. (p. 294)

Similarly, the Alliance for Childhood (2004) makes a strong case for having children focus on the natural world and human relationships, rather than the computer screen. They find little in the way of hard evidence to support the long-term benefits of technology for children.

Impact on Teaching

Although it is difficult to predict accurately the future impact of computer technology on education, it appears that many teachers are changing what they do in the classroom as they increase their reliance on its use. Rather than continuing to use the strategies they found effective in the past, these teachers are rethinking the ways in which they teach. Some are blending technology into their current teaching strategies, and others are using computers and Internet access to fundamentally change the ways in which they teach.

Blending technology and teaching. Most teachers are increasingly willing to combine their current methods of classroom instruction with computer use. Although they are not dramatically changing the teaching that takes place in their classrooms, they are taking advantage of the computer's strengths to supplement what they are already doing. Surveys indicate that many teachers are at least beginning this blending of technology and teaching (Education Week, 2005). This is due, in part to increased access to computers and the Internet in the classroom and the growing level of expertise that teachers have in using this technology. Although new teachers in many states are expected to have strong technology skills in order to receive their initial teacher certification, veteran teachers are continuing to develop technology competencies through in-service training opportunities (Provenzo, Brett, & McCloskey, 2005). In addition, teachers are well aware that students today are a part of what has been called the *digital immediate gratification* or the *DIG generation* (Renard, 2005). Although many may argue that this trend is problematic, it is clear that students embrace digital communications and wise teachers capitalize on this interest as a part of their teaching. Consequently, a large majority of teachers are engaging in at least some instruction via the computer and Internet and providing students with a variety of opportunities to use technology during the school day. Teachers are using computers to show students how to do research, write papers, search for information on the Internet, create presentations, use spreadsheets, visualize new concepts, and find help with homework (Meyer, 2001). They are much more likely to engage in these activities when the computers they use are located in their classrooms. The *Engage in the Debate* feature for this chapter describes the arguments for and against classroom computers as well as discussing the positive and negative aspects of creating computer labs that are used by the whole school. Take some time to reflect on the issues presented in this feature.

Engage in the debate: Computer labs or classroom computers?

Greenacres Elementary is a hypothetical educational setting typical of many elementary schools around the country in terms of computer access and use. The dedicated faculty and staff are working hard to incorporate technology into student learning. Currently, the school has a computer lab set up in a portion of the library. With a block of 28 networked computers, all with Internet access, teachers can use the lab at scheduled times to conduct a number of tasks. Most frequently, lab times are used to teach the whole class skills in computer use. For example, Angela Lopez's third grade class is learning how to use Internet search engines; Devon Martin's fifth-grade class is refining their keyboarding skills. The lab is busy throughout the school day with different groups of students engaged in a variety of learning experiences. Most of the classrooms in Greenacres Elementary have at least one computer and about 80% of the classrooms have Internet access. Because the building is old, it has been difficult to add internet access to all classrooms and the small number of electrical outlets and tiny classrooms limit the number of computers that can be placed in the classrooms. Funding is not only needed to purchase computers, but it's also necessary to improve and adapt the building to facilitate technology usage. Greenacres' teachers find it difficult to fully integrate technology into their teaching since their students typically have access to the computer lab only once a week.

In an ideal world, schools like Greenacres Elementary would have the resources to fully support both a modern computer lab and individual classroom computers. Many schools, however, find they must make difficult choices between the two.

Developing the Habit of Reflective Practice
Gather Information

1. Go to the National Center for Education Statistics home page and search for "Internet Access in U.S. Public Schools and Classrooms."

2. Think back on your own K-12 education. How were computers integrated into your education? What impact did your access (or lack of access) have on your learning?

Identify Beliefs

1. Which benefits students more: a computer lab where whole class instruction can take place or a pod of computers in the back of the classroom?

2. What role should computers play in education? What should students do on computers? What should students *not* do on computers while in school?

Make Decisions

1. Imagine that you are on a committee in a school district. This committee is formed to decide on whether schools will continue using their computer labs or whether those computers should be dispersed into classrooms – which would result in about 2–3 computers per classroom. Which action would you support and why?

Assess and Evaluate

1. If you visited a school with a computer lab, how would you assess and evaluate the effectiveness the teaching and learning taking place with the available technology?

2. If you visited a school with a classroom computer pods, how would you assess and evaluate the effectiveness the teaching and learning taking place with the available technology?

There are numerous ways in which computers and technology are influencing teaching. Many schools, for example, are using **digital field trips** (also referred to as **cyber field trips**) to supplement the more traditional field trips classes take into the community. Elementary students learning about immigration, for example, would be fascinated by the on-line interactive tour of Ellis Island available at Scholastic.com (2005), and high school students taking a biology class may benefit from the Public Broadcast System's cyber field trip to the Galapagos Islands hosted by actor Alan Alda; Texas high school science teacher Sherri Steward; and her student, Mandy Williams (Public Broadcasting System, 2005). Technological tools other than computers are also having an impact on schools. For example, in the teaching of high school mathematics, most high school classrooms use graphing calculators, which allow students to visualize changing equations without having to spend time calculating numbers by hand. Geometer's Sketchpad, an increasingly popular software program that allows students to construct geometric figures electronically, is another example of technology's impact on the teaching of mathematics (Allen, 2003). Finally, read the *Views from the Classroom* feature found on the Companion Website for this text for a powerful story of how a simple phone call and the TV news led to an amazing learning experience.

Views from the Classroom: Sock It to Me

Teacher as facilitator of learning. If most teachers continue to use technology as one of many teaching strategies, the computer will have an important, but limited, impact on the overall directions of schooling. Fundamental changes, like those described by the Blue Ribbon Panel on Technology (Learning Point Associates, 2004), will come about only if teachers reconfigure their roles and interact differently with students. Rather than dispensing information to students, the teacher who makes extensive use of computers can become more of a guide and work with individuals or small groups to facilitate their learning. This is a major shift in emphasis for most teachers and often takes place over several years, if at all. Kellnor (2005) suggests that teachers who want to make this shift must change their mindset about teaching and learning:

> When using technology in the classroom, teachers must become open-minded and recognize that learning new processes and skills is an ongoing necessity. Although this involves added work, there are many imaginative ways of using technology to engage students in the learning process . . . Another shift for teachers comes with adopting a more flexible mindset about how the lesson plan should flow. This means that teachers must get comfortable with the idea of not teaching all their students the same information at the same time (p. 2).

Reflect on the vision of education presented earlier by the Blue Ribbon Panel on Technology and the information discussed in this section. Do you think computers will truly reshape teaching and learning in American schools? What makes you think this way? What will the role of the teacher become? Do you see future teachers blending technology and teaching? Or, do you believe computer technology will transform teachers into facilitators of learning? Given your perspective on the influence of technology, how do you personally feel about this direction? Do you see yourself being comfortable with and excited about these directions?

**Reflection
Opportunity 9.4**

Influence on Learners

Without question, the computer has become a major change agent in the world of work. Every occupation, from grocery clerk to orthopedic surgeon, has been significantly changed through a growing reliance on technology as a tool for everything from the mundane to the extremely complex. Computers have become so essential to all walks of life that every student today will need to develop confidence and competence in using these tools as part of future work efforts in the 21st century. The message from the worlds of business and industry are clear: New workers will need competence in technology to be successful in their jobs. (Partnership for 21st Century Skills, 2008).

Despite the fact that computers are very useful tools in all walks of life, it is important to remember that technology should only be used in teaching and learning when it is an effective tool in meeting the needs of students. There are times when indiscriminate use of technology can be dehumanizing. Jacques Ellul, a 1960s era philosopher who thought deeply about technology's effect on education, argued that as society becomes more technologically advanced it will also become less interested in human beings (Ellul, 1967). Think, for example, about video games. Do they tend to bring people together or isolate them? Can similar criticisms be made about computer use? Consider also a preschool teacher who opts to play videotape episodes of Reading Rainbow, a Public Broadcast System program emphasizing reading activities, instead of taking the time to read aloud to her students. Is this teacher sacrificing a critical literacy activity and human experience? It is important that as technological tools are made available to schools, educators carefully analyze how they incorporate them into teaching and learning. A quote from Ivan Illich, an author who wrote about technology's affect on society, offers us more to reflect upon as we consider the role of technology in student learning (Illich, 1972):

> A good educational system should have three purposes: it should provide all who want to learn with access to available resources at anytime in their lives; empower all who want to share what they know to find those who want to learn it from them; and finally, furnish all who want to present an issue to the public with the opportunity to make their challenge known. (p. 2)

As you read the following information on technology's impact on student learning, remember the words of Illich and Ellul. Make sure that you use technology wisely without allowing it to be a dehumanizing influence in your classroom.

TABLE 9.4   The Computer's Influence on Learning

Influence on Learning	Description
Digital age literacy	Students need to learn how to use the many new technological advances surrounding them effectively.
How students learn	Computers provide real-world contexts for learning, help students make connections with outside experts, provide visualization and analysis tools, create scaffolds for problem solving, and provide opportunities for feedback, reflection, and revision.
Distance learning	Distance learning allows students in diverse locations to take courses from home or in other settings rather than coming to the site where the course is actually being taught.

One of your many responsibilities as a future teacher will be to assist your students in developing the technology understandings and skills they will need to be successful in the world of work. In order to do this, you will need to be aware of the ways in which your students will be influenced by technology. Learners are increasingly affected in three main ways. Each of these influences is summarized in Table 9.4 and described more thoroughly in the paragraphs below.

Digital age literacy. As technology becomes infused into literally every aspect of American life, there is a strong and growing need for a technologically literate citizenry. This has led many schools to change their curricula to include time spent teaching students how to use the many new technological advances surrounding them. Computer labs have been one setting used by schools to help students develop such things as keyboarding skills, effective use of software tools (word processing, data management, etc.), and methods for finding information on the Internet. Many students are learning these skills at home, but others need schools to provide them with the opportunity to familiarize themselves with the many tools needed for success in our digital world. As technological tools continue to change, schools and teachers will need to persist in their efforts to stay up-to-date so that they can assist students in their understanding and use of these options. For example, handheld computers are a recent technological advance that educators are finding useful. In schools where handhelds are being used, teachers work to develop strategies that assist students in understanding and using them (Tooms, Acomb, & McGlothlin, 2004).

How students learn. In addition to changing the curricula of the schools, computers are also having an impact on how students learn. Current researchers and writers are looking at ways in which technology can facilitate the best kinds of learning in students. Roblyer (2006) identifies several ways in which the computer helps facilitate the best learning:

- *Gaining learner attention.* The critical first step in learning is to get the learner interested in what is to be learned. Computers provide a motivating environment that stimulates attention to the learning task.

- *Engaging the learner in meaningful tasks.* Computers allow students to create their own technology-based assignments and projects, making them more meaningful to the learner. While computers can often lead to meaningful learning, the *Ian's Classroom Experiences* feature for this chapter, (found on the Companion Website for this text) discusses instances when computers may not be the best option for some students.

Ian's Classroom Experiences: Implications

- *Increasing perceptions of control.* Because computers allow the learner to make many different choices about the order, sequence, and timing of the events that make up the learning experience, students feel as though they have greater control of their learning. This is seen as especially important for at-risk students and those that have experienced academic failure.

- *Linking learners to information sources.* When computers are linked to the Internet, the wealth of information available to students is limitless. "(T)echnology expands learning environments for students by letting them access primary source materials, obtain information, and have experiences with people and places that they could not otherwise have" (Roblyer, 2006, p. 12).

- *Supporting newer instructional approaches.* Technology-based activities help support the small-group activities that are an essential component of cooperative learning (see Chapter 8). In addition, newer software options for computers encourage general problem solving approaches that are so critical to deeper understandings of curriculum content. Even subjects that one might predict would be influenced very little by technology are being changed indelibly by it. For example, physical education teacher Phil Lawler of Naperville, Illinois (Johnson, 2003) provides his students with heart-monitor watches so he and the students can monitor and record the number of minutes they spend in the optimum cardiovascular pulse-rate range. He downloads the information to his computer and is able to modify his instruction to help each student obtain the most beneficial cardiovascular results.

- *Linking learners to learning tools.* Computers with software options like those described in Table 9.1 provide students with a variety of tools that help facilitate the learning process. For example, quality word-processing software programs allow students to compose, edit, and format reports and papers for class projects quickly and easily. Both the quality and ease of project development are enhanced by this and other learning tools. Another example comes from the classroom of Mary Olson, a visual arts elementary teacher from Illinois (Franklin, 2004). Mary uses a software program called Pictacular which enables her to combine artwork, music, and special effects to make art history come alive for her students. Another tool that Mary uses is Apple's iMovie software, which helps her students set photographs, prints and other visuals to music and voice-overs. To view a video of another example of technology linking learners to learning tools, go to the Companion Website for this text and click on MyEducationLab for Chapter 9.

myeducationlab)
The Power of Classroom Practice

MyEducationLab 9.1

Distance learning. The evidence above suggests that technology is beginning to have a significant impact on the format and content of instruction. In a similar way, computers and the Internet are also influencing where learning takes place.

Distance learning allows students in diverse locations to take courses from home or in other settings rather than coming to the site where the course is actually being taught. It may surprise you to learn that distance education actually came into existence long before computers became prominent in education. For example, the Independent Study High School (ISHS), under the management of the University of Nebraska—Lincoln (University of Nebraska—Lincoln, 2008), began in 1929. Although the ISHS currently offers its courses primarily via the Internet, in its early years courses were taught by sending written assignments back and forth through the mail. Learning through correspondence has been a fairly common educational practice for many years.

Distance learning is a rapidly growing alternative for many school districts trying to meet the needs of increasingly diverse groups of students. Some districts are creating their own virtual courses and offering them over the Internet for students in different schools. This type of distance learning is often referred to as **cyber learning**. For example, a rural school district may not need an advanced calculus course taught in every high school, but rather may find that one class for the entire district can be offered over the Internet. (The *Reflect on Diversity* feature in this section describes the benefits of cyber learning for rural schools). Or, another district may decide to teach Russian through distance learning to meet the needs of the limited number of high school students that may want to take this course for a language elective. Increasing numbers of school districts are also offering cyber learning options in place of more traditional summer school classes (Borja, 2005). Another alternative for distance learning is for school districts to find courses being offered by **virtual schools** and have interested students sign up for appropriate courses through one of these organizations. By September, 2008, 44 states either had full-time programs where students could take all courses online or supplemental programs where a few courses were offered online (Zucker, 2008). Table 9.5 lists some examples of virtual schools.

Reflect on diversity: Cyber education in rural schools

Rural schools face many challenges, including the challenge of offering a wide array of classes to their students with a limited staff. Virtual high schools like those described in Table 9.5 offer web-based courses that create opportunities for students in rural schools to achieve access, excellence, and equity in education. Online courses increase course offerings, alleviate teacher scarcity especially within hard to hire fields (such as math and science), and prevent the possible closures of rural schools.

Cyber education provides students with opportunities to access courses that supplement those available in rural schools. Advanced math and science courses, vocational options, and enrichment experiences are all available over the Internet. Cyber courses are typically developed for students by high school teachers who are certified in the content area. In some instances, during the period scheduled for their online class, students report to a physical classroom in their school—usually the computer lab—and login to their online course. Students typically have frequent interactions with their e-teacher through announcements posted to the class, responses to questions or work submitted the previous class day, or new assignments made available. As in traditional classes, students are responsible for learning course content and completing course requirements. In addition, they participate in group projects, class discussions, and inquiry-based learning.

Alaska is an example of a state that is beginning to use cyber education to meet the needs of rural schools. In addition to enrolling in courses from around the country, the Delta Cyber School (2008), in Delta Junction, Alaska offers an assortment of course work for resident students. High school geometry for example is not offered in many rural Alaskan schools but it is still on the exam required for high school graduation. Rural schools in Alaska that offer geometry are likely to have a non-certified math instructor teach that course resulting in a lower amount of proficiency for the students. Course work through Delta Cyber School provides one way that schools in rural areas can provide equal access to educational opportunities for their students.

Developing the Habit of Reflective Practice
Gather Information

1. Search the Internet for more information on one or more of the high schools described in Table 9.5.

2. Interview someone who has experienced an on-line learning environment and find out more about this type of educational experience.

Identify Beliefs

1. Can cyber learning be an effective experience for most students? Why or why not?

2. Is cyber education an effective way to increase the number, quality and type of course offerings made by rural school districts?

Make Decisions

1. If you were a school board member, would you decide to bring cyber learning into your rural school district? Why or why not?

Assess and Evaluate

1. If your school used cyber education, how would you assess and evaluate the effectiveness of these learning experiences? What information would you gather to help you decide how to improve cyber education in your school?

Source

Delta Cyber School. (2008). Our mission. Retrieved December 19, 2008 from *http://www .dcs.klz.ak.us/about.html*

TABLE 9.5   Sample Virtual High Schools

School	Description and Location
Florida Virtual School	The school began in 1997 and is a national leader in providing K–12 virtual education. It served over 63,000 students in 2007–08.
Illinois Virtual High School	Serving students in Illinois and managed by the Illinois Math and Science Academy, this school aims to increase equity and access to high quality courses.
Insight School of Colorado	A full-time, diploma-granting public high school that is tuition-free for Colorado residents.
Michigan Virtual School	An online resource that allows Michigan middle schools and high schools to provide courses that students wouldn't otherwise have access to.

Source: Information excerpted from school websites.

Educators who teach on-line have unique challenges. For example, in many instances these teachers never have face-to-face contact with their students. Strategies for overcoming this and other challenges need to be considered. Researchers from the Center for Research on Learning and Technology at Indiana University offer the following recommendations for cyber learning experiences (Graham, Cagiltay, Craner, Lim, & Duffy, 2000):

- *Encourage student–faculty contact*—Whether this is through e-mail, discussion boards, video conferencing, occasional phone calls, or periodic face-to-face meetings, it is beneficial for everyone involved to have direct contact.

- *Promote cooperation among students*—Discussion-board assignments should engage students in two-way communications with each other. Encourage students to discuss among themselves a variety of responses based on their understanding of a reading assignment.

- *Foster active learning*—Students can be required to apply what they are learning and report their findings either on-line or face-to-face. For example, an on-line poetry class could require that students attend an open-microphone night at a local bookstore, library, eatery, or literacy club meeting. Students could then share their experiences with classmates.

- *Give prompt feedback*—Instructors should first let students know that assignments have been received. In addition, they should provide students with prompt feedback on such things as answers to student questions, scores on assignments, and comments on work submitted for evaluation.

- *Emphasize time on task*—It is recommended that on-line courses use deadlines rather than a "work at your own pace" style.

- *Communicate high expectations*—Cyber teachers should give challenging assignments, provide examples/models for students to emulate, and publicly praise exemplary work. For example, a teacher could call attention to a quality student posting on a discussion board by saying something like "Make sure to read Ehrin's input on our discussion about the Holocaust. His connection to last week's reading is very insightful. I look forward to reading your responses to Erhin's thoughts."

- *Respect diverse talents and ways of learning*—Give students some choices on assignments and encourage them to share diverse points of view. For example, an on-line class on career education could allow students to explore a variety of career options based on student interests rather than having all students explore the same occupational choices.

Think about your own experiences with distance learning. Have your ever taken a course through any form of distance learning? Describe the format of the experience you had. If you have not taken a course in distance learning, try to imagine yourself in such a setting as you respond to the following questions. What do you see as the potential strengths of this learning option? Can you envision potential weaknesses of teaching and learning through distance education? Are there some learners who may flourish in this setting, whereas others may flounder? What makes you feel this way?

Reflection Opportunity 9.5

What issues must be resolved to strengthen technology's impact?

Although many influential groups such as the International Society for Technology in Education (2005), and the U.S. Department of Education (2004) are promoting computer technology as an important agent for change in America's schools, there are still numerous goals to be met and challenges that must be overcome if technology is to become truly effective in improving education. Table 9.6 summarizes the major issues that must be addressed. As you read this section, think about how these changes can take place.

Technology Costs: Initial and Continuing

One issue that must be resolved if computer technology is to become more integrated into teaching and learning is the initial and continuing costs of the hardware, software, and maintenance that this technology brings to schools. Although many districts are just now reaching the point where they have adequate numbers of computers combined in networks and connected to the Internet, the problems have just begun. Getting computers into classrooms is only the first step in making sure that the technology can be used properly. Beginning in 1999, the Consortium for School Networking (2005) began to educate schools about the actual costs of computers and networks through an initiative called "Taking TCO to the Classroom." TCO is a business-world concept that refers to the total cost of ownership. These costs include not only the initial money required for hardware and software, but also the costs of training, maintenance, and technology support needed to keep the computers and software operating properly.

To meet the budget demands required when schools add computer technology and Internet access, many districts are seeking grant money and training opportunities from large corporations such as IBM, Apple Computers, Dell Computers, and Microsoft. These companies and others have a vested interest in providing schools with computers and software and the expertise needed to use them well. These corporations make it relatively easy for teachers to receive equipment,

TABLE 9.6   Strengthening Technology's Impact

Issue	Description
Technology Costs: Initial and continuing	The costs for hardware, software, and maintenance needed for effective technology use must be included in school district and state budgets.
Equitable Access	In order to eliminate the digital divide, schools need to eliminate funding inequities between high and low-income schools, provide equitable access for all races and both genders, encourage complex computer use for students of all academic ability levels, offer appropriate technology for students with special needs, and provide equitable access for English language learners.
Technology Standards	States must have mechanisms in place to ensure that students develop the knowledge and skills needed to meet the technology standards of professional organizations.
Guiding Internet Use	Teachers and schools need to protect students from inappropriate Internet sites and work with students to understand and avoid Internet plagiarism.
Teacher Training and In-Service	The knowledge and skills needed for using technology in the classroom must be a part of all teacher preparation programs and found in the continuing education programs of all teachers.

materials, and training to assist them in integrating technology into teaching and learning activities. For this reason, it is quite possible that you may someday find yourself writing a grant proposal to a technology corporation in an effort to add needed technology to your classroom or attending a seminar sponsored by a major technology corporation.

One example of a training opportunity available through a major corporation is Intel Corporation's Teach program. To date, this program has trained more than 5 million teachers in over 40 countries (Intel Corporation, 2008). This worldwide effort helps both experienced and pre-service teachers integrate technology into instruction. The major focus of these efforts is to extend students' thinking skills and enhance the learning process through the use of technology. Teachers who participate in the program receive extensive training and resources to promote effective technology teaching and learning in their classrooms.

A relatively small portion of technology training and maintenance comes free of charge from large corporate training sessions. Consequently, when school districts budget for technology improvements, staff development should be a top priority. In addition, districts also need to spend a portion of their technology money to provide for necessary upkeep and maintenance. Faculty members with unreliable technological tools are less likely to use them.

Equitable Access

One issue that is being discussed by many writers is the problem of students having equal access to computer technology. Unfortunately, girls, students in low-income schools, minority students, low-performing students, and students with special needs are receiving fewer opportunities to use computers and the Internet (Warschauer, 2003). This is often referred to in the literature as the **digital divide** to emphasize the inequities that separate the haves from the have-nots in terms of access to technology. This split has been brought about partly as a result of the high costs of equipment and maintenance and partly through the attitudes of teachers and others about who should have access to technology.

Inequities due to funding. As you might expect, schools in poorer areas tend to have students who are less able to use technology in their school and home life. For example, high-poverty schools have a lower percentage of classrooms with access to the Internet (Education Week, 2005). In a recent report, the Henry J. Kaiser Family Foundation (2004) states:

> With wired computers in most schools and libraries and rising home connection rates, almost all children have at least the possibility of basic access. Yet many advocates argue that ongoing inequities in *meaningful* access have real implications for children's educational and economic opportunities. These inequities are reflected in the use of terms such as "digital opportunity" and "digital inequality" as alternatives to "digital divide" (p. 1).

The available data make it clear that schools serving primarily low-income students tend to have fewer computers, less access to the Internet, and older machines (Education Week, 2005; Henry J. Kaiser Foundation, 2004). Teachers in these low-income schools also provide students with fewer opportunities to use computers in their work (Lemke & Martin, 2001).

Racial disparities. Because greater percentages of African American, Hispanic, and Native American students come from situations of poverty, they are less likely to be using computer technology in schools and at home. For example, 42% of Black students, 45% of Hispanic, and 41% of American Indian students reported using the Internet only in school settings, as compared to 27% of white students (Henry J. Kaiser Foundation, 2004). Even when income is taken into account, White students tend to use the computer more than other racial and ethnic groups. For example, only 15% of African American students and just 12% of Hispanic students in one survey indicated having used the Internet in school as compared to 21% of White students (Reid, 2001). Although there are no clear reasons for these differences, some claim it is due to covert racism. Others cite the lack of racially and ethnically diverse content and fewer teachers of color as role models for technology use as reasons for these differences (Monroe, 2004). Although there are signs that this inequity is being addressed in many schools and the gap may be narrowing, racial disparities remain a problem that educators must continue efforts to solve (Henry J. Kaiser Foundation, 2004).

Gender differences and equity. There is a concern by many educators and others that girls are not getting as deeply involved in using computer technology as are boys (Roblyer, 2006). Although there is evidence that there are no significant differences in computer and Internet use for boys and girls, there is a striking contrast in their interest in deeper understandings of technology in the classroom (Dyer, 2004). For example, girls are less likely than boys to enroll in computer science courses. This gap widens in more advanced technology courses. This clear lack of interest is best summarized by the statement "We can but we don't want to" (Dyer, 2004, p. 7). Another statistic that supports this concern is the number of girls taking the advanced placement exam for computer science. In 2000, only 15% of the test takers were girls. Similarly, the percentage of women receiving undergraduate degrees in computer science dropped from 37% in 1984 to 27% in 1998 (Gehring, 2001). One reason cited for this lack of involvement is the greater number of girls who opt out of advanced-level science and mathematics courses. The consequence of this is that the scientific, engineering, and technological fields responsible for designing new technologies remain dominated by men. These men then design products that appeal more to other males and are used less often by girls (Dyer, 2004).

Inequities due to academic performance. Evidence suggests that teachers who have high-achieving classes tend to use more complex computer applications, such as graphics and presentation software, than teachers of low-achieving classes (Lazarus & Wainer, 2005; Manzo, 2001). On the other hand, teachers with low-achieving students tend to use considerably more drill and practice software. For example, limited English proficient students often find themselves using drill and practice software to assist them in language learning, rather than having opportunities to use the Internet to engage in more meaningful experiences (Lacina, 2005). Because teachers are still struggling to figure out how to use computers with low-achieving students effectively, their higher-achieving peers end up with more and better quality time with technology. This continues to accentuate the digital divide that exists between students based on academic performance.

Inequities due to special needs.   Most students with special needs spend at least a part of their school day within the regular classroom. Through inclusion, they are provided with the most effective environment for academic and social learning. Computers and related technologies can provide these students and their teachers with the tools they need to adapt classroom activities to individual needs. Provenzo et al. (2005) identify two broad categories of technology for students with special needs. The first is referred to as **assistive technology** and consists of all technology options that enhance the capabilities of students with disabilities. For example, digitized speech devices are available to help students who are otherwise unable to speak clearly to communicate with peers and teachers. Assistive technology can also include such simple items as a pencil grip that can be used to make that writing device easier to hold. To review additional information on assistive technology, go to the Companion Website for this text and click on MyEducationLab for Chapter 9. The second category of support for students with special needs is called **adaptive computer interface.** This is the computer hardware and software used to help students with special needs overcome a limiting condition and use computers effectively. For example, a trackball is a stationary alternative to a traditional mouse that tends to be less sensitive, allowing students with physical disabilities to manipulate the cursor on a computer screen more successfully.

myeducationlab
The Power of Classroom Practice

MyEducationLab 9.2

Despite the growing efforts of educators to meet the requirements of students with special needs, several hurdles remain to be negotiated before equitable access for this group can be achieved. These include lack of funds to purchase the needed hardware and software, the training of students and teachers to use the technology properly (Provenzo et al., 2005), and software that is incompatible with adaptive technology used by students with special needs (Roblyer, 2004). One promising strategy that is being used to overcome many of the software and hardware issues faced by students with special needs is referred to as **universal design.** This approach has been around for many years in noneducational settings and is perhaps best exemplified by the curb cuts connecting sidewalks and city streets. Designed to give people with disabilities better mobility, they have proven beneficial to people with baby strollers, roller blades, and bicycles. Universal design principles have been applied to classrooms and schools to guarantee that all students can use them without further modifications. More recently, universal-design principles have been applied to computer hardware and software so that technology options can be used by all without the need for further modifications (Roblyer, 2004). This effort is relatively new and continued work will need to be done in the future to ensure that special needs students have the access they need to appropriate technology.

Language barriers.   Many limited English proficient (LEP) students, in addition to frequently encountering the racial disparities associated with technology use described above, also find that they have problems because of language differences. Lacina (2005) and Zehr (2001) identify three issues that make it difficult for LEP students to use computer technology effectively:

- *Lack of teacher training.* Most bilingual and English as a second language (ESL) teachers lack the computer skills needed to select and use appropriate software and to assist students as they use technology in the classroom.

- *Limited hardware.* Most bilingual and ESL programs have limited access to computers and related technology in their classrooms.
- *Lack of quality software and appropriate Websites.* Programs for LEP students suffer because of the limited number of software options available to them and the lack of good Websites designed to accommodate students with limited English proficiency.

Technology Standards

Because computer technology has a relatively brief history in the schools, it is only recently that national and state agencies have identified standards for what students should know and be able to do with computers. Unlike other curriculum areas such as mathematics and social studies, national standards for technology use are a relatively recent addition (International Society for Technology in Education, 2005), with standards for students released in 1998, those for teachers in 2000, and administrators in 2001. Despite being new, these standards are having an impact in individual states, with 49 adopting at least one set as part of their technology plans and teacher-certification programs (International Society for Technology in Education, 2005). As standards for technology become more integrated into the expectations for teachers in individual states and administrators at that level develop ways of promoting technology in K–12 classrooms, the potential influence of computers on instruction and learning should be enhanced. Classroom teachers will be encouraged, personally and by their administrators, to use technology as an important tool for learning. Table 9.7 lists the six student technology standards from the International Society for Technology in Education.

Although the standards presented in Table 9.7 suggest that computers and other technology options can strengthen basic academic skills, some educators and parents have concerns that this may not be the case. For example, students who become reliant on calculators may be less likely to complete basic computational tasks successfully when this technology is not available. Lee Stiff, the past president of the National Council of Teachers of Mathematics, points out that the rote use of calculators is no more appropriate for students than the rote memorization of basic facts that has been a major part of the traditional mathematics curriculum (Stiff, 2005). Rather than an either/or scenario, research indicates that calculators must be used along with strong computational instruction in order to ensure the highest levels of student performance in mathematics (Carnine, Chard, Dixon, Lee, & Wallin, 1998).

In addition to those concerned about the impact of calculators on student learning, some educators and parents are worried that computers are negatively impacting students' writing skills. They are disturbed by poor handwriting skills, spelling errors, inaccurate punctuation, grammatical errors, and the generally poor writing style found in student writing. For example, the use of emoticons (electronic smiley faces and frowns) raises concerns for some educators. Norm Goldstein writes, "These e-mail symbols are the current hieroglyphics, expressing a mood of the writer, who probably is just too lazy (or not interested) to find the right words. These 'smileys,' to be read sideways, diminish clarity and understanding—the underpinnings of good communication" (American Federation of Teachers, 2005). Other educators argue that simply because students are writing in "chat speak" does not mean there is a decline in their ability to write. In fact, they argue that on-line writing technologies actually improve student writing because of the increased amount of written communications.

Guiding Internet Use

Most people who use the Internet regularly find it to be a wonderful source of information and services that enriches both their personal and professional lives. At the same time, however, the huge growth in Websites and the lack of regulations regarding its use have created several problems for educators and students. These issues must be resolved before the Internet can be fully integrated into the daily life of the classroom.

TABLE 9.7   Student Technology Standards

Standard	Exemplars
Creativity and Innovation Students demonstrate creative thinking, construct knowledge, and develop innovative products and processes using technology.	**Students:** a. apply existing knowledge to generate new ideas, products, or processes. b. create original words as a means of personal or group expression. c. use models and simulations to explore complex systems and issues. d. identify trends and forecast possibilities.
Communication and Collaboration Students use digital media and environments to communicate and work collaboratively, including at a distance, to support individual learning and contribute to the learning of others.	**Students:** a. interact, collaborate, and publish with peers, experts, or others employing a variety of digital environments and media. b. communicate information and ideas effectively to multiple audiences using a variety of media and formats. c. develop cultural understanding and global awareness by engaging with learners of other cultures. d. contribute to project teams to produce original works or solve problems.
Research and Information Fluency Students apply digital tools to gather, evaluate, and use information.	**Students:** a. plan strategies to guide inquiry. b. locate, organize, analyze, evaluate, synthesize, and ethically use information from a variety of sources and media. c. evaluate and select information sources and digital tools based on the appropriateness to specific tasks. d. process data and report results.
Critical Thinking, Problem Solving, and Decision Making Students use critical thinking skills to plan and conduct research, manage projects, solve problems, and make informed decisions using appropriate digital tools and resources.	**Students:** a. identify and define authentic problems and significant questions for investigation. b. plan and manage activities to develop a solution or complete a project. c. collect and analyze data to identify solutions and/or make informed decisions. d. use multiple processes and diverse perspectives to explore alternative solutions.
Digital Citizenship Students understand human, cultural, and societal issues related to technology and practice legal and ethical behavior.	**Students:** a. advocate and practice safe, legal, and responsible use of information and technology. b. exhibit a positive attitude toward using technology that supports collaboration, learning, and productivity. c. demonstrate personal responsibility for lifelong learning. d. exhibit leadership for digital citizenship.

TABLE 9.7 Student Technology Standards

Standard	Exemplars
Technology Operations and Concepts Students demonstrate a sound understanding of technology concepts, systems, and operations.	**Students:** a. understand and use technology systems. b. select and use applications effectively and productively. c. troubleshoot systems and applications. d. transfer current knowledge to learning of new technologies.

Source: From International Society for Technology in Education (ISTE) (2007). *National technology standards for students.* Washington, D.C.: Author. All rights reserved.

Protecting students from inappropriate sites. One problem created by the Internet is the accessibility of inappropriate Websites. Unfortunately, a considerable amount of information is available on the Internet that should not be viewed or read by students. Inappropriate language, hate-group propaganda, and sites with strong sexual themes are just some of the problems that teachers and students may encounter. Unsuitable sites for students may also include adult chat rooms where people communicate on-line about personal issues. There have been several well-publicized incidents during the last several years in which children have been befriended by adults with serious mental or emotional problems and been lured away from school or home and into very difficult circumstances. Although software is available to block students from gaining access to most of these sites (Provenzo et al., 2005), teachers must still be vigilant in monitoring students so that they can be sure they are visiting appropriate Internet sites.

Internet plagiarism. Another significant problem associated with Internet use has been student plagiarism. As use of the Internet has expanded, a corresponding increase has been seen in this serious problem. Despite the efforts of many hardworking teachers and professional organizations, the levels of Internet plagiarism remain high (McCabe, 2005). In a study of over 18,000 high school students, about half admitted to having engaged in at least some form of Internet plagiarism. Similarly, colleges and universities face serious challenges around this issue. Two strategies that have proven helpful in curbing plagiarism are the implementation of academic honor codes and allowing students to be involved in addressing academic dishonesty (McCabe, 2005). Teachers and administrators in P–12 schools can also help by continuing their efforts to engage students in thorough discussions about what it means to plagiarize, why it is wrong, and providing honest information about the consequences of engaging in this activity.

Although the Internet has made it easier for some students to use the work of others, it has also provided new services to catch those who plagiarize. For example, Turnitin.com is an Internet business that allows both students and teachers to submit work for electronic assessment. By comparing the material with its database of Websites and previously submitted papers, the company can detect plagiarism with a good level of accuracy. Schools pay a base fee and an additional per-student fee, for services provided (Turnitin, 2008). In addition, Internet search engines such as Google.com are becoming increasingly more sophisticated. Teachers can often type in a sentence or two from a paper suspected of plagiarism and the original Internet source will be revealed. Another site that offers good resources on plagiarism is Plagiarism.org. It provides information for teachers on integrating plagiarism education into the curriculum, help in identifying plagiarism, and handouts that teachers can share with their students.

Consider reflecting on student plagiarism. How do you feel about this issue in general? What constitutes plagiarism in your mind? Is it using a paragraph, page, or an entire document that someone else has written? Where do you draw the line? What are the lessons learned when a student engages in Internet plagiarism? Is this a big problem that should have significant consequences or a smaller one that should be handled more casually? Are you aware of others who were punished for engaging in Internet plagiarism? Do you think the consequences were too harsh or too lenient? How will you deal with plagiarism when it occurs in your classroom?

Cyberbullying. Bullying in schools is changing. In addition to its more traditional forms, some bullies are using technology to antagonize and intimidate their victims. This is referred to as **cyberbullying.** Cyberbullying is carried out through the use of Internet services such as e-mail, chat rooms, discussion boards, blogs, instant messaging, or Web pages. It can also take place when cell phones are used to send intimidating phone calls or text messages. Schools face many challenges when trying to eliminate cyberbullying:

- *Identifying the bully*—A cyberbully can act anonymously, making it difficult for a school to help the victim.

- *Determining where the bullying took place*—Because cyberbullying usually occurs off school grounds, many principals say their options are limited when it comes to disciplining the culprits. Although many states have passed antibullying laws, these laws generally address bullying incidents that occur on school grounds and at school sponsored events.

- *Educating students about the impact*—Cyberbullies are often likely to do and say things in cyberspace that they would be less likely to do in person. Because the bully does not witness the victim's reaction, they do not have opportunities to feel remorse or empathy for their victims.

I-SAFE, an organization promoting safety on the Internet, surveyed 1,500 students in fourth–eighth grade (I-SAFE, 2004) and found that 42% of the students had been bullied on-line with one in four students reporting more than one incidence. Because of the prevalence of cyberbullying, some schools are choosing to take a proactive approach to eliminate its occurrence. For example, faculty members at William Penn School in Philadelphia educate students in appropriate use of technology by emphasizing that cyberspace is an extension of their community (Lisante, 2005). Dean of students Mark Franek tells his students "the school community doesn't begin and end at the door." The faculty uses a variety of creative approaches to remind students of cyberbullying throughout the school year. For example, the school's director of technology has mounted a mirror in the computer lab. As students look in the mirror, they read the caption, "Are you a cyberbully?." Under the mirror is a list of action steps a student can take if he or she is a victim of cyberbullying.

Teacher Training and In-Service

One of the major issues that must be resolved in order to integrate technology more effectively into everyday classroom life is to ensure that all teacher-preparation programs include a strong component of technology education. In addition, once teachers enter the classroom, they need extensive and ongoing in-service training so that they can effectively integrate technology into their teaching and learning experiences. Although the level of training is continuing to improve, many teachers still fail to receive the initial and ongoing training they need to be successful in using technology in the classroom (Education Week, 2005).

Initial teacher preparation. Take a few moments to review the teacher-preparation program for your present college or university. Is course work required in educational technology? If so, what is the content of the course or courses you will take? State teacher-preparation programs are inconsistent in what they require for technology competencies. Although 40 states have standards that must be met before candidates can receive initial certification (Education Week, 2005), only 14 of them require technology training or coursework and 9 require an assessment in technology for certification. Furthermore, the criteria for competency in technology use vary considerably in breadth and scope. Although some states list requirements for what teachers should know and be able to do, others simply state the number of technology courses that teachers must complete for graduation. Consequently, many teachers are entering the profession with limited skills in using computer technology effectively in the classroom.

In-service technology training. Although most school districts are doing the best they can to provide teachers with adequate in-service instruction in technology by spending a larger percentage of their technology budget on teacher training (Education Week, 2005), educators often feel that more needs to be done. Two of the major recommendations of the National Education Technology Plan developed by the U.S. Department of Education (2004) emphasize the importance of in-service training for both teachers and administrators. As school leaders and teachers become more tech-savvy, computers and technology will be more effectively integrated into teaching and learning activities.

Just providing in-service training, however, doesn't guarantee that teachers will develop the skills they need to use technology effectively in their classrooms. Staff in-service activities should focus on how technology can support learning, rather than emphasizing how to use software. Teaching educators how to navigate a piece of software is of little value unless it is also combined with strategies on how to use the software as a teaching tool. Effective in-service training must provide teachers with information on how and when to infuse technological tools into their daily activities.

Before completing the end-of-chapter activities, take time now to reflect on the *Consider This* feature for this chapter. It asks you to think about your own sense of ease around computer technology. Do you feel confident and comfortable around computers, or are you someone who is a little more hesitant to try out computer and software options? Most of the students you will work with in future classrooms will have high levels of computer competence. It is important for you to develop strong skills as well. Go to the Companion Website for this text and reflect on these and other questions as you read and respond to this feature.

**Consider This:
Computer Anxiety**

Summary

In this chapter, four questions were presented to help you learn more about the issues surrounding integrating technology into classroom teaching and learning activities:

How has technology been used in the classroom?

Technology has been an important component of American education from its earliest days and continues to influence classroom life today:

- Early technology options
- Television
- Computers (Praxis II, topic IIa)
- The Internet (Praxis II, topic IIa)

What are schools doing to enhance technology use in the curriculum?

K–12 schools are making many changes that are helping increase computer use:
- Classroom computers with Internet access (Praxis II, topic IIa)
- Quality software (Praxis II, topic IIa)

What is the impact of computers on teaching and learning?

In many schools, computer technology is having a significant effect on what happens in the classroom:
- Impact on teaching (Praxis II, topic IIa)
- Influence on learners (Praxis II, topic Ia)

What issues must be resolved to strengthen technology's impact?

Several significant issues must be addressed before technology can have a stronger impact on teaching and learning:
- Technology costs: initial and continuing
- Equitable access (Praxis II, topics Ib, IIIb)
- Technology standards
- Guiding Internet use (Praxis II, topic Ic)
- Cyberbullying
- Teacher training and in-service (Praxis II, topic IVa)

PRAXIS Test-Preparation Activities

 To review an on-line chapter case study, test your understanding of chapter topics and concepts, and begin preparing for the Praxis II: Principles of Learning and Teaching examination, go to the Praxis Test-Preparation module for this chapter of the Companion Website.

inTASC   Developing the Habit of Reflective Practice

Organizing Questions

Review questions, field-experience opportunities, and activities for building your portfolio are included here for the organizing questions in this chapter.

How has technology been used in the classroom?

Review Questions

1. Broadly defined, what is technology?
2. Name an early technology option used in the schools (prior to the 1980s) and discuss its impact.
3. What is simulation software and how is it used?

Field Experiences

Find a classroom that has computers in it for students to use. Observe how the teacher incorporates technology in her or his teaching.
- What kinds of software are available and how are students using it?
- Does the teacher appear comfortable when using computers in teaching?
- Do students seem to benefit from their use?

Building Your Portfolio: *Software Evaluations*

INTASC Standard 3. For a grade and/or subject of your choice, review two or three pieces of software that students are using.

- Place yourself in the role of a student and evaluate the actual content being taught, the methods used to develop student understanding, and the ease of use.
- Do you think these software programs would be effective learning tools for students? Include these reviews in your portfolio.

What are schools doing to enhance technology use in the curriculum?

Review Questions

1. What must occur so that computers don't become another marginalized technology option?
2. What are the negative aspects of having only computer labs (rather than classroom computers) in schools?

Field Experiences

Spend some time in a school of your choice observing how the computer lab is used.

- Who instructs students during lab time and what is being learned?
- What do you see as the benefits and drawbacks of computer labs?

Building Your Portfolio: *Internet Resource*

INTASC Standard 3. Select a topic that you think could be effectively researched using the Internet for a grade and subject of your choice. Spend time researching the topic using the World Wide Web.

- Describe the topic selected, the methods used in searching the Internet, and the results for inclusion in your portfolio.
- Discuss the usefulness of the Internet for teaching the subject and grade of your choice.

What is the impact of computers on teaching and learning?

Review Questions

1. What are the arguments for computers having the potential to completely reform teaching and learning?
2. What are the reasons given by some for proceeding with caution when using computers in the classroom?
3. How have computers influenced students as learners?

Field Experiences

Talk to a teacher of your choice about technology use in the classroom.

- Have the teacher identify for you both the benefits and problems associated with its use.
- Does this teacher see the computer as a valuable addition to classroom activities or a tool with limited use?

Building Your Portfolio: *Technology in Teaching*

INTASC Standard 3. Create two or three scenarios in which you describe how you would use technology in teaching the grade/subject of your choice.

- In each scenario, describe as specifically as you can how you would use technology as you teach and the ways in which students would learn as they interact with technology.
- Include these scenarios in your portfolio.

What issues must be resolved to strengthen technology's impact?

Review Questions

1. What is the digital divide?
2. What inequities exist in technology use?
3. How significant is the issue of Internet plagiarism?

Building Your Portfolio: *Technology Skills*

INTASC Standard 9. As you develop your technology skills, keep examples of the work you do for your portfolio.

- Clip art used to make your documents more professional, figures and tables created, color documents, spreadsheets, materials located through an Internet search, and digital pictures added to files are just some examples of the types of options you could consider including.
- Continue to update this component of your portfolio as new skills are learned.

Suggested Readings

Alliance for Childhood. (2004). *Tech tonic: Toward a new literacy of technology.* College Park, MD: Author. This report from the Alliance for Childhood suggests that educators and others look carefully at the use of technology and its benefits for children. Although aware that computer technology is here to stay, they make a case for downplaying its use in favor of time spent "with nature, caring adults, the arts, and hands-on work and play" (p. 1).

Education Week. (2005). *Technology counts 2005: Electronic transfer: Moving technology dollars in new directions.* Washington, DC: Author. This and earlier editions of Technology Counts discuss a wealth of issues related to technology use. Much of this issue deals with how school funds are being spent to support learning with technology.

Jossey-Bass (Ed.). (2000). *The Jossey-Bass reader on technology and learning.* San Francisco: Author. This book contains several very thought-provoking articles from other sources about the potential of computers and the Internet to dramatically change how schools operate.

Learning Point Associates. (2004). *Technology in education: Ideas for transformation.* Naperville, IL: Author. The Blue Ribbon Panel on Technology convened by Learning Point Associates describes their vision for using technology to transform education, rather than having technology integrated into the teaching and learning process. They see teachers and students having different work and roles in this transformational process.

Lemke, C., & Martin, C. (2001). *Children and computer technology: Issues and ideas.* Los Altos, CA: The David and Lucile Packard Foundation. Available on the World Wide Web at http://www.futureofchildren.org. This document presents many interesting issues about children and technology use and provides excellent resources for further study.

References

Allen, R. (2003). Technology tools help math learners visualize, make connections. *Curriculum Update,* Fall 2003, Association for Supervision and Curriculum Development. Retrieved November 5, 2005 from: *www.ascd.org/affiliates/articles/cu2003fall_allen_3.html*

Alliance for Childhood. (2004). *Tech tonic: Toward a new literacy of technology.* College Park, MD: Author.

American Academy of Child and Adolescent Psychiatry. (2008). Children and TV violence. Retrieved December 15, 2008 from: *http://www.aacap.org/cs/root/facts_for_families/children_and_tv_violence*

American Federation of Teachers. (2005). Speak out: Does technology hurt student writing? *American Teacher,* March 2005. Retrieved November 5, 2005 from: *www.aft.org/pubs-reports/american_teacher/mar05/speakout.htm*

Baglio, J., Hiller, M., & Zehnder, P. (2005). Kennewick man WebQuest: Seventh grade research investigation module. Retrieved November 7, 2005 from: www.bham.wednet.edu/studentgal/onlineresearch/7th/Kennewick_Man/index.htm

Borja, R. (2005, June 15). Districts add web courses for summer. *Education Week,* pp 1, 15.

Carnine, D., Chard, D., Dixon, R., Lee, D., & Wallin, J. (1998). *Report to the California state board of education and addendum to principal report: Review of high quality experimental mathematics research.* Eugene, OR: National Center to Improve the Tools of Educators.

Children's Technology Review. (2008). *About Children's Technology* Review. Retrieved December 15, 2008 from: *http://www.childrenssoftware.com/aboutcsr.html*

Computer Industry Almanac. (2007). *Worldwide Internet users top 1.2 billion in 2006.* Retrieved December 15, 2008 from: *http://www.c-i-a.com/pr0207.htm*

Consortium for School Networking. (2005). *Taking TCO to the classroom.* Retrieved May 23, 2005 from http://www.cosn.org

Corporation for Public Broadcasting. (2004). Television goes to school: The impact of video on student learning in formal education. Retrieved May 15, 2005 from: http://www.cpb.org

Dyer, S. (ed.). (2004). *Under the microscope: A decade of gender equity projects in the sciences.* Washington, DC: American Association of University Women.

Education Week. (2005). *Technology counts 2005: Electronic transfer: Moving technology dollars in new directions.* Bethesda, MD: Author.

Education Week. (2008). *Technology counts 2008: The push to improve STEM education.* Bethesda, MD: Author.

Ellul, J. (1967). *The technological society.* London: Vintage.

Franklin, J. (2004, Spring). Powerful performances: How technology is transforming K–12 arts classes. *Curriculum Update.* Alexandria, VA: Association for Supervision and Curriculum Development. Retrieved November 1, 2005 from: *www.ascd.org/affiliates/articles/cu2004spring_franklin.html*

Garten, C. (2005). *Assessment, communication and intervention: Linking technology and the standards movement can change education.* Alexandria, VA: Association for Supervision and Curriculum Development.

Gehring, J. (2001). Not enough girls. In *Technology counts 2001: The new divide* (pp. 18–19). Washington, DC: Education Week.

Graham, C., Cagiltay, K., Craner, J., Lim, B., & Duffy, T. (March 1, 2000). Teaching in a web based distance learning environment, an evaluation summary based on four courses. *CRLT technical report no. 13–00.* Center for Research on Learning and Technology. Bloomington: Indiana University.

Henry J. Kaiser Foundation. (2004). *Children, the digital divide, and federal policy.* Menlo Park, CA: Author.

Illich, I. (1972). *Deschooling society.* NY: Harrow Books.

Intel Corporation (2008). Intel Teach Program. Retrieved December 18, 2008 from: http://www.intel.com/education/teach/

International Society for Technology in Education. (2005). Use of NETS by state. Retrieved June 21, 2005 from: *http://cnets.iste.org/docs/States_using_NETS.pdf*

I-SAFE (2005). Cyberbullying: Statistics and tips. Retrieved November 5, 2005 from: *www.isafe.org/channels/sub.php?ch=op&sub_id=media_cyber_bullying*

Johnson, K. (2003, January 13). "New PE" teacher takes students to the max: Every activity stresses cardiovascular fitness. *USA Today.* Retrieved from: www.usatoday.com/usatonline/20030113/4773184s.htm

Kellnor, D. (2005, March). The changing classroom: Challenges for teachers. *Technology Horizons in Education.* Retrieved December 15, 2008 from: *http://www.thejournal.com/articles/17203-4*

Lacina, J. (2005). Promoting language acquisitions: Technology and English language learners. *Childhood Education, 81*(2), 113–115.

Lazarus, W., & Wainer, A. (2005). Measuring digital opportunity for America's children: Where we stand and where we go from here. Retrieved June 20, 2005 from: *http://www.content-bank.org/doms/assets/pdf/highlights.pdf*

Learning Point Associates. (2004). *Technology in education: Ideas for transformation.* Naperville, IL: Author.

Lemke, C., & Martin, C. (2001). *Children and computer technology: Issues and ideas.* Los Altos, CA: The David and Lucile Packard Foundation.

Lisante, J. E. (2005, June 6). Cyberbullying: No muscles needed. *Connect for Kids.* Retrieved November 5, 2005 from: *www.connectforkids.org/node/3116.*

Manzo, K. (2001). Academic record. In *Technology counts 2001: The new divide* (pp. 22–23). Washington, DC: Education Week.

March, T. (2004). The learning power of Webquests. *Educational Leadership, 61*(4), 42–47.

McCabe, D. (2005). CAI research. Center for Academic Integrity. Retrieved June 21, 2005 from: *http://www.academicintegrity.org/cai_research.asp*

McGoogan, G. (2002). Around the world in 24 hours. *Educational Leadership 60*(2), 44–46.

Meyer, L. (2001). New challenges. In *Technology counts 2001: The new divide* (pp. 49–64). Washington, DC: Education Week.

Monroe, B. (2004). *Crossing the digital divide: Race, writing, and technology in the classroom.* New York: Teachers College Press.

Niguidula, D. (November, 2005). Documenting learning with digital portfolios. *Educational Leadership, 63*(3), 44–47.

Norby, S. L. (2004). Hardwired into history. *Educational Leadership, 61*(4), 48–53.

Papert S. (2000). Computers and computer cultures. In *The Jossey-Bass reader on technology and learning.* San Francisco: Jossey-Bass.

Partnership for 21st Century Skills. (2008). Learning for the 21st century. Retrieved December 15, 2008 from: *http://www.21stcenturyskills.org/images/stories/otherdocs/P21up_Report.pdf*

Postman, N. (2000). Some new gods that fail. In *The Jossey-Bass reader on technology and learning.* San Francisco: Jossey-Bass.

Public Broadcasting System. (2005). *Destination: Galapagos Islands cyber field trip.* Scientific American Frontiers Archives. Retrieved November 1, 2005 from: *www.pbs.org/safarchive/5_cool/galapagos/g3_trip.html*

Provenzo, E., Brett, A., & McCloskey, G. (2005). *Computers, curriculum, and cultural change: An introduction for teachers* (2nd ed.). Mahwah, NJ: Erlbaum.

chapter 10

Historical Influences

History can provide you with many important insights into current educational thinking and practice. As you read and reflect on how other educators have responded to the age-old dilemmas of schooling, you will develop new understandings to guide your current thinking and practice. Learning from the successes and failures of the educators who preceded you will help you be more effective in your own educational decision making. In this chapter, four key questions will help you clarify the values of studying history.

Focus Questions

- How does history affect my future teaching?

- What is the history of education for young children?

- What has influenced modern secondary education?

- How has history shaped current educational issues?

Let us look at the general status of the pupil (in southern Negro schools). In the first place approximately 1,000,000, or 30 per cent, of the 3,048,289 children of public school age never entered a school of any kind last year (1930). Of the 2,165,147 who did enroll, 2,038,991, or 94 percent, were in the elementary grades; 107,156, or 5 per cent, in high schools; and 19,000, slightly less than 1 percent, in college . . .

(Of the south's Negro teaching force in 1931), 18,130 (38.7 per cent) . . . have less than high school training; 27,561 (58 per cent) have less than two years beyond high school, which is usually considered minimum for elementary teachers.

From facts and estimates given later in this study it appears that the typical rural Negro teacher of the South is a woman of rural heritage about 27 years of age. She has completed high school and had ten weeks in summer schools. She teaches 47 children through six grades for a term of six months, remaining about two years in the same school. Her annual salary is $360, or $1 a day, and she teaches for about five years (McCuistion, 1932, pp. 16–17).

The study of history is a subject that evokes a negative reaction in many people. Memorizing facts about people and events from the past without making connections to current events makes history appear irrelevant, dry, and dull. If you experienced history from this perspective, you may be wondering about its value in understanding education today. In actuality, however, history provides many important insights into current educational thinking and practice. As can be seen from the article quoted to begin this chapter, many of the issues faced by teachers and schools today are not new. Concerns about adequate teacher preparation, salaries, large class size, high school graduation rates, and teacher turnover are just as real today as they were in 1932. By studying these issues from a historical viewpoint and benefiting from the insights presented, educators can avoid the mistakes and build on the successes experienced by others. History also gives perspective on the progress that educators have made over time.

For example, studying the history of immigrant groups moving to this country provides important insights into current attitudes toward immigrants and their educational experiences. From the earliest colonial days, immigrants moved here with rich histories, diverse languages, and traditions from their homelands. Upon arrival, however, these aspects of their previous lives became less important than the overriding need to adjust to life in America (Cremin, 1970). Thrust into difficult work conditions in communities that had limited tolerance for differences, they were expected to fit in without disrupting the status quo. Polish settlers, for example, brought their own language, foods, and customs to this land and were expected to find jobs, work hard, and learn in the English schools provided for them. In other words, they were expected to assimilate into the culture around them and set aside much of their past heritage. To speak Polish and nurture the old ways was generally discouraged. Early immigrants faced many hardships and found that the best way to overcome them was to adapt to the language, culture, and customs of the majority.

These early immigrants, now part of mainstream American life, often expect new immigrants to do the same. They believe that new immigrants should be ready to set aside much of their past heritage, learn in the predominant language, and assimilate into American culture. Educational approaches like bilingual education are considered unnecessary by many who have struggled through an educational system that did not include this option. If they were able to make the adjustment, they argue, why can't others? Survey results confirm this attitude, with 63% of immigrants stating that all classes for students should be taught in English (Public Agenda, 2003). This historical perspective and its lingering impact today helps us understand some of the resistance many have toward an important educational option available for speakers of languages other than English.

How does history affect my future teaching?

When studied through the lens of current events, history can provide a wealth of important insights. First, it allows you to identify forces that have affected and continue to impact education today. A study of history also helps you learn from past successes and failures so that future progress is enhanced. Finally, learning about past people and events that have influenced education can provide you with useful information about the current status and future directions of educational issues.

Forces Affecting Education

Looking back at the past often allows us to see clearly what was difficult to understand as the events themselves took place. From a personal perspective, most of us can identify actions we have taken that led to problems in our lives. At the time, these actions seemed reasonable. Looking back, however, we can see more clearly the potential pitfalls. The passage of time, combined with the opportunity to reflect on what we did or did not do, gives us important insights into the factors that caused our behavior to have negative consequences. In much the same way, a look at historical figures and events provides you with a better understanding of the forces that influence education today.

Take, for example, the life of Martin Luther (1483–1546). Although he is best known for his efforts in religious reformation, Luther had a significant impact on educational thinking as well. Because of his conviction that the Bible was the key to Christian reform, Luther began to promote improved education, particularly the ability to read, as an essential in German society. To establish a personal relationship with God, he felt everyone needed to be able to read the Bible. Among other things, his influence led to both boys and girls being educated in Germany's schools (Cubberley, 1934). This was an early step that led, after several centuries, to more equitable educational opportunities for girls in this country.

Learning from the Past

We can also learn a great deal from both the successes and failures of past educational efforts. By studying historical figures and events, we can avoid the pitfalls and build on the successes of others. The *Ian's Classroom Experiences* feature for this chapter (found on the Companion Website for this text) discusses the work of Sylvia Ashton-Warner and what can be learned from her work. For another example, consider the work of John Dewey (1859–1952). During the early part of the 20th century, Dewey's ideas formed the basis for a major reform movement known as **progressive education** (Butts & Cremin, 1953). Emphasizing educational relevance and learning through social interactions, this movement added many exciting elements to an American educational climate that many critics found dull and uninteresting (see Chapters 7 and 11 for more information on progressivism as an educational philosophy). Despite its promise, however, progressive education gradually lost much of its momentum as an educational movement.

Ian's Classroom Experiences: Organic Expression

Today, many educators still believe strongly in the principles Dewey proposed and are attempting to implement his philosophy in new and creative ways. For example, *cooperative learning* (see Chapter 8), where students in small groups assume specific group roles and learn through interactions with each other, is based in large part on concepts presented by Dewey. Those attempting to implement these teaching strategies in the classroom can learn much from studying progressive education to understand the reasons for its decreased influence.

Think about this notion of learning from the past. Can you remember a time in your life when you learned from the past actions of someone else? Did you learn from this person's successes or failures? How effective do you think this learning experience was for you? What does this tell you about the importance of learning from the past experiences of others?

Reflection Opportunity 10.1

History's Impact on Current Issues

A third way in which historical figures and events affect your future teaching is through their influence in shaping current educational issues. By understanding the factors that led to the development of current ideas and approaches to education, you will have a better perspective from which to deal with them. For example, one issue facing teachers today is the impact that equitable educational opportunities have on students' abilities to learn. Studying how others have dealt with this issue historically adds further insights into this complex topic. In the early part of the 20th century, Maria Montessori (1870–1952) worked with what were then called "idiot" children in the slums of Rome (Lillard, 1972). Her efforts provide an early example of an attempt to offer more equitable educational opportunities for students with special needs. Montessori's early students came from institutional settings and were viewed by Italian society as very low-functioning individuals with little chance to be successful in life. Following careful observations of these children, however, Montessori felt differently and designed materials and educational experiences to enhance their learning. Within a few short years, these castoffs from society were able to take and complete the examinations for the primary certificate, typically the highest level of education attained by most students at that time (Lillard, 1972).

Other powerful historical events that have had a significant impact on current issues are occurrences of genocide. Throughout the ages, man's inhumanity to his fellow man has had tragic

MyEducationLab 10.1

Views from the Classroom: Collaboration is the Key

consequences. To view a video interview on the history of genocide and its impact on education, go to the Companion Website for this text and click on MyEducationLab for Chapter 10.

Montessori's efforts make it very clear to educators today that students with special needs are capable of achieving considerable success. Rather than focusing on students' disabilities, Montessori identified their abilities and built her curriculum around them. She found that special-needs students, when given tasks that are developmentally appropriate and provided with suitable instructional materials, will learn and grow in powerful ways. As a future teacher, studying the work of Montessori helps provide a framework that you can use to develop similar strategies and attitudes for working with special-needs students in your own classroom. The *Views from the Classroom* feature for this chapter provides additional insights into how teachers today work with students with special needs. Go to the Companion Website for this text and read this teacher's reflections and respond to the questions provided.

What is the history of education for young children?

In Chapter 4, the first two age-related levels of education were defined as early-childhood education and elementary education. Early-childhood education today is typically defined as birth through age 8 (third grade), and elementary education generally includes children from 5 to 12 years of age. The history of schooling at both levels provides important insights into the current theory and practice found in these settings.

Early-Childhood Education

A study of the historical roots of early-childhood education provides a better understanding of the similarities and differences between early childhood and traditional public elementary school education. Beginning with three European educators and continuing into 20th-century America, several key people and events have strongly influenced current directions in early childhood education. This history is summarized in Table 10.1.

European influences. Although many European educators have had a significant impact on early-childhood education, four are discussed here as having made perhaps the most noteworthy contributions to the field. Jean Jacques Rousseau (1712–1778) is the first of these major contributors. In his most well-known book titled *Emile* (Rousseau, 1762/1979), Rousseau described the ideal early education of an imaginary child. He believed that there should be no formal educational experiences until children are 12 years old, and that young children can learn all they need to know from the natural world around them.

Unlike Rousseau's theoretical perspectives on teaching and learning, Johann Pestalozzi (1746–1847) was an educator who established himself among his European peers as a caring, creative teacher. Using many of the ideas proposed by Rousseau (1979), Pestalozzi took charge of an orphanage in Stanz, Switzerland, and was able to make remarkable progress with children who were considered incapable of learning. Characteristics of his teaching included careful observation of children, recognizing the potential in each child, understanding the importance of teacher–student relationships, strengthening peer relations, and learning through the use of the senses. All of these attributes of teaching are seen as essential to early-childhood education today.

Another European educator to significantly influence early education was Friedrich Froebel (1782–1852). Much of Froebel's educational training came from time spent carefully observing Pestalozzi teaching young children. Although he agreed with much of what he saw, Froebel developed his own teaching method (Froebel, 1886). One of his major contributions to early education was the emphasis he placed on play as an important method of learning for young children. He said this about play:

> It gives, therefore, joy, freedom, contentment, inner and outer rest, peace with the world. It holds the sources of all that is good. A child that plays thoroughly, with self-active determination,

TABLE 10.1 History of Early Childhood Education		
Influences	**Key Person/Event**	**Description**
European Influences	Rousseau	Believed that formal education should begin at age 12 and young children could learn all they needed to know from nature
	Pestalozzi	Gifted teacher who based his method on the theories of Rousseau
	Froebel	Emphasized the importance of childhood play; started kindergarten
	Montessori	Developed quality educational materials for use in the early-childhood classroom
American Efforts	Kindergarten Movement	Early kindergarten programs designed to help low-income children become successful in school
	Child Study Movement	Effort to better understand child growth and development
	Cooperative Nursery Schools	Parents assist teacher in implementing preschool program
	Head Start	Begun in 1960s to help low-income preschool children be more successful in school
	Compensatory Education	Research models to assess the effectiveness of special primary classes for low-income students

perseveringly until physical fatigue forbids, will surely be a thorough, determined man, capable of self-sacrifice for the promotion of the welfare of himself and others. (cited in Braun & Edwards, 1972, p. 67)

Froebel spent his career teaching 5-year-old children and named his program the *kindergarten* (meaning "children's garden" in German). His approach gradually spread throughout Germany and later to the United States. Froebel is often referred to as the father of the modern kindergarten, and his ideas about play, the values of singing with children, and circle-time experiences are all considered important parts of kindergarten and early-childhood education today.

Stop for a moment and think about the concept of play as an educational tool. Think back to your own childhood and remember a favorite play experience. What did you do and who did you play with? Besides being fun, this play experience also had learning potential. What social, emotional, intellectual, and language learning possibilities were a part of the play experience you described?

Maria Montessori (1870–1952) is the fourth European educator who had a significant impact on the theory and practice of early childhood education. One example of her influence is the educational materials she developed. Montessori felt very strongly that they should be beautiful (Lillard, 1996). Her educational materials were constructed with care from only the finest woods and other materials and carefully finished to look and feel good to children. Because most of her students were from low-income families, this equipment provided one of the very few opportunities they had to interact with truly beautiful objects.

Reflection Opportunity 10.2

Early American efforts. The kindergarten movement in the United States marked the beginnings of early-childhood education in this country. In 1855, after having studied under Froebel in Germany, Mrs. Carl Schutz opened the first kindergarten classroom in Watertown, Wisconsin (Braun & Edwards, 1972). Throughout the remainder of the 19th century, most kindergarten programs were privately operated and funded through grants from philanthropic organizations to help low-income children become more successful in school (Braun & Edwards, 1972).

In addition to kindergarten education, near the beginning of the 20th century the **child study movement** provided the momentum for new programs for 3- and 4-year-old children (Weber, 1984). This movement was an effort to better understand children and their development through careful observation and study. One setting that became increasingly more common across America for studying child growth and development was the **laboratory nursery school.** Initially funded through federal grants and private foundations, these nursery school and kindergarten programs provided researchers with children to observe and study in a controlled environment.

At about the same time that laboratory nursery schools became more common, **cooperative nursery schools** were also being implemented. Parents of 3- and 4-year-old children would hire a nursery school teacher and then agree to assist her for a portion of the school week so that a low adult–child ratio could be maintained at a minimal cost (Braun & Edwards, 1972). In addition to the quality educational experiences available to children, the parents who spent time in the classroom had many opportunities to see and use good toys and equipment and learn parenting skills as they observed teachers interacting with children.

Project Head Start. During the presidencies of John F. Kennedy and Lyndon B. Johnson, a concerted effort was made to help low-income families break free from the grip of poverty. A cornerstone of this War on Poverty was federal support for early-childhood programs designed to assist young disadvantaged children (Hymes, 1978). The thinking of policy makers was that the cycle of poverty could only be broken by providing young children from low-income families with quality educational experiences. Children provided with early childhood experiences would do better in school, find higher-paying jobs, and break free from poverty's grip. Beginning in 1964, the federal government provided money to local sites for preschool-aged children from low-income families.

The most famous of the programs begun during this period is **Head Start.** Started in 1964 to help low-income 4-year-olds catch up academically with their more advantaged peers, Head Start has stood the test of time as an important program for young children. It currently serves more than 908,000 children from birth through 5 years of age across the United States (Administration for Children, and Families, 2008). The Head Start program is considered comprehensive because of its emphasis on all aspects of the child's development. In addition to focusing on social, emotional, intellectual, language, and physical development, Head Start emphasizes good health and provides resources and assistance with medical, dental, nutritional, and mental health needs.

Reflect on your own early learning experiences. Did you attend a preschool program like one of those described in this section? If so, how did it compare with the programs described here? If you did not attend preschool, what kept you from doing so? Was it the expense? Or were there limited options or other reasons for not attending?

Reflection Opportunity 10.3

Elementary Education

Although today virtually every child attends and completes an elementary school education, during early American history this was not the case. Children from less affluent homes often went to work at a very young age. Through much of early American history, elementary education was offered in private school settings, which were beyond the means of many families. Boys from upper-class families tended to be the only ones receiving formal educational training in either a private school setting or through tutoring experiences. Table 10.2 provides a snapshot of the history of elementary education. Each topic listed is discussed in more detail below.

TABLE 10.2   History of Elementary Education

Time Period	Schooling Options	Description
Early Colonial Times	Dame Schools	Informal programs were run by women from the community who had basic educational skills
	Apprenticeship Programs	Children were taught the skills needed in specific trades by others who had already mastered them
	Charity Schools	Funded by religious groups for poor children to learn basic academic skills along with religious training
Mid-1600s	Town Schools	Funded by tuition paid by parents of children within the local community
	Moving Schools	Teacher traveled between towns and taught children for several months before moving on
	District Schools	Townships were divided into districts, each with its own school
Late 1700s	Common Schools	The idea of universal education and compulsory attendance laws led people such as Horace Mann to promote the establishment of common schools

Colonial origins. Although early American settlers placed a high value on education, the harsh realities of colonial life meant that many children in the 1600s failed to receive any formal educational experiences. Parents were the primary teachers of their own children, passing on their limited knowledge when possible. In addition to home learning, the three most common educational options available to children throughout the colonies were dame schools, apprenticeships, and charity schools. **Dame schools** were informal programs run by women from the community who had some basic skills in reading, writing, mathematics, and religion. They would take children into their homes and, for a small fee, teach them beginning academic and religious skills (Cubberley, 1934). Girls were also frequently given instruction in basic household skills such as cooking and sewing. Less privileged children throughout the colonies often found themselves in **apprenticeship programs** to learn a trade. In addition to the skills needed to be a blacksmith or carpenter, for example, some apprentices learned basic reading, writing, and arithmetic skills that would be helpful in their future occupations (Spring, 2001). Apprenticeship programs lasted from 3 to 10 years and typically ended when the students became young adults, ready to begin work on their own. Another schooling option occasionally available to children from low-income families was the **charity school.** Funded by contributions from religious groups, these programs offered poor children the opportunity to learn basic academic skills in a school setting while strengthening their religious beliefs. In addition to funding these schools, missionary groups were often responsible for providing the teachers as well (Cubberley, 1934).

Although dame schools, apprenticeship programs, and charity schools were available throughout the colonies, other educational options tended to vary somewhat by region. The southern colonies relied heavily on private tutoring to meet the educational needs of children from well-to-do families. In the middle colonies, private-venture schools and church-related school options were common. The New England area provided children with access to community-controlled schools with a religious emphasis (Butts & Cremin, 1953).

The combination of a common religious heritage that valued learning and greater concentrations of children in towns and cities led to the development of a more organized system of schooling in the northern colonies. Religious leaders felt that it was important to educate all children so that they could read and interpret the Bible. This, combined with the demand for skilled and semiskilled workers in the towns and cities, led to the passage of laws emphasizing the importance of education. The most famous of these laws was the *Old Deluder Satan Act,* passed in 1647. This act was so named because Massachusetts Puritans felt that the devil was working hard to keep people from understanding the truths found in the Bible (Spring, 2001). To keep Satan from being successful in deluding people, this act required that every town with 50 or more families had to hire a teacher paid through parental tuition so that children could learn to read and write.

With the passage of similar laws in other New England colonies, the colonial governments for the first time began taking responsibility for the education of children. In towns and cities, these schools were first called **town schools** and were funded by tuition paid by the parents of children (primarily boys) within the local community (Butts & Cremin, 1953). As settlers began to move west in search of good farmland, smaller communities helped fund **moving schools,** where a teacher traveled from one small town to the next and taught children for several months before moving on. Gradually, the **district school** became more common in the northern colonies (Butts & Cremin, 1953). In this system, townships (36 square miles) were divided into districts, each with its own school. Schools were funded by local district revenues (primarily from parents) and provided more consistent schooling options for children within a region.

In addition to stimulating the growth of an organized system of schooling, religious groups also influenced the content and teaching methods used in many classrooms. For example, the discipline techniques used by teachers were based in large part on biblical teachings. Physical punishment, particularly spanking, was the primary discipline strategy used in early elementary school classrooms. The *Explore Your Beliefs* feature for this chapter talks about this issue in more detail. Read this feature now and reflect on your beliefs about spanking.

Explore your beliefs: Spare the rod, spoil the child

The original European settlers who came to America did so in large measure to avoid religious persecution. They brought with them strong views on parenting and human relations that were based in large part on their Christian beliefs as defined in the Bible. It shouldn't surprise you to learn, then, that early colonial schools were strongly influenced by these religious beliefs. One outcome was the common acceptance of what has come to be known as corporal punishment. Physical punishment, primarily in the form of spanking, was the chief means of discipline in colonial schools. The rationale for this approach comes from Proverbs 13:24, which states: "He who spares his rod hates his son, But he who loves him disciplines him diligently."

Corporal punishment has a long tradition in American schools. Corporal punishment is defined as any intervention which is designed to cause physical pain in order to stop or change behavior. The most typical form of school corporal punishment is the striking of a student's buttocks with a wooden paddle by a school authority. The use of corporal punishment has been declining in U.S. schools (Couture, 2001). Public concerns, lawsuits against school boards and educators regarding its use and legislative bans have led to the decline. More than half of the states ban its use. In states where it is allowed, many school boards vote to prohibit it. Still, over 200,000 children are being hit yearly in public schools with a disproportionate number being African-American and Latino children and children with disabilities (Human Rights Watch, 2008).

Many national organizations such as the American Academy of Pediatrics, the National Association of Elementary School Principals, the National Education Association, and the National Parent Teacher Association have spoken out against corporal punishment. Concerns about corporal punishment include how this kind of punishment signals to the child that the way to settle interpersonal conflicts is to use physical force and inflict pain. Children who attend school where corporal punishment is used may fail to develop trusting, secure relationships with their teachers. Despite the concerns of a majority of educators, highly respected professional organizations, many parents, and numerous citizens, corporal punishment remains a viable discipline strategy in many states.

Developing the Habit of Reflective Practice

Gather Information

1. Think back on your own education. How were students disciplined? Did you ever experience or witness corporal punishment in your schooling?

Identify Beliefs

1. What effect do you think corporal punishment has on student learning, performance and behavior?

2. Who do you think should make the decision about regarding corporal punishment being allowed or banned in public schools? Should this be a federal decision? State decision? Local decision? Family decision?

Make Decisions

1. If you were a school board member, would you vote to ban corporal punishment in your local public schools? Why or why not?

Assess and Evaluate

1. If you were comparing two schools, one that practiced corporal punishment and one that banned the use of corporal punishment many years ago, what data would you collect to compare the effects of their discipline strategies?

Resources

Couture, L. A. (2001). Corporal Punishment: Society's Acceptable Violence Towards Children. *http://www.childadvocate.org/1a_research.htm* accessed September 4, 2005.

Human Rights Watch. (2008). *A violent education. Corporal Punishment of children in U.S. Public Schools.* NY: Author.

Common school movement. Beginning with the American Revolution and the unification of the 13 original colonies into the United States of America, ideas about schooling in this country started to change. The **common school movement** was born. It was the beginning of concerted efforts to provide educational opportunities to all children. First, the earlier laws in the northern colonies requiring towns and districts to have schools under the authority of the local government set a precedence for the rest of the union. In addition, there was a growing consensus that not only should these schools exist, but that they should be paid for by the public so that a free basic education would be available to all (Cubberley, 1934). This notion of **universal education** was slowly implemented during the next century through the passage of state and federal laws and the tireless efforts of a leading proponent, Horace Mann.

One significant contribution to the implementation of common schools throughout the United States was the passage of the *Northwest Ordinances of 1785 and 1787* by the federal government. These acts divided the Northwest territories (currently the states of Illinois, Indiana, Michigan, Ohio, Wisconsin, and part of Minnesota) into townships of 36 square miles. One section of each township was set aside for public schools. In addition to promoting the establishment of common schools in the Northwest territories, these acts provided a model for other future states for the creation of common schools.

The second set of legal mandates that had a major impact on universal public education was the implementation of **compulsory attendance laws** in individual states. Massachusetts was the first state to pass such legislation in 1852 and make public school attendance mandatory. Other states followed suit, and by the start of the 20th century, most had passed similar legislation (Cremin, 1980). These laws slowly pushed communities and districts to offer common school options to children, and attendance grew rapidly through this period (Snyder, 1993).

Although many people can be credited with advancing the cause of common schools in the United States, Horace Mann (1796–1859) is unquestionably the most significant contributor. Trained as a lawyer, he became a well-known Massachusetts politician and educational spokesman (Gibbon, 2002). Mann believed strongly in the provision of common schools for all and tirelessly advocated their implementation throughout his career (Butts & Cremin, 1953). In his role as secretary of the Massachusetts State Board of Education and as the editor and founder of *The Common School Journal,* Mann wrote and spoke convincingly about the values of common schools. His writings were distributed throughout the country and had a major impact on the expansion of educational opportunities in the United States.

Thanks to the efforts of individuals like Horace Mann, all students today have access to public educational opportunities. Despite its availability, some people are challenging the requirement that all students must attend some form of schooling. Daniel Pink, for example, sees compulsory school attendance as a concept that has outlived its purpose: "Compared with much of the world, America is a remarkably hands-off land. We don't force people to vote, or to work, or to serve in the military. But we do compel parents to relinquish their kids to this institution (school) for a dozen years, and threaten to jail those who resist" (Noll, 2006, p. 79). The work world, according to Pink, is changing as a large number of workers are becoming what he calls "free agents" in the sense that they are self-employed, freelancers, and telecommuters in their jobs. Pink suggests that education must adjust to these changing demands of the workplace. In fact, he sees the growing numbers of home-schooled children as one indicator that this process has already begun. Pink believes that home schooling and electronic learning will eventually replace much of what has traditionally been accomplished under the guise of compulsory education. Do you agree with Pink's arguments or do you feel that compulsory education still makes good sense?

Reflection Opportunity 10.4

Reflect on your own educational experiences through elementary school. How do your educational experiences compare to those described above? In what ways were they similar to, and different from, the historical programs identified? For much of American history, many American children did not have access to a free, public elementary education. Can you imagine what your life would be like without this most basic educational opportunity?

What has influenced modern secondary education?

Although early forms of secondary education began in colonial times, the availability of this option lagged behind those at the elementary level. The first programs were designed to prepare students for a college education, were funded privately, and only gradually became a part of the public educational system starting in the early 1800s. Access to public high school experiences remained sporadic well into the 20th century, especially in poor and rural areas. Table 10.3 summarizes the history of secondary education, and the following paragraphs describe aspects of this history in more detail.

Early Secondary Options

Three secondary school options were available to students in the American colonies and through the early years of the new nation. The **Latin grammar school** prepared students for the college experience and was the first program available in the colonies. **English grammar schools** were designed

TABLE 10.3   History of Secondary Education

Time Period	Schooling Option	Description
Colonial America	Latin Grammar School	Prepared students for college through the study of Latin and Greek
	English Grammar School	Prepared students who needed formal education beyond the elementary level, but weren't planning to attend college
	American Academy	Prepared students for either college or the business world
Late 1800s	Public High School	Publicly funded high schools for both boys and girls were made available
Early 1900s	Junior High School	Because young adolescents were seen as having different needs, they were separated from high school students for Grades 7–9
1960s	Middle School	The onset of puberty in many sixth grade students led to the growth of schools for Grades 6–8

for those who needed formal education beyond the elementary level for business and commerce, but weren't planning to attend college. The **American Academy** was a combination of the other two options and served the dual purposes of preparing students for college and life in the business world.

Latin grammar schools. Students in the American colonies initially had two choices for a college experience. They could travel to Europe and attend college there or enroll at what is now Harvard University (founded in 1636) in Cambridge, Massachusetts (Cubberley, 1934). In both instances, these institutions demanded that students be trained in Latin and Greek before they could be admitted. The curriculum of the Latin grammar school, whose sole purpose was the preparation of students for the college experience, was thus centered on this classical preparation. Students typically spent 7 years learning both Latin and Greek and then studying classical texts in both languages (Cubberley, 1934). The first Latin grammar school began in Boston in 1635, with others opening soon thereafter in the northern colonies. Gradually, this option spread to the middle colonies. Students in the South were typically tutored at home or traveled to England for training if they were planning on attending college. Latin grammar schools were for boys only. It was some time before girls had similar educational opportunities.

English grammar schools. During the 1700s, the rapid growth of middle-class businesses (particularly in the northern and middle colonies) created the need for a new educational option. The English grammar school was designed to prepare students for work in the business world, with diverse course work to prepare students in such things as bookkeeping, letter writing, marine and military engineering, navigation, and foreign languages (Butts & Cremin, 1953). These programs tended to have more flexible admission policies than the Latin grammar school and some women were able to participate as students.

The American Academy. During the second half of the 18th century, the American academy became a third secondary school option available to students. It combined the college-preparatory experiences found in the Latin grammar school with the more practical and business-oriented education of the English grammar school (Marr, 1959). Over time, the academy began to replace both of its predecessors as the primary form of secondary education found in America. It served as the forerunner for today's modern high school. Benjamin Franklin is credited with starting one of the first American academies in Philadelphia in 1751. Like other similar programs, the academy provided instruction in English, rather than Latin. It included course work that was designed to prepare students for college, and offered a curriculum designed to prepare young people for employment. Subjects taught included writing, geography, history, mental and moral philosophy, music, scientific agriculture, and mechanical arts (Marr, 1959).

Public Secondary Schools

Although most academies were public in the sense that young men with families able to pay the required tuition could attend, publicly funded high schools for both boys and girls became a more common option during the last quarter of the 19th century. The demand for this option grew in the aftermath of the Civil War with the increasing urbanization and industrialization of American life.

Legal support. The growth of public high schools was slow prior to the Civil War. In 1860, there were only 300 nationwide, compared to approximately 6,000 private academies (Binder, 1974). Three legal activities, however, helped speed the implementation of publicly supported options. The first of these was the famous *Kalamazoo case* (Cubberley, 1934). Those opposing a publicly funded high school in Kalamazoo, Michigan, argued that although elementary education should be provided at public expense, a secondary education was a luxury and thus should be funded privately. The Michigan courts, however, disagreed and ruled that school districts could legally tax its citizens for the support of both elementary and secondary schools. The passage of **child labor laws** that made it illegal for business and industry to hire young children, coupled with compulsory attendance laws passed by individual states during the late 19th and early 20th centuries, also led to increased numbers of public high schools around the country (Butts & Cremin, 1953).

Public school growth. Statistics indicate that only a small number of public high schools existed around the country prior to the Civil War. However, conditions in the late 1800s and early 1900s led to a rapid growth in programs. With a change in public attitudes about the value of a high school education and a period of economic growth that provided a larger tax base to support secondary schools, public high schools grew to 2,526 in 1890, as compared to 1,632 private academies (Gutek, 1991). By the end of World War I, most communities and school districts within the United States were providing high school education options to all who wanted them.

Junior High and Middle School Programs

In the early 1900s, elementary schools tended to be for students in Grades 1–8, and secondary schools were set up to accommodate students in Grades 9–12. This format was gradually modified to include junior high programs for students in Grades 7–9. More recently, middle schools options for Grades 6–8 have become popular. Junior high schools were first established in Columbus, Ohio, in 1909 and were common after 1930 (Pulliam & Van Patten, 2007). Middle schools, on the other hand, are a more recent development, having become popular since the 1960s.

Junior high school. This schooling option became popular largely due to the recommendations of a national curriculum review committee looking at what should be taught at the secondary level. In 1892, the National Education Association, in an effort to identify the essential components of the secondary curriculum, convened what came to be known as the *Committee of Ten* (Gutek,

1991). Composed of mostly higher-education personnel, this committee recommended that schools begin at earlier ages to teach subjects such as science, mathematics, history, and English in greater depth. Rather than focus on the basic skills taught in traditional elementary school programs, the Committee of Ten recommended that schools provide an earlier introduction to more specific academic content. This became part of the rationale for separating Grades 7 and 8 from elementary school programs.

With the increased popularity of the junior high school option came a new configuration of public education. Elementary schools were redefined as including Grades 1–6 (with the gradual addition of kindergarten classes), the junior high school consisted of Grades 7–9, and high school programs were shortened to 3 years. This 6–3–3 configuration eventually became the most common pattern for public school systems (Gruhn & Douglass, 1971).

Middle school options. The junior high school option grew in popularity until the 1960s when it began to compete with new middle school programs designed for students in Grades 6–8. A major reason given by educators for this new middle school configuration was the attempt to create an educational climate that better matched the developmental needs of young adolescents (Wavering, 1995). At this age, students are struggling to understand the world in which they live and how they will become a productive part of it. They are transitioning from childhood to adulthood and require both freedom to explore and firm guidance from caring adults. Although children in early adolescence have outgrown the traditional format of elementary education, they are not yet ready for the compartmentalized academic emphasis of the high school curriculum. Middle school programs are designed to help students grow personally and intellectually as they prepare for the high school experience.

Reflect for a moment on the reasons cited above for the creation of junior high and middle school programs. Which rationale makes the most sense to you at this point? Do middle schools or junior high schools seem to better meet the needs of young adolescents? Did you attend a middle school or junior high school? If you had a choice, which option do you think would have been better for you at that age? Why do you think both options continue to exist? Do you think the schooling option you experienced had a positive or negative impact on your success as a student?

Reflection Opportunity 10.5

How has history shaped current educational issues?

One of the lessons we learn from studying historical figures and events is that positive changes in education often take much longer than initially anticipated. At the same time, however, a historical perspective demonstrates that much progress can be made with patience and perseverance. Rather than having big changes occurring rather quickly, history suggests that it is more likely that you will see small incremental growth over longer periods of time. By looking at current educational issues and seeing the growth that has taken place with each, you can better understand the forces that have shaped these issues and have more realistic expectations for future progress.

The historical changes in curriculum presented in Chapter 7 are one example of this type. By studying progressive education, the launch of Sputnik and its curricular implications, the inquiry-based curriculum, options such the open classroom, and the back-to-the-basics movement, you can develop new insights into the current status of curriculum in this country. The tension between educators who wanted to emphasize nontraditional content and methodology and those who stressed mastery of core knowledge in more traditional ways continues to the present day. Recognizing that this is a long-standing issue that may never be fully resolved to the satisfaction of all may help you work with others whose curriculum expectations and teaching methods are different from your own. In the following section, other examples of current educational issues and their historical roots are presented for your review.

Equitable Educational Opportunities for Girls

Historically, girls have had far fewer opportunities for schooling than their male counterparts. In colonial America, only a small number of girls received beginning academic instruction in dame schools and through home training. Most had very little opportunity for formal instruction of any kind. Few expectations were placed on girls beyond learning how to be good mothers and wives (Sadker & Sadker, 1994). It was not until the beginning of the common school movement in the 1800s that girls had more consistent opportunities to participate in what today would be called elementary education (Cremin, 1970).

Girls experienced similar difficulties at the secondary level. They were typically excluded from the Latin grammar schools available in colonial times and only gradually were able to enroll in the English grammar schools that followed. Girls from poor families, particularly in the South, were the least likely to have secondary education available to them. It wasn't until academies were opened specifically for young women in the early 1800s that slow growth began to take place in the secondary education opportunities for girls:

> By the first half of the nineteenth century, some communities in Massachusetts began to experiment with the radical concept of high school education for girls. A high school for boys had already been established in Boston, and in the late 1820s the public demanded one for girls, too. But city leaders underestimated the interest, and there were far more applicants than spaces available. Three out of four girls were turned away. (Sadker & Sadker, 1994, p. 17)

In the 20th century, as educational opportunities became more readily available for young women, the concern shifted to more equitable experiences. With the passage of the Nineteenth Amendment to the U.S. Constitution in 1920, women were given the right to vote for the first time. Although this didn't directly change the educational opportunities available to girls, it began to set the expectation that women should be treated equitably. The Civil Rights Movement of the 1960s and 1970s added further expectations regarding equal opportunities for women in all aspects of life. With the passage of **Title IX** of the Education Amendments Act in 1972, equitable schooling for girls received a major boost. This amendment prohibited discrimination on the basis of sex in any educational program receiving federal assistance for either academics or athletics (Sadker & Sadker, 1994). Table 10.4 shows the progress made since 1972 toward gender equity in high school sports.

Educating Minorities

For much of early American history, educational opportunities for minority children were virtually nonexistent. Religious organizations concerned about the spiritual well-being of all people developed the earliest programs. Gradually, however, educational options became available and

TABLE 10.4   Gender Equity in High School Sports

Year	Boys	Girls
1971	3,700,000	290,000
1978	4,500,000	2,000,000
1985	3,400,000	1,750,000
1993	3,500,000	2,000,000
2000	3,900,000	2,800,000
2005	4,200,000	2,950,000

From: National Coalition for Women and Girls in Education. (2008). *Title IX at 35: Beyond the headlines,* Washington, DC: Author. Reprinted with permission.

minority children had greater access to educational opportunities. Until the famous *Brown v. Board of Education of Topeka* ruling in 1955, however, these opportunities were almost exclusively in segregated schools. The review of early educational experiences of African American, Native American, and Hispanic American students that follows can help you develop new insights about working with minority students and their families in today's classrooms.

African American education. The first schooling opportunities for African American children were established in the northern states in the mid-1700s (West, 1972). These options were segregated, with White students attending separate schools. For the most part, schools for African American students were run by religious organizations for the primary purpose of developing religious understandings (Bullock, 1967). While the North was providing these limited options for African American students, several southern colonies actually prohibited by law the establishment of schools for them. Many in the south believed that educating slaves would lead to open rebellion and threaten an institution that was so financially lucrative to slave owners (Bullock, 1967).

Following the Civil War, the federal government and private philanthropies began promoting schooling options for African American students and increasing numbers of children began attending school. The Freedman's Bureau was established at the end of the Civil War by the federal government to provide many needed services to former slaves, including educational opportunities (Degler, 1959). The creation of this bureau led teachers from northern states to go south to establish schools and teach students. Despite this infusion of federal support, the Southern states remained reluctant to fund and establish schools for African American students and only gradually developed segregated schools for them. Enrollments slowly increased so that by the end of the 19th century approximately 35% of African American children were enrolled in mostly segregated schools (U.S. Department of Commerce, 1975). The programs provided were poorly funded by both federal and state governments, making it difficult for these schools to provide the same quality of experiences found in the better-funded schools for White students (West, 1972).

The problems of inequitable funding and segregated schools continued into the mid-1950s when the Supreme Court ruled in *Brown v. Board of Education of Topeka* (1955) that separate schools for African American students were unfair and must be eliminated. This decision, often viewed as the start of the Civil Rights Movement, was met with strong legal resistance and considerable violence around the country (Ravitch, 1983). Only gradually have segregated schools been replaced with integrated classrooms providing more equitable educational opportunities for African American students. And today, in 21st-century America, although the inequities have decreased, they are far from being eliminated. This issue continues as a distressing reminder of the slowness with which deeply rooted attitudes change over time.

Some are suggesting that rather than decreasing inequities in America we are seeing new growth in segregation and a continuing gap in the funding and support of schools for students of color. Jonathon Kozol, in his book *Shame of the Nation: The Restoration of Apartheid Schooling in America* (2005) makes a strong case for this perspective. He writes:

> Schools that were already deeply segregated 25 or 30 years ago, like most of the schools I visit in the Bronx, are no less segregated now, while thousands of other schools that had been integrated either voluntarily or by the force of law have since been rapidly resegregating both in northern districts and in broad expanses of the South (Kozol, 2005, p. 18).

The *Engage in the Debate* feature for this chapter provides further information about the alarming growth of segregation in America's schools. Read more about this issue now and reflect on the questions posed.

Engage in the debate: The resegregation of America's schools

Over a half a century ago, the U.S. Supreme Court's 1954 decision in *Brown v. Board of Education* aided in the struggle to desegregate public schools. But now, progress has been reversed and segregation is increasing throughout the United States. Jonathan Kozol (2005), an educator and author who focuses on issues of race, poverty and education, visited 60 schools in 30 school districts and 11 states and found that many schools serving black and Hispanic children are comparable to what segregated schools were like before *Brown v. Board of Education.* Kozol explains that the racial and poverty composition of schools is strongly linked to test scores (which influences higher education opportunities), high school graduation rates, the ability to attract and retain talented and experienced teachers, the range of course offerings, student health, school budgets, parental involvement, and the condition of school buildings.

A recent study for The Civil Rights Project at Harvard University (Orfield & Lee, 2003) provided data about the changing levels of school segregation for African American and Latino students. Despite the growing diversity of the school-age population, their research indicated an alarming trend toward school district resegregation. African American and Latino students became more racially segregated from whites in their schools from 1986 to 2000 in virtually every one of the 185 school districts in their sample. The Harvard study found that the average white student in the United States attends a school that is almost four-fifths white. African American students, attend schools that are less than one-third white.

The most segregated minority group, however, is Latino students (Orfield, Frankenberg & Lee, 2005). The average Latino student attends a school where they are in the majority. The segregation is even more prevalent for typical Latino English language learners. They attend schools that are almost two-thirds Latino, making it difficult to interact with English-speaking peers to learn English (Frankenberg, Orfield, and Lee, 2003).

Developing the Habit of Reflective Practice

Gather Information

1. Think back on your own K–12 education. How racially mixed was the student population at the schools you attended? Does your schooling reflect the experiences described by the above researchers?

Identify Beliefs

1. What is causing this resegregation?
2. Why have some school districts that were once so focused on desegregation now allowing resegregation to occur?

Make Decisions

1. Imagine that you are on a committee in a school district. This committee is formed to figure out how to desegregate the schools within the community. What suggestions would you have for accomplishing this task?

Assess and Evaluate

1. What impact did *Brown v. Board of Education* have on our school system?

Sources

Frankenberg, E.D., Orfield, G., and Lee, C. (2003). A multiracial society with segregated schools: are we losing the dream? Cambridge, MA: The Civil Rights Project at Harvard University.

Kozol, J. (2005). *The shame of the nation: The restoration of apartheid schooling in America.* New York: Crown Publishing.

Orfield, G., Frankenberg, E.D. and Lee, C. (2005). Why segregation matters: poverty and educational inequality. Cambridge, MA: The Civil Rights Project at Harvard University.

Orfield, G. and Lee, C. (2003). The Resurgence of School Segregation. *Educational Leadership, 60,* (4), 16–20.

Native American education. From the earliest colonial times, Native Americans have been poorly treated and segregated from the mainstream. For much of this nation's history, this has meant that the educational experiences available to Native American youth have been limited and of poor quality. Through early statehood and the westward expansion of America, Native American children received virtually no organized educational experiences. As tribes were gradually placed on reservations by the federal government, the earliest schools were established by missionaries intent on providing education as an essential tool for religious conversion (Szasz, 1977). In the late 1800s, the federal government slowly began to provide new options in the form of boarding schools and day schools for Native American children. Under the direction of the Bureau of Indian Affairs (BIA), these schools remained the primary options until the 1970s. The *Reflect on Diversity* feature for this chapter provides additional information on the significant challenges and problems faced by students who attended these boarding schools. Read and reflect on these issues now.

Reflect on diversity: The school days of an Indian girl

The following are excerpts from a story written by a Native American woman reflecting back on her early school experiences. She was one of eight who left their homes and traveled by train to the East to live with, and be taught by, missionaries in a boarding school:

The first day in the land of apples was a bitter-cold one; for the snow still covered the ground, and the trees were bare. . . . A paleface woman, with white hair came up after us. We were placed in a line of girls who were marching into the dining room. These were Indian girls, in stiff shoes and closely clinging dresses. The small girls wore sleeved aprons and shingled hair. As I walked noiselessly in my soft moccasins, I felt like sinking to the floor, for my blanket had been stripped from my shoulders. I looked hard at the Indian girls, who seemed not to care that they were even more immodestly dressed than I, in their tightly fitting clothes.

A small bell was tapped, and each of the pupils drew a chair from under the table. Supposing this act meant they were to be seated, I pulled out mine and at once slipped into it from one side. But when I turned my head, I saw that I was the only one seated, and all the rest at our table remained standing. Just as I began to rise, looking shyly around to see how chairs were to be used, a second bell was sounded. All were seated at last, and I had to crawl back into my chair again. I heard a man's voice at one end of the hall, and I looked around to see him. But all the others hung their heads over their plates. As I glanced at the long chain of tables, I caught the eyes of a paleface woman upon me. Immediately I dropped my eyes, wondering why I was so keenly watched by the strange woman. The man ceased his mutterings, and then a third bell was tapped. Every one picked up his knife and fork and began eating. I began crying instead, for by this time I was afraid to venture anything more.

But this eating by formula was not the hardest trial in that first day. Late in the morning, my friend Judewin gave me a terrible warning. Judewin knew a few words of English; and she had overheard the paleface woman talk about cutting our long, heavy hair. Our mothers had taught us that only unskilled warriors who were captured had their hair shingled by the enemy. Among our people, short hair was worn by mourners, and shingled hair by cowards!

A short time after our arrival we three Dakotas were playing in the snowdrifts. We were all still deaf to the English language, excepting Judewin, who always heard such puzzling things. One morning we learned through her ears that we were forbidden to fall lengthwise in the snow, as we had been doing, to see our own impressions. However, before many hours we had forgotten the order, and were having great sport in the snow, when a shrill voice called us . . . Judewin said:

"Now the paleface is angry with us. She is going to punish us for falling into the snow. If she looks straight into your eyes and talks loudly, you must wait until she stops. Then, after a tiny pause, say 'No.' " . . . As it happened, Thowin was summoned to judgment first. . . . Just then I heard Thowin's tremulous answer (to the woman's question), "No." . . . With an angry exclamation, the woman gave her a hard spanking. Then she stopped to say something. Judewin said it was this: "Are you going to obey my word the next time?" Thowin answered again with the only word at her command, "No." (Zitkala-Sa, 1900, pp. 186–188)

Developing the Habit of Reflective Practice

Gather Information

1. Research the internet and your library for further information about our nation's history of Native American education.

2. Think back to a circumstance where everyone else knew and was speaking a language you didn't understand. What do you remember about the experience and how did it make you feel? If you have never had an experience like this, interview someone who has.

Identify Beliefs

1. Have you experienced differences between yourself and others that left you confused about how you should act? Maybe you attended a new place of worship, or you were learning a sport or game that everyone else already knew. How did you feel in these circumstances? Does this give you any insights about what it would be like to be part of a minority culture?

Make Decisions

1. As an educator, you will encounter many linguistic, cultural, and social differences among the students you teach. What will you do to decrease the tension and stress that is associated with these differences?

Assess and Evaluate

1. Why do you think Native American children were educated in this fashion for many years in our U.S. history?

2. How do you think this history of educating Native Americans impacts the views and beliefs that many Native Americans have about public education today?

Source

Zitkala-Sa. (1900). The school days of an Indian girl. *Atlantic Monthly 85* (508), 185–94.

The Civil Rights movement, led by the African American community, created a climate in which it gradually became possible for Native Americans to reclaim more control over the schooling experiences offered to their children. Limited federal money became available for model tribal school programs designed to demonstrate new directions for Native American education. Rather than emphasizing assimilation into the mainstream of American culture, as was the aim of the BIA schools, these tribal schools sought to revive a sense of pride in Native American traditions and included study of such traditions as part of the curriculum (American Indian Education Foundation, 2005).

During the last three decades of the 20th century, the federal government slowly transferred responsibility for most of Native American education from the BIA to the public schools. Today, the vast majority of these students are integrated into the K–12 system, with only 185 remaining elementary and secondary BIA schools nation-wide (Office of Indian Education Programs, 2005). This has reduced the former isolation of Native American students and helped motivate schools to include their unique cultural heritage as part of the curriculum.

Hispanic American education. Much like the African American and Native American students described above, Hispanic American students' earliest schooling opportunities came from religious organizations seeking to convert students and their families to Christianity. Later, when large sections of what are now Texas, California, Arizona, and New Mexico were annexed from Mexico following the Mexican American War of 1848, public schools were made available to them. Although there were no laws prohibiting the education of Hispanic students, they were often taught in segregated schools that were poorly funded and understaffed (Spring, 2001).

In addition to experiencing many of the same difficulties as other minority groups in this country, Hispanic American students also faced another major obstacle. For most of these students, English was their second language. Not only did they face the difficult task of learning in less-than-adequate educational settings, they were also forced to converse and learn in English only classrooms. Speaking Spanish was specifically forbidden and Hispanic American students' rich cultural heritage was simply ignored (Banks, 2009). In short, they were expected to assimilate into the majority culture with no special assistance. It was not until the second half of the 20th century that educational assistance in the form of bilingual education became an option for students.

Students with Special Needs

Students with special needs have always been a part of American society, but the availability of special-educational services for them is a more recent occurrence. Most historians suggest that special education can trace its roots to Europe during the mid-1800s. Primarily through the efforts of Jean-Marc-Gaspard Itard, a French physician, and Edouard Seguin, special education was born (Kanner, 1964). Both men worked with children who were labeled by those around them as "idiots" and were successful in dramatically improving the children's levels of knowledge.

It was not until the mid-1800s that America also began to engage seriously in the process of educating children with special needs. For example, Samuel Howe, a physician by training, was the driving force behind the founding of the Perkins School for the Blind in Watertown, Massachusetts. Similarly, Thomas Gallaudet opened the first school for the deaf in Hartford, Connecticut, in 1817. Other similar programs gradually became available across the country as efforts were made to assist students with special needs (Cubberley, 1934). In all cases, however, these early educational options for children with special needs were separate from those offered to "normal" children and were found in no more than one or two cities in each state.

During the first half of the 20th century, more opportunities for children with special needs were made available in communities across the country. This was followed in the latter half of the century with federal legislation that mandated the integration of regular and special-education efforts whenever possible. The passage of the *Education for All Handicapped Children Act* in 1975 was an important turning point for this movement (see Chapter 13 for more information on this and other legal mandates). The act guaranteed all students with special needs a free and appropriate public education. Whenever possible, their educational experiences were to occur within the regular education classroom. Gradually, then, students with special needs were included in regular instructional settings and special education became an integral part of America's educational efforts (Heward, 2006).

The Professionalization of Teaching

By today's standards, teachers in colonial America were very poorly prepared for their roles (Cubberley, 1934). In almost every case, teachers received no special training at all. If they had been students themselves, knew the content to be taught, saw themselves as teachers, and were accepted by the local community, they were able to teach. Perhaps the biggest reasons for this lack

of preparation were the poor pay and lack of prestige afforded the teaching role. Unfortunately, teachers today still suffer from these same two problems as work to professionalize teaching continues. Reflect on this issue for a moment. Why do you think early teachers needed no special training? How did this influence the pay they received? Do people still believe that teaching requires little training, is an easy job, and shouldn't require highly paid workers? Knowing what you know about teaching at this point, should these attitudes be changed? How can this be accomplished?

Teacher-preparation institutions. As was the case with early secondary programs in the United States, the first schools to train teachers were modeled after their European counterparts. The French and German educational systems both had teacher-training components that Americans studied and gradually implemented as **normal schools.** The word normal has Latin roots and means "model" or "rule." Thus, normal schools were to provide teachers with the "rules for teaching" (Butts & Cremin, 1953). The earliest public normal school in this country was established in 1839 in Lexington, Massachusetts.

Students entered the normal school following the completion of their elementary education and typically spent 2 years taking general knowledge courses similar to those offered in the high schools of the time. A course in pedagogy (teaching) and some practice teaching were also included. It was not until the beginning of the 20th century that students were required to complete a high school education before being admitted into a normal school. Expectations gradually increased, partly because high school teachers needed expertise in subject matter areas. The length of teacher training gradually expanded to 3 and then 4 years as the demands for better training continued. With the granting of baccalaureate degrees, normal schools changed their names and began to call themselves state teachers' colleges. Most states today have several colleges and universities that can trace their roots to the normal school and state teachers' college programs described here.

State control of education. As states gradually increased their financial support for public education, a corresponding effort was made to systematize and unify the training required of teachers and the content of the school curricula. States began developing offices within their governments whose primary responsibility was the education available to students (see Chapter 14 for more information). The offices of state superintendent of education or commissioner of education were created (Butts & Cremin, 1953). Similarly, people from around the state were elected or appointed to state boards of education. These groups were given supervisory responsibilities for education within the state. Following the Civil War, most states had governmental offices and boards to monitor the directions of education. These state offices and boards gradually began to define the requirements for teacher preparation and worked to identify the content that should be taught in elementary and secondary schools. Initially, the powers of these groups were mostly supervisory, but they have gradually come to have primary responsibilities for teacher qualifications and state curriculum guidelines (Lunenburg & Ornstein, 2008).

Before completing the end-of-chapter activities, spend some time with the *Consider This* feature for this chapter found on the Companion Website for this text. Several quotes from historical figures are presented for you to contemplate. Take a few moments to reflect on those that are meaningful to you as you prepare for your role as a future teacher.

Summary

In this chapter, four organizing questions were used to help you understand the value of knowing and studying historical events in education:

How does history affect my future teaching?

History can have a direct impact on your classroom teaching:
- Forces affecting education
- Learning from the past
- History's impact on current issues

What is the history of education for young children?

Teaching children from birth through age 12 has a rich historical tradition:
- Early childhood education
- Elementary education (Praxis II, topic Ic)

What has influenced modern secondary education?

The availability of secondary school education has lagged behind that of elementary education:
- Early options (Praxis II, topic Ic)
- Public secondary schools (Praxis II, topic Ic)
- Junior high and middle school programs (Praxis II, topic Ic)

How has history shaped current educational issues?

Although taking many decades, progress has been made in many important areas:
- Equitable educational opportunities for girls (Praxis II, topic Ib)
- Educating minorities (Praxis II, topic Ib)
- Students with special needs (Praxis II, topic Ib)
- The professionalization of teaching (Praxis II, topic IVa)

PRAXIS Test Preparation Activities

To review an on-line chapter case study, test your understanding of chapter topics and concepts, and begin preparing for the Praxis II: Principles of Learning and Teaching examination, go to the Praxis Test-Preparation module for this chapter of the Companion Website.

inTASC   Developing the Habit of Reflective Practice

Organizing Questions

Review questions, field-experience opportunities, and activities for building your portfolio are included here for the organizing questions in this chapter.

How does history affect my future teaching?

Review Questions

1. Give some examples of how teachers can learn from educational history.
2. How do past educational figures and events impact current issues?

Building Your Portfolio: *Key Historical Figure*

INTASC Standard 9. Choose one historical person that had a significant influence on the age/grade you want to teach.

- Spend some time further researching the contributions that this person made to education today.
- Write a one- or two-page summary of your findings for inclusion in your portfolio.

What is the history of education for young children?

Review Questions

1. What are Froebel's contributions to early childhood education?
2. What were cooperative nursery schools?
3. What was elementary education like in colonial America?
4. What role did Horace Mann play in the implementation of common schools?

Field Experience

Talk to a retired or senior school district administrator or teacher about the addition of kindergarten education to the public school offerings of that district.

- When did it occur and what did classes look like then as compared to now?
- Did parents pay part of the costs? Check to see if prekindergarten programs are offered in this same school district.
- What is available?
- When did these programs begin and how are they funded?

Building Your Portfolio: *Living History Interview*

INTASC Standard 9. Search for an older American (70 + would be best) and talk to that person about his or her own personal educational history.

- Did this person participate in preschool or kindergarten education?
- What were his or her teachers like? What subjects were taught?
- Did any world events influence this person's education?
- Write up your findings for inclusion in your portfolio.

What has influenced modern secondary education?

Review Questions

1. What were the differences between Latin and English grammar schools?
2. What was the American Academy?
3. Describe the differences between junior high and middle school programs.

Field Experience

See if you can find an older administrator or teacher who can describe for you the changes that have occurred in middle school/junior high school programs during the last few decades.

- Were the junior high schools followed by middle schools?
- What reasons were given for the format of schooling available to students during their early adolescent years?

Building Your Portfolio: *Legal Foundations for Secondary Education*

INTASC Standard 9. Choose one of the three legal activities discussed in this chapter that helped promote public secondary education.

- Research this issue in greater depth.
- For your portfolio, describe how this legal action provided momentum for the growing number of public secondary schools in America.

How has history shaped current educational issues?

Review Questions

1. What key 20th-century events helped girls receive more equitable educational opportunities?

2. Describe some of the general characteristics of segregated schools for African American students following the Civil War.

3. What role did normal schools play in professionalizing teaching?

Building Your Portfolio: *History of Current Issue*

INTASC Standard 9. Choose a current educational issue that interests you and study further its historical roots.

- How did this investigation help you to understand the current status of the educational issue better?
- Write up your findings.

Suggested Readings

Braun, S., & Edwards, E. (1972). *History and theory of early childhood education.* Belmont, CA: Wadsworth Publishing. This classic text provides a detailed description of the history of early childhood education.

Cubberley, E. (1934). *Public education in the United States.* Boston: Houghton Mifflin. This is a classic text on the history of American education. Easy to read, and providing its own history, this text gives a strong overview of educational events through the beginning of the 20th century.

Herbst, J. (1996). *The once and future school: Three hundred and fifty years of American secondary education.* New York: Routledge. Herbst provides a comprehensive discussion of the history of American high schools and the social and political forces that shaped them.

Wavering, M. (Ed.). (1995). *Educating young adolescents: Life in the middle.* New York: Garland. This edited book deals with a variety of middle school issues. It also includes a strong chapter on the history and rationale for middle schools.

References

Administration for Children and Families. (2008). Head Start program fact sheet. Retrieved December 29, 2008 from: *http://www.acf.hhs.gov/programs/ohs/about/fy2008.html*

American Indian Education Foundation. (2005). History of Indian education in the U.S. Retrieved July 6, 2005 from: *http://www.aiefprograms.org/history.htm*

Banks, J. (2009). *Teaching strategies for ethnic studies* (8th ed.). Boston: Allyn and Bacon.

Binder, F. (1974). *The age of the common school.* New York: Wiley.

Braun, S., & Edwards, E. (1972). *History and theory of early childhood education.* Belmont, CA: Wadsworth.

Bullock, H. (1967). *A history of Negro education in the south: From 1619 to the present.* Cambridge, MA: Harvard University Press.

Butts, R., & Cremin, L. (1953). *A history of education in American culture.* New York: Henry Holt.

Cremin, L. (1970). *American education: The colonial experience 1607–1783.* New York: Harper & Row.

Cremin, L. (1980). *American education: The national experience.* New York: Harper & Row.

Cubberley, E. (1934). *Public education in the United States.* Boston: Houghton Mifflin.

Degler, C. (1959). *Out of our past: The forces that shaped modern America.* New York: Harper and Row.

Froebel, F. (1886). *Education of man* (J. Jarvis, Trans.). New York: Appleton–Century–Crofts.

Gibbon, P. (2002, May 29). A hero of education. *Education Week,* pp. 33, 36.

Gruhn, W., & Douglass, H. (1971). *The modern junior high school* (3rd ed.). New York: Ronald Press.

Gutek, G. (1991). *Education in the United States: An historical perspective.* Upper Saddle River, NJ: Prentice Hall.

Heward, W. (2006). *Exceptional children: An introduction to special education* (8th ed.). Columbus, OH: Merrill.

Hymes, J. (1978). *Living history interviews.* Carmel, CA: Hacienda Press.

Kanner, L. (1964). *A history of the care and study of the mentally retarded.* Springfield, IL: Charles C. Thomas.

Kozol, J. (2005). *The shame of the nation: The restoration of apartheid schooling in America.* New York: Random House.

Lillard, P. (1972). *Montessori—A modern approach.* New York: Schocken Books.

Lillard, P. (1996). *Montessori today: A comprehensive approach to education from birth to adulthood.* New York: Schocken Books.

Lunenburg, F., & Ornstein, A. (2008). *Educational administration: Concepts and practices* (5th ed.). Belmont, CA: Wadsworth.

Marr, H. (1959). *The old New England academies.* New York: Comet Press.

McCuistion, F. (1932). The south's Negro teaching force. *Journal of Negro Education. 1*(1), 16–24.

Noll, J. (Ed.) (2006). *Taking sides: Clashing views on controversial educational issues* (13th ed.). Dubuque, IA: McGraw Hill/Dushkin.

Office of Indian Education Programs. (2005). Our schools. Retrieved July 6, 2005 from: *http://www.oiep.bia.edu/*

Public Agenda. (2003). *Now that I'm here: What America's immigrants have to say about life in the U.S. today.* Retrieved October 2, 2005 from: *http://www.publicagenda.org/specials/immigration/immigration.htm*

Pulliam, J., & Van Patten, J. (2007). *History of education in America* (9th ed.). Upper Saddle River, NJ: Merrill/Prentice Hall.

Ravitch, D. (1983). *The troubled crusade: American education 1945–1980.* New York: Basic Books.

Rousseau, J. (1979). *Emile* (A. Bloom, Trans.). New York: Basic Books. (Original work published 1762.)

Sadker, M., & Sadker, D. (1994). *Failing at fairness: How America's schools cheat girls.* New York: Charles Scribner's Sons.

Snyder, T. (Ed.). (1993). *120 years of American education: A statistical portrait.* Washington, DC: U.S. Department of Education.

Spring, J. (2001). *The American school, 1642–2000* (5th ed.). Boston: McGraw-Hill.

Szasz, M. (1977). *Education and the American Indian.* Albuquerque, NM: University of New Mexico Press.

U.S. Department of Commerce. (1975). *Historical statistics of the United States, colonial times to 1970.* Washington, DC: Author.

Wavering, M. (Ed.). (1995). *Educating young adolescents: Life in the middle.* New York: Garland.

Weber, E. (1984). *Ideas influencing early childhood education.* New York: Teachers College Press.

West, E. (Ed.). (1972). *The black American and education.* Columbus, OH: Merrill.

chapter 11

Philosophical Foundations

Although philosophy conjures up images of esoteric discussions with little relevance to real life, developing a philosophy of education is a fairly straightforward task that is important for you to work on. You need to begin now to develop and gradually refine your philosophy. In this chapter, you will begin to investigate philosophical foundations of education as you address four organizing questions.

Focus Questions

◢ What is philosophy and why is it important to me as a future teacher?

◢ What key beliefs are associated with different educational philosophies?

◢ How does your choice of educational philosophy impact what you do in the classroom?

◢ How do I develop an educational philosophy?

As part of the lesson on sensory details, Ms. Hyman takes out a small bag of potato chips and says, "After today no more food, I promise." With slight melodrama, she holds the bag up and demonstrates. "I have an ordinary brand of potato chips." The students laugh enthusiastically, as they appreciate the reference to television commercials. "Let's see if we can describe potato chips using sensory details . . . Juan, how would you describe by sight this potato chip?" "It is brown, round, yellow, with a brown burn spot on it," responds Juan. "Maria, touch it, feel it . . . what can you tell me about the feel?" Maria reaches for the chip and describes it as "a little hard, rough . . . I can feel the grains of salt." From the back of the room Roberto calls out, "Hey, over here, I'll try the taste." The class erupts in laughter as the teacher responds to Roberto's offer. The class quiets immediately when Ms. Hyman says, "Listen, boys and girls," and in the silence breaks a single potato chip. "Crunch," says one volunteer; "snap," says another as they try to match the correct word to the sound.

Up at the blackboard, the teacher writes three words on the board and demonstrates their meaning by crushing a potato chip in her hand, letting the pieces fall to the floor, and by shaking the bag. Together they identify "crunchy" (to crush noisily), "crumble" (to break into little pieces), and "rustle" (one thing rubbing softly against the other) (Lawrence-Lightfoot, 1983, pp. 80–81).

In the example presented above, Sara Lawrence-Lightfoot (1983) describes a creative high school teacher by the name of Ms. Hyman who is working with a group of 28 Hispanics, 3 Asians, and 1 Russian student to help them increase their sensory word vocabulary. Clearly, Ms. Hyman didn't just grab a bag of potato chips and begin an extemporaneous lesson. She thought carefully about what she wanted to accomplish and why it was important. After determining her purposes for the activity, and its value, she engaged in planning that included thinking about interesting visuals, motivating demonstrations, and appropriate questions to stimulate the discussion she wanted from her students. In every instance, Ms. Hyman was using her own philosophy of education to make the choices that led to this very creative and captivating lesson. Hyman's beliefs about teaching and learning (her educational philosophy) led to the engaging teaching activity described above.

The topic of educational philosophy seems like one that has little direct connection to the actual activities that take place in the classroom. Nothing could be farther from the truth, however. Your philosophy of education is the foundation stone upon which all of your future teaching will be built. The example above and the discussion that follows it should help you begin to see the direct connection that exists between educational philosophy and your future work with students.

The process of active reflection defined in Chapter 1 and emphasized throughout this book is a fundamental tool you will use as a classroom teacher to develop and refine your philosophy of education. Ms. Hyman's teaching in the example above was almost certainly influenced by active reflection as she made decisions about classroom practice, and in the process refined her own philosophy of education. The following hypothetical description provides one scenario for how Ms. Hyman may have developed her ideas for the lesson:

> Over the past several weeks, Ms. Hyman has been struck by the lack of descriptive details in her students' written assignments. With so many English language learners (ELLs) in her classroom, she recently took the time to sit down with the Teaching English to Speakers of Other Languages (TESOL) instructor for the school and gather information about why this was happening and seek strategies for improving descriptive details in student writing. Ms. Hyman added to her understanding of ELL students when she learned from the TESOL instructor that many students studying a second language appear to have a good grasp of the language when in fact they often have a rather superficial vocabulary and ability to communicate in English. Even though they appear competent and can take part in conversations and engage in written communications, they lack an understanding of the finer points of the English language. These students need assistance in developing the more complex linguistic skills that will help them be successful in the school setting and in later work environments. With this new knowledge, Ms. Hyman plans her lesson on sensory details and refines her philosophy of education based on these new understandings.

Although some people enjoy the intellectual challenges that philosophy presents, many see it as an exercise in deep thinking that, although interesting, has little practical value. **Philosophy,** which can be defined as a seeking after, and love of, wisdom, is in actuality a basic fundamental that is essential for every educator to possess. Robert Heslep (1997), in his book *Philosophical Thinking in Educational Practice,* argues that every teacher must attain a "practical wisdom" as he or she works to prepare the most effective educational experiences for students. Teachers who question and reflect on their selection of goals for teaching and learning and the actions they take in attaining those goals are, in fact, engaging in philosophical thinking and continuing to refine their own philosophy of education. The *Explore Your Beliefs* feature for this chapter provides you with another opportunity to begin thinking about your own philosophy of education. Read the feature now and respond to the questions posed before you move further in the chapter.

Explore your beliefs: Teaching is like . . .

One way to explore your educational philosophy is to develop a metaphor for your beliefs about teaching and learning. When describing something complex, it is often helpful to connect that complex concept to an object or idea that most people know and understand. For example:

Teaching is like tending a garden. Time spent planning your garden helps things run smoothly from planting day through harvest season just as time spent planning how to arrange your classroom physical environment has a big impact on learning from the first day to the final day of the school year. When considering what to plant, a wise gardener chooses vegetables and fruits that she and her family truly will enjoy—why waste time and effort growing things that won't be eaten? This is comparable to a teacher considering students' interests and relevance to the real world when planning her lessons—why waste time and effort learning something that won't be necessary now or in the future? A skilled gardener chooses plant varieties that are compatible with the present climate and soil just as an effective teacher chooses instructional methods that are compatible with the abilities, learning styles and temperaments of his students. A gardener will likely seek advice when dealing with plant diseases and/or pests just as a teacher will collaborate with her colleagues when faced with a student who is challenging to teach. A gardener puts a lot of hours into her garden, but she is able to enjoy the beauty of her garden as it grows and she takes great pride in the success of her garden just as a teacher puts in countless hours at school, taking time to enjoy her students throughout the learning process.

What metaphorical comparison would you make to explain your beliefs about teaching and learning? Consider these ideas or come up with your own:

- Teaching is like walking on the beach.
- Teaching is like painting a masterpiece.
- Teaching is like cooking.
- Teaching is like building a fire.
- Teaching is like fixing a car.
- Teaching is like flying a plane.
- Teaching is like performing a magic show.
- Teaching is like bungee jumping.
- Teaching is like sewing a quilt.

Developing the Habit of Reflective Practice

Gather Information

1. Think back on your own education. Do you have any teachers whose beliefs about teaching and learning seemed to correlate with any of the metaphors listed above?

Identify Beliefs

1. What metaphor do you relate to when describing your beliefs about teaching and learning? Use one of the metaphors listed above or come up with your own and write a paragraph like the one above on gardening to describe your beliefs.

Make Decisions

1. If there was a teacher matched with each metaphor listed above, which teacher would you most like to have? Why?

2. If there was a teacher matched with each metaphor listed above, which teacher would you least like to have? Why?

What is philosophy and why is it important to me as a future teacher?

In a general sense, each of us has a philosophy of life that consists of a set of beliefs and values that consciously and unconsciously govern our actions. Hopefully, we have thought carefully about why we do most of the things we do, and have a clear rationale for the beliefs and values we hold. In a similar way, those who choose to enter the field of teaching have a responsibility to students and their families to spend considerable time and energy in developing a reasoned set of beliefs and values about teaching and learning. This philosophy of education should be grounded in an understanding of philosophy in general, a more specific knowledge of educational philosophy, and a clear grasp of the importance of engaging in the development of this belief system.

As you read this section, reflect on what you expect of other professionals in terms of a belief and value system. Should other professionals such as accountants, sales representatives, lawyers, and doctors have specific values and beliefs that help make them better at what they do? What would you expect, for example, the beliefs and values of a competent lawyer to be? Now apply this same thinking to teaching. Should teachers have a well-defined belief system/educational philosophy to strengthen what they do in the classroom? What kinds of beliefs and values should be a part of an educational philosophy?

Reflection Opportunity 11.1

Philosophy Defined

Although philosophy was briefly defined in the introduction to this chapter, it is important to understand the discipline itself in more depth before looking at its applications to education. As with any field of study, philosophy has its own set of commonly used terms that help people dealing with ideas and problems related to the discipline discuss them with one another. This section identifies some of the terms that help people talk about philosophy.

Philosophy is often conceptualized as consisting of four main branches (Ozmon & Craver, 2008), as shown in Table 11.1. Each branch emphasizes a different focus of attention for philosophical thought. The first such branch is generally referred to as **metaphysics.** Philosophers who are engaging in metaphysical analysis are busy trying to determine what is real. It is an attempt to understand the true nature of existence. The philosopher in this realm struggles with tough metaphysical questions such as these: What is the meaning of life? Does life have a purpose? Are people born good or evil? Does the universe have a design or purpose? Because of the nature of the questions being asked, this branch of philosophy is often considered the most vague and abstract.

Teachers need to be aware of their own metaphysical perspectives so that they can be shared with students as an important part of the teaching/learning process. In addition, the teacher's views on reality help determine the curriculum. For example, Matt Burns, a seventh-grade social studies teacher, believes that a major reality for his students in this ghetto community is the daily encounters with drugs and violence. Because these issues are a fact of life for his students, Matt has invited guest speakers from the community to come in and help students develop effective coping strategies.

TABLE 11.1 Branches of Philosophy		
Branch	**Description**	**Key Questions**
Metaphysics	An attempt to determine what is real	• What is the meaning of life? • Does life have a purpose? • Are people born good or evil? • Does the universe have a design or purpose?
Epistemology	Questions about knowledge and knowing	• What are the limits of knowledge? • Where do we find the sources of knowledge? • How do we acquire knowledge? • Are there ways of determining the validity of knowledge? • What is the truth?
Logic	Procedures for arguing that bring people to valid conclusions	• What is the validity of ideas and how can this be determined? • How can we communicate with others without contradicting ourselves? • What do our arguments mean?
Axiology	Seeking wisdom about the nature of ethical and aesthetic values	*Ethical:* • What are values and why are they important? • How should we live our lives? What is right and what is wrong? *Aesthetic:* • How do we judge what we see, touch, and hear? • What is beauty?

A second branch of philosophy is referred to as **epistemology.** This branch is concerned with issues relating to knowledge and knowing. The epistemologist studies the methods, structure, and validity of knowledge. Some key questions asked by those engaged in epistemological study include the following: What are the limits of knowledge? Where do we find the sources of knowledge? How do we acquire knowledge? Are there ways of determining the validity of knowledge? What is the truth? Clearly, questions of knowledge and knowing are of central importance to teachers. For example, Kendra Hendrickson is a second-grade teacher who has come to the conclusion that it is more important to know how to find information than it is to have that knowledge memorized. So, even though she spends considerable time helping students memorize their addition and subtraction facts, she also allows her students to use calculators in class and on tests. Kendra also believes that students develop mathematical knowledge best when they are actively engaged in learning by doing. She has many manipulative materials available in the room that students can use as they develop conceptual understandings of addition and subtraction. Kendra's understanding of knowledge and knowing strongly influence the ways in which she teaches her students.

The third main branch of philosophy is referred to as **logic.** The emphasis of philosophers engaged in this line of thinking is on understanding the rules and techniques of reasoning. It is an ordered way of thinking that attempts to avoid vagueness and contradictions. Typical questions asked by those in this branch of philosophy are as follows: What is the validity of ideas and how can this be determined? How can we communicate with others without contradicting ourselves? What do our arguments mean?

A major goal of education is to help students communicate and think clearly. Teachers can model logical thinking and communicating as they interact with their students. In addition, they can teach logic informally as they share reasoning strategies with students. Two types of reasoning are typically taught in America's schools. **Deductive reasoning** proceeds from a generalization to the learning of new specific facts and applications. Conversely, **inductive reasoning** proceeds from specific facts to a more generalized conclusion.

A final branch of philosophy is called **axiology.** This philosophical perspective looks at values. Values can be divided into two main categories. One is called **ethics** and represents an attempt to know the correct way to live our lives, to deal with issues of right and wrong, to understand the differences between good and evil, and to internalize principles of right conduct. A second set of values, called **aesthetics,** deals with issues of beauty. Those taking an axiological perspective work to answer the following types of ethical questions: What are values and why are they important? How should we live our lives? What is right and what is wrong? They also consider issues of aesthetics: How do we judge what we see, touch and hear? What is beauty?

Teachers regularly deal with issues of ethics and aesthetics in the classroom. In addition to understanding their own perspectives on these issues, they are responsible for helping students develop their own ability to engage in ethical behavior. For example, Cassandra Hastings is dealing with ethics in her kindergarten classroom as she helps children understand after a related incident that stealing the personal belongings of others is wrong. Denise Black focuses on aesthetic issues with her high school social studies classes when she engages the class in discussions regarding ethnic beauty and perceived differences in beauty across cultures.

The Importance of Educational Philosophy

Although philosophy in a larger sense attempts to answer the most fundamental questions of human existence, **educational philosophy** looks more specifically at questioning the essentials of good teaching. Because education has always been a central element of every society, fundamental questions about effective teaching and learning have been addressed from the earliest of times. Philosophies of education attempt to clarify issues surrounding four essential elements of education, as shown in Figure 11.1. The first of these is our perceptions of

Figure 11.1 Components of an Educational Philosophy

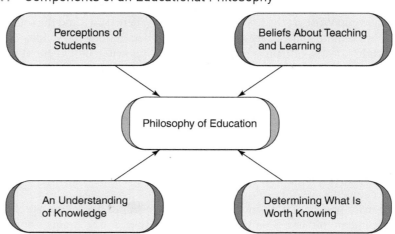

...

students. Educational philosophies work to explain what students are like. Are there differences due to age? What motivates students to learn? Are there identifiable strategies that students use to learn effectively? What differences exist between learners? Secondly, educational philosophies address beliefs about teaching and learning. What does it really mean to teach someone? How do you know when teaching has been effective? What does it truly mean to learn? An understanding of knowledge is another important issue addressed by philosophies of education. Questions about the nature of knowledge, where it comes from, and how it is acquired are all considered. Finally, educational philosophies are helpful in determining what is worth knowing. Because there is so much that could be known about our world, it is important to have some mechanisms for deciding what information has the most value. For example, is it more important to know and be able to describe the parts of a plant or know where to find this information if it is needed?

It should be clear to you at this point that a well-defined perspective on all four of the above elements is needed for good teaching. Can you imagine teaching without first having an understanding of what students are like and how they learn? Must effective teachers have a clear understanding of knowledge and how it is acquired? Is it possible to be an effective teacher if you have not first determined what is worth knowing and how this information should be taught and learned? What are your current beliefs about each of the four components of an educational philosophy?

**Reflection
Opportunity 11.2**

What key beliefs are associated with different educational philosophies?

Throughout history, educational philosophers have worked to define what good teaching and learning should look like. Many different perspectives emerged and have been influential with educators at various times. Currently, five distinct philosophies of education are considered of importance to those working in the classroom. Each has its group of devotees and others who disagree with its basic tenets. As you read about each perspective, think about your own current beliefs about teaching and learning. How well does each philosophy explain why and how people learn? Begin thinking about which philosophy seems to fit your understanding of teaching and learning the best.

Perennialism

Perennialism is an educational philosophy in which the world is seen as unchanging and permanent. Some of the basic beliefs of this philosophy are outlined in Table 11.2. For the perennialist, what was true and right for teachers and students in the past is still the same today. Those who take this perspective feel that education should be geared toward helping students learn

TABLE 11.2   Perennialist Perspectives on Education

Perceptions of Students	Beliefs About Teaching and Learning	Understanding of Knowledge	What Is Worth Knowing
• Human nature is constant • All students learn and grow in similar ways	• Teaching is orderly and carefully articulated • Traditional subjects of study emphasized	• Internalizing wisdom of the ages • Teacher dispenses knowledge, students absorb	• Eternal truths learned through studying great books

about those things that are eternally important. Consequently, classical thought, as expressed through traditional subjects such as history, mathematics, music, science, and art, is the core of the perennialist curriculum. The great works of literature, philosophy, history, science, and the arts are the main texts used for this approach (Kneller, 1971).

An effective perennialist teacher has had a strong education in the liberal arts, a clear understanding of the classical works to be used in the classroom, and the skills needed to engage students in effective dialogue regarding the truths being discussed. Teachers using this educational philosophy see themselves as traditionalists in terms of teaching methodologies. They are in control as they share with students the truths to be learned. Students become the receivers of these truths. Metaphors used to describe the perennialist teacher include "director of mental calisthenics" and "intellectual coach" (Webb, Metha, & Jordan, 2007).

Proponents of perennialism include Mortimer Adler (1982), Allan Bloom (1987), and E. D. Hirsch (1996). All three writers have echoed similar concerns in separate books on education. In his book *The Paideia Proposal,* Adler (1982) promotes a curriculum based on the great books that would be appropriate for all students. He emphasizes high-quality course work in mathematics, literature, the sciences, the arts, and social studies. Hirsch (1996) discusses the importance of schools transmitting to students a body of knowledge that must be understood by them if they are to be considered literate Americans. This knowledge, necessary to understand and function as part of our national culture, has been called **cultural literacy.** Bloom's (1987) book *The Closing of the American Mind* suggests that more and more Americans are becoming culturally illiterate and that this is a major crisis of our time. He feels that a return to a more traditional curriculum is needed to reverse this trend and help the nation become more culturally literate.

Reflect on the perennialist philosophy of education. What important points does this perspective make that you agree with? Do you disagree with any aspects of this philosophy? Do you remember teachers who you think believed in this educational philosophy and used it as the basis of their teaching? How successful do you think these teachers were?

**Reflection
Opportunity 11.3**

Progressivism

A second educational philosophy that has had a major impact on teaching and learning is called **progressivism.** Table 11.3 outlines the progressivist perspectives on education. This philosophy is quite different from the perennialist views just presented. Drawing primarily on the writings of John Dewey (1929, 1938, 1939), the progressive educator believes that education should be considered a part of life itself, rather than a preparation for life in the future. Learning, from a progressive perspective, should be centered on activities that are of interest to the child and are

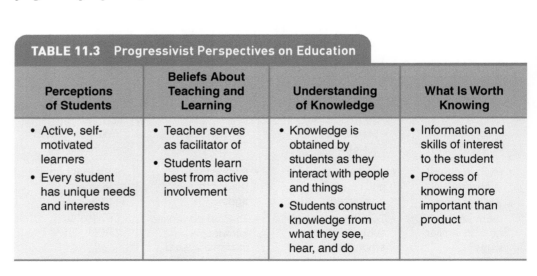

TABLE 11.3   Progressivist Perspectives on Education

Perceptions of Students	Beliefs About Teaching and Learning	Understanding of Knowledge	What Is Worth Knowing
• Active, self-motivated learners • Every student has unique needs and interests	• Teacher serves as facilitator of • Students learn best from active involvement	• Knowledge is obtained by students as they interact with people and things • Students construct knowledge from what they see, hear, and do	• Information and skills of interest to the student • Process of knowing more important than product

frequently selected by children themselves. Teachers using this philosophy act more as guides to learning rather than as dispensers of knowledge. Students frequently engage in problem-solving activities that they do in cooperation with their peers.

The progressive teacher feels that the curriculum should be experience centered. Students learn best when they are engaged in conversations with peers or as they manipulate real-world materials that are relevant to their lives. For example, a teacher using the progressive philosophy in a ninth-grade art class would include considerable opportunities for students to talk with each other regarding the art and artists being studied. A trip to an art museum would add other opportunities for real interactions with materials to make the learning meaningful.

As indicated in Chapter 10, the progressive education movement was most influential from the early 1900s to about the mid-1950s. Although it is less prominent today, many educators continue to center their approach to teaching on the progressive philosophy. The *student-centered curriculum,* where the teacher first determines student abilities and needs before creating the curriculum, and the *integrated curriculum,* which blends disciplines such as science, mathematics, literacy, and the social sciences into integrated learning activities, have strong ties to the progressive philosophy. Both of these curricular approaches are discussed in more depth in Chapter 7. One additional approach to teaching and learning that has been given considerable emphasis in schools is *constructivism.* Grounded in the philosophy of Dewey and the theories of Piaget (1950) and Vygotsky (1978), constructivism is based on the premise that students learn best when they are able to construct their knowledge, often from hands-on interactions with materials or people in their environment.

One philosophy of teaching that has been discussed in earlier chapters and has many connections with the progressive philosophy is Montessori education. To view a video of a Montessori classroom and an interview with a teacher using this approach, go to the Companion Website for this text and click on MyEducationLab for Chapter 11.

Consider reflecting on the progressive educational philosophy. Like the progressivists, do you believe that the curriculum should be experience centered? How important is it to you that students have the opportunity to engage in conversations with each other that can lead to learning? Does the idea of an integrated curriculum make sense to you? What other thoughts do you have about this educational philosophy?

**Reflection
Opportunity 11.4**

myeducationlab
The Power of Classroom Practice

MyEducationLab 11.1

Essentialism

A third educational philosophy that influences teaching and learning is called **essentialism,** which is summarized in Table 11.4. Essentialists believe that every educated person must have developed vital understandings in core areas of the curriculum: reading, writing, mathematics,

TABLE 11.4   Essentialist Perspectives on Education

Perceptions of Students	Beliefs About Teaching and Learning	Understanding of Knowledge	What Is Worth Knowing
• Student motivation frequently comes from teacher • Students need to be disciplined and work hard to learn	• Teacher responsible for motivation students • Teacher dispenses knowledge of traditional subjects, students absorb	• Knowledge comes from memorizing content and internalizing skills of traditional subjects • Knowledge comes from hard work	• Traditional academic subjects, plus technology, seen as valuable • Vocational education not encouraged

social studies, the sciences, and foreign language training. Although this sounds much like the perennialist perspective described earlier, there are differences between the two philosophies. Essentialists, for example, find themselves less concerned with teaching from the great books of the past. Unlike perennialists, the essentialist philosopher is considered an eclectic in terms of teaching methodologies. The essentialist is mainly interested in having an organized, rigorous curriculum that challenges students to do their best and learn as much as possible while in school. Essentialists also are ready to change their core curriculum as needed to keep pace with societal change. For example, the addition of computer literacy to the curriculum would be a sensible option for the essentialist educator.

Essentialism began as an effort to reverse the perceived trend by many of the continued decline in the academic standards of America's schools (Webb et al., 2007). People currently holding this perspective believe that schools have gotten too involved in nonacademic services to students and thus lost sight of their primary purpose, which is training of the intellect. Such things as vocational education, career counseling, and psychological services have taken schools away from their true calling and led to a steady devaluation of scholastic performance. Essentialists believe that the educational system has geared the curriculum to the average student, leaving the brightest and most capable with fewer options for a quality education. In addition, the essentialist believes that the curriculum in many schools is weakened by the introduction of "life adjustment" courses (Webb et al., 2007). The teaching of lessons about self-esteem to children at the elementary level and courses in vocational education at the high school level are both examples that the essentialist would point to as proof of this watering down of the curriculum.

Although essentialism has deep historical roots going back to the time of Plato and Aristotle, its growth in popularity in the 20th century can be traced to reactions against the progressive education movement that became popular in the 1920s and 1930s. Admiral Hyman Rickover (1959) was an early spokesperson for this perspective. He wrote:

> Our schools have done a fine job making Americans out of motley groups of foreigners from all corners of the globe and doing it in record time. This job is finished. The schools must now tackle a different job. They must concentrate on bringing the intellectual powers of each child to the highest possible level. Even the average child now needs almost as good an education as the average middle- and upper-class child used to get in the college-preparatory schools. The talented child needs special schooling to move him rapidly through the period of absorbing knowledge into the period when his fine mind can turn this knowledge into new ideas, new discoveries, new ways of life. (p. 31)

More recently, the educational reform movements of the 1980s have tended to support the essentialist perspective. For example, the National Commission on Excellence in Education's (1983) report titled *A Nation at Risk: The Imperative for Educational Reform* emphasized the need to move back to a more basic core curriculum that was rigorous and espoused high academic standards for all.

Reflection Opportunity 11.5

Reflect on the essentialist philosophy of education. Like others who take this perspective on teaching and learning, do you believe that every educated person must have key understandings in core curriculum areas? What would those areas be and why are they important to you? Are schools too involved in nonacademic services (vocational education, career counseling, psychological services, etc.) and thus avoiding the core curricula that they should be teaching? What nonacademic services should the schools provide and why? What positives and negatives does this philosophy have from your perspective?

Existentialism

A fourth philosophy of education that gained popularity in the last half of the 20th century is **existentialism.** Table 11.5 summarizes key elements of this philosophy. Rather than viewing human beings as having an essential core or some set of universal characteristics, the existentialist views each person as an individual with the freedom and responsibility for her or his own ac-

	TABLE 11.5 Existentialist Perspectives on Education		
Perceptions of Students	**Beliefs About Teaching and Learning**	**Understanding of Knowledge**	**What Is Worth Knowing**
• Every student is an individual • Students should have freedom to choose, take responsibility for actions	• Teacher's role is to demonstrate importance of discipline in pursuing academic goals • Individualized educational experiences promoted	• Knowledge is discovering who we are as individuals • Personalized information is needed to make responsible choices in life	• Individually determined based on life experiences and understanding of the world • That which leads to self-discovery and responsible choice

tions (Wingo, 1974). From the existentialist perspective, if students are to have authentic learning experiences they must be allowed to make choices regarding their goals and the educational curriculum pursued. At the same time, students must learn to make mature decisions and take responsibility for their actions.

Several key principles are associated with the existentialist philosophy of education (Webb et al., 2007). First, students are expected to *take responsibility for their own actions*. They should be given the freedom of choosing much of what they learn and how they learn it, but then be responsible for the results of their actions. Group learning experiences are considered less meaningful by the existentialist philosopher, whereas individualized educational experiences are promoted as the primary vehicle for learning. Another key principle is that the *teacher's role is to demonstrate the value of discipline in pursuing academic goals* rather than trying to force that discipline on students. Unlike the essentialist, existential philosophers believe that discipline must come from within the student and the teacher can merely encourage and model this discipline. Students must voluntarily choose to be disciplined in their studies. Finally, the purpose of education from the existentialist perspective is to *help students discover who they are as individuals* and support their growing awareness of the importance of making responsible choices in life. This process of self-discovery and self-motivation is a lifelong quest in which each person is expected to live each day to its fullest, growing and learning to the best of his or her abilities.

There have been several proponents of the existentialist philosophy of education during the latter part of the 20th century. Perhaps the best-known educational program based on existential principles is A. S. Neill's Summerhill school. Neill (1960) gave students complete freedom to choose when they participated in school activities while encouraging responsibility for the choices made. Another well-known author with an existential perspective is Carl Rogers, who states in his book *Freedom to Learn* (1969):

> I have come to feel that the only learning which significantly influences behavior is self-discovered, self-appropriated learning. Such self-discovered learning, truth that has been personally appropriated and assimilated in experience, cannot be directly communicated to another. As soon as an individual tries to communicate such experience directly, often with a quite natural enthusiasm, it becomes teaching, and its results are inconsequential. It was some relief recently to discover that Soren Kierkegaard, the Danish philosopher, had found this too, in his own experience, and stated it very clearly a century ago. (p. 153)

A third current proponent of the existentialist perspective in education is Nel Noddings (1992, 1995). She promotes the development of schools in which students are encouraged to make their own choices about educational experiences that are personally meaningful while taking responsibility for the options selected. Noddings also describes an alternative model for education that emphasizes the importance of caring relationships in the classroom.

Before continuing on to the final educational philosophy to be discussed in this chapter, consider reflecting on the existential philosophy of education. What do you think of the existentialist view that each of us is a unique individual who needs to take responsibility for his or her own actions? How could you as a future teacher allow opportunities for students taking responsibility for their actions? What do you find appealing about this philosophy? Are there components that you disagree with?

Reflection Opportunity 11.6

Social Reconstructionism

The final philosophy of education discussed here is called **social reconstructionism.** Table 11.6 identifies some key elements of this perspective on teaching and learning. Educators with this philosophy believe that society must make significant changes in how it operates and that the schools are one of the best agents for implementing the transformations needed (Webb et al., 2007). Feminist concerns, racial equality, and gay/lesbian issues are examples of some of the topics that social reconstructionists feel schools should address in order to change societal attitudes. Schools have a significant role to play in helping society free itself from all forms of discrimination, seeing the world as a global village, and working to reconstruct society for the betterment of all.

Although social reconstructionism can be traced back to early Greek times and the writings of Plato, its more modern version is seen as having its roots in the writings of Karl Marx (Jacobsen, 2003). Marx believed that capitalism and the competition that is inherent in it were wrong and that a social revolution was called for in which the working class should rise up and overthrow the ruling class to create a more equitable society. Gradually, the ideas of Marx were blended with those of people such as Kant, Hegel, and Freud to create a philosophy that has focused on social justice issues and the importance of schooling in fundamentally changing attitudes about these matters.

The social reconstructionist teacher places a high value on democracy and sees the classroom as an important place to model democratic ideals. Students explore their own histories and cultures as they work to become more sensitive to, and accepting of, the histories and cultures of

TABLE 11.6 Social Reconstructionist Perspectives on Education			
Perceptions of Students	**Beliefs About Teaching and Learning**	**Understanding of Knowledge**	**What Is Worth Knowing**
• Students are the hope for future growth and change in society • Capable of changing society if given necessary knowledge and skills	• Teachers lead by modeling democratic actions and exciting students about the needs for social change • Much of true learning occurs outside the classroom as students work to change society	• The information and skills needed to be a part of society while working to implement positive change	• Life skills necessary for serving as successful change agents in society

others. Reconstructionists emphasize the importance of human relationships and understanding how to make them work. A problem-solving approach to issues is the preferred mode of addressing concerns in the social reconstructionist classroom (Webb et al., 2007).

Two well-known advocates of social reconstructionism are Ivan Illich and Paulo Freire. In Illich's (1972) book titled *Deschooling Society,* he states that schools are failing in their efforts to help children from poor families break out of the cycle of poverty and lead productive lives. Illich believes that because most true learning actually takes place casually outside of the formal classroom, schools should be "disestablished" or done away with and in their place more appropriate societal structures should be created to assist all students in becoming creative, thoughtful adults. Paulo Freire lived and taught in Latin America and had firsthand experience teaching and working with illiterate peasants. Like Illich, he was primarily concerned with the problems schools created in dealing with the poor (Freire, 1970). Rather than helping them in their efforts to move out of poverty, Freire saw schools as creating mechanisms for keeping the oppressed in their place and the ruling classes in theirs.

Reflect on social reconstructionist perspectives related to teaching and learning. How important is it from your perspective for the schools to play a significant role in reducing all forms of discrimination and helping build a global village? Is this a role that schools should be involved in at all? Why or why not? Do you remember teachers from your own experiences who could be considered social reconstructionists? What did they do or say that made you associate them with this philosophy of education? Were they effective in their roles as teachers? What did you learn in their classrooms and how valuable is the information/attitudes that you learned there?

**Reflection
Opportunity 11.7**

Before reading the section below about ways in which your educational philosophy will impact the curriculum, instruction, and management and discipline in your future classroom, stop and read the *Engage in the Debate* feature for this chapter. It provides you with examples of key issues you will face as a teacher. How you respond to each of these issues may help you determine components of you own educational philosophy. Read and reflect further on this topic now.

Engage in the debate: Philosophical perspectives and real issues

Within the education profession there are many ongoing debates about what approaches should be taken when educating our youth. People on both sides of the issues are influenced by their philosophical perspectives of teaching and learning. Each month, *NEA Today* (a journal published by the National Education Association) features a debate where NEA members take sides on an issue. The following are two examples of the debates published:

Should teachers have the authority to remove disruptive students from their classes permanently? (NEA, 2002).

- A sixth grade teacher in Virginia answered "yes". She argued that disruptive students steal learning away from students who are ready to learn.

- A student services coordinator from Hawaii answered "no". He argued that most teachers who want to remove a disruptive student from the classroom still have interventions that could be tried. He said that teachers should not try to figure these kinds of problems out on their own; it's best to get help from a student support team.

Should teachers express their views on controversial topics in class? (NEA, 2005).

- Rachel Rice, a middle school teacher from Vermont, answered "yes". She argued that this is one way that teachers educate students about the democratic process.

- Lacey Pitts, a NEA student member from Georgia, answered "no". She argued that teachers who attempt to share their views to stimulate conversation often end up alienating students.

Developing the Habit of Reflective Practice

Gather Information

1. Do an Internet search for "NEA Today" and read the two debates referenced in this feature.
2. Read other debates in back issues of *NEA Today*.

Identify Beliefs

1. After reading the debates referenced here take a stand on one of them. What does this tell you about your beliefs?
2. Should teachers debate their opinions based on their educational philosophy? Why or why not?

Make Decisions

1. Imagine that you are a first year teacher eating lunch with fellow faculty members, most of whom have taught at the school for years. An educational issue is being discussed and you have an opinion that is much different from the other teachers in the room. Do you share you opinion? Why or why not?

Assess and Evaluate

1. Look again at the viewpoints expressed in the debates referenced here. What philosophical perspectives do these teachers represent?

Sources

NEA (2002). Debate: Should teachers have the authority to remove disruptive students from their classes permanently? *NEA Today*, January 2002. Retrieved December 31, 2008 from *http://www.nea.org/neatoday/0201/index.html*

NEA (2005). Should teachers express their views on controversial topics in class? *NEA Today*, October 2005. Retrieved December 31, 2008 from *http://www.nea.org/neatoday/0510/ index.html*

How does your choice of educational philosophy impact what you do in the classroom?

In this section, we take a more detailed look at three fundamental components of good teaching and read about how each of the educational philosophies discussed earlier would address them. By describing each philosophy's perspectives on the content of the curriculum, methods of instruction, and classroom management and discipline, you should develop a better understanding of each one and continue to refine your own beliefs about teaching and learning.

Content of the Curriculum

As discussed in Chapter 7, the curriculum taught in American schools is largely determined by local, state, and national guidelines. Yet, every teacher has the opportunity to take the basic curriculum as defined by others and present it to students in a way that reflects his or her personal views of what is valuable to know. Each of the five educational philosophies provides different perspectives on the content of the curriculum that should be taught in schools. Table 11.7 summarizes these views for each of the five philosophies of education presented in the last section.

Perennialist view of curriculum. The driving force in the perennialist curriculum is the training of the mind in traditional subject-matter areas. Every student is expected to complete a core

TABLE 11.7 Philosophical Perspectives on Curriculum Content				
Perennialism	**Progressivism**	**Essentialism**	**Existentialism**	**Social Reconstructionism**
• Training the mind in traditional subjects • Core curriculum of social studies, mathematics, the sciences, music, and art	• Individual topics learned through meaningful experiences • Integrated curriculum around topics of interest to students	• Rigorous common core of traditional courses • Computer literacy also considered important	• Individual curriculum designed to help students understand selves and life's meanings	• Understanding social justice and equity issues • Strategies needed to implement social change

curriculum in social studies, mathematics, the sciences, music, and art. These subjects allow students to develop the intellectual skills needed for success in later life (Adler, 1982). The great books from the past serve as the main vehicle for delivering this classic curriculum. A perennialist high school English teacher, for example, would teach from such literary giants as Shakespeare, Chaucer, and Thoreau to help develop mental abilities in students. In addition to these core subjects, the perennialist educator also believes that character education and issues related to moral development should be included in the curriculum (Webb et al., 2007). The fundamental truths that can be learned from the past also include key values such as honesty, caring about others, and freedom.

Progressivism's perspectives on curriculum.   Unlike the perennialists, whose curriculum is well defined, the progressivist philosophy would suggest a curriculum that is considerably more individualized. Rather than emphasizing a set of universal truths to be learned through carefully crafted core subjects, the progressive teacher emphasizes the importance of learning through experiences that are meaningful to the individual. These teachers also integrate academic subjects into these experiences, rather than separately studying subjects such as mathematics, reading, and social studies. So, for example, Matt and Christie are two fifth-grade students who are interested in the upcoming local elections. They have been given some time each day during the last 2 weeks to work on a report to their peers on the preparations for, and results of, the elections. They are incorporating reading, writing, mathematics, and social studies into this short-term project.

Curriculum from an essentialist perspective.   The essentialist teacher, like the perennialists, believes that the curriculum should focus on a rigorous common core of subjects that all students should complete. Rather than relying solely on the great books from the past, however, the essentialist believes that a variety of materials can be used to teach students this core. The inclusion of more modern curriculum content, such as computer literacy, is also considered valuable to the essentialist. In addition, more recent proponents of essentialism feel that moral/character education is an important part of the core curriculum, and support its inclusion (Bennett, 1993).

Essentialists are primarily concerned with academic rigor. They want the curriculum to be challenging to all students so that they can develop the mental skills needed for success in later life. By holding to high academic standards, the essentialist believes that students can rise to the challenges encountered. Because of these beliefs, these teachers feel comfortable in testing students to make sure they are measuring up to the high standards set by the schools for passage through the system (Webb et al., 2007).

Existentialist curriculum. Existential educators believe that learning is personal and different for each student. Even more so than the progressives, these teachers develop a highly individualized curriculum whose purpose is to help students become more aware of themselves and the meanings surrounding their lives. Existentialists engage their students in dialogues that help them gain insights into the fundamental questions we all face: What is the meaning of life? Is it possible to love and be loved? How should an understanding of death influence the way I live? These questions and others are obviously subjective and are designed to help students come to an understanding that is personally meaningful (Greene, 1988). The results of learning from this curriculum cannot be measured by standardized tests, which would be discouraged by the existentialist.

Literature, biographies, art, music, and film tend to be favored options for discussing the existentialist perspective. A middle school social studies teacher wanting to discuss humankind's struggle between good and evil might consider showing the movie *Schindler's List.* In this film, a German industrialist grapples with his own materialism and the moral dilemma of knowing that most of his Jewish workers will end up facing the Nazi gas chambers. He finally works to save as many workers as he can from this terrible fate. By viewing and then discussing this film, students can develop new insights into the human condition.

Social reconstructionist's perspective on curriculum. The focus of the social reconstructionist curriculum is on understanding the democratic ideals of social justice and equity and helping students develop strategies for implementing social change. Topics of concern to the social reconstructionist, such as poverty, discrimination due to race, sexual preference, or religious affiliation, and world peace, would be addressed at every opportunity in the classroom. For example, an elementary teacher with this perspective could spend time helping students become aware of the problems associated with poverty and get students involved in a project to collect food and clothing to give to local charities involved in assisting low-income families.

To read about one teacher's efforts to implement a curriculum that matches his philosophy of education, go to the Companion Website for this text and read the *Views from the Classroom* feature for this chapter. See if you can identify which of the philosophies of education described above matches best with this teacher's perspectives.

Views from the Classroom: Keeping it Real

Methods of Instruction

A second component of teaching strongly influenced by your choice of educational philosophy is the instructional methods you will use in the classroom. Decisions, for example, about whether to use small- or large-group instructional strategies, direct instruction, cooperative learning, or project learning are all made based on your choice of philosophy. Each of the five perspectives suggests somewhat different techniques to be used in helping students learn. These techniques are summarized in Table 11.8 for each of the five educational philosophies.

Perennialist perspectives on methods of instruction. The perennialist teacher tends toward more traditional methods of instruction. *Direct instruction,* in which the teacher shares information in an organized and motivating manner with groups of students, is often the preferred instructional strategy (see Chapter 7 for more information). The *Socratic method,* in which the teacher uses a series of questions to lead students to an understanding of the chosen topic, is also promoted by perennialists (Adler, 1982).

Progressive methods of instruction. Because the progressivist teacher promotes a more personalized curriculum in which students are actively engaged in their learning, constructivist

TABLE 11.8   Philosophical Perspectives on Instructional Methods

Perennialism	Progressivism	Essentialism	Existentialism	Social Reconstructionism
• Direct instruction, Socratic method • Traditional methods of instruction	• Constructive and cooperative learning preferred	• Traditional methods such as direct instruction and Socratic method • Other methods when they can be effective	• Methods model decision making and choosing between alternatives such as story telling and discussions of existential questions	• Methods vary, with their intent being to guide students to an understanding of social issues and constructive methods of dealing with them.

and cooperative learning (see Chapter 8) are preferred methods of instruction. In constructivist education, the teacher helps students select activities or projects in which they learn from real-world interactions with materials and people that are meaningful to them. *Cooperative learning* engages students in interactions with others in small groups. The learning that takes place through either option is personally meaningful to students and is seen by the progressive educator as the foundation for lifelong learning.

Essentialist perspectives on teaching methods. Much like the perennialists, the essentialist educator tends to emphasize traditional methods of instruction such as direct instruction and the Socratic method. Other techniques are used when they can be justified within an ordered and carefully sequenced curriculum. Students need to be made aware of the purposes and organization of the curriculum through detailed course syllabi and clearly articulated lesson plans. According to the essentialist, this high level of organization in instruction helps make it clear to students what needs to be learned and makes the actual learning experience more effective.

Existentialist methods of instruction. The existentialist's desire to help students decide the major issues of life leads the existentialist to choose methods of instruction that model decision making and choosing between alternatives. Nel Noddings (1993) states it this way:

> In the discussion of religious, metaphysical, and existential questions, teachers and students are both seekers. Teachers tell stories, guide the logic of discussion, point to further readings, model both critical thinking and kindness, and show by their openness what it means to seek intelligent belief or unbelief. (p. 135)

An existentialist middle school science teacher, for example, in a series of discussions on the human life cycle, might address the topic of euthanasia by telling a story about a dying man kept alive solely through the use of medical machines. After seeking feedback from the class on the family's rights to end life and discussing the options with students, the teacher could then provide time for students to reflect on their feelings about euthanasia individually before discussing the issue again as a large group.

Social reconstructionist views on methods of instruction. The social reconstructionist teacher wants to make students aware of the key social issues facing America and the world. The method of sharing may vary, but the passionate need to change how things operate would not. The social reconstructionist would first want to convince students through facts, logic, and emotion that these issues cannot be overlooked and that every individual has a role to play in creating a better world for us all. Having convinced students of the rightness of these causes, the social reconstructionist teacher would then work to get students involved in real-world activities that lead to change. For example, a fifth-grade elementary teacher might choose to convince students that cutting down trees and vegetation creates an imbalance in our ecological system that could eventually lead to a poorer quality of life for us all. Once students are convinced of the problems associated with deforestation, the class can spend some time planting and caring for new trees in a field near the school as a tangible way of improving the situation.

Classroom Management and Discipline

A third component of successful teaching that is strongly influenced by your choice of educational philosophy is classroom management and discipline. Table 11.9 summarizes the management and discipline approaches most closely aligned with each of the five educational philosophies presented in this text. Because of their importance in creating a classroom environment that facilitates good teaching and learning (see Chapter 8), the collection of strategies you use for classroom management and discipline should be based on your understanding of students as learners, your perspectives on what should be learned, and the teaching strategies you will employ. There is a clear link, then, between your choice of educational philosophy and the classroom management and discipline strategies you use.

Perennialist classroom management and discipline. The traditional views of the perennialist educator extend to the management and discipline areas as well. These teachers see themselves as in control and expect students to respect them as educational leaders in the classroom. In addition to training the mind through the great works from the past, the perennialist believes that the teacher's role is to mold the spirit of each student. Students are expected to work hard, obey classroom rules, and respect the authority of adults. It is the responsibility of the teacher to make sure that an orderly and calm environment is available to all who enter the classroom.

Progressive views on management and discipline. The progressive stance on classroom management and discipline is rooted in the belief that students should actively participate in all aspects of classroom life. Students, for example, would be expected to work with the teacher to develop classroom rules and the consequences associated with breaking the rules. Management and

TABLE 11.9 Philosophical Perspectives on Management and Discipline

Perennialism	Progressivism	Essentialism	Existentialism	Social Reconstructionism
• Traditional methods emphasizing control and student respect for the teacher as educational leader	• Students actively participate in planning for, and implementing classroom management and discipline	• Students expected to follow the rules, work hard, and allow others to engage in learning • Character training also emphasized	• Open approach to management and discipline with students given equal responsibility with teacher for dealing with problems and conflict	• Importance of community building • Students need skills for effective group action

discipline problems that had an impact on the entire class would be discussed and resolved with the whole class participating. The teacher would then work to guide individual students who are engaging in inappropriate behaviors in more positive directions. William Glasser's (1969) problem-solving approach (discussed in Chapter 8) is one example of a discipline style that engages students as participants in the management and discipline process.

Essentialist management and discipline. Traditional methods of management and discipline are considered the most valuable strategies to the essentialist. Students are expected to understand and follow the rules as defined by the teacher, work hard to master the content being presented, and allow others to engage in quality learning experiences. Firm management and control are seen as important to the essentialist teacher. In addition, modern essentialists feel strongly about character education and take time as part of their management and discipline efforts to help students understand the reasons for engaging in appropriate classroom behaviors. The academic literacy required of all students is thus supplemented with moral literacy (Bennett, 1993).

Existentialist views on management and discipline. Of all the philosophical perspectives presented here, existentialism has the most open approach to management and discipline. Because considerable responsibility is placed on students for their own learning, freedom of choice and a more student-centered approach are used. Existentialists generally view students as partners in the decision-making processes surrounding management and discipline. Educators using this philosophy would work to understand students' perspectives on areas of conflict within the classroom and interact with them more as equals in determining solutions to the problems encountered. The teacher-effectiveness training program of Thomas Gordon (1974) discussed in Chapter 8 is an example of management and discipline that most closely matches this philosophy.

Social reconstructionist perspectives. The social reconstructionist emphasis on working together to influence society's directions on major social issues positively leads these educators to emphasize the importance of community building. Because everyone needs to understand the problems facing society and work cooperatively to make the necessary changes, it is important for students and teachers to develop a sense of togetherness that leads to effective group action. Considerable time is spent in these classrooms on getting to know one another and understanding the similarities and differences that exist among racial and ethnic groups, males and females, religious affiliations, and people of different sexual orientations. Both planned and naturally occurring team-building activities are used to create a stronger community of learners and social-change agents.

Before reading further in this chapter, stop and reflect on how every student and teacher is different. Because no two of us are exactly alike, it shouldn't be surprising that there is no one philosophy of teaching that is right for all. In fact, a diversity of educational philosophies is considered by many to be an asset. The *Reflect on Diversity* feature for this chapter talks about how schools and teachers can build upon the diversity of educational beliefs that exist among teachers. Read it now and reflect on the questions found in the feature.

Reflect on diversity: Aiming for diverse ideas or consensus?

David Ferrero (2005) points out that great teachers enter the profession not on a mission to raise test scores, but "out of a deep sense of what's good for kids and society, what's worth knowing and thinking about." He points out that individual views on what makes a good education are shaped by beliefs and values that create a sense of what makes life worth living, and therefore what is worth teaching and how it should be taught. Ferrero claims that educators should openly acknowledge their philosophical differences, and create separate schools shaped around beliefs that they share with colleagues. He believes this will create more focused and effective learning communities.

As part of his work at the Bill and Melinda Gates Foundation, Ferrero (2005), visited 8 high-performing small high schools. He discovered that these schools differed profoundly in their curriculum, instruction, and culture. Ferrero describes a crucial but often overlooked source of the distinctiveness among high-performing schools: the educational philosophy held by the teachers. As educators strive to use practices that are research-based, they often forget that between the science of learning and the art of teaching lie important value judgments that affect how teachers interpret and understand the research and the ways in which teaching and learning occur.

Ferrero proposes that large schools be broken down into smaller schools, where teachers with similar philosophies work together towards common goals. He argues that each philosophical perspective has legitimate teaching strategies and that there is no right or wrong way to teach, just different perspectives.

Developing the Habit of Reflective Practice

Gather Information

1. Read the article by David Ferrero (2005) to better understand the position he takes above.
2. Review the philosophical perspectives outlined in this chapter so that you clearly understand their similarities and differences.

Identify Beliefs

1. Do you think it is best that educators seek to teach with people who have similar philosophical perspectives? Why or why not?
2. What are the advantages and disadvantages of having teachers with diverse philosophical perspectives teaching side-by-side?

Make Decisions

1. As an educator, do you expect to share your philosophical perspective with your colleagues?
2. What will you do when a colleague has a philosophical perspective different from your own?

Assess and Evaluate

1. How does an educator's philosophy of teaching and learning impact the way he/she performs on the job? Consider a typical day as a teacher: what teaching decisions are impacted by the teacher's philosophy?

Source

Ferrero, D. (2005). Pathways to reform: Start with values. *Educational Leadership, 62*, (65), 8–15.

How do I develop an educational philosophy?

As you begin to develop an educational philosophy that will guide your future teaching, an initial step you can take is to decide whether you want to be an eclectic philosopher, choosing bits and pieces from several educational philosophies to create your own unique perspectives, or more of a purist who finds one of the defined philosophies that most closely represents your beliefs about students, teaching, and learning and uses it to guide your thinking and actions. In addition to this initial step, there are several activities you can engage in now to begin developing your philosophy of education.

Eclectic or Purist

Many teachers develop their own eclectic educational philosophy. Their reasoning for this approach stems from a deeply held belief that both teachers and students are unique individuals. Because of their uniqueness, no one philosophy can adequately describe the specific teaching and learning strategies needed for all. It makes more sense to the eclectic to create a philosophy of education that takes into consideration the uniqueness of the teacher and the continually changing array of students that enter the classroom each year.

The *Ian's Classroom Experiences* for this chapter (found on the Companion Website for this text) describes Ian's ongoing efforts to refine his own philosophy of education. You may want to read it now for his insights.

Ian's Classroom Experiences: Strategies and Personal Investment

There is a danger, however, in using the eclectic approach. Without careful thought, it becomes easy for teachers to be less concerned about creating a consistent rationale for what they believe and do in the classroom. Eclecticism becomes an excuse for not taking the time and effort it requires to conceptualize a framework for teaching and learning that makes sense and can be articulated to others.

Just as there are many teachers who develop an eclectic educational philosophy, there are large numbers of educators who find that one existing philosophy meshes well with their own way of thinking. After careful study, they adopt it as their own. Although there are clearly elements in each philosophy that appeal to most of these purists, one or two key aspects of the chosen philosophy have deep meaning for these educators and help provide a clear focus to their thinking and actions. The major advantage of selecting one educational philosophy is that it provides a consistent and logical set of perspectives on teaching and learning that was developed through careful analysis by educational leaders both past and present. Each of the five educational philosophies presented in this chapter was developed and refined over many years by bright, articulate writers who have worked to create a systematic, reasoned approach to the education of students of all ages. Teachers who choose one of these five philosophies have ready access to written information that will assist them in understanding the elements of the philosophical perspective and its implications for teaching and learning.

Creating Your Own Educational Philosophy

There are several steps you can take now and in the coming years to develop and refine your own philosophy of education:

- *Learn more about students and teaching.* The more you know, the better able you will be to make good decisions about a philosophy of education.

- *Study educational philosophy.* Either in course work during your initial teacher-preparation program or later, you should take additional opportunities to study educational philosophy in more depth. Use these experiences to add to your existing knowledge of philosophy as you continue to define what seems right to you.

- *Discuss educational philosophy with others.* Don't let the term *educational philosophy* scare you. Remember that it is simply "practical wisdom" (Heslep, 1997) about the teaching and learning process. You should take the time to talk to other teachers and future teachers so that you can refine your own thinking about philosophical issues.

- *Take time to reflect on your own teaching practices.* One of the best ways to refine your thinking is to consider your own teaching practices thoughtfully to determine what is working and what needs to change. As you make decisions about these real-world experiences, your educational philosophy is also being refined.

Creating your own philosophy of education will take time, but you should begin now to identify components of your own approach to education. Listening to, and watching others will

MyEducationLab 11.2

Consider This: What is Your Philosophical Perspective?

help you in this process. To view a teacher discussing her classroom and elements of her philosophy of education, go to the Companion Website for this course and click on MyEducationLab for Chapter 11.

Another activity to help you determine your educational philosophy is found in the *Consider This* feature for this chapter. Go to the Companion Website for this text and read the information presented there. Take a few moments and complete the survey for this feature. As you reflect on your responses, you will find additional insights into your philosophical perspectives on teaching.

Summary

Four organizing questions were used in this chapter to help you develop better understandings of educational philosophies and their importance:

What is philosophy and why is it important to me as a future teacher?

Philosophy is often seen as consisting of four main branches:
- Metaphysics—determining what is real
- Epistemology—issues related to knowledge and knowing (Praxis II, topic Ia)
- Logic—the rules and techniques of reasoning
- Axiology—issues related to ethics and aesthetics

What key beliefs are associated with different educational philosophies?

Five educational philosophies were discussed:
- Perennialism (Praxis II, topic IVa)
- Progressivism (Praxis II, topic IVa)
- Essentialism (Praxis II, topic IVa)
- Existentialism (Praxis II, topic IVa)
- Social reconstructionism (Praxis II, topics IVa, IIIb)

How does your choice of educational philosophy impact what you do in the classroom?

Educational philosophy influences three major elements of classroom life:
- Content of the curriculum (Praxis II, topic IIb)
- Methods of instruction (Praxis II, topics IIb, IIIc)
- Classroom management and discipline (Praxis II, topic IIa)

How do I develop an educational philosophy?

You can begin to take steps now to develop an educational philosophy by:
- Deciding to choose either an eclectic or a specific educational philosophy
- Taking steps to create your own educational philosophy (Praxis II, topic IVa)

PRAXIS   Test-Preparation Activities

To review an on-line chapter case study, test your understanding of chapter topics and concepts, and begin preparing for the Praxis II: Principles of Learning and Teaching examination, go to the Praxis Test-Preparation module for this chapter of the Companion Website.

Developing the Habit of Reflective Practice

Organizing Questions

Review questions, field-experience opportunities, and activities for building your portfolio are included here for the organizing questions in this chapter.

What is philosophy and why is it important to me as a future teacher?

Review Questions

1. What are the four branches of philosophical thought?
2. Why is epistemology an important branch of philosophy for educators?
3. Which branch of philosophy deals with ethics and aesthetics?
4. What four essential elements of education are addressed by educational philosophies?

Building Your Portfolio: *Content of the Curriculum*

INTASC Standard 7. Although your thoughts will probably change over time, what do you currently believe should be the content of the curriculum?

- For the grade or subject of your choice, identify 5–10 broad concepts or understandings that you think students need to have at that level or in that subject area.
- Give a brief rationale for each element of the curriculum you include.

What key beliefs are associated with different educational philosophies?

Review Questions

1. Why do perennialists feel that studying the classics is important?
2. Which educational philosophy is associated with constructivism?
3. Identify one key principle associated with the existentialist philosophy of education.

Field Experience

Observe a teacher in a classroom of your choice. Note what is done and said.

- See if you can determine the educational philosophy that this teacher is using as the basis for his or her actions.
- What did you see or hear that helped you make a decision about the philosophy being used?

Building Your Portfolio: *Educational Philosophy Critique*

INTASC Standard 4. Choose one of the educational philosophies in this chapter that is appealing to you at this point and spend more time reading about it. Once you have developed a deeper understanding of this perspective:

- Summarize what you see to be the strengths and limitations of this philosophy of education.
- Include this critique in your portfolio.

How does your choice of educational philosophy impact what you do in the classroom?

Review Questions

1. What is the perennialist view of curriculum?
2. Which methods of instruction would be associated with the social reconstructionist philosophy of education?
3. What are the existentialist views on management and discipline?

Field Experience

Talk to a teacher about the perceived importance of developing your own educational philosophy.

- Is it seen as important or unimportant by this teacher?
- Does this teacher have a personal philosophy that can be shared?
- How does this person's philosophy impact his or her teaching?

Building Your Portfolio: *Classroom Management and Discipline*

INTASC Standard 5. Describe in a few paragraphs what you currently believe will be the classroom management and discipline strategies you will use in your future teaching.

- Rather than getting too specific, work on identifying general methods that seem to make sense to you.
- Refer to Chapter 8 for more information on specific options.
- Which of the educational philosophies in this chapter most closely aligns with your views?

How do I develop an educational philosophy?

Review Questions

1. What is an eclectic educational philosophy?
2. How can you begin to develop your own educational philosophy?

Building Your Portfolio: *Philosophy of Education*

INTASC Standard 9. Review your responses to the earlier reflective journey activities for this chapter.

- Use this information to begin identifying a framework for your philosophy of education.
- If your current beliefs match one of the educational philosophies presented in this chapter, describe in your own words what that philosophy means to you.
- If you are more eclectic in your current thinking, describe the components of your personal philosophy of education.

Suggested Readings

Kneller, G. (1971). *Introduction to the philosophy of education.* New York: Wiley. This classic text provides a clear description of the educational philosophies described in this chapter.

Noddings, N. (1995). *Philosophy of education.* Boulder, CO: Westview Press. The author presents a strong overview of several philosophies, with a particularly good overview of existentialism.

Ozmon, H., & Craver, S. (2008). *Philosophical foundations of education* (8th ed.). Upper Saddle River, NJ: Merrill/Prentice Hall. This book is a good resource for philosophies not addressed in this textbook, giving detailed descriptions of them.

References

Adler, M. (1982). *The Paideia proposal: An educational manifesto.* New York: Macmillan.

Bennett, W. (1993). *The book of virtues: A treasury of great moral stories.* New York: Simon & Schuster.

Bloom, A. (1987). *The closing of the American mind.* New York: Simon & Schuster.

Dewey, J. (1929). *Democracy and education.* New York: Macmillan.

Dewey, J. (1938). *Experience and education.* New York: Collier Books.

Dewey, J. (1939). *Freedom and culture.* New York: G. P. Putnam's Sons.

Freire, P. (1970). *The pedagogy of the oppressed.* New York: Herder and Herder.

Glasser, W. (1969). *Schools without failure.* New York: Harper and Row.

Gordon, T. (1974). *Teacher effectiveness training.* New York: Wyden.

Greene, M. (1988). *The dialectic of freedom.* New York: Teachers College Press.

Heslep, R. (1997). *Philosophical thinking in educational practice.* Westport, CT: Praeger.

Hirsch, E. (1996). *The schools we need and why we don't have them.* New York: Doubleday.

Illich, I. (1972). *Deschooling society.* New York: Harrow Books.

Jacobsen, D. (2003). *Philosophy in classroom teaching: Bridging the gap* (2nd ed.) Upper Saddle River, NJ: Merrill/Prentice Hall.

Kneller, G. (1971). Introduction to the philosophy of education. New York: Wiley.

Lawrence-Lightfoot, S. (1983). *The good high school.* NY: Basic Books.

National Commission on Excellence in Education. (1983). *A nation at risk: The imperative for educational reform.* Washington, DC: Government Printing Office.

Neill, A. (1960). *Summerhill: A radical approach to child rearing.* New York: Hart Publishing Company.

Noddings, N. (1993). *Educating for intelligent belief or unbelief.* New York: Teachers College Press.

Noddings, N. (1995). *Philosophy of education.* Boulder, CO: Westview Press.

Ozmon, H., & Craver, S. (2008). *Philosophical foundations of education* (8th ed.). Upper Saddle River, NJ: Merrill/Prentice Hall.

Piaget, J. (1950). *The psychology of intelligence* (M. Piercy & D. Berlyne, Trans.). New York: Harcourt, Brace.

Rickover, H. (1959). *Education and freedom.* New York: E. P. Dutton.

Rogers, C. (1969). *Freedom to learn.* Upper Saddle River, NJ: Merrill/Prentice Hall.

Vygotsky, L. (1978). *Mind in society: The development of higher psychological processes.* Cambridge, MA: Harvard University Press.

Webb, L., Metha, A., & Jordan, K. (2007). *Foundations of American education* (5th ed.). Upper Saddle River, NJ: Merrill/Prentice Hall.

Wingo, G. (1974). *Philosophies of education: An introduction.* Lexington, MA: D. C. Heath.

chapter 12

Societal Influences

Students' attitudes, values, and beliefs are shaped in many ways by the society in which they live. In addition, society determines the purposes and directions for institutions such as the public schools. In this chapter, four focus questions will help you better understand these societal influences.

Focus Questions

1. What socializing agents influence students?

2. Are there social issues that affect student behavior?

3. How should teachers and schools respond to social issues?

4. How does society influence schooling?

Courtesy of Laima Druskis/Prentice-Hall, Inc.

Amber, a shy student in your eighth-grade social studies class, has you concerned. Although her classroom comments and writing assignments indicate that she is a very capable student, Amber often disengages herself from classroom activities and stares blankly out the window. You learned from a brief conversation with her seventh-grade language arts teacher that her dad left the family last year to be with another woman and Amber's mom is struggling financially and emotionally to deal with this loss. Having seen Amber's permanent folder, you are aware that she is very bright and has done excellent work in the past. Part of your concern, however, stems from Amber's growing involvement with a group of students who are known to be experimenting with drugs. There have been several times lately when you noticed her talking animatedly with this group before class. You would really like to be able to build a better relationship with Amber and help get her back on track educationally. But you are unsure about where to begin or what to do.

You are planning to enter a profession filled with complex human interactions with people like Amber. Every day you will be challenged to make decisions about each student you teach based on an understanding of that person's background, experiences, and personality. The more you know about what influences human behavior and how that applies to individuals within your classroom, the better able you will be to respond thoughtfully to students' needs.

In addition to influencing individuals' lives, society imparts purpose and value to its institutions. You need to know what those purposes are for American educational institutions and why they are valued by society. This understanding then forms a framework on which all of your teaching experiences are built. For example, one of the purposes for education is the preparation of students for participation in the workforce. Our society needs competent new workers to replace those who retire. Knowing about this purpose and its value helps you as a future teacher to plan learning experiences that can support this objective.

What socializing agents influence students?

As a nation, the United States is a diverse collection of people consisting of numerous subgroups. Each of these groups has its own set of beliefs, traditions, and lifestyles. At the same time, the American people share common institutions, similar governmental structures, and a core set of values. This combination of diversity and shared elements identifies the **society** in which we live. Institutions within society such as the family, peer groups, television, religion, and the schools are all considered **socializing agents** (Cushner, McClelland, & Safford, 2006) that have a significant impact on students' lives. Table 12.1 briefly describes the five key socializing agents discussed in the following sections.

The Family

Literally from the day of birth, families are either directly or indirectly shaping every aspect of a child's life (Berger, 2008). For example, parents who positively respond to their infant's needs for food, shelter, and loving attention are also developing the young child's ability to trust in others (Erikson, 1963). Or, later in a young person's life, parents who discuss and model responsible

TABLE 12.1   Socializing Agents

Socializing Agent	Description
Family	Either directly or indirectly, family life influences every aspect of a child's development. It is the most significant socializing agent for the majority of students through their elementary school years.
Peer Group	By adolescence, many young people question the values and attitudes of family members while embracing the habits, language, and rituals of their peers.
Electronic Media	Because of the high number of hours spent using electronic media, they have an impact on attitudes toward violence, sex roles, consumerism, and sexuality.
Religion	Nearly 80% of all families report that religion has a significant influence on their lives.
Schools	Schools prepare students for the workforce, assist them in becoming effective citizens, and help students reach their full potential as individuals.

consumption of alcohol are influencing that child's attitudes about drinking. Although the family's socializing influences are the greatest during childhood, it continues to have an impact throughout life. In some instances the family's influence is not a positive one, and despite our best efforts as educators is difficult to overcome. For example, Paul is a sophomore at a 4-year college who is taking an introductory course on teaching where he is learning about the diversity that exists in schools today and the importance of future teachers working effectively with students from all walks of life. Unfortunately, Paul comes from a home where his father has consistently denigrated blacks and Hispanics and labeled them as lazy malcontents. Although not totally in agreement with his father, Paul will need to work very hard to overcome the negative stereotypes that he regularly experienced throughout his growing-up years.

Reflect on your own family history. Can you identify ways in which your attitudes, values, and thinking have been influenced by family members? In some instances, you probably recognize where you have accepted the values held by others in your family as personally meaningful. On the other hand, you may remember having consciously chosen to value some things differently than certain members of your family. In either case, your family unit had (and continues to have) a powerful influence on how you view the world. Identify and describe three or four significant ways in which your family has influenced your attitudes, values, and/or thinking. How has your family influenced your potential for future success as a teacher?

**Reflection
Opportunity 12.1**

Peer-Group Influences

Although the family's role as a socializing agent is the greatest in the early years and gradually decreases over time, those young people of approximately the same age that congregate together at school, on the playground, and in other activities such as sports and music experiences have an increasingly stronger influence. The effects of these **peer groups** become readily apparent when children enter elementary school and continue to grow stronger (Gandara, 2005). By adolescence, many young people question the values and attitudes of family members while embracing the habits, language, and rituals of the peer group. Like the family, peer groups can have a significant impact on every aspect of students' lives. For example, many young people choose clothing, speech patterns, hair styles and colors, and jewelry options that distinguish themselves from parents and other adults. These relatively unimportant lifestyle choices are strongly influenced by a student's peer group. More significantly, the peer group often affects student decisions about such things as using drugs and alcohol, engaging in sexual activity, involvement in gangs, and using violence in relating to others. Furthermore, peer groups influence students' attitudes toward diverse people, sex-role expectations, and feelings about education.

Think about the influence of peers on your life to date. Try to remember your own middle school and high school years. How did peers impact your decisions and actions? Did they have more or less influence during this period than your family? Did peers influence your decision to consider teaching as a career? Or, did they have an impact on attitudes and values that may influence your future career choice? Try to identify at least two or three specific examples of peer-group influence.

**Reflection
Opportunity 12.2**

Electronic Media

Electronic media, in all its many forms, is another important socializing agent for students. In addition to television viewing, Rideout (2007) states:

> Over the past few years, media use among children and teens has become more prevalent than ever. With the launch of the iPod, the explosion in instant messaging, the birth of mobile video and YouTube, and the advent of social networking sites like MySpace, young people are rarely out of contact, or out of reach of the media (p. 1).

Although data are incomplete, television viewing appears to consume the most time and probably has the greatest impact. Children in the United States watch an average of over 3 hours of television daily (Kaiser Family Foundation, 2007). Because of these high levels of use, television and other electronic media are often seen as rivaling the home and school as a major socializing agent.

But how does electronic media influence student attitudes and values? Many people are suggesting that one clear connection is that high levels of use are influencing *attitudes toward violence*. Statistics indicate, for example, that by the end of the elementary school years children will have viewed approximately 8,000 murders and 100,000 acts of violence on television (Anderson et al., 2003). Others are concerned about the *stereotypic sex roles* portrayed on television and other electronic media. Male characters, for example, are more prevalent on tv shows for children and are portrayed stereotypically as active, outgoing, and confident, whereas women are typically cast as passive and dependent (Golin, 2004). Television has also been criticized for its *advertising to promote consumerism*. Similar concerns are being expressed when children use the Internet. Children are bombarded with thousands of television advertisements designed to develop brand-name recognition and promote consumerism. It is estimated that children watch approximately 40,000 tv commercials each year (Wilcox et al., 2004). *Sexual content* of television programs and other electronic media is yet another concern. As with televised violence, children are repeatedly exposed to sexual content that may hasten the start of sexual activity in middle school and high school students (Kaiser Family Foundation, 2007).

Religion

Religion plays an important role in the socialization process for many young people in this country. As a nation, the United States leads all wealthy nations with nearly 60% of its citizens stating that religion plays a very important role in their lives (Pew Research Center, 2002). This compares with 30% of Canadians, 27% of Italians, and 11% of the respondents in France indicating that religion is of major importance in their lives. Religion influences such things as people's attitudes about sex roles, discipline, child-rearing practices, the role of the family, and ways of relating to others. For example, traditional Christian teachings would encourage such positive actions as sexual abstinence before marriage and an attitude of respect toward those in authority. On the other hand, strongly held religious beliefs can cause tension and separation between people with divergent perspectives or life experiences. For example, a Christian who believes in the importance of strong family units with both a mother and father may have a difficult time accepting and relating to other family constellations such as single-parent families and gay/lesbian families.

The role of religion in schools has been a topic of intense debate among many different groups over the years. One group to state its opinions on this topic clearly is the Americans United for Separation of Church and State. They make a reasoned case for keeping schools and religion independent from one another:

> Ninety percent of America's youngsters attend public schools. These students come from homes that espouse a variety of religious and philosophical beliefs. Given the incredible diversity of American society, it's important that our public schools respect the beliefs of everyone and protect parental rights. The schools can best do this by not sponsoring religious worship. This principle ensures that America's public schools are welcoming to all children and leaves decisions about religion where they belong with the family. (Americans United for Separation of Church and State, 2005, p. 1)

Reflection Opportunity 12.3

Reflect on your current views regarding religion in the schools. Is there a place for the discussion of religious beliefs in classrooms? If so, in what circumstances could you see this happening? If not, why not? What religious beliefs do you hold? How might these beliefs influence the ways in which you interact with children in your classroom? Can you see yourself relating positively to students whose religious beliefs are different from your own? Why or why not?

TABLE 12.2 Socializing Roles of Schools	
Role	**Description**
Preparation of Capable Workers	Schools prepare students for success in their work lives after high school graduation or following completion of college degrees.
Preparation of Effective Citizens	Schools provide opportunities for students to learn about the U.S. political system and how to change it as well as engaging them in learning experiences that help students understand their roles as productive members of society.
Assistance with Students' Personal Growth	Schools help students develop to their fullest potential as individuals by building self-concept, developing lifelong learning skills, valuing student interests, and encouraging positive attitudes.

From: No Child Left Behind Act. (2002). Retrieved September 26, 2002, from: *http://www.ed.gov/legislation/ ESEA02/pg1.html#sec101*

Schools

Education serves three main roles in socializing students. These roles are summarized in Table 12.2. First is the *preparation of capable workers* to meet the demands of the American economy. This preparation has taken two major directions. One is an education that leads students more directly to work following graduation from high school, and the other has been to prepare students for the college experience. In both instances, the goal is to prepare students for success in later life. The passage of the *No Child Left Behind Act of 2001* specified that this goal should include all children regardless of race, ethnicity, or economic status. The act states: "The purpose of this title [act] is to ensure that all children have a fair, equal, and significant opportunity to obtain a high-quality education and reach, at a minimum, proficiency on challenging state academic achievement standards and state academic assessments" (*No Child Left Behind Act,* 2005).

A second role of the schools is to help prepare students for *effective citizenship.* Being a good citizen means many different things. It includes understanding and valuing the structure of the U.S. political system, making a commitment to democracy, embracing the diversity within American society, and working to promote positive social change. Schools help prepare good citizens in two ways. First, students can learn a great deal through lessons and course work. At the elementary level, for example, students can study diversity and grow in their understanding and acceptance of people different from themselves. Secondly, schools prepare good citizens through a variety of informal learning opportunities. A spontaneous discussion of political corruption following a related news story is an example of this type of learning opportunity.

The third socializing role of the schools is to assist students in *personal growth.* In our society, individuality and personal growth are prized. For this reason, schools are engaged in the task of helping students reach their full potential as individuals. Building self-concept, developing lifelong learning skills, valuing student interests (sports, music, art, hobbies, etc.), and encouraging positive attitudes are some of the ways in which schools assist in this aspect of socialization. Much of the school's ability to influence personal growth occurs informally through interactions between students and school staff. Taking the time to listen to students talk about their interests and giving positive feedback about extracurricular activities are examples of this type.

All of the socializing agents described above influence each of us. Sometimes the impact is positive. At other times, these agents cause people to feel belittled and unworthy. The *Explore Your Beliefs* feature for this chapter talks about oppression and how many people within American society feel oppressed by others. Read this information now and reflect on your beliefs about oppression.

Explore your beliefs: Oppression

How would you define oppression? Do you understand the complexities and impact that it has on various groups of people? In simplified terms, oppression is the cruel use of power by those in authority to subdue those who are in less powerful positions. If you are not a part of a group that is consistently oppressed, you may find it difficult to understand what it is like for many people in this county who are oppressed. The image of a birdcage has been used to explain how oppression works. Cohen (1998) states it this way:

> It isn't possible to understand the nature of oppressive systems by studying any one aspect of discrimination; that would be like trying to understand how a birdcage constrains by examining only one wire in its structure. In order to understand a cage, it is necessary to step back and see all the wires and the webbed pattern they form. Similarly, in order to understand sexism, for instance, one most look at patterns of discrimination in employment, education, family roles, athletics, corporate styles of communication and decision-making, etc. (p. 58)

Oppression can take many forms and affects a variety of groups. For example, racial oppression can take place when the authority and power of the majority are used to control the lives of people from minority groups. Overt forms of oppression are less common today due to legal and moral constraints. More subtle expressions, however, such as the messages being sent through the media regarding minority groups and women and the failure to include the contributions made by different racial groups among the topics taught in the schools, have a significant impact on self concept and motivation. Similarly, lower pay and less prestigious positions in business and industry are examples of gender oppression.

Developing the Habit of Reflective Practice
Gather Information

1. Think back on your own experiences. When have you experienced or observed oppression?
2. Do an Internet search for "National Urban League The State of Black America" and read executive summaries of inequalities between Whites and Blacks (black oppression).

Identify Beliefs

1. Do you think oppression is something that should be of concern to teachers? Why or why not?

Make Decisions

1. What could you do as a future teacher to educate others about oppression?
2. What could you do as a future teacher to educate yourself about oppression?

Assess and Evaluate

1. If you were asked to visit a school setting to look for examples of oppression within the learning environment, what would you look for? (Be sure to consider physical environment, learning materials, student interactions, and teacher actions.)

Source

Cohen, C. (1998). The true colors of the new Jim Toomey: Transformation, integrity, trust, in educating teachers about oppression. In E. Lee, P. Menhart, & M. Okazawa-Rey (eds.) *Beyond heroes and holidays*. Washington, DC: Network of Educators of the Americas.

Are there social issues that affect student behavior?

In today's fast-paced society, students encounter a great many social pressures that influence their attitudes and behavior both in and out of school. Take, for example, 11-year-old Martin, a student in your fifth grade elementary classroom. It is amazing how normal he appears, despite the situations he has faced during the past 2 years. From his former teachers you have learned that Martin is currently living with his mother after a long and bitter custody fight stemming from his parents' divorce. His mother has been unable to find employment and the family has been living on welfare for the past year. To complicate matters, Martin's older brother was seriously injured in a car accident 3 weeks ago. Despite all of these challenges, Martin appears happy, is doing above-average schoolwork, and is well liked by others in the class. Martin's response is unusual. He is considered **resilient** because of his ability to cope with high levels of stress and still function effectively. Researchers have studied the characteristics of students like Martin to see if they can identify coping strategies that can help others manage their own stressful circumstances (Davis, 1999).

Although Martin's stress levels are high, most students face a more limited number of social issues in their lives. When the stress is manageable, students are able to cope and move forward with schooling and the rest of their lives. But as more stressors are added, most students reach the point where they struggle to survive the mounting pressures. At this point, students are **at risk** of tuning out or dropping out of school. In the following sections, the issues students face are discussed so that you can better understand the pressures they encounter. Table 12.3 provides a brief summary of these social issues.

The Changing Family

One social institution that has undergone significant change during the past several decades is the American family. Two-parent families in which Dad works and Mom stays home to raise the children now account for a much smaller percentage of all families, with other configurations taking their place (Berger, 2008). Statistics on families in America today indicate that a common type is the single-parent family. Thirty-two percent of all children live in families with only one parent (Annie E. Casey Foundation, 2008). Approximately 85% of single-parent households are headed by women, with many of these families living at or below the poverty level. From necessity, most single parents work and consequently have more limited opportunities to communicate and interact with teachers (Berger, 2008). Students from single-parent families may have a variety of feelings that cause them stress and can lead to potential problems in the classroom (Gestwicki, 2007). For example, feelings of guilt stemming from an unreasonable belief that they have caused the divorce are common among younger students.

During the past decade, there has also been a dramatic increase in the number of homeless families in the United States (Gollnick & Chinn, 2009). Estimates of numbers vary considerably because it is difficult to identify those that are homeless accurately. One recent estimate, however,

TABLE 12.3   Social Issues Affecting Students

Social Issue	Description
The Changing Family	Growing numbers of single-parent, dual-career, blended, homeless, and gay and lesbian families are influencing the lives of students.
Poverty	Approximately one family in five lives in poverty, which has a significant negative impact on schooling.
Teen Pregnancy	America continues to lead all industrialized nations in the number of teen pregnancies.
AIDS	AIDS is a significant health issue that influences the lives of families and schools.
Child Abuse and Neglect	Students who are abused or neglected experience deep emotional trauma which influences their school performance.
Alcohol and Drugs	Young people may experiment with alcohol and drugs as early as the elementary school years, with many potential social and school-related problems.
Suicide	Suicide is the second leading cause of death among young people between the ages of 15 and 19.
Violence	Violence between students and directed toward teachers is a growing concern to educators and others.
Bullying	Bullying belittles students and is related to increased levels of violence. Schools are working to decrease the incidence of bullying.
School Dropouts	Although school dropout rates have decreased, those who do drop out are even less likely than before of finding productive work.

suggests that there are approximately 1.3 million homeless children in the United States (National Center on Family Homelessness, 2009). Clearly, homeless families are struggling and need a great deal of support from the school and community in order to manage the day-to-day challenges of living. Although teachers and schools cannot be expected to meet all of the needs of homeless families, providing information, support, and understanding can extend an important lifeline to both parents and children in these circumstances. Without this assistance, homeless students may well be one of the most at-risk groups for school failure (Williams, 2005).

Another family structure that is more evident in schools today is the gay and lesbian family with children. In an analysis of the most recent U.S. Census data, Smith and Gray (2001) indicate that the number of reported gay and lesbian families increased by 394% from 1990 to 2000. Although actual numbers of gay and lesbian families are difficult to estimate, The Lesbian and Gay Child Care Task Force (2009) suggests that there are between 6 and 14 million children who are living in gay and lesbian families. Students and parents in these families face many different challenges. Most obvious, perhaps, is that the prejudices of the general public toward gay and lesbian people are often very strong, with social alienation and negative interactions the common result. Many teachers also find these circumstances difficult to accept and consequently relate less positively to both the children and parents in gay and lesbian families. In addition, there is limited legal status for gay and lesbian families, so many either hide their lifestyle from others or avoid contact with the schools and other families (National Center for Lesbian Rights, 2009).

Spend some time thinking about working with parents and families. What skills do you have that will help you establish good relationships with them? Is working with families something you will enjoy or will it be more of a challenge for you? Take a moment to reflect on your attitudes about the diverse families you will encounter in your classroom. How will you feel about working with single-parent, homeless, and gay/lesbian families, for example? Do you think you can work with them in positive ways, or will you bring personal convictions to these interactions that may well get in the way of your relationships? Will your ability to work with all types of families potentially impact your relationships with some of your students?

Reflection Opportunity 12.4

Poverty

Another major social problem facing many students and their families is poverty. Despite numerous governmental and private efforts over the years, the percentage of families living in poverty has remained fairly constant at about one in five (National Center for Children in Poverty, 2008). The problems associated with poverty and extreme poverty are many. Parents frequently feel alienated and powerless and often pass these feelings on to their children. Low levels of parent involvement in the schools and poor school performance from children may well be the result (Berger, 2008). Other common problems associated with poverty are poor health, inadequate health care, increased levels of violence, and higher drug usage (Forum on Child and Family Statistics, 2008).

The impact of poverty on children and families is a serious problem that has major consequences for your work in the classroom. The *Reflect on Diversity* feature found on the Companion Website for this text personalizes these issues by talking about a family in which four children have quality health care, adequate food, etc., while the fifth child in the family has very little. Read this story now and reflect on its impact on your future role as a teacher. How will you respond to America's fifth child?

Reflect on diversity: America's fifth child

Imagine a very wealthy family with five young children under the age of three. Four have enough to eat and comfortable warm rooms in which to sleep. One does not. She is often hungry and lives in a cold room. Sometimes she has to sleep on the streets, in a shelter, and even be taken away from her family and be placed in foster care with strangers.

Imagine this family giving four of their very young children nourishing meals everyday, but letting the fifth child go hungry.

Imagine this very wealthy family making sure four of their young children get all their shots and regular check-ups before they get sick, but ignoring the fifth child who is plagued by chronic infections and respiratory diseases like asthma. (Children's Defense Fund, 2002, p. 3)

While none of us can imagine a wealthy family that would engage in the behaviors described above, American society is in fact allowing approximately one in five children to not have enough to eat, live in substandard housing, and grow up without adequate health care. The richest nation in the world is doing less than it could to combat poverty and assist children as they struggle to deal with its negative consequences.

Poverty is pervasive throughout American society and can be found in small towns as well as large urban areas. It often has a permanent and negative impact on the lives of children and their families. Students from low-income homes frequently find that their life circumstances make it very difficult for them to be successful in school. Consequently, many grow up and live their adult lives in poverty. They often become the parents of the next generation of poor children and the cycle of poverty continues.

Developing the Habit of Reflective Practice

Gather Information

1. Do you know one of America's fifth children? If not, talk to a classroom teacher, school administrator or paraeducator who could describe one for you. What are the circumstances the student faces and how is he or she coping with the stresses of life?

Identify Beliefs

1. What should our schools do to help students and their families who are living in poverty?

2. Some schools offer free meals, free dental care, clothing banks, donations for school supplies, and scholarships for field trips and instruments. Is there a point where schools do too much?

Make Decisions

1. As an educator, what are some of the little things you could do to assist a child whose family is living in poverty?

2. As an educator, what could you do to help students who are not living in poverty have empathy for families who are?

Assess and Evaluate

1. If you were asked to visit a school and evaluate how they are working with "America's fifth child", what would you look for during your visit? What signs would indicate that a school is meeting the needs of students who are living in poverty?

Source

Children's Defense Fund. (2002). *The state of children in America's Union*. Washington, DC: Author.

Teen Pregnancy

Statistics indicate that although the birth rate for teenagers between the ages of 15 and 17 has dropped somewhat, America still leads all industrialized nations in the numbers of teen pregnancies at over 21 per 1,000 (Annie E. Casey Foundation, 2008). Stated another way, each day in the United States 1,154 babies are born to teen mothers (Children's Defense Fund, 2008). Although the stigma associated with teen pregnancy has lessened somewhat, the problems associated with children bearing and raising children are many. In a large majority of cases, teen pregnancies occur outside of marriage and leave the mother with a more limited support system. Teen mothers are more likely to have low–birth-weight babies with greater health-care needs (Annie E. Casey Foundation, 2008). In addition, teen mothers are far more likely to be living in poverty and drop out of high school at higher rates than their peers. Children of teen parents are more likely to drop out of school, get into trouble, and become teen parents themselves (Annie E. Casey Foundation, 2008).

Acquired Immunodeficiency Syndrome (AIDS)

AIDS is a significant health issue that influences the lives of approximately 1.2 million people in the United States. Although only a small percentage of this total are young people, the Centers for Disease Control and Prevention (2009) estimate that over 40,000 young people from 13 to 24 have contracted the disease. Of this number approximately 10,000 have died. Statistics indicate that the HIV virus that causes AIDS is most often spread in the teen years through homosexual activity (Centers for Disease Control and Prevention, 2009). Other significant issues such as heterosexual contact with an HIV carrier, common needles for drug injection, and being born to an AIDS/HIV parent also are factors in contracting this disease. Controlling the spread of the AIDS epidemic requires a continued educational emphasis on eliminating these high-risk behaviors whenever possible.

Child Abuse and Neglect

Four main types of child abuse and neglect are defined by the National Clearinghouse on Child Abuse and Neglect Information (2005). **Physical abuse** is the infliction of physical injury through the punching, beating, kicking, biting, burning, or shaking of a child. **Child neglect** can be either *physical neglect* (e.g., refusal of health care, abandonment, expulsion from the home) or *emotional neglect* (e.g., inattention to the child's need for affection, failure to provide psychological care, allowing alcohol or drug use by the child). **Sexual abuse** includes fondling a child's genitals, intercourse, incest, rape, sodomy, exhibitionism, and commercial exploitation through prostitution. **Emotional abuse** occurs when parents or caregivers engage in behavior that causes or could cause serious behavioral, cognitive, emotional, or mental disorders (e.g., extreme forms of punishment or habitual belittling).

As a future teacher, you are required by law to report suspected cases of child abuse and neglect. You will need to watch for indicators that the child is in distress. The following behaviors may be signs of abuse and neglect:

- Shows sudden changes in behavior or school performance.
- Has not received help for physical or medical problems brought to the parents' attention.
- Has learning problems (or difficulty concentrating) that cannot be attributed to specific physical or psychological causes.
- Is always watchful, as though preparing for something bad to happen.
- Lacks adult supervision.
- Is overly compliant, passive, or withdrawn.
- Comes to school or other activities early, stays late, and does not want to go home (Child Welfare Information Gateway, 2007).

Alcohol and Drugs

Student alcohol and drug use is another serious issue facing teachers and schools (Johnston, O'Malley, Bachman, & Schulenberg 2005). Consumption negatively influences academic achievement, impairs interactions with other students and school staff, and increases the chances of a child dropping out of school. When students engage in alcohol and drug use, the immediate and long-term costs to society are high. Beginning as early as the elementary school years, students place themselves at risk of addiction. Addiction becomes a problem for many teens for three main reasons (Johnston et al., 2005). First, drug use accelerates over time. Gradually, students take larger quantities of drugs at more frequent intervals to get the same "high." Secondly, adolescents tend to use more than one drug at a time. Students experiment with different drugs during a short time period because their friends are trying new options and encourage others to do the same. Finally, adolescents underestimate the power of drugs. Thinking that they are in control of the drugs rather than the other way around, students fail to see the addictive power of drugs.

Reflect back on your own K–12 experiences. Do you remember times when friends or acquaintances experimented with drugs or alcohol? When did you become aware of this activity? How did these experiences influence the students' lives? Based on these remembrances, do you think it will be important for you as a future teacher to be aware of and work to help students who engage in drug and alcohol use?

Reflection Opportunity 12.5

Suicide

For a variety of reasons, young people experience strong feelings of confusion, self-doubt, pressure to succeed, and general stress that can lead to attempted or actual suicide. For example, a high school student struggling with sexual identity may experience significant confusion and feel extreme pressure to conform to the expectations of family and friends. In some instances, this may lead the young person to contemplate suicide as a means of escape. Suicide is the third leading cause of death among young people ages 15–24 (American Psychiatric Association, 2005). The symptoms of young people considering suicide are similar to those of depression. Parents and teachers who become aware of several of the following signs should seek professional assistance to prevent the possibility of suicide:

- Depressed mood
- Substance abuse
- Frequent episodes of running away or being incarcerated
- Family loss or instability; significant problems with parents
- Expressions of suicidal thoughts, or talk of death
- Withdrawal from family and friends
- Difficulty in dealing with sexual orientation (American Psychiatric Association, 2005).

Violence

Violence in schools is a continuing concern that in recent years has received wide media attention. Although it is definitely a problem that must be addressed, the federal government states in a recent report on the nature and scope of school violence: "(T)he percentage of students who reported being victims of crime at school decreased from 10 percent to 5 percent between 1995 and 2003. This included a decrease in theft (from 7 percent to 4 percent) and a decrease in violent victimization (from 3 percent to 1 percent) over the same time period" (U.S. Departments of Education and Justice, 2004, p. 1). At the same time, however, youth violence, once thought to be a problem associated primarily with large urban schools, is now a concern in suburban and rural schools as well. Gang activity, for example, is more common today and can lead to severe violence. Although less than 1% of students are gang members and this percentage has remained relatively constant for larger cities, numbers appear to be growing in the suburbs and smaller cities (Howell & Egley, 2005).

myeducationlab
The Power of Classroom Practice

MyEducationLab 12.1

Gangs and violence can have a negative impact even on the students who work hard to do well. To watch a video about the struggles of a good student in a tough school, go to the Companion Website for this text and click on MyEducationLab for Chapter 12.

Perhaps the most sensational form of violence to surface over the last decade has been school shootings in which students use guns to kill other students, teachers, and school staff. Following the deaths of 12 students at Columbine High School near Denver, Colorado, in April 1999 (Portner, 1999), there has been considerable publicity about violence and safety in America's schools. This heartbreaking event was followed by other shootings that have also received significant national attention. Another incident was on the Red Lake Indian Reservation in Minnesota, where a 16-year-old killed seven others and then turned the gun on himself (Borja & Cavanagh, 2005). Keep in mind, however, that these school shootings, while tragic, occur only very rarely. With over 16 million students enrolled in Grades 9–12 in the United States, the National Center for Education Statistics (2007) reported 14 school-related homicides nationally in one academic year. In comparison, 1,500 young people were homicide victims in cities and towns across the country during that same period.

The U.S. Departments of Education and Justice (2000) suggest that schools respond at three levels in their efforts to prevent violence:

- *Build a school-wide foundation*—By supporting positive discipline, academic success, and mental and emotional wellness through a caring school environment, schools become places where violence is less likely to happen.

- *Intervene early*—Schools need to provide information and support services that will allow teachers and other school personnel to intervene early with students at risk because of significant academic or behavioral difficulties.

- *Provide intensive interventions*—In working with other community organizations, schools should be prepared to provide intensive interventions for the small number of students who engage in violent behaviors.

Reflect on the impact that school violence may have on your future teaching career. Take out your Reflections Journal or open the on-line journal found on the Companion Website for this text and respond to the following questions. First of all, how do you feel about working in an environment where violence is a small but credible risk to you and others? Do you think it will influence the ways in which you may interact with students? Why or why not? What can you do to prepare yourself for this aspect of classroom teaching?

**Reflection
Opportunity 12.6**

Bullying

Another common stressor for students in school settings is **bullying.** Hurst (2005) defines bullying as follows:

> Most scholars generally accept the concept of bullying as an imbalance of power that exists over an extended period of time between two individuals, two groups, or a group and an individual in which the more powerful intimidate or belittle others. Bullying can be both physical and psychological, but physical bullying is not as common as the more subtle forms, such as social exclusion, name-calling, and gossip (p. 8).

Bullying is a significant problem, with one survey indicating that as many as one-third of all students in Grades 6–10 report that they are bullies, were victims of bullies, or both (Bowman, 2001). Bullying often occurs after school hours, or in public areas within the school (such as hallways and bathrooms), and at other times when there is limited teacher supervision (Hurst, 2005). Another type of bullying that is difficult to detect is referred to as "cyber bullying" and occurs when students threaten, tease, and humiliate their peers over the Internet (Blair, 2003).

In addition to its frequency, bullying is a significant problem because of its relationship to violence. Research indicates that students who are bullies and those who are bullied are more likely to engage in violent behavior such as weapons carrying and fighting that leads to injuries (Nansel, Overpeck, Haynie, Ruan, & Scheidt, 2003). A March 5, 2001 school shooting in California provides a more extreme example of the connection between bullying and violence. A 15-year-old who shot and killed two classmates was characterized by his peers as having received constant physical and verbal bullying by other students (Bowman, 2001). Despite the very rare occurrence of school shootings, every effort needs to be made by schools to eliminate bullying behaviors from the classroom not only for the problems it causes directly, but also because of links to violent behaviors.

School Dropouts

The good news about school dropout rates is that they are decreasing. Table 12.4 provides a summary of these trends since 1970. Unfortunately, the bad news is that those who do drop out of school are less likely than ever before to be financially successful. Teens who drop out of high school will find that the advanced skills and knowledge needed for 21st century jobs are available

TABLE 12.4	School Dropout Rates			
Year	Total %	White %	Black %	Hispanic %
1970	15	13.2	27.9	
1980	14.1	11.4	19.1	35.2
1990	12.1	9	13.2	32.4
2001	10.7	7.3	10.9	27.0
2005	9.4	6.0	10.4	22.4

From: National Center for Education Statistics. (2007). *Digest of education statistics*. Washington, DC: Author.

through some form of post-secondary education. Those who haven't completed high school will have fewer and fewer options for good-paying jobs. (Annie E. Casey Foundation, 2008).

Researchers have found five key elements in schools that have been successful in reducing the number of dropouts:

- *Small school size* supports more positive teacher–student relationships and decreases dropouts.
- *Small class size* gives teachers the opportunity to provide a meaningful and challenging curriculum to all students.
- *Intellectual engagement* marks a school as a community of learners where all are encouraged to learn and grow.
- *Portfolio assessments* give students the opportunity to demonstrate their learning in a variety of ways.
- *Committed staff members* understand and support the school's beliefs about teaching and learning (Bhanpuri & Reynolds, 2003).

How should teachers and schools respond to social issues?

Not so many years ago, the social issues discussed in this chapter were considered somehow separate from the work of the schools and were frequently left to others for resolution. During the last 30 or 40 years, however, teachers and schools have recognized the impact that social issues have on schooling and gradually become more involved in supporting students and their families as they work through difficult situations. Although there is great variability in their responses, both teachers and schools today feel responsible for providing support and assistance in dealing with these complex issues.

Your Responses as a Future Teacher

An example of a social issue that is typical of the kind teachers regularly face is that of 6-year-old Kara, a second-grade student. Although she comes from an intact two-parent family, you know from Kara's first-grade teacher that they are struggling financially. Neither parent holds a steady job and you were told at a recent parent–teacher conference that they may be evicted from their apartment at the end of the month because they can't afford to pay the rent. Kara has been doing low–average work in your class, but it seems entirely possible that if she were homeless, her academic pursuits would be overshadowed by the family's financial and housing concerns. Being aware of your community's resources for homeless families, you recommend two community agencies that may be able to help.

TABLE 12.5   Your Responses to Social Issues

Response	Description
Take Time for Relationship Building	Building trust and rapport with students and their families is a key to assisting them.
Accommodate Family Differences	You will need to be aware of, and responsive to, differences in family circumstances.
Know the Warning Signs	Knowing the warning signs for child abuse and neglect, alcohol and drug abuse, and suicide will allow you to refer students for the help they will need.
Understand Your Legal and School-Mandated Responsibilities	Knowing your legal and school-mandated responsibilities will help you know how and when to respond to student and family needs.
Be Aware of Resources	An awareness of school, community, state, and national resources will allow you to direct students and families to the help they need.
Identify Your Personal Limits	You will need to decide how personally involved you can be in the issues students and families face.

Responding to societal pressures like the example above can lead you in two very different directions. One approach that some teachers use is to simply ignore these problems and concentrate on teaching the school curriculum. Although this method allows you to be successful with those students whose problems are relatively minor, it leaves a significant number without adequate support. Your other option is to broaden your role in working with students and families by getting involved at some level in helping resolve the social issues students face. Table 12.5 lists suggestions for getting involved, each of which is discussed in more detail in the subsections below.

Take time for relationship building. Relationships are the key to any helping profession, including teaching. If you take the time to build trust and rapport with your students and their families, it is much more likely that they will come to you for assistance with their problems and listen to your suggestions. Without these strong working relationships, you can do little to help your students with the stresses they face. The challenges of creating good rapport, however, are many. The students and families who need your support and concern the most are often the most difficult to reach. It may be that they have sought out others in the past and been hurt because of it, or their struggles may be so painful and difficult that the situation appears hopeless.

Accommodate family differences. One way in which you can respond effectively to the pressures students face is to be aware of family circumstances and make modifications in your teaching and interactions where possible. If, for example, you know that Amanda's parents are divorced and do not communicate well, it may be necessary to offer them separate parent–teacher conference times. Or, being aware of Bruce's family financial situation, you work to find money to pay for his ticket to the zoo for the upcoming field trip. Finally, knowing that Juanita's parents speak and read only Spanish at home, you could find an adult to translate your written communications into Spanish before sending them to this family. Each of these accommodations requires extra effort on your part, but will pay big dividends in your relationships with both students and families.

Know the warning signs. Child abuse and neglect, alcohol and drug use, and suicide are serious problems that you cannot manage on your own as a teacher. However, if you know the warning signs that indicate these problems may exist, you can refer students and their families to professionals who have the skills needed to deal with them. It is beyond the scope of this text to prepare you to recognize the warning signs for these problems adequately. Although some were provided earlier in this chapter as samples, you should expect to take additional course work or workshops during your teacher-preparation program or as a future teacher to get the more detailed information you will need.

Understand your legal and school-mandated responsibilities. As a teacher, you are legally responsible in all 50 states to report suspected cases of child abuse and neglect. Should you identify clear physical or behavioral indicators, suspected abuse and neglect must be reported to the appropriate state agency. In addition to understanding your legal responsibilities, it is important to be aware of and adhere to school-mandated procedures for dealing with inappropriate student behaviors. Depending on the grade level you teach and the setting of your school, you may be responsible for knowing and following rules for dealing with student alcohol and drug use, procedures for violent student behaviors, and policies on handling students who bring weapons into the school setting. Although these are not commonly occurring events, it is clearly best to be prepared to deal with them if needed.

Be aware of resources. Many times, students' problems go well beyond the abilities of most teachers to resolve. For example, a pregnant student who confides her recently confirmed condition to you is definitely in need of assistance. Without proper counselor training, however, it may be very difficult to provide her with adequate help. Knowing where to go for specialized support, on the other hand, is a more manageable role that most teachers can assume. Resources to assist students can be found in the school setting itself or within the local community. School options may include other teachers with specialized training in dealing with social issues, counselors, specialists (such as a school nurse or psychologist), and administrators. Community resources are often more extensive and include options such as monetary assistance through churches and other organizations, counseling services, support groups (e.g., Alcoholics Anonymous), crisis hotlines, low-cost medical and dental care, and job training/counseling programs.

Identify your personal limits. Think back to your own schooling experiences for a moment. Can you recall one or more teachers that always seemed to have students "hanging out" in their classrooms before or after school to get assistance with nonacademic matters? Most schools have a few teachers that attract students in this way. They consistently help students in need by being a sympathetic listener, serving as a ready resource for good advice, or by providing a few words of encouragement. By taking the time to develop close working relationships with these students and then finding additional opportunities to informally counsel them, these teachers often have a major influence on students' lives. Every teacher must set their own limits as to how much of themselves they can give, based on all aspects of their personalities and personal lives. The *Views From the Classroom* feature for this chapter describes how one teacher works to balance it all so that personal, family, and professional goals can all be met. Go to the Companion Website for this text and read this teacher's perspectives.

Views from the Classroom: Balancing it All

Reflection Opportunity 12.7

You are going to need to decide for yourself how much of a helping person you can be in your teaching career. Although it is essential that everyone get involved to some extent in this aspect of teaching, your level of student support may be different from that of the teachers described above. Take out your Reflections Journal or open the on-line journal found on the Companion Website for this text and think about your feelings on this topic. Can you see yourself being a support and encouragement to students who face the kinds of problems identified in this chapter? Will you be one of those teachers who always has students around seeking advice

TABLE 12.6   The School's Response to Social Issues

Response	Description
Student and Family Support	Free and reduced breakfasts and lunches, vocational counseling, before- and after-school care, interpreters, community services coordinators, medical and dental services are all being offered in school settings.
Educational Awareness Programs	Schools are taking greater responsibility for educating students about the dangers associated with such things as violence, early sexual activity, and drug use.
Implementing Rules and Procedures	Schools are identifying rules and procedures for students and staff in response to violence and drug use.
Counseling	Guidance counselors, a tradition at middle schools and high schools, are now more often available for elementary schools as well.
Alternative Education	For students who are unable to work within the traditional school system, alternate educational opportunities are being provided.

and support? Why or why not? Is this nonacademic helping role something you will feel good about or a part of the job you will resent as a future teacher?

The School's Response to Social Issues

Do you remember times when the schools you attended responded in some way to the many different social issues students face? What programs or people were available to help with these challenges? Try to recall two or three different examples of this type. As you spend more time in the classroom, you will probably find that schools today are continuing to add new options to help students resolve complex social concerns. Table 12.6 summarizes significant ways in which schools are currently responding to social issues. Although considerable debate surrounds the appropriateness of these actions in school settings, there is a growing awareness that these are critical issues that must be addressed by *someone* if students are to be successful in the school setting.

Student and family support.   For quite some time, part of the business of schools has been the support of students and their families. Take, for example, the free and reduced-cost breakfasts and lunches funded by the federal government. The free and reduced-price lunch component began in 1946 and in 2006 served over 28 million low-cost or free lunches each day (U.S. Department of Agriculture, 2008). Another example of the school's long-standing support of students is the vocational counseling opportunities that have been available to many high school students for many decades (Baker & Gerler, 2008).

More recently, schools have become involved in many other strategies to assist students and their families. Examples of this type include:

- *After-school care*—Although schools seldom fund these programs, just having them in the elementary school building is a convenience and service to many families (Education Week, 2005).

- *Interpreters and translators*—Activities such as parent–teacher conferences are more successful when parents with limited English proficiency can have these services available. This allows families to more fully participate in school activities (Zehr, 2004).
- *Home/school/community coordinators*—These coordinators serve families in a variety of ways, such as locating and recommending community services.
- *Full-service schools*—Particularly in low-income urban areas, some schools are providing educational, medical, dental, social, and human services on-site to meet the needs of students and their families (Hurst, 2003).

Educational awareness programs. For many of the issues that young people face, schools are taking greater responsibility for educating students about their dangers. These efforts may include an informal discussion in class, a more formalized lesson or activity, or a long-term educational awareness program. Particularly for violence prevention, sex education, and alcohol and drug use prevention, schools are finding it necessary to implement programs that span several years in an attempt to convince students to avoid these problem behaviors.

Many schools are implementing **violence-prevention programs** as early as the elementary school years to help deter youth violence (U.S. Department of Health and Human Services, 2009). These programs often include strategies for anger management, impulse control, appreciating diversity, and developing conflict-resolution skills. Discussions about the problems associated with gang membership are another important component of many programs. Other attempts to decrease violence in the schools focus on encouraging positive behavior. Teachers and schools work to recognize positive interactions and reward good school citizenship. Rather than discussing what students should avoid, these programs emphasize the importance of creating a school climate in which students and staff get along with one another (U.S. Department of Health and Human Services, 2009).

A second type of educational awareness program found in many schools is sex-education. Despite high teen pregnancy levels and the growing concerns over the AIDS epidemic, the issue of **sex-education programs** in the schools remains a controversial one. The *Engage in the Debate* feature for this chapter provides insights into the reasons for this controversy. Make sure you read more on this topic and respond to the reflection questions provided.

Engage in the debate: Sex education

A long standing dispute in many schools centers on including sex education as a part of the curriculum. Initially, there was much heated discussion between parents and school personnel about the appropriateness of addressing this topic in a school setting. Many people felt that sex education was best done at home where parents and guardians could share their own beliefs and attitudes toward sexuality. These parents and others were suggesting that schools should simply avoid addressing this topic. Those who wanted sex education taught in school settings argued that many families were not talking about issues related to sex and students were either getting no information or inaccurate data on this important subject.

The debate over whether to have sex education in American schools appears to be over. In a 2004 poll (National Public Radio, et. al, 2004), only seven percent of Americans said that sex education should not be taught in schools. The debate now focuses on the perspective schools should take in discussing sexuality. On one end of the continuum are those who support what has come to be known as comprehensive sex education. As the name implies, this approach seeks to educate young people about all aspects of sex and sexuality, including the use of birth control to prevent pregnancy and protect against sexually transmitted diseases. Survey results indicate that parents and guardians strongly support the comprehensive sex education approach. By a margin of five to one, they felt that this approach would be most useful for their children.

A growing movement in sexuality education is the abstinence education option. Programs aligned with this approach emphasize the social, psychological, and health benefits that come from abstaining from sexual activity until marriage. This movement has received the support of the federal government, with Congress appropriating federal funds to promote abstinence until marriage. (National Public Radio, et al, 2004).

Developing the Habit of Reflective Practice

Gather Information

1. Think back on your own K-12 education. Did you have sex education at school? If yes, what grade level(s) do you remember sex education being taught? What topics do you remember being addressed?

Identify Beliefs

1. Should schools be involved in sex education issues? Why or why not?

Make Decisions

1. If you were required to teach either comprehensive sex education or abstinence education, which would you choose? Give a rationale for your decision.

Assess and Evaluate

1. If you were asked to evaluate the effectiveness of a sex education curriculum within a particular school district, what characteristics would you look for to judge the quality of the curriculum? What data would you seek to figure out whether the curriculum is effective?

Source

National Public Radio, The Kaiser Family Foundation, and Harvard University/Kennedy School of Government. (2004). *Sex education in America*. Retrieved January 9, 2009 from *http:// www.npr.org/programs/morning/features/2004/jan/kaiserpoll/publicfinal.pdf*

Although recent surveys indicate that as few as 7% of Americans believe that the family and church should be responsible for dealing with all aspects of sex education, there is considerable disagreement as to the form(s) that these programs should take (National Public Radio, 2004). The three main options that are the most hotly debated are:

- *Abstinence only*—Fifteen percent of Americans believe that schools should teach only about abstinence from sexual intercourse. They believe that schools should not provide information on condoms and other forms of contraception.

- *Abstinence plus*—Forty-six percent of Americans feel that although abstinence is best, many teens continue to engage in sexual activities, so schools should also teach students about safe sex.

- *Responsible sex*—An additional 36% of Americans believe that the main purpose of sex-education programs in the schools should be to help teens make responsible decisions about their sexual activities (National Public Radio, 2004).

A third effort being made by many schools is the implementation of **alcohol and drug awareness programs.** The efforts to prevent student use of alcohol and drugs have been promoted by a variety of state and national groups. The U.S. Department of Education (2009), for example, has established the Office of Safe and Drug-Free Schools Program. As the federal government's primary vehicle for promoting alcohol and drug abuse education and prevention activities, it provides funding to states for these activities and coordinates information development and dissemination at the national level.

In addition to national efforts, there have been numerous state and local programs to help young people become aware of the dangers of drug and alcohol use and provide them with strategies that can be used to prevent their involvement. One example of this type is the Across Ages program developed initially at Temple University's Center for Intergenerational Learning in Philadelphia (Substance Abuse and Mental Health Services Administration, 2005). Designed for students 9–13 years of age, the program's unique feature is the pairing of older adult mentors (age 55 and above) with young adolescents. Through mentoring, community service, social competence training, and family activities the program aims to build each young person's sense of self and responsibility to the community. There are now more than 30 sites using this model in over 30 states.

Implementing rules and procedures. As schools struggle to respond to the many social issues presented by modern society, one important step they have taken is to identify clearly the rules and procedures that both students and staff should follow in responding to these concerns. When rules and procedures are seen as fair and consistently applied, the negative impact of difficult social issues is reduced. Some examples help highlight how schools have responded:

- *Gang attire.* Many schools have implemented rules concerning the wearing of clothing associated with gang membership. By identifying and banning this attire, gang activity in the schools is discouraged (California Attorney General's Crime and Violence Prevention Center, 2005).

- *Weapons ban.* The Children's Defense Fund (2002) estimates that more than 135,000 guns are brought into U.S. schools each day. Based on a federal mandate, schools have implemented a policy of zero tolerance for guns and knives in the school setting and have created heavy penalties for their presence.

- *School safety policies.* Rules and procedures for dealing with violent acts have been implemented by most schools to help curb problem behaviors. Effective policies include steps to prevent violence, strengthen relationships with local law enforcement, and include a plan for crisis management (Joiner, 2002).

- *Monitoring students.* Many schools are committing resources to overseeing students as they congregate in hallways, restrooms, and cafeterias. Although school staff has traditionally served in this role, some schools are hiring security guards or seeking parent volunteers to patrol their buildings. Due to recent gun violence in schools, some are debating the merits of having armed guards (Trotter, 2005).

- *Closed campuses.* On many high school campuses the option of leaving the school grounds during normal hours of operation is severely limited (Henderson, 2003). In particular, these closed campuses hope to decrease student opportunities for drug and alcohol use.

Counseling. Guidance counselors are a vital component of American schooling. Many of the problems facing students today are too complex for teacher assistance. Trained counselors who can talk with students, listen to their concerns, and refer them to appropriate community resources are needed. Guidance personnel can often detect the early warning signs of potential problems and work with families to develop solutions. Working in partnership with teachers and families, counselors can help troubled students receive the assistance they need before it is too late. Traditionally, counseling has been available primarily at the junior high/middle school and secondary levels. More recently, however, elementary schools have begun hiring guidance personnel (Fairfax County Public Schools, 2009).

The American School Counselor Association (2009) identifies the following ways in which school counselors support students in their overall development by:

- *Identifying personal goals*—An important role counselors play is in helping students identify and work toward goals that will help them be successful in school and later life.

- *Engaging in individual or group counseling*—Counselors work with students as needed to assist them in understanding and managing the many stresses they face. For example, a counselor could meet individually with a student to work through the grief associated with the loss of a parent through either death or divorce.

- *Initiating consultations with parents, teachers, and other school personnel*—Another important role of the counselor is to meet with others in the school to share insights about struggling students and provide information that teachers and others can use to identify and support these students.

- *Referring to other professionals*—In some instances, the school counselor needs to refer students to other school personnel or community agencies that can provide resources needed by the student. For example, a counselor may refer a student to a specialist within the school or to a community agency to discuss specifics about teen pregnancy and options available to the student.

Alternative education. For some students, the regular school classroom proves ineffective in meeting their needs. Without specialized programs, they often drop out of school and create further problems for themselves and society. In response to this issue, school districts have developed **alternative-education programs** to meet the needs of these at-risk students. Some options are housed within existing schools, and others are located in separate school or community settings. (See Chapter 4 for more information on alternative school options.) Increasing the number of these programs is being promoted by some as a way to reduce violence in schools, in addition to decreasing dropout rates (Education Week, 2005; U.S. Departments of Education and Justice, 2000).

Alternative education programs are often designed to serve a variety of purposes, including assistance to teen mothers, dropout prevention, and violence education/prevention. With smaller class sizes, specialized curricula, and teachers committed to helping at-risk students, alternative programs are often successful in preventing school dropouts. An example of this type is the Blue Mountain School:

> Blue Mountain School is a place where children are given freedom and encouraged to take responsibility for their own education—and they do. They play, learn, and grow on their own, in small groups, as well as in democratically structured group meetings (Blue Mountain School, 2009). (Alternative Education Resource Organization, 2005).

Other examples of alternative-education options are available on the Website for the Alternative Education Resource Organization (2009).

How does society influence schooling?

In addition to significantly influencing the lives of your future students, society also has a major impact on schools. Both the content of your future classroom curriculum and the strategies you use in instruction will be in large part determined by society. Because schools are institutions created by society to serve its purposes, this statement should not surprise you. Although schools do help shape and refine the directions of society, they primarily reflect the purposes and values assigned it by the larger group. Table 12.7 summarizes society's influence on schooling.

Determining Purposes

Earlier in this chapter, schools were described as socializing students in three main ways: by preparing them for the workforce, creating effective citizens, and facilitating personal growth. Each of these socializing tasks identifies a major purpose for education. And although schools vary in the emphasis placed on each, these core purposes chart a clear course for American education. The *Ian's Classroom Experiences* feature for this chapter (found on the Companion

**Ian's Classroom
Experiences:
Practical Imagery**

TABLE 12.7 Society's Influence on Schooling

Influence	Description
Determining Purposes	Society identifies the three main purposes of education as: preparing students for the work force, creating effective citizens, and facilitating personal growth.
Establishing Values	Society is the driving force behind the values placed on different aspects of the curriculum (art, music, educating the gifted, etc.), the value placed on diversity, and the perceived importance of equal educational opportunity.

Website for this text) describes some of Ian's beliefs about the purposes of education. You may want to read it now for his insights.

It is important to realize that these purposes are not static, but are often redefined as the needs and interests of society vary. For example, in 1957, the launching of Russia's first satellite into space caused great concern in America. We were losing the race into space, and it was assumed that our schools were the main culprit. American students were thought to need stronger mathematics and science skills. Consequently, a major push was made by the schools to improve instruction in these areas (Webb, Metha, & Jordan, 2007). The goal of preparing students for the workforce was modified to accommodate this perceived need by society.

In addition to the broad purposes cited above, society also helps determine other more specific components of American educational efforts, such as the schools' involvement in drug and alcohol awareness, suicide prevention, sex education, and violence-prevention programs. For example, the high U.S. teen suicide rates have led many schools to train staff members to identify students at risk of suicide and refer them to appropriate agencies (American Psychiatric Association, 2005). Although these directions for education are often controversial, most schools are engaged in efforts to assist and educate students in this way.

Establishing Values

In addition to determining the major purposes and directions for education, society is the driving force behind the values placed on certain aspects of schooling. If, for example, American society greatly valued educating the best and brightest students, schools would allocate more of their resources to gifted education. Or, if music, drama, and art were highly prized, more teachers of the arts would be found in American schools. Similarly, society also determines how schools value less tangible things such as diversity and equal educational opportunity. Although they are more difficult to assess, these values play an important role in the directions of American education.

Diversity. In Chapter 2 we established that diversity is a fact of life in American schools. Different family lifestyles, cultures, races, religions, and abilities comingle in educational settings across the country. Urban areas, the suburbs, and rural America are all becoming increasingly diverse. What is not so clear, however, is the value placed on this diversity. Part of the reason for this lack of clarity may be the fact that attitudes are in the process of changing. For much of American history, the United States was viewed as a **cultural melting pot,** where people from diverse backgrounds came together and were assimilated into the dominant culture (Campbell, 2004). By setting aside their traditions, languages, and beliefs, people were "Americanized." More recently, society has begun to recognize the strengths of diverse groups while at the same time striving to create a new mix that is uniquely American. In what is often described as **cultural pluralism,** each group of diverse people adds its own unique traditions and experiences to that of the larger

society. This shift to valuing cultural pluralism is far from universally held and will require much effort and time to accomplish. Over the next several decades, schools will play an important role in making this shift become a reality. To view a video about acting white and its implications for students of color, go to the Companion Website for this text and click on MyEducationLab for Chapter 12.

Equal educational opportunity. A long-standing belief about American education is that it should provide every student with an equal opportunity to develop the knowledge and skills needed to succeed in life. For everyone willing to work hard and spend the time required, success would be assured. On the surface, at least, it would appear that society values equal educational opportunities for all.

It would be naïve, however, to suggest that this is, in fact, a reality. Among other things, the quality of teachers, the quantity and currency of textbooks and curriculum materials, and the home lives of students all vary dramatically from one school to the next. Can a student who takes calculus from a teacher trained in social studies education do as well as one taking the same course from a teacher with a degree in mathematics? Probably not. Does a child from a low-income family with no health care and little money to spend on books and toys have the same likelihood of success in school as her more privileged peers? Clearly, the answer is no. In many instances, American society simply pays lip service to equal educational opportunities. Families who have both money and influence typically have children who are successful in school while families that are poor and powerless typically have children who are much less likely to be successful in school. Much work is yet to done before equal educational opportunity becomes possible for all.

Before completing the end-of-chapter activities which follow, stop and reflect on the *Consider This* feature for this chapter. It addresses the experiences and knowledge you currently have that will help you deal with the many social issues you will face as a future teacher. Your current level of knowledge and experience will help you decide what is yet to be learned and experiences you may still need to have to be successful with these complex human behaviors. Go to the Companion Website for this text to read the feature and respond to the questions presented.

**Consider This:
Preparation for
Responding to
Social Issues**

Summary

In this chapter, four organizing questions were presented to help you better understand the social issues affecting students and learning:

What socializing agents influence students?

Five key socializing agents were presented as having a major impact on student development:
- The family (Praxis II, topic Ia)
- Peer group (Praxis II, topic Ia)
- Electronic Media (Praxis II, topic Ia)
- Religion (Praxis II, topic Ia)
- Schools (Praxis II, topic Ia)

Are there social issues that affect student behavior?

A variety of social issues influence student learning and development:
- The changing family (Praxis II, topic Ia)
- Poverty (Praxis II, topic Ia)

- Teen pregnancy (Praxis II, topic Ia)
- Acquired immunodeficiency syndrome (AIDS)
- Child abuse and neglect (Praxis II, topic Ia)
- Alcohol and drugs (Praxis II, topic Ia)
- Suicide (Praxis II, topic Ia)
- Violence (Praxis II, topic Ia)
- School dropouts

How should teachers and schools respond to social issues?

Both teachers and schools have responsibilities in responding to societal influences on students:
- Your response as a future teacher (Praxis II, topic IVa)
- The school's response to social issues (Praxis II, topic IVb)

How does society influence schooling?

Society influences schooling in two major ways:
- Determining purposes (Praxis II, topic Ib)
- Establishing values (Praxis II, topic IVb)

PRAXIS   Test-Preparation Activities

 To review an on-line chapter case study, test your understanding of chapter topics and concepts, and begin preparing for the Praxis II: Principles of Learning and Teaching examination, go to the Praxis Test-Preparation module for this chapter of the Companion Website.

InTASC   Developing the Habit of Reflective Practice

Organizing Questions

Review questions, field-experience opportunities, and activities for building your portfolio are included here for the organizing questions in this chapter.

What are the key socializing agents influencing students?

Review Questions

1. How does family life influence the students you will teach?

2. In what ways does television affect students?

3. What are the roles of schools in socializing students?

Field Experience

Talk to a classroom teacher about the social forces that impact students.
- What issues are identified and how significantly do they influence student behavior?
- How does the teacher try to help students with these problems?

Building Your Portfolio: *Course Work or Seminars That Deal with Social Issues*

INTASC Standard 2. Keep a careful record of the courses you take or the seminars you attend that give you more detailed information about the social issues students face. This content knowledge should better prepare you to deal with the many issues your future students will encounter.

Are there social issues that affect student behavior?

Review Questions

1. How does poverty impact students' lives?
2. What are the four main types of child abuse and neglect?
3. What signs might indicate that a student is considering suicide?

Field Experience

With the help of a classroom teacher, identify a student who is dealing with a social issue discussed in this chapter. Spend some time observing this student.

- How does the stress being faced seem to influence performance in class?
- Also observe this student's social interactions with peers.
- With the teacher's help, see if you can identify some strategies to help the student work through at least some aspects of the social issue faced.

Building Your Portfolio: *Addressing Complex Social Issues*

INTASC Standard 2. Identify one of the complex social issues described in this chapter that you want to research in more detail.

- Read articles and/or research on the topic of your choice and summarize what you learned for your portfolio.
- Describe several strategies that you could use to help students and their families work through the stressors associated with this issue.

How should teachers and schools respond to social issues?

Review Questions

1. How can you respond to the social issues you will face as a future teacher?
2. What are some of the ways in which schools are responding to the social issues faced by students?

Field Experience

Make an appointment with a school counselor.

- How does she or he develop good working relationships with students?
- What types of problems does this person deal with the most in his or her work with students?
- How are these problems handled?
- What interactions does the counselor have with regular classroom teachers?

Building Your Portfolio: *Identify Key Community Resources*

INTASC Standard 10. Identify two issues addressed in this chapter that you think you will face in your future classroom.

- Identify three–five key community resources that could help students and their families with each issue.
- Briefly describe the services provided by each community organization you have identified.

How does society influence schooling?

Review Questions

1. Why do the purposes for education, as defined by the larger society, change?
2. Compare and contrast the concepts of cultural melting pot and cultural pluralism.

Building Your Portfolio: *Purposes of Education*

INTASC Standard 9. Review the broad purposes of education identified in this chapter.
- Write a position statement in which you make a case for the relative importance of each of these purposes.
- Identify which you see as the most important through the least important.
- Include your responses in your portfolio.

Suggested Readings

Campbell, D. (2004). *Choosing democracy: A practical guide to multicultural education* (3rd ed.). Upper Saddle River, NJ: Merrill/Prentice Hall. This text discusses several of the social issues discussed in this chapter and includes a separate chapter on the impact of culture on the schools.

Children's Defense Fund. (2008). *State of America's Children 2008*. *http://www.childrens defense.org/site/PageServer* This publication provides state and national data on poverty, health, child welfare, youth at risk, early childhood education, nutrition and housing of America's children.

Cushner, K., McClelland, A., & Safford, P. (2006). *Human diversity in education: An integrative approach* (6th ed.). New York: McGraw-Hill. This book provides a broad treatment of the various forms of human diversity found in today's schools, including nationality, ethnicity, race, religion, gender, class, language, sexual orientation, and ability levels.

References

Alternative Education Resource Organization. (2009). AERO member schools organizations. Retrieved January 7, 2009 from: *http://www.educationrevolution.org/aero-member-schools.html*

American Psychiatric Association. (2005). Let's talk facts about teen suicide. Retrieved January 6, 2009 from: *http://www.healthyminds.org/factsheets/LTF-TeenSuicide.pdf*

American School Counselor Association. (2009). Why elementary school counselors. Retrieved January 7, 2009 from: *http://www.schoolcounselor.org/content.asp?contentid=230*

Americans United for Separation of Church and State. (2008). Prayer and the public schools. Religion, education, & your rights. Retrieved December 31, 2008 from: *http://www.au.org/ site/PageServer?pagename=resources_brochure_schoolprayer*

Anderson, C., Berkowitz, L., Donnerstein, E., Huesmann, L., Johnson, J., Linz, D., Malamuth, N., & Wartella, E. (2003). The influence of media violence on youth. *Psychological Science in the Public Interest, 4*(3), 81–110.

Annie E. Casey Foundation. (2008). *2008 Kids count data book*. Baltimore, MD: Author.

Baker, S., & Gerler, E. (2008). *School counseling for the twenty-first century* (5th ed.) Columbus, OH: Merrill/Prentice Hall.

Berger, E. (2008). *Parents as partners in education* (7th ed.). Upper Saddle River, NJ: Merrill/ Prentice Hall.

Bhanpuri, H., & Reynolds, G. (2003). *Understanding and addressing the issue of the high school dropout age*. Naperville, IL: North Central Regional Educational Laboratory.

Blair, J. (2003). New breed of bullies torment their peers on the Internet. *Education Week,* February 5, p. 6.

Blue Mountain School. (2009). Welcome to our virtual home. Retrieved January 7, 2009, from *http://www.bluemountainschool.com*

Borja, R., & Cavanagh, S. (2005). School shootings stun reservation. *Education Week,* March 24, pp. 1, 10, 12.

Bowman, D. (2001). Survey of students documents the extent of bullying. *Education Week,* May 2, p. 11.

California Attorney General's Crime and Violence Prevention Center (2005). Gangs and youth violence. Retrieved August 9, 2005 from: *http://www.safestate.org/index.cfm?navID=69*

Campbell, D. (2004). *Choosing democracy: A practical guide to multicultural education.* (3rd ed.). Upper Saddle River, NJ: Merrill/Prentice Hall.

Centers for Disease Control and Prevention. (2009). HIV/AIDS among youth. Retrieved January 5, 2009 from: *http://www.cdc.gov/hiv/resources/factsheets/PDF/youth.pdf*

Children's Defense Fund. (2002). *The state of children in America's union.* Washington, DC: Author.

Children's Defense Fund. (2008). *Each day in America.* Retrieved December 5, 2008 from: *http://www.childrensdefense.org/data/eachday.aspx*

Child Welfare Information Gateway. (2007). Recognizing child abuse and neglect: Signs and symptoms. Retrieved January 5, 2009 from *http://www.childwelfare.gov/pubs/factsheets/signs.pdf*

Collins, R., Elliott, M., Berry, S., Kanouse, D., Kunkel, D., Hunter, S., & Miu, A. (2004). Watching sex on television predicts adolescent initiation of sexual behavior. *Pediatrics, 114*(3), 280–289.

Cushner, K., McClelland, A., & Safford, P. (2006). *Human diversity in education: An integrative approach* (6th ed.). New York: McGraw-Hill.

Davis, N. (1999). *Resilience: Status of the research and research-based programs.* Retrieved January 5, 2009 from: *http://www.mentalhealth.samhsa.gov/schoolviolence/5–28Resilience.asp*

Education Week. (2005) After-school programs. Retrieved August 9, 2005 from: *http://www.edweek.org/rc/issues/after-school-programs/index.html?querystring=before%20after%20school%20care*

Erikson, E. (1963). *Childhood and society.* (2nd ed.). NY: WW Norton.

Fairfax County Public Schools. (2009). *Guidance and career services.* Retrieved January 7, 2009 from: *http://www.fcps.edu/SS/StudentServices/Guidance/Guidance.htm*

Forum on Child and Family Statistics. (2008). *America's children: Key national indicators of well-being in 2008.* Washington, DC: Author.

Gandara, P. (2005). *Peer group influence and academic aspirations across cultural/ethnic groups of high school students.* Santa Cruz: Center for Research on Education, Diversity, and Excellence, The University of California, Santa Cruz. Retrieved July 29, 2005 from: *http://www.crede.org/research/sfc/intro3_5.html*

Gestwicki, C. (2007). *Home, school, and community relations* (6th ed.). Albany, NY: Delmar.

Golin, J. (2004). Gender representation in television and video programs for children ages 0–6: A literature review. Retrieved August 1, 2005 from: *http://www.dadsanddaughters.org/SeeJane_files/Research%20Summary.pdf*

Gollnick, D., & Chinn, P. (2009). *Multicultural education in a pluralistic society* (8th ed.). Upper Saddle River, NJ: Merrill/Prentice Hall.

Henderson, D. (2003). Closed campus overview. *Greeley Tribune.* February 11 Retrieved August 10, 2005 from: *http://www.greeleytrib.com/article/20030211/SPECIALB01/302110058*

Howell, J., & Egley, A. (2005). *Gangs in small towns and rural counties.* NYGC Bulletin, June No 1. Retrieved August 9, 2005 from: *http://www.iir.com/nygc/publications/NYGCbulletin_June05.pdf*

Hurst, M. (2003). Dental dilemma. *Education Week,* January 8, pp. 27–29.

Hurst, M. (2005). When it comes to bullying, there are no boundaries. *Education Week,* February 9, p. 8.

Johnston, L., O'Malley, P., Bachman, J., & Schulenberg, J. (2005). *Monitoring the future national results on adolescent drug use: Overview of key findings 2004.* Bethesda, MD: National Institute on Drug Abuse.

Joiner, L. (2002). Life-saving lessons. *American School Board Journal, 189*(3), 14–18.

Kaiser Family Foundation. (2007). *Food for thought: Television food advertising to children in the United States.* Menlo Park, CA: Author.

Lesbian and Gay Child Care Task Force. (2009). Our families, our children. Retrieved January 5, 2009 from: *http://www.safeschoolscoalition.org/ocof/ofoc_1needs.html*

Nansel, T., Overpeck, M., Haynie, D., Ruan, J., & Scheidt, P. (2003). Relationships between bullying and violence among US youth. *Archives of Pediatrics and Adolescent Medicine, 157*(4), 348–353.

National Center for Children in Poverty (2008). *Low-income children in the United States.* NY: Columbia University.

National Center for Education Statistics. (2007). *Indicators of school crime and safety: 2007.* Washington, DC: Author.

National Center for Lesbian Rights. (2009). Marriage. Retrieved January 5, 2009 from: *http://www.nclrights.org/*

National Center on Family Homelessness. (2009). For every child a chance. Retrieved January 5, 2009 from *http://www.familyhomelessness.org/*

National Clearinghouse on Child Abuse and Neglect Information. (2003). *Recognizing child abuse and neglect: Signs and symptoms.* Retrieved August 8, 2005 from: *http://nccanch.acf.hhs.gov/pubs/factsheets/signs.cfm*

National Clearinghouse on Child Abuse and Neglect Information. (2005). *Types of child abuse and neglect.* Retrieved August 5, 2005 from: *http://nccanch.acf.hhs.gov/topics/overview/types.cfm*

National Coalition for the Homeless. (2001). *Homeless families with children.* Retrieved August 3, 2005 from: *http://www.nationalhomeless.org/families.html*

National Public Radio. (2004). Sex education in America. Retrieved August 9, 2005 from: *http://www.npr.org/templates/story/story.php?storyId=1622610*

No Child Left Behind Act. (2005). Retrieved August 3, 2005 from: *http://www.ed.gov/policy/elsec/leg/esea02/index.html*

Pew Research Center. (2008). *Among wealthy nations . . . U.S. stands alone in its embrace of religion.* Retrieved December 31, 2008 from: *http://pewglobal.org/reports/pdf/167.pdf*

Portner, J. (1999, April 28). A Colorado community looks for answers after deadly attack. *Education Week,* pp. 1, 16–17.

Rideout, V. (2007). *Parents, children, & media.* Menlo Park, CA: Kaiser Family Foundation.

Smith, D., & Gray, G. (2001). *Gay and lesbian families in the United States: Same-sex unmarried partner households.* Washington, DC: The Urban Institute.

Substance Abuse and Mental Health Services Administration. (2005). SAMSHA model programs: Effective substance abuse and mental health programs for every community. Retrieved August 9, 2005 from: *http://modelprograms.samhsa.gov/template_cf.cfm?page=model&pkProgramID=2*

Trotter, A. (2005). Schools wrestle with the issue of armed guards. *Education Week,* April 6, pp. 1, 16–17.

U.S. Department of Agriculture. (2008). *The national school lunch program: Background, trends, and issues.* Washington, DC: Author.

U.S. Department of Education. (2009). Office of safe and drug-free schools. Retrieved January 6, 2009 from: *http://www.ed.gov/about/offices/list/osdfs/index.html*

U.S. Departments of Education and Justice. (2000). *Safeguarding our children: An action guide.* Washington, DC: Authors.

U.S. Departments of Education and Justice. (2004). *Indicators of school crime and safety: 2004.* Washington, DC: Authors.

U.S. Department of Health and Human Services. (2009). Youth violence: A report of the Surgeon General. Retrieved January 6, 2009 from: *http://www.surgeongeneral.gov/library/youthviolence/report.html*

Webb, L., Metha, A., & Jordan, K. (2007). *Foundations of American education* (5th ed.). Upper Saddle River, NJ: Merrill/Prentice Hall.

Wilcox, B., Cantor, J., Dowrick, P., Kunkel, D., Linn, S., & Palmer, E. (2004). *Report of the APA task force on advertising and children.* Retrieved August 1, 2005 from: *http://www.apa.org/releases/childrenads_summary.pdf*

Williams, D. (2005). A new day for homeless students. *Teaching Tolerance.* Retrieved August 3, 2005 from: *http://www.tolerance.org/teach/printar.jsp?p=0&ar=273&pi=current*

Zehr, M. (2004). Translation efforts a growing priority for urban schools. *Education Week,* October 6, pp. 1, 15.

chapter 13

Legal and Ethical Issues

Every day in the classroom teachers are faced with decisions that have legal and ethical implications. To resolve the many dilemmas they encounter, teachers need to have a clear understanding of their rights and responsibilities under the law and the ethical dimensions of teaching. Four organizing questions will be used in this chapter to assist you in developing your understandings of these aspects of teaching.

Focus Questions

1. What are your legal rights and responsibilities as a teacher?

2. Which legal issues will affect your teaching?

3. What legal issues impact students?

4. How do ethics influence my teaching roles?

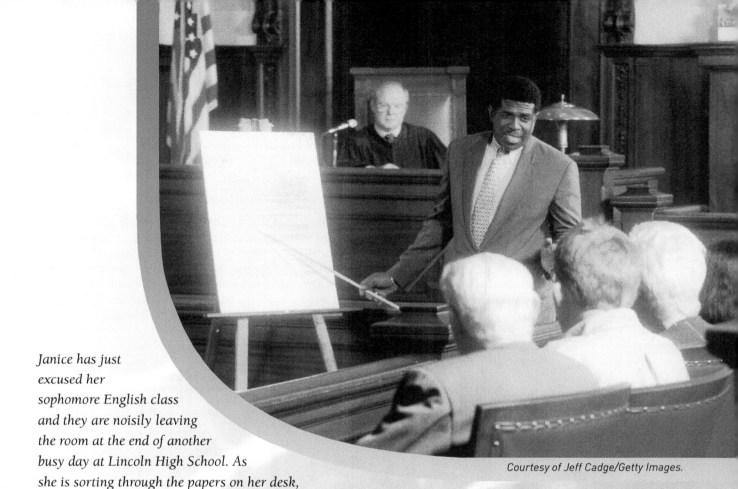

Janice has just excused her sophomore English class and they are noisily leaving the room at the end of another busy day at Lincoln High School. As she is sorting through the papers on her desk, Janice notices that Kimberly has remained behind and is shyly approaching her desk. Over the past 3 months, Janice has been spending extra time working with Kimberly to strengthen her writing skills. The response has been positive and Kimberly has made significant progress.

As Kimberly approaches, Janice notices tears streaming down Kimberly's face as she glances warily around to be sure no one else is near. She is unprepared to hear what spills forth as Kimberly shares with her the troubles she faces. Kimberly tearfully relates her story of being beaten and sexually assaulted by a former boyfriend following a football game 3 weeks ago. She is fearful of the repercussions if her story is told, but also worries that she may be pregnant.

After comforting her as best she can, Janice promises to give Kimberly's situation more thought and get back to her the next day with some possible suggestions. Janice realizes that this is a difficult set of circumstances that may have legal implications. While maintaining confidentiality, she will need to get some help from the school counselor and others so that she can assist Kimberly in the best ways possible.

No teacher wants to hear the kind of story outlined above, but at times these and other less sensational social issues present themselves to teachers in the classroom. This chapter was written to assist you in doing the right thing both legally and ethically in these and other situations. Your responses will be influenced by the system of state and national laws and court decisions that address issues related to schooling. **Educational law** creates a framework that teachers must use in determining appropriate and inappropriate behaviors for both themselves and their students.

What are your legal rights and responsibilities as a teacher?

There are two main sources for the legal guidelines that will have an impact on you as a future teacher: **legislation** and **case law.** Your legal rights and responsibilities are determined in the first instance by either federal or state legislatures empowered to enact laws regarding all aspects of people's lives, including education. In addition, the specific decisions made by federal and state courts on issues relating to education have a major influence on schooling. Referred to as case law, these decisions help schools understand and interpret the educational laws passed by state and federal legislatures. Figure 13.1 outlines these two main sources of legal guidelines for education.

Figure 13.1   Sources of Legal Guidelines

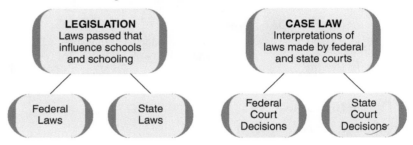

As a future teacher, you will have three main rights defined by law. It is important for you to have a clear understanding of each and then think through how these rights will influence your future work. They include the rights to due process, nondiscrimination, and freedom of expression. Table 13.1 summarizes these rights and the legal foundation for each. The paragraphs that follow provide you with additional information that will help you understand the implications of each right for your work as a future teacher.

Right of Due Process

Legislation and case law have identified many rights that teachers have in their roles as educators. One that is guaranteed to every person, including teachers and students, is the right to **due process** under the law. Basically, due process means that teachers must be treated fairly and that their rights as individuals shall be protected. Both the Fifth and Fourteenth Amendments to our nation's Constitution guarantee every person this right to due process. Various potential situations could arise in which the teacher's right to due process may become an issue. For example, a teacher who discusses creationism as well as evolution as part of the science curriculum and is fired by the school district has the right to due process under the law. Or a nontenured teacher who has received a low performance evaluation by the school principal and is not rehired at the end of the academic year also can expect the opportunity for due process. A final example in which due process can be expected would be an openly gay teacher being asked to resign his position because of sexual orientation. To ensure due process, teachers must be given:

1. Notification of the charges
2. An opportunity for a hearing

TABLE 13.1 Your Legal Rights		
Right	**Legal Foundation**	**Summary**
Due process	• 5th and 14th Amendments to the U.S. Constitution	Every teacher is guaranteed the right to due process when personnel issues such as nonrenewal of contracts and firing are raised.
Nondiscrimination	• Civil Rights Act of 1964 • Section 504 of the Rehabilitation Act of 1990 • Americans with Disabilities Act of 1990	Employers cannot discriminate in the hiring of teachers because of race, color, religion, sex, national origin, or disability.
Freedom of expression	• *Pickering v. Board of Education* (1968)	Freedom to express opinions about actions of administrators, school board when this does not impact the smooth functioning of schools.
	• *Parducci v. Rutland* (1970)	Right of teachers to speak freely about the subjects they teach (academic freedom)

3. Time to prepare a response to the charges
4. The names of witnesses and time to review the evidence
5. An impartial hearing
6. The option of being represented by an attorney
7. The chance to provide their own evidence and to cross-examine witnesses
8. A summary of the procedures and results of the hearing
9. The right to appeal any decisions of the hearing (Thomas, Cambron-McCabe, & McCarthy, 2009)

Right to Nondiscrimination

Another broad right guaranteed to teachers is the **right to nondiscrimination** in employment and retention. The *Civil Rights Act of 1964* protects teachers and others from discrimination when it states:

> It shall be an unlawful employment practice for an employer (1) to fail or refuse to hire or to discharge any individual, or otherwise to discriminate against any individual with respect to his compensation, terms, conditions, or privileges of employment, because of such individual's race, color, religion, sex, or national origin; or (2) to limit, segregate, or classify his employees or applicants for employment in any way which would deprive or tend to deprive any individual of employment opportunities or otherwise adversely affect his status as an employee, because of such individual's race, color, religion, sex, or national origin.

Section 504 of the Rehabilitation Act of 1973 and the *Americans with Disabilities Act* of 1990 extend the legal mandate against discrimination in hiring and retention to individuals with disabilities. More than any other law, the Individuals with Disabilities Education Act (IDEA) has affected the

MyEducationLab 13.1

educational system the most in this country. To study this law further, go to the Companion Web-site for this text and click on MyEducationLab for Chapter 13.

Although these laws have greatly reduced discrimination in the areas defined by law, other potentially discriminatory practices are less well protected. An example of this latter type is discrimination against openly homosexual or bisexual teachers. In Washington State, for example, a high school teacher who admitted being homosexual to the school's assistant principal was dismissed from his teaching position. Upon appeal, the court upheld this dismissal on the grounds that the teacher's presence would interfere with the smooth operation of the school (*Gaylord v. Tacoma School District No. 10,* 1977). Other courts, however, have overruled the firing of homosexual and bisexual teachers when no laws have been broken and sexual conduct has remained private (Fischer, Schimmel, & Stellman, 2007).

Right to Freedom of Expression

On the issue of **freedom of expression,** teachers find themselves struggling to balance their individual right to freedom of speech and writing with the impact that these communications may have on the smooth functioning of the school. Although the U.S. Constitution guarantees individuals freedom of expression, it is important that teachers realize they cannot simply say or write anything they wish in the school environment. Up until the last three decades of the 20th century, teachers who openly criticized their administrators or school board members would likely find themselves dismissed without any opportunity for recourse. An important court case in the late 1960s, however, helped give teachers greater freedom of expression. Marvin Pickering, a high school teacher in Illinois, was fired from his teaching position after a letter he wrote was published in the local newspaper criticizing several actions of the superintendent and members of the school board. Pickering appealed his dismissal, and the U.S. Supreme Court eventually forced the school district to reinstate him and pay his back salary. The court ruled that teachers do have the right as members of American society to be publicly critical of school concerns as long as it does not impact the smooth functioning of the schools (*Pickering v. Board of Education,* 1968; *Stroman v. Colleton County School District,* 1992). Table 13.2 lists the *Pickering* case and others that have dealt with freedom of expression.

TABLE 13.2 Freedom of Expression		
Type	**Legal Basis**	**Description**
Freedom of Speech and Writing	*Pickering v. Board of Education* (1968)	Teachers have the right to be publicly critical of schools as long as they don't disrupt the smooth functioning of the schools.
Freedom of Symbolic Expression	*Guzick v. Debras* (1971)	Posters, buttons worn on clothing, and styles of clothing that express specific opinions about societal issues are allowed as long as they do not significantly disrupt schooling.
Academic Freedom	*Parducci v. Rutland* (1970) *Cary v. Board of Education* (1979)	Teachers may speak freely about the subjects they teach and select materials and methods they feel are appropriate as long as their activity does not disrupt school functioning or conflict with district or government policy.

Symbolic expression. In addition to freedom of speech and writing, it is important for you to be aware of teachers' rights and limits regarding **symbolic expression.** Such things as posters displayed in rooms, buttons worn on clothing to express specific opinions about societal issues, and styles of clothing worn in school settings are all examples of symbolic expression. In general, the courts have supported both teachers and students in their freedom of symbolic self-expression. The exceptions are in situations in which these expressions are sexually suggestive, encourage drug use, or defame a particular group of people (Fischer et al., 2007). For example, it would be inappropriate for a teacher or student to wear a T-shirt emblazoned with the message "Co-Ed Naked Band: Do It with Rhythm" because of its sexual theme.

Academic freedom. Another form of freedom of expression is referred to as academic freedom. This includes:

> the right of teachers to speak freely about their subjects, to experiment with new ideas, and to select appropriate teaching materials and methods. Courts have held that academic freedom is based on the First Amendment and is fundamental to our democratic society. It protects a teacher's right to evaluate and criticize existing values and practices in order to allow for political, social, economic, and scientific progress. (Fischer et al., 2007, p. 169)

In *Parducci v. Rutland* (1970), for example, a teacher was fired for presenting her 11th-grade class with course content that included a satire by Kurt Vonnegut, Jr., titled "Welcome to the Monkey House." The principal and associate superintendent determined that the story encouraged promiscuous sexual activity and the killing of the elderly to make room for younger generations. When the teacher appealed her dismissal to a federal court, she was reinstated when the judge hearing the case decided that the content of the satire did not significantly interfere with school discipline or morale and that the school administration had infringed on the teacher's academic freedom in choosing curricular content.

At the same time, however, the teacher's right to academic freedom must be balanced against other factors within the school and district. For example, if a school board has approved or prohibited a list of books for use in the classroom, teachers must abide by these lists to select materials for instruction. In *Cary v. Board of Education* (1979), for example, a Colorado school board banned 10 books from a list being used by high school teachers in their literature courses. Although the teachers felt that this violated their academic freedom, the court disagreed. Teachers were told they could mention the banned books and discuss them briefly in class, but the school board had the right to select and ban the use of specific books from the school district curriculum.

Spend some time reflecting on the issue of freedom of expression. Are you the type of person who feels strongly about your right to express yourself in whatever ways you feel are appropriate? Do you think that you will find it difficult to accept the decisions that will be made by your school board that influence your freedom of expression? How will you deal with these issues in your future teaching career?

**Reflection
Opportunity 13.1**

Avoiding Liability Due to Negligence or Malpractice

Along with the broad legal rights described above come significant responsibilities that teachers need to accept as part of their teaching role. Table 13.3 summarizes three important legal responsibilities of teachers. The first of these responsibilities is to avoid liability due to negligence or malpractice. **Negligence** occurs when a teacher fails to do what a reasonable and careful person would have done in the same circumstances. For example, Margaret Sheehan, an eighth-grade student, was injured on the playground when her teacher left the class unattended for a few moments and a rock tossed by one of a group of boys struck her in the eye and caused serious injury (*Sheehan v. St. Peter's Catholic Church,* 1971). The court found the teacher guilty of

TABLE 13.3 Teachers' Legal Responsibilities

Responsibility	Legal Foundation	Summary
Avoiding Liability Due to Negligence or Malpractice	• *Sheehan v. St. Peter's Catholic Church* (1971)	Teachers are negligent when they fail to do what a reasonable person would have done in the same circumstances and students are injured.
	• *B.M. by Berger v. State of Montana* (1982)	Teachers and schools engage in malpractice when students are inappropriately placed in special education classes.
Reporting Child Abuse and Neglect	• Child Abuse Prevention and Treatment Act of 1974 • Legal mandates from each of the 50 states	Teachers are required to report suspected cases of child abuse or neglect.
	• *McDonald v. State of Oregon* (1985)	Teachers cannot be sued for libel when they act in good faith to report suspected abuse or neglect.
Observing Copyright Laws	• Copyright Act of 1976	Teachers can make one copy of materials for personal use in preparing for instruction, but must limit the copies they provide to students in their classes.

negligence because a reasonable person in similar circumstances would have realized that there was a significant potential for student injury and would not have left the students unattended. Although teachers cannot be expected to anticipate and prevent all injuries to their students, they are responsible for taking reasonable care to avoid potential mental or physical harm to any of their students.

In addition to negligent behavior in and around the classroom, teachers must avoid educational **malpractice.** Just as lawyers and doctors can engage in inappropriate behaviors that are harmful to their clients, educators can also use strategies and options that can be viewed as harmful to their students. For example, the parents of a student who graduated from high school with fifth-grade reading skills sued the school for educational malpractice (*Peter W. v. San Francisco Unified School District,* 1976). Although the court supported the school district and denied the claim of educational malpractice, in at least one other case a school was held liable for its inappropriate placement of a student in a special education classroom (*B.M. by Berger v. State of Montana,* 1982).

Reporting Child Abuse and Neglect

Teachers are also legally responsible for reporting any suspected cases of child abuse and neglect to the proper authorities. Although this problem is ageless, educators began to address the issue consistently when the federal government passed the *Child Abuse Prevention and Treatment Act* (PL 93–147) in 1974. This law provided financial assistance to states for the creation of programs focusing on the prevention of child abuse. All 50 states have since created their own legal mandates that require teachers to report abuse or suspected cases of abuse (Kelly, 1998). Failure to do so can result in criminal charges of negligence, make the teacher and/or school liable for damages, and may result in a prison term or disciplinary actions by the local school board.

An example of the reporting procedures that teachers follow as mandated reporters of child abuse and neglect comes from the Website for the Department of Children and Families in the state of Connecticut (Connecticut Department of Children and Families, 2009). Teachers, principals, school guidance counselors, paraprofessionals, and any other people paid for caring for children in any public or private facility are considered mandated reporters of suspected child abuse and neglect. Reporters are asked to call a toll-free hotline that is available 24 hours a day. The hotline is staffed by full-time department professionals who process the incoming reports and make sure that the information is received promptly by a case investigator. In addition, a follow-up written report is required by law for mandated reporters. The form is available on-line and confirms the information provided orally over the child abuse and neglect hotline.

Reflect on your reactions to child abuse and neglect. If you were to suspect that a student in your class was being subjected to abuse or neglect, would you know how to report it in your state? In what ways would your suspicions influence your interactions with the student? How do you think you would feel toward the abusing adult or family member? Could you remain professional in your interactions with both the student and the abuser?

**Reflection
Opportunity 13.2**

Avoiding False Allegations

Another important responsibility you will have as a classroom teacher is to avoid putting yourself in situations where you can be accused by students or their families of inappropriate interactions with students. Although this is of concern at all grade levels, it is a critical issue in middle school, junior high, and high school teaching situations. Teachers at these levels need to be sure that all interactions with students are public and appropriate. Although there are exceptions to every rule, certain behaviors or actions should be avoided by teachers so that false accusations do not occur. One example is being alone in a room with a student. In this situation, there are no witnesses to back a teacher's story and confirm the words and actions that take place. A confused or angry student may make an accusation that is difficult to refute in this case. When these charges are made, lingering doubts may remain long past the time that the initial issue is resolved. It is usually best to keep the door open or invite an observer to sit in on a conference that you think in advance may be one in which conflicts or misinterpretations may occur.

A similar situation that you will need to avoid is driving students home at the end of the school day. What may seem to be a courtesy at one level may open you up as a teacher to serious accusations from students or their families. There is the obvious liability issue to consider. If you were in an accident and the student was injured, it is likely that not only you, but also your school, would assume liability for the injuries. Depending on the severity of the injuries, this could be a very significant issue. But a more subtle problem could occur if you drove the student safely home and found that there was no parent or guardian to receive them. Even if there are adults at home, some students may conjure up stories about the conversation or actions that took place on the drive home as a way to get even with the teacher due to a perceived slight or because of anger or frustration over something you have done. As generous and positive as driving a student home may seem, it is full of potential problems that should be avoided.

A third example of a behavior that should be carefully considered before engaging in it is physical touch, specifically in the form of hugs. Most teachers are caring individuals who express their support and concern through touching and hugs, where appropriate. It is a natural response on their part to make contact with others through touch. But hugs and other forms of touch can be problematic in the classroom. Before talking about the potential pitfalls of physical touch, however, it is important to make sure you understand that research and writing over many decades makes it clear that touching is an essential component of healthy development (Field, 2001; Montagu, 1978). At all grades, students typically need and want the reassurance and comfort that only physical touch can give. Teachers who work with young children, in particular,

TABLE 13.4 Photocopying Copyrighted Materials for Classes

Item	Length
Complete Poem	If less than 250 words
Excerpt from Longer Poem	Excerpt must be less than 250 words
Complete Article, Story, or Essay	If less than 2,500 words
Longer Article, Story, Essay, or Book	Excerpt must be less than 1,000 words
Chart, Diagram, or Cartoon	No more than one from a book or magazine

From: Fischer, L., Schimmel, D., & Kelly, C. (2003). *Teachers and the law* (6th ed.). New York: Longman.

have students running up to give them a good morning hug or crawling into laps during story time. It is difficult to avoid touch when working with younger students. At the same time, however, it is important for teachers at all levels to be smart about how, when, and where they touch. Touch should be public, open to all who seek it (rather than available only to a select few in the classroom), and be appropriate to the student and situation. The way in which you hug a close friend, for example, will most likely be different than the hugs you give to students in your classroom. A "high five" or light touch on the shoulder are other examples of physical touch that may be just right for many students. When done appropriately, touching and hugs communicate in very meaningful ways to students while avoiding circumstances that can be misinterpreted by students and others.

Observing Copyright Laws

Another significant legal responsibility that teachers must face is the observance of **copyright laws.** These laws protect authors' intellectual work from unfair use by others that may result in a loss of income. On a daily basis, most teachers use copyrighted materials in a variety of forms and need to be aware of what constitutes **fair use** of these items. The most common area in which copyright laws affect teachers is in the making of photocopies of books or magazines for instructional use. In addition, videotapes, computer software, and materials published on the Internet are also subject to copyright restrictions.

Good teachers are always on the lookout for new materials to use in the classroom. As they read poignant stories, humorous anecdotes, and exciting new information on topics of interest to their students, there is a strong temptation to photocopy the material and share it with them. Although this is an admirable quality, you must temper this inclination with a clear understanding of fair use based on copyright law. The basic federal legislation dealing with this issue is the *Copyright Act,* first enacted in 1906 and later updated in 1976. This act and other more recent guidelines state that teachers can make one copy of a book chapter, an article from a magazine or newspaper, short stories, and poems when this copy is to be used for the teacher's own personal use in preparing for instruction. Specific guidelines are also in place for the fair use of copyrighted materials in classes (see Table 13.4).

Which legal issues will affect your teaching?

The broad legal rights and responsibilities described above help define the ways in which you will teach. In addition, many school-related concerns have been resolved through the courts that will impact your work in the classroom. These legal matters frequently guide what you can and cannot do in your interactions with students, colleagues, and others. In this section, you will learn about several of these legal issues and the impact they are going to have on your life as a teacher.

Certification, Contracts, and Tenure

State laws and court cases have much to say about who can be hired to teach in public school classrooms and what must be done to maintain a contract with a school district. Every state has defined these issues in slightly different ways, so certification issues, teaching contracts, and tenure decisions are all important legal concerns that you should understand before committing to a long-term program of teacher preparation.

Certification. Lupe Perez has just finished her sophomore year at her local university and is interested in completing the teacher certification program there and becoming a fifth-grade teacher. She is surprised to learn of the many requirements that must be met before being admitted and the breadth of course work that students complete for teacher certification. What Lupe may not know is that the initial teacher-certification program is in large part determined by the state in which she lives and varies little from one college or university to the next. Every state has developed a set of legally binding criteria that students must meet before being certified to teach all subjects in an elementary classroom or specialized subjects such as mathematics or English at the middle school and high school levels.

For all states, the expectations for teachers continue to expand as the teaching role itself grows increasingly more complex. For example, a test of basic academic skills is often used as one factor in determining who can enter teacher education programs. A second test is now being required by many states to measure an understanding of the subjects being taught and knowledge of students, learning, and teaching. It is more frequently being required of students completing their certification programs. The Praxis I exam is an example of a test frequently being used as a test of basic skills, and the Praxis II is a common exam of the latter type. Table 13.5 summarizes the elements of each exam.

In addition to initial teacher certification, many states also require teachers to take more course work or engage in further professional development before they receive a permanent teaching credential. For example, the state of Washington now requires new teachers to complete 15 credits of additional course work beyond their initial teaching certificate that leads to a permanent teacher credential. The purpose of this experience is to plan for and complete an individualized professional growth plan designed to assist them in gaining the skills and knowledge needed to be a professional educator (Davis, 2005).

TABLE 13.5 Praxis Exams	
Category	**Description**
Praxis I- Pre-Professional Skills Test	Commonly used as an entrance requirement into teacher education programs. Required in many states, it is a test of basic skills in reading, writing, and mathematics.
Praxis II- Subject Tests	States that use the Praxis II, typically require it at the end of students' programs. It measures their knowledge of the subjects they will teach, principles of teaching, and how students learn.

Teaching contracts. When you seek employment in a school or district, you will be interviewed and initially selected by personnel within the schools. Ultimately, however, local school boards have been given the legal responsibility for hiring new teachers. Because they are the final authority in determining who should receive a contract, these school officials must be careful to avoid violating individual teachers' rights of nondiscrimination described above (Fischer et al., 2007).

In general, school boards issue one of two types of contracts to teachers: term contracts and tenure contracts (Cambron-McCabe, et al., 2009). **Term teaching contracts** are good for a fixed period of time, usually one academic year. At the end of the contract term, the school board can either issue a new contract or decide to end contractual arrangements with the teacher. New teachers are almost always hired on a term contract until such time as they have met the requirements for a more permanent one. This permanent contract is referred to as a **tenure contract** and can only be terminated when the school board can provide evidence that there has been a serious breach of professional conduct. Teachers whose tenure contracts are ended must be granted a fair hearing regarding the charges against them to protect their rights to due process.

Tenure. When you begin your career as a teacher, you will be given a term contract good for one academic year and renewable at the discretion of the school board. During this time, you will be observed and evaluated regarding your teaching effectiveness. Although every attempt will be made to ensure your future success, you are viewed at this point as a probationary employee and as such you will need to prove yourself to fellow teachers and administrators. This probationary period varies between states and districts, but typically extends from 1 to 3 years. Once you are granted tenure and receive a permanent contract, you are fully launched into your teaching career. At this point, a teacher can expect a continuing commitment from the school district for employment. Being tenured gives teachers more flexibility to express their feelings on important issues and to teach in ways they feel are most appropriate for student learning without fear of reprisal from others who may disagree. Although there are clear limits to this freedom, tenure allows more autonomous and creative teaching to take place.

Teacher tenure definitely has benefits, but many have criticized its effectiveness. The primary concern frequently voiced is that tenure makes it very difficult to remove poor teachers from the classroom. Take, as a hypothetical example, Matt LeBlanc. He has taught social studies at the middle school and high school levels for the past 7 years. He did an adequate job during his probationary period, but he has now taken a position as a part-time financial consultant and spends very little time preparing for his classes and participates only minimally in the life of the school. Matt gives few assignments and does a very cursory job in his grading to save time for his part-time position. He seems to be marking time until he can build up his consulting job to the point where he can quit teaching. Students have complained to the administration, but as a tenured teacher, Matt is protected from having his contract terminated because it would be difficult to dismiss him with good cause.

Reflect on teacher tenure. Is tenure a concept you find attractive or do you think of it as an unnecessary facet of teaching? Do you think you will use teacher tenure in the positive ways for which it is intended? How will you feel if you have to work with a tenured teacher who is abusing the system and not really giving his or her all to the profession?

Reflection Opportunity 13.3

Unions, Collective Bargaining, and Strikes

Beginning in the latter part of the 20th century, teachers have increasingly organized into unions for the purpose of collectively seeking better working conditions and improved professional development (see Chapter 5 for more details). One important task teacher unions perform for many educators is to engage in **collective bargaining.** In approximately two-thirds of the states, legislation has been passed to allow unions to negotiate with school districts regarding salary and benefits for their teachers (Fischer et al., 2007). Working together, union officials and teachers in these states have engaged in collective bargaining efforts leading to improved salary and benefit packages.

In about half the states, laws have been passed that allow teachers a limited opportunity to **strike.** In these states, when good-faith negotiations between the union and school district do not lead to an agreement on salary and benefits, teachers are allowed to protest by engaging in a work stoppage until a contract agreement has been reached (Fischer et al., 2007). In many states that do not allow teachers to strike, the law defines specific penalties that can be imposed if teachers engage in an illegal strike. It should be clear that it is important to understand the laws regarding collective bargaining and strikes for the state in which you plan to teach.

Corporal Punishment

Corporal punishment or spanking has been a traditional method of discipline in schools throughout much of American history. Despite its past usage, spanking has become a very controversial issue, with some claiming that it is a form of child abuse and others suggesting that it is an effective discipline strategy when used appropriately. During the last several decades, many states have passed laws to ban this approach. In 1971 one state had banned its use. The most recent statistics indicate that 29 states have now banned corporal punishment, whereas in 9 additional states more than half of all students are in districts with no corporal punishment (Center for Effective Discipline, 2008). Figure 13.2 provides a summary of the current status of corporal punishment in each of the 50 states.

Despite the growing number of states that are banning corporal punishment, approximately 340,000 students are still being spanked and paddled each year in the United States. One reason

Figure 13.2   Corporal Punishment

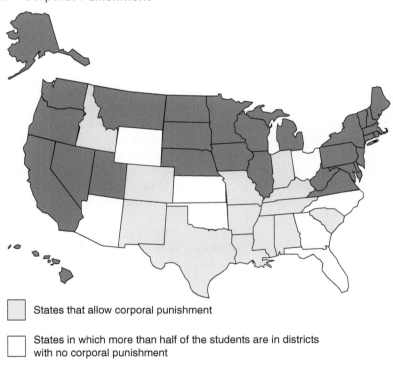

☐ States that allow corporal punishment

☐ States in which more than half of the students are in districts with no corporal punishment

■ States that have banned corporal punishment

From: Center for Effective Discipline. (2008). States banning corporal punishment. Taken from the World Wide Web at: *http://www.stophitting.com/index.php?page=legalinformation#punishment* on January 23, 2009.

for this is that the case law on corporal punishment has sent a mixed message to school districts and states. Although many individual court cases have identified teachers and administrators that have used excessive force in the administration of corporal punishment, the U.S. Supreme Court has ruled that it does not violate a student's constitutional rights (*Ingraham v. Wright,* 1977).

Those opposing corporal punishment have been lobbying state governments for many years to have it abolished. Their rationale is that more recent innovations in discipline are superior in the results they receive and provide better models of how we should interact with one another. Despite a concerted effort on the part of many individuals and groups, the list of states in which corporal punishment is banned has grown slowly over time. The support of groups such as the National Organization of Women, the American School Counselor Association, the American Academy of Pediatrics, and the National PTA has failed to motivate the school districts and states that still use spanking as a form of discipline to abolish its use in the classroom (Center for Effective Discipline, 2008).

What are your thoughts on corporal punishment? If it is legal in your state to use corporal punishment, do you see yourself doing so? If it is banned in your state, do you think this is a mistake? What do you see as the possible strengths and limitations of corporal punishment? Do you remember a situation in which you or someone you knew well was spanked at school? In your opinion, was this an effective form of discipline to use in that situation? Why or why not?

**Reflection
Opportunity 13.4**

Sexual Harassment

Under Title VII of the 1964 Civil Rights act, both students and teachers are protected against sexual harassment and a hostile work environment. The U.S. Equal Employment Opportunity Commission (2009) defines **sexual harassment** as follows:

> Unwelcome sexual advances, requests for sexual favors, and other verbal or physical conduct of a sexual nature constitute sexual harassment when this conduct explicitly or implicitly affects an individual's employment, unreasonably interferes with an individual's work performance, or creates an intimidating, hostile, or offensive work environment.

A **hostile work environment** exists when abusive language, physical aggression, and other demeaning behavior repeatedly occurs in the workplace (Cambron-McCabe, et al., 2009). It is important to know that sexual harassment and hostile work environments do exist in school settings. If, for example, a principal repeatedly makes verbal comments with clear sexual connotations or inappropriately touches a teacher, the principal is engaging in sexual harassment. Or a teacher that angrily and repeatedly verbally derides a student for being "dumb" or "lazy" is creating a hostile work environment for that student. Although not a common occurrence, the day-to-day interactions of school staff and students may lead to either of these two conditions. Teachers need to know their legal rights and take steps to eliminate these problem behaviors.

Religion and Schooling

Until the latter half of the 20th century, religious experiences such as Bible readings and prayer were a common part of life in many schools. During the last several decades, however, the relationship between religion and schooling has become one of the most controversial issues facing teachers and schools. Many people believe that religious experiences and even intellectual discussions about religion have no place in the schools. Those taking this position feel, for example, that prayer in schools, teaching creationism, singing Christmas carols, and celebrating religious holidays should be excluded. This viewpoint is often labeled as **secular humanism.** At the other end of the continuum, those with strong religious beliefs often feel that when all references to religion are eliminated an antireligious bias is created that in some ways becomes its own religion/philosophy. Those taking this position feel that such things as prayer in schools ought to be allowed on a voluntary basis and schools should provide space in their buildings for religious clubs that meet before and after the school day. To view a video on religion and songs sung in the high school choir, go to the Companion Website for this text and click on MyEducationLab for Chapter 13.

myeducationlab
The Power of Classroom Practice

MyEducationLab 13.2

The following are significant issues related to religion and the schools that have been addressed by the U.S. legal system:

- *Separation of church and state*—The First Amendment to the U.S. Constitution states that laws cannot promote or prohibit religious expression.
- *School-sponsored prayer and Bible study*—In *Engel v. Vitale* (1962), the court ruled that schools may not sponsor prayer or Bible study because of student's First Amendment rights.
- *Prayer at public school functions*—The courts, in *Lee v. Weisman* (1962), stated that prayer at public school functions is unconstitutional.
- *Religious clubs*—In *Board of Education of Westside Community Schools v. Mergens* (1990), it was determined that religious clubs can have access to school buildings when other noncurriculum-related student groups are also allowed space.
- *Pledge of Allegiance*—The Supreme Court, in *Elk Grove v. Newdow* (2004), overturned a lower court ruling that teacher-led recitations of the Pledge of Allegiance were unconstitutional when they contained the words "under God." The Pledge therefore remains unchanged.

Schooling Choices

During the last decade of the 20th century, a nationwide effort to give parents and students more options for schooling gained momentum. State and federal legislation has allowed three options to emerge. **Charter schools** "are nonsectarian public schools of choice that operate with freedom from many of the regulations that apply to traditional public schools. The 'charter' establishing each such school is a performance contract detailing the school's mission, program, goals, students served, methods of assessment, and ways to measure success." (U.S. Charter Schools, 2009). **Vouchers** allow parents and students to select schools other than the ones they would normally attend, with the home district transferring to the new school the financial allotment from the state for educating each transferred student. **Home schooling** is an option in which the parents choose to educate their own children in the home environment.

Charter schools. Charter schools (see Chapter 4 for more information) have become a relatively popular option in many states. Between 1992 and 2008, the number of states approving legislation that allowed for the development of charter schools grew from 1 to 40 and the number of schools operating with charters has grow to over 4,500 (Center for Education Reform, 2008). Charter schools were designed to provide the following benefits (U.S. Charter Schools, 2009):

- Increase opportunities for learning and access to quality education for all students
- Create choice for parents and students within the public school system
- Encourage innovative teaching practices
- Create new professional opportunities for teachers
- Encourage community and parent involvement in public education

Although the intended benefits and growing numbers of charter schools are impressive, results on the movement are still unclear. The evidence so far would indicate that most students, parents, and teachers who participate in charter schools are generally pleased with the option, particularly an average school size of approximately 250 students (Center for Education Reform, 2008). The research on student academic performance in charter schools has been less conclusive, however, with most studies finding limited difference between charter schools and other public schools. In some instances, charter schools outperformed public schools, whereas in other situations the reverse was true (Solomon & Goldschmidt, 2004).

Vouchers. The idea of school vouchers has been around since at least the 1950s. At that time, economist Milton Friedman proposed that competition among public schools would have a positive impact on school quality and student performance. He reasoned that if the public schools were more like the free-market system in place for business, teachers would rise to the challenges and provide better instruction and students would consequently engage in higher levels of learning. Friedman advocated for vouchers that parents could use to pay for tuition at the schools of their choice (Latham, 1999). In spite of the efforts of Friedman and many other more recent proponents such as former President Bill Clinton, voucher programs have been considerably more controversial than the charter school movement. One of the major concerns expressed by opponents has been the option of having public school money, in the form of vouchers, being used to fund tuition at private schools. Using vouchers at private schools with strong religious affiliations was seen as a violation of First Amendment guarantees for the separation of church and state. A recent Supreme Court decision, however, has made it clear that this is not the case (*Zelman v. Simmons-Harris,* 2002).

Because of the strong opposition to voucher programs, few states have been able to pass legislation to implement this option. The *No Child Left Behind Act,* however, is being seen by many as a motivation for new efforts to implement voucher programs. The law requires states to provide school options to students in consistently low-rated schools (Richard & Samuels, 2005). A voucher system would provide students and their parents with this choice. Florida, Wisconsin, Ohio, Arizona, Illinois, Iowa, Maine, Minnesota, Pennsylvania, Rhode Island, Utah, and Vermont have implemented voucher plans (Friedman Foundation, 2007). The *Engage in the Debate* feature for this chapter provides addition information on school vouchers.

Engage in the debate: School vouchers

Considerable controversy surrounds the use of vouchers as a method of giving parents and their children choices in the schools they attend. Those who support voucher plans see them as a means of returning to families the tax monies authorized for each student and allowing the family to "spend" this allotment for tuition at public and private schools of their choice. They believe that parents, given this ability to choose, would seek out the best schools for their children and support them financially with their vouchers (Peterson, 2006). These schools would in turn attract the best teachers by rewarding them both financially and by creating even stronger environments for teaching and learning. By having schools compete for voucher money, the best schools would become stronger, while those that are weak would either be required to improve or close their doors. Voucher proponents also see them as a way to equalize educational opportunities for low-income families.

Those who oppose vouchers have equally strong opinions about the problems associated with them. They argue that money and the profit motive in business are very different from the motivations associated with education, making vouchers problematic in schools (Lewis, 2001). They also have strong concerns about private schools receiving public money through a voucher system. Many private schools have a religious affiliation and opponents view this as a means of circumventing the Constitutional prohibitions against subsidizing religious practice and instruction. The Supreme Court, however, ruled that publicly financed tuition vouchers can be used at religious schools without violating the First Amendment (Peterson, 2005).

Developing the Habit of Reflective Practice
Gather Information

1. Go to Stateline.org and search for information on school vouchers.
2. Go to Rethinkingschools.org and search for additional articles and research on school vouchers.

Identify Beliefs

1. Should school vouchers be used to widen educational opportunities for all students? Why or why not?

2. Are vouchers for private school tuition a good idea? Why or why not?

Make Decisions

1. Who should decide whether school vouchers are allowed? Should this be a local school district decision? A state decision? A federal decision?

2. Should politicians or voters decide on the availability of vouchers?

Assess and Evaluate

1. Why do you think so few states use school voucher programs?

2. What would you need to know to determine the success of school vouchers?

Sources

Lewis, J. (2001). Saying no to vouchers: What is the price of democracy? in J. Noll (ed.) *Taking sides: Clashing views on controversial educational issues*. Guilford, CT: McGraw-Hill.

Peterson, K. (2005). *School vouchers slow to spread*. Stateline.org, May 25, 2005. Accessed on September 27, 2005: *http://www.stateline.org/live/ViewPage.action?siteNodeId=142&languageId=1&contentId=297 89*

Peterson, P. (2006). Victory for vouchers? in J. Noll (ed.) *Taking sides: Clashing views on controversial educational issues*. Dubuque, Iowa: McGraw-Hill.

Home schooling. A third schooling option that is steadily growing in popularity is home schooling. There are three main reasons most often cited for the growth of the home schooling movement. The National Center for Education Statistics (2008) surveyed parents of home-schooled children and found:

- *Concern about school environments*—Thirty-one percent of the parents felt that schools were unable to provide high quality and safe learning environments for their children.

- *Lack of religious and/or moral instruction*—Thirty percent of parents surveyed believed that the lack of religious or moral instruction was the primary motivation for home schooling.

- *Perceptions of low-quality public school instruction*—Sixteen percent of the parents chose home schooling as an option so that their children could receive high-quality, individualized instruction in the home setting.

Although the percentage of students and families participating in this option is still small at 2.9% in 2007, home schooling has grown in acceptance and popularity during the last few decades (National Center for Education Statistics, 2008). The approximately 1.5 million home-schooled children in the United States represent a 74% increase from 1999 to 2007. Did you, or someone you knew well experience home schooling? What do you remember as the strengths and limitations of this educational option?

Although home schooling is now legal in all 50 states, there is considerable variation in the level of regulation. For example, only a handful of states have established minimum academic requirements for parents who home school, whereas home-schooled students in about half of the states are required to participate in standardized testing (LaMorte, 2008). An example of state requirements for home schooling is that of California. After reviewing appropriate sections of California state law, Zeise (2005) found the following:

- *Equivalent instruction.* Students who are home schooled are expected to learn the same basic academic content that would be available to them if they were in a regular school setting.
- *Qualified parent instructors.* If the home school registers as a private school or enrolls in an independent study program with a private school, then parent instructors do not need to have California state teacher certification.
- *Systematic reporting.* Parents who home school their own children are expected to keep school authorities apprised annually of students being taught at home and the curriculum that is being followed.
- *Minimum hours of instruction.* Parents and students are expected to engage in a state-mandated minimum number of hours of teaching/learning experiences each day.

What legal issues impact students?

Like you, your students will also have important rights guaranteed by law and through decisions reached by various state and federal courts. You will need to understand these legal issues so that you can advocate on behalf of students whose rights are being violated and conduct yourself in ways that promote these rights. The most basic of these rights may well be the right to a free and appropriate education. The *Reflect on Diversity* feature for this chapter describes this right as it impacts students with special needs. Read and reflect on this issue now. In addition to the right to a free and appropriate education, student rights related to issues of sexual harassment, search and seizure, student records, suspension and expulsion, and freedom of expression are addressed below.

Reflect on diversity: Free and appropriate public education

In 1982, The United States Supreme Court decided a landmark case which impacts the education of all children with special needs (Zirkel and Doe, 2002). The case was *Hendrick Hudson School District v. Rowley*. The plaintiff, Amy Rowley, was a deaf student with an excellent ability to lip-read. An Individual Education Plan (IEP) was prepared for Amy during the fall of her first grade year stating that she should be educated in a regular classroom. The IEP also required that Amy make use of a hearing aid and receive instruction from a tutor for the deaf and a speech therapist. In order to further assist Amy, several school administrators also attended a course in sign-language interpretation and a teletype machine was installed to facilitate communication with Amy's parents who were also deaf.

Amy's parents were unhappy with the IEP because it did not require that Amy be provided with an in-class sign language interpreter. While Amy performed in the top half of her class without an interpreter, she nevertheless missed a substantial portion of what was said. School administrators concluded that no interpreter should be provided, and a district special education committee agreed.

The Rowley Family took the school district to court and the case was eventually reviewed by the United States Supreme Court. They concluded that Amy Rowley was not entitled to a sign-language interpreter. The court found that the school district had complied with all required procedures. Since Amy was doing very well in her class and was advancing easily from grade to grade, they saw no need for a further accommodation. Some special education proponents disagree with the Supreme Court ruling, stating that the law was not meant to be a minimum "floor of opportunity" but rather a ladder to help students reach their maximum potential.

Developing the Habit of Reflective Practice

Gather Information

1. Do an Internet search for Hendrick Hudson School District V. Rowley and read more about this important court case.

Identify Beliefs

1. Should schools provide a minimum "floor of opportunity" or assist students with special needs reach their full potential?

2. How do students with special needs influence the learning potential of all students when they are placed in the regular classroom?

Make Decisions

1. If you were able to decide what should happen in Amy Rowley's case, what would you have decided and why?

Assess and Evaluate

1. What information would you need to assess whether Amy benefited from having a sign language interpreter in the classroom?

Source

Zirkel, P.A. & Doe, J. (2002). Decisions that have shaped U.S. education. *Educational Leadership, 59*, (4), 6–12.

Sexual Harassment

It has been clear for many years that sexual harassment of students by their teachers or other school staff is morally indefensible and grounds for dismissal. Despite the serious consequences for teachers and staff who sexually harass students, the numbers of students who may experience this major problem at least once during their K–12 experience is estimated to be 1 in 10 (Shakeshaft, 2004). In addition to teacher/staff harassment of students, there is considerable concern regarding students sexually harassing other students. In a report by the American Association of University Women (2001), students surveyed indicated that the problem is a significant one for both boys and girls. The AAUW reports that harassment by peers can begin as early as the elementary school years, it occurs regularly in virtually all schools, and is upsetting to both boys and girls. In its survey of more than 2,000 students in the 8th–11th grades, 83% of the girls and 79% of the boys reported having experienced harassment. The most common forms of sexual harassment students face include:

- Sexual comments, jokes, gestures, or looks
- Saying that a person is gay or lesbian
- Spreading sexual rumors about a person
- Touching, grabbing or pinching in a sexual way
- Intentionally brushing up against someone in a sexual way
- Flashing or "mooning" (American Association of University Women, 2001)

Teachers need to address student sexual harassment in two primary ways. First, they need to be aware of the impact of recent court rulings on this issue. In a 1999 U.S. Supreme Court case (*Davis v. Monroe County Board of Education*), it was determined that teachers could be held liable if they fail to implement strategies to end known cases of sexual harassment. It is therefore essential that teachers take the time to work through instances of sexual harassment as they are encountered. Secondly, teachers can work to stamp out harassment by helping students understand the

TABLE 13.6   Responding to Sexual Harassment Among Students

Strategy	Description
Student Education on Harassment	This should begin in elementary school, be age appropriate, and describe what constitutes harassment without creating a climate of fear.
Antiharassment Policy	Every school should have a well-publicized policy that prohibits all forms of verbal and physical harassment.
Responding to Harassment	Everyone involved (including witnesses) should be given the opportunity to describe the harassment in their own words. The targets should be asked about solutions to the problem.
Professional Development	Schools should provide regular training to staff in how to deal with harassment.
Family Involvement	Families should be educated about harassment and their support solicited in dealing with problems as they arise.

legal and ethical problems with this behavior and suggesting more appropriate ways of interacting with each other. By discussing relevant problems as they occur, teachers can help students break out of this inappropriate and harmful mode of interaction. Table 13.6 suggests some ways in which teachers can respond to situations of sexual harassment among students.

Search and Seizure

Under the Fourth Amendment to the U.S. Constitution, all of America's citizens are protected from having their personal belongings and spaces examined without a formal search warrant. This protection from **search and seizure** extends to students as well. Searches are only allowed if there is a strong suspicion that an illegal substance or a dangerous object may be present. So, if school officials have a strong reason to believe that students have drugs, alcohol, or dangerous weapons in their locker, desk, or backpack and use reasonable methods of investigating their suspicions, a legal search can be conducted. For example, two girls in a New Jersey high school were caught smoking in the bathroom and taken to the school office. One girl denied that she was smoking, whereupon the assistant vice principal opened her purse and found not only cigarettes, but also marijuana and related paraphernalia (*New Jersey v. T.L.O.*, 1985). The girl filed suit, claiming that the search of her purse violated her rights, but the court disagreed because of the reasonableness of the investigation under the circumstances.

With prominent national news stories in the last several years on gun violence, search and seizure of guns and other weapons has become a more pressing matter in many schools. One federal law that has had an impact on the consequences of bringing dangerous weapons to school is the *Gun-Free Schools Act* of 1994. The act states: "each State receiving Federal funds under this chapter shall have in effect a State law requiring local educational agencies to expel from school for a period of not less than one year a student who is determined to have brought a weapon to a school." Once a school has determined that there is a strong suspicion that a weapon is on the school grounds, they may search for it and then implement significant consequences to help ensure the safety of both students and staff.

Student Records

American schools have historically kept all sorts of educational records of student progress. Over the years, the list of items included has grown successively longer. Grades on assignments, test scores, records of discipline problems, psychologists' reports, counseling sessions, results of standardized

TABLE 13.7 The Buckley Amendment

Feature	Description
Written Policy	School districts must have a written policy that deals with student records and inform parents annually of their rights under the act.
Reviewing Student Files	School personnel, parents, and eligible students can review their files, but others may not.
Challenging Contents of Files	Procedures are in place for parents and eligible students to challenge the contents of the files.
Meeting Terms of the Act	Parents can contact the Family Right to Privacy Act Office when they feel the school has failed to meet the terms of the act.

From: Fischer, L., Schimmel, D., & Stellman, L. (2007). *Teachers and the law* (7th ed.). New York: Longman.

tests, and attendance records are all examples of the items typically collected. Until the mid-1970s, these records were considered private and neither parents nor students were able to review what was kept in these files. With the passage of the *Family Educational Rights and Privacy Act* (FRPA) in 1974, this policy was changed. Parents with children under 18 years of age and students themselves who are 18 or older are given access to these records under what has now come to be known as the **Buckley Amendment.** Table 13.7 describes the basic features of this important amendment.

Although the Buckley Amendment has clearly benefited both students and their parents, many teachers and administrators have reservations about some aspects of the law. One concern stems from the rights of eligible students and their parents to review letters of recommendation written by faculty and staff. Because they can no longer be considered confidential, many teachers and staff are writing more general and "safe" recommendations, rather than opening themselves up to criticism from parents and students. In similar ways, teachers and school staff may be more guarded in the assessments that end up as part of permanent student records because of parental and student access to these materials.

Have you thought about issues surrounding student confidentiality? Reflect on this aspect of your role as a teacher. Do you feel it is important to protect the privacy of student records? In what circumstances would you need to exercise the most care to avoid violating this right? Can you anticipate situations in which this right may get in the way of your efforts to effectively work with students and their families?

Reflection Opportunity 13.5

Suspension and Expulsion

Not so many years ago, life was simpler in American schools. The serious offenses that led to suspension or expulsion consisted mostly of things like a fistfight in the school parking lot, smoking on school grounds, and swearing at the classroom teacher. An example of this type comes from a 1959 book by Albert Moustakas titled *The Alive and Growing Teacher:*

> We have in our building a boy who is quite a problem with other children. He's well on his way to being a delinquent. He demands money from them or threatens to beat them up. The other children have been instructed to stay away from him and the teachers are almost as afraid of him as the other children. (p. 66)

Although the kinds of difficulties described above are not easy to work through, they are less problematic than the ones faced by teachers today. During the last three or four decades the level of problems encountered has clearly escalated. An indicator of this is that the Bureau of Justice Statistics now gathers information on violent crimes. It reported in 2007 that 78% of all public schools experienced one or more violent crimes during the academic year. Violent deaths, rape, sexual assault, aggravated assault, and threats with a weapon are among the categories now being monitored. Teachers and administrators today must also deal with drugs and alcohol in and around the school, complicating further the lives of teachers and school staff.

Despite efforts at prevention, the serious problems described above continue to occur in schools and make it necessary for teachers and administrators to consider suspension and/or expulsion for students. The most common options used by schools are:

- **In-school suspension**—Removing problem students from regular classes and place them in a special classroom set aside for suspended students. In-school suspension is used for the least serious offenses.
- **Suspension**—Temporarily removing students from the school for a set number of days.
- **Expulsion**—Denying students permanent access to school for an extended period of time. Expulsion is a last resort that schools use when all other options have failed.

Court cases over the years have helped define student and school rights when suspension and expulsion are being considered. In the most serious cases in which longer term suspension or expulsion is being considered, students should receive a written notice specifying the charges and a description of the procedures to be used at the hearing. Furthermore, they should be told what evidence has been collected, the names of any witnesses being called, and know that they can question witnesses and present their own evidence (*Dixon v. Alabama State Board of Education*, 1961). These steps are necessary to honor students' rights to due process.

In a recent attempt to take a firm stance against violence and drug use within the schools, many districts are implementing **zero-tolerance policies** to clarify for students the behaviors that are unacceptable within the schools. Loosely modeled after the strict sentencing laws that have gained popularity within the criminal justice system, zero-tolerance policies for schools clearly state that when students are found with weapons or drugs they face automatic suspension or expulsion. Although this attempt by the schools to get tough against violence and drugs has many positive aspects, there have been repeated examples in national and state news in which students have been suspended for rather inconsequential behaviors such as carrying a squirt gun to school or using mouthwash after lunch. The American Bar Association (2009) cites the following examples:

- Two 10-year-old boys from Arlington, Virginia were suspended for three days for putting soapy water in a teacher's drink. At the teacher's urging, police charged the boys with a felony that carried a maximum sentence of 20 years. The children were formally processed through the juvenile justice system before the case was dismissed months later.
- In Denton County, Texas, a 13-year-old was asked to write a "scary" Halloween story for a class assignment. When the child wrote a story that talked about shooting up a school, he both received a passing grade by his teacher and was referred to the school principal's office. The school officials called the police, and the child spent six days in jail before the courts confirmed that no crime had been committed.

Freedom of Expression

Freedom of expression is considered an important right available to all Americans. This right has been tested in the courts by students and, although not absolute, is available to them in school settings as well. The classic case defining this right was *Tinker v. Des Moines Independent Community School District* (1969). In 1965, as debate over American involvement in the Vietnam War heated up, several students in Des Moines, Iowa, wore black armbands to school to signify their opposition to the war. Some students refused to remove them even though they knew that the bands were specifically banned by district policy. They were suspended and took their case to the courts. The Supreme Court eventually ruled in favor of the students, stating that they didn't "shed their constitutional rights to freedom of speech or expression at the schoolhouse gate."

At the same time, however, schools can legally limit student expression if there is a reasonable expectation that these communications will be disruptive to life in the schools. For example, a federal appeals court supported a Cleveland high school's rule to ban all buttons and badges because they had led to racial friction between Black and White students (*Guzick v. Debras,* 1971). The evidence presented suggested that an escalation of racial tensions and a deterioration of the educational climate would have occurred if the buttons and badges had been allowed. The *Ian's Classroom Experiences* feature for this chapter (found on the Companion Website for this text) provides an interesting example of freedom of expression. You may want to read it now for more insights on this important topic.

Ian's Classroom Experiences: Respect of Power

One area in which students' freedom of expression may be more limited in the future is in their selection of clothing worn to school. Increasing numbers of schools are either requiring student uniforms or implementing school or district dress codes. Colesanti (2008) reviewed individual state policies on uniforms and dress codes and found that 23 give local districts the right to require students to wear uniforms. Four additional states allow districts to establish dress codes, with no mention of uniforms in the state statutes. One state has laws prohibiting dress codes. Clearly, students in schools requiring uniforms or enforcing dress codes are more limited in their freedom of expression. Did you experience either of these circumstances in your own schooling? If so, what were your reactions to it? If not, how do you think you would have felt about it?

How do ethics influence my teaching roles?

Teachers not only must engage in behavior that is in accord with legal mandates, they also need to conduct themselves in ways that are morally defensible. Armed with their own personal belief system and an understanding of the roles and responsibilities of teachers, educators struggle daily with **ethics** as they respond to students, colleagues, and others. As can be seen from the following example, these decisions are often difficult and bring into conflict the rights and responsibilities of several individuals.

> It was only the first week of the new school year and already Sol Goldblum, the sixth-grade teacher, had a problem. For years he had let his students take turns running errands for him—to the principal's office, the custodian, other classrooms. This had always worked well. The students enjoyed the feeling of responsibility this experience gave them, and it helped establish the mutual trust that Sol believed was vital to a healthy classroom community.
>
> The problem started when Billy Baker's turn to do errands came up. Billy had a reputation around school for being a "difficult" student. Billy's fifth-grade teacher had told Sol flat out that Billy was a troublemaker and could not be trusted. Sol thought about this, but he himself had not seen Billy misbehave. It was a new school year, and he thought Billy deserved a fresh start. So, in spite of the teacher's warning, he gave Billy the opportunity to take some papers to the principal's office. On the way, he started a fight with a fourth-grade boy who happened to be in the hallway. This boy had been taunting Billy on the playground the day before.
>
> Now, Sol's principal had called him on the carpet for permitting Billy to go unescorted in the hallway. She told him never to let Billy go unescorted again. She was adamant about this (Hostetler, 1997, p. 1).

Reflect on the situation described above. If you were Sol, how would you respond? What are your responsibilities to Billy? How should you deal with the principal's strong statement about Billy's behavior? Are your own beliefs about teaching and learning being compromised in any way as you decide a course of action? These questions, and more, would be important to address as you make decisions about this complex situation. As you respond to issues like this, you are engaging in ethical decision making, an important part of your role as a professional educator.

Reflection Opportunity 13.6

Another aspect of your ethical decision making is described in the *Explore Your Beliefs* feature for this chapter. It addresses the issue of fairness and equity among students. Read the feature now and respond to the reflection questions presented in the feature.

Explore your beliefs: Is fair equal? Is equal fair?

There is considerable talk in educational circles today about the importance of equity. That is, all students should have equal opportunities to learn and grow in the classroom. For example, students should have equal access to technology, the same opportunity for a safe classroom environment, and equitable interactions with the classroom teacher. This would seem to imply that all students should be treated the same. But, fairness in interactions with students does not mean that teachers always treat them in identical ways. In many circumstances, treating students fairly means that we need to interact with them in somewhat different ways. Here are some examples of situations in which students are treated fairly, but are not treated equally.

Ryan is a gifted student in Lindsay Rieker's fifth-grade classroom. He is currently reading at a tenth-grade reading level. While most of the other students are reading books at the fifth-grade reading level, Lindsay has developed a separate reading list based on Ryan's interests and ability. He is being treated differently in order to meet his academic needs.

Crystal is a low-performing student in Kathy Makoviney's middle school science classroom. She is currently not meeting grade level expectations because she is struggling with recording and interpreting data during lab time. Kathy has found that if she checks frequently on Crystal during lab times, she is able to help her grasp the scientific concepts and Crystal is catching onto writing and understanding lab reports. Crystal is getting more teacher time than some of her more independent peers.

P.J. has chosen the vocational/technical option at her high school and is taking mathematics and science courses that will help prepare her for the technical college she plans to enter next fall. Her twin brother Clifford, however, is enrolled in pre-calculus and physics in preparation for his college course work next year. These two students are being treated differently by their school through the curriculum choices they have voluntarily made.

Developing the Habit of Reflective Practice

Gather Information

1. Think back on your own experiences. Has a teacher ever treated you the same as other students, but you considered it unfair? Has a teacher ever treated you differently in a way that was fair?

2. Go to *http://brownvboard.org*, click on Brown Summary to read about the classic court case confirming the need for equal education opportunities for Black Americans.

Identify Beliefs

1. In what ways do you think all students should be treated exactly the same?

2. For what categories of teacher behavior do you think students should be treated fairly but differently?

Make Decisions

1. How should a teacher explain to students why some students are treated differently in certain circumstances?

Assess and Evaluate

1. Imagine you are a teacher and you have asked a colleague to visit your classroom while you are teaching. You have asked him to observe your teaching and to make sure you are treating students fairly, although not necessarily equally. If he makes a list of what he observes, what might you expect to see on his list?

Defining Ethical Teaching

So, exactly what is ethical teaching? It certainly includes your responses to "crisis situations" like the one Sol faced with Billy above. Doing the right thing in these situations while addressing the rights and responsibilities of a number of different people requires insight and careful deliberation. One way, then, to describe an ethical teacher is as a moral person, that is "a person of good heart; and that means that the moral person cares about others, has a sense of justice, and possesses a sense of social sympathy" (Wagner, 1996, p. 9). But *being* a moral person is not enough. It is also critical for the ethical teacher to *act* as a moral person.

Beyond the crisis situations that all teachers face and must deal with, ethical teaching also includes many day-to-day events that might not initially be considered part of these moral considerations. For "it is in the protracted, everyday, seemingly mundane features of classrooms and teaching that ethical judgment is most often called for. The arrangement of desks, the material on bulletin boards, the rituals schools perpetuate—all these merit ethical reflection and judgment even if their import cannot be neatly packaged in some discrete situation" (Hostetler, 1997, p. 11). Read the *Views from the Classroom* feature on the Companion Website for one teacher's description of this type of ethical teaching.

Views from the Classroom: Brain Surgery

Strike and Ternasky (1993) identify three broad ways in which ethics can be applied to education:

1. *Educational policy.* When teachers create or modify educational policies such as a plan for school-wide discipline, they need to consider whether or not the policy addresses important goals and is fair to all affected parties.

2. *Moral education.* Moral or character education is becoming an increasingly vital part of American education. Ethics should play a key role in the teaching of this part of the curriculum.

3. *Professional ethics.* These are the values and standards of behavior that guide teachers, administrators, and others in carrying out the duties of the profession.

Ethical teaching, then, is a reasoned set of principles for right conduct that is applied to interactions between teachers and students, colleagues, and other stakeholders in education. Although, ultimately, each individual must internalize and act on his or her own beliefs about ethical teaching, the collective wisdom of veteran educators can help guide the development of this belief system. A **code of ethics** is an attempt to summarize this wisdom in ways that can help teachers make the best possible moral decisions in their interactions with students and others. These codes of conduct help refine an understanding of the issues that must be addressed, identify what other teachers believe to be appropriate responses, and lead teachers to reflect on responses to the dilemmas they face. Chapter 5 provides examples of codes of ethics developed by professional organizations.

Engaging in Ethical Teaching

It is important to realize that reading about ethical teaching, taking course work on this topic, and even reflecting daily on ethical issues will not necessarily make you ethical in your teaching. More than any other factor, good behavior is based upon a person's character, which in turn is built slowly after many years of struggling with moral issues (Strike & Ternasky, 1993). As Wagner (1996) puts it, "Assuming that the people coming into a profession are people of good heart, then training in *professional* ethics gives them an eye for subtlety and detail in matters of morality. In particular, training in ethics helps the professional to act as a moral person in the practice of that profession" (p. 8).

The answer, then, to the question "How do I engage in ethical teaching?" seems to have two parts. People of good character must first understand the general principles of ethical conduct for their profession and then struggle to apply them daily to the circumstances that they encounter. As teachers wrestle with the difficult issues of their profession, they grow in their ability to engage in ethical teaching.

With this in mind, two cases are presented below. Each ethical dilemma focuses primarily on a group to which teachers have significant responsibilities. After reading the case, you may wish to refer back to one of the codes of ethics described in Chapter 5 and then make decisions about how you would address the issues presented. Strike and Soltis (1992) suggest a four-step process in dealing with case studies:

1. *Make an initial assessment of the case.* After quickly reading through the case once, make a tentative decision about how you would handle it as the classroom teacher. Think about the principles or concepts that influenced your decision.

2. *Put yourself in the position of others in the case.* As you reread the scenario, think about what you would think or feel from the point of view of others in the case. Does this present other ethical issues for you to consider?

3. *Reconsider your initial decision.* After reflecting on the situation in more depth, is there reason to modify the original decision you made? What factors influenced your maintenance of the original assessment or caused you to rethink it?

4. *Discuss the scenario with your peers.* Try hard to be open to the opinions presented by others. Can a consensus be reached in your discussions with others? Why or why not?

Ethical issues and students. Although it is clear that teachers have ethical responsibilities to their students, the situations educators face make them some of the most complex and demanding to resolve. Read the following example about Fred (Goodlad, Soder, & Sirotnik, 1990), a high school English teacher for the past 15 years who has recently encountered a very difficult situation:

Fred begins to observe trouble in one of his students—a fifteen-year-old boy. Papers usually on time and well done are late and show haste in composition. Changes in the boy's behavior prompt Fred to suggest a meeting with a school social worker. The social worker says that the boy is troubled but will not say why, although he has agreed to continue talking.

Fred hears nothing for several weeks and then receives a call from the social worker. The boy has begun to talk, and the evolving story is that the principal is regularly coercing students into sexual acts in his office. The social worker tells Fred that she was initially skeptical but has become convinced that the students are telling the truth. Fred, too, is skeptical and asks the social worker whether she thinks the boy will talk to him. Under the right circumstances, she says, he will. She agrees to ask him and sets up a meeting out of school hours and off school grounds. As a result, Fred is convinced that the story is true. Fred and the social worker are then left with the question of what to do. The principal is a veteran of the school system; he has a powerful set of connections throughout its many levels. He is known to be skilled in the pursuit of power and occasionally ruthless in its exercise (p. 271).

**Reflection
Opportunity 13.7**

After discussing this matter with other faculty members, Fred finds there is a clear division into three groups. The first can't believe the allegations to be true and side with the principal, others believe that the charges are probably true but are unwilling to do anything about it, and the smallest group stands with Fred and is ready to deal with the problem. How would you respond if you were Fred? Use the four-step approach described on the previous page. By pursuing this problem, Fred would alienate himself from the majority of his colleagues and administrators within the school. Although the case appears straightforward in many respects, it would take moral courage to act responsibly and ethically on behalf of this student. As you write about this situation, be specific and state your rationale for the steps you choose to take.

Ethics and colleagues.   Teachers also have responsibilities toward other members of their professional community. Other teachers, classroom assistants, specialists, and administrators all deserve ethical treatment. In the following case, Jonathan describes his dilemma with a teacher in his high school:

> My friendship with a colleague, Sam, a history teacher, goes back 20 years to the time we were roommates at the state university. I have lately been worried about Sam's behavior, because reports from students and the central office have been alarming, Sam's classes have grown unruly and disrespectful, and one day he even dozed in full view of the students. Sam has become a social recluse, pulling back from all involvement with his colleagues and friends. He has become the talk of the school. On a recent weekend, I was drinking coffee alone at the local mall in a doughnut shop, when, after an awkward entrance, Sam sat down beside me . . .
>
> Sam shared with me that he had become increasingly lonely and despondent over the last few months and had sought psychiatric help. He had also begun self-medicating diazepam, an antianxiety drug, taking more than three times the amount his therapist had recommended. Sam told me that he would be mortified if any of these disclosures were to get out at school. He would work things out in his own best way. He only needed a little more time. Besides, "things weren't really that bad at school, right?" The reason he shared all of this with me, he said, was that he needed to "unload" to the "only friend in the world I can trust." (Nash, 1996, pp. 65–66)

If you were Jonathan, how would you respond in this situation? Should you betray your friendship to this colleague and share what you have learned with others? Do you have a responsibility to the principal to reveal what you have learned? What about Sam's students? What is your ethical responsibility to them? How about Sam himself? Is his drug overdose a serious threat to his physical and mental health? Would revealing this information to others be in Sam's best interests?

Before completing your work for this chapter, go to the Companion Website for this text and respond to the issues presented in the *Consider This* Feature for this chapter. It will challenge you take a stand on the issues of school dress codes, drug testing, weapons in schools, and pregnant students.

Reflection Opportunity 13.8

Consider This: Legal Issues

Summary

In this chapter, four organizing questions were presented to help you develop insights about legal and ethical issues in education:

What are your legal rights and responsibilities as a teacher?

State and federal laws and court cases have determined several legal rights and responsibilities for teachers:
- Right of due process (Praxis II, topic IVb)
- Right to nondiscrimination (Praxis II, topic IVb)
- Right to freedom of expression (Praxis II, topic IVb)
- Avoiding liability due to negligence or malpractice (Praxis II, topic IVb)
- Reporting child abuse and neglect (Praxis II, topic IVb)
- Observing copyright laws (Praxis II, topic IVb)

Which legal issues will affect your teaching?

A number of legal issues will directly impact your role as a teacher:
- Certification, contracts, and tenure (Praxis II, topic IVb)
- Unions, collective bargaining, and strikes (Praxis II, topic IVb)
- Corporal punishment (Praxis II, topic Ic)
- Sexual harassment (Praxis II, topic IVb)
- Religion and schooling (Praxis II, topic IVb)
- Home schooling (Praxis II, topic Ic)

What legal issues impact students?

Students also have rights and responsibilities under the law, providing protections and opportunities to all:
- Sexual harassment (Praxis II, topic Ic)
- Search and seizure (Praxis II, topic Ic)
- Student records (Praxis II, topic IIc)
- Suspension and expulsion (Praxis II, topic Ic)
- Freedom of expression (Praxis II, topic Ic)

How do ethics influence my teaching roles?

Teachers need to conduct themselves in ways that are morally defensible.
- Defining ethical teaching (Praxis II, topic IVb)
- Engaging in ethical teaching (Praxis II, topic IVb)

PRAXIS   Test-Preparation Activities

 To review an on-line chapter case study, test your understanding of chapter topics and concepts, and begin preparing for the Praxis II: Principles of Learning and Teaching examination, go to the Praxis Test-Preparation module for this chapter of the Companion Website.

inTASC   Developing the Habit of Reflective Practice

Organizing Questions
What are your legal rights and responsibilities as a teacher?

Review Questions

1. What are the two main sources for the legal guidelines that will have an impact on your future teaching?
2. What are the different types of freedom of expression?
3. What can happen to you as a teacher if you fail to report a suspected case of child abuse or neglect?

Field Experience

Talk to a classroom teacher of your choice regarding legal issues he or she has either dealt with in the classroom or is concerned about for the future. Summarize your discussion and share it with your peers.

Building Your Portfolio: *A Teacher's Legal Rights*

INTASC Standard 10. Identify a legal right that is of importance to you as a classroom teacher.
- Spend some time reading about the laws and court cases that are relevant to this issue.
- Summarize your findings, including the most important court cases, for inclusion in your portfolio.

Which legal issues will affect your teaching?

Review Questions

1. How have requirements for teacher certification changed over time?
2. What is a hostile work environment and how is it related to sexual harassment?
3. How is a charter school different from a more traditional K–12 school?

Field Experience

Research the policies for teacher tenure in a school district of your choice.
- For how many years is a teacher given a term contract?
- What criteria are used in determining whether or not a teacher should be tenured?
- What are the strengths and limitations of teacher tenure?

Building Your Portfolio: *Signs of Child Abuse and Neglect*

INTASC Standard 10. Search for information about indicators of child abuse and neglect.
- You may choose to contact a school district, mental health agency, or search the Internet for information.
- Develop a one- or two-page handout for your portfolio that describes symptoms of child abuse and neglect that you should be aware of as a future teacher.

What legal issues impact students?

Review Questions

1. Under what circumstances can a school search the personal belongings of students?
2. What issues are addressed by the Buckley Amendment?
3. What is a zero-tolerance policy?

Field Experience

Talk to a school administrator of your choice and find out the procedures used by the school to address sexual harassment, searching for and dealing with drugs/alcohol/weapons, or suspending students from the school.
- If there are written policies, ask for a copy.
- Share your finding with others in your class.

Building Your Portfolio: *A Student's Legal Rights*

INTASC Standard 10. Choose one of the student's legal rights described in this chapter and spend some time reading about the laws and court cases that are relevant to this issue. Summarize your findings, including the most important court cases, for inclusion in your portfolio.

How do ethics influence my teaching roles?

Review Questions

1. How would you define ethical teaching?
2. What are the three broad ways in which ethics can be applied to education?
3. What is a code of ethics?

Building Your Portfolio: *Code of Ethical Behavior*

INTASC Standard 9. Go to the Website of the National Education Association at http://www.nea.org, search for and review the code of ethics of this organization.
- What does this document tell you about ethical behavior of teachers and what are its implications for teaching as a profession?
- Include a copy of this code of ethics in your portfolio along with a brief summary of the key points of the document.

Suggested Readings

Fischer, L., Schimmel, D., & Stellman, L. (2007). *Teachers and the law* (7th ed.). New York: Longman. This book provides a well-organized and thorough description of legal issues that are of importance to teachers and their students.

Thomas, S., Cambron-McCabe, N., & McCarthy, M. (2009). *Public school law: Teachers' and students' rights* (6th ed.). Boston: Allyn and Bacon. The authors present a strong overview of legal mandates and court decisions that impact teaching and learning.

References

American Association of University Women. (2001). *Hostile hallways: Bullying, teasing, and sexual harassment in school.* Washington, DC: The AAUW Educational Foundation.

American Bar Association. (2009). *Zero tolerance policy.* Retrieved January 23, 2009 from *http://www.abanet.org/crimjust/juvjus/zerotolreport.html*

B.M. by Berger v. State of Montana, 649 P.2d 425 (Mont. 1982).

Board of Education of Westside Community Schools v. Mergens, 110 S. Ct. 2356 (1990).

Bureau of Justice Statistics. (2007). *Indicators of school crime and safety: 2007.* Retrieved January 23, 2009 from: *http://www.ojp.usdoj.gov/bjs/abstract/iscs07.htm*

Cary v. Board of Education, Adams-Arapahoe School District, 598 F.2d 535 (10th Cir. 1979).

Center for Education Reform. (2008). *Charter school facts.* Retrieved January 23, 2009 from: *http://www.edreform.com/index.cfm?fuseAction=*

Center for Effective Discipline. (2008). *Discipline at school.* Retrieved January 23, 2009 from: *http://www.stophitting.com/index.php?page=atschool-main*

Civil Rights Act of 1964. Retrieved August 30, 2005 from: *http://www.ourdocuments.gov/doc.php?flash=true&doc=97&page=transcript*

Colasanti, M. (2008). School uniforms and dress codes: State policy. Retrieved January 23, 2009 from *http://www.ecs.org/clearinghouse/77/97/7797.pdf*

Connecticut Department of Children and Families (2009). Q&A about r*eporting child abuse and neglect.* Retrieved January 20, 2009 from: *http://www.state.ct.gov/dcf/cwp/view.asp?a=255649=314388*

Davis, L. (2005). *Professional certification for teachers: What it really means.* Retrieved August 31, 2005 from: *http://www.k12.wa.us/Conferences/JanConf2005/materials/materials13/Professional CertificationForTeacher.doc*

Davis v. Monroe County Board of Education, 526 U.S. 629 (1999).

Dixon v. Alabama State Board of Education, 294 F.2d. 150 (5th Cir. 1961).

Education Week. (2005). Efforts to improve teacher quality. *Quality Counts 2005.* Bethesda, MD: Author.

Elk Grove v. Newdow, No. 02-1624 (2004).

Engel v. Vitale, 370 U.S. 421 (1962).

Field, T. (2001). *Touch.* Cambridge, MA: MIT Press.

Fischer, L., Schimmel, D., & Stellman, L. (2007). *Teachers and the law* (7th ed.). Boston: Allyn & Bacon.

Gaylord v. Tacoma School District No. 10, 559 P.2d 1340 (Wash. 1977).

Goodlad, J., Soder, R., & Sirotnik, K. (1990). *The moral dimensions of teaching.* San Francisco: Jossey-Bass.

Guzick v. Debras, 401 U.S. 948 (1971).

Hostetler, K. (1997). *Ethical judgment in teaching.* Boston: Allyn and Bacon.

Ingraham v. Wright, 430 U.S. 651 (1977).

Kelly, E. (1998). *Legal basics: A handbook for educators.* Bloomington, IN: Phi Delta Kappa Educational Foundation.

LaMorte, M. (2008). *School law: Cases and concepts.* (9th ed.). Boston: Allyn and Bacon.

Latham, A. (1999). School vouchers: Much debate, little research. *Educational Leadership, 56*(2), 28–30.

Lee v. Weisman, 505 U.S. 577 (1992).

Montagu, A. (1978). *Touching: The human significance of the skin* (2nd ed.). New York: Harper and Row.

Moustakas, A. (1959). *The alive and growing teacher.* New York: The Philosophical Library.

Nash, R. (1996). *Real world ethics: Frameworks for educators and human service professionals.* New York: Teachers College Press.

National Center for Education Statistics. (2008). *1.5 million homeschooled students in the United States in 2007. Issue Brief.* Washington, DC: Author.

New Jersey v. T.L.O., 221 Cal. Rptr. 118, 105 S. Ct. 733 (1985).

Parducci v. Rutland, 316 F.Supp. 352 (N.D. Ala. 1970).

Peter W. v. San Francisco Unified School District, 131 Cal. Rptr. 854 (Cal. App. 1976).

Pickering v. Board of Education, 391 U.S. 563 (1968).

Project NoSpank. (2005). *Prominent organizations' position statements opposing corporal punishment.* Retrieved August 31, 2005 from: *http://www.nospank.net/orgs.htm*

Richard, A., & Samuels, C. (2005). Legislatures hit with surge of school choice plans. *Education Week,* February 23, p. 8.

Shakeshaft, C. (2004). *Educator sexual misconduct: A synthesis of existing literature.* Washington, DC: U.S. Department of Education.

Sheehan v. St. Peter's Catholic School, 188 N.W.2d 868 (Minn. 1971).

Solomon, L., & Goldschmidt, P. (2004). *Comparison of traditional public schools and charter schools on retention, school switching, and achievement growth.* Goldwater Institute Policy Report. Retrieved September 2005 from: *http://www.goldwaterinstitute.org/article.php/431.html*

Strike, K., & Soltis, J. (1992). *The ethics of teaching.* New York: Teachers College Press.

Strike, K., & Ternasky, P. (1993). *Ethics for professionals in education: Perspectives for preparation and practice.* New York: Teachers College Press.

Stroman v. Colleton County School District, 981 F.2d 152 (4th Cir. 1992).

Thomas, S., Cambron-McCabe, N., & McCarthy, M., & (2009). *Public school law: Teachers' and students' rights* (6th ed.). Boston: Allyn and Bacon.

Tinker v. Des Moines Independent Community School District, 393 U.S. 503 (1969).

U.S. Charter Schools. (2009). *Overview.* Retrieved January 23, 2009 from: *http://www.uscharterschools.org/pub/uscs_docs/o/index.htm*

U.S. Equal Employment Opportunity Commission. (2009). Sexual harassment. Retrieved January 23, 2009 from *http://www.eeoc.gov/types/sexual_harassment.html*

Wagner, P. (1996). *Understanding professional ethics.* Bloomington, IN: Phi Delta Kappa Educational Foundation.

Zeise, A. (2005). *California educational code for homeschooling.* Retrieved September 1, 2005 from: *http://homeschooling.gomilpitas.com/laws/blCA.htm*

Zelman v. Simmons-Harris, No. 00-1751 (2002).

chapter 14

School Governance and Finance

The rules and regulations that impact how schools operate and are funded come from local, state, and federal sources. Knowing how schools are governed and financed will help you be more effective in your future classroom. In this chapter, three organizing questions will be used to strengthen your understanding of school governance and finance.

Focus Questions

1. Who sets school directions?

2. What other groups shape educational policies?

3. What sources of funds exist for education?

Courtesy of Anthony Magnacca/Merrill Education.

Katy Carmichael has just returned to her second-grade-classroom following a meeting with her school principal. Katy requested new curriculum materials on behalf of the primary teaching team in her school to help students learn mathematics. The Montessori manipulative materials the team wants to purchase are considered by many early childhood educators to be some of the finest available to help students visualize and understand mathematical concepts. Katy and her teaching team feel they would be well worth the nearly $1000 price tag that comes with their purchase. Her principal has explained, however, that because of the cost, this decision would need to first be reviewed by the school curriculum committee. This group consists of three teachers, the principal, and two parents. If approved by the curriculum committee, the local school board could then be approached for final endorsement prior to purchase. Katy has been asked to write a clear rationale for the purchase of these mathematics materials and include examples of how they would be used in the classroom. If the school board is unwilling or unable to fund these materials, the principal has also indicated that another option for funding could be to write a small grant proposal to a regional business that supports educational efforts in mathematics and science.

Katy's request for new materials highlights why it is important for you to understand how schools are run and financed. In many practical ways, a working knowledge of these aspects of schooling helps you be more effective in your future classroom. By knowing how decisions are made, teachers can take the steps needed to discuss issues of importance with appropriate governing bodies. An understanding of financial matters helps teachers find funding sources for the innovative ideas they want to implement. So, what may at first appear to be merely an academic exercise becomes important information for conducting business within the schools.

Who sets school directions?

Decisions about how schools operate and are funded are all a part of what is called school **governance.** Schools are governed by a complex array of local, state, and federal laws, regulations, and agencies. At each level, there are numerous people who individually and collectively help determine the directions taken by schools. Although every district and state is somewhat different, the information shared here should help you develop a much clearer understanding of the people and organizations that will influence the schools in which you teach.

Local Control

In the public schools, most of the day-to-day decision making that occurs regarding such things as curriculum, instruction, financial expenditures, and personnel issues is done at the local school district level. The specific nuts-and-bolts decisions about textbooks to use, curriculum packages to adopt, money to spend, and teachers to hire are ultimately made by the local school board. But other groups, including parents and community members, teachers, and administrators, all have a significant impact on the decisions made. Figure 14.1 summarizes the relationships that exist in local school district governance.

Reflection Opportunity 14.1

Parents and community members. Before reading about the role of parents and community members in local school district governance, think through the following questions about your own schooling experiences. Do you remember parents and/or community members who publicly stated their views about teachers and schools? Your own parents or relatives may be helpful in remembering people and situations. What were the issues that these parents and/or community members raised and how did they share their views with others? Do you remember how the schools responded to the positive and negative issues that were presented? Did parents and community members actually have an impact on teachers and schools? What specific examples come to mind?

Although parents and community members as individuals typically have no legal authority in school governance, they have had a significant, and growing, influence on educational decisions. One option open to parents and community members is participation in any of the organizations that exist to support and influence educational efforts. For example, parents who have children in band and orchestra programs may form a booster club to engage in fund-raising activities. Monies generated from these efforts can then be used to buy new uniforms and pay for travel to performances in the region. Parents and community members also influence educational decisions as they participate in special projects related to the schools. Some examples of this type include volunteering to serve on a curriculum review board for an individual school or the entire school district, being elected to the school board, lobbying the school board for the inclusion or deletion of books and curriculum materials used in the schools, supporting or speaking out against local taxes used to support school activities, and engaging in discussions with others about the importance of quality schools. The *Explore Your Beliefs* feature for this chapter provides further opportunities for you to think about the role of communities in America's schools. Take some time now to read and reflect on the issues presented there.

Figure 14.1 Local School District Governance

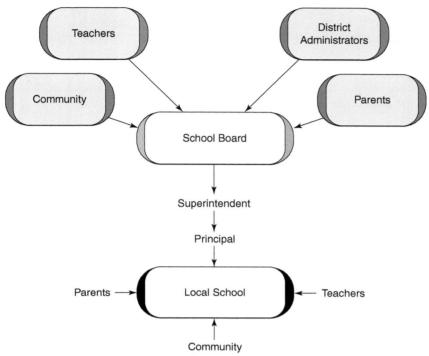

In an effort to improve teaching and learning, schools are taking a hard look at different ways in which they can bring about positive change. One option that is growing in popularity is to build partnerships with community groups.

Recognizing that there is no single solution to school improvement, many schools increasingly rely on collaborative efforts. Relationships with local businesses, universities, medical and religious centers, foundations, and other community-based organizations help enhance both academic and nonacademic skills for schoolchildren.

The challenge is ensuring that teachers, neighbors, parents, and guardians are working together to set and reinforce consistent messages and standards for children. This delicate interchange between schools and communities, experts agree, must be strengthened. Only by working together can these lifelong partnerships hope to salvage young lives and fulfill education's promise of literacy and opportunity.

One example of this growing connection between schools and local communities comes from New Orleans, where newly certified teachers are being offered signing bonuses to teach there. Local businesses are helping by donating money to help pay for these incentives (Hoff, 2002). The Hillsboro, Oregon, schools have made different, but equally valuable, connections with their community to help immigrant families from Mexico transition to life in America (Zehr, 2002). School district personnel help guide students and their families to community resources that provide food, shelter, medical care, and other necessities so that basic needs can be met.

Developing the Habit of Reflective Practice

Gather Information

1. Explore this topic further by going to http://www.ncrel.org/sdrs/areas/pa0cont.htm

Identify Beliefs

1. Do you see community involvement as an important direction for schools? What do you see as the potential benefits and limitations?

Make Decisions

1. Can you see yourself working as a teacher to involve your local community in the activities of your classroom and/or school? Why or why not?

Assess and Evaluate

1. Are there special skills you would need to develop to be successful in involving the community in your class or school?

Teachers' roles. Traditionally, teachers in the United States have been involved in making important decisions that affect schooling at the local level in a variety of ways. For example, Dianne VanderVelde is a high school mathematics teacher who is currently serving on a special task force to identify a textbook series to be used for the teaching of mathematics. Along with three other teachers, two administrators, two parents, and a school board member, she is making an important decision that will influence both teachers and students within the district. Other options for teacher involvement in governance activities have included such things as serving on school or district-wide committees, participating on search committees to select school administrators, working individually or collectively to influence the decisions made by local school boards, and getting involved in union activities to have an impact on the salaries and working conditions for all teachers. In addition, teachers clearly have a very significant role to play in determining the curriculum and instructional methods used in their own classrooms. The *Views From the Classroom* feature for this chapter looks at another factor that influences decision making in classrooms. Go to the Companion Website for this text and read about the male minority in public school classrooms and reflect on the questions posed.

Views from the Classroom: Male Minority

More recently, teachers have been participating in a relatively new approach to school governance called **site-based management.** In close collaboration with the school principal, parents, and community members, teachers are actively engaging in making many of the decisions that were formerly the responsibility of district administrators and school boards. Rather than using the older top-down model, site-based management teams engage in shared decision making that is seen by many as being a more effective approach (Archer, 2005). Using this approach, teachers and administrators at individual schools "pick their own reading programs and their own staff training. They decide how many people to employ, and in what jobs. If they don't like services the district's central office is offering, they can take their money elsewhere" (Archer, 2005, p. 33). In a school using site-based management, teachers have a much higher level of control over decisions that directly impact teaching and learning.

Reflection Opportunity 14.2

Reflect on your future role in school governance. How do you think you would feel about working in a school that used site-based management? If you are in a more traditional school governance situation, do you think you will be willing to do your part in influencing the directions of education in your school and district? Do you see yourself as a person who will be willing to serve on committees, speak out to parents and others, and attend school board meetings for the purpose of influencing decisions being made? Describe your feelings about assuming these roles. How important are these roles to you as a future teacher?

Administrator roles. The role of the school **principal,** who serves as the head administrator in an individual school, has changed dramatically over the years. From a part-time job assumed along with other teaching duties, the principalship has evolved into a complex mix of administrative and instructional leadership tasks (Sergiovanni, 2009). Today's principals have primary responsibility for managing all of the day-to-day operations of their schools. Meetings with parents, teachers, and district administrators, paperwork, student discipline, and facilities maintenance are some of the many management tasks they face on a daily basis. To watch a speech of a principal describing the nature of the job, go to the Companion Website for this text and click on MyEducationLab for Chapter 14.

myeducationlab)
The Power of Classroom Practice

MyEducationLab 14.1

Despite the obvious importance of these administrative tasks, more and more educators are looking to the school principal as an instructional leader as well (Fink & Resnick, 2001). Principals are being asked to spend time in classrooms helping teachers identify areas of strength and those that need improvement, determining and implementing effective assessment strategies, assisting with the selection of curriculum materials, and taking leadership in the development of a school-wide management and discipline program. The use of site-based management further complicates these tasks as principals work to involve teachers, parents, and community members in meaningful decision making within their schools.

Some researchers, as well as principals themselves, are suggesting that current principal-preparation programs at colleges and universities are not adequately preparing their students for the challenging roles they will face (Hess & Kelly, 2005). They suggest that principals need more and better preparation in:

- *Using data for decision making*—Principals are often overwhelmed by the amount of data on teaching and learning they must understand and use. They need to be better prepared to critically use these data.

- *Recruiting, hiring, and evaluating school personnel*—Because teachers are the single most important ingredient in school success, principals must have strong skills in recruiting, hiring, and evaluating.

- *Working with people and organizations outside the school*—Schools are part of the larger community that they serve. Principals need to have skills in building strong relationships with organizations and people in the community.

- *Understanding new trends and directions in education*—As districts consider new options such as becoming a charter school (see Chapter 4), principals need to understand the educational implications of these trends and be prepared to assist the district in making decisions about them (Hess & Kelly, 2005).

Reflect on the role of the school principal. Do you remember any principals from your schooling experiences that either positively or negatively influenced teaching and learning for you and others? Based on your own experiences and what you have read here, what skills are needed to be an effective principal? As you think about your future career in education, can you see yourself being a principal some day? Why or why not? What skills do you think you have (or perhaps don't have) that would either make you a good (or not so good) candidate for this position?

**Reflection
Opportunity 14.3**

Although being a principal is a complex administrative assignment, it is still less taxing than the position of **superintendent of schools.** The superintendent serves as chief executive officer of the school system and must manage a complex array of planning, staffing, budgeting, evaluating, and reporting tasks. Imagine for a moment a relatively small school district that consists of seven elementary schools, two middle schools, an alternative high school, and a traditional high school. The superintendent in this setting is responsible for the education of more than 4,000 students and serves as instructional leader for approximately 350 teachers and paraprofessionals. He or she oversees the efforts of as many as 12 principals, a custodial and maintenance staff of more than 50, and dozens of secretarial employees. Acting on behalf of the school board, the superintendent is responsible for the hiring and firing of faculty and staff, maintaining school buildings and equipment, managing the school district budget, and making decisions about curriculum and instruction.

Because of the complexities of administering an entire school district, one of the issues facing school boards as they seek to recruit and retain top administrators is how to provide competitive salaries and compensation for these individuals in times of very tight budgets. In the very largest and most complex school districts, salary and compensation packages of up to $500,000 have been offered (Glass, 2005). The national average for school superintendent salaries is just over $125,000 and a substantial commitment of school district resources (American Association of School Administrators, 2009).

In addition to the financial challenges of recruiting top candidates to serve as superintendents, it is difficult to find diverse candidates to take on these roles. School districts are trying a variety of innovative strategies to strengthen the diversity of this position. The *Reflect on Diversity* feature for this chapter describes one such approach taken by the Seattle Public Schools. Spend some time thinking about the issues presented in this feature now before moving on in your reading.

Reflect on diversity: Superintendents lack diversity

The lack of diversity among school superintendents across our nation is alarming. While education is a field with a large percentage of women, they account for only twelve percent of superintendents nationwide. Even more disturbing is the lack of minorities in superintendent positions; ninety-six percent of all superintendents are white (Manuel and Slate, 2003).

If school districts want to attract a more diverse applicant pool to superintendent openings, they may want to consider the approach taken by the Seattle Public Schools. In 1995, Seattle recruited African American John Stanford to be their new superintendent. He became one of only a few big-district superintendents without a background in education. In 1991, he had retired as a two-star general from the U.S. Army after 30 years of service. Prior to joining Seattle's public school system, he served as a county manager in Fulton County, Georgia.

It didn't take him long to make big changes in Seattle. On his first day as superintendent, he required central-office staff to spend one day a week helping in the schools. He went on to make numerous practical changes such as providing more places for parents to register their children for school, helping to make the district more accessible to families. He also gave principals more control of their school buildings. Sadly, Stanford only worked 3 years for the Seattle schools before losing a battle to leukemia in 1998. Thousands of Seattle teachers, parents, children and community leaders attended his televised memorial service. President Clinton released a statement commemorating the former general's service both in the Army and as superintendent of Seattle Public Schools:

> *"He streamlined and reinvigorated Seattle's schools, inspiring his students to strive for excellence, and an entire community to believe once again in their public schools."*

As a non-educator, he applied a business model to the bureaucracy of public schools. He was the two-star Army general who absolutely cared about children. "Love 'em and lead 'em" was his personal motto—and he did.

Developing the Habit of Reflective Practice
Gather Information

1. Survey 10 people to find out about the diversity of principals and superintendents in their schooling experience. What are your findings?

Identify Beliefs

1. Do you think it really matters that the majority of school superintendents are white men? Why or why not?

2. Should the number of women superintendents be proportional to the number of women teachers? Why or why not?

Make Decisions

1. If you were on a superintendent hiring committee for your local school district, would you consider looking at candidates who have no experience in education? Give a rationale for your decision.

Assess and Evaluate

1. If you served on a committee of educators for a school district and your mission was to recruit minority teachers within your district to go into administration, what characteristics would you look for in these educators?

Sources

Manuel, M., & Slate, J. (2003). Advancing women in leadership: Hispanic female superintendents in America. *Advancing Women in Leadership Journal*. Fall. Retrieved September 27, 2005 from *http://www.advancingwomen.com/awl/winter2003/MANUEL~1.html*

Seattle Times. (2000). Tribute to John Stanford, Retrieved February 5, 2009 from *http://seattletimes.nwsource.com/special/stanford/*

School board roles. Each state has provisions in its statutes for the selection of community members to serve on **school boards** for local districts. In some states, board membership is determined through public election; other states have an appointment system. School board members come from diverse professional backgrounds and typically have little or no training in the field of education. In fact, the only qualification board members must generally meet in order to serve is that they live within the school district.

Regardless of their public-school knowledge, local school board members have the legal authority to determine educational policy within their districts. Acting on behalf of the community they represent, school board members assume ultimate responsibility for the education of students within the district. This commitment to placing community members in roles of authority regarding all aspects of local educational programming is unique to the American educational system (Lunenburg & Ornstein, 2008). One way in which school boards directly influence educational policy is through their role in selecting textbooks for the schools. To read more about effective textbook selection, go to the Companion Website for this text and click on MyEducationLab for Chapter 14.

myeducationlab
The Power of Classroom Practice

MyEducationLab 14.2

State Authority

Although local school districts make most of the practical decisions that impact teaching and learning within classrooms, states are responsible for enacting the laws and regulations that determine the framework for them. The 10th Amendment to the U.S. Constitution empowers the states to take responsibility for education and each state has responded by creating extensive legal requirements and state agencies to assist with their implementation. Figure 14.2 provides a visual summary of these state agencies and legal organizations influencing local schools.

In recent years, states have increasingly used their "policy muscle" to influence the directions taken by local school districts. As states have increased their share of financial support for K–12 education, there has been a corresponding interest on the part of state governments to make sure that this money is well spent (National Conference of State Legislatures, 2005). Cathy Fernandez, Principal Analyst for the Legislative Finance Committee in New Mexico puts it this way: "the Legislature in New Mexico plays a significant role in public education, especially in terms of funding. They have become increasingly concerned with accountability in education. Putting more

Figure 14.2 State Governance of Schools

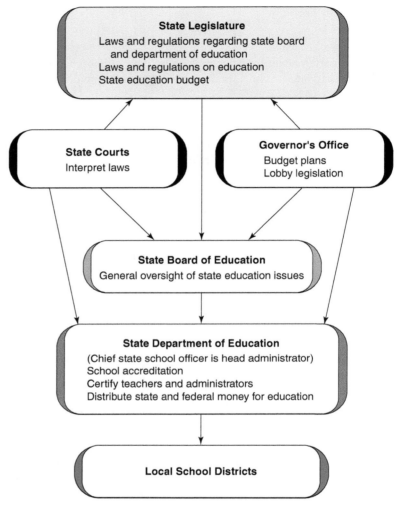

resources towards making our public schools better is not really the issue, but rather what are the citizens getting for the money" (National Conference of State Legislatures, 2009, p. 1).

The following are examples of ways in which states have increased their involvement in the decision making of local schools (Education Week, 2008; National Conference of State Legislatures, 2009):

- *Statewide academic standards.* All fifty states now have statewide academic standards that all schools are expected to meet. Although these standards have been in place in most states for several years, they are now being taken far more seriously due to the mandated testing that frequently accompanies them.

- *Mandated testing.* In all states, the academic standards are aligned with mandated tests that schools are expected to administer. Typically, this is done at the 4th-, 8th-, and 12th-grade levels. Scores on these tests are carefully reviewed by the state, and pressure is being placed on schools to be more accountable for the academic success of their students.

- *School performance.* Thirty-nine states provide assistance to schools that are performing below expectations. Thirty-five provide rewards to those schools who are high performing.

- *Increased regulation.* Virtually every state has greatly expanded the laws and regulations that impact public education. From the 1960s to the present, these regulations have increased from a relatively simple document to several volumes. States are now seen as regulating virtually every aspect of schooling.

The *Ian's Classroom Experiences* feature for this chapter (found on the Companion Website for this text) talks about the relevance of state academic standards. You may want to read it now to learn more.

Ian's Classroom Experiences: Asset Management

State board of education. There are five governmental agencies within states that have a major impact on schools. The first of these is called the **state board of education.** Legislatures grant to state boards of education the authority to engage in general oversight of schools. Every state but Wisconsin has a board of education (Lunenburg & Ornstein, 2008). They are considered the highest-level education agency within each state. In most instances, it is the governor's responsibility to appoint members to the board of education. In many respects, the state board of education operates with similar personnel and in much the same way as local school boards. Lay leaders who have agreed to serve on the state board commit time on a regular basis to meeting, discussing broad issues influencing state public education, and engaging in policy-making activities that impact the schools. Because of the voluntary nature of service on state boards of education, members tend to be older and have the time that it takes to commit to regular meetings during normal working hours.

One common function of the state board of education is the selection of the **chief state school officer.** Sometimes called the state superintendent or commissioner of education, the chief state school officer usually serves both as head of the state board of education and as chief executive of the state department of education (discussed below). This full-time position is funded by the individual states and usually is assumed by a professional educator. In some states, the chief state school officer is an elected position.

State department of education. Although state boards of education are made up of fairly small groups of part-time volunteers, the **state department of education** is a large state agency that consists of numerous full-time staff operating under the direction of the chief state school officer. Although state departments of education generally report to the state board of education, the former tends to be the most influential of the two groups. The full-time nature of the staff, combined with generally better connections to the governor's office and the legislative branches of state government, make state departments of education a powerful player in relation to state education issues. Figure 14.3 shows the key staff and offices of one state's department of education.

Traditionally, the main task of the department of education was to collect and share statistics about education within the state. As states increased the level of regulation over schools, however, departments of education grew in both size and authority. They now typically engage in the following functions:

1. Deciding on school accreditation
2. Certifying teachers
3. Distributing state funds for education
4. Dealing with student transportation and safety issues
5. Checking to make sure state regulations are implemented
6. Engaging in research and program evaluation
7. Overseeing the distribution and proper use of federal funding given to local school districts (Lunenburg & Ornstein, 2008). Have you taken the time to browse your state's department of education website? Doing so would help you better understand the complexities and impact of this important state agency.

Figure 14.3 Key Staff and Offices, California Department of Education

State Superintendent of Public Instruction and Director of Education

Chief Deputy Superintendent

Offices

Assessment & Accountability	School & District Operations
Communications	Child Development
Finance, Technology & Admin	Charter Schools
Data Management	Curriculum Frameworks & Instructional Resources
Fiscal & Administrative Services	Fiscal Policy
Government Affairs	Nutrition Services
Policy Development & External Affairs	Learning Support & Partnerships
Personnel Services	Legal & Audits
School Fiscal Services	Legislative Affairs
Standards and Assessment	School Facilities
Technology Services	Professional Development & Curriculum Support
Accountability & Improvement	State Special Schools
Special Education	Secondary, Postsecondary & Adult Leadership
Curriculum & Instruction	

Source: Retrieved January 28, 2009, from *http://www.cde.ca.gov/re/di/or/*.

State government. Three other groups with considerable influence over educational issues are all housed within the state government itself. To varying degrees, the governor, branches of the legislature, and the state court system are involved in setting directions for public school education. Due to either their visibility within the state, the passing of regulations regarding schooling, or by interpreting the legal requirements affecting education, each has an impact on teaching and learning (National Council of State Legislatures, 2009).

Although the actual influence of state governors varies depending on their interest in and commitment to education, their potential impact is great. For example, in many states the governor appoints both the chief state school officer and members of the state board of education. Governors also are responsible for making budget recommendations to their legislatures on issues such as teacher salaries and overall state funding for education. There are considerable funding disparities across states, based in large part on the leadership and efforts expended by governors and state legislatures. For example, while latest figures indicate that the U.S. average spending per student

Chapter 14   School Governance and Finance   415

is $9,963, Arizona spends just $7,112 and Vermont expends over $15,000 (Education Week, 2009). In addition to their influence on education budgets, governors can often successfully lobby for or against laws being considered that have an impact on public education. They may also choose to use their veto powers to strike down other measures that may adversely affect education. Furthermore, governors can use their public offices to champion education causes. Their support of a specific issue can often influence the thoughts and actions of the general public. Do you know your state governor's level of support for education? What has he or she done to demonstrate a commitment to schools?

State legislatures are given the power to pass laws and regulations that have a far-reaching impact on the schools. These laws commonly fall into three broad categories (Lunenburg & Ornstein, 2008):

- *Issues impacting state education agencies.* For example, legislatures usually are responsible for laws that determine such things as how chief state school officers and state boards of education are selected, others that address the organization and responsibilities of the state department of education, and laws that define the types of local and regional school districts that will exist within the state.

- *Issues related to the financing of public education.* Legislatures determine the annual amount of financial support the state will provide to fund such things as teacher salaries and benefits, district administration, and school building maintenance and construction. In many cases, they also pass laws and provide guidelines that assist cities and counties in raising additional money to support local schools.

- *Issues with broad educational impact.* The length of compulsory education within the state, the general content of the curriculum, the length of the school year, and standards for the construction of school buildings are examples of this type.

Two examples of actions taken by state legislatures should help you see the strong influence these bodies have on teaching and learning. One example of legislative influences on school financing comes from the state of California (Johnston, 2005). A series of laws signed by governor Arnold Swarzenegger in September 2005 require greater financial accountability from schools. In one instance, the law requires school districts to report the salaries paid to staff at individual schools rather than giving out averages of district-wide salaries. Supporters of the new law say that this will make it easier to locate disparities in teacher salaries between schools. A second example of state law and its impact on schools comes from Texas. In 1999, the state passed legislation referred to as the Student Success Initiative (Texas Education Agency, 2008). This legislative action had a significant impact on student testing, creating requirements for passage of the state-mandated reading test during students' third-grade year and both the reading and mathematics tests at Grade 5. The law makes it clear that "a student may advance to the next grade level only by passing these tests or by unanimous decision of his or her grade placement committee" (Texas Education Agency, 2008, p. 1). The Student Success Initiative places heavy responsibility on the schools to make sure that students receive the instruction and support they need to pass the tests and move on to the next grade level.

The laws passed by state legislatures, while making every attempt to be clear and detailed, are open to interpretation by a variety of people. Parents, teachers, schools, and communities often differ in their understandings of the laws relating to education. When various opinions come into conflict, the state court system becomes the arbitrator and assists schools and others in clarifying the actual intent of the laws passed by legislatures. There is no one uniform organization to state court systems across the nation. Typically, however, there are three levels (Drake & Roe, 2003). The first is usually referred to as the **municipal** or **superior court.** Most medium-sized cities have municipal/superior courts and they serve as the initial arbitrator in settling disputes regarding

Engage in the debate: The No Child Left Behind Act

On January 8, 2002, President Bush signed a piece of federal legislation called the "No Child Left Behind Act" (often referred to as NCLB or "nickel-b"). This act is designed to help low-income and minority students perform at the same achievement levels as their peers. The law requires states and school districts to test students annually to assess their academic skills in grades 3 through 8. This powerful piece of legislation couples requirements for testing with a push for higher teacher qualifications and strict sanctions when schools fail to improve test scores for all students.

While no one questions the intent of the No Child Left Behind legislation, many argue with its methods. Alfie Kohn (2004), one of the law's most outspoken critics states:

> NCLB is not a step in the right direction. It is a deeply damaging, mostly ill-intentioned law, and no one genuinely committed to improving public schools (or to advancing the interests of those who have suffered from decades of neglect and oppression) would want to have anything to do with it (p. 576).

The Center on Education Policy (Jennings, 2002), while fully supporting the intent of the No Child Left Behind legislation, describes other potential challenges:

> It is not enough, however, for federal policymakers to simply insist that educators be held accountable and that states and local districts take stronger actions. If the president and the Congress truly expect all students to learn more, all teachers to teach better, and all schools to provide a high-quality education, then all levels of government—including the federal government—must deliver much more. School districts, states, and the federal government must provide additional funding and other meaningful assistance to improve classroom instruction and raise academic achievement. (p. 8)

Developing the Habit of Reflective Practice

Gather Information

1. Do an Internet search for Alfie Kohn and read more about his thoughts on NCLB.
2. Search for The Center on Education Policy and read a more positive view on NCLB.

Identify Beliefs

1. Should teachers be striving to leave no child behind? Is it possible to achieve this goal?

Make Decisions

1. As a future educator, how might NCLB positively influence your teaching? What may be some negative consequences?

Assess and Evaluate

1. What are the strengths and weaknesses of this act?

Sources

Jennings, J. (2002). New leadership for new standards. *The State Education Standard, 3*(2), 7–18. Retrieved April 28, 2003, from *http://www.ctredpol.org/standardsbasededucationreform/stricter federaldemandsbiggerstaterolejune2002.pdf*

Kohn, A. (2004). Test today, privatize tomorrow. *Phi Delta Kappan, 85,* 568–577.

The federal courts are another aspect of American government to strongly influence schooling. This system consists of three main divisions: district courts, courts of appeal, and the Supreme Court (Drake & Roe, 2003). These courts, particularly the U.S. Supreme Court, have had a major impact on the directions of K–12 education. They have repeatedly heard and ruled on a variety of significant issues. Their most influential decisions may well be in the area of protecting teachers and students from too much governmental intervention. A variety of civil rights suits have been reviewed over the years on topics such as the states' authority to compel public school attendance (*Pierce v. Society of Sisters, 1925*), the school's ability to require students to salute the flag (*Minersville School District v. Gobitis, 1940*), teachers' freedom of expression (*Pickering v. Board of Education, 1968*), and students' rights to due process for suspensions and expulsions (*Goss v. Lopez, 1975*). Chapter 13 provides additional information on legal decisions that have had a significant impact on schooling.

The office of president of the United States has also had a strong impact on educational issues as well. For example, Ronald Reagan's two terms in office (1980–1988) saw a scaling back of the government's involvement in education. Federal funding and intervention in the affairs of schools decreased during these years. Other presidents, such as Bill Clinton, have emphasized the importance of excellence in education and provided support for moving toward this goal. George W. Bush, through the *No Child Left Behind Act of 2001* has also had a significant influence on teaching and learning. In addition, his support for school choice and charter schools has been a catalyst for at least a portion of the growth that has occurred with both initiatives (Fuller, 2003). President Barack Obama has pledged to reform the *No Child Left Behind Act,* ensure access to high quality early childhood education programs, and make math and science education a national priority (Obama, 2009). Whether or not you agree with the directions taken by each of these presidents, their impact on your future career has been large.

What other groups shape educational practice?

Although local, state, and federal governmental bodies all have significant roles in educational decision making, other groups also influence what takes place in America's classrooms. Businesses, special interest groups, college and university faculty, and professional education associations provide money, research, and political influence that impact teaching and learning. Table 14.1 summarizes their influence.

Business Organizations

Businesses have been involved in supporting schools since the late 1800s, with more formalized partnerships in existence since the 1970s (Lankard, 1995). The demand for educational reform that began in the 1980s coupled with the need for highly skilled workers entering the workforce led to increased numbers of business/education partnerships. Traditionally, businesses provided such things as grant money for innovative school projects, materials and up-to-date equipment

TABLE 14.1 Other Groups Shaping Educational Policies

Group	Description
Business	The need for highly skilled workers entering the workforce has led to increased numbers of business/education partnerships.
Special-Interest Groups	These organizations have an interest in education and work to influence its direction both locally and nationally.
College and University Faculty	College and university faculty associated with teacher education programs shape the profession through their roles in the preparation of future teachers.
Professional Education Associations	Professional education organizations both lobby for better schooling and also help identify best practices for the profession.

for teaching, and scholarships for students with high academic performance. More recently, businesses also expect to be more directly involved in school reform efforts to make sure that their goals are being addressed. For example, the Microsoft Corporation's Unlimited Potential Program has as its mission "to enable sustained social and economic opportunity for those at the middle and bottom of the world's economic pyramid." The program plans to do this by "transforming education, fostering local innovation, and enabling jobs and opportunities" (Microsoft Corporation, 2009).

Reflection Opportunity 14.4

Reflect on the impact of businesses and corporations on schooling. Do you remember businesses that gave either money or equipment to the schools you attended? What did they give and what influence did this giving have on the effectiveness of your schooling? As you reflect on the role of businesses today in supporting education, what do you see as both the strengths and problems associated with this involvement? Do you think businesses should be more or less involved in supporting schools? Why do you feel this way?

Special-Interest Groups

Special-interest groups are organizations that have a common interest and work collectively to influence the directions of education locally and nationally. These can be as informal as a group of parents working together to raise money for playground equipment or lobbying the local school board regarding specific curriculum materials. Special-interest groups can also be national organizations that have greater resources and a broader influence on the direction of education in America. One example of a national special-interest group is the National Alliance of Black School Educators (NABSE, 2009). The NABSE, founded in 1970 by Dr. Charles Moody and other prominent Black educators, was established to improve the achievement levels of African American youth. The group promotes professional development programs that are designed to enhance the skills of school staff in working with African American students, serves as a forum for the exchange of successful ideas and strategies on diversity topics, and advocates for policies that impact quality education in our schools.

Another example of a special-interest group is the Autism Society of America. At the national level this organization has been actively engaged in advocacy efforts for people with autism and their families:

> The Autism Society of America (ASA) is the leading voice and resource of the entire autism community in education, advocacy, services, research and support. The ASA is committed to meaningful participation and self-determination in all aspects of life for individuals on the autism spectrum and their families. ASA accomplishes its ongoing mission through close collaboration with a successful network of chapters, members and supporters (Autism Society of America, 2009, p.1).

College and University Faculty

College and university faculty in teacher-education programs are another group that influences activities in the public schools in many ways. Perhaps the most significant of these is their role in the preparation of future teachers. Most college professors who instruct teacher-education students have completed a doctoral degree in a discipline related to education and have had experience teaching in public or private schools. The Association of Teacher Educators (ATE), a national professional organization that addresses all aspects of teacher preparation, has identified standards that college and university faculty should meet in order to successfully prepare new teachers. They include

1. Modeling excellent teaching in their instruction of college students
2. Engaging in scholarly activity that is related to teaching or learning
3. Reflecting on their teaching and demonstrating a commitment to lifelong learning
4. Providing leadership in the development of quality teacher-education programs

5. Collaborating in significant ways with the public schools and others in education-related positions

6. Advocating for high-quality education for all students (Association for Teacher Educators, 2009).

Professional Education Associations

A large number of **professional education associations** influence the activities that take place in the K–12 schools. These organizations can be loosely categorized into two broad groups (see Chapter 5 for more information): (1) national teachers' unions (for example, the National Education Association and the American Federation of Teachers) and (2) specialty organizations that address specific aspects of teaching and learning (such as the International Reading Association). The teachers' unions have had a significant impact on education at all levels. At the local level, for example, these organizations often serve as bargaining agents for such things as teacher salaries and benefits, special contracts for additional services (such as driver's education and coaching), and teacher workshop days. Teachers' unions also offer workshops for teachers on current issues at state and national meetings and develop publications on current topics in education (Arizona Education Association, 2009).

Specialty organizations also influence the directions of teaching in many ways. For example, art educators often participate in the National Art Education Association (NAEA), which publishes a long list of pamphlets and books on topics related to art education. A sampling includes books titled *Creating Curriculum in Art, Aesthetics for Young People, The Visual Arts and Early Childhood Learning,* and *Student Behavior in Art Classrooms: The Dynamics of Discipline* (National Art Education Association, 2009). In addition to an annual conference in which art educators learn more about recent issues in their field, 29 states have organizations affiliated with the NAEA and also conduct state meetings on topics of interest to their members. Other examples of important specialty organizations include:

- *National Board for Professional Teaching Standards (NBPTS)*—This organization has developed a set of standards for what accomplished teachers should know and be able to do (National Board for Professional Teaching Standards, 2009). The organization also implemented a rigorous process for national teacher certification that has helped identify a new nation-wide cadre of experienced teachers who have demonstrated their high levels of competence through the creation of an extensive portfolio.

- *Council of Chief State School Officers (CCSSO)*—Bringing together the chief state school officers in each state, "(t)he Council seeks member consensus on major educational issues and expresses their views to civic and professional organizations, federal agencies, Congress, and the public" (Council of Chief State School Officers, 2009). CCSSO was instrumental in the development of the INTASC standards, which are widely used by colleges and universities as benchmarks for what beginning teachers should know and be able to do (see Chapter 1 for more information).

- *National Council for the Accreditation of Teacher Education (NCATE)*—NCATE is the primary national accrediting agency for teacher-education programs throughout the United States. Their goal is to help ensure quality preparation programs for all teachers through an extensive review process (National Council for the Accreditation of Teacher Education, 2009).

What sources of funds exist for education?

The three primary sources of money used to support public education are local, state, and federal funds. Table 14.2 provides a summary of trends since the early 20th century in local, state, and federal funding. Until fairly recently, property taxes assessed at the local level were used to

TABLE 14.2 Financial Support for K–12 Education

School Year	Federal	State	Local
1919–1920	0.3%	16.5%	83.2%
1941–1942	1.4%	31.4%	67.1%
1951–1952	3.5%	38.6%	57.9%
1961–1962	4.3%	38.7%	56.9%
1971–1972	8.9%	38.3%	52.8%
1981–1982	7.4%	47.6%	45.0%
1991–1992	6.6%	46.4%	47.0%
1997–1998	6.8%	48.4%	44.8%
2000–2001	7.3%	49.7%	43.1%
2004–2005	9.2%	46.9%	44%

Source: National Center for Education Statistics. (2007). *Digest of Education Statistics.* Washington, DC: Government Printing Office.

pay the major portion of these expenses. Currently, however, state funds provide the largest share at approximately 47%, local sources account for 44%, and federal spending is just over 9% of the total (National Center for Education Statistics, 2007).

Private-School Funding

Before looking at the funding sources for public education in more depth, it is important to remember that a significant number of students attend private schools in America, and that this attendance directly impacts funding for public schools. As indicated in Chapter 4, approximately 10% of all school-aged children, roughly 5 million students, are currently enrolled in private schools (National Center for Education Statistics, 2007). Most of the funds used to support these students' educational expenses come from the tuition fees paid by their parents. If they were enrolled in local schools that were publicly funded, the increased expenses for school districts would be significant. State and local revenues would need to be increased in order to maintain the levels of service currently provided to public school students.

State and Local Support

As mentioned earlier, the primary source of funding for schools at the local level comes from property taxes. In most instances, these taxes are collected based on the value of the real estate within the school district. All property holders are assessed an annual tax based on the value of the land and buildings they own. So, for example, the elderly couple next door, the couple across the street who have chosen to forego children, and the family with three school-aged children are all homeowners who are assessed an annual tax based on the values of their homes and land as determined by a local assessor. It is quite possible that these homeowners would have differing opinions about using property taxes as a significant source of funding for local schools.

Reflect on each of the families mentioned above. How do you think the childless couple would feel about paying a significant portion of their property taxes for schooling? What attitude would be most likely from the elderly couple, especially if they are living on a small fixed income? Would you expect the parents with three school-aged children to support the use of property

Reflection Opportunity 14.5

taxes for schooling? What other factors besides having school-aged children may determine homeowners' attitudes toward funding schooling through property taxes?

Property taxes have been criticized for creating inequities in school funding. A school located in a low-income area could potentially receive far less tax revenue than a similar sized school in a well-to-do neighborhood. These disparities in funding tend to accentuate the differences that already exist between low-income families and others in the community (Kozol, 2005). With fewer resources, poorer schools tend to have students who score lower on standardized tests of achievement and who take fewer higher level courses in subjects such as mathematics, science, and English. These students are more likely than their more advantaged peers to perpetuate the cycle of poverty by opting out of school at an early age and taking employment in low-paying jobs (Greenwald, Hedges, & Laine, 1996).

Although local support for schools comes primarily from property taxes, state assistance tends to be from either sales taxes on goods and services or a state income tax. In the former situation, when a state resident buys a new shirt or an upgraded computer, he or she pays a sales tax that is used to support a variety of state programs, including the public schools. States that have income taxes typically assess residents a tax based on their adjusted gross income from federal income tax forms, with a portion of that money being used to support the public schools. In some states, residents pay both a sales tax on goods and services and a state tax on their annual income.

Federal Funding

As indicated earlier, the level of federal support for public education is rather small. With just over 9% of the total currently coming from this source, it would appear that the federal government has a minimal impact on the funding for public education. In reality, however, the tight budgeting situations faced by most school districts have made even these relatively small amounts of money a necessity. These funds are used to implement a variety of valuable programs promoted by the federal government. For example, the federal government budgeted $401 million in 2002 to support bilingual education programs (National Center for Education Statistics, 2003). Another example of this type is the commitment of the federal government to support vocational and adult education financially. In 2002, approximately $1.8 billion (approximately 10% of total program costs) was provided by the federal government (National Center for Education Statistics, 2003).

Recent Funding Options

Despite the acknowledged importance of educating America's youth, many citizens have begun to rebel against traditional forms of support for public education. By rejecting efforts by states and local districts to increase taxes and speaking through the power of their votes to elect politicians who promise lower levels of taxation, the American public has made it more difficult to raise the money necessary to fund education. In response to this shrinking pool of traditional support, a variety of newer funding options have been tried. Table 14.3 summarizes these newer approaches.

Schools for profit. One recent trend in education funding is the **schools for profit** movement. Beginning in the mid-1990s, states such as Michigan and Pennsylvania have allowed private enterprise to take over schools that are failing academically as a last-ditch effort to improve the teaching and learning in these settings (Borja, 2004; Cook, 2001). These schools for profit, operated by companies known as education management organizations or EMOs, have struggled to be both profitable and academically successful in very difficult situations. One example is the Pulaski-Edison Junior Academy in Chester, Pennsylvania. Rated by the state of Pennsylvania as the lowest-performing school in the lowest-performing district in the state, the academy was taken over by Edison Schools, the largest education management organization in the country. "Edison is banking on its belief that it can turn around the district with its longer class day, structured curriculum, teacher training, enhanced technology, and overall improved school

TABLE 14.3 Recent Funding Options

Option	Description
Schools for Profit	Private enterprise takes over failing schools in a last-ditch effort to improve teaching and learning
Direct Donations	Gifts of money, goods, and services from corporations, foundations, and individuals
School District Foundations	School districts are creating nonprofit foundations to receive gifts from individuals and corporations
Booster Clubs	Parents and interested community members create a club to provide assistance to a single school and focus their energy and fund-raising efforts on a specific aspect of school activity
User Fees	Certain services such as driver education programs, swimming instructions, certain types of school supplies, participation in athletics, and bus use are being paid for in some schools through fees charged to those using the service
Leasing Facilities and Services	Some schools are leasing unused facilities to community organizations or local businesses to generate revenue
Advertising on School Property	Some schools are allowing advertising on school buses, on homework handouts, and on educational television programming broadcast in the schools as a method of fund-raising

atmosphere" (Cook, 2001, p. 10). Although EMOs like Edison have numerous critics, they continue to be a significant option in many states (Edison Schools, 2009).

School district foundations. An increasing number of school districts are creating their own nonprofit **school district foundations** for the purpose of receiving donations from individuals and corporations. Although it is difficult to get reliable figures on numbers, the National School Foundation Association (2009) provides a list of its members by state. Nebraska, for example, has 13 foundations that are members of the national organization. Some examples of school foundations include the Martinez Education Foundation of Martinez, California. Created in 1984 to supplement the dwindling state funding, the foundation has contributed more than $130,000 in 2008 to help support teachers and learning in the district (Martinez Educational Foundation, 2009). The Harlem School District (2009) offers another example of this type. The district, with approximately 7,750 students, is located in Illinois about 90 miles northwest of Chicago. It has created the Harlem Scholarship Foundation to help meet the needs of the district's students. In addition to providing monetary support to schools within the district, the foundation has created a scholarship program to assist needy students in attaining their higher education goals. It has provided over $250,000 in scholarships to students during its existence.

Booster clubs. Another option for school funding that has been available in many districts for some time and is gaining in nationwide popularity is the **booster club.** Typically, these clubs are created to provide assistance to a single school and focus their energy and fund-raising efforts on a specific aspect of school activity. Most commonly, these booster clubs have supported pursuits such as athletics, band, orchestra, chorus, debate, and drama (Addonizio, 1999). Parents and other booster club members contribute money, solicit financial support and equipment donations from community members, and engage in work tasks that enable these important aspects of schooling to operate successfully with less local and state funding.

User fees. In a growing number of circumstances, users of specific school-provided services are being required by local school districts to pay for them. For example, driver education programs, swimming instruction, certain types of school supplies, participation in athletics, and bus use are being supported by user fees in some districts. Both the number and size of fees continues to grow. For example, in Massachusetts user fees grew from $15.2 to $33.8 million between 2002 and 2006 (Massachusetts Department of Education, 2007). While user fees remain a small proportion of over-all school funding, low income families are often hard-hit when they are implemented. As the number of user fees has grown, their legality has been challenged in both state and federal courts (Dayton & McCarthy, 1992). Typically, the courts have looked at relevant state laws to determine the appropriateness of these fees.

Leasing of facilities and services. Some local school boards are also authorizing schools to lease portions of their facilities to community organizations or local businesses as an additional method of generating revenue or providing services for the district. So, for example, an elementary school with unused classroom space could consider leasing that space to a Head Start program to allow for better connections with this early childhood option while generating additional revenue for the district. Or a school might lease space to a counseling service in exchange for a contracted number of hours of free counseling for students. Some schools also lease portions of school services such as food preparation or transportation to private schools and community organizations as another method of generating income (Pijanowski & Monk, 1996).

Advertising on school property. One final option for increasing revenue available to the schools is the use of advertising on school property. A variety of options have been tried, including the sale of advertising on school buses in New York City and space for advertising on homework handouts in California (Pijanowski & Monk, 1996). Undoubtedly the best known example of revenues generated from advertising on school property is the Channel One television broadcasts. Local school districts that contract with Channel One receive free programming and equipment and then have access to daily news broadcasts that include some advertisements.

Molnar, Boninger, Wilkinson, & Fogarty (2008) have identified seven different ways in which advertising reaches into schools across America:

- **Sponsorship of programs and activities**—Corporations are either paying for, or subsidizing school events so that their name can be associated with them. Sporting events, musical programs, and school clubs (such as chess or second language learning) are examples of activities that corporations are supporting. In addition to name recognition, some advertising of corporate products is frequently allowed.

- **Exclusive agreements**—Schools contract with specific corporations to allow sales of goods and services in the school district. For example, in exchange for a percentage of the profits, schools are contracting with either Pepsi-Cola or Coca-Cola for exclusive rights to sell their products in the district.

- **Incentive programs**—Corporations provide money, goods, or services as "rewards" when students, parents, or staff engage in a specific activity. For example, Campbell's Corporation provides equipment to schools in exchange for proofs of purchase from their products.

- **Appropriation of space**—Spaces in schools (such as scoreboards, bulletin boards, walls, and textbooks) are being "sold" to corporations so that they can put their logos or advertising messages in front of students.

- **Sponsored Educational Materials**—Materials supplied by specific corporations that are used as part of schools' educational efforts. Everything from computers to pencils is being donated by corporations for classroom use. Another example would be Hidden Valley (makers of ranch dressings for salads). They make grants to schools to encourage eating fresh vegetables during lunch. Hidden Valley provides a salad bar for students with their corporate dressings in use and clearly advertised.

- **Electronic marketing**—The Channel One television broadcasting mentioned above is the best known example of this type. In exchange for 10 minutes of daily news programming, students also sit through 2 minutes of advertising for a wide range of products.

- **Fundraising**—Schools and commercial companies work together to raise funds for the schools. For example, McDonald's restaurants hold a McTeacher's Night for specific schools where principals and teachers "work" at McDonald's restaurants greeting customers and staffing the registers in exchange for a portion of the sales. Families and school supporters are encouraged to participate.

Although supporters of advertising in the schools point to the many benefits provided, the immersion of schooling in a setting filled with commercialism is a significant concern to many.

Reflect on the issue of commercialization in schools. Do you remember commercialism as a part of your schooling experiences? If so, what impact do you think this had on your personal behavior? On a broader level, what do you see as the potential problems associated with commercial activities in schools? What are the benefits? Do the benefits outweigh the problems, or should we as a nation move away from this funding source for schools?

Before completing the end-of-chapter activities that follow, take some time to respond to the issues presented in the *Consider This* feature found on the Companion Website for this text. It is designed to get you thinking about the degree to which different groups should be involved in school governance. It is particularly important for you to think about the roles of parents and community members in this process. You will have the most direct contact with these groups and your attitudes about their involvement in school governance will help determine the ways in which you interact with them.

Reflection Opportunity 14.6

Consider This: Who Should Govern Schools?

Summary

To help you understand the ways in which American schools are governed and financed, this chapter was organized around three central questions:

Who sets school directions?

A number of different groups influence the governance of public schools:

- At the local level, parents and community members, teachers, administrators, and school boards influence schooling (Praxis II, topic IVb)
- State authority for schools rests with the board of education, department of education, and state government (Praxis II, topic IVb)
- Federal agencies and the three branches of the federal government all influence schooling (Praxis II, topic IVb)

What other groups shape educational practice?

A number of other groups at the local, state, and national levels also influence educational policy:

- Business organizations
- Special-interest groups
- College and university faculty (Praxis II, topic IVb)
- Professional education associations (Praxis II, topic IVb)

What sources of funds exist for education?

There are three primary sources for school funding, with some newer options gaining in popularity:

- Private-school funding
- State and local support (property taxes, state income taxes, and/or sales taxes) (Praxis II, topic IVb)
- Federal funding (Praxis II, topic IVb)
- Recent developments (schools for profit, school district foundations, booster clubs, user fees, leasing of facilities and services, advertising on school property) (Praxis II, topic IVb)

PRAXIS   Test-Preparation Activities

 To review an on-line chapter case study, test your understanding of chapter topics and concepts, and begin preparing for the Praxis II: Principles of Learning and Teaching examination, go to the Praxis Test-Preparation module for this chapter of the Companion Website.

inTASC   Developing the Habit of Reflective Practice

Organizing Questions

Review questions, field-experience opportunities, and activities for building your portfolio are included here for the organizing questions in this chapter.

Who sets school directions?

Review Questions

1. What roles will you play as a future teacher in school governance?
2. In what ways does a state legislature influence schooling in that state?
3. How does the U.S. Supreme Court help determine directions for schooling?

Field Experience

Attend a school board meeting for a local district.

- Who participated in the meeting?
- What topics were addressed?
- Collect an agenda and any handouts distributed.
- Discuss what you learned with your peers.

Building Your Portfolio: *State Education Agencies*

INTASC Standard 10. Take some time to get to know the structure and organization of your state education agencies.

- Browse library and Internet resources to give you a good idea of their make-up.
- Summarize each of the major agencies by developing an organizational flow chart for each.
- Add these documents to your portfolio.

What other groups shape educational policies?

Review Questions

1. In what ways do special-interest groups influence the directions of education?
2. How do teachers' unions impact schooling?

Building Your Portfolio: *Professional Education Organizations*

INTASC Standard 9. Talk to your college instructors or teachers you know about professional education organizations that you might want to join in the future. Once you have identified several possibilities

- Spend some time on the Internet collecting more information on several options.
- Select three professional organizations that you think may be of future interest.
- Write brief summaries of the services offered by each group and include these summaries in your portfolio.

What sources of funds exist for education?

Review Questions

1. How do private schools influence funding needs for public education?
2. What are the two main methods of school funding at the state level?
3. What is the purpose of a school district foundation?

Field Experience

Schedule and conduct an interview with a principal or assistant principal for a school of your choice.

- Talk to this person about school finances.
- What does this administrator see as the major financial needs and resources of the school?
- Which of the newer funding options described in this chapter are being used in this school?

Building Your Portfolio: *Funding for Local Education*

INTASC Standard 9. Seek additional information about property taxes and other local school fund-raising activities for a district of your choice.

- Talk to a financial officer for that district.
- City or county offices may have additional information about taxes and their use.
- Describe your findings in a two- or three-page paper that you include in your portfolio.

Suggested Readings

Kozol, J. (2005). *The shame of a nation: The restoration of apartheid schooling in America.* New York: Crown Publishers. Read the chapters in this text that deal with the inequitable funding of schools in America. The book describes a growing segregation of students by race and income level that can only be resolved through more equitable educational opportunities for all students.

Lunenburg, F., & Ornstein, A. (2008). *Educational administration: Concepts and practices.* (5th ed.). Belmont, CA: Wadsworth. This text is one used by principal candidates as they prepare for their administrative roles. It provides a clear discussion of school governance issues.

Razik, T., & Swanson, A. (2010). *Fundamental concepts of educational leadership* (3rzd ed.). Upper Saddle River, NJ: Merrill/Prentice Hall. Another textbook for principals, this book has good information on administrators' roles, school governance, and school finance.

References

Addonizio, M. (1999). New revenues for public schools: Alternatives to broad-based taxes. In *Selected papers in school finance.* Washington, DC: U.S. Department of Education. Retrieved from *http://nces.ed.gov/pubs99/1999334/h3*

American Association of School Administrators. (2009). School superintendent salary data. Retrieved January 27, 2009 from *http://www.aasa.org/career/content.cfm?ItemNumber=2295*

Archer, J. (2005). An Edmonton journey. *Education Week,* January 26, pp. 33–36.

Arizona Education Association. (2009). *Calendar of events.* Retrieved January 28, 2009 from: *http://www.arizonaea.org/calendar.php?year=2009&month=1*

Association for Teacher Educators. (2005). *Standards for teacher education.* Retrieved January 28, 2009 from: *http://www.ate1.org/pubs/Standards.cfm*

Autism Society of America. (2009). *Our Mission.* Retrieved January 28, 2009 from: *http://www.autism-society.org/site/PageServer?pagename=asa_princip_mission*

Borja, R. (2004). Education Inc.: K–12 education market appears stable. *Education Week,* November 3, p. 8.

Cook, G. (2001). Searching for miracles. *American School Board Journal, 188*(12), 18–23.

Council of Chief State School Officers. (2009). *Helping our members educate America.* Retrieved January 30, 2009 from: *http://www.ccsso.org/*

Dayton, J., & McCarthy, M. (1992). User fees in public schools: Are they legal? *Journal of Education Finance, 18*(2), 127–141.

Drake, T., & Roe, W. (2003). *The principalship* (6th ed.). Upper Saddle River, NJ: Prentice Hall.

Edison Schools. (2009). *About Edison Schools.* Retrieved February 2, 2009 from: *http://www.edisonschools.com/edison_schools/about-us*

Education Week. (2004). *Private schooling.* Retrieved January 6, 2005 from: *http://www.edweek.org/rc/issues/private-schooling/*

Education Week. (2008). *Quality counts 2008.* Bethesda, MD: Author.

Education Week. (2009). *Quality counts.* Bethesda, MD: Author.

Fink, E., & Resnick, L. (2001). Developing principals as instructional leaders. *Phi Delta Kappan, 82*(8), 598–606.

Fuller, G. (2003). Federalism on the cheap. *Education Week,* January 15, pp. 30–44.

Glass, T. (2005). The big paycheck. *American School Board Journal, 192*(2), 40–42.

Goss v. Lopez, 419 U.S. 565 (1975).

Greenwald, R., Hedges, L., & Laine, R. (1996). The effect of school resources on student achievement. *Review of Educational Research, 66*(3), 361–396.

Harlem School District. (2009). *Harlem scholarship foundation.* Retrieved February 2, 2009 from: *http://www.harlem122.org/education/components/scrapbook/default.php?sectiondetailid=4580+sc_id=1153858382*

Hess, F., & Kelly, A. (2005). Ready to lead? *American School Board Journal, 192*(7), 22–25.

Johnston, R. (2005). California laws heighten fiscal responsibility. *Education Week,* October 5, p. 20.

Kozol, J. (2005). *The shame of a nation: The restoration of apartheid schooling in America.* New York: Crown Publishers.

Lankard, B. (1995). *Business/education partnerships.* ERIC Digest No.156. Washington, DC: ERIC Clearinghouse for Adult, Career, and Vocational Education.

Lunenburg, F., & Ornstein, A. (2008). *Educational administration: Concepts and practices* (5th ed.). Belmont, CA: Wadsworth.

Martinez Educational Foundation. (2009). Martinez Education Foundation. Retrieved January 29, 2009 from: *http://www.martinezedfoundation.com/index.cfm*

Massachusetts Department of Education. (2007). *Education Research Brief,* Issue 1. Retrieved January 29, 2009 from *http://www.doe.mass.edu/research/reports/0907finance.doc*

Microsoft Corporation. (2009). *About Unlimited Potential.* Retrieved January 28, 2009 from: *http://www.microsoft.com/unlimitedpotential/AboutUnlimitedPotential/UnlimitedPotential.mspx*

Minersville School District v. Gobitis, 310 U.S. 586 (1940).

Molnar, A., Boninger, F., Wilkinson, G., and Fogarty, J. (2008). *At sea in a marketing-saturated world: The eleventh annual report on schoolhouse commercialism trends: 2007–2008.* Boulder and Tempe: Education and the Public Interest Center and Commercialism in Education Research Unit. Retrieved February 4, 2009 from *http://epicpolicy.org/publications/Schoolhouse-commercialism-2008*

National Alliance of Black School Educators. (2005). *Our mission.* Retrieved January 28, 2009 from: *http://www.nabse.org/about.htm*

National Art Education Association. (2005). *Publications.* Retrieved January 28, 2009 from: *http://www.arteducators.org/olc/pub/NAEA/store/store_page_2.html*

National Board for Professional Teaching Standards. (2009). *Standards and National Board Certification.* Retrieved January 30, 2009 from: *http://www.nbpts.org/the_standards*

National Center for Education Statistics. (1997). *NAEP 1996 trends in academic progress.* Washington, DC: Government Printing Office.

National Center for Education Statistics. (2003). *Digest of education statistics.* Washington, D.C.: Author.

National Center for Education Statistics. (2007). *Digest of education statistics.* Washington, D.C.: Author.

National Conference of State Legislatures. (2009). *Shifting roles in governance.* Retrieved January 28, 2009 from: *http://www.ncsl.org/programs/educ/K–12Governance.html*

National Council for the Accreditation of Teacher Education. (2009). *About NCATE.* Retrieved February 3, 2009 from: *http://www.ncate.org/public/aboutNCATE.asp*

National Parent Teacher Association. (2005). *Commercialism in the classroom.* Retrieved October 3, 2005 from: *http://search.pta.org/search?ie=&site=ptaprod&output=xmlnodtd&client=ptaprod& lr=&proxystylesheet=ptaprod&oe=&q=commercialism%20in%20the%20classroom*

National School Foundation Association. (2009). *List of foundations by state.* Retrieved February 2, 2009 from *http://www.schoolfoundations.org/en/list_of_foundations_by_state/*

Obama, B. (2009). Barack Obama and Joe Biden's plan for lifetime success through education. Retrieved January 28, 2009 from *http://www.barackobama.com/pdf/issues/PreK–12EducationFact Sheet.pdf*

Pickering v. Board of Education, 391 U.S. 563 (1968).

Pierce v. Society of Sisters, 268 U.S. 510 (1925).

Pijanowski, J. C., & Monk, D. H. (1996). Alternative school revenue sources: There are many fish in the sea. *School Business Affairs,* July, pp. 4–10

Razik, T., & Swanson, A. (2010). *Fundamental concepts of educational leadership* (3rd ed.). Upper Saddle River, NJ: Merrill/Prentice Hall.

Sergiovanni, T. (2009). *The principalship: A reflective practice perspective* (6th ed.). Boston: Allyn and Bacon.

Texas Education Agency. (2008). *Student success initiative.* Retrieved January 28, 2009 from: *http://www.tea.state.tx.us/index3.aspx?id=3230*

U.S. Department of Agriculture. (2008). *Child nutrition programs.* Retrieved January 28, 2009 from: *http://www.ers.usda.gov/Briefing/ChildNutrition/*

U.S. Department of Education. (2009). *Federal role in education.* Retrieved January 28, 2009 from: *http://www.ed.gov/about/overview/fed/role.html*

U.S. Department of Health and Human Services. (2008). *Head Start program fact sheet.* Retrieved January 28, 2009 from: *http://www.acf.hhs.gov/programs/ohs/about/fy2008.html*

part 4

How Do I Grow as a Reflective Practitioner?

Chapter 15: The First Years and Beyond

Courtesy of Jose Pelaez/Corbis Images.

chapter 15

The First Years and Beyond

This chapter is designed to give you a glimpse of what is yet to come in your future career. What will it be like to close the classroom door for the first time and begin your adventure in teaching? What expectations should you have for the first few years in the classroom? You should come away from this chapter with additional understandings of those initial classroom experiences and gain insights into your potential for a long-term teaching career. Four organizing questions will be used to guide you through this process.

Focus Questions

1. What will I need to do to get a teaching position?

2. What must I do to be successful as a beginning teacher?

3. How can I continue to grow personally and professionally?

*Though I think
I learned a lot from
my preteaching
seminars, nothing that was
said or done in education classes
could have prepared me for the gut-
level aspects of day-to-day teaching. You can talk
about it and do everything in your power to psych yourself up for the real thing, but the feeling of having
complete control of a classroom full of students has to be a unique experience for someone just starting out.
Managing your own classroom is totally different from helping in another teacher's class. I couldn't avoid feeling
like a guest during my aiding and student teaching semesters. Now I'm feeling the full force of the responsibility
for my own classroom. It isn't that my knowledge of teaching has increased that much, it's just that overnight
I'm having to behave like a real teacher. Up to this point I've been a student. (MacDonald & Healy, 1999, p. 2)*

Throughout this text you have been reading and responding to features that are designed to help you, the reader, better understand the complexities, challenges, and rewards of the teaching profession. Educators are constantly reflecting on the teaching materials and strategies they use and on deepening their understanding of students and how they learn. As described by a beginning teacher in the above example, there is much on-the-job training that begins the first day you enter the classroom as a full-time teacher and continues throughout the remainder of your career. Although you will have learned a great deal and practiced many different teaching techniques before you complete your teacher-preparation program, the road to mature teaching is a long one that requires even more thought, observation, discussion, and practice. This chapter begins with information on getting that first teaching assignment so that you can experience firsthand the many joys and challenges of the profession.

What will I need to do to get a teaching position?

Somewhere in the not-too-distant future you will be finishing your teacher-preparation program. After reaching this important milestone, an obvious next step will be to locate a job in your chosen profession. You will want to take what you have learned and apply it to the real world of teaching. Finding the best possible match between your interests and skills and available teaching positions can be made easier if you understand the steps that are needed to successfully find a good job. The typical procedures used to find a position are outlined on Table 15.1 and discussed in more detail below.

Know the Job Market

The job market for teachers across the country is generally good and job opportunities are projected to grow in the years ahead. Nationwide, there were 2.8 million elementary and secondary teachers in 1992 (National Center for Education Statistics, 2008). That number increased to 3.5 million in 2005 and is projected to reach 4.2 million in 2017. The American Association for Employment in Education (2002) cites four factors that impact the demand for teachers nationally:

- *Early retirement*—When a state encourages teachers to retire earlier than is normal by offering them financial incentives, the number of new jobs for teachers increases. The state benefits because it can hire new teachers at lower salaries than those who are retiring.

TABLE 15.1 Steps in Finding a Teaching Position

Step	Description
Know the Job Market	Although there are variations between locations and for different subjects and levels taught, the job market for teachers continues to improve.
Locate Openings	College placement services, Internet sites, and direct contact with schools and districts are all possible strategies for locating job openings.
Submit Applications	Most job openings require the submission of a cover letter, résumé, a completed job application form, and letters of reference.
Participate in Interviews	You will participate in interviews conducted by a team of school personnel that may include teachers, administrators, and school board members, who will quiz you about specific aspects of teaching and learning.

- *Regular retirement*—Many teachers hired in the 1970s are ready to retire after having spent 30 or more years in the classroom. As this large population of teachers moves into retirement, new jobs are created.
- *Student enrollment*—The numbers of students entering schools continue to increase, meaning more teachers are needed in schools across the country.
- *Class size*—As states work to reduce class sizes in an effort to provide better learning environments for students, more teachers are needed.

The demand for teachers also varies according to the discipline being taught, the region of the country in which you live, and whether the teaching assignment is in a rural, urban, or suburban setting. Table 15.2 summarizes these differences in teacher supply and demand. The top needs for teachers are in the following subject areas: mathematics, physics, chemistry, special education, and bilingual education (National Center for Education Statistics, 2008).

The region of the country in which you live also influences teacher supply and demand. For example, even though mathematics educators are needed across the country, the Northwest has the lowest demand, and the Northeast portion of the country has the greatest. Similarly, special educators are in highest demand in the Northeast; needs decrease slightly in the Great Lakes region (American Association for Employment in Education, 2008). In addition, some states such as California and Nevada, due to rapid growth in student populations, have high demands for teachers in virtually all subjects and grade levels.

Locate Openings

Once you understand the general job market for teaching, you may wish to consider several options in locating openings of interest to you. Before actually selecting the best strategies, however, consider the level of flexibility you bring to the search process. Are you willing to move anywhere in the state or even across the nation in an effort to find a good position? Or are you "place bound" and only seeking a teaching job in a specific community or area? If you had a choice, would your want to work in an urban, suburban, or rural setting? Do you have thoughts at this point about the characteristics of the students with which you would most like to work? Your answers to these questions will help you begin to decide which strategies you may want to use in seeking a teaching position.

**Reflection
Opportunity 15.1**

For new teachers willing to consider a variety of community settings, an effective job-location strategy is to visit and consult with a college or university **placement service.** Designed to help all students at that institution find employment, these offices typically have up-to-date postings of state and national jobs in education that can be reviewed on a regular basis. With the growth

TABLE 15.2 Teacher Supply and Demand Factors	
Factor	**Description**
Subject Area Taught	Subjects that prospective teachers tend to avoid (such as mathematics) have more job opportunities than others where there are plenty of candidates (such as social studies).
Region of the Country	The demand for teachers varies depending on the region of the country in which you live.
Setting	Urban and rural schools tend to attract fewer teachers and so demands are high for those willing to seek options in these settings. Suburban schools often have more applicants than there are positions.

of Internet access, most placement services also allow you to review these options on their Websites. Normally, the basic services of the placement center are available to students or recent graduates at no cost.

Those who are targeting specific communities in their job search may be more successful in locating a position if they take a more direct and personal approach. By calling, writing, and taking every opportunity to make yourself known to teachers and administrators in districts of interest, the chances of getting hired are increased. Take the time needed to meet school administrators and teachers. If possible, consider volunteering time in the classroom as a way of gaining experience with students while making yourself known to school personnel. Be sure you have as much information as possible about the teaching openings that become available in these schools. Most districts post job openings in a centralized location and many provide this service on their websites.

Submit Applications

Once you have located teaching positions that are of interest to you, the next step is to submit an application. Most applications have four main components:

- *Cover letter.* A **cover letter,** also called a letter of application, is a brief, one-page letter indicating that you are applying for a particular teaching position and states your qualifications for the job. Although each letter has much in common, you should individualize each of them for the specific job for which you are applying.

- *Résumé.* A **résumé** is generally a one- or two-page summary of your life as it relates to teaching and includes such things as your formal education (including teaching certificates earned), experiences related to teaching, awards, memberships in professional organizations, and special interests and skills that make you a strong candidate for a teaching position. College and university placement services often provide guidance in creating an effective résumé. A sample résumé is shown in Figure 15.1.

- *Application.* The job application itself is typically a standardized, multipage document from the local school district that asks for detailed information regarding your teacher preparation and skills in teaching. It often includes an essay question to assess both your writing skills and attitudes toward teaching. A separate application is completed for each teaching position of interest to you.

- *References.* Letters of recommendation from people who have seen you in the classroom working with students or who can speak to your academic preparation are another important element of the application process. You may be able to save time and effort by setting up a **placement file** with your college or university placement service that includes letters of recommendation. On request, this file is mailed to school districts of your choosing for a small fee. Before opening a placement file, check to see if the school districts you are interested in accept these files or instead require references that are completed on district forms.

Participate in Interviews

Once school districts have reviewed all of the written applications submitted for a job vacancy, they select a small number of applicants for face-to-face interviews. Although commonly held in school district buildings, they may also take place at college and university job fairs or as part of professional education meetings. Depending on the circumstances, these interviews can be as short as half an hour or as long as several hours. Teachers, principals, school board members, and district administrators are all potential participants in these interviews.

Job interviews are a critical part of the search process and require careful preparation. Make sure you think about your attire so that you convey the right professional image and consider

Figure 15.1 Sample Résumé

MICHAEL J. HANSEN
1453 Stevens Boulevard
Amherst, MA 01002
Phone: (555) 474-1800

Personal Information
Married Lisa M. Gibbons, June 7, 2004
No children
Age: 23; Health: excellent

Education
B.A. in mathematics, Gettysburg College, 2005
M.I.T. with elementary certification, University of Massachusetts at Lowell, 2007

Experience with Students
Volunteer, Springhill Elementary, Gettysburg, PA, grades 4 and 6, 2004–2005
Tutor in mathematics, elementary through middle school students, Lowell, MA
2005–2006
Student teaching internship, fourth grade, Middleton Elementary, Lowell, MA,
spring 2007

Special Interests
Trombone player through high school and undergraduate degree
High school wrestling and football
Math Olympics coach, 2005–2006

Awards
Dean's List, Gettysburg College, six of eight semesters
Pemberton Scholarship recipient, 2003–2005

References
Placement file available on request, Career Planning and Placement Center,
University of Massachusetts at Lowell, 800 Tower Place, Lowell, MA 02894

materials that you might bring to the interview to highlight your knowledge and skills. You should expect the interviewers to ask several challenging questions about teaching and learning as they seek to gain specific information about your qualifications and skills. Taking the time to think through the possible questions and your answers to them is an effective strategy to use in preparing for the interview. Most interviews also include time for you to ask questions of the district representatives. It is important that you be prepared to ask good questions about the

**Consider This:
Preparing for
a Teacher Interview**

school district and teaching position so that you can make an informed decision if a position is offered. Interviewers also gain important insights about you from the questions asked. The *Consider This* feature for this chapter provides some examples of common interview questions. Go to the Companion Website for this text and respond to these questions so that you will be better prepared for the interview process.

What must I do to be successful as a beginning teacher?

You can take several steps during your early years in the classroom to increase the chances of success. A good starting point is to make sure you have realistic expectations for your first year in the classroom. In addition, you should plan to continually refine and strengthen your personal teaching style, create a community of learners in your classroom, maintain a healthy lifestyle, and understand why some teachers leave the profession. Table 15.3 summarizes these important strategies. Begin now to develop the skills and attitudes you will need to be successful during your beginning years in the classroom and beyond. Before reading the following information, you may want to reflect on the *Views From the Classroom* feature for this chapter. Go to the Companion Website for this text and read about one new teacher's perspectives on beginning her first year in the classroom.

**Views from the
Classroom: The
Clock is Ticking**

Have Realistic First-Year Expectations

Although you will learn a great deal about the realities of teaching as you work in classrooms and talk with teachers throughout your teacher-preparation program, it is still an eye-opening experience to start work with your first group of students. Here are some typical comments made by first-year teachers:

> Though I think I learned a lot from my pre-teaching seminars, nothing that was said or done in education classes could have prepared me for the gut-level aspects of day-to-day teaching. You can talk about it and do everything in your power to psych yourself up for the real thing, but the feeling of having complete control of a classroom full of students has to be a unique experience for someone just starting out. Managing your own classroom is totally different from helping in another teacher's class. I couldn't avoid feeling like a guest during my aiding and student teaching semesters. Now I'm feeling the full force of the responsibility for my own classroom. It isn't that my knowledge of teaching has increased that much, it's just that overnight I'm having to behave like a real teacher. Up to this point I've been a student. (MacDonald & Healy, 1999, p. 2)

> At the beginning, I just wanted to get through my first year of teaching . . . And I changed in my perspective from that kind of survival mode to now where I want to focus on refining everything, and really honing my skills, and trying to do everything a little better every time. (Archer, 2001, p. 52)

> The greatest difference between my expectations and actual classroom experiences has been the arduous task of balancing lessons that target the high achievers and low achievers in the same classroom . . . During the first six weeks of teaching pre-algebra, I altered my teaching strategies to reach those students who counted on their fingers, those who multiplied and divided on a beginner level, and those who have surpassed all eighth grade objectives. (DePaul, 1998, p. 2)

> My first year of teaching has been full of many wonderful surprises. I never knew the average teenage girl's voice could hit such octaves. I never expected to reach a point in my life where I would yearn for my bed at 9:30 every night. I was not prepared for the moment I first heard myself ask, "Does anyone in class not think that spitting on the floor an inappropriate behavior?" But most of all, I never thought that teaching would be such an exhilarating and rewarding career, continually pushing me in quest to be a master educator. (DePaul, 1998, p. 26)

TABLE 15.3 Becoming a Successful Teacher	
Step	**Description**
Have Realistic First-Year Expectations	First-year teachers have many highs and lows as they adjust to the full-time responsibilities of the classroom.
Refine Your Teaching Style	You will need to continue to grow in your understanding of students, clarify your beliefs about good teaching, develop a teaching plan, and monitor the development of your own teaching.
Create a Community of Learners	By being a caring person who takes advantage of naturally occurring opportunities for community building and using teacher-created situations, you can build a community of learners in your future classroom.
Maintain a Healthy Lifestyle	You will need to take the time and energy needed to maintain good physical and mental health so that you can be successful in working with others.
Understand Why Teachers Leave the Profession	It is important for you to understand why some educators leave the profession so that you can better determine if you would be happy working as a teacher.

To hear another first year teacher's description of her beginning teaching experiences, go to the Companion Website for this text and click on MyEducationLab for Chapter 15.

No two teachers or classroom settings are ever exactly alike, so it is difficult to predict with certainty what your first year of teaching will be like. With that said, however, new teachers' reflections on this experience suggest some common responses to the first year of teaching. Four specific elements of beginning teaching will be addressed in more detail here. The physical setting of your classroom and school, the students themselves, parents and families, and colleagues and administrators in your school district will all have a significant impact on your first year of teaching.

myeducationlab
The Power of Classroom Practice

MyEducationLab 15.1

The physical setting. Have you ever taken the time to look carefully at the condition of school buildings in your local community? If you have, it should be clear from these observations that schools tend to be older, overcrowded, and often in need of significant updating. Recent surveys indicate that the average public school was built more than 40 years ago, with approximately one-fourth (28%) built before 1950. (Rowland, 2005). After 40 years school buildings begin to deteriorate rapidly and require far greater maintenance to keep them functional. Table 15.4 summarizes this data for American schools. A report from the U.S. General Accounting Office (2000) estimates that it would cost about $112 billion to bring existing American schools into good overall condition. And although increasing numbers of new schools are being built to accommodate rising student enrollments, the problems of overcrowding are still significant in many areas.

It is also important to realize that the physical setting you will inherit as a new teacher will probably be one of the less desirable classrooms containing fewer pieces of new equipment and

TABLE 15.4 Age of School Buildings

School Characteristic	Built Before 1950	Built 1950–1969	Built 1970–1984	Built 1985 or Later
Elementary	29%	46%	15%	11%
Secondary	24%	46%	23%	8%
Northeastern Schools	30%	49%	15%	6%
Southeastern Schools	23%	43%	20%	14%
Central U.S. Schools	33%	46%	14%	8%
Western Schools	25%	44%	19%	13%

From: National Center for Education Statistics, (2000). *The condition of education.* Washington, DC: U.S. Government Printing Office.

Reflection Opportunity 15.2

more materials that other veteran teachers have left behind. Although this "natural pecking order" can be found in every work situation and can be a negative, it need not hinder your ability to teach effectively (Patterson, 2005). What is important is that you are aware that it is likely to occur and work to compensate for it. How do you think you will feel about getting desks, chairs, teaching supplies, and classroom space that have been passed over by others? What can you do to make the best use of the older, less desirable desks, chairs, and equipment you will likely find in your class-room? Do you think that the physical setting you inherit will affect the ways in which you will teach and your students will learn? What makes you think this?

The students. Most new teachers indicate that students are both their biggest frustration and greatest reward in the first years of teaching. On the one hand, it is frustrating when teach-ers give all that they have in an effort to stimulate learning and some students just do not seem to care. Conversely, most teachers report that there is no greater satisfaction than seeing the light dawn as a student grasps a concept you have worked hard to teach. Susan Palmer was a beginning teacher during the 2000–2001 school year. Susan's story, like many others, is full of many ups and downs. Through it all, however, she found that her relationships with students brought both the greatest joys and the biggest headaches. Susan's experiences are common to many first-year teachers:

> Palmer kept an apple-shaped book on her desk all year long to record the high points of teaching: the day a student gave her an apple; the time one of her most difficult classes really got into a discussion on dreams; the occasions when a struggling student finally engaged in learning. "That's my favorite part," Palmer says. "It's cool when a student writes a note and says, 'Thanks.' It's even better to show me by working, by showing improvements." But by year's end, about half of the apple-shaped notebook was still blank. And the lows of teaching outnumbered the highs. Palmer found herself irritated, even incensed, by student apathy. At the start of the year, she had not realized how tough it would be to motivate them. (May, 2001, p. 2)

Despite the many challenges of first-year teaching and the need to have realistic expectations, you must begin your career committed to the ideals and future directions of the profession. One of these directions is to work hard to close the achievement gap that exists between students of color and low-income students and their more advantaged peers. The *Reflect on Diversity* feature for this chapter asks you to keep this issue at the forefront of your thinking. Read and reflect further on this important topic now.

Reflect on diversity: Closing the achievement gap

As you think ahead to your future as an educator, it is important to understand that one of the key issues you will face relates to the many challenges associated with closing the achievement gap that exists between White middle-class students and the many other diverse groups of students who tend to be less successful in the classroom. Students from low-income families, African American students, Hispanic students, students with special needs and students learning English as a second language are among the many who will need your assistance to perform well in the classroom. The national educational agenda as evidenced in the No Child Left Behind Act of 2002 (see Chapter 14), clearly emphasizes the importance of helping every student learn. Individual states and school districts are working hard to close this achievement gap.

Your role in this effort will be pivotal. It is clear that quality teaching is the essential ingredient needed to leave no child behind (Olson, 2003). No matter where you choose to teach, you interactions with struggling students are critical to their success. You should begin now to develop the attitudes and skills needed to help every child learn.

In addition to developing the skills needed to be successful with all students, you may want to consider taking at least some time during your teaching career to work in a school that has a high percentage of low-performing students. Having quality teachers who can engage all students in effective learning experiences is even more critical for "high-poverty, high-minority, and low-achieving schools" (Olson, 2003, p. 10). Very few schools that fit this profile have been successful in attracting large numbers of well-qualified teachers to join their ranks. This has led to a "teacher gap" in which middle-class schools with mostly White students are able to hire a larger percentage of quality candidates than other less desirable schools. This gap can be effectively closed only when well-prepared teachers commit to working in these settings.

Developing the Habit of Reflective Practice

Gather Information

1. Do an Internet search for "Rethinking Schools Online". In the archives go to volume 15, number 4 and read "Race and the Achievement Gap".

Identify Beliefs

1. What skills and attitudes does a teacher need to have that will help every student learn?
2. What are your personal beliefs that will help every student learn? Are there areas you will need to work on?

Make Decisions

1. If you were planning professional development workshops for a group of teachers who were aiming to close the achievement gap, what would you choose for the workshop topics so that teachers could strengthen their ability to leave no child behind?

Assess and Evaluate

1. If you were judging whether or not a group of teachers were qualified to teach in a low-income, highly diverse school setting, what characteristics would you look for?

Source

Olson, L. (2003). The great divide. *Quality counts 2003*, 22 (17), 9–10.

Parents and families. As with students, most beginning teachers find that working with parents and families can be both challenging and rewarding. It is difficult when parents either don't get involved in the educational process or question every move the teacher makes. Sometimes, for example, parents push their own children too hard and expect them to earn all As. If that doesn't happen, the teacher may receive the blame. Other parents are just too busy or too stressed to participate in their child's education. On the other hand, many parents can be important allies in the educational process and provide much-needed support to you as a beginning teacher. When good relationships with parents have been established, they will work with you to make sure their children are learning and growing. This will make your job as teacher both easier and more rewarding. In addition, having supportive parents can be a big boost to your self-esteem during those periods of uncertainty and doubt that will come your way during those early years of teaching.

Think about working with parents and families. You will be very busy in your first few years of teaching just keeping one step ahead of your students. Do you think that you will be able to take the time needed to work effectively with families? Why or why not? Can you identify some simple strategies that you could use to keep in touch with parents and families that wouldn't over-stress your already busy schedule during these early years of teaching?

Reflection Opportunity 15.3

Mentoring opportunities. If you enter a teacher education program, you will have many opportunities to talk with your professors and other students both in and out of class as you encounter questions or problems related to teaching. Many new teachers are surprised to find that these same opportunities for help and support are not as readily available in most schools (Salvo, Kible, Furay, & Sierra, 2005). Teachers and administrators won't try to avoid you and they will certainly provide support when it is asked for. The realities of school life, however, are that each day you will walk into your classroom, close the door, and spend your teaching day mostly isolated from others who work next door or down the hall (Goodlad, 1984). The few times during the day when you are free from students (lunch periods, planning times, and after school hours) are crowded with other activities that make it difficult for you and others to commit the extra time and energy needed to get together and discuss concerns and successes.

Numerous efforts have been made in recent years to deal with new teachers' feelings of isolation. For example, many states and school districts are implementing **mentoring programs** in which new teachers are paired with veteran educators who serve as guides through the struggles and successes of the beginning years. New teachers are also creating their own informal support systems by seeking out more experienced teachers and other beginning teachers to help them understand and respond to the many problems they encounter in the classroom (Ostrum, 2009). Mentoring programs typically have three major goals as they work to induct teachers into the profession:

1. *Orientation to the district, school, and classroom.* New teachers need to learn the job expectations, the organizational structure and climate, key people, and educational philosophy of others in the district.
2. *Induction to the profession.* Mentors work with new teachers to help them refine their skills in teaching as they move from novice to more experienced educators.
3. *Creating a climate for lifelong learning.* New teachers need to view their profession as a continuing journey of refinement as they strive to become master teachers in their work with students. A quality program assists teachers in this effort (Fulton, Yoon, & Lee, 2005).

In some school districts, veteran teachers work at least part of the school day as a **teacher coach** to new educators. In addition to mentoring their assigned teachers, coaches are given release time from their own teaching so that they can come into the classroom and observe and give feedback that helps the new teacher be more successful (Useem & Neild, 2005). One new teacher describes her coach as follows:

My new teacher coach was a godsend. She was there the day I started. I felt like I was walking in cold, but I got instant support. She helped me set up my room and gave suggestions. She came by once a week, and we talked on the phone and e-mailed. She also modeled lessons and observed in my room (Useem & Neild, 2005, p. 46).

Refine Your Teaching Style

In addition to having realistic first-year expectations, it is important to continue refining your own personal teaching style during your beginning years in the classroom. One message that has been repeated several times throughout this text is that there is no one "right" way of teaching. There are many different styles of good teaching that are based largely on the personality and strengths of individual teachers. As you identify personal strengths and limitations and grow in your understanding of teaching and learning, your personal style will begin to emerge. This process of refinement should start now and continue for most, if not all, of your teaching career.

You will need to take several steps as you hone your personal style. The first is to *continue to grow in your understanding of students.* Your perceptions of students and how they learn (see Chapter 6) should always be an essential foundation for your curriculum planning, teaching strategies, and discipline options. A second step in the development of your personal teaching style is to *clarify your beliefs about good teaching* (Roberts, Kellough, & Moore, 2006). As you read the theory and research of others regarding teaching, work to identify those attitudes and teaching strategies that make the most sense to you. The *Engage in the Debate* feature for this chapter discusses the use of student portfolios as an important teaching/assessment strategy. Read the feature now and respond to the issues presented.

Engage in the debate: Using portfolios to assess student progress

Throughout this text you have been provided with opportunities to develop your own portfolio of materials to demonstrate what you know and can do as a future teacher. As mentioned in Chapter 6, it is also important to realize that portfolios are growing in importance as a student assessment tool. Rather than relying solely on test results to measure student learning, many teachers are working with students to assist them in thoughtfully constructing a portfolio to demonstrate their growth as learners.

A portfolio is a purposeful collection of student work that exhibits the student's efforts, progress, and achievements in one or more areas of the curriculum. The collection must include the following:

- Student participation in selecting contents.
- Criteria for selection.
- Criteria for judging merits.
- Evidence of a student's self-reflection (Prince George's County Public Schools, 2009, p. 1).

Not everyone, however, believes that portfolios can be an effective assessment tool. Berger (1998) emphasizes the difficulties in measuring what students are learning through the use of portfolios. He suggests that "boosters today promote portfolios as 'accurate measures of educational performance, offering 'credible' 'standardized' data. Unfortunately, portfolio scoring simply doesn't work" (p. 1)

Developing the Habit of Reflective Practice
Gather Information

1. Go to *http://www.pgcps.org/~elc/portfolio.html* to read more on portfolios as a tool in student assessment.

Identify Beliefs

1. What do you see as the benefits for the using portfolios as a means of student assessment?

Make Decisions

1. Do you think portfolios should and/or could be used to replace or supplement standardized tests? Give a rationale for your opinion.

Assess and Evaluate

1. What information can you gather from a portfolio that cannot be found on a standardized test? What information can you gather from a standardized test that cannot be found in a portfolio?

Sources

Berger, P. (1998). Portfolio folly. *Education Week*, January 14, pp. 1, 14.

Prince George's County Public Schools. (2009). Portfolio assessment. Retrieved February 27, 2009 from *http://www.pgcps.org/~elc/portfolio.html*

A third component needed to refine your teaching style is to *develop a teaching plan*. After you have identified the elements of teaching that you want to implement, it is then necessary to create from them an overall strategy for how you will approach teaching. A final step is to *monitor the development of your own teaching skills*. Roberts, et. al (2006) identify two effective strategies that you can use to become a better teacher. The first is to engage in self-assessment through reflection, journaling, and continually refining and adding to your professional portfolio. Or, you may want to audiotape or videotape classroom instruction and then use these recordings to critique and improve your teaching. A second strategy is to work closely with your mentor or coach to think about and refine your teaching skills. An additional strategy to consider is to seek direct feedback from your students. You can gather this information through class discussions or simple evaluations following instruction.

Reflect on what you know and what you need to know about your personal teaching style. What do you feel you know about students? What do you think you still need to know? Can you identify basic beliefs you have about teaching at this point in your development? What teaching strategies have you identified as important to you? If you are currently working with students in some capacity, how could you seek feedback about the strengths and areas for growth in your work with these students?

Reflection Opportunity 15.4

Create a Community of Learners

Another factor that will help ensure your success as a classroom teacher is the creation of what is often called a community of learners (Kohn, 1996; Sowers, 2004). When there are strong relationships among students and between students and teachers, the opportunities for learning are greatly enhanced (see Chapter 8 for more information). From the first day of your teaching career, you should work to build good relationships. Creating a learning community where respect and cooperation predominate is not easy, but it is well worth the effort needed to implement.

In a study of 24 elementary schools from around the country, students were asked to what extent they felt their classrooms and schools were supportive communities (Battistich, Solomon, Kim, Watson, & Schaps, 1995). Those students who experienced a positive learning community reported liking school more than those who did not have the advantages of this setting. They were better able to resolve conflicts with others and tended to be more supportive of their peers. In addition, these students were more likely to see learning as valuable and actively engaged in classroom activities. Furthermore, these findings were strongest in schools with high percentages of low-income students.

The fundamental starting point for building a community of learners is for you to be a caring person in your communications with students. As you treat students with the dignity and respect they deserve, they in turn will interact with each other and you more positively. As described in Kohn (1996), a classroom community is a place where:

> . . . care and trust are emphasized above restrictions and threats, where unity and pride
> (of accomplishment and in purpose) replace winning and losing, and where each person is
> asked, helped, and inspired to live up to such ideals and values as kindness, fairness, and
> responsibility. [Such] a classroom community seeks to meet each student's need to feel
> competent, connected to others, and autonomous. . . . Students are not only exposed to basic
> human values, they also have many opportunities to think about, discuss, and act on those
> values, while gaining experiences that promote empathy and understanding of others. (p. 102)

A community of learners also requires strong working relationships with colleagues (Wald & Castleberry, 2000). Other teachers and administrators can provide you with much-needed support, encouragement, and guidance as you begin your teaching career. You, in turn, can provide colleagues with insights that will strengthen their classroom interactions as well. As teachers, administrators, and staff exchange ideas about teaching, learning, and dealing with student behaviors, a school-wide learning community is created. The professional interactions at this level provide opportunities for all the adults involved to grow both personally and professionally. This growth will continue to strengthen the learning communities within individual classrooms. Table 15.5 suggests some ways in which you can begin to build communities of learners.

TABLE 15.5 Examples of Community Building

Example	Description
Getting Acquainted Through Interviews	At the beginning of each school year, many teachers take the time to get students better acquainted by having them interview each other. It is often helpful to begin by asking students to develop the list of questions they would like to ask. Suggest that students pair up with a classmate that they don't know as well and have each pair interview their partner. The information learned can then be shared with the rest of the class.
Class Spirit (Elementary)	To help elementary students develop a better sense of identity and cohesiveness, work with them in developing a list of class favorites. You could have a class animal, name, song, cheer, cartoon character, or other markers that help students see themselves as a cohesive group. Once these class attributes are identified, they can be reinforced throughout the year. For example, a class song could be practiced and sung for parents at an open house or characteristics of the class animal could be researched for a science project and written about as part of a language arts task.
Tower Building (Secondary)	Give groups of four or five students straws and paper clips. Tell them that they have ten minutes to construct the highest tower possible. Once time is completed, have each group identify and share one factor that facilitated their work. Record these responses. Then ask each group to share one thing that blocked the group's effectiveness and list them as well. Use these positives and negatives to have a group discussion of how groups function and the implications for their work together in class.

From: Jones, V., & Jones, L. (2004). *Comprehensive classroom management: Creating communities of support and solving problems* (7th ed.). Boston: Allyn and Bacon.

Maintain a Healthy Lifestyle

Being successful in the classroom also means that you must take the time needed to maintain your own personal health. You will need to be physically, mentally, and emotionally fit in order to manage the many challenges you will face as a teacher. The first year of teaching can be especially difficult for many teachers and every effort must be made to counterbalance the stresses with a healthy lifestyle. Each person has unique ways of taking care of his or her own physical and mental health. Some options to consider include (Kronowitz, 2004):

- Plan a weekend away (or stay home and hibernate)
- Buy yourself flowers
- Read a book you "don't have time for"
- Play with your pet
- Buy a new article of clothing
- Spend some time alone
- Take a walk
- Get more sleep
- Listen to music
- Go to the gym
- Eat healthy foods
- Have your house or apartment cleaned
- Get a babysitter
- Keep a journal
- Play a board game

Reflection Opportunity 15.5

Think about how you can have a healthy lifestyle right now and into your future career as a teacher. What do you do to maintain your own physical well-being? Do you engage in exercise, find time for extra sleep, and vacation to stay physically healthy? Are there other strategies you use? Similarly, how do you maintain your mental health? Review the alternatives presented above, and then write down a list of options that work for you and keep it handy for those times when it will be needed.

Understand Why Teachers Leave the Profession

Teachers can and do cite many good reasons for being satisfied with teaching as a career choice. The National Education Association regularly conducts a survey to assess attitudes of public school teachers. In its most recent survey (2003), they found that the top three reasons teachers gave for continuing were:

1. Desire to work with young people
2. Value or significance of education in society
3. Interest in subject-matter field.

The Metropolitan Life Insurance Company (2005), in a similar survey, found that students are teachers' greatest sources of satisfaction. The other most satisfying component of teaching is a sense of fulfillment and accomplishment.

Although most teachers are satisfied with their career choice, approximately 18% of new teachers surveyed by the Metropolitan Life Insurance Company (2005) are very likely or likely to leave the profession. Based on data collected from the teachers surveyed, Metropolitan Life created a profile of those likely to leave the profession within the next 5 years. These teachers feel:

- Stress from administrator reviews
- Anxiety over low pay, teacher conflicts, and student discipline
- Frustration due to unrealistic demands and heavy workload
- Concern for personal safety
- Worried about lack of resources and financial constraints

Typically, those who end up leaving teaching are those who are dissatisfied with the profession. Table 15.6 summarizes some of the more common reasons given for leaving teaching. In addition, much of this attrition occurs within the first 5 years in the classroom. In a time of increasing personnel shortages, it is of considerable concern to many in education that fairly large numbers of new teachers choose to leave education after only a few years in the classroom. Statistics indicate that nationally approximately 30% of all new teachers and nearly 50% of new educators in urban districts leave the field in the first 5 years (National Commission on Teaching and America's Future, 2003).

One reason for the relatively high turnover rate for new teachers is the *stress of the job*. It takes considerable time and effort to engage in quality instruction. During the first few years of teaching, it can take far longer than many expect to develop the creative lessons needed to motivate and excite students (Kronowitz, 2004). Sam Fisher, who was observed during his first year of teaching in Estacada, Oregon, experienced this problem during an earth science lesson (Boss, 2001). Standing in front of his fourth-grade class a month into the new school year, Fisher realized that the unit on erosion from the textbook was not working out well:

> He snaps his book shut and asks the class, "Is it just me, or is this boring?" That gets their attention. "Tomorrow," he promises, "we'll start a new unit." Then he asks the class to suggest ways that the Earth changes. That's the larger lesson that fourth-graders are supposed to master in science. What do they wonder about? What intrigues them? In the lively discussion that ensues, several students bring up questions about volcanoes. Fisher feels his own curiosity heating up. "Tomorrow," he promises, "we'll start on volcanoes." (Boss, 2001, p. 23)

This promise to his students meant that Fisher was up all night, surfing the Internet to locate materials he could use to teach the promised unit on volcanoes. Not only that, but inventing this new unit required several weeks of additional evening and weekend work.

TABLE 15.6 Why Teachers Leave the Profession

Reason	Description
Stress of the Job	Teaching is a complicated, often difficult job. It takes long hours and a deep commitment to teaching and learning to work through the challenges, especially in the first few years.
Social Issues	Some teachers get discouraged trying to assist students with the many social issues they face. Because these issues have such a strong impact on learning, it can become overwhelming to both students and teachers.
Low Salaries	Although often cited as a major reason for teachers leaving the profession, low salaries may be less important in retention than better teaching conditions.
System Frustrations	Although teachers have considerable freedom within their own classrooms, the constraints placed on them by administrators, budgets, and parents can lead to frustration with the educational system.

Another common stressor for teachers is the challenge of helping students deal with *social issues*. Each situation is complex and typically beyond the teacher's ability to fully resolve. The interactions teachers have with family members, counselors, law enforcement personnel, and students themselves can be emotionally draining. Take, for example, 12-year-old Aramis, a new African American student in your predominantly white middle school. Aramis has received three notes over the last two weeks that are hateful and demeaning. As his teacher, you have seen the notes, talked to Aramis' parents, and discussed the issue in your classes. Despite a concerted effort to reverse this racial intimidation, Aramis is slowly withdrawing from class interactions. This bright, capable young man may be at risk of failure because of the racial intolerance of a small portion of your students. For some teachers, the emotional toll that results from committing significant amounts of personal time and energy helping students deal with these situations may lead to disillusionment and a new career choice.

Reflection Opportunity 15.6

Think carefully about your current life stressors and how you cope with them. First of all, identify what you find stressful in your life today, last week, and/or during the past year. Did you cope successfully with the stressful events you identified? What did you do to manage these stressors? Now reflect on the stressors other teachers identified above. How well do you think you would handle those stressful aspects of teaching? What strategies would you use to work through these and other difficult times in the classroom?

The issue of *low salaries* is often identified as a significant negative factor associated with teaching. It is the most frequently cited reason teachers give for dissatisfaction with their jobs (Markow, Fauth, & Gravitch, 2001). A recent survey of young college graduates also found that nearly 80% of the respondents felt that teachers were seriously underpaid (Farkas, Johnson, & Foleno, 2000). Finally, the 39th Annual Phi Delta Kappa/Gallup Poll of the Public's Attitudes Toward the Public Schools (Rose & Gallup, 2007) determined that 87% of the general public felt that raising teacher salaries would be an important strategy to use in addressing teacher shortages.

Despite consistent perceptions that low teacher salaries contribute to people either avoiding education or leaving the profession, there is at least some evidence that other issues may be more significant in both attracting and keeping good people in the classroom. Although 75% of teachers who had taught for 5 years or less felt they were underpaid, given the hypothetical choice between a significantly higher salary or better student behavior and parental support, 86% chose the latter option. Similarly, 82% hypothetically chose stronger administrative backing over a significantly higher salary (Farkas et al., 2000). While improved salaries would undoubtedly make a difference in attracting and retaining teachers, the other factors just mentioned appear to be much more significant to teachers (Hanushek, Kain, & Rivkin, 2001).

A final reason that some teachers give for leaving teaching is *frustration with the system*. Teachers enter the profession committed to helping students become well-educated, productive citizens. These good intentions can get derailed, however, by the schooling system in which these dedicated individuals find themselves working. The need to follow a curriculum determined by others, the mounds of paperwork to meet local, state, and national mandates; the low levels of financial support; the difficulty of bringing about effective change; and the differing opinions about the goals and directions of education are just some of the many irritants that teachers encounter. Most teachers find ways to cope with these frustrations while continuing to focus on the positive aspects of teaching. For some, however, these annoying elements build to the point that they overshadow all of the good things that are happening in the classroom. Table 15.7 provides some suggestions for dealing with teachers' frustrations with the system.

Other options are available to assist you in being successful in the classroom. Teachers' responses to frequently asked questions about their roles as educators may be one such option. To read these responses, go to the Companion Website for this text and click on MyEducationLab for Chapter 15.

MyEducationLab 15.2

TABLE 15.7 Dealing with System Frustrations

Strategy	Description
Avoid Trouble Areas when Possible	If, for example, you find that attending school board meetings is disturbing, try to avoid attending and spend the time you save in activities that are more productive for you.
Pick Your Battles Carefully	Sometimes it is better to set aside your dissatisfaction over little things so that you can save your energy for those that really matter. By focusing on trying to change a fewer number of these problem areas, you will be more likely to succeed without creating undue personal stress.
Focus on What Really Matters	Every profession, including teaching, has its frustrations. But if you spend the majority of your time thinking about the problems, it means there is less opportunity to focus on the positives. Shifting mentally to an emphasis on things that can help make things better in your classroom and school will make the problem areas seem less troublesome.

How can I continue to grow personally and professionally?

Once you have successfully navigated through those first few years of teaching, there is still much to be done as you continue to mature as an educator. You will have both good days and bad ones. There will be many successes and some failures. The challenges and victories lead to both personal and professional growth and make teaching a career unlike most others. Good teachers experience these highs and lows throughout their careers and use them as the basis for continued growth in their chosen profession. This process of professional development occurs through personal reflection, reflections with others, additional formal learning experiences, and advanced certification options (see Table 15.8).

TABLE 15.8 Growing as a Professional Educator

Strategy	Options
Active Reflection	• Gather information • Identify beliefs • Make decisions • Assess and evaluate
Formal Learning Experiences	• In-service programs • Workshops • Graduate degree programs
Advanced Certification	• Second-stage teacher certification • National Board for Professional Teaching Standards certification

Active Reflection

One way in which experienced teachers continue to grow both personally and professionally is through reflection. Conducted individually or with others, these thoughtful considerations of the teaching/learning process help teachers refine their knowledge and skills. The importance of reflection has been emphasized throughout this book as an essential tool in understanding the content and processes of education. The *Ian's Classroom Experiences* for this chapter (found on the Companion Website for this text) provides you with one more opportunity to read Ian's engagement in active reflection. You may want to read this information now and think about his perspectives on the topic.

**Ian's Classroom
Experiences:
Inherent Attitudes**

Two tools have been integrated into this text to assist you in personal reflection. The first is the use of a journal. Keeping a journal is an excellent method of continuing to grow as an educator. When you write down both the positive and negative things you learned from an experience and include reminders of factors to consider in similar future experiences, this journaling of events becomes a very personal and useful tool in refining your teaching.

Another personal reflection tool emphasized throughout this text has been the teaching portfolio. These samples of student work and teacher activities are another way in which teachers can learn to improve their instruction. But, collecting these artifacts as a future teacher is not enough. You will need to stop and reflect on the materials you have placed in the portfolio (Lyons, 1999). Take a few moments now to think about the portfolio materials you have collected for this text. What do the portfolio materials tell you about the teaching techniques you will probably use? Are these techniques consistent with your developing philosophy of education? What do you need to know and be able to do to improve your teaching and student learning? As you reflect on your answers to these and other questions, continued growth as an educator will take place.

**Reflection
Opportunity 15.7**

For many years, professions such as medicine have required new inductees to complete an apprenticeship period in a real-world setting before becoming fully endorsed to work more independently in their chosen career. This gives the new graduate an opportunity to work in the field while reflecting on effective practice with other more experienced professionals. Recently, educators have grown interested in having new teachers serve a similar apprenticeship under the guidance of experienced teachers. For example, the National Commission on Teaching and America's Future (1996) recommended that the first few years of teaching be restructured so that new teachers can work more closely with master teachers to hone their knowledge and skills.

The first 1–3 years of teaching are often referred to as a period of **teacher induction,** during which you will become acclimated to life in the schools. During this period, you will receive informal and/or formal assistance from other educators so that you can refine the knowledge and skills needed to be successful in the classroom. Informal support includes things like getting advice from the teacher next door on the best ways to manage the paperwork associated with teaching or sitting down with an experienced teacher to discuss ideas for presenting a specific concept to students. Because teachers lead very busy lives, you will probably need to take the initiative in seeking out this assistance from others.

In many school districts today, new teachers also receive more formalized assistance from an expert teacher who serves as a mentor. Mentoring, which emerged in the 1980s as an effort to help novice educators develop the skills they needed to be successful in the classroom, has become an essential component of teacher induction in many schools. Mentors are often either paid additional salary for serving in this role or are given release time from teaching so that they can dedicate more of their energy to providing meaningful assistance to new teachers.

A review of research on mentoring programs (Holloway, 2001) indicates that this activity benefits both novice teachers and those who serve as mentors. In one survey, 96% and 98% of all new teachers and mentors, respectively, believed that they benefited from the experience. In addition, other research shows that new teachers who engage in reflective activities with their mentors both improve their skills in teaching and are less likely to leave the profession. Mentors find that their role allows them to help others while also benefiting from the new teachers' fresh ideas and enthusiasm.

As you collaborate both informally and formally with more experienced colleagues, numerous opportunities will arise to think through with them the many intricacies of the teaching/learning process. This practice of reflection has the potential to lead to significant growth as an educator. These thoughtful considerations of your teaching and student learning will lay the groundwork for a successful career in education. It is also important to remember that this attitude of learning and growing as a teacher will keep you excited and challenged throughout your years in the classroom.

Formal Learning Experiences

Although you will learn a great deal from conversations with other teachers, there are also many opportunities for professional growth that come from additional formal learning experiences. Through in-service programs, workshops, and course work leading to a graduate degree, you will have many options to grow in your understanding of teaching and learning.

In-service programs. Each year, schools and school districts identify specific issues that they feel are important topics for teachers and administrators to study in more depth. For example, a school may choose to review the use of portfolios as an assessment strategy. Or, a district may wish to look at new materials and methods for use in the science curriculum. For the issues selected, schools and districts set aside time for in-service education opportunities. In some instances, school district personnel serve as leaders for these training sessions. For other experiences, state or national experts are called on to conduct the in-service education.

Workshops. Many teachers continue their education by periodically taking additional courses through colleges and universities that are designed to give teachers a deeper understanding of topics that are of interest to them. Many institutions offer courses each term that provide teachers with new learning opportunities. For example, the University of Missouri at Kansas City offered courses in bullying, differentiating instruction, strategies for literacy and learning, and teaching with technology as options for interested teachers during winter semester 2009 (University of Missouri at Kansas City, 2009). In addition to the more traditional workshop courses where students and instructors meet face to face, many colleges and universities (including the University of Missouri at Kansas City) also offer distance learning courses that are either conducted through written correspondence or via the Internet. Although these workshop courses typically cannot be used as part of a graduate degree program, they provide teachers with greater depth of understanding on a wide variety of topics.

Graduate degree programs. Once educators have met the initial challenges of teaching, many find that completing a graduate degree program is another important way in which they can grow as professionals. Approximately 41% of current teachers hold a master's degree, and another 1% possess a doctorate (National Center for Education Statistics, 2007). Graduate degree programs in education are numerous and include specialties in such things as early childhood education, literacy, mathematics education, science education, instructional technology, multicultural education, and special education. In most districts, teachers who receive an advanced degree are usually rewarded with an increase in their annual salary. Although this should not be the primary reason for completing a graduate program, this financial incentive does make the additional study more attractive to many teachers.

Advanced Certification

Because of the complex nature of teaching, more and more states are recognizing the need for teachers to continue their learning throughout their careers. Rather than following an older model in which educators were given a permanent teaching credential that required no further education or development, many states now require teachers to complete a program that leads to an advanced level of teacher certification. The National Association of State Directors of Teacher

Education and Certification (2001) refers to advanced teacher preparation as **second-stage teacher certification.** Others call advanced levels of certification a tiered licensing system (Keller, 2007). You will need to learn all that you can about the certification system in your state.

In addition to state options for advanced teacher certification, the National Board for Professional Teaching Standards (NBPTS) offers a nationally recognized opportunity for teachers to demonstrate competence as master teachers. Created in 1987, the NBPTS has as its mission to enhance teaching and learning by these means:

- Maintaining high and rigorous standards for what accomplished teachers should know and be able to do
- Providing a national voluntary system certifying teachers who meet these standards
- Advocating related education reforms to integrate national board certification in American education and to capitalize on the expertise of national board certified teachers (National Board for Professional Teaching Standards, 2009).

Teachers who seek national board certification work closely with a mentor who helps them complete a rigorous portfolio demonstrating their teaching skills. Thirty-one states currently give teachers with national board certification either one-time or permanent salary increases of several thousand dollars for their demonstrated competence as master teachers. The *Explore Your Beliefs* feature for this chapter provides additional insights into National Board certification.

Explore your beliefs: National board certified teachers

The National Board for Professional Teaching Standards (NBPTS) was established in 1987 to provide a voluntary process that teachers can use to demonstrate advanced teaching skills. Similar to the system medical doctors have for their profession, experienced teachers spend an entire year developing portfolios of their work, providing videotapes of their teaching and taking an exam to assess their knowledge of subject matter and teaching. As of 2006, 42 states are rewarding those who successfully complete the certification process with a raise in salary. (Viadero & Honawar, 2008).

Although most educators support the concept of advanced teacher certification, some concerns are being voiced. One major criticism of the NBPTS system is that it certifies a low percentage of minority teachers (Viadero & Honawar, 2008). Despite the fact that minority teachers account for more than 15% of the workforce, only about 7% are national board certified. The causes for this discrepancy are currently under investigation. Because teachers seeking national board certification spend more than $2,000 in fees and put forth a great deal of personal effort to complete the process, another question being asked is whether it is worth all the effort. A study by the National Research Council found that national board certified teachers are better at improving student achievement than other teachers (Hakel, Koenig, & Elliot, 2008).

Further research is needed to determine the components of the NBPTS system that lead to this positive result.

Developing the Habit of Reflective Practice
Gather Information

1. Do an Internet search for "On the Road to National Certification" and learn from five teachers who documented their personal efforts to achieve national certification.

Identify Beliefs

1. From your readings, do you think national board certification strengthens teaching as a profession? Why or why not?

Make Decisions

1. Can you see yourself completing the process for national board certification at some future point in your career as an educator? Why or why not?

Assess and Evaluate

1. What characteristics do you think most, if not all, nationally board certified teachers have in common?

Sources

Hakel, M., Koenig, J., & Elliot, S. (eds). (2008). *Assessing accomplished teaching: Advanced-level certification programs*. Washington, DC: National Academies Press.

Viadero, D., & Honawar, V. (2008). Credential of NBPTS has impact. *Education Week*, June 18, pp 1, 16.

Summary

In this chapter, three organizing questions were used to guide your thinking about the first years of teaching and beyond:

What will I need to do to get a teaching position?

You will need to follow several key steps in securing your first teaching job:
- Know the job market
- Locate job openings
- Submit applications
- Participate in interviews

What must I do to be successful as a beginning teacher?

Several steps are available that you can take to be more successful as a beginning teacher:
- Have realistic first-year expectations
- Refine your teaching style
- Create a community of learners (Praxis II, topic Ic)
- Maintain a healthy lifestyle
- Understand why teachers leave the profession

How can I continue to grow personally and professionally?

Teaching should be viewed as a lifelong learning experience that can be facilitated by the following:
- Active reflection (Praxis II, topic IVa)
- Formal learning experiences
- Advanced certification

PRAXIS ## Test-Preparation Activities

> To review an on-line chapter case study, test your understanding of chapter topics and concepts, and begin preparing for the Praxis II: Principles of Learning and Teaching examination, go to the Praxis-Test Preparation module for this chapter of the Companion Website.

Developing the Habit of Reflective Practice

Organizing Questions

Review questions, field-experience opportunities, and activities for building your portfolio are included here for the organizing questions in this chapter.

What will I need to do to get a teaching position?

Review Questions

1. What categories of teachers are in greatest and least demand nationally?
2. What are the typical ingredients of a résumé?

Field Experience

Find a teacher or administrator who has participated in interviewing teachers seeking jobs. Discuss with this person what you can expect to take place in the interview process. Based on your discussion, develop a list of tips for making the interview a positive experience.

Building Your Portfolio: *Constructing a Résumé*

INTASC Standard 9. One of the things you will need to do when you begin your future search for a teaching job is to create a résumé summarizing your education, work experience, and personal interests to date. Although you will add many experiences between now and then, constructing a résumé at this point will help you consider engaging in actions that will help you be more competitive in the job market. Consider working with the career planning and placement center at your college or university as you develop an initial draft of your résumé. Include a copy of the results as part of your portfolio.

What must I do to be successful as a beginning teacher?

Review Questions

1. What steps can you take to refine your personal teaching style?
2. Describe strategies you could use to create a community of learners within your future classroom.
3. Why do teachers leave the profession?

Field Experience

Talk to a first-year teacher about the start of his or her teaching career. What does this teacher find to be both the joys and frustrations of the teaching experience? What suggestions does this person have for being successful during the first year? How can you adapt the strategies presented to make your first year more productive?

Building Your Portfolio: *Maintaining a Healthy Lifestyle*

INTASC Standard 9. One of the keys to your initial success as a future teacher is to find ways to stay physically and emotionally healthy despite the regular stress you will face. Develop a list of strategies that you will use to maintain a healthy lifestyle. Include a copy of this list in your portfolio.

How can I continue to grow personally and professionally?

Review Questions

1. What are some strategies you can use to engage in personal reflection about your own teaching?
2. What strategies are schools using to assist with teacher induction?
3. Describe some of the additional formal learning experiences that teachers have throughout their careers.

Field Experience

Find an experienced teacher with 15 or more years of teaching and discuss with that person the keys to success as a teacher. What has helped this person be successful with students and manage the stress of teaching? Ask for tips that would help you be successful as a first-year teacher.

Building Your Portfolio: *A Case for Teaching*

INTASC Standard 9. A portfolio assignment made for Chapter 1 was to create the most persuasive argument you can for teaching as a career. Now that you have completed reading this text and gained additional insights on teaching and learning, go back and review the essay you developed earlier. Revise it so that it reflects your current view on the values of a career in education. Include your revised essay as a component of your portfolio.

Suggested Readings

Codell, E. (1999). *Educating Esmé*. Chapel Hill, NC: Algonquin Books. This book presents the raw and powerful diary of a beginning teacher's first year in an inner city school. Esmé Codell shares her successes, failures, joys, and sorrows in an engaging format that makes it a difficult book to put down. This unconventional teacher has much to say to all teachers.

DePaul, A. (1998). *What to expect your first year of teaching*. Washington, DC: U.S. Department of Education. Available at http://www.ed.gov/pubs/FirstYear/. This publication gives numerous anecdotes from first-year teachers and advice from more experienced teachers and administrators that paint a vivid picture of what that year will be like.

Kronowitz, E. (1999). *Your first year of teaching and beyond* (3rd ed.). New York: Addison Wesley Longman. This book provides a strong overview of the challenges of the first few years of teaching and provides good suggestions for strategies that can help new teachers be successful in their chosen career.

MacDonald, R., & Healy, S. (1999). *A handbook for beginning teachers* (2nd ed.). New York: Addison Wesley Longman. This text has separate chapters on how to work creatively within the educational system and strategies for continuing growth as an educator. It has many good suggestions for the beginning teacher.

References

American Association for Employment in Education. (2008). *Educator supply and demand in the United States*. Columbus, OH: Author.

American Association for Employment in Education. (2002). *Educator supply and demand in the United States*. Columbus, OH: Author.

Archer, J. (2001, September 5). First impressions. *Education Week,* pp. 48–54.

Battistich, V., Solomon, D., Kim, D., Watson, M., & Schaps, E. (1995). Schools as communities, poverty levels of student populations, and students' attitudes, motives, and performance: A multilevel analysis. *American Education Research Journal, 32*(4), 627–658.

Boss, S. (2001). Mr. Fisher finds his calling. *Northwest Education, 7*(2), 20–23, 36–40.

DePaul, A. (1998). *What to expect your first year of teaching.* Washington, DC: U.S. Department of Education.

Farkas, S., Johnson, J., & Foleno, T. (2000). *A sense of calling: Who teaches and why.* NY: Public Agenda.

Fulton, K., Yoon, I., & Lee, C. (2005). *Induction into learning communities.* Washington, DC: National Commission on Teaching and America's Future.

Goodlad, J. (1984). *A place called school.* NY: Macmillan.

Holloway, J. (2001). The benefits of mentoring. *Educational Leadership, 58* (8), 85–86.

Keller, B. (2007). Tiered licensing systems being used by states to help teacher quality. *Education Week,* December 19, pp. 6–7.

Kohn, A. (1996). *Beyond discipline: From compliance to community.* Alexandria, VA: Association for Supervision and Curriculum Development.

Kronowitz, E. (2004). *Your first-year of teaching and beyond* (4th ed.). New York: Longman.

MacDonald, R., & Healy, S. (1999). *A handbook for beginning teachers* (2nd ed.). New York: Longman.

Markow, D., Fauth, S., & Gravitch, D. (2001). *The Metlife survey of the American teacher.* NY: Metropolitan Life Insurance Company.

May, H. (2001, June 11). Highs, lows mark teacher's first year. *Salt Lake Tribune.* Retrieved from: *http://www.sltrib.com/2001/Jun/06112001/utah/10894.htm*

Metropolitan Life Insurance Company. (2005). *The MetLife Survey of the American teacher 2004–2005.* New York: Author.

National Association of State Directors of Teacher Education and Certification. (2001). *The NASDTEC manual on the preparation and certification of educational personnel.* Dubuque, IA: Kendall/Hunt.

National Board for Professional Teaching Standards. (2009). *History of the National Board.* Retrieved February 20, 2009 from *http://www.nbpts.org*

National Center for Education Statistics. (2008). *Projections of education statistics to 2017.* Retrieved February 17, 2009 from: *http://nces.ed.gov/pubs2008/2008078_1.pdf*

National Center for Education Statistics. (2007). *Digest of education statistics.* Retrieved February 17, 2009 from *http://nces.ed.gov/programs/digest/d07/*

National Commission on Teaching and America's Future. (2003). *No dream denied: A pledge to America's children.* Washington, DC: Author.

National Education Association. (2003). *Status of the American public school teacher 2000–2001.* Washington, DC: Author.

Ostrum, E. (2009). How I learned to teach: An expanded 'human capital' model. *Education Week,* February 11, pp. 24, 25.

Parsad, B., Lewis, L., & Farris, E. (2001). *Teacher preparation and professional development: 2000.* Fast Response Survey System. Washington, DC: U.S. Department of Education.

Patterson, M. (2005). Hazed! *Educational Leadership, 62*(8), 20–23.

Roberts, P., Kellough, R., & Moore, K. (2006). *A resource guide for elementary school teaching: Planning for competence* (6th ed.). Columbus, OH: Merrill.

Rose, L., & Gallup, A. (2007). The 39th annual Phi Delta Kappa/Gallup poll of public attitudes toward the public schools. *Phi Delta Kappan, 89*(1), 43–57.

Rowland, C. (2005). How old are America's public schools? *Education Statistics Quarterly, 1*(1). Retrieved October 10, 2005 from: *http://nces.ed.gov/programs/quarterly/vol_1/1_1/4-esq11-h.asp*

Salvo, J., Kibble, L., Furay, M., & Sierra, E. (2005). Surviving day one . . . and beyond. *Educational Leadership, 62*(8), 24–28.

Sowers, J. (2004). *Creating a community of learners: Solving the puzzle of classroom management.* Portland, OR: Northwest Regional Educational Laboratory.

University of Missouri at Kansas City. (2009). Continuing education. Retrieved February 18, 2009 from *http://education.umkc.edu/ce/ce-Spring2009.asp*

Useem, E., & Neild, R. Supporting new teachers in the city. *Educational Leadership, 62*(8), 44–47.

U.S. General Accounting Office. (2000). *School facilities: Construction expenditures have grown significantly in recent years.* Washington, DC: Author.

Wald, P., & Castleberry, M. (2000). *Educators as learners: Creating a professional learning community in your school.* Alexandria, VA: Association for Supervision and Curriculum Development.

Name Index

Subject Index